# READING CRITICALLY, WRITING WELL

## A Reader and Guide

Write observation.
pronoun?

# READING CRITICALLY, WRITING WELL

## A Reader and Guide

### RISE B. AXELROD
California State University, San Bernardino

### CHARLES R. COOPER
University of California, San Diego

ST. MARTIN'S PRESS
New York

*From Rise to her husband Steven, their son Jeremiah, and their parents
—especially to Martha Gould Axelrod, whose writing has always been
an inspiration.*

*From Charles for Suzy and her writing, Laura and her painting,
and Vince and his music.*

Library of Congress Catalog Card Number: 86-60657
Copyright © 1987 by St. Martin's Press, Inc.
All rights reserved.
Manufactured in the United States of America.
10987
fedcb
For information, write St. Martin's Press, Inc.
175 Fifth Avenue, New York, NY 10010

Cover design: Darby Downey
Book design: Nancy Sugihara

ISBN: 0-312-66459-1

## Acknowledgments

Amberg, Jay, "The SAT," *The American Scholar*, vol. 51, no. 4 (Autumn 1982). Copyright ©
1982 by the author. By permission of the publisher.

Baker, Carlos, "The *Nada*-Concept in 'A Clean, Well-Lighted Place,' " from *Hemingway—The
Writer As Artist*, 4th ed. rev. Copyright 1952 © 1956, 1963, 1972, 1980 by Carlos Baker.
Chapter III, pp. 48–74 and 123–125, reprinted with permission of Princeton University Press.

Baker, Russell, "Saving America from Herbert Hoover," from *Growing Up* by Russell Baker.
Copyright © 1982 by Russell Baker. Reprinted by permission of Congdon and Weed, Inc.

Bambara, Toni Cade, "My Man Bavanne." Copyright © 1971 by Toni Cade Bambara. Reprinted from *Gorilla, My Love*, by Toni Cade Bambara, by permission of Random House, Inc.

Benert, Annette, "Survival Through Irony: Hemingway's 'A Clean, Well-Lighted Place,' "
*Studies in Short Fiction*, II (Spring 1974), 181–187. Reprinted by permission of *Studies in Short
Fiction* and Annette Benert.

Bird, Caroline, "The Liberal Arts Religion," from *The Case Against College*. Copyright © 1975
by Caroline Bird.

Bly, Carol, "Enemy Evenings," with deletions from pp. 35, 36, 38, 39 from *Letters from the
Country* by Carol Bly. Copyright © 1981 by Carol Bly. Reprinted by permission of Harper and
Row, Publishers, Inc.

Bok, Sissela, "Intrusive Social Science Research," from *Secrets: On the Ethics of Concealment
and Revelation* by Sissela Bok. Reprinted by permission of Pantheon Books, a division of Random
House, Inc.

*Acknowledgments and copyrights continue at the back of the book on pages 644–646, which
constitute an extension of the copyright page.*

# Preface

*Reading Critically, Writing Well* provides readings for a college writing course. But more than that, it teaches specific strategies for critical reading, enabling students to analyze thoughtfully the readings in this text and in their other college courses. We assume that college students should learn to think and read critically and that as they become better critical readers, they will also become more effective writers. To this instruction in reading, we add comprehensive guidance in writing, helping students to understand and manage the composing process—from invention through planning and drafting to revision.

This text attempts to bring reading and writing together in an ideal relationship: students learn to read a type of discourse with a critical eye and then practice writing that same kind of discourse. It suggests specific questions a good reader uses to analyze each kind of discourse and the criteria for evaluating it—questions and criteria students can apply to the readings in this book as well as to their own writing.

We believe that if students have specific strategies for reading and careful guidance with writing, they can study seriously and compose confidently the types of discourse written by academics and professionals. Instead of exercises in the conventional modes of writing, this text offers real-world writing tasks; students read and write the kinds of discourse they will encounter during college and on the job. They practice the forms of critical analysis, inquiry, and knowledge-making central to research and learning in college. In this way, the text introduces them to writing and learning across the college curriculum. All the major academic disciplines are represented in the readings, which students should find challenging but accessible.

*Reading Critically, Writing Well* opens with a chapter presenting six critical reading strategies: previewing, annotating, summarizing, outlining, taking inventory, and analyzing arguments. This chapter can be studied carefully when the course begins or sampled as it proceeds. The reading and writing chapters, which make up the rest of the book, include

v

two types of personal discourse—autobiography and reflection; two types of explanatory discourse—observation and explanation; and five types of argumentative discourse—evaluation, analysis of cause and effect, proposal, position paper, and literary analysis.

These nine chapters provide students with comprehensive support for reaching the goals stated in our title: reading critically and writing well. Each begins by introducing the type of writing being considered, including a list of its distinguishing features. An annotated sample essay then demonstrates the kinds of questions and comments a good critical reading would yield. Following is a list of questions that can help students to read the type of discourse thoughtfully and critically. This list forms the basis for the annotations of the sample essay.

Next, six or seven published readings and one student piece, of varying length and difficulty, illustrate the wide range of writing situations typical of that type of discourse. Several chapters pair readings in a debate so that students can examine different writers' strategies for approaching the same subject. Each reading is preceded by headnotes that discuss the author and the context in which the selection was written and is followed by questions for analysis. These questions attempt to transcend the division between form and content common in writing courses. They ask students to examine textual features as reflections of writer's decisions, decisions that encompass the writer's understanding of the subject, the rhetorical situation, and the possibilities and constraints of the discourse. The questions for analysis particularize the critical reading questions introduced at the beginning of the chapter. Suggestions for writing also accompany each selection and invite students to compose the type of discourse they have been studying in the chapter. Each chapter briefly discusses the composing process of the student writer whose essay appears in that chapter and concludes with a brief but comprehensive guide to writing. This guide helps students through each stage of the writing process for that particular genre—from finding a topic to revising for readability.

The text concludes with an appendix that discusses library and field research. It includes MLA and APA guidelines for documenting sources, and it offers advice to help students integrate research materials into their own writing. Finally, there are two indexes: one that groups readings by topic and one that lists authors, titles, and subjects.

An Instructor's Manual, prepared with the assistance of Professor Keith Grant-Davie of the University of Maryland, outlines various course plans for using this text and offers suggestions for presenting each reading. It includes, as well, discussion of general teaching strategies that became central to our work as we taught early drafts of these chapters and an annotated bibliography of recent research and theory on learning from text, sources that influenced our choice of critical reading strategies for Chapter 1.

## Acknowledgments

When thinking about our acknowledgments, we confronted a problem. Within the last twenty years composition studies has emerged as an important multidisciplinary scholarly specialty, bringing with it a burgeoning literature. We now possess compelling new theory and research and have more reports of pedagogy than even a diligent composition specialist can follow. Our problem, then, is that so many of our colleagues around the country have influenced this text that acknowledging them all by name would produce a list tediously long to write or read. Instead, we wish to acknowledge our indebtedness generally to colleagues whose work has contributed to our thinking and influenced this book.

This text began when we needed more readings to serve as models of the types of discourse we were assigning in our courses and programs. We have always believed that novice writers must have available a collection of readings of just the type of writing they are attempting, a collection that presents a wide variety of possibilities, strategies, and text patterns for that type of discourse. Cognitive science schema theory supports this belief, as does recent research on the contribution of models to writing development. But novice writers need more. They need to consider models the way writers do in writers' workshops. They need guidance to help them explore how texts are made and achieve their effects, and they need to learn how to read critically or skeptically. In writing the apparatus that introduces and follows the readings in this book, we were influenced by recent work in semiotics, text linguistics, literary criticism, and discourse theory.

Current discourse theorists have helped us think about the composing demands and text features of different types of writing. From these theories, especially theories of argument, and from our own attempts to focus and sequence assignments to make a productive writing course, we have gradually over several years arrived at the chapter divisions and writing assignments found in this book.

Our indebtedness to those who have taught all of us so much about the writing process will be apparent in each chapter of the text. In particular, recent theory and research on invention and revision has transformed our understanding about writing—and about its role in learning and intellectual development.

We also want to thank our students. Students in the Third College Writing Program at the University of California, San Diego, helped us revise early versions of these chapters and have been generous and frank with their advice. Some of them contributed essays to this text. Their instructors also have had a major role in shaping the book, and we are particularly indebted to Cezar Ornatowski, Kate Gardner, Ann Humes, and Michael Pemberton at UCSD, and to Nan Dorsey and Kathryn O'Rourke at UC Riverside.

We owe a debt of gratitude to the many reviewers throughout the country who gave so generously of their time and expertise; their critical reading of earlier drafts of this book helped us enormously. They include Lucien Agosta, Kansas State University; Nancy Barry, University of Iowa; Kathleen Bell, Old Dominion University; Gwendolyn Gong, Texas A & M University; Donald Gray, Indiana University; Richard Jenseth, Pacific Lutheran University; George Miller, University of Delaware; MeMe Riordan, City College of San Francisco; Jeff Schiff, Northern Arizona University; Jenny Sullivan, Northern Virginia Community College; and Richard Zbaracki, Iowa State University. To the crew at St. Martin's Press, we wish to convey our deepest appreciation. We thank Nancy Perry for her encouragement and confidence in us, Marilyn Moller for her incomparable skill and dedication to this project, and Anne McCoy for her careful attention to detail.

Finally, we want to thank our families. The Cooper family provided unwavering enthusiasm and support. Every time one of them asked, "How's it going?" it seemed to come from the heart. The Axelrods, conversely, kept asking, "Are you done yet?"—and for that, too, we are grateful.

# Contents

    A major American novelist recalls her elementary school principal, a woman "impervious to lies or foolish excuses or the insufferable plea of not knowing any better."

CHAPTER THREE

# Reflection

C H A P T E R   F I V E

# Explanation    199

CHAPTER SIX

# Evaluation                                                 263

CHAPTER SEVEN

# Analysis of Cause or Effect

CHAPTER TEN

# Literary Analysis

By examining imagery and characterization in the Hemingway story, a literary critic arrives at an understanding of its theme.

A college student analyzes the contrasting light and dark images in the Hemingway story.

The great American novelist begins at the beginning in this humorous look at the relations between men and women.

# Introduction

*There is no learning to write well without a concomitant
learning to read well.*                                  J. HILLIS MILLER

*Reading Critically, Writing Well* is a collection of reading selections—
examples of good writing for you to enjoy and to study. These selections
illustrate some of the kinds of writing done by college students, historians,
scientists, business executives, and journalists. Studying them will help
you to recognize the decisions writers make and understand why they
make them. You will learn, in particular, how purpose and audience
influence these decisions. You will gain insight into how language works
and how you can use it to discover and to convey meaning.

*Reading Critically, Writing Well* offers both strategies for reading and
guidance for writing. Reading critically means going beyond merely recognizing words and comprehending ideas. Comprehension is only the
beginning of reading. When you read critically, you question, evaluate,
extend, analyze, interpret, and apply what you are reading. Writing well
involves discovering what you want to say and finding ways of saying it
clearly and gracefully. It means exploring your subject, analyzing it systematically, synthesizing information from different sources, anticipating
your readers' questions, arranging your ideas logically, and finding the
right words.

Reading critically and writing well are important to each other. Reading critically, you sometimes notice the text itself—its sentences,
rhythms, and forms. Remembering what you have noticed influences your
writing, making available to you many possibilities for presenting your
own ideas and feelings. You cannot write well without reading critically.
Writing for a particular purpose, as you craft sentences and sequence
them into clear and pleasing patterns, you become aware of the ways all
writers create texts of a certain kind. Remembering what you have
learned enhances your reading, making you a more confident, efficient,
and appreciative reader. You cannot read critically without writing well.

In one further way reading and writing are important to each other: you must read your own texts in order to write them. As your text fills the page, you continually read and reread it to keep your focus. As you revise a completed draft, you read it critically to decide how well it fulfills your purpose. The better you read your own writing, the better your new writing will be. You cannot continue writing or improve your writing without reading critically.

# *Reading Critically*

Since we usually associate the word *critical* with criticism, you might assume that to read critically means criticizing or finding fault with a text. But that is not the word's primary meaning. *Critical* comes from the Greek root *kritos,* meaning to discern, discover, or differentiate.

When you read critically, you read purposefully, with expectations arising from the context and your awareness of the kind of writing you are reading. You read sympathetically, with an appreciation for what the writer is trying to say. You read analytically, examining the different parts of the text to see how they are related. You read systematically, looking for contradictions in logic and shifts in meaning. You read imaginatively, filling in gaps, extending and applying ideas. You become the writer's partner, completing the circuit of communication.

Critical readers do not just read for information, although they do work to notice important details. They do not simply accept the text's authority, but question its assertions and information. For such readers, texts are not merely monologues addressed by active authors to passive readers but dialogues between active authors and active readers. As Walt Whitman once said, this sort of reader "will always have his work to do."

To help you become an active, critical reader, we offer here a repertoire of reading strategies. In Chapter 1, "Strategies for Critical Reading," we present six basic activities for critical reading: previewing, annotating, outlining, summarizing, taking inventory, and analyzing arguments. Chapters 2 through 10 introduce critical reading questions specific to the kind of writing illustrated in that chapter and present questions for analysis to help you apply these genre-specific critical reading questions and the more general critical reading strategies to the reading selections.

# *Writing Well*

According to Greek mythology, Athena, the goddess of knowledge and truth, sprang fully formed and perfect from the head of Zeus. As a metaphor for writing, this myth has much to recommend it: it makes the process seem painless and swift, with a final product that emerges flawless and complete. Yet, all experienced writers know that reality differs markedly from mythology. "Easy writing," as Richard Sheridan once observed, "makes vile hard reading."

Unfortunately, effective writing is not a gift from the muse but the result of labor that can be long and even painful. Writing is a complex intellectual, emotional, and creative process. It requires analyzing and synthesizing diverse bits of knowledge, understanding human psychology so as to anticipate readers' responses, and forging new sentences with unique meanings from the stockpile of words and conventions. It means sometimes having faith in what you have said and how you have said it, and sometimes regarding your own writing skeptically.

To help you handle this challenging process, each of the reading and writing chapters (2 through 10) includes brief guides to writing. These guides divide the writing process into smaller, manageable parts and show ways in which writing can help you discover what you want to say. They will help you to define your purpose and understand your readers—and focus your writing accordingly. Finally, they will help you with your final revision, showing you how to resee your writing—to reconsider what you want to say and reexamine what you have actually said.

## *The Reading Selections*

The selections in this book are exemplary; they represent writing worthy of study and admiration. Yet they are not without fault. Studying them closely will help you learn how others write and how writing conveys meaning to readers. As you come to recognize the many decisions writers must make in the course of composing an essay, you will begin to understand how writers work with and also against conventions, how an understanding of the kind of writing they are doing—and of the way readers read—helps writers to achieve their purpose with grace and originality.

These are selections written by scientists, sociologists, philosophers, politicians, journalists, historians, students, and professional writers. Many of them will introduce you to writing in the academic disciplines you will be studying in college. Some subjects will be new to you, while others will be familiar. Some will be easy to read, while others will be more demanding.

All the selections in this book are examples of what we like to call real-life writing—writing that is actually done in college, the workplace, and the marketplace. To help you learn to read and write some of these common kinds of writing, we group the selections according to type or genre. Within each chapter, there may be a broad range of variation in content, form, and style, yet the selections in each group share the same general aims and basic features. Here is a list of the kinds of writing included in this collection, by chapter:

Chapter 2: Autobiography—writing that relates significant experiences in the author's life

Chapter 3: Reflection—writing that meditates on the meaning of human experience

Chapter 4: Observation—writing that presents firsthand information

Chapter 5: Explanation—writing that presents secondhand information

Chapter 6: Evaluation—writing that defends judgments about the value or worth of something

Chapter 7: Analysis of Cause or Effect—writing that argues for cause and effect relationships

Chapter 8: Proposal—writing that defines problems and argues for solutions

Chapter 9: Position Paper—writing that supports an opinion on a controversial issue

Chapter 10: Literary Analysis—writing that defends an interpretation of a literary work

Each chapter follows the same pattern and is divided into three major sections. The first section discusses the special features of the genre, presents a sample annotated essay, and gives a set of critical reading questions to guide your own reading of the selections in the chapter. Next come the reading selections, which are preceded by headnotes describing the authors and the context for the work and followed by questions for analysis and suggestions for writing. The third section is a guide to writing your own essay of that type.

We hope *Reading Critically, Writing Well* serves you well. If you are intrigued by the readings and learn more effective strategies for reading and writing, then we have accomplished our aim in this book.

# READING CRITICALLY, WRITING WELL

*A Reader and Guide*

# Strategies for Critical Reading

*Serious study of a text requires a pencil in hand*
*—how much pride that pencil carries.*     IRVING HOWE

Critical reading is a rigorous process. It is sometimes slow and always demanding. Reading actively, thoughtfully, and *critically* can be one of the most challenging human activities, for it tests the limits of our energy, patience, and intellect.

Reading critically is often harder than it needs to be, however, because so few readers know how to approach difficult reading. This chapter presents several proven strategies for reading critically, strategies that you can learn readily and then apply not only to the selections in this text but also to your other college reading. Although mastering these strategies will not make the critical reading process an easy one, you will find it much more satisfying and productive and thus will be more able to handle difficult material with confidence.

In order to read critically, you must be prepared to read actively, with pencil in hand, and to perform specific operations on the text as you read. These actions will slow down your reading, but they may save you time in the long run, especially if you must later discuss the reading in class or write about it. New research on how people learn from their reading shows that the active, pencil-in-hand strategies demonstrated in this chapter are far more productive than merely rereading or highlighting or underlining.

In college you will be reading new kinds of material, in forms you may not have had much experience with. Much of this new reading—books, essays, reports—will not have the familiar and helpful cues that textbooks provide, such as headings, summaries, and questions. Your instructors will expect you to handle these unfamiliar texts on your own, and they will assume that you are able to do more with them than you may be accustomed to:

summarize and outline complex material

evaluate a text, deciding whether it is accurate, authoritative, and convincing

gauge a text's importance or significance

compare and contrast different texts

synthesize information from several texts

apply concepts or principles in one text to other texts

analyze the way a text achieves its effects

critically examine a text's reasoning

These expectations call for critical, not casual, reading. When you read a text in this way you must think critically and become an active participant rather than a passive recipient. Instead of listening passively to the author's monologue, you should strive to become actively involved in a dialogue with the author and with other readers of the text. When reading in this special way, you join in a conversation with the writer.

This chapter will demonstrate six strategies for critical reading to help you meet the demands of college studies:

- *previewing:* looking over a text to learn everything you can about it before you start reading
- *annotating:* marking up a text to record your reactions, questions, and conclusions
- *outlining:* identifying the sequence of main ideas
- *summarizing:* stating in your own words the essence of a reading
- *taking inventory:* looking for patterns of meaning
- *analyzing an argument:* evaluating the reasoning and persuasiveness of a text

## Previewing

The first strategy is called previewing because it involves noticing certain features about a text *before* reading it, in order to establish a context and purpose for reading. As you preview, you can write down your observations either on the text itself or on a separate piece of paper.

Previewing answers the following basic questions:

What do I know about the author?
What does the title tell me?
What kind of text is it?
What else do I know about the context of this text?
What can I discover about this text by skimming it?

## What Do I Know About the Author?

Being familiar with the author is not a prerequisite for critical reading, but it can help you determine how much to trust the information and judgments presented. A text's credibility derives in large part from the reader's willingness to accept the author's authority. The author's reputation, credentials, and other publications help establish his or her credibility.

Occasionally a reading may be accompanied by a preface, headnote, or other biographical information. For each selection in this book, for example, a headnote presents vital facts about the writer. Often, however, no special information about the author will accompany an assigned reading. If the name is familiar, recall what you know about the author—the period and the place in which he or she lived, any other publications, anything about his or her life or work that might give clues about this particular reading. If the name is unfamiliar, you might want to learn more by consulting a biographical dictionary, encyclopedia, or index such as *Who's Who, Current Biography, Biographical Index, Dictionary of American Biography,* or *Annual Obituary.*

Throughout this chapter we will refer to "'Letter from Birmingham Jail," a celebrated essay by Dr. Martin Luther King, Jr., to demonstrate each of the critical reading strategies. Notice the headnote about King on page 529. Since Dr. King is so highly respected, even revered, many readers will naturally expect to sympathize with his point of view even if they do not know very much about the situation he is writing about. As a critical reader, however, you should try to remain somewhat skeptical, withholding judgment until you fully understand the issue and realize the opposing argument.

## What Does the Title Tell Me?

Paying some attention to the title before reading the whole selection may provide clues about the subject of the selection, the kind of writing it is, and the circumstances surrounding its composition.

The title of King's essay, "Letter from Birmingham Jail," indicates several things: that it is a letter, that it was written while the author was in jail, and that it was written from the city of Birmingham. Readers who know nothing about the author might discount the letter because it was written by someone in jail, but those familiar with King's career would be likely to assume that the author was imprisoned because of his protest against racial segregation. These readers might further recognize Birmingham as the city in Alabama where dramatic events took place in the civil rights movement.

## What Kind of Text Is It?

Reading unfamiliar text is like traveling in unknown territory. Wise travelers use a map, checking what they see against what they expect to find. In much the same way, previewing for genre equips you with a set of expectations to guide your reading. The word *genre* means "sort" or "type," and is generally used to classify pieces of writing according to their particular style, form, and content. Nonfiction prose genres include autobiography, reflection, observation, explanation, and various forms of argument, such as evaluation, proposal, speculation about causes or effects, and interpretation of opinion about a controversial issue. All these genres are represented in this book.

Some readings, particularly long and complicated ones like King's letter, may be difficult to classify according to genre because they include elements of more than one kind of writing. Such overlap is to be expected since classifying according to genre, like any form of classification, depends on your purpose for classifying, on what features of the reading you choose to emphasize, and on what you think is important in a particular reading. This ambiguity should not be a problem for you as a reader. Indeed, seeing a text as belonging to different genres enables you to look at it from various perspectives, which is one of the goals of critical reading.

By making a tentative decision about the genre of a text, you can guess why the piece was written and how the writing situation affected the particular way it was written. The title "Letter from Birmingham Jail" explicitly identifies this particular selection as a letter. We know that letters are usually written with a particular reader in mind, although they may be addressed to the public in general; that they may be part of an ongoing correspondence, either initiating or responding to an earlier communication; and that they may be personal or public, informal or formal.

The opening of King's letter (p. 529) provides some insight into the situation in which he wrote the letter and some understanding of his specific purpose for writing. The first paragraph makes clear that King wrote the letter in order to rebut or answer criticisms against him by other clergy. The tone he establishes suggests that his rebuttal will not take the form of an angry counterattack but will attempt to explain and justify his position to critics he hopes ultimately to win over to his side. As a public letter written in response to a public statement, "Letter from Birmingham Jail" thus may be classified as a position paper, one that argues for a particular position on a controversial issue. In this case, the issue is racial segregation; King's position is that segregation must end.

Knowing that "Letter from Birmingham Jail" is a position paper allows you to appreciate the controversiality of the subject King is writing about and the sensitivity of the rhetorical situation. You can see how he sets forth his own position at the same time that he tries to bridge the gap separating him from his critics. You can then evaluate the kinds of points King makes and the persuasiveness of his argument.

When you think of a text as belonging to a particular genre, you inevitably recall other examples of that genre. As you read, you hear echoes of other writings and often compare the text with others you have read. Some of these other texts may have influenced the writer you are reading. For instance, King probably knew of the famous public letter "J'accuse" by French author Emile Zola about the notorious Dreyfus case, and as a minister he most certainly knew the Epistles, or letters, in the New Testament. He also must have known some part of the long tradition of writing on civil disobedience: Plato's *Apology*, Thoreau's "Civil Disobedience," and Gandhi's *Nonviolent Resistance*, all advocating the duty to disobey unjust laws. King almost certainly knew, as well, Thomas Hobbes's *Leviathan* and Edmund Burke's *Reflections on the Revolution in France*, both arguing against civil disobedience. These famous documents on civil disobedience must have influenced King's decisions about how to address his readers, what argumentative strategies he might adopt, and the kinds of examples and evidence he might include as he argued the appropriateness of nonviolent direct action.

Whenever you begin a new reading, try to determine as soon as possible what genre you are encountering. You will then be able to read more confidently and productively.

## What Else Do I Know About the Context?

The author, title, and genre provide a good deal of information about the particular context in which a text was written, but there may be still further contexts to be inferred by previewing a selection.

For example, you know that King is responding to a statement made by several clergymen. Although it is not necessary to read their statement, doing so would enlarge your understanding of the context for the letter and also furnish insight into King's argumentative strategy. With a little research, you could find the clergymen's statement, which is printed here:

## Public Statement by Eight Alabama Clergymen

### *April 12, 1963*

We the undersigned clergymen are among those who, in January, issued    1
"An Appeal for Law and Order and Common Sense," in dealing with racial problems in Alabama. We expressed understanding that honest convictions in racial matters could properly be pursued in the courts, but urged that decisions of those courts should in the meantime be peacefully obeyed.

Since that time there had been some evidence of increased forebear-    2
ance and a willingness to face facts. Responsible citizens have undertaken to work on various problems which cause racial friction and unrest. In Birmingham, recent public events have given indication that we all have opportunity for a new constructive and realistic approach to racial problems.

However, we are now confronted by a series of demonstrations by some    3
of our Negro citizens, directed and led in part by outsiders. We recognize the natural impatience of people who feel that their hopes are slow in being realized. But we are convinced that these demonstrations are unwise and untimely.

We agree rather with certain local Negro leadership which has    4
called for honest and open negotiation of racial issues in our area. And we believe this kind of facing of issues can best be accomplished by citizens of our own metropolitan area, white and Negro, meeting with their knowledge and experience of the local situation. All of us need to face that responsibility and find proper channels for its accomplishment.

Just as we formerly pointed out that "hatred and violence have no    5
sanction in our religious and political traditions," we also point out that such actions as incite to hatred and violence, however technically peaceful those actions may be, have not contributed to the resolution of our local problems. We do not believe that these days of new hope are days when extreme measures are justified in Birmingham.

We commend the community as a whole, and the local news media    6
and law enforcement officials in particular, on the calm manner in which

these demonstrations have been handled. We urge the public to continue to show restraint should the demonstrations continue, and the law enforcement officials to remain calm and continue to protect our city from violence.

We further strongly urge our own Negro community to withdraw support from these demonstrations, and to unite locally in working peacefully for a better Birmingham. When rights are consistently denied, a cause should be pressed in the courts and in negotiations among local leaders, and not in the streets. We appeal to both our white and Negro citizenry to observe the principles of law and order and common sense.

*Signed by:*

C. C. J. CARPENTER, D.D., LL.D., *Bishop of Alabama*

JOSEPH A. DURICK, D.D., *Auxiliary Bishop, Diocese of Mobile-Birmingham*

Rabbi MILTON L. GRAFMAN, *Temple Emanu-El, Birmingham, Alabama*

Bishop PAUL HARDIN, *Bishop of the Alabama-West Florida Conference of the Methodist Church*

Bishop NOLAN B. HARMON, *Bishop of the North Alabama Conference of the Methodist Church*

GEORGE M. MURRAY, D.D., LL.D., *Bishop Coadjutor, Episcopal Diocese of Alabama*

EDWARD V. RAMAGE, *Moderator, Synod of the Alabama Presbyterian Church in the United States*

EARL STALLINGS, *Pastor, First Baptist Church, Birmingham, Alabama*

King was already a prominent civil rights leader, and the clergymen knew that he was in Birmingham and had been jailed. Yet they do not mention him, referring only to certain "outsiders." Instead, the clergymen address their remarks to the "responsible citizens" of Birmingham. The date on the letter places the momentous events in Birmingham precisely in the larger historical context of the civil rights movement. King's letter (printed in its entirety in Chapter 9) is dated just four days later.

Looking closely at the clergymen's titles, you can see that they represent the major American religious groups—Jewish, Catholic, and a range of Protestant denominations. Knowing this lets you know precisely who King means when he expresses his disappointment in "the church."

Other background information could also be brought to bear on a reading of King's letter. A general historical knowledge of the period and of the civil rights movement, particularly of the circumstances surrounding the Birmingham demonstrations, would be useful. It might help to know something about King's philosophy of nonviolent civil disobedience and to relate it to some of its sources—Christianity, the Western debate over the rights of individuals versus the rights of the state, the historical treatment of blacks and other minorities in the United States, and the tradition of civil disobedience from Socrates through Christ, Thoreau, and Gandhi.

You can learn about these historical and cultural contexts through reading and library research; the amount you do, of course, depends on how much time you have. You might begin by consulting an encyclopedia under civil disobedience, the civil rights movement, or Martin Luther King, Jr. Other possible sources on any of these subjects can be found by consulting the subject card catalog for books, the *Reader's Guide to Periodical Literature* or a specialized index like *America: History and Life* for journal articles, and *The New York Times Index* for newspaper articles.

## What Else Can I Discover by Skimming the Text?

Before reading a selection carefully, you should skim it to get a sense of what it is about and how it is organized. Skimming is especially useful for long and complicated texts with many headings, subheadings, charts, and figures. Many shorter readings do not provide these cues, but it is still a good idea to look them over quickly in order to get an overview. This kind of superficial first reading is good preparation for a more thoughtful close reading and can also suggest a particular purpose or set of questions to explore while reading.

Even a short text can be informatively skimmed, particularly if you pay attention to the way it unfolds. Since authors often place forecasting and transitional phrases at the beginnings of paragraphs to orient the reader, it is easy to get an overview simply by looking at the first sentence of each paragraph. A quick survey of even a small portion of "Letter from Birmingham Jail" gives a good indication of the main points King takes up: Paragraph 2 indicates why he came to Birmingham; paragraph 3 gives his basic reason for being in Birmingham; paragraph 4 expands on his reasoning; paragraph 5 acknowledges his critics' attitude; and paragraph 6 explains steps in a nonviolent campaign.

If you continue looking quickly at the first sentence of each paragraph, you will be surprised to see how much you can learn about the contents and plan of the essay.

## A Checklist for Previewing

To orient yourself and get the most from your reading, try taking the following steps:

- Consider what you know about the author and how much you should trust him or her.
- Reflect on what the title suggests about the reading.
- Classify the text as to genre, and then speculate about what the piece will be like.
- Determine what the historical and cultural context indicates about the text.
- Skim the reading, noting your first impressions.

# *Annotating*

Previewing is valuable because it prepares you to read closely and critically, but the most fundamental of all critical reading strategies is annotating. As you will see, the strategies of outlining, summarizing, taking inventory, and analyzing an argument all grow out of and extend annotating. This process is essential to critical reading because it focuses your attention on the language of the text. As you read, annotate directly on the page, underlining key words, phrases, or sentences and writing comments or questions in the margins. You can also bracket important sections of the text, connect ideas with lines or arrows, and number related points in sequence. If writing on the text itself is impossible or undesirable to you personally, you can still write notes about the reading on a separate piece of paper.

Most readers annotate in layers, adding further annotations on second and third readings. Annotations can be light or heavy, depending on the reader's purpose and the difficulty of the material. Reading a textbook to prepare for an exam, for example, you might limit yourself to underlining (or highlighting with a colored marker) main ideas and defining new words in the margin. Analyzing a poem or story as a subject for an essay, on the other hand, you would almost certainly annotate more heavily, layering annotations from several readings. You may want to annotate some of the essays in this book heavily in order to analyze the strategies and processes each writer uses as well as to explore ideas and your reactions to them. Learning to read like a writer, you will find annotating to be an invaluable tool to use as you read.

The annotating process is demonstrated here with an excerpt from "Letter from Birmingham Jail." A complete argument in itself, this excerpt expresses King's disappointment in whites who did not support his campaign of nonviolent direct action. We have annotated this excerpt as if we had read only the King headnote on page 529 and the clergymen's letter reprinted earlier in this chapter. We began with three questions to focus the reading: As an outsider, how can King respond in a convincing way to these respected insiders? Will he attack them or show them respect? Will he rely on legal, personal, or historical arguments? The first time through the reading, we annotated with comments, reactions, and questions. Subsequent readings produced annotations of images and oppositions, definitions, and still more questions. In the margin, we outlined the main ideas of the excerpt. The questions that appear after the excerpt express our concluding reflections.

Read the excerpt first without looking at the annotations, and then reread slowly, paying attention to them. Remember that they were accumulated during several readings. The discussion that follows the excerpt comments on the annotations and disentangles the layers.

## An Annotated Reading:

### from *Letter from Birmingham Jail*, Martin Luther King, Jr.

**1. White moderates' shallow understanding and lukewarm acceptance a barrier to racial justice.**
**WCC?**
**KKK: white sheets, nooses, burning crosses—founded after Civil War—white supremacy by terror**

. . . My Christian and Jewish brothers . . . I must confess that over the past few years I have been gravely disappointed with the <u>white moderate</u>. I have almost reached the regrettable conclusion that the Negro's [great stumbling block in his stride toward freedom] is not the White Citizen's Counciler or the Ku Klux Klanner, but the white moderate, who is more devoted to <u>"order"</u> than to justice; who prefers a <u>negative peace</u> which is the <u>absence of tension</u> to a positive peace which is the presence of justice; who constantly says: "I agree with you in the goal you seek, but I cannot agree with your <u>methods</u> of direct action"; who paternalistically believes he can set the timetable for another man's freedom; who lives by a mythical concept of time and who constantly advises the Negro to wait for a "more convenient season." Shallow understanding from people of good will is more frustrating than absolute misunderstanding from <u>people of ill will.</u> [Lukewarm acceptance is much more bewildering than outright rejection.]

**forecasts his main arguments here**

**not sure I agree**

**White moderate— anyone who has not joined King's cause?**

I had hoped that the white moderate would understand that law and order exist for the purpose of establishing

**2. Tension is necessary for progress toward freedom.**

justice and that when they fail in this purpose they become the dangerously structured dams that block the flow of social progress. I had hoped that the white moderate would understand that the present tension in the South is a necessary phase of the transition from an obnoxious negative peace, in which the Negro passively accepted his unjust plight, to a substantive and positive peace, in which all men will respect the dignity and worth of human personality. Actually, we who engage in nonviolent

**Nice contrast of short and long sentences here . . . short ones give emphasis.**

direct action are not the creators of tension. We merely bring to the surface the hidden tension that is already alive. We bring it out in the open, where it can be seen and dealt with. Like a boil that can never be cured so long as it is covered up but must be opened with all its ugliness to the natural medicines of air and light, injustice

**Will light of human conscience and air of national opinion always produce justice?**

must be exposed, with all the tension its exposure creates, to the light of human conscience and the air of national opinion before it can be cured.

In your statement you assert that our actions, even though peaceful, must be condemned because they precipitate violence. But is this a logical assertion? Isn't this like condemning a robbed man because his possession of money precipitated the evil act of robbery? Isn't this like condemning Socrates because his unswerving commitment to truth and his philosophical inquiries precipitated the act by the misguided populace in which they made him drink hemlock? Isn't this like condemning Jesus because his unique God-consciousness and never-ceasing devotion to God's will precipitated the evil act of crucifixion? We must come to see that, as the federal courts have consistently affirmed, it is wrong to urge an individual to cease his efforts to gain his basic constitutional rights because the question may precipitate violence. Society must protect the robbed and punish the robber.

**Who was Socrates? Greek philosopher and teacher, 5th c. B.C. Why quote Socrates and Jesus?**

**3. Peaceful actions can be justified even if they result in violence.**

**Yes!**

**How did white moderates react to King's letter? Did it have any effect?**

I had also hoped that the white moderate would reject the myth concerning time in relation to the struggle for freedom. I have just received a letter from a white brother in Texas. He writes: "All Christians know that the colored people will receive equal rights eventually, but it is possible that you are in too great a religious hurry. It has taken Christianity almost two thousand years to accomplish what it has. The teachings of Christ take time to come to earth." Such an attitude stems from a tragic misconception of time, from the strangely irrational notion that there is something in the very flow of time that will inevitably cure all ills. Actually, time itself is neutral; it can be used either destructively or constructively. More

**4. Must take action now to ensure racial justice.**

"We" must be the white moderates. The clergymen who wrote the letter? Have they repented?

and more I feel that the people of ill will have used time much more effectively than have the people of good will. We will have to repent in this generation not merely for the hateful words and actions of the bad people but for the appalling silence of the good people. Human progress never rolls in on wheels of inevitability; it comes through the tireless efforts of men willing to be co-workers with God, and without this hard work, time itself becomes an ally of the forces of social stagnation. We must use time creatively, in the knowledge that the time is always ripe to do right. Now is the time to make real the promise of democracy and transform our pending national elegy into a creative psalm of brotherhood. Now is the time to lift our national policy from the quicksand of racial injustice to the solid rock of human dignity.

*stagnation:* not moving or flowing

Short words make this stand out.

lots of images: dams, boils, light, wheels, quicksand, rock

Was Birmingham unusual or like most other Southern cities in 1963?
5. two opposing groups of Negroes: complacent and violent

You speak of our activity in Birmingham as extreme.  5
At first I was rather disappointed that fellow clergymen would see my nonviolent efforts as those of an extremist. I began thinking about the fact that I stand in the middle of two opposing forces in the Negro community. One is a force of complacency, made up in part of Negroes who, as a result of long years of oppression, are so drained of self-respect and a sense of "somebodiness" that they have adjusted to segregation; and in part of a few middle-class Negroes, who because of a degree of academic and economic security and because in some ways they profit by segregation, have become insensitive to the problems of the masses. The other force is one of bitterness and hatred, and it comes perilously close to advocating violence. It is expressed in the various black nationalist groups that are springing up across the nation, the largest and best-known being Elijah Muhammad's Muslim movement. Nourished by the Negro's frustration over the continued existence of racial discrimination, this movement is made up of people who have lost faith in America, who have absolutely repudiated Christianity, and who have concluded that the white man is an incorrigible "devil."

Who was Elijah Muhammad?

6. King stands between complacent and violent Negro groups.

How did nonviolence become part of King's movement? Gandhi? Socrates?

I have tried to stand between these two forces, saying  6
that we need emulate neither the "do-nothingism" of the complacent nor the hatred and despair of the black nationalist. For there is the more excellent way of love and nonviolent protest. I am grateful to God that, through the influence of the Negro church, the way of nonviolence became an integral part of our struggle.

How were people trained for nonviolent direct action?

If this philosophy had not emerged, by now many  7
streets of the South would, I am convinced, be flowing with blood. And I am further convinced that if our white

**7. King's movement has prevented racial violence.**

*solace:* comfort
Did this scare tactic really work?

**8. Protest is a natural result of yearning for freedom.**

*Zeitgeist:* spirit of the times

**9. We need extremists for good causes.**

Amos: 8th c. B.C. Hebrew prophet
Paul: 1st c. Christian, now a Catholic saint
Luther: 16th c. German monk who founded Protestantism
Bunyan: 17th c. English preacher

brothers dismiss as "rabble-rousers" and "outside agitators" those of us who employ nonviolent direct action, and if they refuse to support our nonviolent efforts, millions of Negroes will, out of frustration and despair, seek solace and security in black-nationalist ideologies—a development that would inevitably lead to a frightening racial nightmare.

Oppressed people cannot remain oppressed forever.       8
The yearning for freedom eventually manifests itself, and that is what has happened to the American Negro. Something within has reminded him of his birthright of freedom, and something without has reminded him that it can be gained. Consciously or unconsciously, he has been caught up by the *Zeitgeist,* and with his black brothers of Africa and his brown and yellow brothers of Asia, South America and the Caribbean, the United States Negro is moving with a sense of great urgency toward the promised land of racial justice. If one recognizes this vital urge that has engulfed the Negro community, one should readily understand why public demonstrations are taking place. The Negro has many pent-up resentments and latent frustrations, and he must release them. So let him march; let him make prayer pilgrimages to the city hall; let him go on freedom rides—and try to understand why he must do so. If his repressed emotions are not released in nonviolent ways, they will seek expression through violence; this is not a threat but a fact of history. So I have not said to my people: "Get rid of your discontent." Rather, I have tried to say that this normal and healthy discontent can be channeled into the creative outlet of nonviolent direct action. And now this approach is being termed extremist.

But though I was initially disappointed at being categorized as an extremist, as I continued to think about the       9
matter I gradually gained a measure of satisfaction from the label. Was not Jesus an extremist for love; "Love your enemies, bless them that curse you, do good to them that hate you, and pray for them which despitefully use you, and persecute you." Was not Amos an extremist for justice: "Let justice roll down like waters and righteousness like an ever-flowing stream." Was not Paul an extremist for the Christian gospel: "I bear in my body the marks of the Lord Jesus." Was not Martin Luther an extremist: "Here I stand; I cannot do otherwise, so help me God." And John Bunyan: "I will stay in jail to the end of my days before I make a butchery of my conscience." And Abraham Lincoln: "This nation cannot survive half slave

Will creative extremism work in every situation? Did Lincoln and Jefferson consider themselves extremists?

and half free." And Thomas Jefferson: "We hold these truths to be self-evident, that all men are created equal . . ." So the question is not whether we will be extremists, but what kind of extremists we will be. Will we be extremists for hate or for love? Will we be extremists for the preservation of injustice or for the extension of justice? In that dramatic scene on Calvary's hill three men were crucified. We must never forget that all three were crucified for the same crime—the crime of extremism. Two were extremists for immorality, and thus fell below their environment. The other, Jesus Christ, was an <u>extremist for love, truth and goodness,</u> and thereby rose above his environment. Perhaps the South, the nation and the world are in dire need of creative extremists.

I had hoped that the white moderate would see this    10
need. Perhaps I was too optimistic; perhaps I expected too much. I suppose I should have realized that few members of the oppressor race can understand the deep groans and passionate yearnings of the oppressed race, and still fewer have the vision to see that injustice must be rooted

**10. Some whites have supported King.**

out by strong, persistent and determined <u>action.</u> I am thankful, however, that some of our white brothers in the South have grasped the meaning of this social revo-

**How did these whites help the civil rights movement?**

lution and committed themselves to it. They are still all too few in quantity, but they are big in quality. Some— such as Ralph McGill, Lillian Smith, Harry Golden, James McBride Dabbs, Ann Braden and Sarah Patton

**What did these people write?**

Boyle—have written about our struggle in eloquent and prophetic terms. Others have marched with us down nameless streets of the South. They have languished in filthy, roach-infested jails, suffering the abuse and brutality of policemen who view them as "dirty nigger-lovers." Unlike so many of their moderate brothers and sisters, they have recognized the urgency of the moment and sensed the need for powerful "action" antidotes to combat the disease of segregation.

**Where are the 8 clergymen now? What do they think now of their letter and their role in what happened?**
**What do my parents remember about these events and about the civil rights movement of the 1960s?**
**If this were 1963 and I were in Birmingham, what would I be thinking and doing?**
**Did King write his letter expecting immediate results, or was he just making a statement about racial prejudice?**
**Which earlier American writers did King admire?**

As you can see, the annotations on this excerpt are quite diverse. Reactions, comments, definitions, questions, and an outline, attending both to King's ideas and to his argumentative strategies and style, appear in the margin. Within the text itself, key words, phrases, and sentences are underlined, circled, bracketed, and boxed.

Layered annotations like these produce a comprehensive record of a critical reading, a record you can use in class discussion or writing. Such annotations can give you confidence that you understand what a writer is saying and how it is being said. By persisting with demanding, time-consuming annotations and rereadings, you will gradually master the critical reading strategies with which you can approach any difficult text confidently.

In the following analysis of the annotations, we comment separately on the marginal questions, definitions, reactions, outlining, and underlining. In this discussion, the numbers in parentheses indicate the paragraph number of the annotated text.

## Questions

Questions are the most notable aspect of the annotations: the more than twenty questions in the margins help focus the reading, identify needed information and definitions, and express confusion. These questions emerged gradually through several readings. Three questions were written even before the first reading, in the previewing stage. During the first reading, most of the questions reflecting lack of knowledge arose: WCC (1), Socrates (3), moderates' reaction (4), identity of white moderates (4), typicality of Birmingham (5), source of King's nonviolence (6), training for nonviolence (6), and identity and writings of whites who supported King (10). Questions written during later readings express doubts, reflections, and reactions. These appear at many points. The five concluding questions, written after the last reading, identify final reflections.

All these questions reflect an inquiring, critical reader, one who is willing to admit what he or she does not know and unwilling to accept passively a revered American's argument. This questioning stance can lead to useful reflection—and to questions that may later suggest topics for research and writing.

## Definitions

On our first reading, imagining ourselves to be college freshmen, we encountered several unfamiliar words and names; since none of them seemed essential to a general understanding of the reading, we did not stop to look them up. We did, however, write down impressions of the

Ku Klux Klan (1) and ask "Who was Socrates?" (3). During the second reading, we looked up words and people in an unabridged college dictionary: Ku Klux Klan (1), Socrates (3), stagnation (4), solace (7), *Zeitgeist* (8), Amos, Paul, Luther, and Bunyan (9). Identifying the individuals revealed that King is relying in part on a wide range of historical figures to support his argument. The dictionary did not provide definitions of White Citizen's Counciler (1) or Elijah Muhammad (5), but these could be tracked down in the library.

## Reactions

The annotations on this excerpt react to both ideas and style. Some annotations record agreement ("Yes!" in 3) or disagreement (1) with King's statements. At other times, annotations point out King's writing strategies, such as forecasting (1), contrast (5), or referring to authorities (3). Other annotations comment on aspects of his style: contrast of short and long sentences, with short sentences used for emphasis (2), short words for emphasis (4), and use of images (4). Within the text, several of King's attempts at concise, quotable statements are boxed (1, 3, 4, 8).

## Outlining Main Ideas

An outline of the sequence of main ideas appears in the margin as a series of numbered points, one point for each paragraph. The next section will examine this outline and discuss the strategy of outlining. We mention it here as a reminder that annotating leads naturally to outlining, which can join other annotations in the margin.

## Underlining

Knowing that we eventually wanted to make an inventory of images and oppositions (strategies illustrated later in this chapter), we bracketed images and underlined oppositions. These annotations enable us to produce the word and phrase lists that are essential for taking inventory.

## A Checklist for Annotating

To focus and sustain a critical reading, annotate as you read and reread. In the margin, write any

- questions
- comments and reactions
- definitions
- main ideas

On the reading itself, underline, circle, or box any

- special uses of language, such as images or oppositions
- features of style
- words to be defined or people and events to be identified

Each chapter of this book provides critical reading questions to guide you in annotating essays of the particular type treated in that chapter. In addition, a brief annotated selection appears in each chapter to introduce you to the special features of the genre and to demonstrate how your annotating can reflect the focus and scope of those special features.

# Outlining

Outlining may be a part of the annotating process, or it may be a separate critical reading activity that follows and extends your annotation of a text. Making an outline on a separate piece of paper is especially helpful when you need to remember the reading or when it is complicated and hard to follow.

When you write, you probably do some outlining to sort through and organize your ideas. In the same way, outlining as you read leads you to focus on a text's most important ideas, separating what is central from what is peripheral. Outlining also reveals just how the selection is organized and may help you identify any shortcomings in its organization or logic. Since it displays just the main points, an outline presents only the framework of an essay and hence is quite general, even abstract.

Outlining a reading is a two-step process. First, you must identify the main ideas. Look for the sequence of main points that carries the reading along. Some paragraphs may contain no main ideas, while others may contain one or more. Then, you should underline (or otherwise highlight) the main ideas on the text or list them in your own words in the margin.

In the King excerpt, the numbered list in the margin is a scratch, or informal, outline that captures the movement of King's argument and the main points of the essay. Though it is complete within the annotations, listing it separately enables us to see the framework of the reading more easily. The outline is printed here, slightly reworded for consistency:

1. White moderates' shallow understanding and lukewarm acceptance are a barrier to racial justice.

2. Tension is necessary for progress toward freedom.

3. Peaceful actions can be justified even if they result in violence.

4. People must take action now to ensure racial justice.

5. There are two opposing groups of Negroes: complacent and violent.

6. King stands between complacent and violent Negro groups.

7. King's movement has prevented racial violence.

8. Protest is a natural result of yearning for freedom.

9. We need extremists for good causes.

10. Some whites have supported King.

The main ideas are expressed in our own sentences. This outline captures the movement of King's argument and the main points of the essay. A later section in this chapter will demonstrate a more formal and specialized kind of outline that results from a logical analysis of an argument.

Scratch outlining adequately identifies the sequence of main ideas or events in all kinds of writing. It can increase your understanding of a difficult reading and ensure that you will remember it longer. As you attempt to produce the kinds of writing you read in this book, outlining will enable you to reflect on the decisions other writers have made about organizing and ordering their materials.

## Summarizing

Like outlining, summarizing unfamiliar or difficult information is an excellent way to learn from your reading and remember what you have read. Whereas annotating immerses you in a reading and outlining produces an overview, summarizing a reading gives you its essence. When you summarize a text, you handle the ideas and information not as the author did, but in your own way, in your own words. Writing a good summary is a test of intelligence and persistence, difficult but extraordinarily satisfying. When you finish a coherent summary, you know that you have mastered new material, reduced it to its essentials, and made it your own. Since summarizing is time-consuming and challenging, you should reserve it for material that is unusually hard to understand, perhaps material on which you will be tested or material about which you must write convincingly. Here is a plan which will help you summarize:

1. Read and reread the material, annotating as you go. At this stage you are trying to become thoroughly familiar with the material.

2. Identify the main ideas, either by making a scratch outline or by underlining the main ideas.

3. Write a summary that includes only the main ideas, not illustrations or examples or quotations, and make sure that it is coherent and reads smoothly. Although your summary will rely on key terms and concepts in the material, it must be stated entirely in your own words.

To summarize the King excerpt, for example:

> King expresses his disappointment with white moderates who, by opposing tension-producing nonviolent direct action, become a barrier to racial justice. He explains that tension is often necessary for social progress and that nonviolent direct action can be justified even if it results in violence. He argues that racial justice will come about only by taking action now. Responding to charges of extremism from white moderates, King claims that he has actually prevented extreme racial violence by directing the frustrations of oppressed blacks into nonviolent protest. He asserts that extremism for a good cause is justified.

This summary relies on key words from King's writing, but all the sentences are our own. We have abstracted the main ideas and woven them into a coherent summary.

There is no exact formula about how long a summary should be in relation to the original. Some readings are dense with new concepts, while others intersperse concepts with quotations, charts and tables, and illustrations. A summary should be long enough to present the main ideas coherently.

## Taking Inventory

Like outlining and summarizing, taking inventory builds on and extends annotating. Taking inventory involves analyzing and classifying your annotations, searching systematically for patterns in the text, and interpreting their significance. An inventory is basically a list. When you take inventory, you make various kinds of lists to explore their meaning. You will surely want to use this strategy when you are preparing to write about a reading, but you can also use it simply as a means of reading critically.

This section presents three basic kinds of inventories: (1) inventory of annotations to discover and interpret patterns, (2) inventory of oppositions to reveal contrasting perspectives within the text, and (3) inventory of figurative language to uncover the author's feelings and attitudes.

## Inventory of Annotations

Inventorying annotations is a three-step process:

1. First, examine your annotations for patterns or repetitions of any kind. Here are some possibilities:

   recurring images

   noticeable stylistic features

   repeated descriptions

   consistent ways of characterizing people or events and of defining terms

   repeated words and phrases

   repeated subjects or topics

   repeated examples or illustrations

   reliance on particular writing strategies

2. List and group the items in the pattern.
3. Finally, decide what the pattern indicates about the reading.

The patterns you discover will depend on the kind of reading you are analyzing and on the care and thoroughness of your annotations. In our annotations of the King excerpt, we noted several different patterns, including images, quotable statements, and authorities. In order to learn more about why King cited these particular authorities, we listed and grouped them as follows:

*Philosopher:* Socrates
*Religious leaders:* Jesus, Amos, Paul, Luther, and Bunyan
*Political leaders:* Lincoln and Jefferson

In an encyclopedia, we read the entry about each person on the list, trying to connect the individual's particular philosophy to King's criticism of moderates and his justification for tension-producing direct action. With just a little reading, we found enough material for a brief paper analyzing King's argumentative strategy of quoting and aligning himself with revered authorities. When you read King's complete letter, you will see that he relies on this strategy throughout the letter, mentioning and quoting many more authorities.

## Inventory of Oppositions

Another way to take inventory is to study the pattern of oppositions within the text. All texts carry within themselves voices of opposition. These voices may echo the views and values of critical readers the writer anticipates or predecessors to which the writer is responding in some way; they may even reflect the writer's own conflicting values. To fully understand a text's meaning and how it is carried in the language, you may need to look closely for such a dialogue of opposing voices within the text.

When we think of oppositions, we ordinarily think of polarities such as *yes* and *no, up* and *down, black* and *white, new* and *old.* Some oppositions, however, may be more subtle. The excerpt from the "Letter from Birmingham Jail" is rich in such oppositions: *moderate* versus *extremist, order* versus *justice, direct action* versus *passive acceptance, expression* versus *repression.* These oppositions are not accidental; and they form a significant pattern that gives a critical reader important information about the essay.

A careful reading will show that one of the two terms in an opposition is nearly always valued over the other. In the King passage, for example, *extremist* is valued over *moderate.* This preference for extremism is surprising. The critical reader should ask why, when white extremists like the Ku Klux Klan have committed so many outrages against blacks, King would prefer extremism. If King is trying to convince his readers to accept his point of view, why would he represent himself as an extremist? Moreover, why would a clergyman advocate extremism instead of moderation?

Only by studying the pattern of oppositions can you answer these questions. Then you will see that King sets up this opposition to force his readers to examine their own values and realize that they are in fact misplaced. Instead of working toward justice, he says, those who support law and order maintain the unjust status quo. Getting his readers to think of the white moderate as blocking rather than facilitating peaceful change brings them to align themselves with King and perhaps even embrace his strategy of nonviolent resistance.

Taking inventory of oppositions is a four-step method of analysis:

1. Divide a piece of paper in half lengthwise by drawing a line down the middle. In the left-hand column, list those words and phrases from the text that you think indicate oppositions. Enter in the right-hand column the word or phrase that is the opposite of each term in the left-hand column. You may have to paraphrase or even supply this opposite term if it is not stated directly in the text.

2. For each pair of terms, put an asterisk next to the one that seems to be preferred by the writer.

3. Study the list of preferred terms and identify what you think is the predominant system of values put forth by the text. Do the same for the other list, identifying the alternative system or systems of

values implied in the text. Take around ten minutes to describe the oppositions in writing.

4. To explore these conflicting points of view, write for about five minutes presenting one side, and then for another five minutes presenting the other side. Use as many of the terms from the list as you can—explaining, extending, and justifying the values they imply. You may also, if you wish, quarrel with the choice of terms on the grounds that they are slanted or oversimplify the issue.

The following inventory and analysis of the King excerpt demonstrates the four-step method for inventorying oppositions.

LISTING OPPOSITIONS. This list of oppositions with stars next to the author's preferred term in each pair demonstrates steps 1 and 2:

| | |
|---|---|
| white moderate | *extremist |
| order | *justice |
| negative peace | *positive peace |
| absence of justice | *presence of justice |
| goals | *methods |
| *direct action | passive acceptance |
| *exposed tension | hidden tension |
| *robbed | robber |
| *individual | society |
| *words | silence |
| *expression | repression |
| *extension of justice | preservation of injustice |
| *extremist for love, truth, and justice | extremist for immorality |

ANALYZING OPPOSITIONS. Step 3 produced the following description of the conflicting points of view:

In this reading, King addresses as "white moderates" the clergymen who criticized him. He sees the moderate position in essentially negative terms, whereas extremism can be either negative or positive. Moderation is equated with passivity, acceptance of the status quo, fear of disorder, perhaps even fear of any change. The moderates believe justice can wait, whereas law and order cannot. Yet, as King points out, there is no law and order for blacks who are victimized and denied their constitutional rights.

The argument King has with the white moderates is basically over means and ends. Both agree on the ends but disagree on the means that should be taken to secure those ends. What means are justified to achieve one's goals? How does one decide? King is willing to risk a certain amount of tension and disorder to bring about justice; he suggests that if progress is not made, more disorder, not less, is bound to result. In a sense King represents himself as a moderate caught between the two extremes—the white moderates' "do-nothingism" and the black extremists' radicalism.

At the same time, King substitutes the opposition between moderation and extremism with an opposition between two kinds of extremism, one for love and the other for hate. In fact, he represents himself as an extremist willing to make whatever sacrifices—and perhaps even to take whatever means—are necessary to reach his goal of justice.

CONSIDERING ALTERNATIVE POINTS OF VIEW. Step 4 entailed five minutes of writing exploring the point of view opposed to the author's and five more minutes of writing presenting King's possible response to this point of view:

> *The moderates' side:* I can sympathize with the moderates' fear of further disorder and violence. Even though King advocates nonviolence, violence does result. He may not cause it, but it does occur because of him. Moderates do not really advocate passive acceptance of injustice, but want to pursue justice through legal means. These methods may be slow, but since ours is a system of law, the only way to make change is through that system. King wants to shake up the system, to force it to move more quickly for fear of violence. That strikes me as blackmail, as bad as if he were committing violence himself. Couldn't public opinion be brought to bear on the legal system to move more quickly? Can't we elect officials who will change unjust laws and see that the just ones are obeyed? The *vote* should be the weapon in a democracy, shouldn't it?

> *King's possible response:* He would probably argue that this viewpoint is naive. One of the major injustices at that time was that blacks were prevented from voting, and no elected official would risk going against those who voted for him. King would probably agree that public opinion needs to be changed, that people need to be educated, but he would also argue that education is not enough when people are being systematically deprived of their legal rights. The very system of law that should protect people was being used as a weapon against blacks in the South. The only way to get something done is to shake people up, make them aware of the injustice they are allowing to continue. Seeing their own police officers committing violence should make people question their own values and begin to take action to right the wrongs.

## Inventory of Figurative Language

Inventorying can also be used to analyze figurative language patterns in a text. Figurative language (metaphor, simile, and symbol), which takes words literally associated with one object or idea and transfers them to another object or idea, communicates more than direct statement can convey. Such language enhances meaning because it embodies abstract ideas in vivid images. For example, King uses the image of a dam to express the abstract idea of the blockage of justice. Figurative language also enriches meaning by drawing upon a complex of feeling and association. Connotations associated with one thing are transferred to the other, as when King compares the injustice suffered by blacks to a boil. Most people associate boils with throbbing pain and would do almost anything to relieve the discomfort.

As oppositions indicate relations of contrast and difference, figures of speech indicate relations of resemblance and likeness. Here are definitions and examples of the most common figures of speech:

*Metaphor* implicitly compares two different things by identifying them with each other. For instance, when King calls the white moderate "the Negro's great stumbling block in his stride toward freedom," he does not mean that the white moderate literally trips the Negro who is attempting to walk toward freedom. The sentence makes sense only if understood figuratively: the white moderate trips up the Negro by frustrating every effort to eliminate injustice.

*Simile*, a more explicit form of comparison, uses the word *like* or *as* to signal the relation of two seemingly unrelated things. King uses simile when he says that injustice is "like a boil that can never be cured so long as it is covered up." This simile makes several points of comparison between injustice and a boil. It suggests that injustice is a disease of society as a boil is a disease of the body and that injustice, like a boil, must be exposed or it will fester and worsen.

*Symbolism* compares two things by making one stand for the other. King uses the white moderate as a symbol for supposed liberals and would-be supporters of civil rights who are actually frustrating the cause.

How these figures of speech are used in a text reveals something of the writer's feelings about the subject and attitude toward prospective readers. It may even suggest the writer's feelings about the act of writing itself. Taking inventory of patterns of figurative language can provide insight into the tone of the writing and the text's emotional effect on its readers.

Taking inventory of figurative language is a three-step procedure:

1. List all the figures of speech you find in the reading—metaphor, simile, and symbol.

2. Group the figures of speech that appear to express similar feelings and attitudes, and label each group.

3. Write for ten to fifteen minutes, exploring the meaning of these patterns.

The following inventory and analysis of the King excerpt demonstrates the three steps for inventorying figurative language.

LISTING FIGURES OF SPEECH. Step 1 produced this inventory:

order is a dangerously structured dam that blocks the flow

social progress should flow

stumbling block in the stride toward freedom

injustice is like a boil that can never be cured

the light of human conscience and air of national opinion

time is something to be used, neutral, an ally, ripe

quicksand of racial injustice

the solid rock of human dignity

human progress never rolls in on wheels of inevitability

men are co-workers with God

groups springing up

promised land of racial justice

vital urge engulfed

pent-up resentments

normal and healthy discontent can be channeled into the creative outlet of nonviolent direct action

root out injustice

powerful action is an antidote

disease of segregation

GROUPING FIGURES OF SPEECH. Step 2 yielded three groups:

*Sickness:* segregation is a disease; action is healthy, the only antidote; injustice is like a boil

*Underground:* tension is hidden; resentments are pent-up, repressed; injustice must be rooted out; extremist groups are springing up; discontent can be channeled into a creative outlet

*Blockage:* forward movement is impeded by obstacles—the dam, stumbling block; human progress never rolls in on wheels of inevitability; social progress should flow

EXPLORING PATTERNS. Step 3 entailed about ten minutes of writing to explore the meaning of the groups listed in step 2:

The patterns of blockage and underground suggest a feeling of frustration. Inertia is a problem; movement forward toward progress or upward toward the promised land is stalled. There seems to be a strong need to break through the resistance, the passivity, the discontent and to be creative, active, vital. These are probably King's feelings both about his attempt to lead purposeful, effective demonstrations and his effort to write a convincing letter.

The simile of injustice being like a boil links the two patterns of underground and sickness, suggesting something bad, a disease, is inside the people or the society. The cure is to expose, to root out, the blocked hatred and injustice and release the tension or emotion that has so long been repressed. This implies that repression itself is the evil, not simply what is repressed.

## A Checklist for Taking Inventory

To recapitulate, it is helpful when reading closely to make inventories of the following:

- your annotations, in order to summarize and expand your observations about the reading
- oppositions within the text, in order to discover the conversations taking place between the author and other writers and readers, and even between the author's own ideas and values
- figurative language, in order to uncover clues about the author's attitudes and feelings on the subject, the writing situation, and even about writing itself

# *Analyzing an Argument*

An argument is basically a group of statements that have a special relationship to one another: one of the statements (the claim or conclusion) is asserted as true on the basis of the other statements (reasons, evidence, or assumptions). Reading and thinking about argument critically requires first identifying the claim and the supporting statements and then evaluating the argument.

## Outlining the Parts of an Argument

In order to analyze an argument, you must first decide which statement is the claim and which statements support the claim. Cues within an argument sometimes indicate the role the various statements play. The following words or phrases signal that claims are being made: therefore, thus, then, it follows that, hence, (which) shows that, implies that, so, you see that, points to, as a result, one can conclude that, consequently, demonstrates that, suggests that. Other cues indicate that supporting statements are being presented: because, since, for the reason that, in view of, for, in the first place, given that, as shown by, assuming that, insofar as, first, second, the following reasons.

If an argument provides few or no cues, you can identify the role of the statements by asking certain questions. To identify the claim, ask: What point is the writer attempting to establish? What is being asserted as true? What is the writer trying to convince me of? To identify the supporting statements, ask: Why should I accept this claim as true? What reasons or evidence does the writer give for this claim? On what basis should I accept this claim?

When looking for cues in the excerpt from "Letter from Birmingham Jail," we found the word "conclusion" in the first paragraph: "I have almost reached the regrettable conclusion that the Negro's great stumbling block in his stride toward freedom is not the White Citizen's Counciler or the Ku Klux Klanner, but the white moderate . . . ." Once we had found this claim, we were able to identify the statements supporting it. Notice that the sentence continues with a series of *who* clauses that define characteristics of the white moderate. Since each *who* clause in the opening paragraph forecasts a reason developed in the following paragraphs, we concluded that each one could be restated as a *because* clause.

Following this analysis, we made an outline of King's argument, using Roman numerals for the claims, capital letters for the major supporting statements, and Arabic numerals for additional supporting reasons, evidence, or assumptions.

I. The Negro's great stumbling block in his stride toward freedom is . . . the white moderate
   A. *Because* the white moderate is more devoted to "order" than to justice (paragraph 2)
      1. Law and order should exist to establish justice
      2. Likens law and order to dangerously structured dams that block the flow of social progress
   B. *Because* the white moderate prefers a negative peace (absence of tension) to a positive peace (justice) (paragraph 2)
      1. The tension already exists
      2. It is not created by nonviolent direct action
      3. Boil simile: Compares society that does not eliminate injustice to a boil that hides its infections. Both can only be cured by exposure.
   C. *Because* even though the white moderate agrees with the goals, he does not support the means to achieve them (paragraph 3)
      1. Rebuts the argument that the means—nonviolent direct action—are wrong because they precipitate violence

       2. Analogy of the robbed man condemned because he had money
       3. Comparison with Socrates and Jesus
    D. *Because* the white moderate paternalistically believes he can set a timetable for another man's freedom (paragraph 4)
       1. Rebuts the white moderate's argument that Christianity will cure man's ills and man must wait patiently for that to happen
       2. Argues that time is neutral and that man must use time creatively for constructive rather than destructive ends
II. Creative extremism is preferable to moderation
    A. Classifies himself as a moderate (paragraphs 5–8)
       1. I stand between two forces: the white moderate's complacency and the Black Muslim's rage
       2. If nonviolent direct action were stopped, more violence, not less, would result
       3. "Millions of Negroes will, out of frustration and despair, seek solace and security in black-nationalist ideologies" (paragraph 7)
       4. Repressed emotions will be expressed—if not in nonviolent ways, then through violence (paragraph 8)
    B. Redefines himself as a "creative extremist" (paragraph 9)
       1. Extremism for love, truth, and goodness is creative extremism
       2. Identifies himself with creative extremists like Jesus, Amos, Paul, Martin Luther, John Bunyan, Abraham Lincoln, and Thomas Jefferson
    C. Not all white people are moderates, many are creative extremists (paragraph 10)
       1. Lists names of white writers
       2. Refers to white activists

## Evaluating an Argument

Once you have identified the claim and the supporting statements and have outlined the argument, you may begin to evaluate it. A successful argument appeals to the readers' sense of logic, their emotions, and their sense of the author's credibility. In evaluating an argument, you should examine how these appeals are made and decide how convincing they are. An argument need not make all three appeals, but those that do tend to be stronger and more convincing.

LOGICAL APPEAL. Logic refers to the way we make inferences or draw conclusions from supporting evidence. When judging the logic of an argument, you must decide three things: (1) whether the supporting evidence is reliable, (2) whether it is appropriate, and (3) whether the argument is consistent.

*Testing for Reliability.* By reliability, we mean simply that the supporting evidence is dependable, that you can rely on it. Some common kinds of supporting evidence and guidelines for judging their reliability follow:

*Facts* are based on actual experience or observation. The reliability of facts depends on their accuracy (they should not distort or misrepresent reality), completeness (they should not omit important details), and the trustworthiness of their sources (sources should be qualified and unbiased). King, for instance, asserts as fact that the American Negro will not wait much longer for racial justice (paragraph 8). His contemporaries might question the factuality of this assertion by asking: Is it true of all American Negroes? How much longer will they wait? How does King know what the American Negro will or will not do?

*Statistics* are often assumed to be factual but are really only interpretations of data. The reliability of statistical evidence depends on the comparability of the data (apples cannot be compared to oranges), the accuracy of the methods of gathering and analyzing data (representative samples should be used and variables accounted for), and the trustworthiness of the sources (sources should be qualified and unbiased). There are no statistics in the excerpt, but earlier in the essay King writes: "There have been more unsolved bombings in Negro homes and churches in Birmingham than in any other city in the nation" (paragraph 6 of the full version in Chapter 9). King's contemporaries were certainly aware that Birmingham had endured many bombings, even if they doubted the comparison. By not citing his source or stating actual figures, King gives hostile readers an excuse to doubt his authority.

*Examples and anecdotes* are primarily useful as illustrations and can be quite persuasive. A vivid example or gripping anecdote can bring home the point dramatically. The reliability of examples and anecdotes depends on their representativeness (whether they are truly typical and thus generalizable) and their specificity (particular details make them memorable). To illustrate what he means by black nationalist extremists, King refers in the excerpt to Elijah Muhammad's Muslim movement (paragraph 5). Conversely, in paragraph 9, he refers to Jesus, Paul, Martin Luther, and others as examples of good extremists. These examples clarify by specifying what King means when he distinguishes between extremism for hate and extremism for love.

*Comparisons and analogies* also serve as illustrations, and although they are not conclusive, they can be persuasive. Their reliability depends primarily on the closeness of the correspondence (the points of similarity must outweigh the points of difference). In paragraph 3, King uses a series of analogies comparing nonviolent protesters to a robbed man, to Socrates, and to Jesus. Critical readers might question, for example, the comparison between the protester and the robbed man since the former is active while the latter is passive. Nevertheless, the analogy serves to identify King and his supporters with innocent victims wrongly blamed for crimes committed against them.

*Authorities* can also be cited as support. The reliability of the authorities depends chiefly on the relevance and credibility of each particular authority. King cites authorities repeatedly throughout the essay. In this brief excerpt, for instance, he refers not only to religious leaders like Jesus and Martin Luther but also to American political leaders like Lincoln and Jefferson. These figures are highly respected, and King makes clear on what basis he associates himself with them.

*Testing for Appropriateness.* No matter how reliable the evidence is, it will not support the claim unless it is deemed appropriate under the particular circumstances. Readers make judgments all the time about the appropriateness of arguments when they consider whether the evidence really supports the claim. To judge appropriateness, ask yourself these questions: Does the support really lead me to accept the claim? If so, why? If not, why not?

King's use of examples, as indicated above, is appropriate for his readers, but they might give modern readers a problem. Not only were King's original audience certain to be familiar with figures like Elijah Muhammad and Jesus, but they were also sure to accept King's classification of these people as bad and good extremists. Because of their appropriateness, the examples served King's purpose by convincing readers that his nonviolent movement was the only real alternative to the violent Black Muslims.

*Testing for Consistency.* To be consistent, all the evidence must work together to support the claim. If any piece of evidence contradicts another, then the argument is inconsistent or contradictory. To judge the consistency of an argument, look for logical contradictions.

A critical reader might regard as contradictory King's characterizing himself first as a moderate between the forces of complacency and violence, and later as an extremist opposed to the forces of violence. Shifting terms or meanings of a central term often signals a contradiction. King attempts to reconcile this apparent contradiction by explicitly redefining extremism in paragraph 9.

EMOTIONAL APPEAL. By appealing to readers' emotions, the writer tries to excite readers and involve them emotionally in the argument. Sometimes, however, a writer may use slanted, highly charged language to manipulate the reader's emotions. Even though this kind of manipulative argument might seem convincing, it is unacceptable because it is unfair.

All words have connotations, associations that enrich their meaning. These connotations give words much of their emotional power. In the preceding paragraph, for example, the word *manipulate* arouses an emotional response as well as an intellectual one. Being manipulated implies being treated like a puppet. No one wants to be manipulated. We used this word to make readers see why manipulative arguments are unfair even if they seem to be convincing.

When you evaluate an argument's emotional appeal, you are basically asking yourself: Do I feel manipulated by this argument? Knowing that figurative language can arouse strong emotions and that arguments based on such language may be questionable, we asked ourselves just this question in regard to King's use of the dam metaphor in paragraph 2. This is what our question produced:

> When King equates law and order with dams, he is trying to change his readers' understanding of the situation. The dam metaphor represents law and order negatively rather than positively. Dams are holding places that serve a positive function but they can also be seen as obstacles that block the natural and free flow of water. When water is equated to social progress, the dams clearly become obstacles. Why he describes the dams as "dangerously structured" is unclear. Perhaps, he wants to suggest the possibility that they are a threat to safety and peace. This would be a surprising turn since dams are supposed to protect us. Also, since King is a minister writing to other clergymen, is there any connection between the words "dam" and "damn"? Anyway, the dam metaphor makes the white moderate, who thinks of himself as advancing the cause of justice by upholding law and order, see himself instead as actually blocking progress. It doesn't seem to be an unfair or manipulative use of language, though the implied threat could be seen as unfair.

ETHICAL APPEAL. Through this appeal, writers try to persuade readers to respect and believe them. Because readers may not know them personally or even by reputation, they must present an image of themselves in their writing that will gain their readers' confidence. This image cannot be made directly but must be made indirectly, through the arguments, language, and the system of values and beliefs implied in the writing.

One way to gauge the author's credibility is to identify the tone of the argument. Tone is concerned not so much with what is said as with how it is said. It conveys the writer's attitude toward the subject and toward the reader. By reading sensitively, you should be able to evaluate the writer's stance and attitude through the tone of the writing. To identify the tone, list whatever descriptive adjectives come to mind in response to either of these questions: How would you characterize the tone of this selection? Judging from this piece of writing, what kind of person does the author seem to be? Here is an answer to the second question, based on the excerpt from "Letter from Birmingham Jail":

> I know something about King from TV programs on the civil rights movement. But if I were to talk about my impression of him from this passage, I'd use words like patient, thoughtful, well educated, moral, confident. He doesn't lose his temper, but tries to convince his readers by making a case that is reasoned carefully and painstakingly. He's trying to change people's attitudes; no matter how annoyed he might be with them he treats them with respect. It's as if he believes that their hearts are right, but they're just confused. If he can just set them straight, everything will be fine. Of course, he also sounds a little pompous when he compares himself to Jesus and Socrates, and the threat he appears to make in paragraph 8 seems out of character. Maybe he's losing control of his self-image at those moments.

## A Checklist for Analyzing an Argument

To identify the claim, ask yourself,

- What point is the writer attempting to establish?
- What is being asserted as true?
- What is the writer trying to convince me of?

To identify the support, ask yourself,

- Why should I accept this claim as true?
- What reasons or evidence does the writer give for this claim?
- On what basis should I accept this claim?

To evaluate the logical appeal of an argument,

- Identify the kinds of support offered.
- Apply the test for reliability.
- Apply the tests for appropriateness and consistency.

To evaluate the emotional appeal of an argument, ask yourself,

- Do I feel manipulated by this argument?

To evaluate the ethical appeal of an argument, ask yourself,

- How would I characterize the tone of this argument?
- What kind of person does the author seem to be?

# CHAPTER TWO

## *Autobiography*

Everyone enjoys hearing a story. Nearly every day we encounter stories in one form or another—a friend's account of something that happened, a TV soap opera, a prime-time TV drama, a movie, a novel, a short story.

Autobiographers are storytellers too. They share their remembered experience of events, people, and places significant in their lives. This form of writing is important to both writers and readers. Writers value the way autobiography records and clarifies their experience. They treasure the insight that comes from exploring their personal histories through writing. Readers take special pleasure in the engaging stories offered in autobiography. They enjoy comparing others' lives to their own, and they savor the reflections on human experience such accounts inspire.

Autobiography is a centuries-old form of writing. Literary scholars have studied it respectfully, tracing its changes through time and describing its modern variations. The autobiographies of Benjamin Franklin, Frederick Douglass, Mark Twain, Henry Adams, Zora Neale Hurston, Richard Rodriguez, Maya Angelou, Lillian Hellman, and Russell Baker are important works of American literature.

In addition to its value to individual readers and writers and its importance as literary art, autobiography plays a role in documenting cultural and intellectual history. In business, the arts, and academic disciplines, influential persons describe in their autobiographies what it was like to engage in a particular kind of work and professional life. Here,

33

autobiography shades off into memoir, which is not so frankly personal as autobiography. Still, most memoirs reveal something of a person's values and character.

Participating in this ancient and valued form of writing, you will be creating art from your life, shaping a story that can give great pleasure to readers. By vividly recalling an important topic or event in your life, you may discover how it contributed to making you the person you are.

## A GUIDE TO READING AUTOBIOGRAPHICAL WRITING

Learning to recognize the basic features of autobiography will enable you to read this kind of writing more critically. This section presents a discussion of these basic features, an annotated essay, and a list of key questions to guide your reading of autobiography.

# *Basic Features of Autobiographical Writing*

Autobiography derives from a particular way of reflecting on experience. Relying on memory, autobiographers try to recall in detail what happened at key points in their lives; from these details they hope to discover the *meaning* of what happened. Their central purpose, then, is to discover meaning or significance in their experience and communicate it to their readers.

These readers expect to be shown how this personal meaning was arrived at, and they anticipate many of the features readers of novels expect. Consequently, autobiography must present the full story and include relevant details so that readers can imagine what happened, what things looked like, and who was there. Autobiographical writing thus includes the following features: *an engaging story, a vivid scene and memorable people,* and *autobiographical significance.*

AN ENGAGING STORY. Autobiographical essays tell an engaging, memorable story, usually one that has some tension or suspense: we are anxious to know what will happen. As a storyteller, the writer is careful to realize all the dramatic possibilities of the story—an engaging beginning, a pace that quickens or slows at appropriate places, and a satisfying ending. The writer also includes specific narrative actions, namely, people moving, talking, and gesturing.

Some autobiographical essays focus on events and are specifically organized around the story. Even autobiographies that focus on places or people, however, may be embedded with one or more brief stories or anecdotes.

A VIVID SCENE AND MEMORABLE PEOPLE.  Readers of autobiographical essays can readily imagine the scene and people. An autobiography may present a panoramic view of the whole scene, identifying several particular objects or people. Or it may focus closely on one object or person, providing many details of appearance, size, shape, color, or texture. An autobiography may also compare a person to similar or dissimilar persons. Writers of modern autobiography, in particular, may reconstruct conversations with people at the scene, resulting in dialogues like those found in novels.

Some autobiographical essays focus primarily on scenes or people and thus essentially consist of description of memorable places or significant individuals. But even essays concerned with narrating events nearly always depict the scene (or scenes) and the people present.

AUTOBIOGRAPHICAL SIGNIFICANCE.  Stories of remembered experiences may entertain and please readers, but that is not their primary purpose. Autobiographers write to understand their experience, to understand themselves. They seek meaning, and they want to share that meaning, knowing that readers will respond appreciatively because we are all constantly striving to understand our own lives.

Writers often state autobiographical significance directly by commenting on what seemed important in the events, scenes, or people they present to us. They may evaluate or judge what happened, examine it reflectively but inconclusively, or tell us confidently what they think it meant. Even if they state the significance directly in these ways, they will also imply it through the details they include in the essay. They may, however, let the story speak entirely for itself, refraining from any direct commentary about significance.

## An Annotated Reading:
### *Saving America from Herbert Hoover*, Russell Baker

We read autobiography primarily for the pleasure it provides, a pleasure not unlike that derived from novels or movies. We watch the story unfold, people move and talk, the scene become recognizable. We come to understand the unique life and times of the writer.

When reading the autobiography of someone's childhood and adolescence, we will probably compare our own life to the writer's. We may read the autobiography or memoirs of an American president or senator to learn specific cultural and historical information. We might even read the autobiographies of several scientists, artists, composers, or novelists to discover what they reveal about creativity. Whatever the purpose, reading autobiography provides the pleasure of looking in on another's life—and the simultaneous reward of reflecting on our own lives.

The following brief selection illustrates the basic features of autobiography. The selection has been annotated as it might have been by any critical reader. These annotations will enable you to note many of the important features of autobiography. Before you look at the annotations, however, read the selection all the way through to familiarize yourself with it.

The selection comes from Russell Baker's *Growing Up,* winner of the Pulitzer Prize for Autobiography in 1983. For many years Baker was a journalist for the *Baltimore Sun* and *The New York Times,* covering the White House, Congress, and national politics. Since 1962 he has written a column for the *Times,* meriting the Pulitzer Prize for Distinguished Commentary in 1979.

Baker was born in 1924 and grew up in small towns in Virginia and in the cities of Newark and Baltimore. When his father died, he and his mother and sister lived for a short time with his Uncle Allen and Aunt Pat. The incident described in this excerpt occurs at Uncle Allen's house when Baker was eight, a presidential election year when America was in the depths of a great economic depression. As you read, notice how Baker relies on dialogue and how he reveals the significance of this incident in his life.

## Saving America
## from Herbert Hoover

| | |
|---|---|
| Belleville a suburb or a small town? | Uncle Allen moved us out of Newark and up to Belleville in 1932. I liked Belleville. There were big grassy 1 |
| *canopied:* covered | lawns and streets canopied with trees. We lived on the first floor of a two-family house across the street from |
| contrast of rich and poor, Republicans and Democrats begins here | Public School Number 8. The landlady lived on the second floor. Aunt Pat detested her for being a landlady. The propertied classes ranked high in Aunt Pat's catalogue of natural enemies. |
| dramatic beginning— shouting, arguing— makes me curious | Coming in from play one evening at dusk, I heard Aunt 2 Pat shouting in the kitchen. |
| | "She's got her nerve!" 3 |

conflict between Pat and Allen

Uncle Allen tried his customary soothing refrain. 4
"Calm down now, Pat. Just calm down."

"Calm down! Not with that thing on the front door! 5
Jesus, Mary, and Joseph, Allen! What are the neighbors
going to think?"

I tiptoed outside to see what terrible thing was on the 6
front door. In fact there were two front doors side by side.

parlor/quarters—old-fashioned way to talk about a house

One opened directly into our parlor, the other opened
onto a staircase that led up to the landlady's quarters.
Our front door looked the same as always, but fixed to
the landlady's door was a large head-and-shoulders por-

*genial:* friendly

trait of a genial-looking man with hair parted down the
middle.

There was printing under the picture. I could read eas- 7
ily now. My mother had spent so much time teaching me

smart kid

to read that the principal at P.S. Number 8 had agreed
to let me skip second grade and go on to the third, which
didn't satisfy my mother, who thought I should have been
skipped at least to the fourth. Reading the material under
the picture gave me no trouble, but I couldn't understand
why it should anger Aunt Pat.

Hoover the only one described—contrast between his sweet looks and Pat's hatred of him

It identified the man in the picture as Herbert Hoover. 8
It said something to the effect that he should be reelected.
I studied the picture carefully and was impressed by the
gentleness of Herbert Hoover's expression. He had round,
chubby cheeks that reminded me of babies. He certainly
didn't look like a man to make your blood boil. I went

Uncle Allen a sexist— wants Pat to cook instead of engage in politics

back in the house, where Uncle Allen was trying to focus
Aunt Pat's mind on making supper.

"How can I cook with that damn thing on the front 9
door?" she cried.

people in the incident: Allen, Pat, Baker, his mother

My mother was sitting at the table smiling and enjoying 10
the excitement. As meekly as possible, I asked her,
"What's wrong about Herbert Hoover?"

"Great mother of God!" cried Aunt Pat. "You poor 11
child!" And she told me what was wrong about Herbert
Hoover. He was destroying America, that was one thing
wrong about him.

"Now just a second, Pat—" 12

But Uncle Allen's plea for calm was lost in the gale. 13
People were starving because of Herbert Hoover. My
mother was out of work because of Herbert Hoover. Men

list of problems in the Depression

were killing themselves because of Herbert Hoover, and
their fatherless children were being packed away into orphanages—Aunt Pat's dread of orphanages made this the
worst offense of all to her—because of Herbert Hoover.

"Now, Pat, be fair—" 14

How old are Pat and Allen? What do they look like? Is he older than she is? They must not have children.

"I'll be fair. I'm going to tear that thing off the front 15 door."

She was in motion now. Uncle Allen stepped between 16 her and the parlor. "You can't do that, Pat. It's her house. She has a right to put up a poster if she wants."

"We pay the rent that keeps her, it's our house too," 17 Aunt Pat roared, but for the first time she seemed ready to defer to Uncle Allen's sense of what was right.

Seeing that he had averted a crisis for the moment, 18 Uncle Allen adopted the foxy-grandpa style he sometimes used when he wanted to win a point by persuasion. Tak-ing a toothpick out of his vest pocket, he chewed it thoughtfully for the longest while, a gesture we all rec-ognized. He was thinking; he had an idea aborning. When all was silent, he smiled a canny smile and spoke in his deepest down-home southern drawl.

shows several specific actions—getting toothpick, chewing, smiling, drawling

*canny:* shrewd, clever

"Waal, Pat, I'll tell you," he said. "Down in Lancaster 19 Court House where I come from, we always liked to settle things peaceable. Kind of keep the blood cool, y'know. I remember one time old Mr. Charlie Nickens had a fight with a fellow down there whose cows kept getting into his orchard"—Uncle Allen remembered nothing of the sort. He was making it up out of the whole cloth, hoping to get Aunt Pat soothed sufficiently to get on with making the chipped-beef gravy for supper—"and old Mr. Nickens swore he was going to shoot the next cow he caught in there eating his apples off the ground, because he fed those apples to his hogs, you know. But I had a better idea. 'Lord, Mr. Nickens, you don't want to shoot that man's cows,' I told him. 'A hole in the fence is a two-way street. If his cows come over to your side, why don't you encourage your hogs to go over to his side and wallow around in his vegetable garden?' I think that's what we ought to do about Mr. Hoover out front."

slowest part

"I don't get it," said Aunt Pat. I didn't either. 20

"We've got a front door too," Uncle Allen said. "It's 21 a two-way street. Instead of tearing down her Hoover poster, why don't we get a Roosevelt poster and stick it up right alongside hers on our own door?"

lots of dialogue

Roosevelt won the election.

scene limited to kitchen until now

Aunt Pat was delighted with the idea. She headed for 22 the door.

"Where are you going, Pat?" he asked. 23

"To talk to the Dunleavys," she said. "I want to find 24 out where to get a Roosevelt poster."

"Can't it wait till after supper?" 25

It couldn't. Aunt Pat headed out to canvass the neigh- 26 bors. The Dunleavys, the O'Connells, the Quinns, the

all Irish names

*rabid:* fanatical

many contrasts of poor and rich

What a sexist!

information about characters mainly in what they say

eager kid

Why didn't Baker describe the trip? Or taping the poster?

tells significance of the event

upper level/lower level

Is he still one?
Story covers just a few hours of real time.

O'Learys. They were all rabid Democrats. One of them would guide her to the source of Franklin Roosevelt posters. We had no telephone; telephones were luxuries for the rich. She traveled from neighbor to neighbor in search of someone wise in the mechanics of politics and came back with the address of a storefront campaign office where posters were available free.

The office lay a mighty distance, down on Washington 27 Avenue, and we had no car. Cars were also luxuries for the rich. That was all right; Aunt Pat would walk.

"Supper," Uncle Allen pleaded. 28

My mother could cook the chipped beef, Aunt Pat 29 said, and have it ready on her return.

"It's dark," Uncle Allen said. "It's too far to go alone." 30

By now I was totally involved. I too wanted to save 31 America from Herbert Hoover. I wanted to defeat the landlady upstairs who lived off Uncle Allen's money. Above all I wanted to be part of the excitement. "I'll go with her," I cried.

Off we went. The walk seemed endless, the trip back 32 even longer, but when we returned and Aunt Pat taped the picture of Franklin Roosevelt to our front door I forgot exhaustion. I felt like a hero of liberty. I had discovered the joys of politics. If I had lived upstairs with the land-lady I would probably have become a hard-money Re-publican, but chance had put me on the lower level where the Depression stirred such passion that even a child could not resist. In my first venture into politics, I became a Roosevelt Democrat.

## Critical Reading Questions

Experienced critical readers read actively, with specific questions in mind that reflect their knowledge of the particular kind of writing they are considering. The following questions can guide your reading of the autobiographical essays in this chapter and of other autobiographical writing as well. These questions will enable you to increase your knowledge of how autobiographies work. This knowledge will, in turn, greatly bene-fit your own writing of autobiographical essays. As an example of how such questions can make your reading more purposeful and more focused, we have applied each one to the Baker piece.

1. *What is the story (or stories)?*

This is an easy but important question to answer, reminding you to identify the main story or the separate brief stories. Consider the basic narrative story line, noting how much of the essay is devoted to narrative and how much to other features—presenting the scene and people or commenting on significance. Also note, as a time frame for the essay, where the story begins and ends.

Baker's story is complete within just two or three hours of clock time, beginning as young Baker enters the house at dusk and ending when Pat tapes the Roosevelt poster to the door. Baker concentrates more on people and their interactions than on summarizing what happened. After the brief orientation in paragraph 1, he opens the incident with dramatic dialogue and concludes by stating the autobiographical significance.

2. *How does the writer present the story?*

As you gain more experience with autobiography in this chapter, you will gradually be able to answer this question more fully. Story is a complex feature of fictional and autobiographical texts, involving a good deal more than the simple narrative line, the basic statements that assert what happened.

To answer this question, notice as you read and reread an essay how the writer creates tension or suspense, making you anxious (or eager or just curious) to know what will happen. Observe how the writer uses dialogue and specific narrative action. Notice where the pace of the story seems to quicken or slow, and consider what the writer is doing at those points. Finally, decide whether the writer presents a full, comprehensive narrative, one that answers all your questions about what happened.

Baker creates interest immediately through the argument between Pat and Allen. We might think the incident concerns Pat and Allen, but Baker uses the story to disclose his own earliest memories of political awareness. Pat creates the drama through argument, self-assertion, and action; Baker joins in the crucial actions and is changed by them.

Throughout the selection, Baker relies on dialogue to present people and move the story along. He notes Uncle Allen's specific actions (paragraph 18) and slows the pace as Uncle Allen relates his small story (paragraph 19).

3. *What is the scene (or scenes)?*

Identify the scene or scenes in the essay. Notice the actual physical location for the event, person, or place. Observe the size of the scene. Consider whether the writer remains located in one scene or shifts from one scene to another. Decide which scene is the most important one in the essay.

Baker limits the scene to the kitchen and to the entrance of the house with its two doors, one to Allen and Pat's apartment, the other to the stairs leading to the landlady's apartment. He does not show us

Pat's search through the neighborhood for information about a Roosevelt poster, Pat and Baker's trip downtown, or the taping up of the poster.

4. *How does the writer present the scene?*

Consider first the point of view from which the writer presents the scene (or scenes), viewing it from one fixed position, moving through the scene, or alternating between fixed and moving points of view. Notice whether the writer provides a distant, panoramic view of the scene as well as a close-up view of particular objects in the scene. Notice the extent of the exact details provided—color, size, texture, location.

Reflect on what you have observed, and conjecture why the writer has presented the scene in just this way. Imagine the writer deciding what to leave out, what to put in, whether to mention an object or describe it in detail, whether to shift point of view and when to do it, whether to stay at a distance or move in close. Remember that the writer chose to present the scene in a way that would support his or her larger purpose of sharing personal meaning.

Baker orients us briefly to the neighborhood and the two-story house and then takes us inside to the kitchen. He goes to the entryway to describe the poster, then returns to the kitchen. Later, he goes downtown with Pat and then watches her tape the poster to the door. Keeping the focus on the political activity (the posters and the arguing), he describes only the Hoover poster and devotes most of the essay to the conversation between Allen and Pat. He does not describe the kitchen or the people (though he does describe them elsewhere in the book from which this selection comes). Baker observes, participates offstage (the trip downtown), and finally reflects on the personal significance of the incident.

5. *Who are the significant people?*

Notice how many people other than the writer play a role in the essay, and observe the relations of these people to the writer and to each other. Where are the antagonistic, the loving, and the indifferent relations?

Uncle Allen, Aunt Pat, Baker, and Baker's mother are the participants in this scene. The landlady and Hoover are absent antagonists, while Roosevelt, also absent, is an ally. Like Baker, his mother is only an observer of the kitchen conversation. Pat is angry about Hoover and resists Allen's attempts to keep her in the kitchen, yet everyone seems friendly, even loving.

6. *How does the writer present these people?*

Notice whether the writer describes people or merely identifies them. Observe the kind of description the writer offers: looks or dress, movements or gestures or postures, ways of talking. Consider how much the writer leaves to the reader to infer about the person and how much is offered directly.

From these observations, decide how successfully the writer has presented other people. Keep in mind that, except in autobiographical essays concerned mainly with significant other people, the writer will be the central figure, with other people having only minor roles. Do you want to know more about a person? Do you remain puzzled about a person even though the writer describes this person in some detail? Are you uncertain about the motives for a person's actions?

Baker describes no one but Hoover, but he does show people moving and talking. Dialogue is particularly important in this selection. From the dialogue, we can infer a great deal about Allen and Pat, especially their relationship and their political convictions.

7. *What do I learn about the writer, and how is the autobiographical significance disclosed?*

Consider all the cues available to you about the writer. What different kinds of information do you have about the writer? How much do you learn? What seems to be the significance for the writer of the event, person, or place?

Consider just how the writer discloses autobiographical significance in the material you are reading. Must you infer it, or is it stated? Are you satisfied that the writer has realized the significance? Is it possible the writer has distorted or overlooked certain personal meanings of the event, person, or place? In general, what can you conclude about the writer's handling of autobiographical significance?

Baker wants us to see the young Baker as bright (he skipped a grade and is able to read the Hoover poster), sociable, and eager for adventure and knowledge. At the end of the selection, Baker announces the significance of the incident: it introduced him to the joys of politics and made him a Roosevelt Democrat.

8. *In what ways does this piece lead me to reflect on my own experience?*

This quite personal question reminds you of your own interests in reading autobiography. You may be entertained by the essay, and you may learn something about another person. Even more important, you may find that the essay causes you to reflect on your own life. What events, persons, or places come to mind? What feelings do you remember? Does the writer remind you of other people you know?

The Baker essay might have caused you to think about your earliest awareness of politicians and political events. It might have led you to reflect on just how you arrived at your current political preferences. It might even have caused you to remember an aunt or uncle who influenced your life.

# Eudora Welty

An important American writer of the twentieth century, Eudora Welty (b. 1909) has been awarded the Pulitzer Prize (1973) and American Book Award for fiction and the Gold Medal for the Novel from the National Institute of Arts and Letters. Her major works include four collections of short stories (brought together in *The Collected Stories of Eudora Welty*, 1980) and several novels, including *Delta Wedding* (1946), *The Ponder Heart* (1954), *Losing Battles* (1970), and *The Optimist's Daughter* (1972). She has published a collection of photographs entitled *One Time, One Place* (1971) that she took in Mississippi during the 1930s when she worked in the Depression years' Works Progress Administration. She has also published many essays, reviews, and critical articles.

# *Miss Duling*

Welty was born in the Jackson, Mississippi, house in which she still lives. In this selection from her autobiography, *One Writer's Beginnings* (1984), she recalls the principal of the grammar school across the street from her house. Although the selection focuses on Miss Duling, it also reveals a great deal about Welty and her family. Welty is not simply reporting on Miss Duling; she is probing Miss Duling's impact on her own life. Anticipating this selection, you might want to recall teachers or principals who have been important in your life. How would you present one of them in writing? What would you want readers to know about the significance of this person in your life? Knowing that Welty writes short stories and novels, how would you predict she might present the real-life Miss Duling?

As you read, notice how Welty presents Miss Duling and what Welty learns about herself by remembering the place the principal occupied in her life.

From the first I was clamorous to learn—I wanted to know and begged    1
to be told not so much what, or how, or why, or where, as when. How soon?

> Pear tree by the garden gate,
> How much longer must I wait?

This rhyme from one of my nursery books was the one that spoke for me. But I lived not at all unhappily in this craving, for my wild curiosity was in large part suspense, which carries its own secret pleasure. And so one of the godmothers of fiction was already bending over me.

44

When I was five years old, I knew the alphabet, I'd been vaccinated 2
(for smallpox), and I could read. So my mother walked across the street
to Jefferson Davis Grammar School and asked the principal if she would
allow me to enter the first grade after Christmas.

"Oh, all right," said Miss Duling. "Probably the best thing you could 3
do with her."

Miss Duling, a lifelong subscriber to perfection, was a figure of au- 4
thority, the most whole-souled I have ever come to know. She was a
dedicated schoolteacher who denied herself all she might have done or
whatever other way she might have lived (this possibility was the last
that could have occurred to us, her subjects in school). I believe she
came of well-off people, well-educated, in Kentucky, and certainly old
photographs show she was a beautiful, high-spirited-looking young lady—
and came down to Jackson to its new grammar school that was going
begging for a principal. She must have earned next to nothing; Mississippi
then as now was the nation's lowest-ranking state economically, and our
legislature has always shown a painfully loud reluctance to give money
to public education. That challenge *brought* her.

In the long run she came into touch, as teacher or principal, with 5
three generations of Jacksonians. My parents had not, but everybody
else's parents had gone to school to her. She'd taught most of our leaders
somewhere along the line. When she wanted something done—some
civic oversight corrected, some injustice made right overnight, or even
a tree spared that the fool telephone people were about to cut down—
she telephoned the mayor, or the chief of police, or the president of the
power company, or the head doctor at the hospital, or the judge in charge
of a case, or whoever, and calling them by their first names, *told* them.
It is impossible to imagine her meeting with anything less than compli-
ance. The ringing of her brass bell from their days at Davis School would
still be in their ears. She also proposed a spelling match between the
fourth grade at Davis School and the Mississippi Legislature, who went
through with it; and that told the Legislature.

Her standards were very high and of course inflexible, her authority 6
was total; why *wouldn't* this carry with it a brass bell that could be heard
ringing for a block in all directions? That bell belonged to the figure of
Miss Duling as though it grew directly out of her right arm, as wings
grew out of an angel or a tail out of the devil. When we entered, marching, into her school, by strictest teaching, surveillance, and order we
learned grammar, arithmetic, spelling, reading, writing, and geography;
and she, not the teachers, I believe, wrote out the examinations: need
I tell you, they were "hard."

She's not the only teacher who has influenced me, but Miss Duling,   7
in some fictional shape or form, has stridden into a larger part of my
work than I'd realized until now. She emerges in my perhaps inordinate
number of schoolteacher characters. I loved those characters in the writing. But I did not, in life, love Miss Duling. I was afraid of her high-
arched bony nose, her eyebrows lifted in half-circles above her hooded,
brilliant eyes, and of the Kentucky R's in her speech, and the long steps
she took in her hightop shoes. I did nothing but fear her bearing-down
authority, and did not connect this (as of course we were meant to) with
our own need or desire to learn, perhaps because I already had this wish,
and did not need to be driven.

She was impervious to lies or foolish excuses or the insufferable plea   8
of not knowing any better. She wasn't going to have any frills, either,
at Davis School. When a new governor moved into the mansion, he
sent his daughter to Davis School; her name was Lady Rachel Conner.
Miss Duling at once called the governor to the telephone and told him,
"She'll be plain Rachel here."

Miss Duling dressed as plainly as a Pilgrim on a Thanksgiving poster   9
we made in the schoolroom, in a longish black-and-white checked
gingham dress, a bright thick wool sweater the red of a railroad lantern—
she'd knitted it herself—black stockings and her narrow elegant feet in
black hightop shoes with heels you could hear coming, rhythmical as a
parade drum down the hall. Her silky black curly hair was drawn back
out of curl, fastened by high combs, and knotted behind. She carried
her spectacles on a gold chain hung around her neck. Her gaze was in
general sweeping, then suddenly at the point of concentration upon you.
With a swing of her bell that took her whole right arm and shoulder,
she rang it, militant and impartial, from the head of the front steps of
Davis School when it was time for us all to line up, girls on one side,
boys on the other. We were to march past her into the school building,
while the fourth-grader she nabbed played time on the piano, mostly to
a tune we could have skipped to, but we didn't skip into Davis School.

Little recess (open-air exercises) and big recess (lunch-boxes from   10
home opened and eaten on the grass, on the girls' side and the boys' side
of the yard) and dismissal were also regulated by Miss Duling's bell. The
bell was also used to catch us off guard with fire drill.

It was examinations that drove my wits away, as all emergencies do.   11
Being expected to measure up was paralysing. I failed to make 100 on
my spelling exam because I missed one word and that word was "uncle."
Mother, as I knew she would, took it personally. "You couldn't spell
*uncle*? When you've got those five perfectly splendid uncles in West
Virginia? What would *they* say to that?"

It was never that Mother wanted me to beat my classmates in grades; 12 what she wanted was for me to have my answers right. It was unclouded perfection I was up against.

My father was much more tolerant of possible error. He only said, as 13 he steeply and impeccably sharpened my pencils on examination morning, "Now just keep remembering: the examinations were made out for the *average* student to pass. That's the majority. And if the majority can pass, think how much better *you* can do."

I looked to my mother, who had her own opinions about the majority. 14 My father wished to treat it with respect, she didn't. I'd been born left-handed, but the habit was broken when I entered the first grade in Davis School. My father had insisted. He pointed out that everything in life had been made for the convenience of right-handed people, because they were the majority, and he often used "what the majority wants" as a criterion for what was for the best. My mother said she could not promise him, could not promise him at all, that I wouldn't stutter as a consequence. Mother had been born left-handed too; her family consisted of five left-handed brothers, a left-handed mother, and a father who could write with both hands at the same time, also backwards and forwards and upside down, different words with each hand. She had been broken of it when she was young, and she said she used to stutter.

"But you still stutter," I'd remind her, only to hear her say loftily, 15 "You should have heard me when I was your age."

In my childhood days, a great deal of stock was put, in general, in the 16 value of doing well in school. Both daily newspapers in Jackson saw the honor roll as news and published the lists, and the grades, of all the honor students. The city fathers gave the children who made the honor roll free season tickets to the baseball games down at the grandstand. We all attended and all worshiped some player on the Jackson Senators: I offered up my 100's in arithmetic and spelling, reading and writing, attendance and, yes, deportment—I must have been a prig!—to Red McDermott, the third baseman. And our happiness matched that of knowing Miss Duling was on her summer vacation, far, far away in Kentucky.

## QUESTIONS FOR ANALYSIS

1. Welty chooses a bell as the symbol of Miss Duling's authority. Skim the selection and decide what use Welty makes of the bell each time it appears.

2. How does Welty illustrate Miss Duling's authority in the community?

3. Welty does not mention Miss Duling at all in paragraphs 11–15 and not until the last sentence in paragraph 16, about a third of the total selection. What is Welty doing in these paragraphs? What relation do they have to her presentation of Miss Duling in the other parts of the selection?

4. How would you describe Welty's attitude toward Miss Duling? Point to specific evidence in the selection to support your answer.

5. How does Welty present Miss Duling's physical appearance? Underline each visual detail, specific movement or gesture, and quoted statement. Take inventory of these references to identify Welty's choices and strategy. (See Chapter 1 for a discussion of taking inventory.)

6. What do you learn about Welty in this selection? How does she disclose the significance of Miss Duling in her life?

## SUGGESTIONS FOR WRITING

1. Recall some of the people who have been significant in your own life. Select one of these people, and write an essay describing this person and showing how he or she was significant for you.

2. Write an essay about someone you know well right now. Identify this individual's chief character trait, and illustrate it with several anecdotes.

3. Which teacher has contributed most to your intellectual development? Write an essay presenting this teacher through characterization and anecdote to explain why this teacher was so influential.

# Richard Feynman

Richard Feynman was born in 1918 in Far Rockaway, New York, near New York City. During the 1940s he was part of the group that developed the atomic bomb. Since 1946 he has taught physics at Cornell University and the California Institute of Technology, where he is professor of theoretical physics. In 1965 he won the Nobel Prize for physics. Feynman has published several books and many research reports. Among physicists, he is best known for his contributions to solving problems of quantum electrodynamics, beta decay, and liquid helium.

## *He Fixes Radios by Thinking*

This selection comes from Feynman's autobiography, *Surely You're Joking, Mr. Feynman.* The title of the book comes from the response of a college dean's wife to Feynman's clumsy request for both cream and lemon in his tea.

Fascinated with electricity and all kinds of electrical gadgets, Feynman became an expert at repairing radios when he was only twelve, in 1930, at the beginning of the Depression. In this selection, he describes this phase in his life, when he became known in his town as the kid who could fix anything wrong with a radio.

Writers of book-length autobiographies commonly describe phases in their lives telling how they changed or what they learned during a certain period of weeks or months. The phase has a point—the autobiographical significance of the change or learning—and it usually focuses on just a few important incidents.

As you read, notice how Feynman selects and arranges important incidents. Notice too how he presents the significance of this phase. What does he learn about himself during this time in his life, and how does he convey it to the reader?

I enjoyed radios. I started with a crystal set that I bought at the store, 1 and I used to listen to it at night in bed while I was going to sleep, through a pair of earphones. When my mother and father went out until late at night, they would come into my room and take the earphones off—and worry about what was going into my head while I was asleep.

About that time I invented a burglar alarm, which was a very simple- 2 minded thing: it was just a big battery and a bell connected with some wire. When the door to my room opened, it pushed the wire against the battery and closed the circuit, and the bell would go off.

One night my mother and father came home from a night out and ₃
very, very quietly, so as not to disturb the child, opened the door to
come into my room to take my earphones off. All of a sudden this
tremendous bell went off with a helluva racket—BONG BONG BONG
BONG BONG!!! I jumped out of bed yelling, "It worked! It worked!"

I bought radios at rummage sales. I didn't have any money, but it ₄
wasn't very expensive—they were old, broken radios, and I'd buy them
and try to fix them. Usually they were broken in some simple-minded
way—some obvious wire was hanging loose, or a coil was broken or partly
unwound—so I could get some of them going. On one of these radios
one night I got WACO in Waco, Texas—it was tremendously exciting!

On this same tube radio up in my lab I was able to hear a station up ₅
in Schenectady called WGN. Now, all of us kids—my two cousins, my
sister, and the neighborhood kids—listened on the radio downstairs to a
program called the Eno Crime Club—Eno effervescent salts—it was *the*
thing! Well, I discovered that I could hear this program up in my lab on
WGN one hour before it was broadcast in New York! So I'd discover
what was going to happen, and then, when we were all sitting around
the radio downstairs listening to the Eno Crime Club, I'd say, "You know,
we haven't heard from so-and-so in a long time. I betcha he comes and
saves the situation."

Two seconds later, *bup-bup*, he comes! So they all got excited about ₆
this, and I predicted a couple of other things. Then they realized that
there must be some trick to it—that I must know, somehow. So I owned
up to what it was, that I could hear it upstairs the hour before.

You know what the result was, naturally. Now they couldn't wait for ₇
the regular hour. They all had to sit upstairs in my lab with this little
creaky radio for half an hour, listening to the Eno Crime Club from
Schenectady.

We lived at that time in a big house; it was left by my grandfather to ₈
his children, and they didn't have much money aside from the house. It
was a very large, wooden house, and I would run wires all around the
outside, and had plugs in all the rooms, so I could always listen to my
radios, which were upstairs in my lab. I also had a loudspeaker—not the
whole speaker, but the part without the big horn on it.

One day, when I had my earphones on, I connected them to the ₉
loudspeaker, and I discovered something: I put my finger in the speaker
and I could hear it in the earphones; I scratched the speaker and I'd hear
it in the earphones. So I discovered that the speaker could act like a
microphone, and you didn't even need any batteries. At school we were
talking about Alexander Graham Bell, so I gave a demonstration of the

speaker and the earphones. I didn't know it at the time, but I think it was the type of telephone he originally used.

So now I had a microphone, and I could broadcast from upstairs to 10 downstairs, and from downstairs to upstairs, using the amplifiers of my rummage-sale radios. At that time my sister Joan, who was nine years younger than I was, must have been about two or three, and there was a guy on the radio called Uncle Don that she liked to listen to. He'd sing little songs about "good children," and so on, and he'd read cards sent in by parents telling that "Mary So-and-so is having a birthday this Saturday at 25 Flatbush Avenue."

One day my cousin Francis and I sat Joan down and said that there 11 was a special program she should listen to. Then we ran upstairs and we started to broadcast: "This is Uncle Don. We know a very nice little girl named Joan who lives on New Broadway; she's got a birthday coming— not today, but such-and-such. She's a cute girl." We sang a little song, and then we made music: "*Deedle leet deet, doodle doodle loot doot; deedle deedle leet, doodle loot doot doo . . .*" We went through the whole deal, and then we came downstairs: "How was it? Did you like the program?"

"It was good," she said, "but why did you make the music with your 12 mouth?"

One day I got a telephone call: "Mister, are you Richard Feynman?" 13
"Yes." 14
"This is a hotel. We have a radio that doesn't work, and would like 15 it repaired. We understand you might be able to do something about it."
"But I'm only a little boy," I said. "I don't know how—" 16
"Yes, we know that, but we'd like you to come over anyway." 17
It was a hotel that my aunt was running, but I didn't know that. I 18 went over there with—they still tell the story—a big screwdriver in my back pocket. Well, I was small, so *any* screwdriver looked big in my back pocket.

I went up to the radio and tried to fix it. I didn't know anything about 19 it, but there was also a handyman at the hotel, and either he noticed, or I noticed, a loose knob on the rheostat—to turn up the volume—so that it wasn't turning the shaft. He went off and filed something, and fixed it up so it worked.

The next radio I tried to fix didn't work at all. That was easy: it wasn't 20 plugged in right. As the repair jobs got more and more complicated, I got better and better, and more elaborate. I bought myself a milliammeter in New York and converted it into a voltmeter that had different scales on it by using the right lengths (which I calculated) of very fine copper wire. It wasn't very accurate, but it was good enough to tell whether things were in the right ballpark at different connections in those radio sets.

The main reason people hired me was the Depression. They didn't 21 have any money to fix their radios, and they'd hear about this kid who would do it for less. So I'd climb on roofs to fix antennas, and all kinds of stuff. I got a series of lessons of ever-increasing difficulty. Ultimately I got some job like converting a DC set into an AC set, and it was very hard to keep the hum from going through the system, and I didn't build it quite right. I shouldn't have bitten that one off, but I didn't know.

One job was really sensational. I was working at the time for a printer, 22 and a man who knew that printer knew I was trying to get jobs fixing radios, so he sent a fellow around to the print shop to pick me up. The guy is obviously poor—his car is a complete wreck—and we go to his house which is in a cheap part of town. On the way, I say, "What's the trouble with the radio?"

He says, "When I turn it on it makes a noise, and after a while the 23 noise stops and everything's all right, but I don't like the noise at the beginning."

I think to myself: "What the hell! If he hasn't got any money, you'd 24 think he could stand a little noise for a while."

And all the time, on the way to his house, he's saying things like, 25 "Do you know anything about radios? How do you know about radios— you're just a little boy!"

He's putting me down the whole way, and I'm thinking, "So what's 26 the matter with him? So it makes a little noise."

But when we got there I went over to the radio and turned it on. 27 Little noise? *My God!* No wonder the poor guy couldn't stand it. The thing began to roar and wobble—WUH BUH BUH BUH BUH—A *tremendous* amount of noise. Then it quieted down and played correctly. So I started to think: "How can that happen?"

I start walking back and forth, thinking, and I realize that one way it 28 can happen is that the tubes are heating up in the wrong order—that is, the amplifier's all hot, the tubes are ready to go, and there's nothing feeding in, or there's some back circuit feeding in, or something wrong in the beginning part—the RF part—and therefore it's making a lot of noise, picking up something. And when the RF circuit's finally going, and the grid voltages are adjusted, everything's all right.

So the guy says, "What are you doing? You come to fix the radio, but 29 you're only walking back and forth!"

I say, "I'm thinking!" Then I said to myself, "All right, take the tubes 30 out, and reverse the order completely in the set." (Many radio sets in those days used the same tubes in different places—212s, I think they were, or 212-As.) So I changed the tubes around, stepped to the front of the radio, turned the thing on, and it's as quiet as a lamb: it waits until it heats up, and then plays perfectly—no noise.

When a person has been negative to you, and then you do something 31 like that, they're usually a hundred percent the other way, kind of to compensate. He got me other jobs, and kept telling everybody what a tremendous genius I was, saying, "He fixes radios by *thinking*!" The whole idea of thinking, to fix a radio—a little boy stops and thinks, and figures out how to do it—he never thought that was possible.

Radio circuits were much easier to understand in those days because 32 everything was out in the open. After you took the set apart (it was a big problem to find the right screws), you could see this was a resistor, that's a condenser, here's a this, there's a that; they were all labeled. And if wax had been dripping from the condenser, it was too hot and you could tell that the condenser was burned out. If there was charcoal on one of the resistors you knew where the trouble was. Or, if you couldn't tell what was the matter by looking at it, you'd test it with your voltmeter and see whether voltage was coming through. The sets were simple, the circuits were not complicated. The voltage on the grids was always about one and a half or two volts and the voltages on the plates were one hundred or two hundred, DC. So it wasn't hard for me to fix a radio by understanding what was going on inside, noticing that something wasn't working right, and fixing it.

Sometimes it took quite a while. I remember one particular time when 33 it took the whole afternoon to find a burned-out resistor that was not apparent. That particular time it happened to be a friend of my mother, so I *had* time—there was nobody on my back saying, "What are you doing?" Instead, they were saying, "Would you like a little milk, or some cake?" I finally fixed it because I had, and still have, persistence. Once I get on a puzzle, I can't get off. If my mother's friend had said, "Never mind, it's too much work," I'd have blown my top, because I want to beat this damn thing, as long as I've gone this far. I can't just leave it after I've found out so much about it. I have to keep going to find out ultimately what is the matter with it in the end.

## QUESTIONS FOR ANALYSIS

1. Feynman begins his description of this phase with two brief incidents involving his parents. Why do you think he begins in this way?

2. List the specific incidents that Feynman selects to illustrate this significant phase in his life. Given what he wants to reveal about himself during this phase, how do you assess his selection of incidents? Do all

the incidents reveal the same thing about Feynman? Why do you think he sequenced the incidents as he did?

3. Which incident did you find most interesting and memorable? Why is it your favorite?

4. Feynman does not describe scenes or people, but he does use reconstructed dialogue effectively. Skim the essay, looking for dialogue. When does Feynman use dialogue, and with what results?

5. What does Feynman say he learned about himself during this phase in his life? Where and how does he reveal this?

6. From what he says and does, what impression do you get of the young Feynman? What kind of a twelve-year-old was he? Support your answer by referring to specific parts of the selection.

## SUGGESTIONS FOR WRITING

1. Think about phases in your childhood or adolescence during which you learned something new, something that has influenced your life. Write a brief essay about one such phase, presenting specific incidents that will help your readers see what you learned and why it was important to you.

2. Consider phases during which significant changes occurred in your life. Perhaps your parents divorced, or you moved to a new city or neighborhood, were seriously ill, took your first part-time job, or experienced a religious conversion. Choose one of these phases, and write a brief essay describing what happened, how you changed, and how the change significantly influenced your life.

# Richard Rodriguez

Richard Rodriguez (b. 1944) describes himself as "a full-time writer." He is also a popular lecturer. His essays have appeared in *The American Scholar, College English*, and *Change* magazine. An autobiography of his school years, *Hunger of Memory: The Education of Richard Rodriguez* (1982), won the Christopher Award.

# Gains and Losses

The following selection is an excerpt from Rodriguez's autobiography, *Hunger of Memory, written* when he was in his middle thirties.

At the age of seven, speaking only Spanish, Rodriguez started school at a Catholic elementary school in Sacramento, California. His teachers spoke only English and expected him to learn—and use—English immediately. Writing as an adult, Rodriguez tells the story of these first months in school, revealing not only their significance in his life but also his views on bilingual education in American schools. This controversial program permits students to use languages other than English in school and to be taught in their own language, while also learning to speak English.

As you read, notice how Rodriguez and other members of his family changed during his first months in school.

Supporters of bilingual education today imply that students like me   1
miss a great deal by not being taught in their family's language. What they seem not to recognize is that, as a socially disadvantaged child, I considered Spanish to be a private language. What I needed to learn in school was that I had the right—and the obligation—to speak the public language of *los gringos*. The odd truth is that my first-grade classmates could have become bilingual, in the conventional sense of that word, more easily than I. Had they been taught (as upper-middle-class children are often taught early) a second language like Spanish or French, they could have regarded it simply as that: another public language. In my case such bilingualism could not have been so quickly achieved. What I did not believe was that I could speak a single public language.

Without question, it would have pleased me to hear my teachers ad-   2
dress me in Spanish when I entered the classroom. I would have felt much less afraid. I would have trusted them and responded with ease. But I would have delayed—for how long postponed?—having to learn the language of public society. I would have evaded—and for how long

could I have afforded to delay?—learning the great lesson of school, that I had a public identity.

Fortunately, my teachers were unsentimental about their responsi-   3
bility. What they understood was that I needed to speak a public language. So their voices would search me out, asking me questions. Each
time I'd hear them, I'd look up in surprise to see a nun's face frowning
at me. I'd mumble, not really meaning to answer. The nun would persist,
'Richard, stand up. Don't look at the floor. Speak up. Speak to the entire
class, not just to me!' But I couldn't believe that the English language
was mine to use. (In part, I did not want to believe it.) I continued to
mumble. I resisted the teacher's demands. (Did I somehow suspect that
once I learned public language my pleasing family life would be changed?)
Silent, waiting for the bell to sound, I remained dazed, diffident, afraid.

Because I wrongly imagined that English was intrinsically a public   4
language and Spanish an intrinsically private one, I easily noted the
difference between classroom language and the language of home. At
school, words were directed to a general audience of listeners. ('Boys and
girls.') Words were meaningfully ordered. And the point was not self-
expression alone but to make oneself understood by many others. The
teacher quizzed: 'Boys and girls, why do we use that word in this sentence?
Could we think of a better word to use there? Would the sentence change
its meaning if the words were differently arranged? And wasn't there a
better way of saying much the same thing?' (I couldn't say. I wouldn't
try to say.)

Three months. Five. Half a year passed. Unsmiling, ever watchful, my   5
teachers noted my silence. They began to connect my behavior with the
difficult progress my older sister and brother were making. Until one
Saturday morning three nuns arrived at the house to talk to our parents.
Stiffly, they sat on the blue living room sofa. From the doorway of another
room, spying the visitors, I noted the incongruity—the clash of two
worlds, the faces and voices of school intruding upon the familiar setting
of home. I overheard one voice gently wondering, 'Do your children
speak only Spanish at home, Mrs. Rodriguez?' While another voice
added, 'That Richard especially seems so timid and shy.'

*That Rich-heard!*   6

With great tact the visitors continued, 'Is it possible for you and your   7
husband to encourage your children to practice their English when they
are home?' Of course, my parents complied. What would they not do for
their children's well-being? And how could they have questioned the
Church's authority which those women represented? In an instant, they
agreed to give up the language (the sounds) that had revealed and ac-
centuated our family's closeness. The moment after the visitors left, the

change was observed. '*Ahora*, speak to us *en inglés*,' my father and mother united to tell us.

At first, it seemed a kind of game. After dinner each night, the family 8 gathered to practice 'our' English. (It was still then *inglés*, a language foreign to us, so we felt drawn as strangers to it.) Laughing, we would try to define words we could not pronounce. We played with strange English sounds, often over-anglicizing our pronunciations. And we filled the smiling gaps of our sentences with familiar Spanish sounds. But that was cheating, somebody shouted. Everyone laughed. In school, meanwhile, like my brother and sister, I was required to attend a daily tutoring session. I needed a full year of special attention. I also needed my teachers to keep my attention from straying in class by calling out, *Rich-heard*— their English voices slowly prying loose my ties to my other name, its three notes, *Ri-car-do*. Most of all I needed to hear my mother and father speak to me in a moment of seriousness in broken—suddenly heartbreaking—English. The scene was inevitable: One Saturday morning I entered the kitchen where my parents were talking in Spanish. I did not realize that they were talking in Spanish however until, at the moment they saw me, I heard their voices change to speak English. Those *gringo* sounds they uttered startled me. Pushed me away. In that moment of trivial misunderstanding and profound insight, I felt my throat twisted by un-sounded grief. I turned quickly and left the room. But I had no place to escape to with Spanish. (The spell was broken.) My brother and sisters were speaking English in another part of the house.

Again and again in the days following, increasingly angry, I was obliged 9 to hear my mother and father: 'Speak to us *en inglés*.' (*Speak*.) Only then did I determine to learn classroom English. Weeks after, it happened: One day in school I raised my hand to volunteer an answer. I spoke out in a loud voice. And I did not think it remarkable when the entire class understood. That day, I moved very far from the disadvantaged child I had been only days earlier. The belief, the calming assurance that I belonged in public, had at last taken hold.

Shortly after, I stopped hearing the high and loud sounds of *los gringos*. 10 A more and more confident speaker of English, I didn't trouble to listen to *how* strangers sounded, speaking to me. And there simply were too many English-speaking people in my day for me to hear American accents anymore. Conversations quickened. Listening to persons who sounded eccentrically pitched voices, I usually noted their sounds for an initial few seconds before I concentrated on *what* they were saying. Conversations became content-full. Transparent. Hearing someone's *tone* of voice—angry or questioning or sarcastic or happy or sad—I didn't distinguish it from the words it expressed. Sound and word were thus tightly wedded. At the end of a day, I was often bemused, always relieved, to realize how 'silent,' though crowded with words, my day in public had been. (This public silence measured and quickened the change in my life.)

At last, seven years old, I came to believe what had been technically  11 true since my birth: I was an American citizen.

But the special feeling of closeness at home was diminished by then.  12 Gone was the desperate, urgent, intense feeling of being at home; rare was the experience of feeling myself individualized by family intimates. We remained a loving family, but one greatly changed. No longer so close; no longer bound tight by the pleasing and troubling knowledge of our public separateness. Neither my older brother nor sister rushed home after school anymore. Nor did I. When I arrived home there would often be neighborhood kids in the house. Or the house would be empty of sounds.

Following the dramatic Americanization of their children, even my  13 parents grew more publicly confident. Especially my mother. She learned the names of all the people on our block. And she decided we needed to have a telephone installed in the house. My father continued to use the word *gringo*. But it was no longer charged with the old bitterness or distrust. (Stripped of any emotional content, the word simply became a name for those Americans not of Hispanic descent.) Hearing him, some-times, I wasn't sure if he was pronouncing the Spanish word *gringo* or saying gringo in English.

Matching the silence I started hearing in public was a new quiet at  14 home. The family's quiet was partly due to the fact that, as we children learned more and more English, we shared fewer and fewer words with our parents. Sentences needed to be spoken slowly when a child addressed his mother or father. (Often the parent wouldn't understand.) The child would need to repeat himself. (Still the parent misunderstood.) The young voice, frustrated, would end up saying, 'Never mind'—the subject was closed. Dinners would be noisy with the clinking of knives and forks against dishes. My mother would smile softly between her remarks; my father at the other end of the table would chew and chew at his food, while he stared over the heads of his children.

My *mother*! My *father*! After English became my primary language, I  15 no longer knew what words to use in addressing my parents. The old Spanish words (those tender accents of sound) I had used earlier—*mamá* and *papá*—I couldn't use anymore. They would have been too painful reminders of how much had changed in my life. On the other hand, the words I heard neighborhood kids call *their* parents seemed equally unsat-isfactory. *Mother* and *Father; Ma, Papa, Pa, Dad, Pop* (how I hated the all-American sound of that last word especially)—all these terms I felt were unsuitable, not really terms of address for *my* parents. As a result, I never used them at home. Whenever I'd speak to my parents, I would try to get their attention with eye contact alone. In public conversations, I'd refer to 'my parents' or 'my mother and father.'

My mother and father, for their part, responded differently, as their children spoke to them less. She grew restless, seemed troubled and anxious at the scarcity of words exchanged in the house. It was she who would question me about my day when I came home from school. She smiled at small talk. She pried at the edges of my sentences to get me to say something more. (What?) She'd join conversations she overheard, but her intrusions often stopped her children's talking. By contrast, my father seemed reconciled to the new quiet. Though his English improved somewhat, he retired into silence. At dinner he spoke very little. One night his children and even his wife helplessly giggled at his garbled English pronunciation of the Catholic Grace before Meals. Thereafter he made his wife recite the prayer at the start of each meal, even on formal occasions, when there were guests in the house. Hers became the public voice of the family. On official business, it was she, not my father, one would usually hear on the phone or in stores, talking to strangers. His children grew so accustomed to his silence that, years later, they would speak routinely of his shyness. (My mother would often try to explain: Both his parents died when he was eight. He was raised by an uncle who treated him like little more than a menial servant. He was never encouraged to speak. He grew up alone. A man of few words.) But my father was not shy, I realized, when I'd watch him speaking Spanish with relatives. Using Spanish, he was quickly effusive. Especially when talking with other men, his voice would spark, flicker, flare alive with sounds. In Spanish, he expressed ideas and feelings he rarely revealed in English. With firm Spanish sounds, he conveyed confidence and authority English would never allow him. [16]

The silence at home, however, was finally more than a literal silence. Fewer words passed between parent and child, but more profound was the silence that resulted from my inattention to sounds. At about the time I no longer bothered to listen with care to the sounds of English in public, I grew careless about listening to the sounds family members made when they spoke. Most of the time I heard someone speaking at home and didn't distinguish his sounds from the words people uttered in public. I didn't even pay much attention to my parents' accented and ungrammatical speech. At least not at home. Only when I was with them in public would I grow alert to their accents. Though, even then, their [17] sounds caused me less and less concern. For I was increasingly confident of my own public identity.

I would have been happier about my public success had I not sometimes 18 recalled what it had been like earlier, when my family had conveyed its intimacy through a set of conveniently private sounds. Sometimes in public, hearing a stranger, I'd hark back to my past. A Mexican farmworker approached me downtown to ask directions to somewhere. '¿Hijito . . . ?' he said. And his voice summoned deep longing. Another time, standing beside my mother in the visiting room of a Carmelite convent, before the dense screen which rendered the nuns shadowy figures, I heard several Spanish-speaking nuns—their busy, singsong overlapping voices—assure us that yes, yes, we were remembered, all our family was remembered in their prayers. (Their voices echoed faraway family sounds.) Another day, a dark-faced old woman—her hand light on my shoulder—steadied herself against me as she boarded a bus. She murmured something I couldn't quite comprehend. Her Spanish voice came near, like the face of a never-before-seen relative in the instant before I was kissed. Her voice, like so many of the Spanish voices I'd hear in public, recalled the golden age of my youth. Hearing Spanish then, I continued to be a careful, if sad, listener to sounds. Hearing a Spanish-speaking family walking behind me, I turned to look. I smiled for an instant, before my glance found the Hispanic-looking faces of strangers in the crowd going by.

QUESTIONS FOR ANALYSIS

1. Change—and its gains and losses—is the theme of this essay. What is the autobiographical significance of Rodriguez's change? How does he reveal this significance?

2. What contrast seems most important in this selection? How does Rodriguez develop this contrast throughout the essay?

3. How many people play roles in this selection? List them, and consider Rodriguez's strategy in presenting each person. Given his purpose in the essay, what advantages or disadvantages do you see in his way of presenting each person?

4. What kind of voice do you hear in this selection? How is it like or unlike the voice in the Feynman selection? How do the two writers achieve these voices? What produces the voice in each selection?

5. Feynman relies on a sequence of specific incidents to present his radio-repairing phase. How would you describe Rodriguez's strategy for presenting his public-language–learning phase?

6. Both Rodriguez and Feynman use dialogue, but they insert it into their texts in different ways. What is the difference? What advantages or disadvantages do you see in the two different ways of using dialogue?

7. In his sentences, Rodriguez makes notable use of dashes and parentheses. Analyze the use of dashes first and then the use of parentheses. What does Rodriguez accomplish in his sentences with each of these types of punctuation?

## SUGGESTIONS FOR WRITING

1. Consider phases of your life in which you changed in some significant way, a change with both gains and losses. Write an essay about one of these phases, describing what happened and how you changed, weighing the gains and losses, and evaluating the autobiographical significance of the change.

2. Think about phases of schooling or training in which you learned something important about a subject or skill, as well as about yourself. Write an essay about this phase, describing what you learned and how you learned it and disclosing the autobiographical significance of this learning.

# Susan Allen Toth

Susan Allen Toth (b. 1940) grew up in small-town Ames, Iowa, during the 1940s and 1950s. Since 1969 she has taught in the English Department at Macalester College in St. Paul, Minnesota. She has published two autobiographies, *Blooming: A Small-Town Girlhood* (1981) and *Ivy Days: Growing Up Back East* (1984).

# Blaine's Pool

Autobiographers write about significant events and people, as Baker, Welty, Feynman, and Rodriguez do. They also write about memorable, meaningful places. Previewing this selection, you see immediately from the title that it focuses on a remembered place, a local public swimming pool to which Toth and her girlfriends returned again and again each summer. How might Toth present this place vividly to her readers? If you were to write about a pool, playground, or other place you used to visit frequently, how would you describe it? Looking back on these visits to the pool from her perspective as a grown woman in *Blooming: A Small-Town Girlhood*, Toth remembers what happened there and what it meant to her. As you read, notice how she presents this place and discloses its autobiographical significance.

Even the setting of Blaine's Pool made it a place apart. Outside the city limits, it was dug out of the ground in a small hollow surrounded by a scraggly woods and a dirty, meandering river. Blaine's had a remote air about it, a kind of isolation. As one of our mothers drove, very carefully, down a steep hill that curved sharply, we heard the noise of splashing and confused shouts, screams, and the lifeguard's whistle before we could see the pool itself. We bounced up and down on the back seat, giggling and chattering in high-pitched voices, until the mother, made nervous by the hot rods that zoomed past her up the hill, snapped crossly. We subsided and clutched our rolled-up bathtowels in anticipation.

As we pulled into the parking lot, where the mother would pick us up a few hours later, we all strained to see what faces we could make out at the poolside, in the bleachers, or at the pop stand. Much of our anticipation depended on just this uncertainty. Who was here? Would Bob O'Brien and Lon Sell have already come? Or gone? Were we too late? Or too early? Was that Tommy Sandvig on the diving board? The mother was probably glad to escape from our gasps, pointings and smothered cries. No matter whose mother she was, though, she never commented on this aspect of the swimming pool ritual. By eleven or twelve, we were all expected to have boyfriends, or at least to want to have them. Blaine's Pool was a proper place to find them.

I sometimes think I learned about sex at Blaine's Pool. Oh, not the ³ hard facts (it was years before I knew what they really were, and there are still some days when I don't feel too sure). So what jagged bits of knowledge did I take home from Blaine's, along with a bent locker key and someone's used Tangee orange lipstick, rescued from the dressing-room floor? Mostly stinging bits of intense physical sensation. Looking back to those green, dreaming summers, I always think of blistering heat and ice-cold water. Some afternoons, when I couldn't go to Blaine's, I sat in my shorts and halter in our steaming living room, damply reading, feeling the old wool upholstery of the comfy Morris chair rub against my thighs, while I sucked and chewed on ice cubes and balanced the glass, painfully cold, on my knee for as long as I could stand it. That was the kind of intensity I felt at Blaine's. Emerging from the shaded dressing room, I always blinked, temporarily blinded, in the dazzling light that reflected from the white bleachers, shining metal slides, and of course the glittering blue water. It was as though all the colors had been turned up just a bit too bright.

As the sun beat down on my head, shoulders and thighs, I had to ⁴ decide how to get into the water. It was inviting, but very cold. So my friends and I edged gingerly into the shallow end, stepping daintily down the little children's steps, and then began rubbing our tummies cautiously with the cold water. We seldom got the chance to edge much farther, because by that time one of the boys saw us. Whooping and splashing, he leaped into the water, scooping up water with the palm of his hand in a practiced, skidding gesture, covering our exaggerated screams with shock waves. By the time the lifeguard blew his whistle and shook a finger at us, we were wet, initiated, ready to paddle down to the deep end and continue the Blaine's ritual. Some afternoons I was braver. Standing for only a few moments on the pool's edge, before anyone could push me in, I looked down and anticipated with a delicious shudder how the water would feel, closing over me in a total embrace. Then I jumped. For one brief moment as I went under I wondered if I would ever come up again. Then I surfaced, blowing, laughing, and waited for the others to join me.

Then, of course, we swam. We girls never did laps, and we seldom ⁵ even swam in a straight line. Instead we darted back and forth, moving to parts of the pool where someone we hoped would notice us had last dived in. As we hung, treading water, chatting together in brief gasps, Tommy or Bob or Lon glided under water toward us, often in twos or threes, as though they needed support. We girls pretended not to notice them coming until they spouted to the top, with loud shouts, and pounced on us to dunk us. The lifeguards were supposed to stop any horseplay (a sign by the pool read: "No running. No bottles by the pool. NO HORSEPLAY."). But they usually looked the other way at such simple stuff as dunking. Being shoved under water was recognized as a sign that a boy had noticed you. He had at least taken the trouble to push you down. We certainly never complained, though I sometimes swallowed water and came up coughing. At other times the boys would ignore us and engage in their own elaborate games, diving for pennies or playing tag. We girls clung to the side, hanging on to the gutters, and watched.

When I grew older, I heard for the first time about something called    2
the battle of the sexes. It brought to mind an image that would doubtless seem ludicrously inappropriate to Millett or Mailer, but that's because neither one of them ever held on for dear life to the giant tops at Blaine's Pool.

Once there must have been two tops; one rusting anchor was still    3
fastened to the bottom, a melancholy reminder of summers long gone. But by the time I was there, only one top was left intact, and we all wrestled and struggled to be among the few its surface could hold. The top was maybe six feet in diameter, with a steering wheel at the center that you turned to make the top revolve as you stood on its slanting, slippery surface. It spun on a slightly askew axis, so that as you turned the wheel faster, and the top whirled faster, it was harder and harder to hang on. The boys always had control of the steering wheel; at least, they felt they had a right to it, so that if we girls climbed on board when the top was empty, they soon spied us from wherever they were in the pool and came splashing noisily over to assume charge. Those of us girls who were sturdy, not easily scared off, or perhaps a bit foolhardy, stayed on the top. As the boys turned the wheel, we clung to whatever part of its metal rim we could grab. Faster and faster it spun, and before long girls would begin to fall off, like bits of spray dashed away from a fierce centrifugal force. Even a boy or two might lose hold, pretending, if possible, that he had just decided to dive from the edge, or that he wanted to jump on one of the girls who had just fallen off, cannonballing on top of her.

Whoever stayed on the top longest won. When competition got down    4
to the last two swimmers, anything was acceptable, from prying someone's fingers off the wheel to tripping and pushing. The boys had fewer inhibitions about those tactics, and consequently one of them always won. I wish I could say I was often one of the last girls to leave the top,

but I wasn't. I got dizzy quickly, and, stomach churning, ended up gulping mouthfuls of chlorine as I tumbled ignominiously into the water.

Climbing out, waterlogged, I felt heavy and washed out, so tired I forgot to hold in my stomach as I walked away. Stretching out on a wooden bleacher, I closed my eyes and listened to the shouting and splashing, which seemed dimmer and far away, even though the pool was just a few feet off. With dulled vision, I occasionally squinted at the swimmers hurrying along the pool deck to see who was still in action. But I was warm, drying, and strangely invisible. I can still feel how comforting the sun seemed then, how blissfully tired and somehow virtuous I felt, worn out by all my social exertions. As I shifted position, very carefully, I could feel the rough grain of the wood. The paint was worn off in many spots, and once when I moved too fast, I got a splinter in my hand. There I lay in the sun and baked, letting time pass over me.

When I finally got up, I could look down and see damp cool stains on the wood where I had been. Tired, but still anxious to extract the last bit of possible pleasure from the afternoon, I jumped in quickly. Soon we had to trudge to the dressing room; it was almost time for the mother to return.

Not everything connected with Blaine's Pool is illuminated in my memory with the blinding glare of sun and water. Though it was by day filled with open games, battles on the top, flirtations in the water, Blaine's Pool was reputed to be quite another sort of place at night. Its hidden location, surrounded by trees, naturally made it a favorite spot for "parking," or so the stories went. None of us girls had ever parked anywhere yet, so we didn't know. But sometimes, floating on my back in a quiet moment, I would look up at the overhanging trees and wonder. Occasionally a lifeguard left his post for a few minutes and walked over to the rattly stands placed just outside the pool enclosure for observers. Once I saw the guard talking to a pretty girl with red lipstick who stood, casually brushing back her hair, on the lowest step. After a bit he returned to his chair, and she left. I thought they were probably arranging to meet later that night, somewhere in the trees.

This suggestive air of illicit sex that hung over the pool, or so I thought, crystallized for me one late afternoon when we were still halfheartedly messing about in the almost empty pool. Most of the boys had gone home. Among the stragglers were an older girl with long black hair and lots of curves that owed nothing to elastic, and her boyfriend, who we knew was a football player on the high-school team. They were swimming lazily in the deep end, diving under water, tagging and laughing. As I bounced on the bottom of the shallow end, wondering if I

could rub out the seat of the new swimsuit I now hated, Peggy O'Reilly
came striding through the water toward me as fast as she could. "Susan!"
she said breathlessly. "Guess what! I just saw Cindy and Steve! Do you
know what they were *doing?*" No, I said, I didn't know. "Well," she
announced with a sense of real importance, "they were *kissing under
water.*" We were both silent. With one instinct, we turned to look at
the deep end. Holding hands, Cindy and Steve were climbing out of the
water. They walked toward the dressing rooms, and we watched them
until they passed out of sight.

Soon we too left the pool. Dressing hurriedly in a tiny cubicle, I kept    9
a close watch on the floor. A few of the booths had gaps in the floor-
boards, and a few weeks earlier they had caught some boys underneath
the girls' dressing room, peering up. If you dressed in the open, walled
section, where the sun could dry your hair, you had to look above the
wall toward the trees. Sometimes a few boys shinnied up the trunks in
order to be able to get a good view. It is only now as I remember these
small terrors, our automatic precautions, that I realize with surprise we
never dreamed of invading the boys' dressing room in return.

After we were all ready, we turned in our locker baskets and rolled    10
our damp suits in our towels. Then we loitered around the pop stand,
hung on the fence, or made patterns in the dust with our sneakers, talking
about everyone we'd seen that day and what he had done and what we
had said in return. The mother was later than she'd promised. I walked
around the pool enclosure to the bleachers near the trees. The ground
was littered with torn popcorn boxes, green Coke bottles, and candy
wrappings. The grass there and under the trees was sparse and brown. It
was hard to imagine anyone wanting to linger there, even at night. When
I finally heard a horn honk, impatiently, I was glad to hurry over to the
parking lot and squeeze comfortably into the back seat with my friends.

Whatever impressions I soaked in with the chlorine or sun . . . must    11
have stained me somewhere ineradicably. For ever since then, at bad
times I have headed, like a lemming, to the water. When in pain, I can
be found in a pool. Perhaps the noise of yelling children reminds me of
happy afternoons at Blaine's, or perhaps I am obscurely pleased that I no
longer need to be part of that boisterous group and that I can just swim,
by myself, with my own thoughts. I don't know. Last summer, when a
man I had much loved and I suddenly parted, I fled the house every
afternoon at five for the new municipal pool in the city where I now
live. This pool is much bigger than Blaine's; quite an impressive place,
and at that hour the guards cordon off lengths for laps. I felt the tightness
in my chest and stomach begin to ease the minute I stepped out of my
car and saw that huge pool, almost empty, waiting for me. A few swim-

mers, whom I didn't know, already churned up and down the black lines: company, without the responsibility of conversation. They might comment on the weather, or the temperature of the water, but they wouldn't know or care about what I was feeling. As I undressed in the shower room, I could pat my snug, now familiar body, to reassure myself that it was still there.

Once in the pool, doing my laps, I felt a kind of anesthetic set in. Cold water slithered over me, a numb caress, promising relief. It seemed to wash off some of the unhappiness that clung to me all over like mosquito repellent. Even the chlorine helped: as I mechanically stroked, back and forth, I hoped it would disinfect my brain. Clinging to the pool edge between laps, breathing hard, I could look up at the empty sky and see blue peace mirroring back to the pool. Everything seemed far away, except the water, the cold tile I grasped, the blue of sky and water. No one knew who I was, and I didn't have to remember. When I climbed out, tired, after an hour, I had the same feeling I used to have after an afternoon at Blaine's: exhausted, satisfied, with the hope of perhaps yet another hot afternoon before the summer ended. I was glad to be tired. I could tell I was still alive. Tomorrow I could go back to the swimming pool.

### QUESTIONS FOR ANALYSIS

1. What does Toth disclose about herself in this excerpt from her autobiography? Does the disclosure strike you as honest and convincing? Explain your judgment.

2. Autobiographers try to present significant places so that we can imagine them vividly. Underline specific details of Blaine's Pool in Toth's essay—sentences, phrases, or words that give any information about the location, appearance, smells, or sounds of the pool. Take inventory of these details in order to understand Toth's strategy for presenting the pool. (See Chapter 1, which presents a plan for taking inventory.)

3. In conveying the significance of the pool in her life, Toth relies mainly on typical events that happened often, such as the drive to the pool (paragraphs 1 and 2). Sometimes, however, she includes specific single incidents. The first of these comes toward the end of paragraph 11—the guard talking to the girl with red lipstick. Locate the other specific incidents and decide what each contributes to the essay. What seems to be the advantage of specific incidents? How would the essay be different if Toth had used more specific and fewer typical incidents?

4. Toth remarks that what she learned about "intense physical sensation" at Blaine's Pool was an indirect introduction to sex. Beginning with paragraph 3, underline every intense physical sensation Toth mentions. Underline only specific sensations ("painfully cold" glass). Take inventory of these sensations and analyze how they are used.

5. Autobiographers sometimes describe what they thought and felt at the time of an early event, as Toth does in paragraph 3; they may also reflect on these early events from their present perspective, describing what they now think and feel, as Toth does in the last two paragraphs. What does Toth reveal about Blaine's Pool in this final reflective disclosure?

## SUGGESTIONS FOR WRITING

1. Think about the places that have been important in your life. Choose one of these places, and write an essay presenting it vividly and showing its special qualities and its significance in your life.

2. From your childhood, think of places you frequently visited—for instance, a pool, park, gym, movie theater, video game room, shopping center, or church camp. Select a place you associate with some important insight or knowledge. Write an essay about this place, presenting it vividly, telling incidents that happened there, and showing its importance in your life.

# Alice Walker

Alice Walker was born in 1944 in the small town of Eatonton, Georgia. She has taught for short periods at Jackson State College, Wellesley College, Brandeis University, and the University of California at Berkeley. She is best known for her Pulitzer Prize-winning novel, *The Color Purple* (1982), and the movie based on it. Some consider her first novel, *Meridian* (1976), the best novel of the civil rights movement. She has published two collections of short stories, *In Love and Trouble: Stories of Black Women* (1973) and *You Can't Keep a Good Woman Down* (1981), and three collections of poems, *Once* (1968), *Revolutionary Petunias and Other Poems* (1973), and *Goodnight, Willie Lee, I'll See You in the Morning* (1979). Her essays, written between 1967 and 1982, have been published in *In Search of Our Mothers' Gardens* (1983). Her stories, poems, and essays are often anthologized.

# Beauty: When the Other Dancer Is the Self

This selection is the final chapter in Walker's *In Search of Our Mothers' Gardens*. In this essay, Walker ranges across many years of her life, from her early childhood to her mid-thirties, when she is writing the selection. Though she moves around in time, she keeps returning to a single traumatic incident that influenced her life.

1　It is a bright summer day in 1947. My father, a fat, funny man with beautiful eyes and a subversive wit, is trying to decide which of his eight children he will take with him to the county fair. My mother, of course, will not go. She is knocked out from getting most of us ready: I hold my neck stiff against the pressure of her knuckles as she hastily completes the braiding and then beribboning of my hair.

2　My father is the driver for the rich old white lady up the road. Her name is Miss Mey. She owns all the land for miles around, as well as the house in which we live. All I remember about her is that she once offered to pay my mother thirty-five cents for cleaning her house, raking up piles of her magnolia leaves, and washing her family's clothes, and that my mother—she of no money, eight children, and a chronic earache—refused it. But I do not think of this in 1947. I am two and a half years old. I want to go everywhere my daddy goes. I am excited at the prospect of riding in a car. Someone has told me fairs are fun. That there is room

69

in the car for only three of us doesn't faze me at all. Whirling happily in my starchy frock, showing off my biscuit-polished patent-leather shoes and lavender socks, tossing my head in a way that makes my ribbons bounce, I stand, hands on hips, before my father. "Take me, Daddy," I say with assurance; "I'm the prettiest!"

Later, it does not surprise me to find myself in Miss Mey's shiny black    3
car, sharing the back seat with the other lucky ones. Does not surprise me that I thoroughly enjoy the fair. At home that night I tell the unlucky ones all I can remember about the merry-go-round, the man who eats live chickens, and the teddy bears, until they say: that's enough, baby Alice. Shut up now, and go to sleep.

It is Easter Sunday, 1950. I am dressed in a green, flocked, scalloped-    4
hem dress (handmade by my adoring sister, Ruth) that has its own smooth satin petticoat and tiny hot-pink roses tucked into each scallop. My shoes, new T-strap patent leather, again highly biscuit-polished. I am six years old and have learned one of the longest Easter speeches to be heard that day, totally unlike the speech I said when I was two: "Easter lilies/ pure and white/blossom in/the morning light." When I rise to give my speech I do so on a great wave of love and pride and expectation. People in the church stop rustling their new crinolines. They seem to hold their breath. I can tell they admire my dress, but it is my spirit, bordering on sassiness (womanishness), they secretly applaud.

"That girl's a little *mess*," they whisper to each other, pleased.    5

Naturally I say my speech without stammer or pause, unlike those who    6
stutter, stammer, or, worst of all, forget. This is before the word "beautiful" exists in people's vocabulary, but "Oh, isn't she the *cutest* thing!" frequently floats my way. "And got so much sense!" they gratefully add . . . for which thoughtful addition I thank them to this day.

*It was great fun being cute. But then, one day, it ended.*    7

I am eight years old and a tomboy. I have a cowboy hat, cowboy boots,    8
checkered shirt and pants, all red. My playmates are my brothers, two and four years older than I. Their colors are black and green, the only difference in the way we are dressed. On Saturday nights we all go to the picture show, even my mother; Westerns are her favorite kind of movie. Back home, "on the ranch," we pretend we are Tom Mix, Hop-along Cassidy, Lash LaRue (we've even named one of our dogs Lash LaRue); we chase each other for hours rustling cattle, being outlaws, delivering damsels from distress. Then my parents decide to buy my brothers guns. These are not "real" guns. They shoot "BBs," copper pellets my brothers say will kill birds. Because I am a girl, I do not get a gun. Instantly I am relegated to the position of Indian. Now there

appears a great distance between us. They shoot and shoot at everything with their new guns. I try to keep up with my bow and arrows.

One day while I am standing on top of our makeshift "garage"—pieces 9 of tin nailed across some poles—holding my bow and arrow and looking out toward the fields, I feel an incredible blow in my right eye. I look down just in time to see my brother lower his gun.

Both brothers rush to my side. My eye stings, and I cover it with my 10 hand. "If you tell," they say, "we will get a whipping. You don't want that to happen, do you?" I do not. "Here is a piece of wire," says the older brother, picking it up from the roof; "say you stepped on one end of it and the other flew up and hit you." The pain is beginning to start. "Yes," I say. "Yes, I will say that is what happened." If I do not say this is what happened, I know my brothers will find ways to make me wish I had. But now I will say anything that gets me to my mother.

Confronted by our parents we stick to the lie agreed upon. They place 11 me on a bench on the porch and I close my left eye while they examine the right. There is a tree growing from underneath the porch that climbs past the railing to the roof. It is the last thing my right eye sees. I watch as its trunk, its branches, and then its leaves are blotted out by the rising blood.

I am in shock. First there is intense fever, which my father tries to 12 break using lily leaves bound around my head. Then there are chills: my mother tries to get me to eat soup. Eventually, I do not know how, my parents learn what has happened. A week after the "accident" they take me to see a doctor. "Why did you wait so long to come?" he asks, looking into my eye and shaking his head. "Eyes are sympathetic," he says. "If one is blind, the other will likely become blind too."

This comment of the doctor's terrifies me. But it is really how I look 13 that bothers me most. Where the BB pellet struck there is a glob of whitish scar tissue, a hideous cataract, on my eye. Now when I stare at people—a favorite pastime, up to now—they will stare back. Not at the "cute" little girl, but at her scar. For six years I do not stare at anyone, because I do not raise my head.

Years later, in the throes of a mid-life crisis, I ask my mother and sister 14 whether I changed after the "accident." "No," they say, puzzled. "What do you mean?"

*What do I mean?* 15

I am eight, and, for the first time, doing poorly in school, where I 16 have been something of a whiz since I was four. We have just moved to the place where the "accident" occurred. We do not know any of the people around us because this is a different county. The only time I see the friends I knew is when we go back to our old church. The new school is the former state penitentiary. It is a large stone building, cold and drafty, crammed to overflowing with boisterous, ill-disciplined children. On the third floor there is a huge circular imprint of some partition that has been torn out.

"What used to be here?" I ask a sullen girl next to me on our way past 17 it to lunch.

"The electric chair," says she.                                                    18

At night I have nightmares about the electric chair, and about all the 19 people reputedly "fried" in it. I am afraid of the school, where all the students seem to be budding criminals.

"What's the matter with your eye?" they ask, critically.                           20

When I don't answer (I cannot decide whether it was an "accident" 21 or not), they shove me, insist on a fight.

My brother, the one who created the story about the wire, comes to 22 my rescue. But then brags so much about "protecting" me, I become sick.

After months of torture at the school, my parents decide to send me 23 back to our old community, to my old school. I live with my grandparents and the teacher they board. But there is no room for Phoebe, my cat. By the time my grandparents decide there *is* room, and I ask for my cat, she cannot be found. Miss Yarborough, the boarding teacher, takes me under her wing, and begins to teach me to play the piano. But soon she marries an African—a "prince," she says—and is whisked away to his continent.

At my old school there is at least one teacher who loves me. She is 24 the teacher who "knew me before I was born" and bought my first baby clothes. It is she who makes life bearable. It is her presence that finally helps me turn on the one child at the school who continually calls me "one-eyed bitch." One day I simply grab him by his coat and beat him until I am satisfied. It is my teacher who tells me my mother is ill.

My mother is lying in bed in the middle of the day, something I have 25 never seen. She is in too much pain to speak. She has an abscess in her ear. I stand looking down on her, knowing that if she dies, I cannot live. She is being treated with warm oils and hot bricks held against her cheek. Finally a doctor comes. But I must go back to my grandparents' house. The weeks pass but I am hardly aware of it. All I know is that my mother might die, my father is not so jolly, my brothers still have their guns, and I am the one sent away from home.

"You did not change," they say.                                                    26

*Did I imagine the anguish of never looking up?* 27

I am twelve. When relatives come to visit I hide in my room. My 28 cousin Brenda, just my age, whose father works in the post office and whose mother is a nurse, comes to find me. "Hello," she says. And then she asks, looking at my recent school picture, which I did not want taken, and on which the "glob," as I think of it, is clearly visible, "You still can't see out of that eye?"

"No," I say, and flop back on the bed over my book. 29

That night, as I do almost every night, I abuse my eye. I rant and rave 30 at it, in front of the mirror. I plead with it to clear up before morning. I tell it I hate and despise it. I do not pray for sight. I pray for beauty.

"You did not change," they say. 31

I am fourteen and baby-sitting for my brother Bill, who lives in Boston. 32 He is my favorite brother and there is a strong bond between us. Understanding my feelings of shame and ugliness he and his wife take me to a local hospital, where the "glob" is removed by a doctor named O. Henry. There is still a small bluish crater where the scar tissue was, but the ugly white stuff is gone. Almost immediately I become a different person from the girl who does not raise her head. Or so I think. Now that I've raised my head I win the boyfriend of my dreams. Now that I've raised my head I have plenty of friends. Now that I've raised my head classwork comes from my lips as faultlessly as Easter speeches did, and I leave high school as valedictorian, most popular student, and *queen*, hardly believing my luck. Ironically, the girl who was voted most beautiful in our class (and was) was later shot twice through the chest by a male companion, using a "real" gun, while she was pregnant. But that's another story in itself. Or is it?

"You did not change," they say. 33

It is now thirty years since the "accident." A beautiful journalist comes 34 to visit and to interview me. She is going to write a cover story for her magazine that focuses on my latest book. "Decide how you want to look on the cover," she says. "Glamorous, or whatever."

Never mind "glamorous," it is the "whatever" that I hear. Suddenly 35 all I can think of is whether I will get enough sleep the night before the photography session: if I don't, my eye will be tired and wander, as blind eyes will.

At night in bed with my lover I think up reasons why I should not 36 appear on the cover of a magazine. "My meanest critics will say I've sold out," I say. "My family will now realize I write scandalous books."

"But what's the real reason you don't want to do this?" he asks.    37

"Because in all probability," I say in a rush, "my eye won't be straight."    38

"It will be straight enough," he says. Then, "Besides, I thought you'd    39
made your peace with that."

And I suddenly remember that I have.    40

*I remember:*

I am talking to my brother Jimmy, asking if he remembers anything    41
unusual about the day I was shot. He does not know I consider that day
the last time my father, with his sweet home remedy of cool lily leaves,
chose me, and that I suffered and raged inside because of this. "Well,"
he says, "all I remember is standing by the side of the highway with
Daddy, trying to flag down a car. A white man stopped, but when Daddy
said he needed somebody to take his little girl to the doctor, he drove
off."

*I remember:*

I am in the desert for the first time. I fall totally in love with it. I am    42
so overwhelmed by its beauty, I confront for the first time, consciously,
the meaning of the doctor's words years ago: "Eyes are sympathetic. If
one is blind, the other will likely become blind too." I realize I have
dashed about the world madly, looking at this, looking at that, storing
up images against the fading of the light. *But I might have missed seeing
the desert!* The shock of that possibility—and gratitude for over twenty-
five years of sight—sends me literally to my knees. Poem after poem
comes—which is perhaps how poets pray.

ON SIGHT

I am so thankful I have seen
The Desert
And the creatures in the desert
And the desert Itself.

The desert has its own moon
Which I have seen
With my own eye.
There is no flag on it.

Trees of the desert have arms
All of which are always up
That is because the moon is up
Ths sun is up
Also the sky
The stars
Clouds
None with flags.

If there *were* flags, I doubt
the trees would point.
Would you?

*But mostly, I remember this:*

I am twenty-seven, and my baby daughter is almost three. Since her  43
birth I have worried about her discovery that her mother's eyes are different from other people's. Will she be embarrassed? I think. What will
she say? Every day she watches a television program called "Big Blue
Marble." It begins with a picture of the earth as it appears from the
moon. It is bluish, a little battered-looking, but full of light, with whitish
clouds swirling around it. Every time I see it I weep with love, as if it is
a picture of Grandma's house. One day when I am putting Rebecca down
for her nap, she suddenly focuses on my eye. Something inside me
cringes, gets ready to try to protect myself. All children are cruel about
physical differences, I know from experience, and that they don't always
mean to be is another matter. I assume Rebecca will be the same.

But no-o-o-o. She studies my face intently as we stand, her inside and  44
me outside her crib. She even holds my face maternally between her
dimpled little hands. Then, looking every bit as serious and lawyerlike
as her father, she says, as if it may just possibly have slipped my attention:
"Mommy, there's a *world* in your eye." (As in, "Don't be alarmed, or do
anything crazy.") And then, gently, but with great interest: "Mommy,
where did you *get* that world in your eye?"

For the most part, the pain left then. (So what, if my brothers grew  45
up to buy even more powerful pellet guns for their sons and to carry real
guns themselves. So what, if a young "Morehouse man" once nearly fell
off the steps of Trevor Arnett Library because he thought my eyes were
blue.) Crying and laughing I ran to the bathroom, while Rebecca mum-
bled and sang herself off to sleep. Yes indeed, I realized, looking into the
mirror. There *was* a world in my eye. And I saw that it was possible to
love it: that in fact, for all it had taught me of shame and anger and
inner vision, I *did* love it. Even to see it drifting out of orbit in boredom,
or rolling up out of fatigue, not to mention floating back at attention in
excitement (bearing witness, a friend has called it), deeply suitable to
my personality, and even characteristic of me.

That night I dream I am dancing to Stevie Wonder's song "Always"  46
(the name of the song is really "As," but I hear it as "Always"). As I
dance, whirling and joyous, happier than I've ever been in my life,
another bright-faced dancer joins me. We dance and kiss each other and
hold each other through the night. The other dancer has obviously come
through all right, as I have done. She is beautiful, whole and free. And
she is also me.

## QUESTIONS FOR ANALYSIS

1. How would you explain the significance for Walker of the central incident in this selection?

2. What impression do you get of Walker from this selection? Point to specific parts of the selection that support your impression.

3. Outline this selection by listing each specific incident and indicating Walker's approximate age at the time of that incident. Why do you think Walker chose each of these incidents? What seems to be the relevance of each incident to Walker's autobiographical disclosure?

4. Choose the one incident that for you is most memorably presented. How exactly does Walker present this incident? Explain why you find it so effective.

5. Analyze how Walker uses the repeated phrases "You did not change" and "I remember." When does Walker use these phrases, and to what effect? What advantages or disadvantages do you see in this strategy of repetition?

6. Except for the school (paragraphs 16–18), Walker does not describe scenes; neither does she describe people. She does, however, describe people's clothes. Examine paragraphs 2, 4, and 8. What do you notice about her descriptions of clothing in these paragraphs? Why do you suppose she pays so much attention to clothes?

7. How does Walker begin (paragraph 1) and end (paragraph 46) this essay? What relation do you see between the beginning and ending?

8. Select at least three paragraphs from the selection that contain dialogue. Keeping in mind that Walker could have summarized rather than quoted, decide why she might have chosen to use dialogue in each of these paragraphs.

## SUGGESTIONS FOR WRITING

1. Consider your scars, emotional or physical, and choose one to write about. Tell your readers how you got this scar and what it has meant in your life.

2. Think about the crucial events and turning points in your life. Select one to write about. Describe carefully what happened and show how this event has continued to be important in your life.

# Brad Benioff

Brad Benioff, a freshman, rows for the crew team of the University of California at San Diego. In high school in Westlake, California (near Los Angeles), he played water polo and basketball. He took piano lessons for many years and now plays for enjoyment, although he still composes songs that he plays and sings. During the summer, with the help of several friends, he runs a day camp for about fifty neighborhood children. Benioff has not yet chosen a major or decided on a career.

# *Rick*

Benioff wrote this essay in his freshman composition class. Like the Welty selection earlier in this chapter, Benioff's essay focuses on a single memorable person, his high school water polo coach, Rick Rezinas. As you read, notice how Benioff uses reconstructed dialogue to dramatize his relation to Rick and how he discloses Rick's significance in his life.

I walked through the dawn chill, shivering as much from nervousness as from the cold. Steam curled up from the water in the pool and disappeared in the ocher morning light. Athletes spread themselves about on the deck, lazily stretching and whispering to each other as if the stillness were sacred. It was to be my first practice with the high school water polo team. I knew nothing about the game, but a friend had pushed me to play, arguing, "It's the most fun of any sport. Trust me." He had awakened me that morning long before daylight, forced me into a bathing suit, and driven me to the pool.

"Relax," he said. "Rick is the greatest of coaches. You'll like him. You'll have fun."

The mythical Rick. I had heard of him many times before. All the older players knew him by his first name and always spoke of him as a friend rather than a coach. He was a math teacher at our school, and his classes were very popular. Whenever class schedules came out, everyone hoped to be placed in Mr. Rezinas's class. He had been known to throw parties for the team or take them on weekend excursions skiing or backpacking. To be Rick's friend was to be part of an exclusive club, and I was being invited to join. And so I looked forward with nervous anticipation to meeting this man.

My friend walked me out to the pool deck and steered me toward a man standing beside the pool.

"Rick," announced my friend, "I'd like you to meet your newest   5
player."

Rick was not a friendly looking man. He wore only swim trunks, and   6
his short, powerful legs rose up to meet a bulging torso. His big belly was
solid. His shoulders, as if to offset his front-heaviness, were thrown back,
creating a deep crease of excess muscle from his sides around the small
of his back, a crease like a huge frown. His arms were crossed, two
medieval maces placed carefully on their racks, ready to be swung at any
moment. His round cheeks and chin were darkened by traces of black
whiskers. His hair was sparse. Huge, black, mirrored sunglasses replaced
his eyes. Below his prominent nose was a thin, sinister mustache. I
couldn't believe this menacing-looking man was the legendary jovial
Rick.

He said nothing at first. In those moments of silence, I felt more   7
inadequate than ever before in my life. My reflection in his glasses stared
back at me, accusing me of being too skinny, too young, too stupid, too
weak to be on his team. Where did I get the nerve to approach him with
such a ridiculous body and ask to play water polo, a *man's* game? Finally,
he broke the silence, having finished appraising my meager body. "We'll
fatten him up," he growled.

Thus began a week of torture. For four hours a day, the coach stood   8
beside the pool scowling down at me. I could do nothing right.

"No! No! No!" He shook his head in disgust. "Throw the damn ball   9
with your whole arm! Get your goddamn elbow out of the water!"

Any failure on my part brought down his full wrath. He bellowed at   10
my incompetence and punished me with push-ups and wind sprints. Even
when I was close to utter exhaustion, I found no sympathy. "What the
hell are you doing on the wall?" he would bellow. "Coach . . . my side,
it's cramped."

"Swim on it! If you can't take a little pain, then you don't play!" With   11
this, he would push me off the wall.

He seemed to enjoy playing me against the older, stronger players.   12
"Goddamn it, Brad! If someone elbows or hits you, don't look out at me
and cry, 'It's not fair.' Push back! Don't be so weak!" I got elbowed
around until it seemed that none of my internal organs was unscathed.
He worked me until my muscles wouldn't respond, and then he demanded
more.

"You're not trying! Push it!"   13

"Would you move? You're too slow! Swim!"   14

"Damn it! Get out and give me twenty!"   15

It took little time for me to hate both the game and the man who 16 ruled it.

I reacted by working as hard as I could. I decided to deprive him of 17 the pleasure of finding fault with me. I learned quickly and started playing as flawlessly as possible. I dispensed with looking tired, showing pain, or complaining of cramps. I pushed, hit, and elbowed back at the biggest of players. No matter how flawless or aggressive my performance, though, he would find fault and let me know it. He was never critical of other players. He would laugh and joke with the other players; but whenever he saw me, he frowned.

I decided to quit. 18

After a particularly demanding practice, I walked up to this tyrant. I 19 tried to hold his gaze, but the black glasses forced me to look down.

"Coach Rezinas," I blurted, "I've decided that I don't want to play 20 water polo." His scowl deepened. Then after a moment he said, "You can't quit. Not until after the first game." And he walked away. The dictator had issued his command.

There was no rule to keep me from quitting. Anger flushed through 21 me. Somehow I would get revenge on this awful man. After the first game? Okay. I would play. I would show him what a valuable player I was. He would miss my talents when I quit. I worked myself up before the first game by imagining the hated face: the black glasses, the thin mustache, the open, snarling mouth. I was not surprised that he placed me in the starting lineup because I was certain he would take me out soon. I played furiously. The ball, the goal, the opposition, even the water seemed to be extensions of Rick, his face glaring from every angle, his words echoing loudly in my ears. Time and time again I would get the ball and, thinking of his tortures, fire it toward the goal with a strength to kill. I forgot that he might take me out. No defender could stand up to me. I would swim by them or over them. Anger and the need for vengeance gave me energy. I didn't notice the time slipping by, the quarters ending.

Then, the game ended. My teammates rushed out to me, congratu- 22 lating and cheering me. I had scored five goals, a school record for one game, and shut out the other team with several key defensive plays. Now I could get revenge. Now I could quit. I stepped out of the pool prepared with the words I would spit into his face: "I QUIT!"

As I approached him, I stopped dead. He was smiling at me, his glasses 23 off. He reached out with his right hand and shook mine with exuberance.

"I knew you had it in you! I knew it!" he laughed. 24

Through his laughter, I gained a new understanding of the man. He   25
had pushed me to my fullest potential, tapping into the talent I may
never have found in myself. He was responsible for the way I played that
day. My glory was his. He never hated me. On the contrary, I was his
apprentice, his favored pupil. He had brought out my best. Could I really
hate someone who had done that much for me? He had done what he
had promised: he had fattened me up mentally as well as physically. All
this hit me in a second and left me completely confused. I tried to speak,
but only managed to croak, "Coach . . . uh . . . I, uh . . . " He cut me
off with another burst of laughter. He still shook my hand.

"Call me Rick," he said.                                                       26

## QUESTIONS FOR ANALYSIS

1. In autobiographical writing, personal disclosure can be direct or indirect. What do you learn about Benioff in this essay? Does he state
   what he is like directly or reveal himself only indirectly? Point to
   specific parts of the essay to explain your conclusion.

2. How would you summarize the significance of Rick in Benioff's life?

3. Benioff includes scenes, incidents, and people. Which one of these
   features receives most emphasis? Given Benioff's purpose, how do you
   assess this emphasis?

4. Benioff includes typical interactions with his coach as well as specific
   dramatic confrontations. Identify these confrontations. What role do
   they play in the essay? What is Benioff's strategy in presenting them?

## SUGGESTIONS FOR WRITING

1. Consider school coaches and professional teachers outside of school
   who have influenced your life. Choose one of these people and write
   an essay describing what the individual taught you and how he or she
   went about it. Your essay should reveal your reaction and what you
   learned about the person and about yourself.

2. Consider the adults with whom you had continuing disagreements or
   conflicts when you were a child or teenager. Choose one of these
   adults—a parent, relative, teacher, or neighbor, for example—to
   write about. In your essay, present this adult and show the nature of
   the disagreement through specific incidents. Disclose what you
   learned about the adult and about yourself.

# A Look at Brad Benioff's Writing Process

As suggested in the Guide to Autobiographical Writing in the next section, Benioff readily listed several topics, finding most promise in his list of persons who had influenced his life. In order to choose a person to write about, he tried to think of one memorable thing each had said to him. For his high school water polo coach, Rick Rezinas, he remembered "We'll fatten him up." He recalled both how much this statement scared him when he first heard it and how significant it was in their relationship. He knew that he wanted to explore Rezinas's importance in his life, and he felt confident that Rezinas's unusual appearance and coaching style would interest readers.

In probing his topic, Benioff was able to generate large amounts of specific material about feelings, scenes, and remembered conversations and statements. Exploring his present thoughts and feelings, he realized how much his father and Rezinas were alike. As he reconstructed dialogues with Rezinas—an especially productive invention activity that contributed significantly to his first draft—he could not be certain whether his father or Rezinas had said some of the things he wrote down.

Benioff explained that he always tried to include more in his drafts than he thought he could use in a revision. This time, after productive invention, he had more material than he could use even in a markedly inflated first draft. In this first draft, he included nearly all possibly relevant episodes and conversations, producing a draft nearly twice as long as the revision printed above. In conference, he and his instructor worked on reducing episodes to those that contributed most to characterizing Rezinas and disclosing his significance in Benioff's life. They also worked on making the ending more dramatic, dropping a paragraph of reflection on the talk with Rezinas after the dramatic first game and concluding with dialogue, the final statement appropriately coming from Rezinas and providing a title for the essay.

## A GUIDE TO AUTOBIOGRAPHICAL WRITING

From the autobiographical selections you have read and analyzed in this chapter, you have learned that autobiographical essays include engaging stories; vivid scenes; memorable people; and personal disclosure by the writer, indicating the autobiographical significance of the event, person, or place. Having learned to question, evaluate, and appreciate autobiography as a reader, you can now approach autobiography more confidently as a writer. You can more readily imagine the problems autobiographers must solve, the materials and possibilities they have to work with, the choices and decisions they must make. This section offers specific guidelines for writing autobiographical essays and suggestions to help you solve the special problems this kind of writing presents.

## *Invention*

The following activities will help you to find an autobiographical topic to write about, to recall details of this topic, and to explore its significance in your life. Completing these activities will produce a record of remembered details and thoughts that will be invaluable as you draft your essay.

FINDING AN AUTOBIOGRAPHICAL TOPIC. The readings in this chapter illustrate many possible autobiographical topics, as do the Suggestions for Writing that follow each reading. You might want to review these quickly before you begin. It is more likely that you will find a promising topic if you have many diverse possibilities to choose from. You might therefore begin your search by listing potential subjects, using the four autobiographical categories illustrated in this chapter as a starting point. List as many specific topics as you can under each of these categories: incident, developmental phase, person, place. The growing list may suggest still further topics that might not have come to mind immediately.

For *incidents*, list especially memorable brief incidents of a few hours or, at most, a day in length. Think of the first time you did something; of accidents, surprises, victories, defeats; of moments of discovery or awareness.

For *phases*, list periods of several weeks or months when something important was happening in your life, when you were changing in a significant way. Perhaps participating in a particular group, class, or team challenged you in some way or changed your beliefs or ideas. You may have moved to a new city or school and had to make a difficult adjustment, or you may have been ill for a long time. Maybe you learned something new or developed a new interest. Think of recent phases as well as ones much earlier in your life.

For *persons*, list significant people in your life. Think of people who taught you something about yourself, who surprised or disappointed you, or who had authority over you.

For *places*, list important places in your life, places you think of often. Try to recall places where something joyful or traumatic happened, or places where you learned something unforgettable. Consider places you knew well for a long time as well as those you visited only once, places you still see every day as well as those you have not seen for years. Focus on places that are small enough to be presented vividly to your readers: a room, rather than a building; a neighborhood or park, rather than a city; one trail or vantage point, rather than a national forest; one museum or cafe, rather than an entire country. You can list quite ordinary places (a kitchen, basement workroom, park bench) if they have personal significance for you.

This list-making process will almost certainly produce a number of possible topics for your autobiographical essay. The topic you ultimately choose should be one you truly care about, one that will give you the pleasure of recalling past experience and deciding what it means to you. Your topic should also be one that is likely to engage your readers, who will enjoy reflecting on their own lives as they read about yours. Finally, and of the greatest importance, your topic should have rich autobiographical significance. In autobiographical writing, you will describe events, places, and people; but you will do so in an expressive and revealing way. Readers expect to hear a personal voice in autobiography. They expect personal disclosure—even risky and surprising disclosure—not just amiable reporting. Fulfilling this expectation is the special challenge of autobiographical writing.

PROBING YOUR TOPIC. Once you have selected a topic, probe your memory to recall details and feelings. You should explore your present perspective on this topic from your past and attempt to establish its autobiographical significance. The following activities will guide you in probing your subject, in order to produce a fuller, more focused draft. Each activity takes only a few minutes to complete.

*Recalling First Impressions.* Write for a few minutes about your very first thoughts and feelings about the event, place, or person. What happened? Who was there? How did you react? What thoughts did you have? What feelings can you remember? What do your first impressions reveal about you as a person?

*Exploring Your Present Perspective.* Next, shift your focus from the past to the present. From your present perspective, what ideas do you have about the event, place, or person? Write for a few minutes, trying to express your present thoughts and feelings. How have your feelings changed? What insights do you now have? What does your present perspective reveal about you as a person?

*Stating Autobiographical Significance.* Readers want not only to hear your story but also to know what it means to you, what you learned from it, how it changed you. Now that you have explored your first impressions and present perspective of the event, person, or place, try writing two or three sentences that state its significance in your life. These sentences may eventually help you to focus your draft, providing a purpose and a main point for your writing.

*Identifying Particulars of the Scene.* If readers are to imagine the particulars of your story, you must show them who was there and what the scene looked like. Think of your topic and the important people and particular objects in the scene (or scenes). In your mind's eye, survey the location of your topic, trying to visualize again all the important particulars. List the most important objects and people.

*Detailing the Scene.* In order to make the scene vivid and memorable for readers and to understand its significance for you, try moving in close and presenting details of some particulars in the scene. Choose two or three objects or people from your list, and write about each for a few minutes, detailing each object or person as fully as you can. Try to recall specific sensory details: size, appearance, dress, way of walking and gesturing, posture, and mannerisms of a person; size, shape, color, condition, and texture of an object. Imagine the object or person seen from the side, from behind, from a distance, and close up. Write down what you see.

*Reconstructing Dialogue.* Reconstructed conversations are often important in modern autobiography. If another person plays a role in your topic— even a minor role—reconstruct what the two of you might have said to each other. Keep your dialogue as close to informal talk as you can, and use the following format:

[Your name]: [What you said]
[Other person's name]: [What the other person said]
[Continue alternating contributions down the page.]

*Restating Autobiographical Significance.* Now that you have explored your topic in several ways, write two or three sentences restating its significance in your life. Why is this event, person, or place still important to you? What do you think you might learn about yourself as you write? What do you want to disclose about yourself to your readers?

This final restatement of autobiographical significance will help you to focus your thoughts before you begin drafting. It will also guide you in selecting details to include in your essay.

# *Drafting*

Before you begin drafting, review the invention writing you have completed. Reread your notes, searching for promising ideas and notable details; then jot down any further ideas and details your notes suggest to you.

You are now ready to proceed to your first draft. The following guidelines will help you set goals to focus your writing, make specific plans for your essay, and decide how to begin.

SETTING GOALS. Establishing specific goals before you begin and keeping them in mind as you write will enable you to draft more confidently. The following questions may help you to set goals for your draft: What do I want to accomplish with this autobiographical essay? How can I present my topic vividly and memorably to my readers? Like Baker, should I rely on reconstructed conversation to dramatize an incident; or, like Toth, should I concentrate on sensory details and activities to present a place? To describe a person, should I attempt Welty's variety of details about Miss Duling—her walk, dress, place in the community, standards for students, imperious manner, and ringing bell?

How will I tell readers why this event, person, or place is important to me? For example, Benioff leaves us to infer how Coach Rick Rezinas has been a significant influence in his life, Walker in part presents the significance of her struggle with disfigurement through a dream, and Rodriguez tells us directly that learning English gave him a public identity.

What will readers learn about me from this essay? You will recall that we learn of Feynman's playfulness and creativity, Benioff's determination, and Rodriguez's and Welty's eagerness to learn.

How will I begin engagingly and hold my readers' interest? (See the Getting Started section for a discussion of beginnings.) How can this essay about my experience lead readers to reflect on their own experience?

PLANNING YOUR ORGANIZATION. The particular goals you have established will determine the plan of your draft. Although this plan can unfold as you write, many writers find it helpful to sketch out a tentative plan before they begin drafting. If you plan to narrate a single event, for example, you could outline briefly what happens from beginning to end. If you plan to describe a person or place, you might plan the order in which major features of your description will appear. Reviewing plans of selections in this chapter will suggest possibilities. Be prepared to depart from your plan once you have started writing since drafting nearly always produces unexpected discoveries that may make it necessary to change direction.

BEGINNING. A strong beginning will immediately engage readers' interest, so consider beginning your essay with dialogue, with an unusual detail of a person or scene, or with an action. You might also begin by presenting the context for your essay, orienting readers in a general way to the event, person, or place. For example, Baker opens with an argument between Aunt Pat and Uncle Allen. Toth opens with unusual details about Blaine's Pool, locating it in a hollow within a remote, scraggly wood. Walker begins with activity—getting ready for the county fair, competing with brothers and sisters for a place in the car, driving off down the road. Benioff begins with a specific scene, the school's swimming pool in the early morning light. Feynman begins more conventionally, though no less successfully, by giving us the context for his interest in radios.

You might have to try two or three different beginnings before finding a promising way to start, but do not agonize for too long over the first sentence. Try out any possible beginning and see what happens.

CHOOSING RELEVANT DETAILS. If you have had a successful period of invention, you probably already have more particular details than you can use in one essay. Well-prepared writers must spend a great deal of time deciding which details and information to leave out. As you draft, remember to include enough details so that readers can imagine the person or scene but only those details that support the autobiographical disclosure you are making.

# Revising

Once you have completed a first draft, you should try to find ways to strengthen it so that it comes closer to achieving your goals. The critical reading questions at the beginning of this chapter will guide you in reading your draft critically and determining how it can be improved. You should also try to have someone else read your draft in light of these critical reading questions.

As you revise an autobiographical essay, concentrate on clarifying the autobiographical significance, strengthening particularity, and improving readability.

REVISING TO CLARIFY AUTOBIOGRAPHICAL SIGNIFICANCE. Remember that readers of autobiography want to know why the event, person, or place was important in the writer's life. They also want to reflect on similar episodes in their own lives. Try to clarify and focus the autobiographical significance in your draft, and remove any details that do not contribute to it. Reconsider your tone of voice and emotional distance or perspective. Consider adding further details, scenes, or anecdotes to demonstrate the importance of the episode in your life.

REVISING TO STRENGTHEN PARTICULARITY. Reconsider how well you have presented the scene and people to your readers. You may need to reduce the number of particular details in order to keep the essay in focus, or you may want to add details to enable readers to imagine the scene and people more vividly. Keeping in mind that any additional details should support the autobiographical significance, try to identify other objects or people in the scene and provide specific details about them. Consider whether you should include a fuller range of sensory details—sounds and smells, in addition to sights. Decide whether you should recreate dialogues to particularize your summaries of conversations or to dramatize relations between people.

REVISING TO IMPROVE READABILITY. Imagine a reader reading your essay for the first time, sentence by sentence. This reader's inevitable first question will be, do I really want to read this? Decide whether you can improve your beginning to engage this reader immediately. Look for any gaps in your essay, and think about how you might smooth the transition from one part to the next. Find any overly complicated or slow sections from which you could delete unnecessary material. Look for sentences that could be clarified or perhaps combined with adjacent sentences. Decide whether you can improve your ending to provide a more dramatic, memorable, and satisfying conclusion.

When you have a final version of your essay, check it closely for mistakes in spelling, usage, and punctuation. If possible, have someone else examine your essay for such mistakes too.

# CHAPTER THREE

# *Reflection*

The reflective essay, like autobiography, derives from the writer's personal experience. What distinguishes the reflective essay, however, as the noted author Virginia Woolf once said, is its "fierce attachment to an idea." While autobiographers tell us about significant events, people, and places in their lives, writers of reflection tell us what they are thinking.

The source of the reflective essay can be traced to the writing of the French nobleman Michel Eyquem de Montaigne. When Montaigne published his reflections in 1580, he called them *Essays,* a word that in French means tests or trials. The word *essay* underscores the exploratory nature of all writing, but it is especially descriptive of reflective writing because reflecting is a process of thinking. When reflection is committed to paper, the writing itself becomes a process of discovery, a process of trying out or testing ideas.

The movement of reflective writing is generally from experience to idea. Reflective essays usually begin with some personal experience that leads to reflection upon human experience in general. Even though they treat the most far-reaching subjects—self-esteem, intimacy, fear, death— writers of reflection have modest goals. They do not attempt to exhaust their subjects, nor do they set themselves up as experts. They simply explore their own understanding.

As you read the reflective essays in this chapter and begin writing one of your own, you might find Montaigne's description of his own efforts helpful:

I take the first subject that chance offers. They are all equally good to me. And I never plan to develop them completely. For I do not see the whole of anything, nor do those who promise to show it to us. Of a hundred members and faces that each thing has, I take one, sometimes only to lick it, sometimes to brush the surface, sometimes to pinch it to the bone. I give it a stab, not as wide but as deep as I know how. And most often I like to take them from some unaccustomed point of view. . . . I want to be seen in my simple, natural, ordinary fashion, without straining or artifice; for it is myself that I portray.

Like Montaigne, the writers you will read in this chapter strive for simplicity and grace. Their styles, though highly individual, share with Montaigne a kind of naturalness, free of ostentation and pomposity. These elegant little essays charm readers as they stimulate their thinking. You will enjoy reading reflective essays for their substance as well as for their style. The subjects they touch upon may be weighty but their touch is light.

## A GUIDE TO READING REFLECTIVE WRITING

Reflective writing can be so enchanting that it is sometimes hard to read it critically. To maintain a critical stance, you should be alert for the basic features and strategies of reflective writing. This section discusses these features, presents a sample annotated essay, and recommends some critical reading questions to keep in mind as you read.

# Basic Features
# of Reflective Writing

Whereas we normally think of reflection as private musings, reflective writing is definitely public, intended not only to try out ideas but also to convey them to others. At its best, reflective writing is also an art form that pleases and inspires its readers.

The following are the five essential features of reflective writing: *a general subject, a particular occasion, a controlling idea, a clear organization,* and *an appropriate tone.*

A GENERAL SUBJECT. Reflective writing is philosophical in that it treats subjects basic to human experience. These subjects have to do with how we live our lives, the fears that haunt us, and the dreams that inspire us. In fact, anything that relates to the human condition and how we cope with it qualifies as a subject of reflective writing.

A PARTICULAR OCCASION. As the essayist E. B. White once remarked, the writer of reflective essays is "sustained by the childish belief that everything he thinks about, everything that happens to him, is of general interest." Reflective writers take something they did, saw, read, or overheard and use it as the occasion for their general reflections. This occasion serves not only as a starting point for reflection but also as a concrete example—a memorable anecdote or vivid image—that helps readers grasp the writer's more abstract ideas.

A CONTROLLING IDEA. The essence of the reflective essay is the writer's development of the subject. It is not enough merely to raise the subject. The writer must also examine, define, compare, analyze, and classify the subject, figuring out what it means and why it is important. At the heart of all this exploration and conjecture is a single, controlling idea that brings the essay into focus. This idea is usually stated directly, but in some essays it may only be implied.

A CLEAR ORGANIZATION. Because they are basically an assemblage of ideas, anecdotes, and images, reflective essays need to be clearly organized. Readers should be able to understand, for example, how the essay's opening relates to its ending. They should see the connections between anecdotes and generalizations. Above all, they must be aware of the progression of ideas, the thread of logic that connects one point to the next and that relates back to the essay's controlling idea.

AN APPROPRIATE TONE. The tone of a reflective essay deserves special attention because so much of the essay's meaning is conveyed by its tone. Although the reflective essay, as essayist Edward Hoagland says, is "like the human voice talking," the essayist modulates this voice to fit the writing situation. Some essays are witty and entertaining, for example, while others are serious and contemplative. Even within a particular essay, the tone may vary enormously, reflecting the writer's different attitudes toward the subject.

## An Annotated Reading:
### *Fear of Families,* Phyllis Theroux

Readers enjoy reading reflective writing because it is entertaining as well as interesting. They delight in the imaginative ways writers use particular occasions as points of departure for their meditations. They find general observations about the human condition fresh as well as fascinating. And often they marvel at the insight they gain into the human psyche.

The following brief reflective essay has been annotated to show how you might read this kind of writing critically. Try reading the essay first, and then reread it as you look at the annotations. "Fear of Families" was written by Phyllis Theroux, a professional writer whose reflective essays appear in newspapers like *The Washington Post* and magazines like *Mademoiselle* and *Reader's Digest.* A collection of her early essays, *California and Other States of Grace,* was published in 1980. "Fear of Families" originally appeared in *The New York Times* and was later published in a second collection, *Peripheral Visions* (1982).

Theroux particularizes her general subjects by discussing them in the context of common domestic experiences. For example, writing about piano lessons in one essay enables her to reflect more generally on communication between parent and child. In another essay, she writes about shopping obsessively as a way to ward off anxiety about money. As you read "Fear of Families," notice how Theroux uses common domestic experiences to reflect on a more general subject. Also, ask yourself why she titled her essay "Fear *of* Families" instead of "Fear *in* Families." What difference does this choice of words make?

## Fear of Families

**Oppositions:**
**independence/survival**
**pride/fear**

**Occasion: observation of another family**
**Subject: fear of families**

**Ha! Play on words suggests you are on trial at home.**

**apartness/togetherness**
**reunion/face-off**
**Describes interaction in general terms**

**Particular example**

**Real-sounding dialogue**

As life goes on and independence becomes necessary for survival, pride of family can turn into fear of family, and during this past Christmas and New Year's season, which I celebrated with a number of other people's relatives, it appeared that fear of families is not a unique problem. To sit around a table with all those faces that give back the truth, the whole truth, and quite possibly nothing but the truth about ourselves, can give one a "so help me God" feeling.

Twelve months of apartness culminating in a week of togetherness can turn a family reunion into a family face-off. The odds are that somebody will "say something," a stiffness will descend over the table, and several people will excuse themselves to make early plane reservations home. At one family dinner it got so hot that I retreated into the kitchen, only to be followed by a couple who squared off before the microwave oven, where he said to her, "You want to know what really tees me off about you . . . ?" I went back into the dining room where his mother had just said, "Well, I don't think that Sadat acted like a politician but a statesman!" To which her mother replied archly, "And what's wrong with that?"

| | |
|---|---|
| Drawing conclusions | There were a lot of small vignettes like these going on ³ all over town during the holidays, and the first conclusion to draw is that relatives are better off not relating to each |
| vivid image | other if blood is going to gush all over the rug. But I can't help but think that beneath all the double-edged remarks |
| What is this anxiety? | and devastating toasts was a lot of anxiety that had no place to go. |
| Feelings are reciprocal— parallel structure of sentence | If the son is threatened by his mother, so also is the ⁴ mother threatened by the son. Her loneliness, his un-willingness to identify with it, his guilt, her bitterness— |
| Not everything on surface | this is only one of the combinations that sit above and below the salt, and I wonder whether family reunions |
| Controlling idea: relationships involve risk | don't turn into disasters so quickly because we're only willing to relate to each other when it's safe. |
| dam image vivid | To embrace the whole of another person is to take the ⁵ risk that their dam will break and overwhelm us with |
| Fear of losing oneself in the other | responsibility and anxiety. To recognize another person's frailty may somehow sap whatever strength we've man- |
| See own needs and frailties in the other | aged to build up for ourselves. The anger comes from sensing that the support we need is not so different from the support the other person needs. But to acknowledge that is so painful that some people would rather drink |
| Bourbon | themselves into the bottom of a bottle of Old Grand-Dad |
| Twist: strain of *not* relating | and count the hours left before everyone will go home. The strain of not relating is what provokes the blood- ⁶ |
| Irony: kill for love | shed, and some people will kill each other for love, par-ticularly during the holidays when we're supposed to love each other to death. But perhaps the reason it's so hard to relate is because it's so hard to be disappointed, to |
| Range of family weirdos—hard to admit you're one also | know that the schizoids, compulsive cleaners, alcoholics, and dullards, all the relatives who come home to roost, are not so different from us. |
| Accepting others = accepting yourself | To embrace them is to embrace these tendencies in ⁷ ourselves, which is a difficult task. And so anger deflects |
| Vivid image: opposite of holding hands | love, hands are clenched behind backs, and we walk the tightrope of the holidays praying the wrong prayer for the |
| Ends on sad note | wrong reason instead of saying, "What the hell, we're all in this together. . . ." |

# Critical Reading Questions

Keep the following questions in mind as you read the reflective essays in this chapter and as you evaluate your own writing. They will help you to identify the essay's basic features and to examine the writing strategies with a critical eye. To indicate how these questions might be used to guide your reading of reflective writing, each one has been applied to the Theroux essay.

1. *What is the general subject of this essay?*

Although this question seems obvious, people's answers often differ markedly. For instance, one reader might say that Theroux is writing about fear, while another might say she is writing about families. Both are right, of course, but an even better answer would combine the two subjects, as Theroux does in her title. Her subject is the special kind of fear that occurs in families and other close relationships, the fear of intimacy. What makes this subject of general interest is the fact that we all experience it in one way or another.

2. *What occasioned this reflection? How is this occasion presented? Is it particularized enough to make the general subject understandable?*

Reflective writing usually specifies its general subject with particulars. The writer might tell an anecdote or describe a scene. This example serves to make the general idea concrete and meaningful. As a critical reader, you should examine the occasion to determine how well it illustrates the general point. Theroux begins by describing a visit with someone else's family during the holidays. This experience gives her the objectivity to see family life in general and to recognize how her own family resembles other families. Her vivid description of the interactions between family members, particularly the conversations that dramatize the exasperation and absurdity of family arguments, awakens in readers the memory of similar experiences and enables them to share Theroux's more objective perspective.

3. *How is the subject developed? What is the controlling idea? Is the organization clear and easy to follow?*

Writers develop their subjects in many different and surprising ways. In fact, what is most interesting is not the subject itself, but the way the writer develops it. Some writers analyze the subject, breaking it into stages or parts which they might then classify and label. Others present a series of concrete examples—anecdotes and scenes—to show different facets of the subject. Another common strategy is to place the subject in a broader context by comparing it to a related subject. Another possibility is to examine what the causes or effects are. Often, writers of reflection combine several of these strategies. As a critical reader, you will want to see which strategies are used and determine how appropriate and well developed they are.

Theroux begins with a dramatic example she calls a vignette and then goes on to examine the causes of her subject. She suggests, for example, that family arguments are not significant in themselves but as expressions of repressed feelings. This notion leads to her controlling idea that family interactions are risky because they expose powerful, hidden feelings. Finally, she points to a connection between loving others and loving ourselves, comparing our attitudes toward others' emotions and our own unacknowledged feelings.

4. *What tone does the writer adopt? Is the tone consistent, or does it change? How appropriate is the tone?*

Readers are usually very responsive to tone, sensing it even if they cannot describe it. As a critical reader, you should become more aware of how tone affects your reaction to a piece of writing. While "Fear of Families" makes nearly every reader smile, it also makes some wince. Theroux plays with language and exaggerates. She is witty and calls attention to her wit. At the same time, she touches a nerve, exposing readers' secret fears. She does this with such delicacy, however, that they usually feel relieved to learn that others harbor fears like their own.

# Laurence Shames

A free-lance writer, Laurence Shames has had articles published in such diverse journals as *World Tennis* and *Saturday Review*. In 1982, he was a contributing editor for *Esquire*, writing the monthly "Ethics" column. Some of the subjects he touched upon were success and failure, fidelity, the fear of losing, and the desire to win.

# *The Eyes of Fear*

As the title of this selection indicates, Shames—like Theroux—is writing about the general subject of fear. While Theroux treats fear in families, Shames focuses on fear in sexual relationships, but both are ultimately concerned with fear of intimacy. Reflective essays often deal with similar subjects, but they approach these subjects from different angles because of the subjective nature of reflective writing. The occasions out of which reflections arise are bound to differ, as are the conclusions that writers draw from their reflections.

Reflective essays also differ from one another because they are written for different purposes and audiences. "The Eyes of Fear" (1982), for example, was originally written for the "Ethics" column in *Esquire*, a magazine with a well-defined audience composed primarily of young professional men. As you read this essay, consider how writing on ethics for this particular audience may have shaped Shames's essay. What seems to you to be his immediate purpose? How might this essay have been different if Shames had written it for another magazine, such as *Ms.* or *Family Circle?*

Remember how they did it in *1984?* 1

They studied you until they'd learned your deepest fear—rats, bats, 2 darkness, whatever—and then they used that fear to turn you. The premise was that while human beings might be expected to behave with some degree of dignity and moral sense under normal circumstances, they'd crumble when confronted with their personal demons; courage and resolve would slip away, and people would become abject, malleable, capable of any sort of betrayal.

A sobering proposition—but one that, in Orwell's nightmare world, 3 proved only too accurate. How about in our world?

We, too, occasionally have our worst fears thrown in our face, are 4 confronted with situations in which the choice is between staring down our private bogeymen and skulking away in safe but ignoble retreat. True, most of us will never have to deal with the primordial horror of having

rodents nibble at us, but we will face other fears: the fear of intimacy, which, for many of us, is truly scarring and which can lead us to be dishonest, unfair, and self-defeating in our relationships; the fear of taking an uncharted course in a career—a fear that can turn us into morally hollow yes-men or cause us to be untrue to our real ambitions; and, in every aspect of our lives, the basic fear of change—a timidness about growth and risk that, in the long haul, can make us bitter, disappointed, and mean.

Consider, for example, the fear of intimacy. Intimacy offers itself as     5
one of life's great comforts, but for all its tender appeal, many of us find it terrifying. And not without reason: intimacy means reckless self-exposure, a bold baring of the soft white underbelly, an offering of the jugular. It demands more trust than many of us grow up believing the world deserves. Yet few of us choose to be hermits or celibates; the difficulty, then, is in reconciling our need for closeness with our fear of it. And, ethically, the danger is that we may go halfway, then balk, inevitably hurting people in the process, deceiving them without intending to, being helplessly dishonest to others because we're being untrue to ourselves.

In college I hung around with a group of guys for whom meeting women     6
was a major preoccupation. Some of us liked having one girlfriend at a time, in a sort of puppy-love version of what has come to be known as serial monogamy. Others preferred to juggle several entanglements at once, with results that ranged from the comical to the cruel. Then there was this fellow I'll call Arty. Arty had a style all his own. Forward, eccentric, and dapper, he insinuated himself into the favor of more young ladies than any of us could win. Yet he never seemed the slightest bit entangled. He was the consummate hit-and-run man, as adept at ending things as at starting them.

For a while, of course, this capacity of his impressed the rest of us no     7
end. Compared with the blistering pace of Arty's escapades, our humble efforts seemed sluggish and mundane. Gradually, however, even to us die-hard adolescents, it became clear that the fellow had a problem. His fear of getting close to women was so pronounced that it led him to all sorts of caddish behavior. Whatever his intentions may have been, he ended up misleading every woman he met, and he left behind, if not exactly a string of broken hearts, then certainly a number of ladies who had good reason to feel baffled, angry, and used. Arty was a classic case of a guy letting himself be bullied into shabbiness by his fears, not even truly enjoying his encounters because they were laced with so much anxiety. After a while, the rest of us didn't know whom to feel sorrier

for—the women who crossed Arty's path, or Arty himself. *They* were victimized by Arty's fear only once; *he* was doomed to repeat the pattern again and again.

After college, some of us old friends stayed in touch, staging informal 8 reunions at various taverns in the cities where we'd ended up. True to form, we'd still discuss, among other things, our dealings with women, but the emphasis was different now. In spite of ourselves, we were getting serious. We were at the age when the question of marriage was beginning to bear down on us with the slow portentousness of a distant but oncoming train. We'd flirt with the subject and sometimes make goading conjectures about who would be the first to take the plunge. There was no consensus on this point; as to who would be the *last*, however, there was general and confident agreement.

We were wrong, of course. Arty was the first of us to wed. To me, 9 this was more than a surprise; it represented a moral victory of a high order.

I still remember when he told me of his plans. The revelation literally 10 took my breath away. This was *Arty*—the guy so scared of closeness that he'd hardly leave an imprint on a paramour's pillow. But people change—or *can* change. "Look," Arty said to me, "don't you think I know what I've been doing all these years? I've just been jerking around, wasting everybody's time, acting like the kind of person I really hope I'm not. I've got to take the chance and try to be different. I think I've found someone who understands how tough it's gonna be for me and who'll be able to handle it, and I've got to take a shot."

That was around three years ago, and Arty and his wife are still fighting 11 the good fight against Arty's fear of intimacy. It hasn't been easy. It's not the sort of fear you stand up to once and conquer; it requires a more durable sort of courage, the sort that renews itself every day.

Arty—so he admits—is still clutched at times by the old terrors; he 12 clams up, broods, gets moody and aloof. His wife, when frustrated, throws tantrums. The two of them have been known to make scenes and to indulge in extended sulks. Yet, beneath the turbulent surface of their marriage, there is a true adventure going on.

It's an adventure whose basis is a moral contract, a mutual pledge not 13 to retreat into halfheartedness. And while the contract's demands are unyielding, its rewards are rich and irreplaceable. "I no longer try to get away with the sort of evasions that I never *wanted* to get away with in the first place," Arty says. "Marriage is like boxing: you can run but you can't hide. Sooner or later, you're going to end up in a clinch—and it's in the clinches where you learn the most about yourself, where your strength is really tested."

But the challenge of marriage is one that Arty still wonders if he's 14 equal to. "You know," he said to me a while back, during a particularly bumpy phase, "I didn't exactly pave the way for this. I mean, I'd always been too scared even to really have a girlfriend, and all of a sudden this little voice starts telling me that maybe I should take this giant leap all the way to marriage, and I *listen*. Maybe it was just a crazy thing for me to do."

I disagreed with him, and told him so. To me, it was his finest hour. 15 Because if duking it out with our personal demons is full of potential pitfalls, it also offers opportunities for real self-transcendence, for genuine heroics. Where's the virtue, after all, in taking a stand when we're *not* afraid? What's the value of a moral contract that doesn't cost us anything?

Big Brother, in his perverse wisdom, was correct in his assumption 16 that every person has his private fear, his exposed nerve. But it doesn't take an all-seeing autocrat to discover that vulnerable point and to probe it—the circumstances of ordinary life will do that just as well. The way we hold our ground when that sensitive place is tweaked, when that anxiety-drenched subject is foisted on us, is the surest test of what we're made of.

## QUESTIONS FOR ANALYSIS

1. Shames opens and closes this essay with allusions to George Orwell's novel *1984*. In what way are these references an appropriate frame for the essay? What does framing allow Shames to accomplish?

2. Most of this essay is devoted to a story about Arty. What do you learn about Arty and the author from this anecdote? How does Shames use this strategy of narrating to develop his subject?

3. Shames quotes Arty at a few points in the essay. Find these quotations, and rewrite one of them as a summary of what Arty said rather than a direct quote. From this example, what can you conclude about the advantages of quoting over summarizing?

4. Why do you think Shames calls Arty's decision to marry "a moral victory of a high order"? What ethical or moral issue is involved? What part, if any, does ethics play in Shames's controlling idea?

5. Describe Shames's tone in this essay, pointing to specific examples. Does the tone remain the same throughout, or do you detect any changes? How does the tone affect your response to the essay?

6. Even though this essay deals with fear of intimacy, it contains many instances of figurative language suggesting conflict—for example, the simile "Marriage is like boxing." Review the essay, making an inventory of the figurative language under two headings: "Intimacy" and "Conflict." Then ask yourself why Shames might be concerned with conflict in an essay on intimacy. What is the relationship between conflict and intimacy? (Chapter 1 gives a plan for taking inventory.)

7. How do you think Shames would have Arty respond to Theroux's statement in "Fear of Families" that "to embrace the whole of another person is to take the risk that their dam will break and overwhelm us with responsibility and anxiety"?

### SUGGESTIONS FOR WRITING

1. In this essay, Shames identifies several kinds of private fears: the fear of intimacy, the fear of taking an uncharted course in a career, the basic fear of change. What other fears do people experience? Write a reflective essay that examines one of these common fears.

2. This essay on fear appeared in *Esquire*'s "Ethics" column. Many other human qualities also have ethical dimensions. Egotism, for example, can lead people to be untruthful and to use others. Think of a quality that affects people's moral behavior negatively or positively and write a reflective essay about it.

# Virginia Woolf

Virginia Woolf (1882–1941) is one of this century's greatest novelists. Her father, Leslie Stephen, was a writer and intellectual, and Woolf enjoyed a childhood full of literature and ideas. As a girl growing up in Victorian England, however, she was deprived of a formal education. Taking advantage of her father's extensive library, Woolf educated herself. By the time she was twenty-three, she regularly reviewed books for the respected *Times Literary Supplement* and taught an evening college course for working men and women. She was also one of the founders of the Bloomsbury Group, a gathering of free-thinking artists, writers, and philosophers who exchanged ideas and inspired one another's creativity.

Among Woolf's most popular and critically acclaimed novels are *Mrs. Dalloway* (1925), *To the Lighthouse* (1927), and *The Waves* (1931). She is also known for her many essays: biographical and critical pieces on British literary figures and reflective essays collected in several volumes, beginning with *The Common Reader* (1925). An outspoken feminist, Woolf wrote a book-length essay, *A Room of One's Own* (1929), on the status of women, particularly female intellectuals and artists.

## *The Death of the Moth*

As the title suggests, this essay was occasioned by an incident that the writer observed. Ordinary events like this usually go unnoticed, but when they catch a writer's eye, they often lead to reflections. What is interesting is not the fact that Woolf derives from the incident a reflective essay about death, but how she writes this essay. Her style of reflective writing differs markedly from the discursive styles of Theroux and Shames. As a novelist, Woolf was critical of discursive essayists whom she said "scold" readers. Her goal was to "sting us awake" by presenting the incident vividly and dramatically. Instead of discussing the event, she develops her controlling idea primarily through description and contrast. As you read, notice how much space Woolf devotes to showing the scene as opposed to telling the reader what she is thinking or feeling.

Moths that fly by day are not properly to be called moths; they do not excite that pleasant sense of dark autumn nights and ivy-blossom which the commonest yellow-underwing asleep in the shadow of the curtain never fails to rouse in us. They are hybrid creatures, neither gay like butterflies nor sombre like their own species. Nevertheless the present specimen, with his narrow hay-coloured wings, fringed with a tassel of the same colour, seemed to be content with life. It was a pleasant morning, mid-September, mild, benignant, yet with a keener breath than that of the summer months. The plough was already scoring the field opposite the window, and where the share had been, the earth was pressed flat and gleamed with moisture. Such vigour came rolling in from the fields and the down beyond that it was difficult to keep the eyes strictly turned upon the book. The rooks too were keeping one of their annual festivities; soaring round the tree tops until it looked as if a vast net with thousands of black knots in it had been cast up into the air; which, after a few moments sank slowly down upon the trees until every twig seemed to have a knot at the end of it. Then, suddenly, the net would be thrown into the air again in a wider circle this time, with the utmost clamour and vociferation, as though to be thrown into the air and settle slowly down upon the tree tops were a tremendously exciting experience.

The same energy which inspired the rooks, the ploughmen, the horses, and even, it seemed, the lean bare-backed downs, sent the moth fluttering from side to side of his square of the window-pane. One could not help watching him. One was, indeed, conscious of a queer feeling of pity for him. The possibilities of pleasure seemed that morning so enormous and so various that to have only a moth's part in life, and a day moth's at that, appeared a hard fate, and his zest in enjoying his meagre opportunities to the full, pathetic. He flew vigorously to one corner of his compartment, and, after waiting there a second, flew across to the other. What remained for him but to fly to a third corner and then to a fourth? That was all he could do, in spite of the size of the downs, the width of the sky, the far-off smoke of houses, and the romantic voice, now and then, of a steamer out at sea. What he could do he did. Watching him, it seemed as if a fibre, very thin but pure, of the enormous energy of the world had been thrust into his frail and diminutive body. As often as he crossed the pane, I could fancy that a thread of vital light became visible. He was little or nothing but life.

Yet, because he was so small, and so simple a form of the energy that was rolling in at the open window and driving its way through so many narrow and intricate corridors in my own brain and in those of other human beings, there was something marvelous as well as pathetic about him. It was as if someone had taken a tiny bead of pure life and decking it as lightly as possible with down and feathers, had set it dancing and zigzagging to show us the true nature of life. Thus displayed one could not get over the strangeness of it. One is apt to forget all about life, seeing it humped and bossed and garnished and cumbered so that it has to move with the greatest circumspection and dignity. Again, the thought of all that life might have been had he been born in any other shape caused one to view his simple activities with a kind of pity.

After a time, tired by his dancing apparently, he settled on the window ledge in the sun, and, the queer spectacle being at an end, I forgot about him. Then, looking up, my eye was caught by him. He was trying to resume his dancing, but seemed either so stiff or so awkward that he could only flutter to the bottom of the window-pane; and when he tried to fly across it he failed. Being intent on other matters I watched these futile attempts for a time without thinking, unconsciously waiting for him to resume his flight, as one waits for a machine, that has stopped momentarily, to start again without considering the reason of its failure. After perhaps a seventh attempt he slipped from the wooden ledge and fell, fluttering his wings, onto his back on the window sill. The helplessness of his attitude roused me. It flashed upon me he was in difficulties; he could no longer raise himself; his legs struggled vainly. But, as I stretched out a pencil, meaning to help him to right himself, it came over me that the failure and awkwardness were the approach of death. I laid the pencil down again.

The legs agitated themselves once more. I looked as if for the enemy against which he struggled. I looked out of doors. What had happened there? Presumably it was midday, and work in the fields had stopped. Stillness and quiet had replaced the previous animation. The birds had taken themselves off to feed in the brooks. The horses stood still. Yet the power was there all the same, massed outside indifferent, impersonal, not attending to anything in particular. Somehow it was opposed to the little hay-coloured moth. It was useless to try to do anything. One could only watch the extraordinary efforts made by those tiny legs against an oncoming doom which could, had it chosen, have submerged an entire city, not merely a city, but masses of human beings; nothing, I knew had any chance against death. Nevertheless after a pause of exhaustion the legs fluttered again. It was superb this last protest, and so frantic that he succeeded at last in righting himself. One's sympathies, of course, were all on the side of life. Also, when there was nobody to care or to know, this gigantic effort on the part of an insignificant little moth, against a power of such magnitude, to retain what no one else valued or desired to keep, moved one strangely. Again, somehow, one saw life, a pure bead. I lifted the pencil again, useless though I knew it to be. But even as I did so, the unmistakable tokens of death showed themselves. The body relaxed, and instantly grew stiff. The struggle was over. The insignificant little creature now knew death. As I looked at the dead moth, this minute wayside triumph of so great a force over so mean an antagonist filled me with wonder. Just as life had been strange a few minutes before, so death was now as strange. The moth having righted himself now lay most decently and uncomplainingly composed. O yes, he seemed to say, death is stronger than I am.

## QUESTIONS FOR ANALYSIS

1. In the opening paragraph, Woolf refers to the moth as "the present specimen." What does this choice of words suggest about her attitude toward the moth? Take inventory of the language Woolf uses to describe the moth throughout the essay. How does her attitude toward the moth change? Point to specific word choices to illustrate your answer. (Chapter 1 outlines procedures for taking inventory.)

2. In the beginning of the essay, Woolf uses the pronoun "one." Where does she shift to "I"? Why do you think she makes this shift? What does it signify?

3. In her description, Woolf triangulates among three distinct points: the window, beyond the window, and inside the room. What is going on in each? How do these places relate to one another? What does Woolf gain by moving her focus among these three points?

4. Briefly summarize what you think Woolf is saying in this essay. What is her controlling idea?

5. What does Woolf mean by this sentence: "He was little or nothing but life"? How does this statement relate to the essay's controlling idea?

6. At several points, Woolf anthropomorphizes nature by attributing human characteristics to it. Find these places, and explain how Woolf uses anthropomorphizing to develop her controlling idea. What can you conclude about Woolf's use of this writing strategy?

7. Woolf is widely respected for her writing style. Select one sentence or passage from the essay that you think is especially well written, and explain why you found it exceptional.

## SUGGESTIONS FOR WRITING

1. Sometimes the most insignificant events cause us to reflect on the most weighty subjects, such as when the death of a moth leads Woolf to reflect on life and death. In a journal, keep a record of everything that happens during one twenty-four-hour period. From this record, select an occasion that leads you to reflect on some profound topic.

Then write an essay on this subject, using this occasion as your starting point.

2. Write a reflective essay on some aspect of nature. Ground your reflection in a particular occasion. Describe a scene or relate an anecdote that reveals the significance of nature for you.

# Lewis Thomas

Lewis Thomas is a physician, medical administrator, and researcher as well as a distinguished writer. Born in New York in 1913, he was educated at Princeton University and Harvard Medical School. Thomas has served as chairman of the departments of pathology and medicine at the New York University-Bellevue Medical Center and as chairman of pathology and dean of Yale Medical School. After leaving Yale, he assumed the prestigious position of president of Memorial Sloan-Kettering Cancer Center.

Thomas is a prolific writer, and his articles have appeared in many journals, both scientific and popular. He regularly writes a column, "Notes of a Biology Watcher," for the *New England Journal of Medicine* and has collected these essays in two volumes: *The Lives of the Cell: Notes of a Biology Watcher* (1974), winner of the National Book Award, and *The Medusa and the Snail: More Notes of a Biology Watcher* (1979). In 1983, he published two books, *Late Night Thoughts on Listening to Mahler's Ninth Symphony* and *The Youngest Science*, an autobiography in which he parallels his own growth and maturation with that of the science of medicine.

# *On Natural Death*

Previewing the title can reveal a great deal about the essay you are about to read. The title of this essay indicates that Thomas, like Woolf, is reflecting upon the general subject of death, but he narrows this broad subject by focusing on something he calls "natural" death. The word "natural" also suggests that Thomas has an opposition in mind between death that is natural and death that is unnatural in some way. As you read, ask yourself what Thomas means by "natural" and what values he associates with it and with its opposite.

This essay was originally written for the *New England Journal of Medicine*, a journal that is widely read by doctors, and was later reprinted in *The Medusa and the Snail*. How might writing for this particular audience influence Thomas's style? How might being a scientist, particularly a doctor, affect his thinking about death?

There are so many new books about dying that there are now special shelves set aside for them in bookshops, along with the health-diet and home-repair paperbacks and the sex manuals. Some of them are so packed with detailed information and step-by-step instructions for performing the function that you'd think this was a new sort of skill which all of us are now required to learn. The strongest impression the casual reader gets, leafing through, is that proper dying has become an extraordinary, even an exotic experience, something only the specially trained get to do.

Also, you could be led to believe that we are the only creatures capable of the awareness of death, that when all the rest of nature is being cycled through dying, one generation after another, it is a different kind of process, done automatically and trivially, more "natural," as we say.

An elm in our backyard caught the blight this summer and dropped stone dead, leafless, almost overnight. One weekend it was a normal-looking elm, maybe a little bare in spots but nothing alarming, and the next weekend it was gone, passed over, departed, taken. Taken is right, for the tree surgeon came by yesterday with his crew of young helpers and their cherry picker, and took it down branch by branch and carted it off in the back of a red truck, everyone singing.

The dying of a field mouse, at the jaws of an amiable household cat, is a spectacle I have beheld many times. It used to make me wince. Early in life I gave up throwing sticks at the cat to make him drop the mouse, because the dropped mouse regularly went ahead and died anyway, but I always shouted unaffections at the cat to let him know the sort of animal he had become. Nature, I thought, was an abomination.

Recently I've done some thinking about that mouse, and I wonder if his dying is necessarily all that different from the passing of our elm. The main difference, if there is one, would be in the matter of pain. I do not believe that an elm tree has pain receptors, and even so, the blight seems to me a relatively painless way to go even if there were nerve endings in a tree, which there are not. But the mouse dangling tail-down from the teeth of a gray cat is something else again, with pain beyond bearing, you'd think, all over his small body.

There are now some plausible reasons for thinking it is not like that at all, and you can make up an entirely different story about the mouse and his dying if you like. At the instant of being trapped and penetrated by teeth, peptide hormones are released by cells in the hypothalamus and the pituitary gland; instantly these substances, called endorphins, are attached to the surfaces of other cells responsible for pain perception; the hormones have the pharmacologic properties of opium; there is no pain. Thus it is that the mouse seems always to dangle so languidly from the jaws, lies there so quietly when dropped, dies of his injuries without a struggle. If a mouse could shrug, he'd shrug.

I do not know if this is true or not, nor do I know how to prove it if it is true. Maybe if you could get in there quickly enough and administer naloxone, a specific morphine antagonist, you could turn off the endorphins and observe the restoration of pain, but this is not something I would care to do or see. I think I will leave it there, as a good guess about the dying of a cat-chewed mouse, perhaps about dying in general.

Montaigne had a hunch about dying, based on his own close call in a  8
riding accident. He was so badly injured as to be believed dead by his companions, and was carried home with lamentations, "all bloody, stained all over with the blood I had thrown up." He remembers the entire episode, despite having been "dead, for two full hours," with wonderment:

> It seemed to me that my life was hanging only by the tip of my lips. I closed my eyes in order, it seemed to me, to help push it out, and took pleasure in growing languid and letting myself go. It was an idea that was only floating on the surface of my soul, as delicate and feeble as all the rest, but in truth not only free from distress but mingled with that sweet feeling that people have who have let themselves slide into sleep. I believe that this is the same state in which people find themselves whom we see fainting in the agony of death, and I maintain that we pity them without cause. . . . In order to get used to the idea of death, I find there is nothing like coming close to it.

Later, in another essay, Montaigne returns to it:    9

> If you know not how to die, never trouble yourself; Nature will in a moment fully and sufficiently instruct you; she will exactly do that business for you; take you no care for it.

The worst accident I've ever seen was on Okinawa, in the early days  10
of the invasion, when a jeep ran into a troop carrier and was crushed nearly flat. Inside were two young MPs, trapped in bent steel, both mortally hurt, with only their heads and shoulders visible. We had a conversation while people with the right tools were prying them free. Sorry about the accident, they said. No, they said, they felt fine. Is everyone else okay, one of them said. Well, the other one said, no hurry now. And then they died.

Pain is useful for avoidance, for getting away when there's time to get  11
away, but when it is end game, and no way back, pain is likely to be turned off, and the mechanisms for this are wonderfully precise and quick. If I had to design an ecosystem in which creatures had to live off each other and in which dying was an indispensable part of living, I could not think of a better way to manage.

## QUESTIONS FOR ANALYSIS

1. What is the occasion for this reflection? How does Thomas use this occasion to set up his meditation on the general subject? By using this particular occasion, what attitudes and values does he evoke in you, as one typical reader?

2. In your own words, identify this essay's controlling idea. Then locate the place in the essay where this idea is most explicitly stated.

3. Throughout the essay, Thomas uses personal anecdote to develop his subject. Find the anecdotes, and choose one to examine closely. Why do you suppose he chose this particular anecdote? What purpose do the details serve? How does this anecdote enable Thomas to particularize his controlling idea?

4. In this essay, Thomas relies on the strategy of comparison and contrast. Take inventory of the instances of comparison and contrast. From this analysis, what conclusions can you make about how Thomas uses this writing strategy to develop his controlling idea? (Chapter 1 presents a plan for taking inventory.)

5. Why do you suppose Thomas quotes Montaigne? Look closely at the quotations. What images does Montaigne use to describe his experience? How do these images correspond to the images Thomas uses to describe the experiences of the elm, mouse, and soldiers?

6. Thomas could have concluded the essay with Montaigne. What does he gain from including the last two paragraphs in the essay? How are they essential to his overall plan?

7. At several points in the essay, Thomas uses colloquial language, like "dropped stone dead." He also uses technical terms, like "hypothalamus." Take inventory of the essay, listing instances of colloquial and of technical language. Then conjecture on the effect of combining these two kinds of language in the same essay. What do these word choices suggest about the writer's tone?

8. Does Thomas ever reveal in the essay his personal feelings about dying? If so, where? If not, why do you think he avoids mixing personal revelation with reflection?

9. How might a scientific paper on the subject of natural death differ from this reflective essay? What can you conclude about the differences between scientific and reflective writing?

### SUGGESTIONS FOR WRITING

1. Death is not only the subject of many how-to books, but is also the subject of many reflective essays. In an essay entitled "That to Philosophize is to Learn to Die," Montaigne writes: "The goal of our career is death. It is the necessary object of our aim. If it frightens us, how is it possible to go a step forward without feverishness? The remedy of the common herd is not to think about it."

Spend some time thinking about death, and then write your own reflective essay on the subject.

2. In our culture, there are many books and courses to teach us how to perform "natural" functions such as dying, loving, and child-raising. What is meant by "natural"? If a process is "natural," does that mean that we cannot learn anything about managing it? Write a reflective essay examining these questions, or others you might have in response to Thomas's essay.

# E. M. Forster

Widely regarded as one of the most important British writers of this century, E(dward) M(organ) Forster (1879–1970) is probably best known for his novel A *Passage to India* (1924). Forster began his writing career as a journalist contributing to the liberal journal *The Independent Review*. He published five novels, a collection of short stories (*The Celestial Omnibus* in 1911), a highly respected book of literary criticism (*Aspects of the Novel* in 1927), and two collections of essays (*Abinger Harvest* in 1926 and *Two Cheers for Democracy* in 1951).

# My Wood

The title "My Wood" (from *Abinger Harvest*) refers to the occasion that gave rise to this essay, the author's purchase of some land. Buying land, of course, is fairly common, but Forster takes this particular event and demonstrates that it has general significance. He does this by studying the effect ownership has had on him personally. Before you begin reading, reflect for a moment on your own attitudes toward owning things—a car, a pet, a book. How do you feel about your possessions? How do you feel when other people handle or borrow things you own?

In this essay Forster claims to resist generalizing from his own experience, yet his purpose for writing is not likely to be personal expression. As you read, conjecture about what Forster's purpose really is. Moreover, ask yourself why he would deny that his essay generalizes about the effects of ownership.

A few years ago I wrote a book which dealt in part with the difficulties 1 of the English in India. Feeling that they would have had no difficulties in India themselves, the Americans read the book freely. The more they read it the better it made them feel, and a cheque to the author was the result. I bought a wood with the cheque. It is not a large wood—it contains scarcely any trees, and it is intersected, blast it, by a public footpath. Still, it is the first property that I have owned, so it is right that other people should participate in my shame, and should ask themselves, in accents that will vary in horror, this very important question: What is the effect of property upon the character? Don't let's touch economics; the effect of private ownership upon the community as a whole is another question—a more important question, perhaps, but another one. Let's keep to psychology. If you own things, what's their effect on you? What's the effect on me of my wood?

111

To watch a moth fluttering @ the window I almost feels a sense of pity.

In the first place, it makes me feel heavy. Property does have this effect. Property produces men of weight, and it was a man of weight who failed to get into the Kingdom of Heaven. He was not wicked, that unfortunate millionaire in the parable, he was only stout; he stuck out in front, not to mention behind, and as he wedged himself this way and that in the crystalline entrance and bruised his well-fed flanks, he saw beneath him a comparatively slim camel passing through the eye of a needle and being woven into the robe of God. The Gospels all through couple stoutness and slowness. They point out what is perfectly obvious, yet seldom realized: that if you have a lot of things you cannot move about a lot, that furniture requires dusting, dusters require servants, servants require insurance stamps, and the whole tangle of them makes you think twice before you accept an invitation to dinner or go for a bathe in the Jordan. Sometimes the Gospels proceed further and say with Tolstoy that property is sinful; they approach the difficult ground of asceticism here, where I cannot follow them. But as to the immediate effects of property on people, they just show straightforward logic. It produces men of weight. Men of weight cannot, by definition, move like the lightning from the East unto the West, and the ascent of a fourteen-stone bishop into a pulpit is thus the exact antithesis of the coming of the Son of Man. My wood makes me feel heavy. 2

In the second place, it makes me feel it ought to be larger. 3

The other day I heard a twig snap in it. I was annoyed at first, for I 4 thought that someone was blackberrying, and depreciating the value of the undergrowth. On coming nearer, I saw it was not a man who had trodden on the twig and snapped it, but a bird, and I felt pleased. My bird. The bird was not equally pleased. Ignoring the relation between us, it took fright as soon as it saw the shape of my face, and flew straight over the boundary hedge into a field, the property of Mrs. Henessy, where it sat down with a loud squawk. It had become Mrs. Henessy's bird. Something seemed grossly amiss here, something that would not have occurred had the wood been larger. I could not afford to buy Mrs. Henessy out, I dared not murder her, and limitations of this sort beset me on every side. Ahab did not want that vineyard—he only needed it to round off his property, preparatory to plotting a new curve—and all the land around my wood has become necessary to me in order to round off the wood. A boundary protects. But—poor little thing—the boundary ought in its turn to be protected. Noises on the edge of it. Children throw stones. A little more, and then a little more, until we reach the sea. Happy Canute! Happier Alexander! And after all, why should even the world be the limit of possession? A rocket containing a Union Jack, will, it is hoped, be shortly fired at the moon. Mars. Sirius. Beyond which

. . . But these immensities ended by saddening me. I could not suppose that my wood was the destined nucleus of universal dominion—it is so very small and contains no mineral wealth beyond the blackberries. Nor was I comforted when Mrs. Henessy's bird took alarm for the second time and flew clean away from us all, under the belief that it belonged to itself.

In the third place, property makes its owner feel that he ought to do 5 something to it. Yet he isn't sure what. A restlessness comes over him, a vague sense that he has a personality to express—the same sense which, without any vagueness, leads the artist to an act of creation. Sometimes I think I will cut down such trees as remain in the wood, at other times I want to fill up the gaps between them with new trees. Both impulses are pretentious and empty. They are not honest movements towards money-making or beauty. They spring from a foolish desire to express myself and from an inability to enjoy what I have got. Creation, property, enjoyment form a sinister trinity in the human mind. Creation and en-joyment are both very very good, yet they are often unattainable without a material basis, and at such moments property pushes itself in as a substitute, saying, "Accept me instead—I'm good enough for all three." It is not enough. It is, as Shakespeare said of lust, "The expense of spirit in a waste of shame": it is "Before, a joy proposed; behind, a dream." Yet we don't know how to shun it. It is forced on us by our economic system as the alternative to starvation. It is also forced on us by an internal defect in the soul, by the feeling that in property may lie the germs of self-development and of exquisite or heroic deeds. Our life on earth is, and ought to be, material and carnal. But we have not yet learned to manage our materialism and carnality properly; they are still entangled with the desire for ownership, where (in the words of Dante) "Possession is one with loss."

And this brings us to our fourth and final point: the blackberries. 6

Blackberries are not plentiful in this meagre grove, but they are easily 7 seen from the public footpath which traverses it, and all too easily gath-ered. Foxgloves, too—people will pull up the foxgloves, and ladies of an educational tendency even grub for toadstools to show them on the Mon-day in class. Other ladies, less educated, roll down the bracken in the arms of their gentlemen friends. There is paper, there are tins. Pray, does my wood belong to me or doesn't it? And, if it does, should I not own it best by allowing no one else to walk there? There is a wood near Lyme Regis, also cursed by a public footpath, where the owner has not hesitated on this point. He has built high stone walls each side of the path, and has spanned it by bridges, so that the public circulate like termites while he gorges on the blackberries unseen. He really does own his wood, this able chap. Dives in Hell did pretty well, but the gulf dividing him from Lazarus could be traversed by vision, and nothing traverses it here. And perhaps I shall come to this in time. I shall wall in and fence out until I really taste the sweets of property. Enormously stout, endlessly avaricious, pseudo-creative, intensely selfish, I shall weave upon my forehead the quadruple crown of possession until those nasty Bolshies come and take it off again and thrust me aside into the outer darkness.

### QUESTIONS FOR ANALYSIS

1. According to Forster, what are the effects of owning property? Identify the effect that you think is most important, and explain why ownership might have that particular effect.

2. Forster sets up many different sets of oppositions in this essay: private property versus the public footpath, heavy versus light. Make an inventory of the oppositions you find in the essay. Then decide what systems of attitudes and values you think these oppositions imply. (See Chapter 1 for a discussion of taking inventory.)

3. What is the controlling idea of this essay? Where does Forster come closest to stating this idea explicitly?

4. Forster makes several allusions to the Bible, to history, and to literature. Identify as many of these references as you can. Then select one of them and explain how Forster uses it to develop his subject.

5. Most of Forster's paragraphs are quite long and developed, yet he has two single-sentence paragraphs. Find these two paragraphs. What advantages or disadvantages do you see in this paragraphing strategy?

6. In paragraph 4, Forster tells an anecdote about a bird that flew from his wood to Mrs. Henessy's. Why do you think he tells this story? What purpose does it serve in the essay as a whole? How does Forster use this narrative to illustrate his controlling idea?

7. In paragraph 5, Forster's writing seems especially dense and abstract. Analyze the style—sentence structure and word choices—of this paragraph to see how it differs from the style of paragraph 4. Why do you suppose Forster's style differs so much in these two paragraphs?

8. What effect do the last few sentences of the essay have? Why do you think Forster mentions the Communists ("those nasty Bolshies")? What does he mean by the "sweets of property"?

9. How would you characterize the tone of this essay? Is it consistent, or do you find the tone changing? Cite specific language from the text to illustrate your response.

## SUGGESTIONS FOR WRITING

1. Many young people today are criticized for being concerned only with material possessions. Do you think this criticism is accurate and fair? Write a reflective essay exploring some aspect of this subject.

2. In this essay, Forster suggests that the "desire to express" one's personality is "foolish" and often mistaken for artistic impulse. How would you define creativity? Does it stem from a desire for self-expression or from some other source? Write a reflective essay in which you ponder what creativity means to you.

# E. B. White

Most children known E(lwyn) B(rooks) White (1899–1985) as the author of *Stuart Little* (1945) and *Charlotte's Web* (1952), but adults chiefly regard him as an essayist and fine prose stylist. He is perhaps best known for his revision of *The Elements of Style*, by William Strunk, Jr. Over the years, White's many essays have appeared in *The New Yorker*, *Harper's Magazine*, and the *Atlantic Monthly* and have been collected in three volumes—*One Man's Meat* (1944), *The Second Tree from the Corner* (1954), and *The Points of My Compass* (1962). In 1976, White selected his favorites, "along with a few" that he said "seemed to have the odor of durability clinging to them," to appear in *The Essays of E. B. White*.

White received many awards, including the Gold Medal for Essays and Criticism of the American Academy of Arts and Letters (1960), the Presidential Medal of Freedom (1963), the Laura Ingalls Wilder Award (1970), and the National Medal for Literature (1971). The citation accompanying the Gold Medal praised White with these words: "When he writes of large subjects he does not make them larger and windier than they are, and when he writes of small things they are never insignificant."

# *The Ring of Time*

E. B. White wrote "The Ring of Time" after watching a circus performer practice her act. The practice session itself was uneventful. No one fell from the high wire, nor did a lion go berserk. All that happened was that a young girl rode around the ring on a horse and did some rather uninspiring tricks. Yet this experience occasioned one of the best reflective essays ever written. What White captures in this essay is a moment in time, making it mean something larger, something universal and transcendent. As you read the essay, ask yourself how White infuses this incident with meaning. How does he make the scene come alive?

Fiddler Bayou, March 22, 1956

After the lions had returned to their cages, creeping angrily through the chutes, a little bunch of us drifted away and into an open doorway nearby, where we stood for a while in semidarkness, watching a big brown circus horse go harumphing around the practice ring. His trainer was a woman of about forty, and the two of them, horse and woman, seemed caught up in one of those desultory treadmills of afternoon from which there is no apparent escape. The day was hot, and we kibitzers were grateful to be briefly out of the sun's glare. The long rein, or tape, by

116

which the woman guided her charge counterclockwise in his dull career formed the radius of their private circle, of which she was the revolving center; and she, too, stepped a tiny circumference of her own, in order to accommodate the horse and allow him his maximum scope. She had on a short-skirted costume and a conical straw hat. Her legs were bare and she wore high heels, which probed deep into the loose tanbark and kept her ankles in a state of constant turmoil. The great size and meekness of the horse, the repetitive exercise, the heat of the afternoon, all exerted a hypnotic charm that invited boredom; we spectators were experiencing a languor—we neither expected relief nor felt entitled to any. We had paid a dollar to get into the grounds, to be sure, but we had got our dollar's worth a few minutes before, when the lion trainer's whiplash had got caught around a toe of one of the lions. What more did we want for a dollar?

Behind me I heard someone say, "Excuse me, please," in a low voice. 2 She was halfway into the building when I turned and saw her—a girl of sixteen or seventeen, politely threading her way through us onlookers who blocked the entrance. As she emerged in front of us, I saw that she was barefoot, her dirty little feet fighting the uneven ground. In most respects she was like any of two or three dozen showgirls you encounter if you wander about the winter quarters of Mr. John Ringling North's circus, in Sarasota—cleverly proportioned, deeply browned by the sun, dusty, eager, and almost naked. But her grave face and the naturalness of her manner gave her a sort of quick distinction and brought a new note into the gloomy octagonal building where we had all cast our lot for a few moments. As soon as she had squeezed through the crowd, she spoke a word or two to the older woman, whom I took to be her mother, stepped to the ring, and waited while the horse coasted to a stop in front of her. She gave the animal a couple of affectionate swipes on his enormous neck and then swung herself aboard. The horse immediately resumed his rocking canter, the woman goading him on, chanting something that sounded like "Hop! Hop!"

In attempting to recapture this mild spectacle, I am merely acting as 3 recording secretary for one of the oldest of societies—the society of those who, at one time or another, have surrendered, without even a show of resistance, to the bedazzlement of a circus rider. As a writing man, or secretary, I have always felt charged with the safekeeping of all unexpected items of worldly or unworldly enchantment, as though I might be held personally responsible if even a small one were to be lost. But it is not easy to communicate anything of this nature. The circus comes as close to being the world in microcosm as anything I know; in a way, it puts all the rest of show business in the shade. Its magic is universal and complex. Out of its wild disorder comes order; from its rank smell rises the good aroma of courage and daring; out of its preliminary shabbiness comes the final splendor. And buried in the familiar boasts of its advance agents lies the modesty of most of its people. For me the circus is at its best before it has been put together. It is at its best at certain moments when it comes to a point, as through a burning glass, in the activity and destiny of a single performer out of so many. One ring is always bigger than three. One rider, one aerialist, is always greater than six. In short, a man has to catch the circus unawares to experience its full impact and share its gaudy dream.

The ten-minute ride the girl took achieved—as far as I was concerned,    4
who wasn't looking for it, and quite unbeknownst to her, who wasn't even striving for it—the thing that is sought by performers everywhere, on whatever stage, whether struggling in the tidal currents of Shakespeare or bucking the difficult motion of a horse. I somehow got the idea she was just cadging a ride, improving a shining ten minutes in the diligent way all serious artists seize free moments to hone the blade of their talent and keep themselves in trim. Her brief tour included only elementary postures and tricks, perhaps because they were all she was capable of, perhaps because her warmup at this hour was unscheduled and the ring was not rigged for a real practice session. She swung herself off and on the horse several times, gripping his mane. She did a few knee-stands— or whatever they are called—dropping to her knees and quickly bouncing back up on her feet again. Most of the time she simply rode in a standing position, well aft on the beast, her hands hanging easily at her sides, her head erect, her straw-colored ponytail lightly brushing her shoulders, the blood of exertion showing faintly through the tan of her skin. Twice she managed a one-foot stance—a sort of ballet pose, with arms outstretched. At one point the neck strap of her bathing suit broke and she went twice around the ring in the classic attitude of a woman making minor repairs to a garment. The fact that she was standing on the back of a moving horse while doing this invested the matter with a clownish significance that perfectly fitted the spirit of the circus—jocund, yet charming. She just rolled the strap into a neat ball and stowed it inside her bodice while the horse rocked and rolled beneath her in dutiful innocence. The bathing suit proved as self-reliant as its owner and stood up well enough without benefit of strap.

The richness of the scene was in its plainness, its natural condition—    5
of horse, of ring, of girl, even to the girl's bare feet that gripped the bare back of her proud and ridiculous mount. The enchantment grew not out of anything that happened or was performed but out of something that seemed to go round and around and around with the girl, attending her,

a steady gleam in the shape of a circle—a ring of ambition, of happiness, of youth. (And the positive pleasures of equilibrium under difficulties.) In a week or two, all would be changed, all (or almost all) lost: the girl would wear makeup, the horse would wear gold, the ring would be painted, the bark would be clean for the feet of the horse, the girl's feet would be clean for the slippers that she'd wear. All, all would be lost.

As I watched with the others, our jaws adroop, our eyes alight, I became painfully conscious of the element of time. Everything in the hideous old building seemed to take the shape of a circle, conforming to the course of the horse. The rider's gaze, as she peered straight ahead, seemed to be circular, as though bent by force of circumstance; then time itself began running in circles, and so the beginning was where the end was, and the two were the same, and one thing ran into the next and time went round and around and got nowhere. The girl wasn't so young that she did not know the delicious satisfaction of having a perfectly behaved body and the fun of using it to do a trick most people can't do, but she was too young to know that time does not really move in a circle at all. I thought: "She will never be as beautiful as this again"—a thought that made me acutely unhappy—and in a flash my mind (which is too much of a busybody to suit me) had projected her twenty-five years ahead, and she was now in the center of the ring, on foot, wearing a conical hat and high-heeled shoes, the image of the older woman, holding the long rein, caught in the treadmill of an afternoon long in the future. "She is at that enviable moment in life [I thought] when she believes she can go once around the ring, make one complete circuit, and at the end be exactly the same age as at the start." Everything in her movements, her expression, told you that for her the ring of time was perfectly formed, changeless, predictable, without beginning or end, like the ring in which she was traveling at this moment with the horse that wallowed under her. And then I slipped back into my trance, and time was circular again—time, pausing quietly with the rest of us, so as not to disturb the balance of a performer.

Her ride ended as casually as it had begun. The older woman stopped the horse, and the girl slid to the ground. As she walked toward us to leave, there was a quick, small burst of applause. She smiled broadly, in surprise and pleasure; then her face suddenly regained its gravity and she disappeared through the door.

It has been ambitious and plucky of me to attempt to describe what is indescribable, and I have failed, as I knew I would. But I have discharged my duty to my society; and besides, a writer, like an acrobat, must occasionally try a stunt that is too much for him. At any rate, it is worth reporting that long before the circus comes to town, its most notable performances have already been given. Under the bright lights of the finished show, a performer need only reflect the electric candle power that is directed upon him; but in the dark and dirty old training rings and in the makeshift cages, whatever light is generated, whatever excitement, whatever beauty, must come from original sources—from internal fires of professional hunger and delight, from the exuberance and gravity of youth. It is the difference between planetary light and the combustion of stars.

### QUESTIONS FOR ANALYSIS

1. Reread the opening paragraph and underline the words that help to set the mood of the essay. Then, in your own words, describe the mood. Why is this an effective opening?

2. Why do you think White is fascinated by the girl on the horse? Find the passages in which he describes her. What impression does this description give you? What general significance does White attach to her?

3. White's essay is not merely about the circus. What else is it about? How does he use "this mild spectacle" to say something more general? In other words, what would you say is this essay's controlling idea?

4. White says that "a man has to catch the circus unawares to experience its full impact and share its gaudy dream." What do you suppose he means? How has White caught the circus unawares in this essay?

5. In paragraph 3, White interrupts his narrative to discuss his own role of "recording secretary." Skim the essay, noting other places where he describes himself. What do you think White gains from calling attention to himself in this way? What is your impression of him?

6. White is a masterful stylist who uses a wide variety of sentence structures to great effect. Find a sentence that you think is especially well written, and explain why you like it.

7. Take inventory of the figurative language in this selection. What values and attitudes does White convey through these images? (A plan for taking inventory appears in Chapter 1.)

### SUGGESTIONS FOR WRITING

1. In this essay, White describes himself as an "onlooker," describing a scene he witnessed. Writers often find occasion for reflection in their observations, yet it is not the occasion that must be special but the writer's way of seeing it.

Write a reflective essay centering, as White does, upon a particular scene. Try to make this scene come to life and, at the same time, let your reader know what larger meanings it carries for you.

2. In this essay, White is reflecting from an adult's perspective on something that is usually associated with childhood. Think of something you associate with childhood, and write a reflective essay about it.

# Joan Didion

Joan Didion is a novelist, a screenwriter, and an essayist. Her most successful novels have been *Play It As It Lays* (1971), *The Book of Common Prayer* (1977), and *Democracy* (1984). With her husband John Gregory Dunne, Didion wrote the screenplays for *A Star Is Born* (1976) and *True Confessions* (1981). In addition to the controversial book-length essay *Salvador* (1983), she has published two collections of essays: *Slouching Towards Bethlehem* (1968) and *The White Album* (1979).

After graduating from college, Didion wrote for *Mademoiselle*, *Saturday Evening Post*, and *Life*. She even worked for a time on the editorial staff of *Vogue*, where a senior editor taught her how to write: "Every day I would go into her office with eight lines of copy or a caption or something. She would sit there and mark up with a pencil and get very angry about extra words, about verbs not working. . . . In an eight-line caption everything had to work, every word, every comma."

# *On Self-Respect*

The following selection may seem unusual in that it was occasioned by something that did not happen. In this piece, Didion writes about the memory of her failure to be elected to Phi Beta Kappa, the college honorary society. As Didion looks back, she reflects not only on what this failure meant to her but also on what self-respect means more generally.

A recognized master of the reflective essay, Didion writes occasionally about her art. In one essay, she commented: "We live entirely, especially if we are writers, by the imposition of a narrative line upon disparate images, by the 'ideas' with which we have learned to freeze the shifting phantasmagoria which is our actual experience." As you read this selection, consider how Didion uses ideas to order and understand her experience. Ask yourself what her controlling idea is and how it works to organize the essay.

Once, in a dry season, I wrote in large letters across two pages of a 1 notebook that innocence ends when one is stripped of the delusion that one likes oneself. Although now, some years later, I marvel that a mind on the outs with itself should have nonetheless made painstaking record of its every tremor, I recall with embarrassing clarity the flavor of those particular ashes. It was a matter of misplaced self-respect.

I had not been elected to Phi Beta Kappa. This failure could scarcely 2 have been more predictable or less ambiguous (I simply did not have the grades), but I was unnerved by it; I had somehow thought myself a kind of academic Raskolnikov, curiously exempt from the cause-effect relationships which hampered others. Although even the humorless nineteen-year-old that I was must have recognized that the situation lacked real tragic stature, the day that I did not make Phi Beta Kappa nonetheless marked the end of something, and innocence may well be the word for it. I lost the conviction that lights would always turn green for me, the pleasant certainty that those rather passive virtues which had won me approval as a child automatically guaranteed me not only Phi Beta Kappa keys but happiness, honor, and the love of a good man; lost a certain touching faith in the totem power of good manners, clean hair, and proven competence on the Stanford-Binet scale. To such doubtful amulets had my self-respect been pinned, and I faced myself that day with the nonplused apprehension of someone who has come across a vampire and has no crucifix at hand.

Although to be driven back upon oneself is an uneasy affair at best, 3 rather like trying to cross a border with borrowed credentials, it seems to me now the one condition necessary to the beginnings of real self-respect. Most of our platitudes notwithstanding, self-deception remains the most difficult deception. The tricks that work on others count for nothing in that very well-lit back alley where one keeps assignations with oneself: no winning smiles will do here, no prettily drawn lists of good intentions. One shuffles flashily but in vain through one's marked cards— the kindness done for the wrong reason, the apparent triumph which involved no real effort, the seemingly heroic act into which one had been shamed. The dismal fact is that self-respect has nothing to do with the approval of others—who are, after all, deceived easily enough; has nothing to do with reputation, which, as Rhett Butler told Scarlett O'Hara, is something people with courage can do without.

To do without self-respect, on the other hand, is to be an unwilling 4 audience of one to an interminable documentary that details one's failings, both real and imagined, with fresh footage spliced in for every screening. *There's the glass you broke in anger, there's the hurt on X's face; watch now, this next scene, the night Y came back from Houston, see how you muff this one.* To live without self-respect is to lie awake some night, beyond the reach of warm milk, phenobarbital, and the sleeping hand on the coverlet, counting up the sins of commission and omission, the trusts betrayed, the promises subtly broken, the gifts irrevocably wasted through sloth or cowardice or carelessness. However long we postpone it, we eventually lie down alone in that notoriously uncomfortable bed, the one we make ourselves. Whether or not we sleep in it depends, of course, on whether or not we respect ourselves.

To protest that some fairly improbable people, some people who *could*      5
*not possibly respect themselves,* seem to sleep easily enough is to miss the
point entirely, as surely as those people miss it who think that self-respect
has necessarily to do with not having safety pins in one's underwear.
There is a common superstition that "self-respect" is a kind of charm
against snakes, something that keeps those who have it locked in some
unblighted Eden, out of strange beds, ambivalent conversations, and
trouble in general. It does not at all. It has nothing to do with the face
of things, but concerns instead a separate peace, a private reconciliation.
Although the careless, suicidal Julian English in *Appointment in Samarra*
and the careless, incurably dishonest Jordan Baker in *The Great Gatsby*
seem equally improbable candidates for self-respect, Jordan Baker had it,
Julian English did not. With that genius for accommodation more often
seen in women than in men, Jordan took her own measure, made her
own peace, avoided threats to that peace: "I hate careless people," she
told Nick Carraway. "It takes two to make an accident."

Like Jordan Baker, people with self-respect have the courage of their      6
mistakes. They know the price of things. If they choose to commit adultery, they do not then go running, in an excess of bad conscience, to
receive absolution from the wronged parties; nor do they complain unduly
of the unfairness, the undeserved embarrassment, of being named co-
respondent. In brief, people with self-respect exhibit a certain toughness,
a kind of moral nerve; they display what was once called *character,* a
quality which, although approved in the abstract, sometimes loses ground
to other, more instantly negotiable virtues. The measure of its slipping
prestige is that one tends to think of it only in connection with homely
children and United States senators who have been defeated, preferably
in the primary, for reelection. Nonetheless, character—the willingness
to accept responsibility for one's own life—is the source from which self-
respect springs.

Self-respect is something that our grandparents, whether or not they      7
had it, knew all about. They had instilled in them, young, a certain
discipline, the sense that one lives by doing things one does not particularly want to do, by putting fears and doubts to one side, by weighing
immediate comforts against the possibility of larger, even intangible,
comforts. It seemed to the nineteenth century admirable, but not remarkable, that Chinese Gordon put on a clean white suit and held Khar-
toum against the Mahdi; it did not seem unjust that the way to free land
in California involved death and difficulty and dirt. In a diary kept during
the winter of 1846, an emigrating twelve-year-old named Narcissa Corn-
wall noted coolly: "Father was busy reading and did not notice that the
house was being filled with strange Indians until Mother spoke about it."

Even lacking any clue as to what Mother said, one can scarcely fail to be impressed by the entire incident: the father reading, the Indians filing in, the mother choosing the words that would not alarm, the child duly recording the event and noting further that those particular Indians were not, "fortunately for us," hostile. Indians were simply part of the *donnée*.

In one guise or another, Indians always are. Again, it is a question of recognizing that anything worth having has its price. People who respect themselves are willing to accept the risk that the Indians will be hostile, that the venture will go bankrupt, that the liaison may not turn out to be one in which *every day is a holiday because you're married to me*. They are willing to invest something of themselves; they may not play at all, but when they do play, they know the odds.

That kind of self-respect is a discipline, a habit of mind that can never be faked but can be developed, trained, coaxed forth. It was once suggested to me that, as an antidote to crying, I put my head in a paper bag. As it happens, there is a sound physiological reason, something to do with oxygen, for doing exactly that, but the psychological effect alone is incalculable: it is difficult in the extreme to continue fancying oneself Cathy in *Wuthering Heights* with one's head in a Food Fair bag. There is a similar case for all the small disciplines, unimportant in themselves; imagine maintaining any kind of swoon, commiserative or carnal, in a cold shower.

But those small disciplines are available only insofar as they represent larger ones. To say that Waterloo was won on the playing fields of Eton is not to say that Napoleon might have been saved by a crash program in cricket; to give formal dinners in the rain forest would be pointless did not the candlelight flickering on the liana call forth deeper, stronger disciplines, values instilled long before. It is a kind of ritual, helping us to remember who and what we are. In order to remember it, one must have known it.

To have that sense of one's intrinsic worth which constitutes self-respect is potentially to have everything: the ability to discriminate, to love and to remain indifferent. To lack it is to be locked within oneself, paradoxically incapable of either love or indifference. If we do not respect ourselves, we are on the one hand forced to despise those who have so few resources as to consort with us, so little perception as to remain blind to our fatal weaknesses. On the other, we are peculiarly in thrall to everyone we see, curiously determined to live out—since our self-image is untenable—their false notions of us. We flatter ourselves by thinking this compulsion to please others an attractive trait: a gist for imaginative empathy, evidence of our willingness to give. *Of course* I will play Francesca to your Paolo, Helen Keller to anyone's Annie Sullivan: no expectation is too misplaced, no role too ludicrous. At the mercy of those we cannot but hold in contempt, we play roles doomed to failure before they are begun, each defeat generating fresh despair at the urgency of divining and meeting the next demand made upon us.

It is the phenomenon sometimes called "alienation from self." In its advanced stages, we no longer answer the telephone, because someone might want something; that we could say *no* without drowning in self-reproach is an idea alien to this game. Every encounter demands too much, tears the nerves, drains the will, and the specter of something as small as an unanswered letter arouses such disproportionate guilt that answering it becomes out of the question. To assign unanswered letters their proper weight, to free us from the expectations of others, to give us back to ourselves—there lies the great, the singular power of self-respect. Without it, one eventually discovers the final turn of the screw: one runs away to find oneself, and finds no one at home.

### QUESTIONS FOR ANALYSIS

1. Didion relies on her reading as well as her personal experience to develop her ideas about self-respect. Underline all of the references to books and authors. Why do you think Didion relies so often on this kind of development? Choose one reference that you recognize and explain what it contributes to the essay.

2. At one point in the essay, Didion indicates that she is aware of a question some readers might have about her ideas. Find this point, and analyze how Didion responds to the question. Consider also why she would interrupt her reflections to respond to such a question.

3. Throughout the essay, Didion surprises us with references to common objects and everyday events: lights turning green, crossing a border, well-lit back alleys, marked playing cards, for example. Make an inventory of these references. What can you conclude about their role in the essay? (Chapter 1 contains a plan for taking inventory.)

4. In this essay, Didion regularly presents examples in threes: in paragraph 2, for example, she asserts that she lost faith in "good manners, clean hair, and proven competence on the Stanford-Binet scale [an intelligence test]." Skim the essay, underlining other instances where examples come in threes. Why do you think Didion relies on this strategy? What advantages or disadvantages do you see in it?

5. Throughout the essay Didion contrasts what it is like to have self-respect and what it is like to lack it. Make an inventory of these

references in two lists, one headed "With Self-Respect," the other "Without Self-Respect." What can you conclude about Didion's strategy of contrast? How does she use it to develop her ideas?

6. Didion also relies on the invaluable strategy of explaining causes and effects. Review the essay, looking for places where Didion explains the causes of self-respect and its effects. What does this cause-effect strategy contribute to the essay?

7. A consummate stylist, Didion maintains a lively, interesting pace by varying sentence length and sentence structure. Choose a paragraph that you think is especially well written, and count the number of words in each sentence. Then identify the kinds of sentence structures she uses. Which sentences follow the basic subject-verb-object pattern? Which are simple, compound, complex? Which use coordination? Which subordination?

8. What is your impression of the author from reading this essay? What gives you this impression?

## SUGGESTIONS FOR WRITING

1. In this essay, Didion generalizes about self-respect from her own experience of failure. Think of an experience you have had, and generalize from it about some quality or virtue that you think people should cultivate.

2. At one point in this essay, Didion writes: "The dismal fact is that self-respect has nothing to do with the approval of others." Write a reflective essay of your own in response to this statement. Why should this be a "dismal fact"? Is it really even a "fact"? Don't children develop a sense of self-respect from the way others treat them? Why do you think Didion makes this statement? Do you think she believes it? Does her essay support it?

# Neda Rose Baric

When Neda Rose Baric applied to college she intended to become a history major, but she has now decided to major in English, largely because she loves to read. Baric claims she'll read anything—including cereal boxes—but her favorite authors are Sylvia Plath, Nathaniel West, and Henry James.

Although Baric reads constantly, she seldom writes, except as classwork. She feels fairly confident about writing essays, however, believing that writing is a natural extension of reading: "I can write logically because I've seen it done so many times."

# *On Reading* The Bell Jar

Baric's reflective essay derives from a different kind of occasion than the other selections in this chapter. Her essay was inspired by her reading, specifically by Sylvia Plath's novel *The Bell Jar* (1963), which was assigned in an English class. Baric's class was asked to reflect upon its response to one of the works assigned in class.

*The Bell Jar* tells the story of a young woman's coming of age in the early 1950s. Baric felt a strong association with the main character, Esther Greenwood (comparable to the identification Esther has with another character named Doreen), even though the events in her own life do not even roughly parallel the events in Esther's life. What struck Baric so forcefully was how little conditions have changed from the 50s to the 80s, particularly for bright, aspiring young women. Notice to what extent Baric's reflections concern the condition of women in general and not just her own experience.

No book has ever affected me the way *The Bell Jar* did. The situations seem to address me personally, to reach out to me. Even though my background differs from hers and I live in a different era, I can empathize with Esther Greenwood. The resemblances between us are not superficial. We share many of the same beliefs, and I have had many of the same problems Esther faces. Esther's comment about Doreen expresses my own feelings about Esther: "Everything she said was like a secret voice speaking straight out of my own bones."

I appreciate Esther's frustration with all of the "weird old women" who "wanted to adopt me in some way, and, for the price of their care and influence, have me resemble them." I have encountered this same problem—on a smaller scale, perhaps—since grade school. To be an intelligent, advanced child can be a curse when you must continually live up to someone else's expectations. This phenomenon seems to occur primarily when successful older women see bright, young girls becoming trapped in the ghetto of traditional female careers. These women try to program girls for achievement and competition, and they expect the girls to adhere to their beliefs and principles. In junior high school, a history teacher reprimanded me whenever she felt that I wasn't living up to her standards. When I got tired of her demands and refused to comply with them, she called me rebellious and sulked. A friend of mine faced a similar situation. An otherwise wonderful woman took my friend under her wing but never forgave her for deciding to attend a state college instead of a prestigious private university. To this day, she still nags my friend about that decision—even though it is far too late to change it. It is difficult to satisfy yourself and others simultaneously. Esther is pulled by so many forces that she no longer has a will of her own. Certainly it is flattering when people take an interest in you, but when you have to make important decisions just to please others, you start to feel suffocated.

I also sympathize with Esther's paranoia over schoolwork and fully    3 understand her fears about taking chemistry. When I began considering majoring in English, my desire to study American literature was dampened by the realization that I would finally have to read *Walden*. I hate *Walden*. I absolutely loathe and fear *Walden*. I should have already read it for several classes, but I've only read the first chapter—and that was years ago. Something in me simply refuses to take this book in. I've faked it successfully in the past, but I know that I'll be exposed the next time I am assigned the book. Like Esther, I also feel like a moron whenever I thumb through the college catalog. Even if I took all the undergraduate classes offered, I would still feel stupid. Just the fact that so many classes are listed makes me feel inadequate, as though I should be taking more. I frequently have nightmares (especially toward the end of the term) in which I either forget to turn in an important paper or sleep through the final. I know that these dreams stem from fear of failure, and the fear that my stupidity will be revealed.

What affects me most about *The Bell Jar* is that Esther's feminist ideas    4 are almost exactly like my own. It's more like the 1950s than the 1980s in my family right now, so I know what Esther had to face. Often I look at my parents, my sister and brother-in-law, and my brother and his two almost-but-not-quite wives, and I heartily agree with Esther's cynical statement:

And I knew that in spite of all of the roses and kisses and restaurant dinners a man showered on a woman before he married her, what he secretly wanted when the service ended was for her to flatten out under his feet like Mrs. Williard's kitchen mat.

Not long ago my sister, who recently celebrated twelve years of marriage, told me that equality in a relationship ends at the altar. She wasn't angry about it, just long ago resigned. I wonder how many real advances women have made since Sylvia Plath wrote those lines. I, who was born after the publication of *The Bell Jar*, have always been steered by my parents toward the traditional female occupations of nurse, teacher, and secretary—all of which I naturally despise. The last thing I want to do is "transcribe letter after thrilling letter." In fact, the idea of serving men appalls me. It would truly be, as Esther so beautifully states, "a dreary and wasted life for a girl with fifteen years of straight A's." The fact that traditional women's jobs generally require less education only fuels my desire to continue in school. Many of my plans are driven by an inner anger at the disparity between women's expectations and men's. Since I've been at the university, I've noticed with increasing dismay that male undergraduate English majors are vastly outnumbered by females, yet among graduate students the number of males and females is about equal and nearly all the professors are men. Why? Because men are smarter than women? No. It's because women have been taught to have modest goals. They are told, as Esther was told by her mother, to be content with being "the place the arrow shoots off from" rather than the arrow itself. Women become grade school teachers while their male counterparts become university professors. Even women who intend to pursue an advanced degree are often diverted by the need to earn a living or by the ticking of the biological clock that tells them they had better have children while they still can. The world only *seems* less male-dominated today than it was in Esther's time. Actual improvements are negligible.

Esther and I are most similar in our tendency to get angry. Esther is   5 angered by the execution of the Rosenbergs and the sexual double standard. In the delivery room, Esther becomes indignant as she watches a woman giving birth. The scene is nightmarish—the woman on "an awful torture table," looking like a spider. Instead of the miracle of birth, we see a painful, poorly orchestrated ritual run by men who have no concern for the woman's feelings. Through her anger Esther recognizes the injustices of society. Without anger, she would be complacent with her lot. I too get angry in order to fight off complacency. Although people tell me I am too intense for my own good, I know that I have to allow myself to care passionately.

Esther Greenwood is my sister. That she and I have lived such similar 6
lives is due in part to the artistry of Sylvia Plath. The fact that Esther
and I have so much in common shows that not much has changed for a
female college student since the 1950s. Esther is my sister, Sylvia Plath
is my sister, and all the women who came between are my sisters. We
are related by the common effort to live with others yet at the same time
become most fully ourselves.

## QUESTIONS FOR ANALYSIS

1. What parallels does Baric find between Esther and herself? Choose
   one parallel and explain how Baric uses it as the starting point for
   her general reflections.

2. In paragraph 2, Baric sets up an opposition between being "trapped"
   and being "rebellious." Take inventory of the other words in the essay
   that fit under these two headings. Then explain how these oppositions
   convey the essay's controlling idea. (Chapter 1 outlines a plan for
   taking inventory.)

3. What writing strategy does Baric use to help readers understand her
   "paranoia over schoolwork"? How effective is this strategy? Recommend one addition, deletion, or other change that you think would
   make this paragraph work better.

4. Early in paragraph 4, Baric discusses the lack of equality in marriage,
   and later she shifts to the kinds of jobs women are likely to have.
   Summarize this paragraph, explaining how Baric connects these two
   apparently unrelated points.

5. Skim the essay, annotating Baric's quotations from *The Bell Jar*. From
   your analysis of Baric's use of quotation, what seems to be the advantage of quoting rather than paraphrasing? Point to specific examples
   from the essay to illustrate your answer.

6. How does Baric use comparison and contrast in this essay?

7. Describe how Baric concludes her essay. What advantage or disadvantage do you see in this way of ending a reflective essay? What
   generalization can you make about conclusions to essays of reflection?

8. Choose one sentence that you think is especially well written and
   explain what makes it so good. Or, if you prefer, choose a sentence
   that you think is poorly written and rewrite it, explaining why your
   revision is better.

SUGGESTIONS FOR WRITING

1. Recall a story, poem, play, or film that led you to reflect about your own life and about life in general. Write an essay presenting your reflections in a way that lets your readers see how the reflections came out of the particular occasion.

2. Baric writes eloquently in this essay about her feelings of suffocation under the weight of other people's expectations. Young men—as well as women—often have similar problems coping with their elders' expectations. Write an essay that reflects on these problems. How, for instance, do they differ for men and women?

# A Look at Neda Rose Baric's Writing Process

Baric felt confident when her instructor assigned a reflective essay on any of the readings in the course. She had read some reflective essays by Joan Didion and had already written a reflection on a book—her instructor called it a meditation—in high school. Baric described the genre as "very expressive, requiring you to delve into yourself, to show how the work touches you." As she recalled, Didion once defined writing as "the act of saying I."

Baric had no trouble selecting a reading. She had been so struck by *The Bell Jar* that she had read it a second time and could not seem to get the novel out of her mind. Because she felt so confident, Baric did not bother with invention. She started right away to write a rough draft. Yet her first attempt to draft the essay was frustrating. She persisted for several hours—writing, reading what she had written, crossing out, making changes but not improving it. Although she had written a page and a half, she doubted that she could use any of it.

The next day, Baric carefully reread her writing and tried to figure out why her draft had gone awry. She had written about events in the novel and about her own similar experiences but had failed to organize these events in a meaningful way or to generalize about them. What she needed, she realized, was to find a controlling idea, to answer the question "So what?" She had become so involved in telling her stories that she had forgotten why she was telling them. She also had no sense of who she was telling them to. Once she began to think about readers, she grasped the importance of using the parallels between Esther's experiences and her own—not as an end in themselves but as a way of generalizing about women's experience.

# A GUIDE TO REFLECTIVE WRITING

The essays in this chapter suggest the richness and diversity of reflective writing. Reflection can be philosophical, focusing on ethical issues or touching on interpersonal relationships; it can be serious or tongue-in-cheek, lyrical or prosaic.

Writers of reflective essays try not to be pompous or pretentious or to lecture or scold their readers. They try to make their essays insightful and interesting, even entertaining. Above all, they try to write with grace and simplicity.

Many students are reluctant to share their ideas or disclose their feelings to their teachers and classmates, preferring to keep their reflections to themselves. But to be a writer, particularly a writer of reflective essays, you must overcome your reluctance and say as simply and directly as possible, "This is what I think."

The following section offers general guidelines on invention, drafting, and revising a reflective essay.

## *Invention*

The following activities should spur your thinking, helping you to find a particular occasion and general subject, analyze your readers, develop your subject, and identify your controlling idea. Taking some time now to consider a wide range of possibilities will pay off later when you draft your essay because it will give you confidence in your choice of subject and in your ability to develop it effectively.

FINDING A PARTICULAR OCCASION AND GENERAL SUBJECT. As the readings in this chapter illustrate, writers usually begin their essays with a particular event or observation that occasions their reflections upon a general subject. In the process of invention, however, the particular occasion does not always come before the general subject. Sometimes writers set out to reflect upon a general subject such as envy or friendship and must search for just the right image or anecdote with which to particularize it.

To help you find an occasion and subject for your essay, make a chart like the one that follows by matching particular occasions to general subjects. In the left-hand column, list particular occasions—a conversation you have had or overheard, a scene you have observed, a quotation you recall, an incident in your own or someone else's life—that might lead you to reflect more generally. In the right-hand column, list general subjects—human qualities like compassion, vanity, jealousy, faithfulness;

social customs and mores for dating, eating, working; abstract notions like fate, free will, the imagination—that suggest themselves to you.

Move from left to right and also from right to left, making your lists as long as you can. You will find that a single occasion might suggest several subjects and that a subject might be particularized by a variety of occasions. Each entry will surely suggest other possibilities for you to consider. If you are having trouble getting started, review the Suggestions for Writing following each reading in this chapter. Your chart of possibilities is likely to become quite messy, but do not censor your ideas. A full and rich exploration of topics will give you confidence that the one you finally choose is the most promising.

| *Particular Occasions* | *General Subjects* |
|---|---|
| Saw jr. high girls wearing makeup as thick as a clown's | Make-up: make-over, mask the real self; Ideas of beauty; Changing fashions: conformity or rebellion? |
| Punk styles of the 80s/ zoot suits of the 40s | |
| Rumor of Paul McCartney's death | Rumors: Sources? Purpose? Malicious like gossip? How do they start? stop? Friendship & betrayal |
| Rumor about Diane and Tom spread by a friend of theirs | |
| Saw film called *Betrayal* | |
| Buying clothes, I couldn't decide and let salesperson pressure me. | Decisions & indecisiveness; Bowing to outside pressure; Low self-esteem; Can't or won't think of self— conformity again! |
| Take friends to help me make a decision | |
| Saw bumper sticker: "Don't Californicate Oregon" | Bumper stickers—a kind of writing, very expressive |
| "Truckers Do It On the Road" | Political, sexual, just funny |
| "Nuke the Gay Whales" | Propaganda, offensive |

As further occasions and subjects occur to you over the next two or three days, add them to this chart.

CHOOSING A SUBJECT. Review the chart and select an occasion and subject you now think looks promising.

To test whether this selection will work, write for fifteen minutes exploring your thoughts on it. Do not make any special demands on yourself to be profound or even to be coherent. Just put your ideas on paper as they come, letting one idea suggest another. Your aim is to determine whether you have anything to say and whether the topic holds your interest. If you discover that you do not have very much to say or that you quickly lose interest in the subject, choose another one and try again. It might take you a few preliminary explorations to find the right subject.

ANALYZING YOUR READERS. Before going on to develop your ideas, you should spend some time thinking about who will be reading your essay and how you can make your ideas understandable and appealing to them. Will your readers primarily be people your own age with similar experiences and views? Will they be older or younger? Are they likely to have thought or read about your subject? What ideas do you think they already have about the subject? Will they be likely to regard your ideas as new? as threatening? as unreasonable?

Ask yourself these and any other questions you can think of; then write a brief description of your readers, focusing on what you think they already know and how you might engage their interest and help them to understand your view of the subject.

DEVELOPING YOUR SUBJECT. Once you have chosen a subject with which you feel comfortable and have given some thought to your readers' knowledge and expectations, you can begin to develop your subject systematically.

Take each of the following strategies—illustrating, giving examples, narrating anecdotes, describing scenes and people, explaining causes or effects, comparing and contrasting—and write for at least five minutes using the strategy to develop the occasion or some aspect of your general subject. For instance, if you are writing about rumors, you might give several examples of rumors you have heard, tell an anecdote about a particular rumor, describe a person who has spread a rumor or been the subject of one, explain how a particular rumor came about or what effect it had, and compare spreading rumors to malicious gossip in small communities.

You will probably decide not to use all these strategies in your essay, but trying them now will help you explore your reflections and think of ways to communicate them to your readers.

IDENTIFYING YOUR CONTROLLING IDEA. Reread what you have written and briefly state what you think should be the controlling idea of your essay. Specifically, ask yourself "So what?" "What point am I trying to make about this subject?"

Then write a few more sentences explaining why this idea is a good one. What makes it interesting to you and will make it interesting to your readers?

# *Drafting*

After completing the preceding invention activities, you should feel confident in your choice of subject even though you may also feel a little overwhelmed by the chaos of ideas your invention has generated. The following suggestions for setting goals, planning your organization, and deciding how to begin your essay should prepare you to write your first draft with confidence.

SETTING GOALS. Setting goals for your essay can help you as you draft by reminding you of what you want your essay to accomplish. In particular, you will want to consider what your readers ordinarily think about your subject and how you can make your ideas acceptable to them. If, for example, you think your readers are likely to have thought about your subject, you will want to extend their understanding by taking a new tack on the subject. Thomas helps readers reflect on death by giving them a global perspective, while Woolf helps her readers to see death in sharp contrast to life.

If, on the other hand, you think your ideas will be surprising or hard for readers to accept, ask yourself how you can present your train of thought so that readers are carried along inevitably from one small point to the next. Forster, for example, leads readers to accept his revolutionary ideas about ownership by telling amusing anecdotes and explaining how owning property has affected him personally. Theroux sets up oppositions throughout her essay to get readers to see that things are not always what they seem to be in family relationships.

Consider also how you can make your generalizations concrete and specific. Can you dramatize the subject for your readers by telling an anecdote with lively dialogue either about someone else as Shames and Theroux do or about yourself as Forster and Thomas do? Can you describe a scene, like Woolf and White, so vividly that readers can almost see it? Can you enrich your writing as Baric and Didion do with quotations which tap your readers' memories and associations?

PLANNING YOUR ORGANIZATION. If you have completed the preceding writing and thinking activities carefully, you have probably done a good deal of planning already. Although many writers continue to plan as they draft, letting their ideas organize themselves naturally, you may prefer to prepare an outline before you begin to draft. Indicate in your outline how the essay will open, which strategies you plan to use, and in what order.

In some essays, one strategy predominates over the others. Forster, for example, organizes his essay around the effects of owning property. Shames centers his on an extended anecdote. White devotes his essay to describing a single scene, while Woolf juxtaposes several different scenes. Yet, even these essays usually weave other strategies into and around the central strategy. Forster describes scenes and people, tells little anecdotes, and fills his essay with allusions. In attempting to define the general concept of self-respect, Didion builds a structure of contrasts and personal anecdotes.

BEGINNING. Although most reflective essays open with a particular occasion, some begin right away by generalizing about the subject. Baric tells us about her strong identification with *The Bell Jar*, while Theroux tells us what she learned from observing someone else's family interact during Christmas. Even when writers open with generalizations, they ground their ideas in specifics: Baric's experience reading a particular novel and Theroux's observations of a particular family at a particular time and place.

Didion grabs her readers' attention with an arresting opening sentence: "Once, in a dry season, I wrote in large letters across two pages of a notebook that innocence ends when one is stripped of the delusion that one likes oneself." Shames surprises his readers with a question: "Remember how they did it in *1984?*" White engages his readers with an enchanting image: "After the lions had returned to their cages, creeping angrily through the chutes, a little bunch of us drifted away and into an open doorway nearby, where we stood for a while in semidarkness, watching a big brown circus horse go harumphing around the practice ring."

# Revising

Reflective essays may look casual and improvised, as if the writer's thoughts had just flowed from one point to another, but they are actually carefully structured and usually extensively revised. You can never predict where your drafting will take you. Even if you work from an outline, ideas will beget other ideas and you will make new discoveries in the process of putting your ideas on paper. This can be the most exciting and creative aspect of writing, but it means that your draft will probably require substantial revision.

Begin your revision by reading your draft critically, using the critical reading questions at the beginning of this chapter. (If possible, have someone else read it critically too.) As you revise, concentrate on developing the subject further, making the writing clearer, and eliminating any errors.

REVISING TO DEVELOP YOUR SUBJECT FURTHER. Begin by rereading your draft and making an outline of it to see its structure more objectively. Then, using words that do not already appear in the essay, restate its controlling idea. This will help you decide whether the draft is too superficial, leaving out important ideas and implications, or too cluttered and unfocused. Be prepared to reorder your points to make them flow more smoothly, to cut parts that stray too far from the main idea, and to add more details. Most drafts of reflective essays need more elaboration—fuller development of anecdotes and descriptions, further explanation of causes and effects, a richer fabric of comparisons and contrasts, for example. Remember that the difficulty most readers have with reflective writing is that it tends to become too abstract. As you revise your essay, look for places where you can make your generalizations more concrete by embodying them in vivid images and pointed anecdotes.

REVISING TO IMPROVE READABILITY. If you think that your draft is not as clear as it could be, get some distance before you begin to revise. Put your draft away for a few days so that you can return to it with a fresh eye. Then look for any abstract words (particularly those ending in *-ion*) and try to find another way of stating them. Examine the verbs you have used. Can you substitute concrete active verbs for any *is* forms? Can you change any of your sentences from passive to active, so that the subject performs the action rather than receives it?

When you have a final copy, proofread it carefully for any errors in spelling, usage, and punctuation.

# *Observation*

Certain kinds of writing are based on direct investigation done by the writer. Travel accounts, descriptions of natural phenomena, profiles of people or places, and original research reports are some familiar examples. In all of these, writers depend mainly, if not solely, on what they can learn for themselves. Whether by visiting a place, participating in an activity, interviewing a person, or conducting an experiment, these writers all carry out firsthand research to find the information they then present to readers. Travel writers, for example, may write about a place they have visited; naturalists may describe phenomena they have observed. Investigative reporters or clinical psychologists may write about a person they have talked to many times; anthropologists may write about a group with whom they have lived for several months or years.

A great deal of what we know about people and the world comes from this kind of writing—in fact, it establishes much of the basic knowledge in both the natural and social sciences. Because it often deals with unfamiliar subjects, it can be enormously interesting.

Writing up your own observations can offer special challenges and rewards. You can visit places on or off campus and interview people who interest you—and write extended profiles of those places or people. You can write up original research done for another class, or you can even devise questionnaires in order to survey people's perceptions and attitudes and then report on your findings.

This kind of writing allows you to explore the complex relations among the activities of observing, taking notes, and writing them up. Essentially, you will be translating your own experiences and perceptions into writing to be shared with others—a profoundly important act. Moreover, such activities form the basic strategies of inquiry and knowledge-making in many of the academic disciplines you will study as a college student.

## A GUIDE TO READING OBSERVATIONAL WRITING

You will be able to read observational writing more critically—questioning, analyzing, and evaluating it—by recognizing its basic features. This section contains a discussion of these features followed by an annotated essay and a list of key questions that should help you as a reader to get the most out of this kind of writing.

# Basic Features of Observational Writing

Writers of observational accounts are usually motivated by curiosity to learn about unusual subjects or to find a unique angle on ordinary subjects. They share what they learn with their readers in order to inform and intrigue them. To achieve this end, they include special features: *a well-focused subject, a vivid presentation of the subject,* and *a clear pattern of organization.*

A WELL-FOCUSED SUBJECT. The subject of an observation can be ordinary or extraordinary, but the way in which it is treated is paramount to its interest. This subject may be so unusual or fascinating—a dangerous place, a well-known but mysterious person, a forbidden yet terribly appealing activity, the surprising results of a survey or experiment—that readers cannot help but be drawn in. Even if the subject is fairly ordinary, the writer will probably emphasize what is new or unusual about it. This novel perspective on the subject provides the focus for the essay.

A VIVID PRESENTATION OF THE SUBJECT. An observational piece presents its subject vividly, with much specific descriptive detail. We watch people moving and hear them talking. We see actual places. If carefully chosen, these details add up to create a dominant impression that reinforces the writer's novel perspective on the subject.

A CLEAR PATTERN OF ORGANIZATION. Observational writing needs to be clearly and obviously patterned, making it easy for readers to follow the presentation; it must impose order on a jumble of notes about things the writer noticed or heard. A travel article may tell about a writer's visit chronologically—what was seen first, next, and so on—while a profile of a person can be organized around the person's traits (or around a series of anecdotes about the single most important trait). A report of an experiment typically explains how the research was done before relating the results. An effective plan holds readers' interest. Information can alternate with anecdotes, descriptions, and comments to keep readers interested in the report and receptive to the new information.

## An Annotated Reading:
### *Fire in the Lake,* Frances FitzGerald

People usually read observational pieces because they are interested in or curious about the subject. They anticipate sharing the writer's close observations of the person, place, or activity and expect well-chosen details to help them imagine what the writer saw. As they read, however, they will be evaluating the believability of the material and the credibility of the writer.

Look now at one brief observation. The piece is annotated as it might be by any careful, curious reader, noting important features, identifying key terms, and posing certain questions. It is helpful to read the selection first before comparing it to the annotations.

This selection begins the final chapter in *Fire in the Lake,* Frances FitzGerald's remarkable study of the Vietnamese and of the American influence in Vietnam. FitzGerald was a free-lance journalist there in 1966, and she continued studying its history when she returned to the United States. Published in 1972, *Fire in the Lake* won the Pulitzer Prize, the National Book Award, and the Bancroft Prize for History.

The selection here illustrates the important role firsthand investigation can play in historical writing about recent events. From the first sentence we know that FitzGerald studied Vietnam both as a reader and as a visitor. She begins with a panoramic view of traffic entering Saigon (now Ho Chi Minh City), the capital and largest city in Vietnam. Immediately she zooms in close to a narrow bridge, piles of garbage, a mysterious girl in high heels, and a waiting Buick.

# Fire in the Lake

begins with a distant view—then moves in close

opens with a specific scene
*pedicabs*: bicycle cabs

action, people
Who is this girl?

special subject: refugee villages

point of view shifts to a tour through Bui Phat

instead of mud- and garbage-lined

repetition of compost and garbage images

Chaos, maze pattern

nice visual details: colors, lights, furniture —concrete, neon, and plastic

only two specific people: girl and this American

NLF: National Liberation Front (Viet Cong)

American war cause of Bui Phat (what about NLF war?)

contrast: tanks vs. tombs

contrast: U.S. and Vietnamese armies

organic image

Before entering Saigon, the military traffic from Tan 1
Son Nhut airfield slows in a choking blanket of its own
exhaust. Where it crawls along to the narrow bridge in a
frenzy of bicycles, pedicabs, and tri-Lambrettas, two piles
of garbage mark the entrance to a new quarter of the city.
Every evening a girl on spindle heels picks her way over
the barrier of rotting fruit and onto the sidewalks. Triumphant, she smiles at the boys who lounge at the soft-drink
stand, and with a toss of her long earrings, climbs into a
waiting Buick.

Behind her, the alleyway carpeted with mud winds 2
back past the façade of the new houses into a maze of
thatched huts and tin-roofed shacks called Bui Phat. One
of the oldest of the refugee quarters, Bui Phat lies just
across the river from the generous villas and tree-lined
streets of French Saigon. On its tangle of footpaths,
white-shirted boys push their Vespas past laborers in black
pajamas and women carrying water on coolie poles. After
twelve years and recurrent tides of new refugees, Bui Phat
is less an urban quarter than a compost of villages where
peasants live with their city children. The children run
thick underfoot. The police, it is said, rarely enter this
quarter for fear of a gang of teen-age boys, whose leader,
a young army deserter, reigns over Bui Phat.

Most of Bui Phat lives beyond the law, the electricity 3
lines, and the water system, but it has its secret fortunes.
Here and there amid the chaos of shacks and alleyways,
new concrete buildings rear up in a splendor of pastel-
faced walls, neon lights, and plastic garden furniture. In
one of them there is a half-naked American who suns
himself on a porch under a clothesline draped with military uniforms. He does not know, and probably never
will know, that the house just down the alleyway is owned
and inhabited by an agent of the NLF.

Bui Phat and its likenesses are what the American war 4
has brought to Vietnam. In the countryside there is only
an absence: the bare brown fields, the weeds growing in
the charred earth of the village, the jungle that has swept
back over the cleared land. The grandest ruins are those
of the American tanks, for the Vietnamese no longer
build fine stone tombs as did their ancestors. The U.S.
First Infantry Division has carved its divisional insignia
with defoliants in a stretch of jungle—a giant, poisonous
graffito—but the Vietnamese have left nothing to mark
the passage of their armies and an entire generation of
young men. In many places death is not even a physical
absence. The villages that once again take root in the

| | |
|---|---|
| ironic comparison of villages and bomb craters | rich soil of the Delta fill up with children as quickly as the holes made by the five-hundred-pound and thousand-pound bombs fill up with paddy silt. The desire for sur- |
| Life somehow thrives amid the war's wreckage but diminished | vival has been greater than the war itself, for there are approximately two million more people in the south today than there were before the war. But the balance of the nation has changed, and Saigon is no longer the village, it is Bui Phat. |
| paradoxical: new slum | From Dong Ha in the north to Rach Gia, the slow port at the base of the Delta, these new slums, these crushed villages, spread through all of the cities and garrisoned towns. They are everywhere, plastered against sandbag forts, piled up under the guns of the provincial capitals, overwhelming what is left of the Delta's yellow stucco towns. Seaward of Da Nang the tin huts of the refugee settlements lie between the ammunition and the garbage dumps, indistinguishable from either. These huts have |
| contrasts U.S. military structures (permanent) with Vietnamese villages (transitory) | been rebuilt many times during the war, for every year there is some kind of disaster—an airplane crash or an explosion in the ammunition depot—that wipes out whole hamlets. Around Qui Nhon, Bien Hoa, and Cam |
| *surrealist:* artist; surrealistic art dreamlike, with puzzling imagery | Ranh bay, where the Americans have built jetports and military installations to last through the twentieth cen- tury, the thatched huts crowd so closely that a single neglected cigarette or a spark from a charcoal brazier suf- fices to burn the settlements down. On the streets of tin |
| babies—dead soldiers keeps mentioning babies and children contrasts birth and death | shacks that run straight as a surrealist's line past the run- ways and into the sand, babies play naked in the dust and rows of green combat fatigues hang over the barbed wire like dead soldiers. |
| How can so much life come out of so much destruction and chaos? main point: to show what has happened to South Vietnam because of the war | Out of a population of seventeen million there are now five million refugees. Perhaps 40 or 50 percent of the population, as opposed to the 15 percent before the war, live in and around the cities and towns. The distribution is that of a highly industrialized country, but there is almost no industry in South Vietnam. And the word |
| *bidonvilles:* shanty- towns? Concludes with strong image of shattered nation. Supports garbage motif. | "city" and even "town" is misleading. What was even in 1965 a nation of villages and landed estates is now a nation of *bidonvilles,* refugee camps, and army bases. South Vietnam is a country shattered so that no two pieces fit together. |

5

6

# Critical Reading Questions

Good critical readers approach a piece of writing with an inquisitive eye. Reading alertly, they anticipate key concepts and features. Here are some questions that should enable you to read observational material insightfully and critically. They should help to guide your reading of selections in this chapter and of any other observational writing as well, including your own. As an example of how such questions might be used, we have applied each one to the FitzGerald piece.

1. *What is the subject, and what special focus does the writer adopt?*

Ordinarily easy to answer, this question ensures that you do, in fact, know what the writer hopes to inform you about. FitzGerald, for example, writes about the effects of the war, and in this brief excerpt focuses on the ramshackle refugee villages that sprang up around the Vietnamese cities.

2. *What is the writer's purpose in presenting this subject to readers? What is he or she saying about the subject?*

Even with a well-focused subject presented in a swiftly paced, engaging way, you may not immediately see the writer's reason for writing about the subject. To understand the writer's purpose, consider the tone of the piece. Is it playful? serious? angry? What seems to be the writer's attitude toward the subject? Can you guess what motivated the writer to address this subject? What does the writer seem to assume about his or her readers? From these conjectures, decide what you think the writer's purpose might be.

FitzGerald seems to be trying to reveal the shocking disruptions to Vietnamese culture caused by the war. To achieve her goal here, she concentrates on the most visible of the disruptions: the refugee villages where millions of people from the countryside were forced to live.

3. *How does the writer engage and sustain readers' interest in the subject?*

Consider how effectively the writer draws you in from the very beginning. Look for places where the pace slows and your attention wanders. Pacing information provides a context in which readers can understand and remember new information and thus plays a very important part in observational writing. Does the writer present too much new information too fast? Are there any long factual stretches that need to be broken by descriptive details or anecdotes?

You rightfully expect to be intrigued by the writer's observations. Was your interest captured by the FitzGerald excerpt? Which were the most and least compelling parts? Even academic research reports should aim to keep readers attentive and interested. If you are reading one that seems dull, consider whether the sentence structure is repetitive and whether the piece is overloaded with difficult concepts or information.

FitzGerald easily engages readers' interest with action, visual detail, and specific people. She could have begun with a generalization about refugee villages, but instead, she shows us one all-too-real village. Even as she expands her view to include the whole country, she continues to hold our attention with details of actual people and places.

4. *How are important scenes and people presented?*

Decide how many actual places and people there are (you might want to list them), and then consider how the writer presents them. Are scenes described or merely mentioned? Does the writer point out any small parts of the scenes? Are you given many visual details? Look for information about size, shape, position, color, texture. Are people described or merely named? Do you see them moving, gesturing, and talking? Are you aware of what they're wearing? Do you have any sense of their personalities?

Try to assess how successfully the writer has presented scenes and people, and then analyze whether they seem relevant to the writer's purpose. Do details contribute to your understanding of the subject, or do they seem irrelevant?

FitzGerald opens with a specific scene at the entrance to Bui Phat. Except for the mysterious girl in the high heels and the half-naked American in the sun, she does not show us specific people. She mentions several groups of people: boys at the soft drink stand or pushing their Vespas, women carrying water, children running. It is probably fair to assume that she is not so much concerned with specific people as with giving an overall impression of the refugee villages.

5. *What point of view and plan does the writer use?*

Look to see whether the writer views a scene from a distance or moves in close. Also notice whether he or she presents a scene from a fixed point of view (looking at it from one perspective), or takes you on a tour through a scene, or both. Scrutinize the way in which the writer has planned the piece by considering whether it is organized like a narrative (telling a story) or like a statement with examples. Of special importance is how the piece begins and ends. With these considerations in mind, decide whether you think the writer chose the point of view most appropriate to his or her intention and whether the writer's plan produced a well-paced essay, easy and satisfying for you to follow.

FitzGerald begins with specifics and ends with generalizations. She does this by looking directly at a single small scene and then moving on to a tour through one village. After that she shifts to a topographic viewpoint and shows us the whole country in one paragraph, from Dong Ha to Rach Gia. Finally, she offers summary statistics about the refugees.

6. *What do I learn from the writer's observations?*

Whatever the writer's purpose and strategies, your own aim as a reader of an observational piece is to be informed about subjects and to find satisfaction in their manner of presentation. Were you informed by this piece, and did you really learn anything of importance? Is it something you are likely to remember? What did you learn?

# John McPhee

John McPhee (b. 1931) lives in Princeton, New Jersey, where he occasionally teaches a writing workshop in the "Literature of Fact" at Princeton University. He is very highly regarded as a writer of profiles—in-depth reporting about people, places, and activities—and is a shrewd observer and masterful interviewer. In his profiles he ingeniously integrates information from observations, interviews, and research into engaging, readable prose. Readers marvel at the way he explains clearly such complex subjects as experimental aircraft or modern physics and captures interest in such ordinary subjects as bears or oranges. Among his eighteen published books are *Oranges* (1967), *Coming into the Country* (1977), *In Suspect Terrain* (1983), and *Table of Contents* (1985).

# *The New York Pickpocket Academy*

This selection comes from *Giving Good Weight* (1979), a long profile of the New Jersey farmers who sell produce at a farmers' market in New York City. McPhee spent several weeks working at Rich Hodgson's produce stand, gathering material for his essay. Among other things, he observed pickpockets at work; from these observations came this profile of pickpocketing and other crimes, focusing on the criminals, their victims, and the reactions of the farmers.

Right away, as we begin reading, we meet two pickpockets and three farmers, Melissa Mousseau, Bob Lewis, and Rich Hodgson, who get the story—this "narrative of fact"—underway. The narrator of the story is McPhee himself, weighing and sacking produce, all the while looking beyond the zucchini and tomatoes for material that might interest readers.

As you read, notice the many details McPhee provides about the people and the scene: the vegetables and trucks and hats and colors and sounds of the market. Notice, too, the great variety of examples he presents of crime—and honesty. Do these diverse examples add up to anything special? What would you say McPhee's purpose is in sharing his observations with us?

Brooklyn, and the pickpocket in the burgundy jacket appears just before noon. Melissa Mousseau recognizes him much as if he were an old customer and points him out to Bob Lewis, who follows him from truck to truck. Aware of Lewis, he leaves the market. By two, he will have made another run. A woman with deep-auburn hair and pale, nervous hands clumsily attracts the attention of a customer whose large white

147

purse she is rifling. Until a moment ago, the customer was occupied with the choosing of apples and peppers, but now she shouts out, "Hey, what are you doing? Your hand is in my purse. What are you doing?" The auburn-haired woman not only has her hand in the purse but most of her arm as well. She withdraws it, and with intense absorption begins to finger the peppers. "How much are the peppers? Mister, give me some of these!" she says, looking up at me with a gypsy's dark, starburst eyes. "Three pounds for a dollar," I tell her, with a swift glance around for Lewis or a cop. When I look back, the pickpocket is gone. Other faces have filled in—people unconcernedly examining the fruit. The woman with the white purse has returned her attention to the apples. She merely seems annoyed. Lewis once sent word around from truck to truck that we should regularly announce in loud voices that pickpockets were present in the market, but none of the farmers complied. Hodgson shrugged and said, "Why distract the customers?" Possibly Fifty-ninth Street is the New York Pickpocket Academy. Half a dozen scores have been made there in a day. I once looked up and saw a well-dressed gentleman under a gray fedora being kicked and kicked again by a man in a green polo shirt. He kicked him in the calves. He kicked him in the thighs. He kicked him in the gluteal bulge. He kicked him from the middle of the market out to the edge, and he kicked him into the street. "Get your ass out of here!" shouted the booter, redundantly. Turning back toward the market, he addressed the curious. "Pickpocket," he explained. The dip did not press charges.

People switch shopping carts from time to time. They make off with     2
a loaded one and leave an empty cart behind. Crime on such levels is a part of the background here, something in the urban air, so many parts per million. The condition is accepted with a resignation that approaches nonchalance. . . . We lost . . . [a cash box] once in Brooklyn, with something like two hundred dollars. For various reasons, suspicion immediately attached itself to a part-time employee who was selling with us and probably handed the box in a bag to a confederate. The previous Wednesday, he had been working for another farmer, who discharged him for dishonesty. Now, just after our cash box disappeared, he began saying, and repeating, in an excited voice, "It's real, man. It's real. We don't like it but that's reality—reality, man—and there is nothing we can do." Rich felt there *was* something he could do. He said, "You're fired."

Politely, the man inquired if he could know the reason for his dismissal.     3
"Sure," Rich said. "I don't trust you."     4
"That's cool, man, cool," said our ex-employee. He took off his apron     5
and was gone.

Most thievery is petty and is on the other side of the tables. As Rich 6 describes it, "Brooklyn, Fifty-ninth Street, people rip off stuff everywhere. You just expect it. An old man comes along and puts a dozen eggs in a bag. Women choosing peaches steal one for every one they buy—a peach for me, a peach for you. What can you do? You stand there and watch. When they take too many, you complain. I watched a guy one day taking nectarines. He would put one in a plastic bag, then one in a pocket, then one in a pile on the ground. After he did that half a dozen times, he had me weigh the bag."

"This isn't England," Barry Benepe informed us once, "and a lot of 7 people are pretty dishonest."

Now, in Brooklyn, a heavyset woman well past the middle of life is 8 sobbing pitifully, flailing her arms in despair. She is sitting on a bench in the middle of the market. She is wearing a print dress, a wide-brimmed straw hat. Between sobs, she presents in a heavy Russian accent the reason for her distress. She was buying green beans from Don Keller, and when she was about to pay him she discovered that someone had opened her handbag—even while it was on her arm, she said—and had removed several books of food stamps, a telephone bill, and eighty dollars in cash. Lewis, in his daypack, stands over her and tells her he is sorry. He says, "This sort of thing will happen wherever there's a crowd."

Another customer breaks in to scold Lewis, saying, "This is the biggest 9 rip-off place in Brooklyn. Two of my friends were pickpocketed here last week and I had to give them carfare home."

Lewis puts a hand on his forehead and, after a pensive moment, says, 10 "That was very kind of you."

The Russian woman is shrieking now. Lewis attends her like a working 11 dentist. "It's all right. It will be O.K. It may not be as bad as you think." He remarks that he would call the police if he thought there was something they could do.

Jeffrey Mack, eight years old, has been listening to all this, and he 12 now says, "I see a cop."

Jeffrey has an eye for cops that no one else seems to share. (A squad 13 car came here for him one morning and took him off to face a truant officer. Seeing his fright, a Pacific Street prostitute got into the car and rode with him.)

"Where, Jeffrey?" 14

"There." Jeffrey lifts an arm and points. 15

"Where?" 16

"There." He points again—at trucks, farmers, a falafel man. 17

"I don't see a policeman," Lewis says to him. "If you see one, Jeffrey, 18 go and get him."

Jeffrey goes, and comes back with an off-duty 78th Precinct cop who    19
is wearing a white apron and has been selling fruits and vegetables in the
market. The officer speaks sternly to the crying woman. "Your name?"

"Catherine Barta."    20

"Address?"    21

"Eighty-five Eastern Parkway."    22

Every Wednesday, she walks a mile or so to the Greenmarket. She    23
has lived in Brooklyn close to half her life, the rest of it in the Ukraine.
Heading back to his vegetables, the officer observes that there is nothing
he can do.

Out from behind her tables comes Joan Benack, the baker, of Rocky    24
Acres Farm, Milan, New York—a small woman with a high, thin voice.
Leaving her tropical carrot bread, her zucchini bread, her anadama bread,
her beer bread, she goes around with a borrowed hat collecting money
from the farmers for Catherine Barta. Bills stuff the hat, size 7—the
money of Alvina Frey and John Labanowski and Cleather Slade and Rich
Hodgson and Bob Engle, who has seen it come and go. He was a broker
for Merrill Lynch before the stock market imploded, and now he is a
blond-bearded farmer in a basketball shirt selling apples that he grows in
Clintondale, New York. Don Keller offers a dozen eggs, and one by one
the farmers come out from their trucks to fill Mrs. Barta's shopping cart
with beans and zucchini, apples, eggplants, tomatoes, peppers, and corn.
As a result, her wails and sobs grow louder.

A man who gave Rich Hodgson a ten-dollar bill for a ninety-five-cent    25
box of brown eggs asks Rich to give the ten back after Rich has handed
him nine dollars and five cents, explaining that he has some smaller bills
that he wants to exchange for a twenty. Rich hands him the ten. Into
Rich's palm he counts out five ones, a five, and the ten for a twenty and
goes away satisfied, as he has every reason to be, having conned Rich
out of nine dollars, five cents, and a box of brown eggs. Rich smiles at
his foolishness, shrugs, and sells some cheese. If cash were equanimity,
he would never lose a cent. One day, a gang of kids began taking Don
Keller's vegetables and throwing them at the Hodgson truck. Anders
Thueson threw an apple at the kids, who then picked up rocks. Thueson
reached into the back of the truck and came up with a machete. While
Hodgson told him to put it away, pant legs went up, switchblades came
into view. Part of the gang bombarded the truck with debris from a nearby
roof. Any indication of panic might have been disastrous. Hodgson
packed deliberately, and drove away.

Todd Jameson, who comes in with his brother Dan from Farmingdale,    26
New Jersey, weighed some squash one day, and put it in a brown bag.
He set the package down while he weighed something else. Then, reach-

ing for the squash, he picked up an identical bag that happened to contain fifty dollars in rolled coins. He handed it to the customer who had asked for the squash. Too late, Todd discovered the mistake. A couple of hours later, though, the customer—"I'll never forget him as long as I live, the white hair, the glasses, the ruddy face"—came back. He said, "Hey, this isn't squash. I didn't ask for money, I asked for squash." Whenever that man comes to market, the Jamesons give him a bag full of food. "You see, where I come from, that would never, never happen," Todd explains. "If I made a mistake like that in Farmingdale, no one—no one—would come back with fifty dollars' worth of change."

Dusk comes down without further crime in Brooklyn, and the farmers 27 are packing to go. John Labanowski—short, compact, with a beer in his hand—is expounding on his day. "The white people are educating the colored on the use of beet greens," he reports. "A colored woman was telling me today, 'Cut the tops off,' and a white woman spoke up and said, 'Hold it,' and told the colored woman, 'You're throwing the best part away.' They go on talking, and pretty soon the colored woman is saying, 'I'm seventy-three on Monday,' and the white says, 'I don't believe a word you say.' You want to know why I come in here? I come in here for fun. For profit, of course, but for relaxation, too. I like being here with these people. They say the city is a rat race, but they've got it backwards. The farm is what gets to be a rat race. You should come out and see what I—" He is interrupted by the reappearance in the market of Catherine Barta, who went home long ago and has now returned, her eyes hidden by her wide-brimmed hat, her shopping cart full beside her. On the kitchen table, at 85 Eastern Parkway, she found her telephone bill, her stamps, and her cash. She has come back to the farmers with their food and money.

## QUESTIONS FOR ANALYSIS

1. In order to evaluate McPhee's plan, make a brief outline of the selection, listing the separate crimes in the order they occur and noting key people and incidents. What advantages do you see in the way McPhee sequences the various crimes? What other order might he have tried? (Chapter 1 presents a discussion of outlining.)

2. Using your outline, review the separate crimes in the selection, noticing which ones McPhee relates in the present tense and which in the past tense. All the crimes, of course, occurred in the past. Why do you think he presents some in the present tense, and how does it influence your response?

3. This selection includes many remembered or reconstructed statements and conversations. Skim the selection, noticing how often direct dialogue (that set within quotation marks) is used. Instead of quoting exactly, McPhee could have paraphrased what people said. What contribution does direct dialogue make to the essay? (You might try paraphrasing one of the quotes to judge the different effects.)

4. The heavyset woman in the print dress, Catherine Barta, appears twice. What roles does she play in the selection? Why do you think McPhee gives her such prominence?

5. McPhee includes many specific details of the market scene—we learn people's names, see what they're wearing, hear their voices, and listen in on their conversations. Choose a brief part or episode that you think has especially notable and memorable details. What details did you notice, and what do you think they contribute to the essay?

6. What do you think was McPhee's purpose in writing about crime at the Brooklyn market? What would you say is the main point of this profile?

## SUGGESTIONS FOR WRITING

1. Visit a farmers' market, flea market, or department store. You may not observe anything as sensational as an "academy" of pickpockets, but you will very likely find some unifying point for your observations. Report on this place vividly—so that your readers can see it and hear it as you did.

2. Think of a scene filled with people and action, a place you can visit easily two or three times. While you are there, talk to people and, if possible, participate in what they are doing. Take notes on what you see and hear, and then compose a profile of the scene. Be sure that your report has a clear focus—so that your purpose in writing is unmistakable.

   Some places you might consider visiting are a used-car lot, an auction hall, a soup kitchen, a fast-food restaurant, a small-claims court, or the campus computer center.

# David Halberstam

David Halberstam (b. 1934) began his writing career as a newspaper reporter in Mississippi and Tennessee, moving on to the *New York Times* in 1960. He specializes in comprehensive reporting on special events, activities, and people. In 1964 he won the Pulitzer Prize for his reporting from Vietnam. He is probably best known for *The Best and the Brightest* (1972), his best-selling book about John F. Kennedy and his close advisers.

# *Tiff Wood, Sculler*

This reading comes from *The Amateurs* (1985), a book about four single-scull rowers competing to represent the United States in the 1984 Olympics. Competitive rowing takes place in one-, two-, four-, and eight-person boats. A single scull is a slender boat weighing only about thirty pounds, which one rower powers with two long oars mounted in special brackets on its side. This selection is a profile of Tiff Wood, the oldest of the four competitors. Read to learn as much as you can about Wood and single-scull rowing, but also try to decide what Halberstam is really trying to tell us. What does he seem to be saying about amateurs who persist at a challenging sport that brings them neither wide recognition nor money?

As Tiff Wood walked among the other young businessmen in Boston, he appeared to be just another modest young man in Ivy League clothes, the actuarial expert with a consulting firm that he in fact was. Despite his six-one height and his 185 pounds, he did not look tall and powerful as one might imagine a great oar. In his street clothes, he seemed almost slight of build. But there was no fat on him, he was all muscle. If the normal body fat was somewhere around 18 percent, his level of fat varied between 7 and 8.5 percent (skater Eric Heiden's was 7 percent). Only in his rowing clothes did the power in his body show his enormously strong arms and his immensely thick and awesomely muscled legs. The power in them was unmistakable; and when John Biglow spoke of Tiff Wood and his ability, he spoke first of his legs. Tiff Wood, in classic terms of muscularity, was much stronger than John Biglow.

In addition to his strength, Wood had an exceptional capacity to bear pain. Rowing, particularly single sculling, inflicts on the individual in every race a level of pain associated with few other sports. There was certainly pain in football during a head-on collision, pain in other sports on the occasion of a serious injury. That was more the threat of pain; in rowing there was the absolute guarantee of it every time. Pain in championship single-scull rowing is a given. Each race is like a sprint. But unlike a sprint, which usually lasts 10 or 20 or 45 seconds, a two-thousand-meter sculling championship lasts 7 minutes and is roughly the length of a two-mile run. The body quickly burns out its normal supplies of oxygen and then demands more. But less and less oxygen is available. That means the body is still producing high levels of energy, but it is making the sculler pay for it by producing a great deal of lactic acid as well. With the lactic acid comes greater and greater pain. In addition, the scullers are unable to pace themselves, as long-distance runners can. They might try to hold back a little bit of energy so they will not burn out at the end, but in truth they go all out from the very beginning. It is an advantage to lead in a sculling race; the leader can see the other boats behind him and does not get caught in their wash.

When a race was over and Tiff Wood had rowed at his peak, it took ₃ almost five days before his body was physically replenished. When he thought of rowing, the first thing that came to mind was pain. After the first twenty-five strokes of a race, his body ached. His lungs and his legs seemed to scream at him to stop. On occasion the temptation was almost irresistible. The ability to resist the impulse, to keep going in spite of it, to reach through it and summon extra resources of power while others, stronger and smoother of technique, were fading, made him a champion. But he could not think of racing without thinking of the pain. It was hard for him in advance of a race to sit and plan out what he intended to do because the very thought of racing filled him with dread of the pain.

But he was also aware that his ability to absorb that pain had made ₄ him an exceptional competitor. He had rationalized all of it very carefully, going over and over in his mind the pluses and minuses of what he was doing. The race itself was a terrible ordeal. The pain bordered, he thought, on a kind of torture. The worst part of the torture was that it was self-imposed. There was no need to go through with it. But he had willed himself to deal with it; he wanted to measure himself against the best, and the only way to do that was to bear the pain.

In truth, deep down, he liked this aspect of the sport because it permitted ordinary and not particularly talented young men and women to reach beyond themselves. "I think," he once said, "that what I like about it is the chance to be a hero. Every day in what seem like a very ordinary setting there are heroes in every boat, people reaching down to come up with that much more energy to make it work. I like that, I honor it and I think that is special in this world." In the end, rowing made him feel good about himself.

Parker, his coach and a former Olympic sculler himself, thought that    6
Tiff Wood was particularly good at calibrating exactly how much energy
he had left and giving every single bit. Part of his strength, Parker
thought, was in coming across a finish line on the surge of his last possible
stroke, absolutely depleted. This was true even in practice, and Parker
recently had a graphic illustration of it. He had, near the end of a long
and punishing workout, asked Wood for a final twenty power strokes,
and Wood had given them. But Parker had not been paying attention,
and he had asked Wood for ten more, ten more strokes from a body that
was finished; and Wood, the most modest and proper young man imaginable, had screamed at Parker in a kind of elemental rage, "Fuck you!"

Early in Wood's college career Parker had decided that any attempt to    7
make him row with greater finesse would be counterproductive. He was
impatient with technique. The best way to coach him, Parker decided,
was not to coach him but to leave him to his furies. What set Wood
apart was will, the power of the mind to bend the body to its uses. There
was a certain madness to that, Wood knew, but there was also a purpose.
He had, after all, been raised in a tradition in which sacrifice, if not
pain, was an essential ingredient. He believed, he said, in the Puritan
ethic, not the leisure society. A world where people sought only leisure
seemed empty to him. The best thing about rowing was in the obstacles
it presented, even if these were, in his words, manufactured obstacles.

He was, of course, intensely competitive. Rowing indoors on the tanks    8
during the long, boring winter months, he invented competitive games
to keep him going—he would try to row a larger puddle than the oarsman
just ahead of him. (He was scrupulous about not cheating, though of
course the other oarsman did not know the contest was going on.) When
Wood graduated from college he had gloried in taking the tests for both
business and law school and had done exceptionally well. He always
tested well. Some friends had teased him about the fact that he should
have taken the tests for medical school as well. Just one more group of
applicants to compete against, they said.

His fiancé, Kristy Aserlind, also a rower, liked going for long, aimless    9
walks. Tiff Wood did not. If Tiff went for a walk, there had to be a form
to it, 3½ times around the block. It would be even better if there were
an existing record for those 3½ blocks that he could compete against.

There had to be form and purpose to the walk because there had to    10
be form and purpose to life. That was one of the interesting things about
rowing. Those who competed at this level did so with a demonic passion.
Yet there was no overt financial reward at the end, nor indeed was there
even any covert financial reward, a brokerage house wanting and giving
special privilege to the famed amateur. Yet the athletes were almost

always the children of the upper middle class, privileged, affluent, a group that in this society did not readily seek hardship. One could understand the son of a ghetto family playing in the school yard for six hours a day hoping that basketball was a ticket out of the slum; it was harder to understand the son of Beacon Hill spending so much time and subjecting himself to so much pain to attain an honor that no one else even understood. Perhaps in our society the true madness in the search for excellence is left for the amateur.

For Tiff Wood was a son of Beacon Hill, the home of the American 11 establishment, and he had gone to the best schools, as had his father before him. The Woods were not very old Boston. Reginald Wood, the grandfather, who had quit school at fourteen to be a runner on the floor in Wall Street, had been successful in the stock market. Very much a self-made man, he had been determined that his children would have the best in education.

Richard Wood, Tiff's father, had gone to Harvard, and in his early 12 sixties, he was as lean as his son. He still ran three or four miles a day, and on weekends he usually ran ten miles a day. In his late fifties, he had run in three marathons. In the first one he quit after seventeen miles. In the second, when he made twenty-three miles and could no longer run, he alternately walked a block and ran a block, finishing in 5½ hours. The next year, better prepared, he made it home without limping, in 4½ hours. He loved the outdoors, and he was the first one on the ski slopes in the morning, the last one off in the evening. He took a special pleasure in being on the slopes on days when it was ten degrees below zero and no one else would go out except, from the time he was eight years old, his son Tiff. There had never been a doubt in Richard Wood's mind that the boy was determined to stay with his father on all occasions, to push himself as hard as he could even if he had to absorb an unusual amount of punishment in the process. If he was not competing with a father (for the question of whether an eight- or nine-year-old competes with a parent is a difficult one to answer), he was certainly proving something to his father, again and again. Even as a little boy he had been obsessive. In kindergarten, he had become so voracious a reader that the school at the end of the year had given him a handsomely lettered certificate proclaiming him "the World's Greatest Reader." His father thought his willingness to take on excessively harsh challenges bordered on a form of masochism.

When he was ten, he had stayed at the home of a friend named David 13 Hansen and they had decided to sleep outside in the simplest kind of tent. It was early spring and cold. That night there was a horrendous rainstorm. In the middle of the storm David Hansen had come inside, but the next morning Richard Wood was appalled to find his son asleep in four inches of water. From then on he had realized that his son was always going to push himself to the limits in terms of physical risk, that he was not just proving something but gaining recognition as well.

A year later they had gone mountain climbing in New Hampshire, 14 and very high up they had come to a tiny pool of water that was at most twenty feet in diameter. The water was absolutely ice cold. Above it stood a very steep mountain cliff, perhaps thirty feet high. Anyone diving from it to the pool would have to make an almost perfect dive or be splattered on the rocks. Richard Wood had taken one look at the cliff and known exactly what was going to happen. Tiff was going to want to dive in, but the pool was so small that he could easily miss it. "It'd really be something to dive in from there," Tiff had said. "I think I'll pass," Richard Wood had said. He had watched as Tiff had measured the distance and he thought, Do I tell him not to do it? He had decided, no, he could not forbid him, and Tiff had made one dive and done it cleanly, a dive into water that no one in his right mind would want to swim in in the first place.

Those were not particularly happy years for Tiff Wood. His parents' 15 marriage was coming apart and they were about to get a divorce. He found himself painfully shy, and his feelings about things were completely internalized: It was not that he was without feelings, it was that he found no way to express them. Just after his parents had been divorced, he had once started to cry over some minor incident. When his stepmother had tried to comfort him, he had turned away from her abruptly. "I don't want anyone to feel sorry for me," he had said. Given a chance by his father to stay at home or go away to boarding school, he had seized the chance to go away.

He had arrived at St. Paul's School in 1967, thirteen years old, small 16 for his age, unsure of himself, confused. He was, he realized later, a very shy little boy who kept all of his pain inside. At St. Paul's he had not done well in the beginning. He was smart, but he had realized immediately that too strenuous a use of his intelligence and the accumulation of exceptional grades did not bring popularity. He was rebellious and wore his hair long. Popularity eluded him. "The people I wanted to be my friends were not interested in being my friends," he said of that time. "I thought they were making a mistake. But it was not easy to show this to them."

At St. Paul's popularity and status were in some indefinable way tied 17 to things that might well be outside his reach, such as looks and size and athletic accomplishment. He had never been a particularly gifted athlete. His eyesight was terrible, and in those days there were no soft contact lenses. He felt clumsy and awkward at almost everything, and then he tried rowing. On the first two days he had gone out, the conditions had been appalling, cold and snowy. The boat had been filled with water and he had loved it. The harsh weather, which drove off most of his contemporaries, drew him in. He had always felt comfortable in such weather. From the start he had had a sense that this was a sport in which he could excel, for it required only strength and dedication, not skill or grace or timing.

At St. Paul's, rowing had a particular prestige, it was bound into the tradition of the school as much as football was. Besides, football was out. He could barely see the ball. But in rowing the athletes looked behind them. His mother, aware of his problem, encouraged him in crew; his father still preferred football. Tiff Wood's instincts told him crew was his sport. Whatever price was required to succeed in rowing, he decided he would pay it. He had been rowing what were called club boats, which were like intramural boats, and had noticed that the coach of the crew, Richard Davis, was very popular with the more senior rowers. Davis was young, just out of the Air Force, and at night he ate with the students; Tiff Wood by chance had been assigned to his dinner table, and Tiff quietly sat there night after night, absorbing as much of this cherished atmosphere as he could. He sat there torn between desperately wanting to be noticed and just as desperately wanting not to be noticed. He was aware that he was almost too small to be in the company of such important and accomplished young men. He was so silent that he was not even sure that Davis had noticed him.

In his second year at St. Paul's another boy broke his collarbone, and Davis had reached down and placed Wood in the third varsity boat. After that his life centered on rowing. He was awkward at everything else, but about this he felt strong and confident. It was his one chance of asserting himself. If almost everyone else had better technique, Tiff Wood would compensate for lack of finesse by simple determination and will. His instinct, when something went wrong, was simply to pull harder, to punish himself a little more. That became his trademark. Richard Davis was the perfect coach for a young man like him. Davis had coached for a time at Harvard while a graduate student, and he patterned himself after Harry Parker. Davis was less interested in technique than in conditioning and attitude. If his rowers were in better shape and had worked harder, he taught them, they would win. "You have to row until it hurts," he told them. That was perfect for Tiff Wood. The key was not God-given, it was in the rowers themselves. If, at the end of a grueling afternoon on the water, Davis called for a run back to the school, which was a mile away, there were perceptible groans from the other kids; but Tiff Wood would lead the run back with pleasure showing on his face, for this was his territory, these were his rules.

Soon he began to build a reputation as a very strong oar. On some days he thought he was rowing so well that he could move a boat all by himself. If he pushed himself to his absolute outer limit, pushed the level of pain above any acceptable limit, he could make his boat win. Knowing this, he punished himself that much more. His mother faithfully came to all his races. "I'll see you at Henley one day, Tiff," she said. 20

The next year he returned to St. Paul's and was assigned a new dorm. As he approached the form on the first day, he saw one of the most admired boys in the hip, irreverent crowd he hoped to join, one of those golden boys for whom everything seemed to come easily and who had seemed a thousand social levels above him in the past. "Hello, Tiff," the boy had said. Tiff had arrived. If, in years to come, he stayed with rowing much longer than any of his contemporaries, it was partly out of gratitude and partly because rowing was so crucial to him. At a time when he was most vulnerable, rowing had given form to his life and brought him confidence. 21

He was not a pretty rower—indeed, he was rough and elemental. "I am," he said, "propelled by a sense of urgency." His nickname, befitting his style, was The Hammer. That was a term, slightly pejorative, for a rower who used brute strength to cover up technical deficiency. He was the quintessential hammer. Because he had a knack for moving boats— his boats *won*—his coaches both in prep school and college had been reluctant to tamper with his style and add technique. It was as if he were too impatient to use his power to bother to learn technique, for in the transition to greater finesse, at least at the start, power would have to be sacrificed. When he drove his oars into the water, he did it with such fury and strength that it virtually drove a physical shock into his body. He was rough at the catch, the moment when the oar hits the water; he knew that, but he was forgiven even that flaw. When his boat was behind, his response was always to punish himself a little more. "Which one is Tiff?" his stepmother, Jane Wood, quite new to the sport, had once cried while watching a Harvard boat race. "I can't pick him out." "He's the one who keeps moving his head," answered one of her friends, more sophisticated about rowing. 22

Some traditional scullers were offended by the crudeness of his technique. For a long time this did not bother him. If anything, he disdained those who placed a premium on form. "Form is for gymnastics and figure skating and diving, not rowing. I want to win. Rowing is about winning. If you win, then everyone says your form is good anyway," he once said. He was quick to summon historical precedents for the defeat of finesse 23 crews by strong but crude crews. He took pleasure in talking about a famed (and victorious) University of Washington crew that was so rough it was known in the sport as "Lurch, Wobble and Gobble." He liked to quote Steven Fairbairn, an Australian oarsman who had been a critic of the traditional view of rowing that style was more important than power and endurance. "Drive at your blade," Fairbairn had said, "and let your body and slide take care of themselves." Tiff Wood took solace in those words.

## QUESTIONS FOR ANALYSIS

1. What would you say is Halberstam's purpose in profiling Tiff Wood? Which parts of the profile best show or demonstrate this purpose?

2. Though Halberstam learned about Wood by observing and interviewing him, he rarely quotes him or describes his present activities. Notice his use of the past tense in presenting Wood. What advantages do you see in this strategy, given his purpose?

3. Halberstam tells us many things about Wood in this profile. What two qualities does he focus on right away in the first four paragraphs, and why do you think he starts with these particular qualities? How did this beginning influence the way you read the remainder of the profile?

4. In this excerpt, Halberstam includes other people, some of them like Wood, some different from him. Reread the profile quickly, making an inventory of those who are like Wood and those who are unlike him. After reflecting on these lists, determine what you learn about Wood from those *unlike* him, whom Halberstam intentionally contrasts with him. How do you assess Halberstam's strategy of comparisons and contrasts?

5. In addition to making direct assertions about the kind of athlete and person Wood is, Halberstam shows us what he is like in various other ways: visual details, dialogue, comparisons and contrasts with others, anecdotes. Skim the essay, taking inventory of specific anecdotes about various incidents or events in Wood's life. Reread each anecdote and decide what it reveals about Wood. Then, pick the anecdote you find most engaging, and analyze how Halberstam presents that anecdote to make it so appealing to you.

6. Does Tiff Wood remind you of a character in a novel? In what way is this profile like or unlike a chapter in a novel and Wood like or unlike a character in a novel?

## SUGGESTIONS FOR WRITING

1. Think of people you know (or know about) who have some striking characteristic or quality. It could be determination, intelligence, creativity, courage, foolhardiness. Choose one person to observe and interview. Write a profile, focusing on this person's special quality.

2. Profile someone engaged in an activity that interests you. Observe your subject carefully while he or she is involved in the activity, and then interview appropriate people—your subject, and others who participate in the activity or who know him or her. Decide on a point of view toward this individual and on a purpose for your profile—the purpose should be apparent to your readers by the anecdotes, details, and dialogue you select.

# Alexander Petrunkevitch

Alexander Petrunkevitch (1875–1964), a Russian zoologist, gained an international reputation as an authority on spiders. He devoted more than 25,000 hours to amassing a famous collection of spiders, including many tarantulas. From 1910 to 1944, he taught at Yale University. He published over a hundred books about insects, including *Index Catalogue of Spiders of North, Central, and South America* (1911) and *Principles of Classification* (1952); he has also published several translations of Russian poetry. Twelve insects are named for him.

# The Spider and the Wasp

In this essay, Petrunkevitch writes as a specialized scientist for a general but educated readership. He knows that most of these readers are not trained as scientists, but he assumes they all have some interest in scientific findings. The essay was first published in 1952 in *Scientific American*, a magazine that reports on new developments in the physical, biological, and social sciences. In *Scientific American*, specialists do not document their sources by citing other published work within their articles; instead, they include a list of important references at the end of their articles.

In this essay, Petrunkevitch reports a good deal of information about tarantula spiders and digger wasps. Though he never says so directly in the essay, he discovered much of the information himself by observing these insects in the field and in his laboratory. Much of what we know about the earth and its living organisms comes from reports and essays based on this kind of patient observation and careful note taking. As you read, notice the various ways Petrunkevitch presents what he has learned while watching these insects.

In the feeding and safeguarding of their progeny insects and spiders 1 exhibit some interesting analogies to reasoning and some crass examples of blind instinct. The case I propose to describe here is that of the tarantula spiders and their archenemy, the digger wasps of the genus *Pepsis*. It is a classic example of what looks like intelligence pitted against instinct—a strange situation in which the victim, though fully able to defend itself, submits unwittingly to its destruction.

Most tarantulas live in the tropics, but several species occur in the 2 temperate zone and a few are common in the southern U.S. Some varieties are large and have powerful fangs with which they can inflict a deep wound. These formidable-looking spiders do not, however, attack man; you can hold one in your hand, if you are gentle, without being bitten. Their bite is dangerous only to insects and small mammals such as mice; for man it is no worse than a hornet's sting.

Tarantulas customarily live in deep cylindrical burrows, from which ³ they emerge at dusk and into which they retire at dawn. Mature males wander about after dark in search of females and occasionally stray into houses. After mating, the male dies in a few weeks, but a female lives much longer and can mate several years in succession. In a Paris museum is a tropical specimen which is said to have been living in captivity for 25 years.

A fertilized female tarantula lays from 200 to 400 eggs at a time; thus ⁴ it is possible for a single tarantula to produce several thousand young. She takes no care of them beyond weaving a cocoon of silk to enclose the eggs. After they hatch, the young walk away, find convenient places in which to dig their burrows and spend the rest of their lives in solitude. The eyesight of tarantulas is poor, being limited to a sensing of change in the intensity of light and to the perception of moving objects. They apparently have little or no sense of hearing, for a hungry tarantula will pay no attention to a loudly chirping cricket placed in its cage unless the insect happens to touch one of its legs.

But all spiders, and especially hairy ones, have an extremely delicate ⁵ sense of touch. Laboratory experiments prove that tarantulas can distinguish three types of touch: pressure against the body wall, stroking of the body hair, and riffling of certain very fine hairs on the legs called trichobothria. Pressure against the body, by the finger or the end of a pencil, causes the tarantula to move off slowly for a short distance. The touch excites no defensive response unless the approach is from above where the spider can see the motion, in which case it rises on its hind legs, lifts its front legs, opens its fangs and holds this threatening posture as long as the object continues to move.

The entire body of a tarantula, especially its legs, is thickly clothed ⁶ with hair. Some of it is short and wooly, some long and stiff. Touching this body hair produces one of two distinct reactions. When the spider is hungry, it responds with an immediate and swift attack. At the touch of a cricket's antennae the tarantula seizes the insect so swiftly that a motion picture taken at the rate of 64 frames per second shows only the result and not the process of capture. But when the spider is not hungry, the stimulation of its hairs merely causes it to shake the touched limb. An insect can walk under its hairy belly unharmed.

The trichobothria, very fine hairs growing from disklike membranes ⁷ on the legs, are sensitive only to air movement. A light breeze makes them vibrate slowly, without disturbing the common hair. When one

blows gently on the trichobothria, the tarantula reacts with a quick jerk
of its four front legs. If the front and hind legs are stimulated at the same
time, the spider makes a sudden jump. This reaction is quite independent
of the state of its appetite.

These three tactile responses—to pressure on the body wall, to moving    8
of the common hair, and to flexing of the trichobothria—are so different
from one another that there is no possibility of confusing them. They
serve the tarantula adequately for most of its needs and enable it to avoid
most annoyances and dangers. But they fail the spider completely when
it meets its deadly enemy, the digger wasp *Pepsis*.

These solitary wasps are beautiful and formidable creatures. Most species    9
are either a deep shiny blue all over, or deep blue with rusty wings. The
largest have a wing span of about 4 inches. They live on nectar. When
excited, they give off a pungent odor—a warning that they are ready to
attack. The sting is much worse than that of a bee or common wasp, and
the pain and swelling last longer. In the adult stage the wasp lives only a
few months. The female produces but a few eggs, one at a time at intervals
of two or three days. For each egg the mother must provide one adult
tarantula, alive but paralyzed. The mother wasp attaches the egg to the
paralyzed spider's abdomen. Upon hatching from the egg, the larva is many
hundreds of times smaller than its living but helpless victim. It eats no
other food and drinks no water. By the time it has finished its single
Gargantuan meal and become ready for wasphood, nothing remains of the
tarantula but its indigestible chitinous skeleton.

The mother wasp goes tarantula-hunting when the egg in her ovary is    10
almost ready to be laid. Flying low over the ground late on a sunny afternoon,
the wasp looks for its victim or for the mouth of a tarantula burrow, a round
hole edged by a bit of silk. The sex of the spider makes no difference, but
the mother is highly discriminating as to species. Each species of *Pepsis*
requires a certain species of tarantula, and the wasp will not attack the
wrong species. In a cage with a tarantula which is not its normal prey, the
wasp avoids the spider and is usually killed by it in the night.

Yet when a wasp finds the correct species, it is the other way about.    11
To identify the species the wasp apparently must explore the spider with
her antennae. The tarantula shows an amazing tolerance to this exploration. The wasp crawls under it and walks over it without evoking any
hostile response. The molestation is so great and so persistent that the
tarantula often rises on all eight legs, as if it were on stilts. It may stand
this way for several minutes. Meanwhile the wasp, having satisfied itself
that the victim is of the right species moves off a few inches to dig the
spider's grave. Working vigorously with legs and jaws, it excavates a hole
8 to 10 inches deep with a diameter slightly larger than the spider's girth.

Now and again the wasp pops out of the hole to make sure that the spider is still there.

When the grave is finished, the wasp returns to the tarantula to complete her ghastly enterprise. First she feels it all over once more with her antennae. Then her behavior becomes more aggressive. She bends her abdomen, protruding her sting, and searches for the soft membrane at the point where the spider's legs join its body—the only spot where she can penetrate the horny skeleton. From time to time, as the exasperated spider slowly shifts ground, the wasp turns on her back and slides along with the aid of her wings, trying to get under the tarantula for a shot at the vital spot. During all this maneuvering, which can last for several minutes, the tarantula makes no move to save itself. Finally the wasp corners it against some obstruction and grasps one of its legs in her powerful jaws. Now at last the harassed spider tries a desperate but vain defense. The two contestants roll over and over on the ground. It is a terrifying sight and the outcome is always the same. The wasp finally manages to thrust her sting into the soft spot and holds it there for a few seconds while she pumps in the poison. Almost immediately the tarantula falls paralyzed on its back. Its legs stop twitching; its heart stops beating. Yet it is not dead, as is shown by the fact that if taken from the wasp it can be restored to some sensitivity by being kept in a moist chamber for several months.

After paralyzing the tarantula, the wasp cleans herself by dragging her body along the ground and rubbing her feet, sucks a drop of blood oozing from the wound in the spider's abdomen, then grabs a leg of the flabby, helpless animal in her jaws and drags it down to the bottom of the grave. She stays there for many minutes, sometimes for several hours, and what she does all that time in the dark we do not know. Eventually she lays her egg and attaches it to the side of the spider's abdomen with a sticky secretion. Then she emerges, fills the grave with soil carried bit by bit in her jaws, and finally tramples the ground all around to hide any trace of the grave from prowlers. Then she flies away, leaving her descendant safely started in life.

In all this the behavior of the wasp evidently is qualitatively different from that of the spider. The wasp acts like an intelligent animal. This is not to say that instinct plays no part or that she reasons as man does. But her actions are to the point; they are not automatic and can be modified to fit the situation. We do not know for certain how she identifies the tarantula—probably it is by some olfactory or chemo-tactile sense—but she does it purposefully and does not blindly tackle a wrong species.

On the other hand, the tarantula's behavior shows only confusion. Evidently the wasp's pawing gives it no pleasure, for it tries to move away. That the wasp is not simulating sexual stimulation is certain because male and female tarantulas react in the same way to its advances. That the spider is not anesthetized by some odorless secretion is easily shown by blowing lightly at the tarantula and making it jump suddenly. What, then, makes the tarantula behave as stupidly as it does?

No clear, simple answer is available. Possibly the stimulation by the wasp's antennae is masked by a heavier pressure on the spider's body, so that it reacts as when prodded by a pencil. But the explanation may be much more complex. Initiative in attack is not in the nature of tarantulas; most species fight only when cornered so that escape is impossible. Their inherited patterns of behavior apparently prompt them to avoid problems rather than attack them. For example, spiders always weave their webs in three dimensions, and when a spider finds that there is insufficient space to attach certain threads in the third dimension, it leaves the place and seeks another, instead of finishing the web in a single plane. This urge to escape seems to arise under all circumstances, in all phases of life, and to take the place of reasoning. For a spider to change the pattern of its web is as impossible as for an inexperienced man to build a bridge across a chasm obstructing his way.

In a way the instinctive urge to escape is not only easier but often more efficient than reasoning. The tarantula does exactly what is most efficient in all cases except in an encounter with a ruthless and determined attacker dependent for the existence of her own species on killing as many tarantulas as she can lay eggs. Perhaps in this case the spider follows its usual pattern of trying to escape, instead of seizing and killing the wasp, because it is not aware of its danger. In any case, the survival of the tarantula species as a whole is protected by the fact that the spider is much more fertile than the wasp.

## QUESTIONS FOR ANALYSIS

1. What seems to be Petrunkevitch's purpose in telling us about tarantulas and the digger wasps? What general strategy does he use to achieve his purpose?

2. Outline the essay in order to discover what plan Petrunkevitch follows in presenting the information. In your view, is it an ideal plan? What different plans for presenting the same information could you imagine? (Chapter 1 presents a plan for outlining.)

3. In his first paragraph, what exactly does Petrunkevitch forecast about his essay? What advantages or disadvantages do you see in such a beginning for this type of essay? How did this beginning influence the way you read the essay?

4. Reread the essay, underlining all words, phrases, or sentences at the beginning of each paragraph that provide a transition from the previous paragraph; then notice the different kinds of transitions Petrunkevitch employs. What can you conclude about his transitional strategies?

5. Nearly all readers for whom the information in this essay is new would say that it is clear and accessible on first reading, that it is richly informative and yet not hard to read. Unfortunately, not all the observational and explanatory reading material you encounter in college or on the job will be this accessible—this clear and graceful. To determine how Petrunkevitch achieves this balance, analyze paragraphs 4 and 9. What makes them clear to you? What decisions did Petrunkevitch make as a writer to produce this informative yet easy reading?

6. Skim the essay, circling all the words you did not know when you first read them. Then consider what clues are available in the piece to provide at least a partial definition of each of these words. In general, what kinds of clues does Petrunkevitch provide to help you understand unfamiliar words?

## SUGGESTIONS FOR WRITING

1. Write an essay about some activity in nature you are familiar with and can observe closely. Describe and interpret a specific activity of insects, birds, animals, even household pets. You may want to do some library research on the subject you observe, but the focus of your essay should be on what you observe firsthand. (Hold on to your observation notes in case your instructor or other students want to see them or in case you need to revise your essay.)

2. Write an essay about a process you know extremely well—one that you or someone else can repeat several times while you take notes on it. Choose a process that interests you greatly and will probably interest your readers. It would be best to avoid overly familiar activities: baking a cake, tying a shoe, driving a car. Consider something like editing a section in a newspaper (writing, editing, choosing headlines, planning layout), performing some small and especially difficult part of a sport, composing music, cleaning or tuning some unusual piece of equipment. (Hold on to your observation notes in case you need them for revision or your instructor wants to see them.)

# Annie Dillard

Annie Dillard (b. 1945) is a poet, reporter, essayist, and literary theorist. Since 1974, when she won the Pulitzer Prize for *Pilgrim at Tinker Creek,* she has been considered one of America's finest nonfiction prose writers. She has published a book of poems, *Tickets for the Prayer Wheel* (1982), and one book of literary theory, *Living by Fiction* (1982).

# *Solar Eclipse*

This selection comes from a chapter in *Teaching a Stone to Talk* (1982). Subtitled *Expeditions and Encounters,* the book presents Dillard's observations of unusual and interesting places, events, and people. In this selection, she reports her observations of a total eclipse of the sun. Assume she is writing for readers who have never seen a total eclipse; and as you read, notice her strategies for presenting this event in ways that will help readers imagine it for themselves. Dillard is not an astronomer, and you will sense right away that she is attempting something different from scientific reporting. What seems to be her interest in reporting this eclipse beyond helping readers imagine what happened?

It began with no ado. It was odd that such a well-advertised public 1 event should have no starting gun, no overture, no introductory speaker. I should have known right then that I was out of my depth. Without pause or preamble, silent as orbits, a piece of the sun went away. We looked at it through welders' goggles. A piece of the sun was missing; in its place we saw empty sky.

I had seen a partial eclipse in 1970. A partial eclipse is very interesting. 2 It bears almost no relation to a total eclipse. Seeing a partial eclipse bears the same relation to seeing a total eclipse as kissing a man does to marrying him, or as flying in an airplane does to falling out of an airplane. Although the one experience precedes the other, it in no way prepares you for it. During a partial eclipse the sky does not darken—not even when 94 percent of the sun is hidden. Nor does the sun, seen colorless through protective devices, seem terribly strange. We have all seen a sliver of light in the sky; we have all seen the crescent moon by day. However, during a partial eclipse the air does indeed get cold, precisely as if someone were standing between you and the fire. And blackbirds do fly back to their roosts. I had seen a partial eclipse before, and here was another.

What you see in an eclipse is entirely different from what you know. ₃ It is especially different for those of us whose grasp of astronomy is so frail that, given a flashlight, a grapefruit, two oranges, and fifteen years, we still could not figure out which way to set the clocks for Daylight Saving Time. Usually it is a bit of a trick to keep your knowledge from blinding you. But during an eclipse it is easy. What you see is much more convincing than any wild-eyed theory you may know.

You may read that the moon has something to do with eclipses. I have ₄ never seen the moon yet. You do not see the moon. So near the sun, it is as completely invisible as the stars are by day. What you see before your eyes is the sun going through phases. It gets narrower and narrower, as the waning moon does, and, like the ordinary moon, it travels alone in the simple sky. The sky is of course background. It does not appear to eat the sun; it is far behind the sun. The sun simply shaves away; gradually, you see less sun and more sky.

The sky's blue was deepening, but there was no darkness. The sun was ₅ a wide crescent, like a segment of tangerine. The wind freshened and blew steadily over the hill. The eastern hill across the highway grew dusky and sharp. The towns and orchards in the valley to the south were dissolving into the blue light. Only the thin river held a trickle of sun.

Now the sky to the west deepened to indigo, a color never seen. A ₆ dark sky usually loses color. This was a saturated, deep indigo, up in the air. Stuck up into that unworldly sky was the cone of Mount Adams, and the alpenglow was upon it. The alpenglow is that red light of sunset which holds out on snowy mountaintops long after the valleys and table-lands are dimmed. "Look at Mount Adams," I said, and that was the last sane moment I remember.

I turned back to the sun. It was going. The sun was going, and the ₇ world was wrong. The grasses were wrong; they were platinum. Their every detail of stem, head, and blade shone lightless and artificially dis-tinct as an art photographer's platinum print. This color has never been seen on earth. The hues were metallic; their finish was matte. The hill-side was a nineteenth-century tinted photograph from which the tints had faded. All the people you see in the photograph, distinct and detailed as their faces look, are now dead. The sky was navy blue. My hands were silver. All the distant hills' grasses were finespun metal which the wind laid down. I was watching a faded color print of a movie filmed in the Middle Ages; I was standing in it, by some mistake. I was standing in a movie of hillside grasses filmed in the Middle Ages. I missed my own century, the people I knew, and the real light of day.

I looked at Gary. He was in the film. Everything was lost. He was a ₈ platinum print, a dead artist's version of life. I saw on his skull the darkness of night mixed with the colors of day. My mind was going out; my eyes were receding the way galaxies recede to the rim of space. Gary was light-years away, gesturing inside a circle of darkness, down the wrong end of a telescope. He smiled as if he saw me; the stringy crinkles around his eyes moved. The sight of him, familiar and wrong, was something I was remembering from centuries hence, from the other side of death: yes, *that* is the way he used to look, when we were living. When it was our generation's turn to be alive. I could not hear him; the wind was too loud. Behind him the sun was going. We had all started down a chute of time. At first it was pleasant; now there was no stopping it. Gary was chuting away across space, moving and talking and catching my eye, chuting down the long corridor of separation. The skin on his face moved like thin bronze plating that would peel.

The grass at our feet was wild barley. It was the wild einkorn wheat 9 which grew on the hilly flanks of the Zagros Mountains, above the Euphrates valley, above the valley of the river we called *River*. We harvested the grass with stone sickles, I remember. We found the grasses on the hillsides; we built our shelter beside them and cut them down. That is how he used to look then, that one, moving and living and catching my eye, with the sky so dark behind him, and the wind blowing. God save our life.

From all the hills came screams. A piece of sky beside the crescent 10 sun was detaching. It was a loosened circle of evening sky, suddenly lighted from the back. It was an abrupt black body out of nowhere; it was a flat disk; it was almost over the sun. That is when there were screams. At once this disk of sky slid over the sun like a lid. The sky snapped over the sun like a lens cover. The hatch in the brain slammed. Abruptly it was dark night, on the land and in the sky. In the night sky was a tiny ring of light. The hole where the sun belongs is very small. A thin ring of light marked its place. There was no sound. The eyes dried, the arteries drained, the lungs hushed. There was no world. We were the world's dead people rotating and orbiting around and around, embedded in the planet's crust, while the earth rolled down. Our minds were light-years distant, forgetful of almost everything. Only an extraordinary act of will could recall to us our former, living selves and our contexts in matter and time. We had, it seems, loved the planet and loved our lives, but could no longer remember the way of them. We got the light wrong. In the sky was something that should not be there. In the black sky was a ring of light. It was a thin ring, an old, thin silver wedding band, an old, worn ring. It was an old wedding band in the sky, or a morsel of bone. There were stars. It was all over.

The world which lay under darkness and stillness following the closing 11
of the lid was not the world we know. The event was over. Its devastation
lay round about us. The clamoring mind and heart stilled, almost indifferent, certainly disembodied, frail, and exhausted. The hills were
hushed, obliterated. Up in the sky, like a crater from some distant cataclysm, was a hollow ring.

You have seen photographs of the sun taken during a total eclipse. 12
The corona fills the print. All of those photographs were taken through
telescopes. The lenses of telescopes and cameras can no more cover the
breadth and scale of the visual array than language can cover the breadth
and simultaneity of internal experience. Lenses enlarge the sight, omit
its context, and make of it a pretty and sensible picture, like something
on a Christmas card. I assure you, if you send any shepherds a Christmas
card on which is printed a three-by-three photograph of the angel of the
Lord, the glory of the Lord, and a multitude of the heavenly host, they
will not be sore afraid. More fearsome things can come in envelopes.
More moving photographs than those of the sun's corona can appear in
magazines. But I pray you will never see anything more awful in the sky.

You see the wide world swaddled in darkness; you see a vast breadth 13
of hilly land, and an enormous, distant, blackened valley; you see towns'
lights, a river's path, and blurred portions of your hat and scarf; you see
your husband's face looking like an early black-and-white film; and you
see a sprawl of black sky and blue sky together, with unfamiliar stars in
it, some barely visible bands of cloud, and over there, a small white ring.
The ring is as small as one goose in a flock of migrating geese—if you
happen to notice a flock of migrating geese. It is one 360th part of the
visible sky. The sun we see is less than half the diameter of a dime held
at arm's length.

When the sun appeared as a blinding bead on the ring's side, the 14
eclipse was over. The black lens cover appeared again, backlighted, and
slid away. At once the yellow light made the sky blue again; the black
lid dissolved and vanished. The real world began there. I remember now:
we all hurried away. We were born and bored at a stroke. We rushed
down the hill. We found our car; we saw the other people streaming
down the hillsides; we joined the highway traffic and drove away.

We never looked back. It was a general vamoose, and an odd one, for 15
when we left the hill, the sun was still partially eclipsed—a sight rare
enough, and one which, in itself, we would probably have driven five
hours to see. But enough is enough. One turns at last even from glory
itself with a sigh of relief. From the depths of mystery, and even from
the heights of splendor, we bounce back and hurry for the latitudes of
home.

### QUESTIONS FOR ANALYSIS

1. Dillard consistently presents her observations by comparing them to familiar objects and events. Beginning with "kissing" in paragraph 2, make an inventory of the comparisons in the essay. In these comparisons, what kinds of knowledge and experience does Dillard assume that her readers have? Did she over- or underestimate your own knowledge and experience? (Chapter 1 discusses taking inventory.)

2. In her last two paragraphs, Dillard continues to report her observations, but she comments as well. What is included in these comments? How effective do you find her strategy of concluding by integrating observations and comments, rather than concluding only with comments?

3. Dillard regularly describes what she is seeing by saying what it is not. Skim the essay looking for the *no*'s and *not*'s that set up these contrasts. What advantages do you see in this strategy?

4. In paragraphs 7–9, Dillard's perspective shifts. How would you describe this shift? What is she doing in these three paragraphs that is different? What effect does this shift have on you?

5. Look closely at the sentences in paragraph 10. Why do you think Dillard wrote these kinds of sentences at this point in her report?

6. Which part of this selection did you like best? Identify one part (a paragraph or several sentences) and explain why it appeals to you.

7. Dillard relies heavily on the semicolon in this selection. It appears in nearly every paragraph. Examine closely each use of the semicolon. How does she use it? What advantages or disadvantages do you see in her decision to rely so heavily on the semicolon?

8. Both Petrunkevitch and Dillard report observations of natural phenomena, Petrunkevitch of a particular species of spider and wasp, Dillard of a solar eclipse. What similarities and differences do you notice in their strategies for reporting observations?

### SUGGESTIONS FOR WRITING

1. Observe some dramatic natural phenomenon like a thunderstorm, snow squall or blizzard, hurricane, tornado, flood, river ice thaw, Santa Ana wind, blue norther, sandstorm, or high surf. Take notes of your observations, and then write an observational report for readers in a part of the country where the phenomenon never occurs.

2. Observe some urban phenomenon like rush hour on the subway, grid-lock on the streets, fast food restaurants at lunch hour, weekday happy hour in bars, building construction, street repairs, street peddlers, homeless people on the streets, or students hanging out before or after school across the street from a high school. From your observational notes write a report for readers who live in small towns or who rarely visit large cities.

# Judith S. Wallerstein and
# Joan B. Kelly

Judith Wallerstein and Joan Kelly are psychologists specializing in family counseling and social work. They gained fame for a five-year study of sixty families who had undergone divorce. For their study they interviewed all the family members three times: just as the divorce was occurring, eighteen months later, and then again in five years. Their first reports from this study were published between 1975 and 1979 in scholarly journals and then summarized for a wider audience in *Surviving the Breakup: How Children and Parents Cope with Divorce* (1980).

# *California's Children of Divorce*

It is not at all unusual for academic research to appear first in specialized research journals, then as a book, and finally in popular publications for the nonspecialist reader. This is just the publication history of Wallerstein and Kelly's California Children of Divorce Project. The selection presented here appeared in 1980 in *Psychology Today*, a monthly magazine that summarizes and interprets psychological studies for college-educated adults. For this report Wallerstein and Kelly present their major findings by selecting the most relevant evidence from their hundreds of hours of interviews with members of divorced families. It is like many you will read as a college student, especially in sociology, psychology, and education courses.

Nearly everyone has experienced the effects of divorce, either as a family member or as a close friend. How do you think psychologists might study the effects of divorce? Before you begin reading, preview the selection, looking closely at headings and sampling first sentences in paragraphs.

As you read, notice how Wallerstein and Kelly collect information and report it to you. How convincing do you find their work?

The conventional wisdom used to be that unhappily married people should remain married "for the good of the children." Today's conventional wisdom holds, with equal vigor, that an unhappy couple might well *divorce* for the good of the children; that an unhappy marriage for the adults is unhappy also for the children; and that divorce that promotes the happiness of the adults will benefit the children as well. 1

Testing that new dogma was among our goals in 1971 when we started what became known as the Children of Divorce Project. We interviewed all the members of 60 families with children that had recently gone 2 through divorce, and reinterviewed them 18 months later. Recently, we saw them again, after a lapse of five years. Our study has no counterpart in the United States or in Europe in the span of years it covers, in the participation of so many children of different ages, and in the kinds of questions that were posed.

Our results called into sharp question much more than the idea that what is good for the parents is always good for the kids. For example, we thought that by five years after the initial separation, new family structures would be an accepted part of life, and our observations would be made within a social and psychological landscape that had come to rest. Yet we found more people than we expected to find still in various degrees of turmoil.

Our overall conclusion is that divorce produces not a single pattern in people's lives, as the conventional wisdom of any era tends to claim, but at least three patterns, with many variations. Among both adults and children five years afterward, we found about a quarter to be resilient (those for whom the divorce was successful), half to be muddling through, coping when and as they could, and a final quarter to be bruised: failing to recover from the divorce or looking back to the predivorce family with intense longing. Some in each group had been that way before and continued unchanged; for the rest, we found roughly equal numbers for whom the divorce seemed connected to improvement and decline.

What made the biggest difference for the children was not the divorce itself, but the factors that make for good adjustment and satisfaction in intact families: psychologically healthy parents and children who are involved with one another in appropriate ways. Yet providing these optimal conditions is difficult in the postdivorce family, with its characteristic climate of anger, rejection, and attempts to exclude the absent parent.

**Changing Family Circumstances**   News of their parents' divorce clearly had been an unhappy shock to most of the children. We found that although many of them had lived for years in an unhappy home, they did not experience the divorce as a solution to their unhappiness, nor did they greet it with relief at the time, or for several years thereafter.

To be sure, as many of the children matured, they often acquired a different perspective. But at the time of the family disruption, many of the children considered their situation neither better nor worse than that of other families around them. They would, in fact, have been content to hobble along. The divorce was a bolt of lightning that struck them when they had not even been aware of a need to come in from the storm.

Five years later, there had been little shifting of the children from the    8
custody of one parent to the other. Seventy-seven percent of the youngsters continued to live in the custody of their mothers. Eight percent
now lived with the fathers, a slight increase; another 3 percent shuttled
back and forth from one home to the other, usually not in a planned
joint-custody arrangement, but under duress when their relationship with
one or the other parent became overwhelmed with ill will. An additional
11 percent of the children—adolescents—were now living on their own.

Almost two-thirds of the youngsters had changed their place of resi-    9
dence, and a substantial number of these had moved three or more times.
The moves were generally within a radius of 30 miles, however; very few
families left the region. The fathers tended to stay close by as well. One-
half continued to live within the same county as their children, some
still within biking distance. An additional 30 percent of the fathers were
within a one-hour drive.

Twenty-four (43 percent) of the fathers had remarried in the inter-    10
vening four years, of whom five were then redivorced and two subsequently remarried. Thus, 44 percent of the youngsters had a new stepmother. Nineteen of the mothers—one-third—had remarried; two of
these women were then redivorced, and two widowed. Hence, nearly a
quarter of the children lived with a stepparent.

The majority of the fathers (68 percent) had made their child-support    11
payments with considerable regularity, and an additional 19 percent paid
some support, but irregularly and in varying amounts. (Nationally, the
estimated figures are considerably lower.) Only 13 percent were completely delinquent. Still, far more of the mothers than the fathers had
traveled downward from their former economic status.

At the time of divorce, two-fifths of the families had been solidly upper    12
class or upper middle class, whereas two-thirds of the women and their
children were now either solidly middle class or lower middle class.

**The Children's Differing Reactions**    Hardly a child of divorce we came    13
to know did not cling to the fantasy of a magical reconciliation between
his parents. Danny, age seven, whose parents had been divorced for
several years when we first saw him, softly confided his "best" fantasy.
He had, he said, always wanted to fix up Hazel Street and Pine Street.
"They're all filled with mud and they don't join, but a long time ago,
they did, and I'd like to cut the two streets so they join. But this," he
sighed, "will be a long time off."

When we saw Danny again, he was 11. "Divorce is not as bad as you    14
think . . . not near as bad as it looks in movies or on television," he
said. He had thought a lot about divorce, he told us; and had just recently

figured it all out. "It's something like if you break a glass and pick the pieces up right away, they will fit back together perfectly, but if you take one piece and sand the edge, it will never fit again."

Five years after the separation, 28 percent of the children strongly 15 approved of their parents' divorce, 42 percent were somewhere in the middle, accepting the changed family but not taking a strong position for or against the divorce, and 30 percent strongly disapproved—a major shift from the initial count. Then, three-quarters of the children strongly disapproved. Still, the faithfulness of so many youngsters to their predivorce families was unsettling, and more loyal than many parents welcomed.

Nancy, now in the second grade, said, "when they first divorced, I 16 was kind of sad." Then, she said, she found out life was still fun because "we got to see Daddy in his house. . . . There are lots of good things to do. . . . Things are not so different. . . . You can meet a lot of new dogs and new people."

Thirty-four percent of the children and adolescents appeared to be 17 doing especially well psychologically at the five-year mark. Their self-esteem was high and they were coping competently with the tasks of school, playground, and home. There were no significant age or sex differences among these resilient youngsters. The boys appeared to have caught up with their sisters in the years since the first follow-up, which had found the boys lagging behind. Characteristic of these children was their sense of sufficiency: the divorce had not depleted their lives by removing a loving parent, or by pairing them with an angry, disturbed one. At times, they still felt lonely, unhappy, or sorrowful about the divorce, but these misgivings did not make them aggrieved or angry at either parent.

Roughly 29 percent of the children were in the middle range of psy- 18 chological health. They were learning at grade level at school and showing reasonably appropriate social behavior and judgment in their relationships with adults and children. They were considered average by their teachers. Nevertheless, islands of unhappiness and diminished self-esteem or anger continued to demand significant portions of their attention and energy, and sometimes hampered the full potential of their development.

Sonja, age 11, was typical of the middle group. "I don't think about 19 the divorce as much as I used to," she said. "Before, I wasn't right. I was all mad and yelling at Mom. . . . Usually, I still yell at her. I tell her I don't mean it, but I can't control myself." Disquietingly, Sonja talked with considerable pleasure about hurting and slapping people. She laughed excitedly as she recounted several stories of people, adults and children, getting into difficulties. Recently, Sonja was caught stealing some things from a shopping center and also from the school. Yet Sonja's mother indicated that the child is not as demanding as she used to be, and that, overall, her behavior is improving.

We found a final third of the children and adolescents to be consciously  20 and intensely unhappy and dissatisfied with their life in the postdivorce family. Among this group were those with moderate to severe depression, although at least half of the depressed children had islands of relatively unburdened development within them and were able to move ahead in ways appropriate for their age in several important parts of their lives, such as school.

We were struck as well by the high incidence of intense loneliness  21 that we observed in 27 percent of the children, a little higher than at the 18 month mark. These children complained of coming home to empty houses after school to await the return of the working parent. On weekends, these youngsters often felt left out of the social life of both divorced parents. Several also complained of loneliness within a remarriage, while recognizing ruefully that the newly married adults wanted privacy and time away from curious children.

Anger played a significant role in the psychological life of 23 percent  22 of the children and adolescents, who were not coping well. Most of the anger was defensive and reflected the underlying fear, sorrow, and sense of powerlessness of these youngsters. Anger at the father was especially likely to be sustained, especially in older boys and adolescents. Three children had rejected their fathers' overtures, including Paul, who returned unopened his father's birthday present to him on his 14th birthday. Other children's anger took other forms, including explosive outbursts of temper and delinquent behavior, such as drug involvement and stealing.

**The Importance of Involved Fathers**   What accounted for the successful  23 outcomes? Some children improved simply by escaping a disturbed and cruel parent to be left in the custody of a concerned and loving one. Some of these youngsters developed good relationships with a stepparent. Little boys, especially, appeared to spurt ahead with excitement and new growth with a stepfather whom they grew quickly to love.

A number of other factors seemed common to the children who dealt  24 most resiliently with divorce. One factor, not surprisingly, was having a strong personality to start with. As we followed the course of the children whom we had placed initially within the ranks of the very well adjusted, it appeared that two-thirds of these resilient, successful copers were still functioning very well five years later. Sad to say, some boys and girls in all age groups who had been able to cope during a conflict-ridden marriage deteriorated notably in the post-separation period.

The most unpredictable change occurred among those children whose 25 adjustment initially was a mixed bag of successes and failures. Very few of the boys and girls who were originally at the midpoint of the scale were still there after five years. Those youngsters were the most vulnerable to change, and stood in equal measure to either deteriorate or improve.

Perhaps the most crucial factor influencing a good readjustment was a 26 stable, loving relationship with both parents, between whom friction had largely dissipated, leaving regular, dependable visiting patterns that the parent with custody encouraged. . . . Forty percent of the mother-child relationships were adequate to very good, with an additional 20 percent at the adequate mark. Occasionally, when the father had been abusive or was psychologically disturbed, a strong mother bore the emotional load by herself and seemed able to give the children all the emotional support they needed. Usually, however, it took two, and a custodial parent's efforts to improve the child's life were burdened by the seeming disinterest of the other parent.

The contribution that the out-of-home parent could make emerged 27 with clarity at five years. Frequent, flexible visiting patterns remained important to the majority of the children. Nearly one-quarter of the youngsters continued to see their fathers weekly, if not several times weekly. An additional 20 percent visited two to three times a month. Thus, 45 percent of the children and adolescents continued to enjoy what society deems "reasonable visitation," although many of the children continued to complain of not enough contact.

The 17 percent of youngsters with erratic visits (less than once a 28 month) continued to be anguished by the father's inconstancy; the passage of five years had not lessened their wish to be loved by both parents. The same percentage as before (9 percent) had no contact.

Overall, we found that 30 percent of the children had an emotionally 29 nurturant relationship with their father five years after the marital separation, and that this sense of a continuing, close relationship was critical to the good adjustment of both boys and girls.

These men had worked hard to earn the parenthood that fathers in 30 intact families customarily take for granted. Some had persevered despite such irritations as one former wife who, four years after the separation, was still regularly calling her former husband during their son's visits with him to order the boy to shower. One man described the special personalities of his three children so vividly that hearing him talk, one would have been hard put to know that there had been a divorce in the family five years earlier. The children of these men, in turn, were spared the sense of loss and rejection that many less fortunate children experienced.

In contrast to the youngsters who yearned for more visits, almost one- 31 fifth of the youngsters did not find the visits pleasurable or gratifying. A number of them resented being used to carry hostile messages between parents. Noted Larry, a 13-year-old, "My father has to understand that when he shoots arrows at my mother, they first have to go through our bodies before they reach her."

In the most unsatisfactory visiting arrangements, a range of parental 32 behavior, from outright abandonment to general unreliability, often disappointed a child repeatedly, usually leading the child to feel rejected, rebuffed, and unloved and unlovable. Anger at the rejecting father usually did not undo the child's unhappy conclusion about his or her essential unlovability to the father. Lea, for example, was an abnormally quiet girl whose teacher said she did not believe she could succeed at anything. We interviewed her at home. When asked about her father, she brought out a box containing all of the letters her father had written to her during the past three years. These letters, possibly 15 in number, were dog-eared, folded and refolded, and the interviewer couldn't help but be reminded of a precious collection of love letters that had been read and reread with tears. The father had actually visited only once in the past two years.

Peter, age nine, had not seen his father, who lives nearby, more than 33 once every two to three months. We expected that he would be troubled, but we were entirely unprepared for the extent of this child's misery. The interviewer observed: "I asked Peter when he had last seen his dad. The child looked at me blankly and his thinking became confused, his speech halting. Just then, a police car went by with its siren screaming. The child stared into space and seemed lost in reverie. As this continued for a few minutes, I gently suggested that the police car had reminded him of his father, a police officer. Peter began to cry and sobbed without stopping for 35 minutes."

Even though the majority of fathers and children continued to see 34 each other fairly often, by the five-year mark three-quarters of these relationships offered the children little in fully addressing the complex tasks of growing up. Yet, paradoxically, by his absence a father continued to influence the thoughts and feelings of his children; most particularly, the disinterested father left behind a legacy of depression and damaged self-esteem.

Except in extreme cases in which a father was clearly abusing children 35 or seriously disturbed, some contact seemed better than none at all. The father's presence kept the child from a worrisome concern with abandonment and total rejection and from the nagging self-doubts that follow such worry. The father's presence, however limited, also diminished the child's vulnerability and aloneness and total dependency on the one parent.

A few other factors that we had expected to be significant in helping 36 children adjust turned out not to be. Children were incapable of using friends to make up for troubled conditions at home; rather, those with comparatively stable homes were the ones most likely to have friends outside. Grandparents provided some solid supports for both divorced mothers and their children—when they supported the idea of the divorce—but were not a strong enough influence to make up for problems elsewhere. Most children did not seem to be influenced either for good or ill if their mother worked, although some of the youngest boys appeared to do significantly better in school and in their overall adjustment when the mother did not work full time.

One-third of the children once again confronted far-reaching change 37 in their daily lives when one or both of their divorced parents remarried. (Only two of the fathers with custody remarried.) The arrival of a stepfather seemed to create particular friction for a short while. Most of the stepfathers had been married before, expected to assume the role of parent to their wives' children, and, encouraged by the women, moved quickly into the prerequisites, prerogatives, and authority that this position traditionally conveyed. Only a few men appeared sensitive to the need to cultivate a relationship with stepchildren gradually and to make due allowance for suspiciousness and resistance in the initial stages.

Still, after some early tensions, the relationships with the children 38 from two to eight years old took root fairly quickly and were happy and gratifying to both child and adult. Yet children with a stepfather seemed particularly sensitive to friction between parents.

Many people expect children to experience conflict as they turn from 39 father to stepfather during their growing-up years. This was not borne out by our observations. Nor was the expectation that in the happily remarried family the biological father was likely to fade out of the children's lives. The great majority of fathers in the remarried families continued to visit, much as they had earlier. Mostly, children enlarged their view of the family and made room for three major figures. Jerry, age 10, when asked how often he saw his father, responded, "Which dad do you mean?" When a child did experience painful psychological conflict between the father and the stepfather, the adults were likely to be jealous or competitive, pulling hard in opposite directions.

The most tragic situations for the child were those in which mother 40 and stepfather demanded that the child renounce his or her love for the father as the price for acceptance and affection within the remarried family. Such children were severely troubled and depressed, too preoccupied with the chronic unresolvable conflict to learn or to develop at a normal pace.

***Eventual Softening of the Strains***    Most of the adults in our study, 41 especially the women, were feeling better five years after divorce than they had when we first saw them, despite the greater economic pressure and the many stresses of the postdivorce family. But among the children, although individuals had improved or worsened, the percentages within broad categories of good and poor adjustment had remained relatively stable. Hence, it seems that a divorced family per se is neither more nor less beneficial for children than an unhappy marriage. Unfortunately, neither unhappy marriage nor divorce is especially congenial for children. Each imposes its own set of differing stresses.

Our other major finding about how important it is for a child to keep 42 a relationship with both original parents points to the need for a concept of greater shared parental responsibility after divorce. In this condition, each parent continues to be responsible for, and genuinely concerned about, the well-being of his or her children, and allows the other parent this option as well.

The concept of joint legal custody, in which each parent has the right 43 to make important decisions about the life of the child, is a step in the right direction. The newer idea of shared *physical* custody, whether parents share the children 50–50, 80–20, or in other proportions, may also be a positive step, but it needs to be studied to determine its advantages and disadvantages for children at different developmental stages. Many people object that parents who cannot agree during marriage certainly cannot be expected to reach agreement on child-related matters after divorce. Indeed, some infuriated or disturbed parents will never chart a rational course with regard to their children. Yet it seems clear that our society must encourage fathers and mothers to accept the importance of continuity in parent-child relationships after divorce. Perhaps in changing legal expectations, we can take the first steps in a necessary re-education about meeting the needs of children in the postdivorce family.

Unfortunately, it seems clear that the divorced family is, in many ways, 44 less adaptive economically, socially, and psychologically to the raising of children than the two-parent family, or at least the two-adult family. This does not mean that it cannot be done. But the fact remains that the divorced family in which the burden falls entirely or mostly on one parent is more vulnerable to stress, has more limited economic and psychological reserves, and lacks the supporting or buffering presence of another adult for the expected and unexpected crises of life.

In order to fulfill the responsibility of child-rearing and provide even  45
minimally for the needs of the adult, many divorced families are in urgent
need of a network of services that are not now available in most communities, ranging from educational, vocational, and financial counseling
to enriched child care and after-school programs. At the five-year point
in our own study, two-fifths of the men and a somewhat greater number
of the women characterized the brief counseling we offered as useful and
supportive and were still following suggestions that we had made at the
first meetings five years earlier.

Divorcing with children requires in adults the capacity to maintain  46
entirely separate social and sexual roles while they continue to cooperate
as parents. This is very difficult. We began our work with the conviction
that divorce should remain a readily available option to adults who are
locked into an unhappy marriage. Our findings, although somewhat
graver than expected, have not changed our conviction. They have given
greater impetus to our interest in easing the family rupture for children
and adults alike.

## QUESTIONS FOR ANALYSIS

1. Research reports answer specific questions or explore hypotheses.
   What question do Wallerstein and Kelly propose to answer? Summarize their answer briefly, and decide how convincing you find it.

2. To understand the conventional strategy of introductions in research
   reports, analyze paragraphs 1–5, labeling the function of each one in
   relation to the whole report. What can you conclude about introductions in research reports?

3. As in most research reports, the major sections in Wallerstein and
   Kelly's report are signaled by headings. Review the section under each
   heading, deciding on its relation to the other parts. Do the sections
   each seem to be fulfilling a necessary and predictable function in a
   research report, or do they have some other relation you can discern?
   Why do you think the authors sequence the parts as they do?

4. Wallerstein and Kelly's findings derive from their interviews with divorced families. What kinds of information from the interviews do
   they include in their report? Evaluate the appropriateness of each.

5. Readable research reports provide readers with clear transitions, especially at the beginning of paragraphs. Analyze paragraphs 23–32, underlining the specific beginning-of-paragraph transitional elements
   that connect each paragraph to the preceding one. How many different kinds of transitions do you find? For you as one reader, which
   transitions do you think work best?

6. Some people believe that social science research only confirms the obvious. Do the findings of this report surprise you in any way? If so, what are the surprises?

7. Statistics play an important role in social science research, especially that based on questionnaires or interviews with large groups of people. Examine paragraphs 6–12 carefully, and comment on what kind of statistics appear and how they are used.

### SUGGESTIONS FOR WRITING

1. Consider the following nuggets of conventional wisdom: successful students are exceptionally well-organized; good writing comes from inspiration; today's college students are interested only in job training; studying the humanities makes you a better person; private schools provide better preparation for college than public schools; college athletes are rarely serious as students; the most creative students lead very different lives from other students. Examine one of these statements by interviewing several people, and write a report about what you learn.

2. Identify a school or community controversy, and interview several people on both sides in order to discover the issues and differences. Write a report on what you learn.

# Kimberley Duran

An undergraduate with a special interest in clinical and counseling psychology, Kimberley Duran hopes to be a counselor at a high school or social agency. She keeps a diary and often writes letters to friends and family. In her spare time, Duran likes to be with her friends, especially at the beach. She lives in California.

## *Reality at the County Morgue*

For a profile assignment in her freshman composition course, Kimberley Duran decided to visit the morgue at a county medical center. On her visit, she made herself look carefully at everything her guides showed her, including some things she was not expecting to see. She in turn passes along to her readers all the details of her experience, including a good bit we may not be prepared to read about.

As in all good investigative writing, we learn much about the subject. As you read, notice how much actual information you are picking up. More important, read to find out why Duran presents the morgue in just this way: What does she want us to think and feel? Is she merely trying to shock us? What seems to be her main point?

Speeding along the freeway en route to the hospital, I wondered if I 1 should have my seat belt on. I was, after all, going to a morgue. How ironic it would be if I got into an accident on my way there and arrived at the morgue in some vehicle other than my own Toyota. I was not convinced of the danger, though, and my seat belt remained unfastened.

The weather was a perfect prelude for my visit to the morgue. Dark 2 low clouds loomed overhead. The only other preparation I need is dark clothes, I thought. Glancing at my outfit, I had to smile. A black sweater and dark skirt was the outfit I had absentmindedly chosen to wear that day. For a moment I debated whether to go home and change. No, I can't, I thought. I'm late already. Besides, what else would one wear to a morgue? Profiling a morgue—I don't know about this, I thought. I wonder what dead people look like. I've never seen a dead body before.

As I walked into my mom's office at the County Medical Center, I 3 reminded myself how lucky it was that she worked there. I would never have been able to get access to the morgue without this connection.

"Kim, I need to tell you a couple of things," she said in a quiet tone. 4 "First, when you are down there, you have to be very strong and very mature about what you see. Dr. Russell is going to pass you off as a medical student. You have to keep quiet about who you are, because Dr. Russell and I could get into a lot of trouble for this."

"Well, I don't want to get you into trouble for . . ."                                    5

"No, no," she interrupted. "It'll be okay. Just don't let them know     6
who you really are. We really lucked out in that Herman is going to show you two the morgue." Then she laughed.

"I don't get it, who's Herman?"                                                         7

"Herman is just a clerk. He'll never be suspicious of you. Dr. Stewart,     8
the pathologist, was supposed to give Dr. Russell and his 'medical student' a tour, but he had to leave early, so now you'll be able to investigate all you like."

Somehow, I wasn't as thrilled as she was. I was becoming a little     9
nervous. Just what kinds of things were there to see that I had to be "sneaked" in?

Just then Dr. Russell arrived. "Well, are we all ready to visit the     10
morgue?"

Dr. Russell—an ears, nose and throat specialist—is a small man, stand-     11
ing only 5'5" tall and weighing a mere 130 pounds. There is an air of friendliness about him. He is very quick-witted and quick-paced. The times I had seen him at the hospital he was always moving: he seemed to work at a rapid pace, reading charts, grabbing instruments here and there, all the while maintaining a lively conversation. The interesting thing about Dr. Russell is that he is afraid of dead bodies.

After my mom, his secretary, explained to him that Herman was to     12
show us around, they both laughed in unison. They seemed to get a thrill out of being so sneaky and fooling everyone. I was not able to join in the joke. I was too nervous.

As Dr. Russell helped me into a white doctor's coat, my mom said     13
dreamily, "My daughter, the medical student," and looked at me with a twinkle in her eye.

"You know, Kimberley," Dr. Russell said, "I am so glad that you are     14
coming with me down there; otherwise, I wouldn't go. I'm scared of that place."

That's comforting to hear, I thought. The butterflies in my stomach     15
were turning into bats.

As we were about to leave, Dr. Russell turned to my mom. "Where's     16
the morgue?" he asked. Just then Herman showed up to escort us. Herman wore glasses, and his face was unshaven. The morgue is not even attached to the hospital. It is a small beige building with brown trim about two blocks behind the hospital. Bodies are taken there in a special van.

"Not much is going on down there right now," Herman said with a 17 shrug. "I think they're doing an autopsy."

Not much going on? As I walked up the stairs to the small beige 18 building, I wondered what I had gotten myself into, and how I could get myself out of it within the next two seconds. Too late. Herman had already unlocked and opened the door for us. Hesitantly, I stepped inside and immediately noticed a most unpleasant odor, a lot like that of a fish market. I had expected to see large drawers built into the walls where the bodies are stored. Instead, I was in a hallway. A large steel door that resembled the door to a bank vault lay directly in front of me. A small unlocked padlock dangled on the handle. "That's the refrigerated room," Herman told us. "Where the bodies are kept," added Dr. Russell. Herman slowly opened the door for us to see. A dense mist rolled out. Peering into the dimly lit room, I saw table after table of corpses covered with white sheets. Their white feet protruding from under the sheets made my stomach turn. The only evidence that blood had ever pulsated through them was revealed by their blue toenails.

Dr. Russell took a firm hold of my arm, as much for his benefit as for 19 mine, and led me in. To my surprise, the fish smell was even stronger in there. The chilling cold invaded my body, as scenes from "Invasion of the Body Snatchers" flashed through my mind. It was silently eerie in that room. I did not like it. For a moment, I imagined myself being locked in there. At the sounds of my screams, the bodies would slowly rise off the table and come after me.

Dr. Russell's voice brought me back to reality, but I still glanced over 20 my shoulder to make sure that Herman was holding open the door. "The ones on the right are the done ones," Herman stated, referring to the bodies with completed autopsies.

"Would you like to see one, Kimberley?" Before I could say "No, not 21 really," he began uncovering the nearest corpse. It was a black male. There were stitches all across his chest where he'd been sewn up after the autopsy. With a slightly shaky hand, Dr. Russell started to uncover the face, but a securely tied black plastic bag prevented us from viewing the face.

I found it hard to believe that only a few days—or hours—earlier these 22 corpses were walking, talking, thinking individuals. It was strange being in a room where Dr. Russell and I were the minority: the living. The shocking reality was that I too would be a corpse lying in an eerie room like this one day. This room is also where bodies are identified by the next of kin. When a body is horribly disfigured, the next of kin is refused permission to view the body. Bodies are then identified by other means such as fingerprints or dental records. In one case, the parents of a particularly disfigured dead twenty-year-old pleaded to view the body and spend a final few minutes with their beloved son. Permission to view the entire body was still denied because of the disfigurement; the body was securely covered except for an arm. The parents were allowed in the morgue to hold their son's hand for five minutes.

Bodies remain in the morgue only until the family can arrange for a 23 mortician to pick up the body and prepare it for burial or cremation.

I was more than glad to leave that room. "How many bodies would 24 you say were in there—about fifteen?" I asked. Dr. Russell reopened the door and counted. "Fifteen exactly. Boy, are you observant," he said. Herman escorted us down the hall so Dr. Russell could wash his hands after touching the corpse. Out of the corner of my eye I saw a garish flash of red as we passed by a room.

"There's an autopsy going on in there," Dr. Russell told me. "Do you 25 think you can handle it?" he asked. I don't remember my answer. I just remember the shock I felt as I entered the room. Only my great curiosity kept me from fainting or becoming nauseated or screaming "Oh, God! Get me out of here!!" Surely, the sight of that skinned carcass was enough to unnerve any person. Lying on a long steel table was a nude male corpse. The red that I had seen was the inside of his chest, completely exposed. He had been cut from waist to neck and all the chest skin had been pulled to his sides so as to expose the chest cavity. Most of his organs had already been removed. The coroner was slicing and examining a lung when I arrived. The man's brain and liver lay on the table down by his knees. His ribs protruded and, amazingly, resembled a side of beef. The muscles of his neck and shoulders looked like steak. Everything exposed was so red it seemed the inside of the body knew no other color.

As I peered inside his empty chest, I could see a pool of blood.       26

Looking at the man's head, I did not understand what I saw first, for 27 the man had no visible face, only a smooth pale surface. What I didn't realize was that the face pulls down just like a mask. The man had a face; it was conveniently peeled down from the forehead and tucked under the chin. The smooth pale surface I was looking at was the tissue that lies directly below the skin of the face. The inside of his head was completely empty. The top of the skull had been opened, and the brain had been taken out. The coroner picked up the brain and sliced it as neatly as a loaf of bread with what appeared to be an ordinary kitchen knife. I saw the white and gray matter of the brain that I had learned about in my high school physiology class.

All the while the coroner was examining and dissecting organs, he 28 spoke into a microphone that hung from the ceiling, noting for the record details of what he was finding. A scale, similar to those found in the produce department of a grocery store, hung above the corpse's feet. It was used for weighing human organs. I looked around. There were many cabinets on the white walls; across the room was a cluster of four useless windows, tinted so that no one could see in or out. Three other workers dressed in green "scrubs" were also in the room, but only the coroner spoke. He used many technical terms to describe each organ's condition as he dissected and examined it. He paused a few moments for Herman to introduce Dr. Russell and me. "Can you tell me how this man died?" Dr. Russell asked.

"Well," said the coroner, "he was coming down the mountain from 29 Big Bear when his car went off the mountain. I believe he was ejected through the sun roof," he said, with a touch of sadness in his voice. He then sliced through the liver.

Autopsies are not performed on every person who dies, only those who 30 die under suspicious circumstances. Some of these circumstances include death while taking a prescribed medication or when under a nurse's care, or the sudden unexpected death of a "healthy" person. Autopsies are also performed when the cause of death is unknown. Car accident victims are always given autopsies to determine whether they died of brain damage, a snapped spinal cord, a heart attack, or from another cause. Also determined is whether alcohol, drugs, or possibly poison was in the victim's system, and if it was a determining factor in his or her death. This is why the organs are sliced and examined. Samples of blood, tissue, urine, and saliva are taken for evaluation. Life insurance companies also have a great interest in determining the exact cause of death.

I was amazed at how much the colors varied on this man's battered 31 body. His legs were large and inhumanly white, his arms dark pink, and his chest cavity incredibly red. Large and small dark purple scratch marks covered his body. His left arm was slightly bent at the elbow. His last desperate attempt to save his life was horrifyingly preserved in his tightly clenched fist.

Unlike the bodies in the refrigerated room, this body drew my atten- 32 tion. My eyes could not take in enough. After the initial shock, I was fascinated to see what the inside of a human body actually looked like. I wanted to learn all I could.

I was not scared of this corpse as I had been of the ones in refrigeration. 33 Hidden by white sheets, the bodies there seemed more like ghouls than human beings. The cold, the darkness, and the silence had made my skin crawl. This corpse, in contrast, was illuminated by bright fluorescent lamps and surrounded by living human beings. Instead of silence, this room brought the comforting sounds of human voices. The corpse was by no means hidden, either. One glance at this corpse, and I, a stranger, had seen more of his body than even his parents ever would.

There were some parts of this man that the doctor could never ex- 34 amine. His personality, his feelings, his likes and dislikes would not be announced into the hanging microphone. Not even his name was mentioned.

"Autopsy completed at 16:05 hours," stated the coroner.        35

As an assistant proceeded to pull the skin back into place, I saw the 36 face for the first time. How horribly purple it was from hemorrhaging. The same scratches that covered his body also covered his face. With his large nose and half-opened eyes and mouth, the face reminded me of a scary Halloween mask.

"How long has he been dead?" I asked.        37

"Well, his father reported him missing three days ago. He was found 38 yesterday. He's been dead long enough for flies to lay eggs in his mouth and eyes." With that statement, I realized I had observed enough.

Dr. Russell and I thanked the coroner for letting us watch and pro- 39 ceeded down the hall to the door.

"Wow, I can't believe we made it through all that," I said. Looking 40 over at Dr. Russell, I started to laugh. He had clutched his chest and thrown his arm across the wall so as to steady himself. "We made it, we made it, Kimberley," he said, taking deep breaths.

As we got outside, he said to me seriously, "I can work with the living 41 but not the dead. I'm scared of dead bodies." I then realized that all the while I was inside the room observing, Dr. Russell stood back a few feet, in the doorway.

Rushing into my mom's office a few minutes later, I was fairly bursting 42 with the details of what I had witnessed. I was very anxious to tell her and the whole world of the experience I had just been through. After hearing my story, she pulled out a newspaper. On the front page was a picture of a wrecked Porsche. The headline read, "Father Finds Missing Son's Body in Wrecked Car on Mountainside."

"That's the young man you saw," she said.        43

Reading the article and the man's name turned my excitement to 44 sadness and remorse. Somehow he had never seemed like a real person until then. I had not thought of the man's family or the pain they must have been going through.

Walking my mom out to her car, I was still a little shaky.        45

"Are you okay?" she asked.        46

"Yeah, I'm okay," I said. "I'll see you at home."        47

Walking to my own car, I was struck by a moment of panic. "Put your 48 seat belt on," I demanded of my mom.

I got into my car and did the same—securely fastened my seat belt.   49

Driving home carefully, I couldn't help thinking how glad I was to   50
have that experience over with. It was fascinating all right, but once was
enough. Then suddenly I realized that this would not be my last visit to
the morgue. Unfortunately, we would meet again someday. Only then
it would be under completely different circumstances.


## QUESTIONS FOR ANALYSIS

1. Consider how Duran beings her profile (through paragraph 15). How
   well does this beginning work? As a strategy for beginning profiles of
   places, what advantages and disadvantages do you see in Duran's beginning? How else might she have begun?

2. Sometimes writers will frame a composition by making the ending
   repeat some element of the beginning. How does Duran frame her
   profile? In your view, how appropriate and effective is the frame in
   the context of her profile?

3. Locate paragraphs that present information Duran could have acquired only in follow-up interviews or by reading. What part of the
   total information in the profile do these paragraphs present? Why do
   you think Duran places these paragraphs where she does in the profile?

4. Duran paragraphs often. Why do you think she chose that paragraphing strategy? Did you find her strategy helpful or unhelpful? Notice
   that not all her paragraphs are journalistically brief. What role do the
   longer paragraphs play in the profile?

5. Certainly Duran makes a vivid presentation of the county morgue,
   but just how does she do it? Select one part of the profile that seems
   particularly striking to you, and analyze it carefully. Exactly what
   information does Duran include? What details do you imagine she
   decided to leave out?

6. Do you find Duran's profile authoritative and believable? If so, how
   would you account for its authority? If not, how would you explain
   its failure?

7. What do you think is the main point of this essay?


## SUGGESTIONS FOR WRITING

1. Think of forbidding, mysterious, or exotic places in your community,
   places you have been curious about but have not ever visited. Arrange
   to visit one such spot so that you can observe what goes on and talk

to people there. Then write a profile of this place, presenting it vividly to your readers and reporting what you learned.

2. Places of life and death have great dramatic possibilities and natural appeal to readers and thus hold special appeal for profile writers. Consider visiting some unit of a hospital or clinic—a newborn nursery or an emergency room, for instance. Write a profile of this place.

3. Profile writers sometimes visit perfectly ordinary places. Usually, they look for something extraordinary about it, hoping to show it freshly or humorously or ironically. Go to a very ordinary place—a gas station, a supermarket, an elementary school. Observe and talk to people, looking for an unusual angle that will allow you to write an engaging profile of the place.

# A Look at Kimberley Duran's Writing Process

As she was listing possible profile subjects, Duran knew immediately that she had her place when she wrote "county hospital." When she got the idea to write about the morgue, she felt both excited and anxious: this was the place at the hospital she knew least about and feared most. At the same time, she was almost certain it would be the most unusual and compelling part of the hospital for her—and her readers as well. Her mother worked at the hospital and had from time to time brought home stories about the morgue. Though she had never been there herself, she was able to arrange for her daughter to see it, thereby eliminating the time and effort involved in getting access to a place that discouraged casual visitors, including students working on writing projects.

Since she was unable to anticipate much of what she would see on her visit, Duran could not prepare interview questions in advance. At the morgue she was so overwhelmed by what she saw that she didn't take any notes except to write down people's names. On her way back home, she stopped in a coffee shop and spent over an hour making notes on everything she could remember seeing and hearing. She recorded specific sights, sounds, smells, and actions and reconstructed some of the conversations. These notes roughly followed the order in which she had seen things and later suggested the plan for her profile: moving from scene to scene chronologically.

Two days later she returned to the hospital to interview Dr. Stewart and Herman. For those interviews she was able to draw up in advance many questions about why autopsies were performed and how they were carried out. She also wanted to know how bodies got into and out of the morgue, and she was curious about the people who worked there.

Very little of this follow-up information found its way into her draft, because she decided she wanted to focus on what she had actually seen on her first visit. She wanted to take her readers on a tour of the place, to show them the morgue just as she saw it.

She wasn't certain about how to begin, and so she decided to draft separately the three principal scenes—office, refrigerated room, and autopsy room—and think later about how to put them together. This decision was very fruitful: she started drafting immediately, and she later put the scenes in the order in which she encountered them at the hospital. Although she was pleased with the three sketches, she still did not know exactly how she would set them into the context of a full profile. It was when she remembered that she had buckled her seat belt as soon as she got back into her car that she discovered the frame for her profile: driving to the hospital without her seat belt fastened and leaving with it securely fastened. Finally, in a workshop discussion of her first draft in her composition class she recognized the larger theme: her own mortality.

## A GUIDE TO OBSERVATIONAL WRITING

From the readings in this chapter, you can see that profiles and observations present special challenges. Since writers necessarily collect large amounts of original material of diverse kinds—some of it from visits, some from interviews, some from other direct research—all of it must be sorted through, organized, and integrated into a readable draft. The guide to invention, drafting, and revising that follows is designed to assist you in solving the special problems you encounter in this kind of writing.

## *Invention*

The following activities can help you choose a subject, plan and carry through your research, find a main point or thesis, and analyze your readers. If you complete them all before you write your first draft, you will have collected all, or nearly all, the information you will need—and you will then be free to focus well on your actual writing.

CHOOSING A SUBJECT. Finding just the right subject is critical. A good way to begin is by listing the widest possible variety of subjects. It is advantageous to make the list cumulative, allowing yourself to add more items as they come to mind. After a while your list should be long enough to ensure that you have not overlooked a possible subject. Just laying it out on the page and scanning your options are a visual aid to choosing what subject you want to write about.

For an essay based on personal observation, interviews, or other research, your subject should be a person, a place, or a question for study. All these types of essays are illustrated by the readings in this chapter.

You might begin by listing possible subjects in each category. For a *person*, list activities or professions you want to study closely by profiling someone in the event or field. You need not have a particular person in mind. For a *place*, list places you are curious about and would be able to visit and study. If you can think of unusual places, fine, but consider also places from everyday life—a computer center, a weight-reduction clinic, a small-claims court, a nursery school. For a *research study*, list research questions you could answer through close observation, surveys, or experiments. You might first consider subjects from other courses you're taking. Some students find that they are unable to list subjects in one or more of these three categories, so if this happens to you just concentrate on the ideas that do come to mind.

After reflecting on your lists, choose a subject you are genuinely curious about, one which will hold your interest for a week or two of study. Try also to find a subject that readers may want to learn about. For a person or place subject, select one you can visit several times, and for a research subject, pick something you can complete and write up within the time available. Most important, choose a subject that interests you—and that you think might appeal to your readers.

PROBING YOUR SUBJECT. Before you study your subject, it might be helpful to jot down everything you presently know and feel about it. You may discover that you know more than you think you do.

Start by writing for several minutes without stopping, putting down everything you know about your subject. Include personal memories, facts, anecdotes, statistics, visual details—anything that comes to mind. How would you define or describe this subject? What is its purpose or function? What does it remind you of?

Next, try to state something about your attitude toward your subject. What feelings do you have about it? Do you feel neutral, anxious, eager? Why does it interest you? What preconceptions do you have about it? How do other people feel about it?

Continue with your expectations. What do you expect to discover? Do you anticipate being surprised, amused, shocked? What kind of profile or report would you really like to write about this subject? What readers do you want to address?

This initial probing of your subject will probably help you decide whether you are interested enough to continue with it.

INVESTIGATING YOUR SUBJECT. This kind of writing requires that you go out and gather original information. You may need to visit a site, interview someone, or collect data. To guarantee that you complete the information gathering within the time available, take time now to plan. Decide what times you have open within the next few days, then make phone calls to schedule visits. When you write down your appointments, be sure to include names, addresses, phone numbers, dates and times, and any special arrangements you have made for a visit.

*Visiting a Place.* If you profile a place or a person engaged in an activity at a particular place, you will need to make one or more visits to the place to gather information. The appendix on research and documentation provides useful guidelines for observing a place, taking notes on the spot, supplementing your notes later, and reflecting on what you have seen.

*Interviewing a Person.* If your profile requires that you interview someone, you will find the guidelines for interviewing in the appendix to be invaluable. These guidelines will help you plan and set up an interview, take notes during an interview, supplement your notes immediately after an interview, and reflect on what you have learned.

*Gathering Published Information.* If you are profiling a person or place, you may be able to pick up appropriate fliers, brochures, or reports, and you may want to do background reading on a particular kind of work or activity. If you are reporting on research, you might want to review related studies. Take careful notes from your reading, and keep accurate records of sources.

DECIDING ON YOUR MAIN POINT. You will need to find a focus in the material you have collected and then to decide on exactly what you want to say about it. Review all your notes and impressions, with the following kind of questions in mind. What is the single most important thing you learned? What surprises or contradictions did you encounter? What larger social or personal implications do you see in your material? What do you most want readers to know about your subject? What will be your purpose in writing about this subject? What are your feelings about the subject?

From your reflections on these questions, you should be able to write a few sentences that identify the main point you want to make to your readers.

ANALYZING YOUR READERS. Before you begin drafting, you will find it helpful for planning and selecting material to analyze your readers carefully—who they are will very much influence your writing. You could try to write for several minutes about your readers, just to see what turns up. What do they know or perceive about your subject? Why would they want to read about it? How can you interest them in it? What parts of your material might especially interest them?

# Drafting

If you have completed the preceding invention activities, you will probably have made many discoveries about your subject and with your substantial notes in hand will be ready to proceed to a first draft. The following discussion describes how to set goals for drafting, plan your draft, and decide how to begin.

SETTING GOALS. Establish specific goals with your readers and purpose in mind. Consider how much your readers already know about the subject. If they are familiar with it, you will need to find an engaging angle to present it to them. If they are likely to be unfamiliar with the subject, you may need to define special terms or describe fully unusual procedures or activities. Considering how you will enable them to visualize the subject for themselves should lead you to determine a larger strategy for engaging and holding their interest throughout your essay. Notice, for instance, how Dillard emphasizes the drama of the solar eclipse and Duran appeals to our morbid fascination with dead bodies. Both writers count on our curiosity about the unfamiliar to pull us into their narrative.

Not only should you keep your readers' expectations in mind as you draft, but you should also make sure to include everything that serves your own purposes of presentation. McPhee, for example, chose from a wealth of sights and sounds just those details that serve his purpose: telling about crime at the farmers' market. Concentrating on your thesis or main point as you draft should help this process.

PLANNING YOUR ORGANIZATION. If you are profiling a person or place, you will have many choices of plans. You can organize around features (of a person or place), around subtopics, or around ideas. Halberstam, for example, organizes around Tiff Wood's strength, ability to bear pain, and competitiveness. You can also organize narratively, taking the reader on a tour of a place in just the order you followed on your visit. Both McPhee and Duran organize narratively. Whatever plan you decide on should reflect your purpose and your readers' needs.

Some writers find it helpful to outline a tentative plan before beginning to draft. You may change direction once you start drafting, but some sort of plan is necessary if your draft is to be well organized and coherent.

BEGINNING. It is sometimes difficult to know how to begin writing about personal observations. You may have so much interesting material that it could be difficult to decide how to lead the reader into it. As you begin to draft, you can start with any part of the material, but it is usually best to start with an easy part—something you know you want to include or information you understand particularly well. Eventually you will want to open with something that will capture readers' attention, but there's no reason you must write it first. Petrunkevitch opens his essay by stating his main point, but all the other writers (except Wallerstein and Kelly) in this chapter begin with specific scenes or actions: McPhee focuses immediately on two pickpockets at work; Duran starts out speeding along the freeway on her way to the morgue.

# Revising

Since a first draft is an initial attempt to discover the possibilities in your material, it will nearly always need substantial revision. A good starting point would be to read your draft critically (and have someone else read it, as well) in light of the critical reading questions at the beginning of this chapter. These questions should enable you to reconsider what you have achieved in your draft and to decide what you can do to strengthen it. When revising observational writing, you will want to be particularly concerned with the main point and informativeness, as well as with readability.

REVISING TO FOCUS YOUR MAIN POINT. To provide a clear focus for your revision, consider whether you want to make your purpose more explicit. Be sure that readers will see the point of your essay. Decide whether all the details in your draft support your purpose, and eliminate any material that does not. Consider whether any additional anecdotes, visual details, or dialogue might sharpen the focus.

REVISING FOR INFORMATIVENESS. Once you have a draft and perhaps some response to it from readers, you may see other ways you need to inform readers still further about your subject. Does anything still need clarification, explanation, or definition? Again, decide whether you want to revisit the place or reinterview the person or otherwise gather still more data. Consider whether you might have given readers more information than they need about parts of your subject, thereby blurring the focus of your essay.

REVISING TO IMPROVE READABILITY. Since a clear, engaging beginning is essential, consider alternatives to what you have chosen, on the chance that some other part of your information would make a stronger opening. You might look at the beginnings of the selections in this chapter to see whether one of them suggests a different way you might open your piece. Outline your draft to discover its basic plan, and then consider whether you can improve on the plan by moving or deleting any parts. Reread your draft, looking for gaps and slow spots. Finally, decide whether adding anything or taking out any details would help keep readers on track and hold their interest.

Once you have a revision, proofread it carefully for mistakes in usage, punctuation, and spelling. Careless errors will reduce the readability of your essay and undermine your authority with your readers.

# CHAPTER FIVE

# *Explanation*

Explanatory essays explain a subject in order to inform readers. We all depend on the information we learn from reading such essays. For certain kinds of writing—encyclopedia entries, textbooks, and summaries—writers themselves rely mainly, if not entirely, on what they have learned from reading explanatory essays by other writers. Writers may summarize what they have learned from various sources about certain subjects or present the results of their library research on a historically important person or event. They may also review recent studies on a particular issue or topic, summarizing the research and stating conclusions about what is known and what is yet to be determined.

Needless to say, as a college student you will be reading and composing this kind of writing frequently. In all academic disciplines, knowledge accumulates through continuous summary and review of previous knowledge. This essential accumulation depends on writers' knowing how to locate information, read it carefully, and summarize it accurately. In this chapter, you will be practicing these basic activities of learning and explaining; in so doing, you will be participating in the centuries-old tradition of passing along in writing all that we humans have learned.

Writing explanations will give you the opportunity to explain a concept or principle to less informed readers. As you prepare to write, you may need to read more about this concept, interview an expert, or conduct research. This kind of writing also involves exploring the relationships among critical reading, taking notes, selecting relevant information for particular readers, and explaining and reviewing what others have written. You will have to decide when to summarize, reducing information to essentials; when to paraphrase, restating significant information in your own words; and when to quote, repeating exactly what another writer has said. Handling the information others have written will, of course, engage you in documenting your sources. All these writing strategies will be important not only in the writing you will do in the remaining chapters of this text but also in your other college courses.

## A  GUIDE  TO  READING
## EXPLANATORY  WRITING

Because explanation will be an important part of your assigned reading in college, it is important to be able to read it confidently and critically. To do so, you will want to know the basic features of this kind of writing. This section outlines these basic features, presents a brief annotated sample, and includes a list of questions that will help you to analyze and evaluate this kind of writing.

# *Basic Features of*
# *Explanatory Writing*

Writers of explanations strive to present well-established information to their readers as clearly as possible. In order to produce readable, informative explanations, they generally include these special features: *a specific subject and main point, an obvious plan of organization, careful definitions of unfamiliar terms and concepts, numerous illustrations,* and *documentation of sources.*

A SPECIFIC SUBJECT AND MAIN POINT.  An explanation (at least one of essay length) must maintain its focus on a single specific subject, one that is not too broad or general. Instead of considering all the wildlife in Pennsylvania, for example, an explanatory essay might focus on wild bears. And the essay should not simply catalogue information but should usually make a particular point, perhaps showing how bears have adapted to man's presence.

AN OBVIOUS PLAN OF ORGANIZATION.  An explanatory essay should be easy for readers to follow. To this end, the writer may immediately forecast the essay's content and organization, provide easily discernible transitions between paragraphs or sections, and emphasize the most significant information. A long article may even include occasional summaries that recapitulate the main points.

DEFINITIONS OF UNFAMILIAR TERMS AND CONCEPTS.  Since explanatory essays so often introduce readers to new subjects, such essays must define any technical terms and concepts that will be unfamiliar to readers. One of the most crucial decisions facing a writer of explanation is which concepts readers already know and which must be defined.

NUMEROUS ILLUSTRATIONS. Explanatory essays should contain a great many more illustrations than generalizations. Instead of a series of general statements about bears, for example, an experienced writer of explanations will provide one generalization followed by several illustrations (facts, examples, anecdotes). When the next generalization appears, it too will be followed by illustrations. Readers need such illustrations to be able to understand and remember new information.

DOCUMENTATION OF SOURCES. Relying as they must on published information, writers of explanatory essays must know when and how to document their sources. If summarized or paraphrased information in the essay is well-established common knowledge, for example, documentation of its source is probably not necessary. If, however, the information is new, its source probably should be cited. The sources of all direct quotes must, of course, be provided.

Documenting a source involves identifying the author, title, and certain facts of publication. (A guide to documenting sources can be found in the appendix at the back of the book.)

## An Annotated Reading:
### *The Remarkable Mississippi River,* Mark Twain

When you read explanatory writing, you are seeking information. You may want to know how to rebuild an engine, find cheaper air fares to Acapulco, care for a newborn infant, or cook fried chicken. You may want to learn more about an individual or about the history of your state, or to find out what a quark is, what research says about allergies and asthma, or which careers will be open to you if you major in biology. When you read explanatory writing, you will be pleased to be entertained; but you do not require it. You want mainly to learn new information.

Because you are reading for information, you should monitor your understanding continually, deciding whether you understand what you have read or whether you should reread, look up unfamiliar words, or even read a different writer on the same subject. You will also want to judge the completeness and accuracy of the information, in effect deciding whether you trust the writer as an authority on the subject.

Look now at one brief explanatory selection, with annotations of the kind any careful reader, guided by the critical reading questions that follow the excerpt, might have made. Be sure to read the selection first before you examine the annotations.

This selection constitutes the opening paragraphs of Mark Twain's *Life on the Mississippi*, first published in 1883. Much of the book is based on firsthand observation and memory (Twain grew up on the river and piloted steamboats on it), but this selection reflects Twain's careful research into the river and its history. He not only reports what he has learned but also shares his love of the river and his fascination with everything about it. He assumes that any American reader will want to read about the greatest river in the country.

It will be immediately apparent that this is not an engineering report or a navigation handbook. Twain selects his facts, not for us to memorize, but to leave us with an impression about the river.

## The Remarkable Mississippi River

The Mississippi is well worth reading about. It is not a commonplace river, but on the contrary is in all ways remarkable. Considering the Missouri its main branch, it is the longest river in the world—four thousand three hundred miles. It seems safe to say that it is also the crookedest river in the world, since in one part of its journey it uses up one thousand three hundred miles to cover the same ground that the crow would fly over in six hundred and seventy-five. It discharges three times as much water as the St. Lawrence, twenty-five times as much as the Rhine, and three hundred and thirty-eight times as much as the Thames. No other river has so vast a drainage basin: it draws its water supply from twenty-eight States and Territories; from Delaware, on the Atlantic seaboard, and from all the country between that and Idaho on the Pacific slope—a spread of forty-five degrees of longitude. The Mississippi receives and carries to the Gulf water from fifty-four subordinate rivers that are navigable by steamboats, and from some hundreds that are navigable by flats and keels. The area of its drainage basin is as great as the combined areas of England, Wales, Scotland, Ireland, France, Spain, Portugal, Germany, Austria, Italy, and Turkey; and almost all this wide region is fertile; the Mississippi valley, proper, is exceptionally so.

It is a remarkable river in this: that instead of widening toward its mouth, it grows narrower; grows narrower and deeper. From the junction of the Ohio to a point halfway down to the sea, the width averages a mile in high water:

*Marginal annotations:*

forecasts main point

1. drainage

comparison to other rivers

*drainage basin*: the area from which water flows into a river

impressive list

2. narrowness, depth at mouth

1

2

thence to the sea the width steadily diminishes, until, at the "Passes," above the mouth, it is but little over half a mile. At the junction of the Ohio the Mississippi's depth is eighty-seven feet; the depth increases gradually, reaching one hundred and twenty-nine just above the mouth.

*keeps repeating*
*remarkable*

3. *rise in lower river*

*not sure what* rise
*means here*

4. *mud deposits*

*refers to authorities*

5. *how mud deposits*
*have extended land*

*very informal language*

6. *moves by cutting*
*through*

*enthusiasm—seems to*
*want me to share his*
*amazement at the river*

*humorous examples*

The difference in rise and fall is <u>also remarkable</u>—not in the upper, but in the lower river. The rise is tolerably uniform down to Natchez (three hundred and sixty miles above the mouth)—about fifty feet. But at Bayou La Fourche the river rises only twenty-four feet; at New Orleans only fifteen, and just above the mouth only two and one half. [3]

An article in the New Orleans *Times-Democrat*, based upon reports of able engineers, states that the river annually empties four hundred and six million tons of mud into the Gulf of Mexico—which brings to mind Captain Marryat's rude name for the Mississippi—"the Great Sewer." This mud, solidified, would make a mass a mile square and two hundred and forty-one feet high. [4]

<u>The mud deposit</u> gradually extends the land—but only gradually; it has extended it not quite a third of a mile in the two hundred years which have elapsed since the river took its place in history. The belief of the scientific people is that the mouth used to be at Baton Rouge, where the hills cease, and that the two hundred miles of land between there and the Gulf was built by the river. This gives us the age of that piece of country, <u>without any trouble at all</u>—one hundred and twenty thousand years. Yet it is much the <u>youthfulest batch</u> of country that lies around there anywhere. [5]

The Mississippi is <u>remarkable in still another way</u>—its disposition to make prodigious jumps by cutting through narrow necks of land, and thus straightening and shortening itself. More than once it has shortened itself thirty miles at a single jump! These cutoffs have had curious effects: they have thrown several river towns out into the rural districts, and built up sand bars and forests in front of them. The town of Delta used to be three miles below Vicksburg: a recent cutoff has radically changed the position, and Delta is now *two miles above* Vicksburg. [6]

<u>Both of these river towns</u> have been retired to the country by that cutoff. A cutoff plays havoc with boundary lines and jurisdictions: for instance, a man is living in the State of Mississippi today, a cutoff occurs tonight, and tomorrow the man finds himself and his land over on the other side of the river, within the boundaries and subject to the laws of the State of Louisiana! Such a [7]

thing, happening in the upper river in the old times, could have transferred a slave from Missouri to Illinois and made a free man of him.

**7. moves by shifting sideways**

**I like the way he names specific towns and places.**

The Mississippi does not alter its locality by cutoffs alone: it is always changing its habitat *bodily*—is always moving bodily *sidewise*. At Hard Times, La., the river is two miles west of the region it used to occupy. As a result, the original *site* of that settlement is not now in Louisiana at all, but on the other side of the river, in the State of Mississippi. *Nearly the whole of that one thousand three hundred miles of old Mississippi River which La Salle floated down in his canoes, two hundred years ago, is good solid dry ground now.* The river lies to the right of it, in places, and to the left of it in other places.

**main point: seems to be how unusual the river is**

**painless piece to read—Twain seems determined that I will enjoy it**

8

# Critical Reading Questions

The following questions will help you to read explanatory writing more efficiently and critically. They will enable you to sort through the information, noting the main points and supporting illustrations, and to evaluate the completeness and accuracy of the explanation. To illustrate how these questions might be used, each one has been applied to the Twain selection.

1. *What are the subject and main point?*

The subject of an explanation can nearly always be identified with ease; usually it will be announced in the title of the selection. You should also be able to identify without difficulty the main point the writer is making about the subject, since it too is usually stated explicitly.

If the writer's main point is not apparent, however, you may have to infer it by considering the writer's purpose. Besides seeking to inform readers, why is the writer presenting this subject? Consider the tone of the selection. How would you describe the writer's voice? What seems to be the writer's attitude toward the subject and toward readers?

On the basis of your conclusions about the author's subject and main point, decide whether the subject is appropriately focused—not too broad or too narrow. Is the main point consistently supported by all the information? Is the writer's tone appropriate for this subject?

Twain's subject is the Mississippi River, in particular the characteristics, extensiveness, and results of its drainage. His main point seems to be just how remarkable, how huge and distinctive, the Mississippi River is. Taking a light tone, he seems to want to entertain readers as much as inform them.

2. *How well is the essay organized?*

To answer this question, examine the plan of the essay and outline its major parts. Then underline in the text the main signals and transitions—words or phrases that provide cues about the organization. Notice whether the writer forecasts the plan and contents at the beginning of the essay.

After you have completed this analysis, decide whether the writer's plan enables you to understand the information offered. Were you able to move smoothly through the essay without confusion? Would a fuller forecast at the beginning of the essay of its plan and contents have helped you? Can you imagine a different and better ordering of the parts?

Was information too densely packed at some points, slowing or interrupting your reading? Did the writer provide the necessary signals (paragraphing, transitions, emphasis, summaries) to keep you on track? Should there have been stronger signals at any point in the essay?

Twain begins by announcing and forecasting his main point: how remarkable the Mississippi River is. He repeats the word *remarkable* at the beginning of paragraphs 2, 3, and 6 and presents a series of remarkable features of the river: the size of its drainage basin, its narrowness and depth towards the mouth, its erratic rise at certain points, the amount of mud it carries, and its changing course. To keep the reader on track, Twain makes a direct connection to the previous paragraph in the first sentence of each new paragraph (with the exception of paragraph 4).

3. *How effectively does the writer define special terms or difficult concepts?*

Identify all the terms or concepts that the writer defines and notice the different ways in which they are explained. These definitions may be either direct (expressly stated in phrases, sentences, or longer passages) or indirect (understandable from the context of a sentence or passage). Sometimes large sections of an explanatory essay will be taken up with definitions of various kinds.

Did you find all the definitions you need? Are the definitions clear? Did any definitions seem unnecessary? Indicate those places where definitions should have been provided or better ones supplied.

For most readers, Twain's essay contains only one technical term— *drainage basin*—that needs explanation, and this term is fully defined in the context of the first paragraph. Twain uses words that may be unfamiliar to you (*disposition, prodigious, havoc, jurisdictions*) in paragraphs 6 and 7, but they are all easy to understand in context.

4. *What kinds of information and illustrations has the writer included? How effectively is this information presented?*

Analyze the kinds and diversity of information in the essay. Notice whether the writer uses facts, statistics, anecdotes, comparisons or contrasts, descriptions of objects or processes, extended definitions, developed examples, lists, scenarios (imagined events), or quotes from authorities. Observe any tables, charts, graphs, drawings, photographs, and maps; consider what kinds of information they offer and their relation to the text of the eassay.

This analysis will enable you to identify the strategies the writer has chosen to present the information and the effectiveness of these strategies. Do you have all the information you need to understand the subject and main point? Are there any places where you need more information? Conjecture about what kinds of additional information would be most helpful. Is any information not clear to you?

Part of the task of evaluating explanatory writing is to decide for yourself whether the information seems trustworthy. Does it seem complete and comprehensive, given the writer's point about the subject? Does the writer's stance or tone seem confident and authoritative? Do you trust this person to inform you about this subject? In the case of a research review, should you read for yourself some of the key original sources cited?

Twain relies on facts and statistics throughout his essay. He compares the Mississippi to other rivers. To impress readers with the size of its drainage basin, he lists countries whose combined area equals that of the basin. He also refers to engineering research.

5. *How does the writer appeal to readers' interests?*

One way writers appeal to readers' interests is by trying to maintain an optimum balance between familiar and new information. They may also include an engaging beginning, humor, or startling or sensational facts and examples. Readers of explanatory writing do not require such appeals to their interests, but they are grateful for them.

Look for instances of direct appeals to readers' interests in the essay, and notice how the writer makes them. How well do you think they work in the essay? What other kinds of appeals do you think might strengthen the essay?

Twain seems to go out of his way to entertain readers and hold their interest in his subject. He addresses readers directly in the first sentence and continually tries to astound them with amazing facts about the Mississippi. He also includes humor, even telling a tall tale (paragraph 7) like those told by Mississippi boatmen.

# Richard E. Leakey and Roger Lewin

Richard Leakey (b. 1945) studies ancient man from fossil records dating back nearly three million years. Over the past several years, with his wife Meave and a team of other anthropologists, he has concentrated his search along the eastern shores of Lake Turkana, Kenya, in East Africa. Searching for fossil bones at a site called Koobi Fora, Leakey's team has discovered bones belonging to nearly two hundred of our early ancestors. From these discoveries come Leakey's theories about man's early history.

Son of famous British anthropologists Louis and Mary Leakey, Leakey is a third-generation Kenyan. He directs the National Museum of Kenya and chairs the Foundation for Research into the Origins of Man.

Roger Lewin has been science editor of *New Scientist* in London. He is coauthor with Richard Leakey of *Origins: What New Discoveries Reveal About the Emergence of Our Species* (1977) and *People of the Lake* (1978) and the author of four other books.

# *People of the Lake*

This selection is from *People of the Lake*, which chronicles Leakey's research at Lake Turkana. The authors are ingenious at engaging readers' interest in what some consider a dry subject—finding and reassembling bone fragments and conjecturing about their meaning. They begin by conveying a feeling for their work and its geological context; then, as a strategy for presenting information, they devise a scenario, what they call a "pure fantasy."

You prospect for fossils by walking around looking for signs of them 1 on the surface: a glint of bone may be the only visible trace of a complete skull buried just under the surface. Or it may be a disappointing fragment. With every season's rains new fossils may be exposed. But if they lie on the surface too long, they rapidly disintegrate, to be lost forever. . . . The continued geologic stirrings have helped give us a glimpse of the past by heaving some of the sediments upward, exposing them to the ravages of erosion and the inquisitive attentions of modern archaeologists.

Suppose, now, we are back on the eastern shores of Lake Turkana, 2 two and a half million years ago. What might we see?

Standing by the shores we'd be aware of crocodiles basking in the 3 tropical heat on sandspits pointing fingerlike into the shallow waters. Hippos wallow, occasionally exploding watery sighs and making waves as they jostle each other lazily. The air is punctuated by the slap of wings as a group of pelicans take noisily to the air, squawking crossly for reasons best known to themselves.

A little more than five miles away to the east, savanna-covered hills 4 rise up from the lake basin, sliced here and there by forest-filled valleys. At one point the hills are breached by a large river that has snaked its way down from the Ethiopian mountains. We can't see the river because its path is followed by a lush growth of trees and bushes: wild figs, acacia, and Celtis grow thickly. As the river reaches the floodplain of the lake it shatters into a delta of countless streams, some small, some large, but each fringed by an attentive line of trees and bushes.

As we walk up one of the stream beds—dry now because there have 5 been no rains for months—we might hear the rustle of a pig in search of roots and vegetation in the undergrowth. As the tree cover thickens, we catch a glimpse of a colobus monkey retreating through the treetops. Lower down, mangabeys feed on the ripening figs. In the seclusion of the surrounding bushes, small groups of impala and waterbuck move cautiously. By climbing a tree we could see out into the open where herds of gazelle graze and troops of geladalike baboons forage in the grass and under stones and bushes.

After we've gone about a mile up the stream, we come across a scene 6 that is strangely familiar but which, nevertheless, we have never seen before: a group of about eight creatures—definitely humanlike, but definitely not truly human—are before us, some on the stream bed, some on its sandy bank. Two adult females are making piles of roots and nuts; they are emptying what appear to be containers made from animal skins. Another adult, a male, has just finished digging a hole in the stream bed, partly with his hands, partly with a stick. Children crowd around him, going down on their hands and knees to scoop up the water his excavation has reached. He shoos them away and then fills a folded leaf with the cool water which he then gives to another adult male who is lying on the bank—he looks ill.

The scene is a mixture of industry and leisure: children play, some 7 digging in the stream as the big male had just done, others inexpertly knocking two stones together at the feet of an adult who makes a simple tool with ease, and others just have fun chasing through the bushes.

Suddenly there is a shout—at least it sounds like a shout. Everyone 8 turns in the direction of the call to see a group of adults, mostly males, walking excitedly toward the camp. They are carrying hunks of hippo flesh, and they are obviously pleased with themselves. They had been wandering along a tree-lined stream bed about a mile south of their camp early that morning and had stumbled across the freshly dead animal. So, after collecting some lava cobbles from some distance away toward the hills, they made some cutting tools and proceeded to slice off generous pieces of meat. And when they'd eaten some of the tasty liver in celebration, they carried the meat triumphantly to the camp. The departure for the camp came none too soon as the steadily growing numbers of hyenas were rapidly losing patience at being kept away from a meal they clearly thought was rightfully theirs.

The hippo was so big that it made good sense to butcher the carcass  9
in this way rather than stagger back to the camp with the meat still clinging to a heavy leg bone, something they would have had no hesitation in doing with, say, a gazelle—just as they had done a few days previously.

Two females and a youth who were just about to set off, carrying skin  10
containers and newly sharpened digging sticks in search of roots, berries, and nuts, changed their minds and stayed for the feast. It's a feast in which everyone joins, the meat being sliced up with razor-sharp stone flakes by the males who found the animal. A latecomer, a male who comes down the stream holding a bunch of roots in one hand and a dead hare in the other, also gets a share.

Compared with the tranquillity of just a little while ago, the camp  11
scene is now alive with the hubbub, excitement (and some squabbling) of eating meat; it doesn't happen every day, and they clearly enjoy it. Judging by the variety of noises they are making and the responsive interactions, we can say that they are communicating with each other. They touch each other a lot too.

Some days later the group moves on, one of the older males helping  12
his sick companion, for he is still weak. Behind they leave their stream bed campsite littered with broken stones, tools, flakes, old digging sticks, splintered nutshells, and one or two molding uneaten tubers. They go in search of another sandy place that is also free from the vicious spike grass that thrives on the lake's floodplain; and they will want the shelter of trees again too, not just to escape from the glare of the sun, but also to flee into if they are threatened by predators. Probably they will camp in another dry stream bed. And perhaps they might be lucky again and find another bonanza of meat as part of their primitive hunting-and-gathering economy.

The story is, of course, pure fantasy, but we construct it around as  13
many facts and inspired guesses that we can. There *is* an ancient living site in the place we describe. (It is called the KBS site, KB being the initials of Kay Behrensmeyer, the scientist who found the site.) And the

bones of a hippo *do* lie surrounded by stone tools about a mile to the south. Although the two sites are about the same age (somewhat more than two million years), we do not suggest that the occupants of the one really did butcher the animal at the second site. But as a reconstruction of life-style, the scenario stands as a valid view.

The rains must have come shortly after the hominids left their living site; and the water filling the water course must have risen slowly and steadily. We know this because even tiny flakes of stone, light enough to blow away in a strong wind, remained to be buried by silt, together with the bigger flakes and stone tools—and a fig leaf! The leaf subsequently decayed, leaving only an impression in the fine deposits to remind us of the cool shade its parent tree must have thrown on our ancestors. Or perhaps it is a reminder that, with the inexorable advance toward humanity, the innocence of the Garden of Eden stops here? But such mystical views are best left to other authors.    14

During the past ten years more than one thousand fragments of fossil hominids have been unearthed by research teams at the major sites in the Rift Valley. This is less impressive than it may appear at first because many of the specimens are isolated or broken teeth. (The lower Omo appears to be a particularly rich source of these specimens.) If we were to discard the more fragmentary cranial material, we would be left with perhaps twenty or so "good" skulls (usually lacking the lower jaw). These skulls are from individuals who lived between about three million and one million years ago.    15

As far as we can tell from the East Turkana deposits, the hominids were to be seen about as frequently around the Pliocene and Pleistocene landscapes as were the carnivores. We can therefore make a *conservative* guess that, during that two-million-year period, somewhere between thirty and fifty million hominids lived in the geological corridor that runs from the Hadar, through the Omo valley, past Lake Turkana, and down to Olduvai.    16

Only a tiny proportion of these creatures' skeletons would have survived the ravages of a combination of scavengers and the elements, thus having a chance of becoming fossilized. And only a tiny fraction of these will ever see the light of day again. Most will be buried forever, a mute and frustratingly inaccessible record of our past.    17

## QUESTIONS FOR ANALYSIS

1. Leakey and Lewin present anthropological information by devising a scenario. What information do they include in the opening orientation and setting (paragraphs 3–7)? What information do they incor-

porate into the central dramatic event of the scenario (paragraphs 8–11)?

2. This anthropological information could easily have been presented in a report or textbook, summarized concisely and objectively as established facts about camp life, hunting, and food consumption of ancient man two-and-a-half million years ago at Lake Turkana. As a means of presenting anthropological evidence to nonspecialists, what advantages do you see in Leakey and Lewin's scenario? What disadvantages?

3. Which facts and actions of the scenario probably come from established anthropological evidence and which from the authors' imaginations, their "inspired guesses"? How do you think they would justify the inspired guesses?

4. The authors assert that "as a reconstruction of life-style, the scenario stands as a valid view"? How would you determine whether you agree with them?

5. What impression of the Turkana people's quality of life do the authors want us to have? Reread the scenario, taking inventory of language that suggests quality of life. What can you conclude from this analysis? (See Chapter 1 for a plan for taking inventory.)

6. Look closely at the opening and closing paragraphs, and decide how they are related.

7. Skim the essay, looking for unfamiliar words. Now that you have read the entire essay, which of these words do you think you could define, even partially? Which definitions do you think are essential in order to understand the information in the essay?

## SUGGESTIONS FOR WRITING

A scenario enables readers to understand unfamiliar information. By helping them to imagine what might have happened, it informs readers about what actually is known. The academic subjects you have studied in high school and in college and the specialized information you have acquired from jobs you have held offer many possibilities for writing scenarios. Here are some suggestions:

A scenario about some biological process that involves particular interactions among organisms

A scenario about a geological or astronomical event that is not yet well understood

A scenario describing to new employees some part of a job you have held

A scenario explaining some social or political process to a recent immigrant to America

# Fawn M. Brodie

Fawn Brodie (1915–1981) was a professor of history at the University of California, Los Angeles, and a well-known biographer. Her books include *No Man Knows My History* (a biography of the Mormon prophet Joseph Smith published in 1945), *Thaddeus Stevens: Scourge of the South* (1959), *Thomas Jefferson: An Intimate History* (1974), and *Richard Nixon: The Child and the Man* (1981).

# The Semi-Transparent Shadows

This selection is the opening section in Brodie's biography of Thomas Jefferson, America's third president, who lived from 1743 to 1826. It is both a pointed biographical sketch and an analysis of some of the difficulties in writing about prominent people.

Before you begin reading, pause to consider what you know about Jefferson. What do you know about his character, life and times, or political leadership? How was he different from our other early presidents? Consider, as well, a biographer's motives and inspiration. Why might a contemporary historian want to write still another biography of Jefferson? Finally, puzzle for a moment over Brodie's title for the chapter from which this selection is taken.

Thomas Jefferson of all our great presidents was the most orderly and the most acquisitive. He was also the most controlled. The celebrated equanimity of his temper, crystallized in his pronouncement "Peace is our passion," extended to his private as well as his public life; his daughter Martha described how he lost his temper in her presence only two times in his life. Once was when a long trusted slave twice defied an order concerning the use of a carriage horse, the second when two quarreling ferrymen let the boat in which Jefferson and his daughter were being carried across a river drift dangerously toward some rapids. Then, Martha said, her father, "his face 'like a lion' told the ferrymen 'in tones of thunder' to row for their lives or he would pitch them into the stream."[1]

Jefferson's acquisitiveness particularly in regard to books was legendary in his own lifetime. All his friends knew how he accumulated one of the great private libraries of the young United States, how he sold it far below its value to replace the Library of Congress when the British army burned it in the War of 1812, and then promptly began building up another library to match the old. Few, however, knew that he was so enraged by the senseless act of military vandalism that he suggested paying incendiaries in London to set British buildings afire in return.[2] The rage was momentary; he had believed from the beginning that the war was unnecessary and after initial acquiescence came to see it as a disaster for his country, but he was too loyal to his intimate friend and successor, James Madison, to say so publicly. During his own presidency, faced with the same European imbroglio that sucked Madison into his fatal declaration of war against the British, Jefferson had lived by his own admonition concerning peace, and had avoided war in the face of exasperating provocation. To John Langdon he had written in 1808, when war seemed imminent, "I think one war enough for the life of one man." And to a group of citizens in Maryland, speaking briefly on his way home to retirement in 1809, he had said, "The care of human life and happiness, and not their destruction, is the first and only legitimate object of good government."[3]

Still, in the same year, 1808, Jefferson was capable of issuing an order for one private act of destruction. When he learned that dogs were killing his prize Merino sheep at Monticello he wrote to his overseer: "To secure wool enough, the negroes dogs must all be killed. Do not spare a single one. If you keep a couple yourself it will be enough for the whole land. Let this be carried into execution immediately." And in a letter to a friend he suggested that the world would be better off were the whole canine species to be exterminated.[4]

Jefferson had a superb sense of history and an exact understanding of his own role in it. He preserved a legacy of over 25,000 letters from his friends and acquaintances, as well as copies of his own letters, made with letter presses and on the polygraph machines he delighted in, that numbered 18,000. These letters he indexed in his extraordinary Epistolary Record, extending from 1783 to 1826, which in itself numbered 656 pages. Still, he destroyed what would have been among the most revealing letters of his life, his correspondence with his mother and with his wife. He never finished his autobiography and halfway through this mere fragment of his life numbering only 120 pages, he complained, "I am already tired of talking about myself."[5]

His orderliness reached such proportions that it can be properly called compulsive. He began his famous *Garden Book* in 1766 with the cheerful line, "March 20. Purple hyacinth begins to bloom," and continued this record of flowering and planting for fifty-eight years. His early biographer Henry Randall was confounded at the discovery among Jefferson's papers of a neatly made chart, "A Statement of the Vegetable market in Washington, during a period of 8 years, wherein the earliest & latest appearance of each article within the whole 8 years is noted." Jefferson had taken the time to note the exact beginning and ending of the season for twenty-nine vegetables and seven fruits. "Never was there a more methodical man from great matters down to the merest seeming trifles," Randall wrote, "never so diligent a recorder of them!" It is in his fantastically detailed account books, however, that Jefferson's orderliness and passion for recording details begin to seem compulsive. Here in these books he listed almost every expenditure of his adult life. Still, this attention to detail did not prevent his going steadily ever deeper into debt. In a careful reading one can follow the intricate path leading him ever more certainly into the final swamp—owing over $100,000—in which he was hopelessly mired when he died.

Jefferson kept a *Farm Book* with intermittent records of fifty-two years 6 of plantation management, including inventories and distribution lists concerning more than a hundred slaves. In this enormously valuable source book, which tells us how much fish and beef, how many beds and blankets, were doled out to each slave and in what year, and which gives the date of almost every slave's birth, and often the date of his death, one can learn more about detailed relations between Jefferson and his slaves than in any other document. It is also a record of extraordinary concealment. Nowhere is there any hint, for example, that the two slaves Harriet and Beverly, listed in the *Farm Book* on page 130 as runaways in 1822, and believed by many of his neighbors and slaves to be his own children, were treated with any special indulgences. This we learn from other sources. And Beverly and Harriet's famous mother, Sally Hemings, celebrated in bawdy ballads during Jefferson's presidency as his slave mistress, is nowhere in the *Farm Book* treated with special attention, as she is in his account books. She is not even given a last name, simply appearing as "Sally" in over thirty listings.

Even though the total record of Jefferson's writings, and the letters 7 written to him, promise to reach fifty-two volumes, there are many mysterious lacunae. This every previous historian or biographer, whether idolatrous or critical, protective or scurrilous, has sensed quickly once he let himself be drawn into the labyrinth of Jeffersonian literature, lured by the mysteries, baffled by Jefferson's ambivalences, and captured by his special genius. Unlike Lincoln's image, which emerges solid, well-defined, a great craggy statue whose proportions are familiar and whose lineaments defy distortion, Jefferson's image remains unfinished. He is like one of Michelangelo's great marble slaves, emerging but still partly trapped in the unchiseled marble. If a biographical portrait of Lincoln is at variance with the true man, it is the biographer who is pitilessly exposed, not Lincoln. And thanks to the industry of an unending parade of Lincoln scholars, there are almost no important mysteries left.

Jefferson, for all his prodigious industry in writing, collecting, index-    8
ing, and preserving his personal record in what he understood perfectly
to be a "heroic age," and so described it to John Adams,[6] has always
defied definitive portraiture. Biographer Albert J. Nock, writing in 1926,
stated that Jefferson "was the most approachable and the most impene-
trable of men, easy and delightful of acquaintance, impossible of knowledge." Nathan Schachner called him "the delight and despair of biographers," of all the great American statesmen, "the most fascinating"
and "the most difficult."[7] Dumas Malone, who has come closer than
anyone with his expert biographical brush, admitted ruefully after finishing the first of his volumes, "In my youthful presumptuousness I flattered
myself that sometime I would fully comprehend and encompass him. I
do not claim that I have yet done so, and I do not believe that I or any
other single person can."[8] . . .

Jefferson's secrecy about his intimate life pervades every kind of docu-    9
ment he left behind. Although as attentive to the preservation of the
early records of his young republic as to his own, he did not keep a diary,
as did John and John Quincy Adams, and was persuaded only with great
difficulty to embark on his autobiography. "Nothing could be more re-
pugnant to my feelings," he wrote on his retirement from the presidency
in 1809, than writing "the history of my whole life."[9] What he wrote
down at age seventy-seven was a confounding exercise in concealment,
containing only skeletal hints of one of the most richly endowed men in
our history. Why he abandoned his memoir at the precise point he did—
after describing his five years in France—is in itself a clue to his continuing need for secrecy concerning his private life. Moreover, he did not
feel the necessity of amplifying his reputation with a long memoir, as did
Ulysses S. Grant, Herbert Hoover, Harry Truman, Dwight Eisenhower,
and Lyndon Johnson, or even the necessity of leaving a political statement. This he had done already in his Virginia constitution, Declaration
of Independence, and Statute of Virginia for Religious Freedom, the
latter two of which he asked to be mentioned on his tombstone.

Like Lincoln and Franklin Roosevelt, Jefferson kept his intimate feel-    10
ings hidden from the public, either in triumph or in crisis. All three in
this respect were unlike Andrew Jackson, who paraded his affections and
his hatreds, or Theodore Roosevelt, who articulated almost everything
openly in terms of grand adventure. The essential nature of Lincoln's
melancholy still resists analysis; during his life he disguised it and ame-
liorated it by his storytelling and remarkable gift for political parable.
"Were it not for these stories I should die," he once confided, "they are
vents through which my sadness, my gloom and my melancholy escape."[10] A sensitive study of the Lincoln marriage will not always defy

biographers, just as the truth about Franklin Roosevelt's feelings toward several women who served importantly to shape his life must one day be captured in print, as Joseph Lash succeeded in capturing the feelings of his remarkable wife.

Despite hundreds of volumes about Jefferson, there remain unexpected 11 reserves of unmined ore, particularly in relation to the *connections* between his public life and his inner life, as well as his intimate life. There is important material which has been belittled; controversial material flatly rejected as libelous, and abundant psychological material which is dismissed as "unhistorical" or simply not seen at all. Still, one must admit that what Henry Adams called the "semi-transparent shadows" particularly defy the biographical brush. With Jefferson there is always a shadow behind the obvious. Jefferson was ambivalent not only about love but also about revolution, religion, slavery, and power. He abominated slavery but continued all his life—in Peter Gay's phrase—to "live with, and off it." He was never truly comfortable with power, and his avowal that "that government is best which governs least" was a personal as well as a political statement. Yet he had the habit of command, an instinct for leadership, and a superb capacity for political writing.

## NOTES

1. Henry S. Randall, *The Life of Thomas Jefferson*, 3 vols. (New York, 1858), III, 510.

2. Jefferson to General Thaddeus Kosciusko, June 1812, *Writings of Thomas Jefferson*, Paul L. Ford, ed., 10 vols. (New York, 1892–99), IX, 362.

3. Jefferson to John Langdon, August 2, 1808, and "Address to the Republican Citizens of Washington County, Maryland," March 31, 1809, *Writings of Thomas Jefferson*, Andrew Lipscomb and Albert Bergh, eds., 20 vols. (Washington, D.C., 1903), XVI, 310, 359; hereafter designated as *Writings*, L. and B.

4. Jefferson to Edmund Bacon, December 26, 1808, *Thomas Jefferson's Garden Book, 1766–1824*, Edwin M. Betts, ed. (Philadelphia, 1944), 383; Jefferson to Peter Minor, September 24, 1811, *Thomas Jefferson's Farm Book* (Princeton, 1953) [138]. A photographic record of the *Farm Book* was published by Edwin Morris Betts, with commentary and relevant extracts from Jefferson's other writings, including letters concerning his slaves. The page references in the *Farm Book* are the same as Jefferson's own. Other pagination, by Betts, is indicated in this volume in brackets for purposes of distinguishing it from that of the photographic record.

5. *Autobiography of Thomas Jefferson, with an Introductory Essay by Dumas Malone*, adapted from *Jefferson the Virginian* (Boston, 1948), 62.

6. Jefferson to John Adams, March 25, 1826, *The Adams-Jefferson Letters*, Lester J. Cappon, ed. (Chapel Hill, N.C., 1959), 614.

7. Albert J. Nock, *Jefferson* (New York, 1926), 33: Nathan Schachner, *Thomas Jefferson: A Biography* (New York, 1951), vii.

8. Malone, *Jefferson the Virginian*, vii.

9. Jefferson to Skelton Jones, July 28, 1809, *Writings*, L. and B., XII, 302.

10. Quoted in Emanuel Hertz, *The Hidden Lincoln, from the Letters and Papers of William H. Herndon* (New York, 1938), 230.

## QUESTIONS FOR ANALYSIS

1. Take inventory of the contrasts or contradictions in this selection. (Chapter 1 outlines a procedure for taking inventory.) Use this inventory to discover the point Brodie is making about Jefferson.

2. Make a brief outline of this selection to discover Brodie's plan of organization. (Chapter 1 offers guidelines for outlining.) Given the point Brodie seems to be making, what advantages or disadvantages do you see in her plan? How does the plan make the selection easier or harder to read?

3. How does the first paragraph forecast the topics and plan of the selection? What advantages do you see for explicit forecasting in explanations?

4. Skim the essay, underlining words that were unfamiliar to you when you encountered them on first reading. Decide how many of these words you can confidently understand from context. How does the context provide these understandings?

5. Analyze Brodie's citations and references. What can you conclude about the range of sources available to a historical biographer? Are you aware of still other sources biographers might rely on?

## SUGGESTIONS FOR WRITING

1. Identify a historical figure you would like to know more about. Research this figure and write a biographical essay about him or her. Instead of relying only on one other writer's biography of this figure, try to integrate several sources of material into your essay. You will find it especially rewarding if you can use the individual's own writings—books, letters, manuscripts. Reference specialists in your college library can help you locate such materials.

2. Write about a deceased relative you never knew personally, a relative who has left a journal or diary or letters. Characterize this relative through these documents, presenting details from them and making inferences about what is and is not there.

3. Ask your college or community librarian about collections of letters
   and other documents you could examine that have been left by prominent local people. Choose a person to write about. Analyze some
   portion of the documents in order to reach conclusions about this
   person.

# Daniel Goleman

Daniel Goleman (b. 1946), a science writer, covers the behavioral sciences for the *New York Times* and is also a senior editor at *Psychology Today* magazine. His books include *Varieties of Meditative Experience* (1977), *Frames: Attentional Politics* (1984), and *Vital Lies, Simple Truths: The Psychology of Self-Deception* (1985). He has published over fifty articles in psychology journals. For two of these articles he won national media awards from the American Psychological Association.

# *The Intelligent Filter*

In his book *Vital Lies, Simple Truths: The Psychology of Self-Deception*, Goleman explains that our minds apparently have an "intelligent filter" that chooses what we will be aware of at any moment. This filter enables us to survive: if we were aware at all times of every sound and sight and smell, we would probably go mad. Although this filter provides a sense of security and reduces anxiety, it also contributes to self-deception, enabling us to censor insights, memories, observations, and ideas we would be better off addressing.

In the following selection from the book, Goleman reviews recent research in psychology to establish the existence of such a filter and to explain how this filter operates.

What words do these fragments suggest to you?    1
　s—x
　shi—
　f——k

Reading these, you should have no trouble completing them, more    2
likely than not, as suggestive or off-color words. But imagine yourself in a room with a stranger, repeating aloud the words you make of these fragments. Your responses might take another turn, if only to avoid embarrassment. Your thoughts might, too.

Over more than two decades following World War II, researchers con-    3
ducted a gargantuan number of studies to test ways in which what one perceives can be muted or heightened depending on its emotional salience. Several hundred published studies dealt with this question, for the most part without resolving anything. The problem was not so much with the studies themselves, as with the then-current understanding of how the mind processes information.[1]

Take the words in the list above. If I ask you to complete the fragments 4
and you tell me they represent the words "six," "shin," and "fork," I can
surmise that you either did not allow yourself to *perceive* the more suggestive alternatives, or that you suppressed *reporting* them to me. In more
technical terms, the question is one of the locus of bias: is it in perception
or in response?

If the bias was in your response, then I can assume the suggestive 5
words first came to mind but you quickly thought of more acceptable
alternatives. But if the bias was in your original perception and you *never*
were aware of the suggestive words, your mind somehow engineered its
censorship outside your awareness.

The implications for how the mind's workings are orchestrated are 6
quite different for each of these alternatives. Bias in response suggests
that this is merely an instance of social dissembling—nothing very startling. But a bias in perception implies an unconscious center at work in
the mind, imposing its judgments on all we perceive, shaping our experience to fit its priorities.

For many years these two possibilities vied with each other as mutually 7
exclusive alternatives. An exhaustive review in 1966 of two decades of
experimental results pro and con was unable to resolve the debate.[2] The
reviewer's conclusion, after failing to settle the battle, was a conciliatory
suggestion: since the two possibilities are not incompatible, perhaps, just
perhaps, both may be correct. There may be censors in perception as
well as in response.

That suggestion fits well with what is today the commonly accepted 8
view of how information moves—and fails to move—through the mind.

There was a half-century lapse before experimental psychologists se- 9
riously addressed the proposals Freud made in the seventh chapter of *The
Interpretation of Dreams*. From the 1920s on, the ascendancy of behav-
iorism made what went on within the mind a taboo topic for most psychologists. When the mechanics of mind finally re-entered psychological
research, one immediate impetus was most unlikely: the rise of aviation.

The next major volley in the debate over how the mind handles in- 10
formation was fired in 1958 by Donald Broadbent, a British psychologist.[3]
His interests were very different from Freud's. Broadbent worked with
the British Royal Navy in the years after World War II. Because of the
explosive growth of aviation in that era, the volume of air traffic besieged
controllers. The controllers, Broadbent realized, took in far more information through their eyes and ears than they could deal with. He wondered just how the mind sorted out this barrage.

Broadbent, like Freud, used a flow chart to describe how the mind 11
handles information. His chart showed that people receive more data

through the senses than they can handle (see Figure 1). This information gets to a short-term store—akin to the sensory store—and then flows on to a "selective filter," where most of it is weeded out. This filter somehow blocks all but those messages that merit fuller attention. The passage is seemingly instantaneous. But the few thousandths of a second it takes allow ample time for the mind to sort through the mass of data in sensory storage and filter out irrelevancies before the information passes into conscious awareness.

Broadbent assumed that the mind needs to filter the information that impinges on it through the senses because it has only a limited capacity. The selective filter, he believed, is essential here because of a bottleneck: there is a sharply limited channel capacity at the next stage of processing, often called "short-term" or "primary" memory.

Primary memory is the region of perception that falls under the beam of attention. For our purposes we will call it "awareness." The contents of the zone of awareness are what we take to be "on our minds" at a given moment; it is our window onto the stream of consciousness. This zone is quite fragile, its contents fleeting.

The traffic between awareness and long-term memory is two-way, according to Broadbent's model; what is in long-term memory can be called into awareness, what is in awareness finds a place in memory. Only information that reaches awareness, he proposed, will be retained for very long—that is, we remember only what we first pay attention to. Awareness, then, is the gateway to memory, and a filter controls what enters awareness. But what controls the filter?

For Broadbent, only the gross physical aspect of a message—its loudness or brightness, say—determined whether it would get through, not its meaning. That view was put to rest soon after he proposed it by experiments on the "cocktail party effect." At a cocktail party or in a

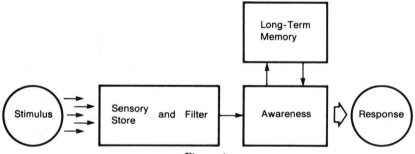

**Figure 1.**
*Broadbent's model of the mind, slightly modified: Sensory stimuli are analyzed as they reach the sensory store and sorted and filtered on their way to awareness (or short-term memory).*

crowded restaurant there is typically a din of competing conversations, all carried on at high volume within earshot of the others.

Contrary to Broadbent's prediction, you don't hear simply the loudest 16 voice. For example, if you are stuck listening to a bore recount the gruesome details of his last vacation, rocky relationship, or nearly con-summated deal, it is easy to tune him out and tune in on a more inter-esting conversation nearby—particularly if you hear your own name men-tioned. During the course of these tune-outs and tune-ins, the *sounds* coming to your ears may be identical in volume. What changes is the focus of your *attention*.

This means that information is scanned for *meaning* before it reaches 17 the filter, contradicting Broadbent's assertion that the filter tunes in or out based solely on physical aspects of a message. The filter seems to have some intelligence; it is tuned by the importance to a person of the message.

This has major consequences for how the mind's architecture must be 18 arranged. In order for an intelligent filter—one that reads meaning—to operate during the few moments of sensory storage, the arrangement of the mind's elements must be modified in a critical fashion. If the filter is intelligent, then there must be some circuit that connects the part of the mind that cognizes—that recognizes meanings—with the part that takes in and sorts through initial impressions. A simple, linear model such as Freud and Broadbent proposed would not work.

Meanings are stored in long-term memory. What is required is a *loop* 19 between long-term memory and the earlier stages of information process-ing. That loop is shown in Figure 2. Such a feedback loop allows for the sensory store to sort its contents by drawing on the vast repertoire of experience, on the meanings and understandings built up over a life span,

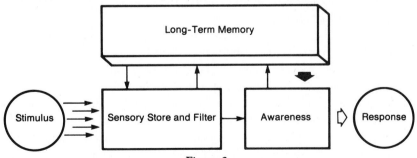

**Figure 2.**
*A simplified model of the mind, loosely adapted from Donald Norman: Memory screens perception at the earliest stage of information flow, filtering for salience what is allowed through to awareness.*

stored in long-term memory. The judgment "salient" or "irrelevant" can be made only on the basis of the knowledge in long-term memory. With access to the mind's lifelong store of experience, preferences, and goals, the filter can sift through the mass of impressions that assail it at each successive moment, and immediately tune in or out what matters.

Indeed, contemporary theorists now assume that information passing 20 through the sensory store is subjected to scrutiny and filtered on the basis of its meaning and relevance. "Essentially," sums up Matthew Erdelyi, a cognitive psychologist, "long-term memory itself becomes the filter, deciding what to block from short-term storage (and therefore awareness), thereby determining indirectly what to accept for eventual storage in long-term memory itself."[4]

That means the contents of awareness come to us picked over, sorted 21 through, and pre-packaged. The whole process takes a fraction of a second.

There are compelling reasons for this arrangement in the design of the 22 mind. It is much to our benefit that the raw information that passes from sensory storage to awareness sifts through a smart filter. The region of consciousness would be far too cluttered were it not reached by a vastly reduced information flow. While the information in consciousness seems limited, it also seems to be the case that before getting there, that information—and an even vaster amount left behind, seemingly to evaporate—has gone through a massive amount of analysis.

The more thoroughly information in sensory storage can be sorted out, 23 the more efficiently the next way station—awareness—can operate. If too much gets through, awareness is swamped. . . . It is of critical import that this filter operate at a peak, in order to save us from continuous distraction by a mass of irrelevant information. If the filter were much less thorough we might literally be driven to distraction by distractions, as happens in schizophrenia.

The idea that information passes through an intelligent filter led to 24 what has become the prevailing view of how information flows through the mind. The most commonly pictured flow chart was proposed by Donald Norman in 1968; Figure 2 is a simplified version of his model.[5] In this model what enters through the senses gets a thorough, automatic scan by long-term memory—specifically by "semantic" memory, the repository of meanings and knowledge about the world. For example, every bundle of sounds automatically is directed to an "address" in semantic memory that yields its meaning. If you hear the word "grunt," semantic memory recognizes its meaning; if you hear a grunt, semantic memory also recognizes that that sound is not a word.

All this filtering goes on out of awareness. What gets through to aware- 25 ness is what messages have pertinence to whatever mental activity is current. If you are looking for restaurants, you will notice signs for them and not for gas stations; if you are skimming through the newspaper, you will notice those items that you care about. What gets through enters awareness, and only what is useful occupies that mental space.

Perception, says Norman, is a matter of degree. In scanning incoming 26 information, semantic memory need not go into every detail; it need only sort out what is and is not relevant to the concern of the moment. Irrelevant information is only partly analyzed, if just to the point of recognizing its irrelevancy. What *is* relevant gets fuller processing. For example, if you casually scan a newspaper page and suddenly see your name, it will seem to "leap out" at you. Presumably the words you saw as you skimmed were partly processed and found irrelevant; your name— which is always relevant—rated full processing.

This model of the mind has several important implications. For one, 27 it posits that information is screened by memory at every stage of its processing, and that memory scans information and filters it for salience. All this processing goes on *before* information enters awareness; only a small portion of the information available at a given moment filters through to consciousness.

That is not to say that attention is entirely passive. We can, after all, 28 decide to scan for something, and so awareness can modify how the filter operates. But awareness does so indirectly, through the services of long-term memory: the activity of the filter is never directly evident to aware-ness. We can, however, bring information into awareness from long-term memory. There is two-way traffic, then, between awareness and long-term memory, but there is only one-way traffic between the filter and awareness. There is a very real sense in which long-term memory—the sum total of experience one has about life—has a more decisive say in the flow of information than we ordinarily realize.

## NOTES

1. The best review of this saga and the issues dealt with in modeling the mind is in Matthew Hugh Erdelyi, "A New Look at the New Look: Perceptual Defense and Vigilance," *Psychological Review* 81 (1974), 1–25. Also recommended: Colin Mar-tindale, *Cognition and Consciousness* (Homewood, Illinois: Dorsey Press, 1981).

2. R. N. Haber, "Nature of the Effect of Set on Perception," *Psychological Review* 73 (1966), 335–351.

3. Donald E. Broadbent, *Perception and Communication* (London: Pergamon Press, 1958).

4. Erdelyi, op. cit., 19.
5. Donald A. Norman, "Toward a Theory of Memory and Attention," *Psychological Review* 75 (1968), 522–536.

## QUESTIONS FOR ANALYSIS

1. Two figures play an important role in this selection. Examine these illustrations again closely. How do the two models of the mind differ? Why do you think Goleman included both figures? How did the figures help you to understand the information in the text?

2. What do you think of Goleman's opening strategy? Did you find it engaging? What seems to you to be its point?

3. The title of this selection directs us to Goleman's main point: the mind contains an intelligent filter. He does not make this point until paragraph 17, however. Why do you think he waits so long to announce it? What is he doing up to that point?

4. For most readers, this selection is not especially easy to read. If you found it hard to read (all of it or parts of it), what do you think made it hard for you? Which of the critical reading strategies described in Chapter 1 would make this selection easier for you to read?

5. Successful explanatory writing keeps the reader on track with shrewd paragraphing and obvious transitions from one paragraph to the next. Look again at paragraphs 10–16, and indicate why you think Goleman decided to paragraph where he did. Then underline any words or phrases at the beginnings of paragraphs 11–16 that refer back to the previous paragraph. Do you find such transitions in each paragraph?

6. What is the relation of the final two paragraphs to the rest of the selection? What is Goleman trying to accomplish in each of these paragraphs?

## SUGGESTIONS FOR WRITING

1. Choose an important concept or principle in one of your college courses that can be explained successfully only with figures, charts, drawings, or tables of data. Explain this concept or principle to readers who have not studied it closely. You might want to read more than one source on the subject or even consult an expert. Consider carefully the relation of your figures (or other graphics) to your written explanation.

2. Think about the kinds of information that are important in your present job (or in a previous job). Explain some part of this information to someone new to the job.

# Gary Zukav

Gary Zukav is a professional writer with broad interests in both the humanities and the sciences. During three years of work, in consultation with physicists in America and England, he wrote the book from which the following selection is taken. One of these physicists remarked that Zukav "puts the reader in touch with all the various ways that physicists have worked out for talking about what is so hard to talk about." This physicist also commented, "It is more stimulating to talk physics with him [Zukav] than with most professionals." Zukav seems to be one of those writers who can explain the work of specialists (in all fields) to nonspecialists, interested laymen as well as college students, taking their first course in an unfamiliar academic specialty.

## *Heisenberg's Uncertainty Principle*

This selection comes from *The Dancing Wu Li Masters: An Overview of the New Physics* (1979), Zukav's book introducing nonspecialists to the new physics, quantum mechanics. In this selection, he attempts to explain a fundamental principle of the new physics, the uncertainty principle, first formulated in 1927 by the German physicist Werner Heisenberg.

Quantum mechanics studies physical properties of matter at the subatomic level. Since subatomic particles cannot be seen, physicists must study them with sensitive measuring instruments. The uncertainty principle explains what happens when physicists try to take these measurements. As part of his explanation, Zukav mentions the work of several other physicists—Newton, Planck, Bohr, and Born.

Read this selection to learn about the uncertainty principle and to discover why it is so important to the new physics.

Heisenberg's remarkable discovery was that there are limits beyond 1
which we cannot measure accurately, at the same time, the processes of nature. These limits are not imposed by the clumsy nature of our measuring devices or the extremely small size of the entities that we attempt to measure, but rather by the very way that nature presents itself to us. In other words, there exists an ambiguity barrier beyond which we never can pass without venturing into the realm of uncertainty. For this reason, Heisenberg's discovery became known as the "uncertainty principle."

The uncertainty principle reveals that as we penetrate deeper and 2
deeper into the subatomic realm, we reach a certain point at which one part or another of our picture of nature becomes blurred, and there is no

way to reclarify that part without blurring another part of the picture! It is as though we are adjusting a moving picture that is slightly out of focus. As we make the final adjustments, we are astonished to discover that when the right side of the picture clears, the left side of the picture becomes completely unfocused and nothing in it is recognizable. When we try to focus the left side of the picture, the right side starts to blur and soon the situation is reversed. If we try to strike a balance between these two extremes, both sides of the picture return to a recognizable condition, but in no way can we remove the original fuzziness from them.

The right side of the picture, in the original formulation of the uncertainty principle, corresponds to the position in space of a moving particle. The left side of the picture corresponds to its momentum. According to the uncertainty principle, we cannot measure accurately, at the same time, both the position *and* the momentum of a moving particle. The more precisely we determine one of these properties, the less we know about the other. If we precisely determine the position of the particle, then, strange as it sounds, there is *nothing* that we can know about its momentum. If we precisely determine the momentum of the particle, there is no way to determine its position.

To illustrate this strange statement, Heisenberg proposed that we imagine a super microscope of extraordinarily high resolving power—powerful enough, in fact, to be able to see an electron moving around in its orbit. Since electrons are so small, we cannot use ordinary light in our microscope because the wavelength of ordinary light is much too long to "see" electrons, in the same way that long sea waves barely are influenced by a thin pole sticking out of the water.

If we hold a strand of hair between a bright light and the wall, the hair casts no distinct shadow. It is so thin compared to the wavelengths of the light that the light waves bend around it instead of being obstructed by it. To see something, we have to obstruct the light waves we are looking with. In other words, to see something, we have to illuminate it with wavelengths smaller than it is. For this reason, Heisenberg substituted gamma rays for visible light in his imaginary microscope. Gamma rays have the shortest wavelength known, which is just what we need for seeing an electron. An electron is large enough, compared to the tiny wavelength of gamma rays, to obstruct some of them: to make a shadow on the wall, as it were. This enables us to locate the electron.

The only problem, and this is where quantum physics enters the picture, is that, according to Planck's discovery, gamma rays, which have a much shorter wavelength than visible light, also contain much more energy than visible light. When a gamma ray strikes the imaginary electron, it illuminates the electron, but unfortunately, it also knocks it out of its orbit and changes its direction and speed (its momentum) in an unpredictable and uncontrollable way. (We cannot calculate precisely the angle of rebound between a particle, like the electron, and a wave, like the gamma ray.) In short, if we use light with a wavelength short enough to locate the electron, we cause an undeterminable change in the electron's momentum.

The only alternative is to use a less energetic light. Less energetic 7 light, however, causes our original problem: Light with an energy low enough not to disturb the momentum of the electron will have a wavelength so long that it will not be able to show us where the electron is! There is no way that we can know simultaneously the position *and* the momentum of a moving particle. All attempts to observe the electron alter the electron.

This is the primary significance of the uncertainty principle. At the 8 subatomic level, *we cannot observe something without changing it.* There is no such thing as the independent observer who can stand on the sidelines watching nature run its course without influencing it.

In one sense, this is not such a surprising statement. A good way to 9 make a stranger turn and look at you is to stare intently at his back. All of us know this, but we often discredit what we know when it contradicts what we have been taught is possible. Classical physics is based on the assumption that our reality, independently of us, runs its course in space and time according to strict causal laws. Not only can we observe it, unnoticed, as it unfolds, we can predict its future by applying causal laws to initial conditions. In this sense, Heisenberg's uncertainty principle is a *very* surprising statement.

We cannot apply Newton's laws of motion to an individual particle 10 that does not have an initial location and momentum, which is exactly what the uncertainty principle shows us that we cannot determine. In other words, it is impossible, even in principle, ever to know enough about a particle in the subatomic realm to apply Newton's laws of motion which, for three centuries, were the basis of physics. *Newton's laws do not apply to the subatomic realm.*\* (Newton's *concepts* do not even apply in the subatomic realm.) Given a beam of electrons, quantum theory can predict the probable distribution of the electrons over a given space at a given time, but quantum theory cannot predict, even in principle,

---

\*Strictly speaking, Newton's laws do not disappear totally in the subatomic realm: they remain valid as operator equations. Also, in some experiments involving subatomic particles Newton's laws may be taken as good approximations in the description of what is happening.

the course of a single electron. The whole idea of a causal universe is undermined by the uncertainty principle.

In a related context, Niels Bohr wrote that quantum mechanics, by   11
its essence, entails:

> . . . the necessity of a final renunciation of the classical ideal of causality and a radical revision of our attitude toward the problem of physical reality.[1]

Yet there is another startling implication in the uncertainty principle.   12
The concepts of position and momentum are intimately bound up with our idea of a thing called a moving particle. If, as it turns out, we cannot determine the position and momentum of a moving particle, as we always have assumed that we could, then we are forced to admit that this thing that we have been calling a moving particle, whatever it is, is *not* the "moving particle" we thought it was, because "moving particles" always have both position and momentum.

As Max Born put it:   13

> . . . if we can never actually determine more than one of the two properties (possession of a definite position and of a definite momentum), and if when one is determined we can make no assertion at all about the other property for the same moment, so far as our experiment goes, then we are not justified in concluding that the "thing" under examination can actually be described as a particle in the usual sense of the term.[2]

Whatever it is that we are observing *can* have a determinable momen-   14
tum, and it *can* have a determinable position, but of these two properties, *we must choose,* for any given moment, which one we wish to bring into focus. This means, in reference to "moving particles" anyway, that we can never see them the way they "really are," but only the way we choose to see them!

As Heisenberg wrote:   15

> What we observe is not nature itself, but nature exposed to our method of questioning.[3]

The uncertainty principle rigorously brings us to the realization that   16
there is no "My Way" which is separate from the world around us. It brings into question the very existence of an "objective" reality, as does complementarity and the concept of particles as correlations.

The tables have been turned. "The exact sciences" no longer study an   17
objective reality that runs its course regardless of our interest in it or not, leaving us to fare as best we can while it goes its predetermined way. Science, at the level of subatomic events, is no longer exact, the distinction between objective and subjective has vanished, and the portals through which the universe manifests itself are, as we once knew a long

time ago, those impotent, passive witnesses to its unfolding, the "I"s, of which we, insignificant we, are examples. The Cogs in the Machine have become the Creators of the Universe.

If the new physics has led us anywhere, it is back to ourselves, which, [18] of course, is the only place that we could go.

### NOTES

1. Niels Bohr, *Atomic Theory and Human Knowledge*, New York, John Wiley, 1958, p. 60.
2. Born, *op. cit.*, p. 97.
3. Heisenberg, *Physics and Philosophy*, *op. cit.*, p. 58.

### QUESTIONS FOR ANALYSIS

1. Since this selection seeks to explain a single concept, it is an excellent candidate for summary. Following the guidelines outlined in Chapter 1, write a summary of this selection. How does writing a summary influence your understanding of this selection?

2. In paragraphs 2 and 3, Zukav uses an extended analogy to explain the uncertainty principle. What is this analogy, and how did it help you to understand uncertainty? Specifically, what does it add to your understanding?

3. Zukav quotes three physicists (Bohr, Born, and Heisenberg) and documents the sources of the quotes. Look again at these three quotes, and decide what role each plays in the essay. Why do you think Zukav chose these quotes and placed them where he did?

4. In the introduction to the book from which this selection is taken, Zukav writes, "I suggest that you read this book for your pleasure, and not to learn what is in it. . . . By enjoying yourself, you probably will remember more than if you had set about to learn it all." What do you think of this advice? As you consider your answer, reflect on your reading of this selection, other selections in this chapter, and still other explanations you may be reading now in other courses.

5. Reflect on the strategies Zukav in this essay and Goleman in "The Intelligent Filter" use to explain complicated subjects to nonspecialists. Consider their plans of organization, use of illustrations, appeals to readers' interests, and success in informing the reader. What can you conclude about explanatory writing from these two essays?

## SUGGESTIONS FOR WRITING

1. Identify a principle or concept you are now studying in another course. Choose one that is quite challenging, one you are still struggling to master, one that you must read about further either in your textbook or in other sources. Write an essay explaining this principle or concept to someone unfamiliar with it.

2. Write an essay explaining the uncertainty principle to readers unfamiliar with it. Illustrate your essay by applying the principle to any subject or activity. For example, how does it apply to news reporting, medical research, studies requiring observation of people or animals?

# Jon D. Miller

Jon D. Miller (b. 1941) teaches and directs the Public Opinion Laboratory at Northern Illinois University. He specializes in studies of public attitudes toward science and technology. He has published numerous articles on public participation in the formation of science policy and on scientific literacy. His books include *Citizenship in an Age of Science* (1980) and *The American People and Science Policy* (1983).

# *Scientific Literacy: A Conceptual and Empirical Review*

This selection constitutes one chapter in a book-length collection of essays on scientific literacy. People who are scientifically literate understand how scientists work and think, know about key scientific discoveries and concepts, and value the work of scientists. Miller surveys the research on scientific literacy and summarizes the current level of scientific literacy in America. He then conjectures about the implications of this level for our society.

Miller's essay is a good example of a research review in the social sciences, the kind of review you will be asked to read from time to time in sociology, psychology, political science, or education courses. It is lengthy and encompasses a great deal of information; the tone is detached and academic.

In approaching this formidable essay, reflect on your own attitudes toward science and scientists and your own scientific knowledge. How many different sciences have you studied? Do you know most about biology, chemistry, physics, geology, or astronomy? Which of the sciences do you most want to know more about?

Before you begin reading, preview the selection by skimming the headings and subheadings. Notice how much information they give you about the topics and plan.

In a democratic society, the level of scientific literacy in the population ₁ has important implications for science policy decisions. As this essay will show, the level of scientific literacy in the United States is deplorably low; thus any measures we can take to raise this level, to foster informed and intelligent participation in science policy issues, will improve the quality of both our science and technology and our political life.

The development of scientific literacy by a broader public did not    2
become the subject of systematic study until the 1930s, when John
Dewey, in a paper entitled "The Supreme Intellectual Obligation," declared that

> the responsibility of science cannot be fulfilled by methods that are chiefly
> concerned with self-perpetuation of specialized science to the neglect of in-
> fluencing the much larger number to adopt into the very make-up of their
> minds those attitudes of openmindedness, intellectual integrity, observation,
> and interest in testing their opinions and beliefs, that are characteristic of the
> scientific attitude.[1]

Following Dewey's charge, a number of science educators began to    3
think about the formal definition and measurement of the scientific attitude. Ira C. Davis, for one, believed that the individual who possesses
this attitude will "show a willingness to change his opinion on the basis
of new evidence; . . . search for the whole truth without prejudice; . . .
have a concept of cause and effect relationships; . . . make a habit of
basing judgment on fact; and . . . have the ability to distinguish between
fact and theory."[2] Victor H. Noll and A.G. Hoff came up with similar
definitions, and they began the task of developing items for use in testing.[3] Virtually all of the empirical work done before the Second World
War had as its focus the development of a scientific attitude.

With the postwar growth of standardized testing, a number of science    4
educators and test developers began to focus on the level of comprehension of basic scientific constructs and terms. A growing number of studies,
epitomized by the standardized tests of the Educational Testing Service
(ETS) and the College Board, attempted to chart the level of cognitive
scientific knowledge among various groups in the population.

Beginning in the mid-sixties, the National Assessment of Educational    5
Progress (NAEP) started to collect data from national random samples
of precollegiate students concerning, among other categories, their level
of scientific knowledge. These studies were the first to measure systematically both the understanding of the norms, or processes, of science
and the cognitive content of the major disciplines. These two dimensions
together—an understanding of the norms of science and knowledge of
major scientific constructs—constitute the traditional meaning of scientific literacy as applied to broader populations. But if scientific literacy is
to become truly relevant to our contemporary situation, one additional
dimension must be added: awareness of the impact of science and technology on society and the policy choices that must inevitably emerge.

About fifteen years ago, concern about the public's knowledge of vari-    6
ous scientific or technological public policy issues began to surface. En-

vironmental groups, for example, found that some minimal level of scientific knowledge was necessary if individuals were to understand debates about pollution of the environment. In addition, the increasing number of state referenda on issues such as nuclear power and laetrile were generating apprehension in the scientific community about the public's ability to understand the issues and to make an informed judgment. These concerns echo those of the fifties, when groups opposed to fluoridation of water were able to win referenda on this issue, primarily because the majority of those voting were not scientifically literate. Not able to comprehend the arguments about fluoridation, many voters appeared to prefer not to drink something whose potential effects they did not understand.

In summarizing the case for a broader public understanding of public 7 policy issues—what Benjamin Shen has recently characterized as "civic science literacy"[4]—Robert Morison wrote:

> Science can no longer be content to present itself as an activity independent of the rest of society, governed by its own rules and directed by the inner dynamics of its own processes. Too many of these processes have effects which, though beneficial in many respects, often strike the average man as a threat to his autonomy. Too often science seems to be thrusting society as a whole in directions in which it does not fully understand and which it certainly has not chosen.
>
> The scientific community must redouble its efforts to present science—in the classroom, in the public press, and through education-extension activities of various kinds—as a fully understandable process, "justifiable to man," and controllable by him.[5]

SOME PREVIOUS EMPIRICAL MEASURES

Despite the lively discourse that surrounded the issue of scientific lit- 8 eracy, few efforts were made to measure it for the population broadly, or even for major segments of it. Until the last decade, nearly all the important efforts that were made focused on school populations, most often on small selected sets of schools or classrooms. For a nation generally disposed to social measurement, this was a somewhat disappointing database.

Before analyzing its current levels and distribution, it might be useful 9 to review briefly the previous efforts made to measure scientific literacy from the perspective of its three constitutive dimensions.

*The Norms and Methods of Science*

Most of the early empirical work in this area had as its focus the 10 definition and measurement of the scientific attitude as described by Dewey. Davis, using examples from the everyday experience of the student, sought to develop sets of items that would create situations to force a judgment. By providing a set of rational, intuitive, or superstitious alternatives, Davis attempted to measure the student's utilization of the scientific attitude. For example, students were presented with statements such as "Red hair means that a person has a fiery temperament," "A disease is a punishment for some particular moral wrong," or "Air is composed of molecules." Davis collected data from approximately one thousand Wisconsin high-school students and teachers, and reached the following conclusions:

1. High-school pupils in Wisconsin are not superstitious.
2. High-school pupils make almost as good records as the teachers.
3. Many of the theories in science are being taught as facts by many of our best teachers.
4. Pupils seem to have a fairly clear concept of the cause and effect relationship, but they do not seem to be able to recognize the adequacy of a supposed cause to produce the given result.
5. Many teachers tend to propagandize their material when there is no scientific evidence for the statements they make.
6. Teachers do not consciously attempt to develop the characteristics of a scientific attitude. If pupils have acquired these characteristics, it has come about by some process of thinking or experiences outside of the science classroom.[6]

Tests similar to those used by Davis, stressing the use of everyday examples to measure the use of scientific thinking, were developed by Noll and Hoff.[7]

In its science testing program, NAEP included a number of items concerning knowledge of scientific norms and the ability to reason to conclusions from relatively simple data. These studies provide the only national estimates of the knowledge levels of scientific norms or the ability of young people to think in logical and ordered terms.

In its 1972-73 assessment of science achievement, students of nine, thirteen, and seventeen years of age were asked to perform a set of simple tests and experiments and to explain the results. Each student, for example, was shown unlabeled pieces of sandstone, quartz, and granite, and asked to select the stone that would "most likely [be] formed under water." The sandstone was selected by 60 percent of the nine-year-olds, 71 percent of the thirteen-year-olds, and 78 percent of the seventeen-year-olds. When asked to explain why they had selected the sandstone, however, only 7 percent of the first group, 15 percent of the second, and 26 percent of the third were able to describe the process of sedimentation, even vaguely, or to provide other acceptable explanations.[8] That similar patterns were found in several other experiments, such as color mixing, temperature mixing, relative volume, rotation and revolution, and simple circuit boards, suggests that much of what may appear to be scientific knowledge in multiple-choice testing is not supported by an *understanding* of the underlying scientific principles and processes.

Unfortunately, the National Assessment did not use multi-item scales [13] extensively, which would have provided more reliable summary measures, preferring instead to collect and report sets of individual test items from year to year. Most of these data are available for secondary analysis, and there is much work to be done in converting this very important archive into analyses to provide a portrait of the level and distribution of pre-collegiate and young adult understanding of the norms and methods of science.[9]

## Cognitive Science Knowledge

As the use of standardized testing expanded during the fifties and six- [14] ties, a number of tests were developed to measure a student's knowledge of basic scientific constructs.[10] A majority were used by teachers and school systems to evaluate individual students, to determine admission or placement, or for related academic counseling purposes. While some test score summaries have been published by the ETS and other national testing services, these reports reflect the scores of only those students who plan to attend college or who for some other reason have elected to take the test; and it is this self-selected nature of the student popu-lations involved that continues to raise substantial problems for inter-pretation and analysis. (The NAEP studies cited previously are note-worthy in that they are the only national data collection program in which the bias of self-selection inherent in voluntary testing programs has been eliminated.)

The only national data set that provides scores of cognitive science [15] knowledge for broad and randomly selected populations is the National Assessment, which for over a decade has periodically collected cognitive science knowledge data from national samples of nine-, thirteen-, and seventeen-year-olds. In some years, a national sample of young adults twenty-six through thirty-five was also used to assess the continuing im-pact of formal study.

On the basis of three assessments between 1969 and 1977, NAEP [16] found declining science achievement scores for all age groups and almost all socioeconomic subgroups. Female students, black students, students whose parents did not complete high school, and students who live in large central cities were all substantially below the national average in science achievement. [11]

*Attitudes toward Organized Science*

The third dimension of the scientific literacy typology is an individual's [17] knowledge about what may be generally called organized science—that is, basic science, applied science, and development—and includes both general information about the impact of science on the individual and society and more concrete policy information on specific scientific or technological issues.

The first national study that included a meaningful set of measures of [18] attitudes toward organized science and knowledge about it was a 1957 science news survey conducted by the Survey Research Center at the University of Michigan for the National Association of Science Writers. Although the purpose of the survey was to study the public's interest in science news and its information consumption patterns, the interview schedule also included measures of general attitudes toward organized science and knowledge of it, as well as some issues that were then current. [12]

The survey found that only a minority of the public was strongly in- [19] terested in scientific issues and that the level of public knowledge about science was relatively low. It found, too, that the public tended to hold high expectations for the future achievements of science and technology, but were aware of the two-edged nature of the scientific enterprise. Stephen Withey summarized the public mood: "On the surface the natives are quiet, supportive, and appreciative but there is some questioning, some alert watching, and considerable mistrust. The public will wait and see; they have no reason to do anything else, and many have no other place to turn."[13]

Beginning in 1972, the National Science Board initiated a biennial [20] survey of public attitudes toward science and technology, [14] which found that the public retained a high level of appreciation and expectation amid signs of an increasing wariness. Yet, there was no evidence to indicate the development of a strong antiscience sentiment.

In subsequent surveys in 1979 and 1981, the focus changed to a more [21] structured approach, in an attempt to identify the segment of the population interested in, and knowledgeable about, science policy matters, and to examine the attitudes of this "attentive public."[15] The results showed that about 20 percent of American adults followed scientific matters regularly and that their attitude toward organized science was more favorable as a rule than that of the general population groups previously measured.

The attitudes of young adults toward organized science was even more 22
positive. In a 1978 national survey of high-school and college students,
researchers identified the developmental roots of adult attentiveness to
science matters, and determined that the attitudes of these young adults
were generally positive and supportive of science.[16] Like older Americans
surveyed, however, substantial segments of these young adults were not
very interested in, and had little information about, scientific and technological matters. Approximately 90 percent of the high-school students
who did not plan to attend college failed to meet minimal criteria for
interest in scientific issues or for cognitive knowledge of basic scientific
constructs. There is no reason to believe that the next generation will
be antiscientific; more likely, it will continue to hold the same attitudes—
corrected for the rising levels of educational achievement of the new
generation—as do adults today.

That there has been little consensus on a comprehensive definition of 23
scientific literacy seems obvious from the relatively uncoordinated efforts
to measure its dimensions. And although a number of partial measures
have been developed, we are still without one that will help delineate
that segment of the American population that we can call scientifically
literate. It is to the task of constructing and analyzing a single measure
of scientific literacy that we now turn.

LEVELS AND DISTRIBUTION OF SCIENTIFIC LITERACY

The 1979 National Science Foundation survey of adult attitudes to- 24
ward science and technology, on which the following examination of the
current level of scientific literacy and its distribution in the population
is based, included all of the items necessary to measure each of the three
dimensions of scientific literacy, and utilized a national probability sample
from which valid generalizations can be made.[17] We will look first at the
public's ability to understand the process of scientific study, then at their
comprehension of selected disciplinary constructs, and finally, examine
the public's understanding of some contemporary political issues that
involve science and technology. Once each of the dimensions has been
measured appropriately, the three facets will be combined into a single
measure of scientific literacy.

*Understanding the Scientific Approach*

The first national survey to measure adult comprehension (as opposed 25
to that of schoolchildren and young adults) of the process of scientific
study—what Dewey termed the scientific attitude—was the University

of Michigan science news study of 1957. Each respondent was asked to define the meaning of "scientific study," and the open-ended response was coded into a set of categories that reflected various perceptions of scientific study. In reviewing the data, Withey concluded that only about 12 percent could be said to have a reasonable understanding of the term.[18]

The NSF survey included the same question: it asked each respondent to assess whether he or she had a clear understanding of the meaning of scientific study, a general sense of its meaning, or little understanding of its meaning. Those who said they had a clear understanding of the term were asked to explain its meaning in their own words, and the response was recorded verbatim.[19] (The responses were later coded by two coders independently, and those cases that involved disagreements in coding were judged by the coding supervisor.)

Approximately 14 percent of those surveyed were able to provide a minimally acceptable definition[20] of the meaning of scientific study (Table 1), a level of understanding that is not statistically different from the 12 percent previously recorded. There has apparently been little improvement over the last twenty-two years in the proportion of American adults who correctly understand the meaning of scientific study.

Following the multiple measurement principle,[21] the 1979 survey also included a short battery of items about astrology. Each respondent was asked, first, how often he or she read astrology reports, and then to

**TABLE 1.**
*Adults Who Understand the Scientific Approach*

|  | % | N |
| --- | --- | --- |
| *All adults* | 9 | 1,635 |
| *Age* |  |  |
| 17–34 | 14 | 670 |
| 35–54 | 8 | 492 |
| 55 and over | 4 | 473 |
| *Gender* |  |  |
| Female | 8 | 862 |
| Male | 11 | 773 |
| *Education* |  |  |
| Less than high school | 1 | 465 |
| High-school degree | 5 | 550 |
| Some college | 16 | 382 |
| Baccalaureate degree | 24 | 146 |
| Graduate degree | 32 | 92 |

characterize astrology as very, "sort of," or not at all scientific. Eight percent thought astrology was very scientific; 34 said it was sort of scientific; and half recognized that it is not scientific at all. In general, these responses allowed correction of the results obtained from the question about the meaning of scientific study, because any person who correctly understood the scientific process would have rejected the notion of astrology as scientific. Following this logic, a final measure of understanding of scientific study was constructed: to qualify as understanding the process of scientific investigation, a respondent would have to be able to provide a reasonable definition of scientific study *and* to recognize that astrology is not scientific. Using this yardstick, only 9 percent of those sampled could meet this rather minimal test.

The 1979 data pointed to a strong association between formal educa- 29 tion and an understanding of the scientific approach, yet only a third of those with graduate degrees qualified as understanding the process of scientific inquiry. A separate multivariate logic analysis indicated that most of the differences observed by age and gender could be attributed to the level of formal education.

From these data, only one in ten American adults, it appears, under- 30 stands the meaning of the scientific approach, but other data from the same survey suggest that the majority of the public *can* differentiate between science and pseudoscience in more concrete terms. When asked if the results of animal studies on the safety and efficacy of chemical food additives had induced them to change their eating or food buying habits, 74 percent of the respondents answered in the affirmative, compared to 5 percent who said that astrology reports had prompted them at one time or another to change their plans. As Table 2 shows, although the influence of astrology reports on behavior was significantly associated with low levels of formal education, there was a uniformly high acceptance of the results of animal studies regardless of the level of educational attainment.

In 1979, then, only one in ten American adults understood the mean- 31 ing of the scientific approach, but a substantially larger proportion of the population did have a high level of confidence—or faith—in what they perceived to be scientific studies.

*Understanding Basic Scientific Constructs*

The argument here is clear and simple. The individual who does not 32 comprehend basic terms like atom, molecule, cell, gravity, or radiation will find it nearly impossible to follow the public discussion of scientific

**TABLE 2.**

*Influence of Scientific Studies and Pseudoscientific Reports on Decision-Making
(percentage reporting a change in personal behavior)*

|  | ANIMAL STUDIES | ASTROLOGY REPORTS | N |
|---|---|---|---|
| *All adults* | 74 | 5 | 1,635 |
| *Age* | | | |
| 17–34 | 73% | 7% | 670 |
| 35–54 | 77 | 4 | 492 |
| 55 and over | 74 | 6 | 473 |
| *Gender* | | | |
| Female | 79 | 7 | 862 |
| Male | 69 | 3 | 773 |
| *Education* | | | |
| Less than high school | 71 | 9 | 465 |
| High-school degree | 75 | 7 | 550 |
| Some college | 76 | 3 | 382 |
| Baccalaureate degree | 75 | 0 | 146 |
| Graduate degree | 78 | 1 | 92 |

results or public policy issues pertaining to science and technology. In short, a minimal scientific vocabulary is necessary to be scientifically literate.

The 1979 NSF survey included three items—radiation, GNP, and [33] DNA—that may be said to represent basic science and social science terminology. Again, respondents were asked whether they held a clear understanding of each term, a general sense of its meaning, or little understanding of its meaning. Although the accuracy of these self-assessments was not verified, as it was for the understanding of the meaning of scientific study, there is little reason to believe that such checks would not have shown the same discrepancy.[22]

According to the data, about half the respondents thought they had [34] a clear understanding of radiation, about a third thought they understood GNP, and only one in five claimed knowledge of the meaning of DNA (Table 3). Again, there was a strong correlation between knowledge of these terms and the level of formal education.

To provide a single measure of this dimension, a summary index was [35] constructed: a respondent would have to report a clear understanding of at least one of the three constructs and not less than a general sense of a second to be classified as knowledgeable about basic scientific constructs. Exactly half met this requirement. Formal education was once again the key determinant: 96 percent of those holding graduate degrees

**TABLE 3.**
*Adults Reporting a Clear Understanding of Basic Scientific Concepts*

| | RADIATION | GNP | DNA | HIGH ON INDEX | N |
|---|---|---|---|---|---|
| All adults | 49 | 31 | 22 | 50 | 1,635 |
| Age | | | | | |
| 17–34 | 44% | 43% | 21% | 64% | 670 |
| 35–54 | 49 | 30 | 17 | 47 | 492 |
| 55 and over | 39 | 23 | 10 | 34 | 473 |
| Gender | | | | | |
| Female | 41 | 21 | 20 | 43 | 862 |
| Male | 58 | 43 | 26 | 59 | 773 |
| Education | | | | | |
| Less than high school | 30 | 7 | 3 | 18 | 465 |
| High-school degree | 47 | 23 | 15 | 45 | 550 |
| Some college | 60 | 47 | 37 | 72 | 382 |
| Baccalaureate degree | 70 | 67 | 52 | 88 | 146 |
| Graduate degree | 78 | 80 | 57 | 96 | 92 |

met the criterion in contrast to only 18 percent of those without a high-school diploma.

## Understanding of Science Policy Issues

As science becomes increasingly dependent upon public support, and as public regulation reaches deeper into the conduct of organized science, the frequency and importance of science policy issues on the national agenda will undoubtedly increase. Slightly over half the bills introduced in Congress involve science or technology in some degree,[23] and the establishment of the standing Committee on Science and Technology in the House of Representatives attests to the importance of scientific and technological issues in the national political system. 36

The 1979 NSF survey provides a useful measure of the third dimension of scientific literacy—the understanding of some of the major public policy issues that involve or directly affect the conduct of science and technology. The survey includes separate batteries of items about three controversies—the use of chemical additives in food, nuclear power, and space exploration. For each, respondents were asked to cite two potential benefits and two potential harms. Approximately two thirds cited at least two benefits or dangers (or one of each) for food additives and nuclear power, but only a third were similarly knowledgeable about the potential benefits and harms of space exploration (Table 4). As with the other two dimensions of scientific literacy, the level of formal education related positively to how well informed the respondent was. 37

**TABLE 4.**

*Adults with High Score on Selected Science-Related Public Policy Issues*

| | NUCLEAR POWER | FOOD ADDITIVES | SPACE PROGRAM | HIGH ON INDEX | N |
|---|---|---|---|---|---|
| *All adults* | 68 | 61 | 32 | 41 | 1,635 |
| *Age* | | | | | |
| 17–34 | 71% | 68% | 42% | 51% | 670 |
| 35–54 | 70 | 63 | 30 | 38 | 492 |
| 55 and over | 62 | 52 | 20 | 30 | 473 |
| *Gender* | | | | | |
| Female | 62 | 60 | 26 | 34 | 862 |
| Male | 73 | 63 | 38 | 48 | 773 |
| *Education* | | | | | |
| Less than high school | 50 | 37 | 16 | 16 | 465 |
| High-school degree | 66 | 62 | 28 | 37 | 550 |
| Some college | 80 | 75 | 43 | 55 | 382 |
| Baccalaureate degree | 87 | 84 | 47 | 68 | 146 |
| Graduate degree | 89 | 91 | 58 | 81 | 92 |

To be counted among those knowledgeable about scientific and tech- 38 nological public policy issues, a respondent had to name a minimum of six potential benefits or harms out of a possible twelve—the single criterion devised to measure this dimension of scientific literacy. Approximately 41 percent qualified.

Using the three dimensions described in the preceding section, a single 39 measure of scientific literacy was constructed that required a minimally acceptable score in all three areas for an individual to be considered scientifically literate. On the basis of this measure, only 7 percent of the respondents—primarily males, individuals over thirty-five, and college graduates—qualified (Table 5). But even among holders of graduate degrees, only a quarter could be called scientifically literate.

IMPLICATIONS FOR A DEMOCRATIC SOCIETY

Assuming that this estimate is correct, that the overwhelming majority 40 of the American adult population is scientifically *illiterate*, what are the implications for our political system? How is science policy to be made? Can the basic tenets of a participatory political system be maintained? These issues can only be addressed, I believe, by placing them in the context of the general process of political specialization that has become the hallmark of American politics in recent decades.

*Political Specialization*

No individual today, no matter how good his or her intentions, can 41 hope to acquire and maintain a mastery of more than a few political

**TABLE 5.**

*The Percentage of the Public Classified as Scientifically Literate*

|  | SCIENTIFICALLY LITERATE | N |
|---|---|---|
| *All adults* | 7 | 1,635 |
| *Age* | | |
| 17–34 | 11% | 670 |
| 35–54 | 7 | 492 |
| 55 and over | 3 | 473 |
| *Gender* | | |
| Female | 6 | 867 |
| Male | 9 | 773 |
| *Education* | | |
| Less than high school | 0 | 465 |
| High-school degree | 2 | 550 |
| Some college | 14 | 382 |
| Baccalaureate degree | 22 | 146 |
| Graduate degree | 26 | 92 |

issues at one time. Thus the modern citizen who chooses to follow political affairs opts for political specialization—that is, selects out of the myriad issues those few in which he or she is willing to invest the time and other resources necessary to become and remain informed.

The need for specialization springs from a combination of two basic [42] forces. First, participation in the political process is but one of the many demands on the time of contemporary men and women. That many adults choose to devote a smaller share of their time to political affairs, in favor of more attractive, perhaps more personally satisfying alternatives, can be seen in the steady decline of public participation in the political system over the last four decades. Even presidential elections, which command the highest levels of public concern and participation, attract barely half the eligible adults in the United States.

Second, the specialized information required to be knowledgeable [43] about almost any given political issue is increasing rapidly. Issues involving science fall into this category, as do most of the issues on the national political agenda. For example, an area like economic policy—often referred to as the pocketbook issue—has become increasingly complex and is beyond the ken of a substantial majority of American adults. If only 31 percent of the adult population professed to have a clear understanding of a term like GNP,[24] how many citizens, then, might be expected to comprehend the current debate over "supply-side economics" or the fate of the dollar in international monetary markets?

Both forces have worked to narrow the political horizon of most Amer- 44
ican adults. Unlike "single-issue" politics, where the interest of the participant revolves totally around one strongly felt political position, political specialization is a rational and gradual narrowing of the number of
topics on which an individual can hope to remain adequately informed.
Even then, they are not nearly as well informed about an issue as their
interest would imply.

How does this specialization process affect the more general political 45
system? Three decades ago, Gabriel Almond described the process as it
applied to public attitudes toward foreign policy and public participation
in its formulation. In his original work, he illustrated, in stratified py-
ramidal form, the types of public participation in the political process
that were likely to occur under conditions of issue specialization (Figure
1).[25] At the pinnacle are those who have the power to make binding
policy decisions, a group that would include a mix of executive, legislative, and judicial officers. In the case of science policy, the officers
would be primarily at the federal level.

Nongovernmental policy leaders, often referred to as elites in political 46
science, comprise the second level. This group interacts regularly with
the decision-makers, and from time to time, as noted by James Rosenau
and others, there is some flow of elites into decision-making posts, and

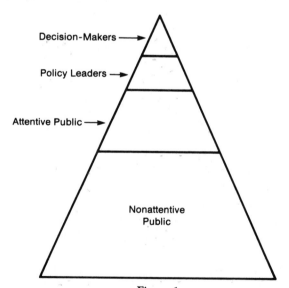

**Figure 1.**
*A Stratified Model of Science and Technology Policy Formulation*

of decision-makers into the leadership group.[26] When there is a high level of concurrence between the decision-makers and the leadership group, policy is made, and normally there is no wider public participation in the policy process. The policy leadership group may itself divide on some issues. In this case, appeals may be made to the attentive public—the third level—to join in the policy process and to try to influence decision-makers by contacting them directly and by persuasion. The attentive public is composed of individuals interested in a particular policy area and willing to become and remain knowledgeable about the issue. In 1979 the attentive public for science policy included about 27 million adults, or about 18 percent of the adult population.[27]

Although the processes for mobilizing the attentive public for science 47 policy are only now being studied, the flow of appeals from leaders to the attentive public apparently takes place through professional organizations, specialized journals and magazines, and employment-related institutions. The flow of concerns from the attentive public to the decision-makers, on the other hand, undoubtedly goes through the traditional avenues of letter writing and telephone and personal contacts.

The attentive public also becomes involved when there is a high degree 48 of consensus among the leadership group but a lack of concurrence by some or all of the decision-makers. In this case, the leadership groups work to mobilize the attentive public to contact the decision-makers and to argue directly for the preferred policy. The recent discussions of federal funding for science illustrate this case.

At the bottom of the pyramid is the general, or nonattentive, public. 49 For the most part, these individuals have little interest in science policy and a low level of knowledge about organized science. Two very important points must be understood about this group, however. First, should the general population become sufficiently unhappy about the policies that the decision-makers, leaders, and the attentive public have fostered in any area, it can exercise a political veto. The public's role in ending the wars in Korea and Vietnam illustrate how powerful this option can be. It is this very ability of the general population to intervene and veto that sustains the democratic nature of the policy formulation process.

Second, it is important not to equate nonattentiveness to science pol- 50 icy with ignorance or lack of intellectual activity. We are all nonattentive to a vast number of issues. Many of the nonattentive public may be well educated, interested in other issues and knowledgeable about them, and politically active. According to the data from the 1979 NSF survey, about half of the adult population in the United States at the time of the survey were attentive to one or more political issues.[28]

*Scientific Literacy and the Formulation of Science Policy*

Given this stratified decision-making process, the low level of scientific 51
literacy raises two important problems. First, among the 80 percent of
the population not attentive to science policy, the level of scientific
literacy is extraordinarily low—in the 2 to 3 percent range. In the context
of the political specialization process, we would not expect a very high
rate of scientific literacy in the nonattentive public, and few voters would
be expected to make their choices primarily on the basis of scientifc or
technological issues. Yet in recent years, an increasing number of referenda have concerned issues related to science or technology—nuclear
power, laetrile, recombinant DNA facilities, fluoridation—and it is apparent that a substantial majority of the general electorate will not be
able to make informed judgments on these issues.

Second, approximately 70 percent of the attentive public for science 52
policy did *not* meet the minimal criteria for scientific literacy. This is a
surprising result, but not an inexplicable one. Almost half of the adult
population had a minimal facility with basic scientific terms (Table 3),
and 40 percent had at least a minimal level of issue information (Table
4). Many of these individuals may have had a high level of interest in
one or more science-related issues and may have followed them through
popular magazines such as *Science 83, Smithsonian, National Geographic,
Discover,* or *Omni,* without understanding the scientific processes involved. They would perhaps have more difficulty comprehending articles
in *Science, Scientific American,* or in professional or disciplinary journals,
but can undoubtedly write very clear letters to their congressmen and
senators. They would appear to be dependent upon science journalists to
"interpret" the scientific debate on most issues.

As more appeals are made to the attentive public to pressure directly 53
for public policy outcomes, the importance of this group will grow. Yet,
the situation is a fragile one. Given the large numbers in this group who
are dependent on "translators," the personality or philosophical perspective of the translator may become as important—if not more so—than
the substance of the scientific arguments.

There are compelling cultural, economic, and political arguments for 54
a major effort to expand scientific literacy in both the general and attentive publics. In my opinion, the most effective place to start is in the
elementary and secondary schools. . . . Beyond improved science education at this level, I would urge that high priority be placed on the
expansion of scientific literacy among the attentive public for science
policy, both in terms of increasing their overall numbers and in aug-
menting their basic level of literacy. What makes political specialization

possible is just this basic level of literacy in any given issue area. There is an interested audience searching for more sophisticated information than is normally available in the news media. The extraordinary growth of semisophisticated science magazines like *Discover, Omni,* and *Science 83,* for example, represents in large part the desire for more and better information among the attentive public for science policy.

From Dewey to Morison, the scientific community has been urged to 55 communicate more effectively and openly with the public, especially the informed public — and scientists and engineers are responding by showing a new level of willingness to explain their problems and aspirations to interested lay audiences. But if this communication is to continue and expand so that the science policy process can function effectively, there must be an audience capable of understanding both the substance of the arguments and the basic processes of science. We can accomplish this by addressing, without delay, the educational needs of the attentive public for science policy.

## NOTES

1. John Dewey, "The Supreme Intellectual Obligation," *Science Education* 18 (1934): 1–4.

2. Ira C. Davis, "The Measurement of Scientific Attitudes," *Science Education* 19 (1935): 117–22.

3. A.G. Hoff, "A Test for Scientific Attitude," *School Science and Mathematics* 36 (1936): 763–70; Victor H. Noll, "Measuring the Scientific Attitude," *Journal of Abnormal and Social Psychology* 30 (1935): 145–54.

4. Benjamin Shen, "Scientific Literacy and the Public Understanding of Science," in *Communication of Scientific Information,* edited by S. Day (Basel: Karger, 1975).

5. Robert S. Morison, "Science and Social Attitudes," *Science* 165 (1969): 150–56.

6. Davis, "The Measurement of Scientific Attitudes."

7. Hoff, "A Test for Scientific Attitude," and Noll, "Measuring the Scientific Attitude."

8. National Assessment of Educational Progress, *Selected Results for the National Assessments of Science: Scientific Principles and Procedures,* Science Report No. 04-S-02 (Denver: Educational Commission of the States, 1975).

9. Jon D. Miller, "Secondary Analysis and Science Education," *Journal of Research in Science Teaching* 19 (1982): 719–25.

10. Oscar K. Buros, *The Sixth Mental Measurements Yearbook* (Highland Park, New Jersey: Gryphon Press, 1965).

11. National Assessment of Educational Progress, *Three National Assessments of Science: 1969–1977,* Science Report No. 08-S-00 (Denver: Educational Commission of the States, 1978a); and *Science Achievement in the Schools,* No. 08-S-01 (Denver: Educational Commission of the States, 1978b).

12. Robert C. Davis, *The Public Impact of Science in the Mass Media*, Survey Research Center, Monograph No. 25, University of Michigan, Ann Arbor, 1958; and Stephen B. Withey, "Public Opinion about Science and the Scientists," *Public Opinion Quarterly* 23 (1959): 382–88.

13. Withey, Ibid.

14. National Science Board, *Science Indicators 1972*; *Science Indicators 1974*; *Science Indicators 1976*; and *Science Indicators 1980* (Washington, D.C.: Government Printing Office, 1973, 1975, 1977, 1981).

15. Jon D. Miller, *The American People and Science Policy* (New York: Pergamon, 1983); Jon D. Miller, Kenneth Prewitt, and Robert Pearson, *The Attitudes of the U.S. Public toward Science and Technology*, a final report to the National Science Foundation, 1980.

16. Jon D. Miller, Robert W. Suchner, and Alan V. Voelker, *Citizenship in an Age of Science* (New York: Pergamon, 1980).

17. The 1979 survey collected personal interviews from a national stratified cluster sample of 1,635 adults. The field work was performed by the Institute for Survey Research at Temple University, and the interviews averaged fifty-five minutes in length. For a full description of the sample selection methods and the interview instrument, see Miller et al., *The Attitudes of the U.S. Public toward Science and Technology*.

18. Withey, "Public Opinion about Science."

19. The questions concerning the understanding of scientific study are illustrative of the limitations and utility of survey measurements. Asking an individual if he or she has a clear understanding of the meaning of scientific study is inherently subjective. Undoubtedly some individuals overestimated their level of understanding, while others underestimated it. Yet, the subjective nature of the response is also its strength, since a person who does not think that he or she understands the term would be unlikely to utilize it in communicating with others. The pairing of this subjective query with the more objective and substantive follow-up definition and astrology questions allowed for a correction for overestimates of understanding in the subjective query. The resulting estimate of the proportion of adults with an understanding of the meaning of scientific study should be taken as an upper limit on the occurrence of this understanding under more rigorous measurement methods.

20. To be classified as understanding the process of scientific study, a respondent had to report that scientific study involved (1) the advancement and potential falsification of generalizations and hypotheses, leading to the creation of theory, (2) the investigation of a subject with an open mind and a willingness to consider all evidence in determining results, or (3) the use of experimental or similar methods of controlled comparison or systematic observation. Responses that characterized scientific study as the accumulation of facts, the use of specific instruments (i.e., looking at things through a microscope), or as simply careful study, were coded as incorrect.

21. Donald T. Campbell and Donald W. Fiske, "Convergent and Discriminant Validation by the Multitrait-Multimethod Matrix," *Psychology Bulletin* 56 (1959): 81–105.

22. As I pointed out in note 19, it is important to note the limitations inherent in these measures. If probes had been employed for this second question, some of the respondents who rated their understanding of these terms to be high would have been reclassified downward. These estimates should be taken as upper limits of the true value in the population.

23. Shen, "Scientific Literacy and the Public Understanding of Science."

24. Miller et al., *The Attitudes of the U.S. Public toward Science and Technology.*

25. Gabriel Almond, *The American People and Foreign Policy* (New York: Harcourt Brace, 1950).

26. James Rosenau, *Citizenship Between Elections* (New York: Free Press, 1974).

27. Miller, *The American People and Science Policy;* Miller et al., *The Attitudes of the U.S. Public toward Science and Technology.*

28. Miller et al., *The Attitudes of the U.S. Public toward Science and Technology.*

## QUESTIONS FOR ANALYSIS

1. Miller's subject is scientific literacy. What is the main point he wants to make about this subject?

2. In the opening paragraphs (1–7), what strategies does Miller employ to interest readers in his subject? Did he succeed in interesting you? What advantages and disadvantages do you see in Miller's introductory strategies?

3. Like most research summarizers and textbook writers, Miller uses headings and subheadings effectively. Review these headings and explain what they contributed to your understanding of the information.

4. In a long selection such as this, readers find repeated summaries and forecasts very helpful. Skim the selection, looking for summaries of preceding sections and forecasts of upcoming ones. What specific information does Miller include in each of these summaries and forecasts? Which ones do you find most helpful?

5. Miller includes five tables in his report. What problems (if any) did you have understanding the data in these tables? Why do you think Miller included them? What is the relation of the tables to the surrounding text?

6. Research reviews nearly always conclude with a summary of what is known about the subject under review; they may also conclude with implications, usually a summing up of the subject's significance. Miller's essay includes both these features. What does he attempt to do with these features? How would you evaluate this method of presenting the summary and implications?

## SUGGESTIONS FOR WRITING

1. Choose a current educational, environmental, social, or political problem that interests you. Review the research on this problem, and report what you learn. Write for readers who have an interest in the problem but who have not read any of the research you are reviewing. Your purpose will be simply to summarize the research. You do not have to analyze the problem yourself or propose a solution to it, although you may conjecture about the implications of what the researchers have to say.

2. Review recent research on some common or highly publicized health problem like emphysema, AIDS, high blood pressure, obesity, or bulemia. Focus your review on medical journals, not popular magazines. Write up what you learn for readers who would not ordinarily have access to medical journals.

# Scott Holz

Scott Holz is a freshman at the University of California, San Diego, where he races for the cycling team. His hobbies include scuba diving, writing song lyrics, and playing electric bass guitar. Each summer he teaches swimming for the school district in his home town of Covina, California (near Pasadena). Students in his classes range from three-year-olds to adults. A history major, Holz hopes to go to law school.

## Swimming Pool Physics

In this essay, written for his freshman composition class, Holz explains some laws of physics by analyzing the familiar motions of floating, sinking, and swimming. As you read, consider what knowledge of physics and swimming Holz needed in order to write this essay.

When swimmers perform certain motions, they take for granted that they will float and move through water. They never think of themselves as working models of many of the laws of classical physics. When people swim, however, they are applying Archimedes' principle, the center of gravity law, and the laws of inertia and action and reaction. Although swimmers do not have to be physics majors to be able to swim, applying their knowledge of swimming can help them understand these physical laws.

Before people can swim, they must be able to float. Floating can be understood in terms of Archimedes' principle and the laws of gravity and buoyancy. Archimedes' principle states that a body is buoyed up by a force equal to the weight of the fluid that the body displaces. The body will sink of its weight when the immersed body is greater than the weight of the displaced fluid. On the other hand, if the body weighs less than the displaced fluid, it will float. When swimmers inhale deeply and hold a large quantity of air in their lungs, their buoyancy is increased. Contrary to common belief, the increase in buoyancy is not caused by the air in the lungs raising the body to the surface. Actually, as the body takes in air, the chest expands and displaces more water. Since the body's weight does not change with the expansion, the buoyancy is increased. Thus, the buoyancy of a swimmer immersed in water can be controlled by the amount of air that is inhaled and held by the body.

The position in which a body floats is determined by centers of gravity and buoyancy. On land or in the air, a person rotates around a point that is the center of weight distribution. This center point is located near the hips in the human body. However, in the water, where a person is almost weightless, the body does not rotate around the center of gravity. Instead, the swimmer rotates around a center of buoyancy that is located in the chest. A swimmer can float motionlessly only when the center of gravity is aligned directly under the center of buoyancy. This normally occurs when a swimmer floats on his back or in a vertical position. Gravity tends to pull on each body part separately. When the buoyancy of a specific part of the body is greater than that of water, it will float. For example, an arm may float while a leg may sink, a difference we can understand through the idea of body composition.

Body composition, in relation to swimmers, is the amount of heavy    4 bone and muscle tissue in proportion to the amount of fatty tissue present in the body. Fat is lighter than water and therefore tends to float, while bones and muscles are heavier than water and tend to sink. Consequently, men normally have more difficulty floating than women do because the average man's body composition has less fat than does the average woman's body. An easy test called the jellyfish float can determine how buoyant a person is. While in chest-deep water, the person submerges to the neck, takes a deep breath of air, bends forward at the waist, and places his head in the water face down. He then bends his knees enough to get his feet off of the bottom, holds his breath, and relaxes as much as possible. If the person sinks, his weight is greater than the buoyant force of the water. If a portion of the head or back remains above the surface, the person's weight is less than that of the displaced water.

After a person is floating, the next step is to swim, to move through    5 the water in an efficient way. The law of inertia has much to do with the way a body moves through water. This law states that a body remains at rest or in uniform motion unless it is acted upon by some external force. In the case of swimming, the external forces are those that act to retard the motions of the swimmer. These forces cannot be eliminated, but they can be minimized through effective stroking to reduce frontal resistance and eddy resistance. When swimmers glide through the water, they will eventually stop. According to the law of inertia, if frontal and eddy resistance were not present, swimmers could glide forever.

Frontal resistance is caused by water pushing on the front of the moving    6 body and is directly proportional to the amount of frontal surface area in motion. For example, it is much more difficult for a swimmer to move forward through the water in a vertical position than in a horizontal one. In the vertical position, the body is forming frontal resistance with the shoulders, chest, hips, arms, and legs. When a body moves through the water in a horizontal position, only the shoulders present resistance.

The second type of resisting force is eddy resistance (drag). Drag is    7
formed by the layer of water that flows along the body while it is in motion. The negative effects of the flow are reduced when the body is kept in a straight, streamlined position. The texture of the surface along which the water flows also plays an important factor in eddy resistance. The water does not flow as well around a rough surface as it does around a smooth one. For this reason, many competitive swimmers shave their arms and legs because hair increases drag, whereas smooth skin offers very little resistance.

Probably the most important physical law that applies to swimming is    8
Newton's law of action and reaction, which explains why movement through water is possible. Newton's theory states that for every action there is an equal and opposite reaction. Thus, by pushing water backward with the hands and feet, the swimmer moves forward. However, the movements of swimmers are not one hundred percent efficient. Some reaction force is lost as water slips around the arms, hands, legs, and feet, if they are not positioned properly during their propulsive movements. Also, any force that is not applied in exactly the opposite direction to where the swimmer wishes to move will result in loss of efficiency. Newton's law also implies that if the underwater recovery actions of the arms and the legs are too rigorous, the water will "push back," again with equal force, and the swimmer will lose momentum.

We normally take for granted the reasons why an activity like swim-    9
ming is possible. However, by analyzing a swimmer's motions, we see that the laws of classical physics explain almost all the swimmer's actions and reactions.

## QUESTIONS FOR ANALYSIS

1. How successful do you find Holz's explanations of physical laws? Which is most successful? least successful? What did you learn from this essay?

2. To discover Holz's plan, make a brief outline of his essay. (Chapter 1 provides guidelines for outlining.) Given his informative purpose, what advantages do you see in his plan?

3. Holz does not cite references for the laws of physics he discusses. Why do you think he omits such references? Was his decision wise?

4. Did you find this essay hard to read or easy to read? How would you account for its level of difficulty?

5. Goleman, Zukav, and Holz all attempt to explain scientific concepts. How do their approaches and strategies differ? What can you conclude about scientific explanation from these three selections?

### SUGGESTIONS FOR WRITING

1. Select a difficult law, principle, or concept from a subject you are studying, and explain it in terms of a familiar activity. Write for readers who have not studied the subject you are explaining.

2. Research a familiar phenomenon like ocean waves, thunder, eye blinks, sneezing, sleep or dreams, wind, fall leaf colors, TV reception. Explain this phenomenon to a much younger reader (ten to twelve years old) who has never examined it but has only noticed it. Consider explanatory strategies like analogy, scenario, comparison/contrast, and definition. Try to engage young readers' interest in the phenomenon.

# A Look at Scott Holz's Writing Process

Following the guide to writing in the next section, Holz began by listing subjects in several categories. His longest list was of ordinary activities or events he wanted to know more about; swimming was among these activities. As he explored this subject in writing, he concentrated on describing specific dives and swimming strokes. As a result, he tentatively decided that his main point would be how different the main swimming strokes really are.

Later, talking with friends looking for subjects for the same assignment, he thought about how he might explain swimming scientifically. He decided that he wanted to do more than explain certain swimming strokes on the basis of his own experience and observations. He then remembered explanations of the physics of swimming in manuals he had studied to qualify as a swimming instructor. Rereading those and reviewing principles he had learned about in high school physics, he found many that could explain swimming.

When he analyzed his readers—other students in his composition class—he realized that all or nearly all of them could swim and had probably taken swimming lessons. He guessed they had all watched parts of the 1985 summer Olympics swimming competition. He decided that the physics of swimming really would be a more informative subject for these readers than a description of swimming strokes that were already familiar to them. As he set goals for drafting, he recognized that he could approach his draft as an introduction to some principles of classical physics for beginning science students as easily as he could direct it to swim-mers. That decision led him to refocus his main point on presenting physics concepts, with swimmers' activities as the basic explanatory strategy.

Holz reports that he was very disappointed in his first draft. He was enthusiastic about his subject and had more than enough information to choose from, but the draft was not interesting. It read like a dry textbook presenting physics principles like a catalog or list. In a conference on the draft, his instructor suggested he organize around the sequence for teach-ing a beginner to swim. He liked the suggestion even though it meant substantive rewriting. The new plan increased the likelihood that the essay would hold readers' interest, and he was surprised to find that it made the information more readable, "made it flow," as Holz said.

## A GUIDE TO EXPLANATORY WRITING

This guide to writing will support your planning, drafting, and revising of an explanatory essay.

# *Invention*

A period of thoughtful exploration and research before you begin draft-ing will enable you to produce a more readable, informative draft. The following invention activities can help you to choose a subject, explore it fully, decide on your main point, analyze your readers, and research your subject. With the exception of the research you may need to carry out, each of these activities takes only a few minutes to complete.

CHOOSING A SUBJECT. Since explanations encompass nearly any subject you could imagine, the possibilities may seem dizzying. How do you go about finding a subject? Experienced writers begin the process by listing likely subjects.

Before you start your own list, first review the suggestions for writing that follow each reading selection in this chapter. On your list, include subjects that you already know about as well as those you would like to learn about. Try listing possible subjects in the following categories, which other students have found very helpful for finding a subject.

an academic principle or concept from a course you are now taking

a current issue or problem that has been the topic of recently published research studies a historical figure you would like to learn more about

an ordinary event or activity or object you have always been curious about: bird migration, espresso machines, coughing, automatic transmissions, clarinets, volleyballs, bookbinding, hang gliding

a current danger to public health, the environment, or the social order: acid rain, winter depression, illegal disposal of waste materials, poor schools, alcoholism, child abuse

Once you have compiled a list of possible subjects, choose one that truly interests you, one you feel eager to write about and to learn more about. Consider too whether you will be able to interest readers in the subject.

EXPLORING YOUR SUBJECT. When writers are drawn to a subject, they will often invest some time exploring it in writing before they begin drafting. In this way, they can discover what they already know about the subject and determine whether they are truly interested in it. Take a few minutes now to write down whatever you know about the topic you have chosen. Write quickly, without planning or organizing. Feel free to write in phrases or word lists, as well as in sentences. You might also want to make drawings or charts. Write without stopping for several minutes, putting down everything you know about this subject.

DECIDING ON A SPECIFIC SUBJECT AND MAIN POINT. A well-written explanatory essay presents a specific, limited subject and makes a well-focused point about that subject. Achieving this focus is a challenging decision for any writer. Generalizing about your subject and writing questions about it may help you to decide on your focus.

Begin by rereading what you wrote when you explored your topic. Then try to write a few general statements about the subject, defining it, stating its importance, identifying anything unusual or surprising about it. Also write a few questions about the subject, questions that you would like answered or that you suspect readers would want to see answered.

These statements and questions may help you decide on a specific subject and the point you want to make about it. Try now to restate it, narrowing your focus if possible to a particular part of the subject you can write about informatively in a brief essay. Write down the point you think you will want to make about this specific subject. Keep in mind that you may want to refocus the subject after you have analyzed your readers and done research. You may even decide on a different point you want to make about it.

ANALYZING YOUR READERS. Once you have decided on your focus, you will need to determine who your readers will be. This decision is important in all kinds of writing, and particularly so in explanatory writing. In order to know what terms to define and what information to include, writers of explanations must estimate what their readers already know about the subject. Writers of explanations must also figure out how to appeal to readers' interest in the subject and related subjects and to hold their interest throughout the essay.

Write now for several minutes about your readers. Describe them, indicate what they know about your subject, and explore ways you might interest them in it.

RESEARCHING YOUR SUBJECT. Having determined what information your readers will need to know, you can now begin to research your subject. Read or reread anything you may already have at hand about it. Go to the library to search for further information; talk to an expert. Because you may later need to document your sources, be sure to take careful notes. (The appendix outlines a proven strategy for library research.)

# *Drafting*

After you have completed a period of thoughtful exploration and research, you are ready to draft. Before you begin, however, you will want to set goals and plan your organization.

SETTING GOALS. Setting goals enables you to draft more confidently and to maintain your focus. Consider your readers and your purpose. What terms will you need to define for your readers? Can you assume readers will know the meaning of words like *equanimity, acquiescence,* and *lacunae,* as does Brodie? Will you be able to define key words in context, as Twain defines *drainage basin* in his first paragraph? Or will you want to offer explicit definitions of key words, as Goleman defines *sensory store, primary memory,* and *long-term memory* for his readers?

What do your readers already know? How can you present new information without boring or confusing them? How can you create interest in your subject? Leakey and Lewin, for example, present anthropological information through a scenario. Goleman relies on figures to illustrate components of memory, and Miller depends on tables of data about scientific literacy. Goleman attempts to create interest with three shocking words, and Miller hopes to engage our interest by emphasizing the importance of scientific literacy.

Remember that your purpose is to present well-established information to your readers as clearly as possible, making a particular point about this information. You therefore want your presentation to sound informed and authoritative.

PLANNING YOUR ORGANIZATION. Your drafting will usually proceed more smoothly if you outline your plans before beginning to draft. Once you start drafting, however, you may need to depart from your plan. At this point, you should devise a tentative plan that arranges your information in a sensible way and sequences the information for maximum clarity and informativeness. Notice, for instance, Twain's simple sequence of remarkable features of the Mississippi, Holz's plan for presenting physics concepts by the stages in which one learns to swim, and Brodie's plan for organizing around Jefferson's personal traits. Be sure that this tentative plan supports your main point.

KEEPING THE READER ON TRACK. Explanations and research reviews should provide numerous cues to keep readers on track. Plan your introduction so that it states your subject and main point and clearly forecasts the plan of your essay. Remember to provide transitions between paragraphs and between major sections to enable the reader to follow your essay. Notice, for example, how in their first paragraphs Twain forecasts the remarkableness of the Mississippi and Brodie forecasts Jefferson's personal traits. Notice, too, how Twain repeats his key word (*remarkable*), Miller segments with topic headings, and Goleman uses paragraph transitions to keep readers on track.

# Revising

You might begin your revision by analyzing your draft in light of the critical reading questions at the beginning of this chapter. If possible, ask someone else to analyze your draft in the same way. As you revise, be especially attentive to ways in which you can strengthen your focus, organization, content, and readability.

REVISING TO SHARPEN THE FOCUS. Read your draft carefully, looking for ways to sharpen the focus of your essay. As you were drafting, you may have decided to make a different main point about the information. If necessary, remove any information not directly related to your main point.

REVISING TO CLARIFY THE ORGANIZATION. Make an outline of your draft so that you can consider its underlying structure. Decide whether this structure is appropriate for your information, readers, and main point. Consider other ways in which the essay might be organized. Try moving parts of your essay around to determine if another organization might be more effective.

REVISING TO STRENGTHEN THE CONTENT. Your draft should be complete and authoritative, telling readers everything they need to know—but no more than they need to know—to convey your point about the subject. Determine whether you have provided enough substance in your essay or whether you should do further research in order to locate additional information. Decide whether all the material in your present draft is relevant and informative. Consider replacing overly familiar content with new or surprising content.

REVISING TO IMPROVE READABILITY. In order to grasp and remember the new information presented, readers should be able to proceed through an explanation efficiently. Consider whether your beginning helps readers to understand the plan of your essay. Be sure you have provided enough cues in the body of the essay to keep readers on track—timely paragraphing, forecasts, transitions, brief summaries. Read your draft slowly, sentence by sentence, looking for gaps and digressions. Do whatever you can to help your readers move smoothly through your essay.

When you have a revision, proofread to correct all errors in punctuation, usage, and spelling. Careless mistakes will detract from the readability of your essay.

# CHAPTER SIX

# *Evaluation*

Should we see the new Spielberg film? Is Kurt Vonnegut's latest novel as good as *Slaughterhouse Five*? Does Ms. Johnson deserve a promotion? Which of these explanations of tropism is better, and why? How's the food in that new Vietnamese restaurant? If I buy that car will I get my money's worth? Which college is best for me?

These are some of the many occasions when evaluations are made—at home, at work, in school. We evaluate people, films, books, ideas, objects, and places; often we are the ones being evaluated—by teachers, employers, the IRS.

Most of these everyday evaluations are casual, offhand expressions of taste such as "I liked *Out of Africa*. It's a good film." Usually, we state what we like or dislike without bothering to explain our judgment. Occasionally, however, someone asks the reason for an opinion and we can either say, "I don't know—I just know what I like," or we can offer an explanation and in so doing discover the basis for our judgment.

As a college student, you will be asked to write evaluations in many situations. You might be asked to evaluate a book or an article, judge a scientific hypothesis against the results of an experiment, evaluate the impact of a theory, or assess the value of two conflicting interpretations. You will also undoubtedly read evaluative writing in your courses and be tested on what you have read.

Written evaluations will almost certainly play an important part in your work. On the job, you will probably be evaluated periodically and

263

may have to evaluate people whom you supervise. It is also likely that you will be asked your opinion of various plans or proposals under consideration, and your ability to make fair and reasonable evaluations will affect your chances for promotion.

Learning to write and read evaluative writing is valuable in a more general way as well. Writing evaluations builds your confidence in your own judgment. By supporting your opinions instead of merely asserting them, you gain practice in reasoning systematically. You learn to examine your own assumptions, to discover what you think and why, and come to understand better your own values and to discover which ones others share. Finally, you learn to think critically, to question rather than simply accept what you are told. In this way, you learn to rely on your own authority.

# A GUIDE TO READING EVALUATIVE WRITING

To gain confidence as a critical reader of evaluative writing, you should learn to recognize its basic features and know what questions to ask as you read. This section presents the basic features of evaluative writing and a sample annotated essay that illustrates these features. The list of key questions appearing after the essay should help you read evaluative writing with a critical eye.

# *Basic Features of Evaluative Writing*

Just as an evaluation prompts readers to examine their own values, so too does it give writers the opportunity to convince others to accept their views. To accomplish these ends, evaluative essays generally include four basic features: *an adequately described subject, a definitive judgment, a convincing argument,* and *pointed comparisons.*

AN ADEQUATELY DESCRIBED SUBJECT. An evaluation always identifies the subject and usually describes it in some detail, depending on what the writer thinks readers need to know. In general, writers of evaluations provide only enough information to allow readers to understand and accept their judgment; they seldom include more information than is necessary to support their argument. Film and book reviews, however, may include more information than other kinds of evaluations because reviewers assume their readers want not only an evaluation but also a description of the film or book. Readers of film reviews, for example, usually want to know who the actors and director are, where the film takes place, and generally what happens in it.

A DEFINITIVE JUDGMENT.   An evaluation asserts a judgment about the value of the subject. This judgment is the main point, or thesis, of the evaluation. Although an evaluation may weigh the subject's good and bad qualities in order to give a balanced appraisal, a well-written evaluation does not equivocate but states its judgment directly.

A CONVINCING ARGUMENT.   An evaluation cannot merely state its judgment but must present a convincing argument. In order to be convincing, an evaluative argument must be based on reasonable criteria, provide supporting evidence, and gain the readers' confidence in the writer's authority.

Even the most casual evaluative statement—"that was a lousy film"—is based on certain criteria, the general standards by which a particular kind of subject like a film is commonly judged. An unfavorable film review might mention the film's unbelievable plot and the stiffness of the actors, implying that the reviewer's criteria for a good film include a believable plot and convincing acting. Occasionally, writers may need to define and defend their criteria. Some might argue, for instance, that whether a film's plot should be believable depends on the kind of film being evaluated. Most would agree that realistic films, as opposed to science fiction or fantasy, should have believable, realistic plots.

To apply these criteria to the particular subject of an evaluation, evidence must be cited. To support the assertion that a film's plot is unbelievable, the reviewer might cite as evidence a summary of the plot, highlighting the most unlikely incidents. Description, examples, facts, statistics, and testimony of witnesses and authorities can all be used as evidence in evaluative writing.

An evaluative argument also depends on the readers' confidence in the writer's expertise and fairness. Writers instill trust in their authority by demonstrating their knowledge of the subject and by showing their credentials—specialized training, advanced degrees, or years of experience. To demonstrate that their judgment is fair, writers of evaluation may also need to establish that they are impartial. A tone of reasonableness and authority in a writer's voice does a great deal to gain readers' trust.

POINTED COMPARISONS. Comparisons are not a requirement of evaluative writing, but they are often made because of the relative nature of this kind of writing. Particular subjects are judged in terms of the general category to which they belong and are usually compared to other instances of that category. In judging the believability of a film's plot, for example, a reviewer might compare that film to other similar films. You could compare the plots of two science fantasy films like *Star Wars* and *The Empire Strikes Back* or compare *Star Wars* to other stories about a young boy's coming of age like *Huckleberry Finn* and *Great Expectations*.

## An Annotated Reading:
### *Saint Ralph,* Michael Kinsley

Recognizing the basic features of evaluative writing helps you decide whether the selection you are reading is an evaluation and also immediately gives direction to your reading. As a critical reader, you should pay special attention to the writer's judgment and determine whether you accept it. Look now at one brief essay that has been annotated with the help of the critical reading questions that follow the selection. Read the selection all the way through, and then reread it while looking at the annotations.

"Saint Ralph," by Michael Kinsley, is an evaluation of Ralph Nader, the attorney and self-appointed consumer advocate, who began his career in 1965 by attacking auto industry executives for marketing a car (the Chevrolet Corvair) that they knew to be a safety hazard. Nader's book, *Unsafe at Any Speed*, contributed to the commercial failure of the Corvair and led to a series of laws mandating auto safety features. His activities spawned a generation of idealistic young consumer advocates, dubbed Nader's Raiders.

Kinsley, a former Nader's Raider, is now the editor of *The New Republic*, the journal in which this essay was first published. "Saint Ralph" is not a piece of personal reminiscence, however, but a hard-nosed evaluation of Nader as a public figure, written on the twentieth anniversary of Nader's landmark exposé of the auto industry. Even though Kinsley takes Nader seriously, he can't resist poking fun at him. As you read, notice the way he has seasoned his praise with a few grains of satire.

## *Saint Ralph*

| | |
|---|---|
| **Subject: Ralph Nader** Heard of him, but don't know much | Henry James wrote the meanest description of <u>Ralph Nader</u> (though one not perhaps without a certain measure of accuracy, as the master himself might put it) in his |

1886 novel, *The Bostonians*. James called the character Miss Birdseye:

| | |
|---|---|
| James's description satiric | "She always dressed in the same way: she wore a loose 2 black jacket, with deep pockets, which were stuffed with papers. . . . She belonged to the Short-Skirts League, as |
| backs any cause | a matter of course; for she belonged to any and every league that had been founded for almost any purpose |
| ignorant about people helping mankind | whatever. [Yet she] knew less about her fellow-creatures, if possible, after fifty years of humanitary zeal, than on |
| fervor for a cause | the day she had gone into the field to testify against the |
| gross injustice | iniquity of most arrangements. . . . No one had an idea |
| self-sacrificing | how she lived; whenever money was given her she gave it away. . . . There was a legend that an Hungarian had once possessed himself of her affections, [but] it was open |
| serious | to grave doubt that she could have entertained a senti- |
| can't love people, only causes | ment so personal. She was in love . . . only with causes. . . ." |
| satirized | Thus the social reformer, skewered. I worked several 3 |
| knows him personally | years for Ralph Nader, and he's actually quite warm and |
| fanatic | funny in person. Nevertheless, his is the classic zealot's |
| damning criticism | worldview (paranoid) and humorless, and his vision of the |
| thinks everyone's his enemy | ideal society—regulations for all contingencies of life, warning labels on every french fry, and a citizenry on hair-trigger alert for violations of its personal space—is not one many others would care to share with him. |
| Nader not a reasonable person | But reasonable people don't move the world. On the 4 20th anniversary of *Unsafe at Any Speed*, his tract against |
| High praise for a social reformer! | dangerous automobiles, no living American is responsible for more concrete improvements in the society we actually do inhabit than Ralph Nader. |
| directly addresses reader | In all statistical probability, at least several dozen of 5 you who are reading this issue of TNR would be dead today if Nader hadn't single-handedly invented the issue |
| lists Nader's reforms | of auto safety. His long campaign for mandatory air bags may bore most people and enrage a few. But would even these people want cars without seat belts, padded dashboards, collapsible steering wheels, and shatter-resistant |
| Even though he assumes reader would know who Nader is, he tells a lot. | glass? On matters ranging from the Occupational Safety and Health Administration to the Freedom of Information Act (just two of his monuments), Nader stands ac- |
| extremity maybe necessary | cused—sometimes justly—of going "too far." But without the people who go too far, we wouldn't go far enough. |
| | Although Nader's personal popularity has diminished, 6 |
| unchangeable | and the causes he favors are out of fashion, his achieve- |
| comparison to FDR's New Deal | ments are as immutable as FDR's. President Reagan may |
| attack, rail against | inveigh against burdensome government regulation, just as he inveighs against government spending. He may at- |

What did Nader do for clean air?

Times have changed, but even the most conservative politician or businessman appreciates Nader's reforms—or at least some of them.

impracticable, visionary—like Don Quixote

return to comparison with Miss Birdseye

N's weaknesses

1. blind to benefits

Ha! He has a sense of humor.

2. legal mind-set

true

giant, hero

N's status today

Ha!

tempt changes at the margin. But he would no more get the government out of the business of protecting consumers, workers, and the environment than he would dismantle Social Security. Americans like clean air and water, safe transportation, open government, honest advertisements, uncontaminated meat. No electable politician would attempt to push back the clock by 20 years.

I wonder how many conservative businessmen, even, 7 would care to return to the days when anyone could light up a cigarette next to you on a long airplane flight, and when an airline could overbook and bump you with no explanation or compensation. No-smoking sections and airline bumping rules—minor bits of Naderism—seemed like quixotic obsessions when first proposed. Now they are taken for granted.

Like James's Miss Birdseye, Nader knows little of or- 8 dinary human appetites. This gives him his fanatic's strength of purpose. But it also sometimes leads him astray by blinding him to the benefits that come with the risks he campaigns against. The pleasure of a hot dog means nothing to Ralph. (He calls it "America's most dangerous unguided missile.") If everyone lived like Ralph Nader, we could dispense with nuclear power and not worry about replacing the energy. In this world of sinners, though, not everyone wants to live on raw vegetables and set the thermostat at 60. Intelligent public policy requires trade-offs that the fanatic is ill-equipped and indisposed to make.

Nader's other great weakness as a reformer is that he's 9 a prisoner of the legal mind-set. He believes in the infinite power of lawyers to achieve both bad and good. "The ultimate goal of this movement," says a recent Nader press release, "is to give all citizens more rights and remedies for resolving their grievances and for achieving a better society." But it's open to doubt, to say the least, whether the better society is one where all grievances are thought of as a matter of legal rights and remedies, to be enforced by lawyers and judges.

These days Ralph Nader is something less than a co- 10 lossus bestriding American society, but still something more than another colorful Washington character. Over two decades he and his ever-replenished band of disciples have operated out of a series of ratty offices, generally moving in shortly before the developers arrive to tear the place down and put up another fancy building for fancy lawyers (some of them, no doubt, getting rich off the very laws and agencies Ralph created).

He still wears those awful suits and lives in that same   11
studio apartment. Some cynics think the asceticism is an
act. And it's true that his story about wearing shoes
bought at the Army PX in 1959 is wearing as thin as
those shoes must be. But if a good marketing sense were
a bar to canonization there would be few saints.

*self-denial*

*people who believe everyone has selfish motives*

*Ha! procedure by which person is declared a saint*

At age 52, Nader may be softening a little. He some-   12
times shows up at those business parties that pass for social
life in Washington. I even think I saw him eating a piece
of cheese at one a few weeks ago. His narrow lapels,
pointy shoes, and skinny ties are now the height of fashion, offering some hope that the day will come when his
clothes will be out again and his politics will be back.

*getting to be like everyone else*

For 20 years Washington has been wondering, Where's   13
the catch? Will he sell out for money, or will he run for
office? Those are the normal options. But Ralph Nader is
not a normal person. Operating on the mental fringe
where self-abnegation blurs into self-obsession, Ralph is
living proof that there isn't much difference between a
fanatic and a saint. I'll bet you Mother Teresa is impossible to deal with, too.

*criticism or praise?*
*self-denial*

*Who's she? another comparison*

**Final judgment: Nader is a great social reformer even if he is odd.**

# Critical Reading Questions

These questions focus attention on the basic features of evaluative
writing and raise critical issues to be aware of as you read and analyze
this kind of writing.

1. *Does the writer provide enough information about the subject? What kind
of information is presented?*

As a critical reader, you must determine whether you are told what
you need to know about the subject. Begin by skimming the essay to see
just how much information is provided and how much the writer assumes
readers already know about the subject. Note where important details
are left out or where you are told more than you need to know.

Kinsley apparently assumes that his readers have heard of Ralph Nader
(an appropriate assumption about readers of a magazine such as *The New
Republic*) and know something about his work. The essay opens not with
background information but with a satirical description, implying that
Kinsley assumes his readers are somewhat critical or at least bemused by
Nader's social reforming fervor. Kinsley does remind readers of Nader's
landmark exposé and mentions some of the reforms for which Nader is
responsible.

2. *What is the writer's judgment?*

The judgment is usually easy to find because most evaluations explicitly state and even restate it several times. Some evaluations, however, list good and bad qualities without appearing to make a definitive judgment. The writer may not be trying to equivocate or be obscure but may be genuinely ambivalent. Critical readers must find the evaluative statements and decide which are given the most weight.

Kinsley, for example, seems to be quite genuinely fond and admiring of Nader and just as genuinely exasperated by him. The evaluation is certainly a mixture of praise and criticism: it begins negatively with satire and name-calling, turns to praise in paragraph 4, and returns to criticism by paragraph 8. The marginal annotations note the evaluative statements—both positive and negative—and conclude that Kinsley's final judgment is more positive than negative.

3. *What are the criteria on which the judgment is based? How appropriate are they?*

As a critical reader, you should examine the criteria underlying the argument in order to determine what they are and whether they are appropriate for judging this kind of subject. Even if the criteria are not stated explicitly, you should be able to infer them from the essay.

Kinsley relies on three criteria: real accomplishments, personality, and mind-set. The criterion most appropriate for evaluating a social reformer, in our view and apparently in Kinsley's as well, is responsibility for actual improvements in society. On that score, Nader comes out very well. In terms of personality, Kinsley's judgment is surprising. He acknowledges that Nader's paranoia makes him a difficult person but points out that "reasonable people don't move the world." Finally, Kinsley suggests that Nader's greatest shortcoming is his legal mind-set, his belief that the only way to get things done is through legislation. This last criterion could have been developed further since it is not obvious what problems arise from this particular mind-set and what advantages other mind-sets might have.

4. *How well is the judgment supported?*

Evaluative arguments rely on many different kinds of evidence. Your job as a critical reader is to determine whether the evidence supplied is reliable, appropriate, and consistent—in a word, whether it is convincing.

In paragraph 5, Kinsley lists reforms for which Nader is responsible and indicates the wide range of Nader's influence. He also suggests the statistical probability, without actually citing statistics, that some of these reforms may have saved readers' lives. In discussing Nader's public and private personality, Kinsley is able to give eyewitness testimony.

5. *If comparisons are used, what do they add to the argument?*

Writers of evaluations typically use comparison to assess the subject's value relative to the value of another well-known subject. Comparison may be used in this way to praise or to condemn.

Kinsley uses comparison for both of these purposes. By quoting Henry James's satiric description of the social reformer, he draws attention to those aspects of Nader's character that most people regard as eccentric and unpleasant. But by comparing Nader's achievements to those of President Franklin D. Roosevelt, Kinsley reminds readers of the astonishing fact that Nader, without the power of public office, has been able to accomplish so much. Finally, by suggesting a parallel between Nader and Mother Teresa, the Roman Catholic nun who won the Nobel Peace Prize for her work with the poor in India, Kinsley implies that Nader's strange and difficult personality may in fact be one reason for his success.

6. *How confident are you of the writer's authority? What impression do you have of the writer from the tone of the essay?*

When you read an evaluative piece, you make your own evaluation of the subject, and you do this partially by judging the writer. If you trust that the writer knows the subject and is fair and unbiased, then you will be likely to accept the judgment. As a critical reader, therefore, you form an opinion of the writer both from what is said and how it is said.

Kinsley's satiric treatment demonstrates from the start that although he once worked with Nader, he can be objective and even critical of him. Although his wit is sharp, it does not seem cruel or unjust. It is clear, moreover, that not only does he know Nader personally, but he also understands how Nader operates and how he uses his public personality to get things done.

7. *How effectively is the evaluation organized?*

There are no formats or simple rules that writers of evaluation can follow. In general, they try to emphasize their strongest arguments by placing them either at the beginning or at the ending of the essay. Most evaluations set out their judgment early in the essay and restate it in summary form at the end. A brief description of the subject may open the essay, but evaluations usually weave information about the subject into the argument as evidence to support the judgment. To guide the reader—particularly if the essay is long and complicated—statements forecasting the main points of the argument and signaling shifts from one point to another may be injected at crucial intervals.

Although Kinsley does not explicitly forecast his argument at the beginning of the essay, the James quotation in effect serves as a kind of forecast, suggesting some of the criteria by which social reformers like

Nader might be judged. In particular, it points to the apparent contradiction between the typical reformer's "humanitarian zeal" and inability to get along with or care about people. Kinsley focuses on just this paradox when he discusses Nader's paranoid personality and his effectiveness as a social reformer. This opening also enables Kinsley to disarm readers who have already formed a negative judgment of Nader. He follows this opening with his strongest arguments for praising Nader, and then returns at the end to some minor criticisms. Thus, as you can see, Kinsley breaks even the most general rule about placing your best arguments in the beginning or ending—the positions of greatest emphasis—rather than in the middle where they could get lost.

# Stanley Kauffmann

Stanley Kauffmann (b. 1916), one of America's premier film critics, has written a weekly column for *The New Republic* since 1958 and occasionally teaches film criticism at the New School for Social Research in New York. Both the Ford Foundation and Yale University have honored him for his film criticism. In addition to being a film critic, Kauffmann has been an actor, director, playwright, and novelist. His books include several collections of film and theater criticism—*A World on Film* (1966), *Figures of Light* (1971), *Persons of the Drama* (1976), *Before My Eyes* (1980), and *Theater Criticisms* (1983)—as well as a few novels and plays.

A scholar with a vast knowledge of film, Kauffmann speaks authoritatively on every facet of film-making from screenwriting to acting to cinematography. At the same time, he is interested in film as a reflection of and an influence upon cultural values and attitudes.

# Dr. Strangelove

This selection is an example of a common kind of evaluative writing—the film review. The subject of Kauffmann's review is *Dr. Strangelove: Or How I Learned to Stop Worrying and Love the Bomb*, a film released late in 1963. This review first appeared in *The New Republic* and was later published in *A World on Film*.

A popular success, *Dr. Strangelove* received Academy Award nominations for best picture, best screenplay, best director, and best actor (Peter Sellers). It was also a highly controversial film. The controversy revolved around the film's subject—nuclear war—and how the film, which offers a bizarre vision of a world gone mad, treats this subject. Some reviewers praised *Dr. Strangelove* as a forceful antiwar film, while others thought it too self-indulgent and hopeless. Pauline Kael, the influential film reviewer for the *New Yorker*, criticized the film for being too pessimistic, for "chortling over madness" without "any possibilities for sanity."

Before reading the essay, reflect on the criteria you typically use when evaluating films. How appropriate does it seem to you to judge a film according to whether it is optimistic or pessimistic? If a film makes a political statement, on what basis do you think it should be judged?

Stanley Kubrick's film *Dr. Strangelove* is the best American picture that 1 I can remember since Chaplin's *Monsieur Verdoux* and Huston's *Treasure of the Sierra Madre* (both 1947). The screenplay is by Kubrick, Terry Southern (whose touch is tartly manifest), and Peter George, and is derived from George's novel *Red Alert* (originally published as *Two Hours to Doom* by "Peter Bryant"), which had roughly the same plot basis as *Fail-Safe* and had it earlier. A nuclear attack is accidentally launched on Russia; in order to avert retaliation and total war, the American President calls the Soviet Premier to warn him that the unintended attack is coming and to help him destroy the US planes. But one plane gets through, drops its megaton message, and detonates the Soviet Doomsday Machine, a thermonuclear device which, once triggered, cannot be untriggered and which will blanket the earth with radioactive material for ninety-three years. This film is a comedy.

A comedy, not a satire. Satire, in Fowler's good definition, is aimed ₂ at amendment. It is written by men about men for the improvement of their world. *Dr. Strangelove* has been made, quintessentially, from the viewpoint of another race on another planet or in another universe, observing how mankind, its reflexes scored in its nervous system and its mind entangled in orthodoxies, insisted on destroying itself. The film, therefore, does not hope to alter men; it is simply a (distant?) future report on what happened; as recounted by Mark Twain's Satan to a moderately interested Lord or by an amused scout to Hardy's President of the Immortals. It is so truthful a film, so unsparing, so hopeless in the last pit-bottom depths of that word, that the very blackness has a kind of shine. It is to the vestige or promise of the Olympian in us that it speaks, and it is that possibly saving remnant in us that it makes laugh.

Thus the comedy, which might also be called *Whatever Happened to* ₃ *Man?*, is that, as we watch man's fate overtake him and vice versa, we note his ingenuity (very cute), his irrationality (incredible), his idealism (pathetic). Tragedy might have been possible in this history of his if perfection had been possible in his future, but the point seems to be that this is "the promised end." There is nothing to prevent the film's being seen as a cautionary tale; still its subject matter is the so-far incurable in us. The text might have been taken from Shaw's Devil in *Man and Superman*:

> The power that governs the earth is not the power of Life but of Death; and the inner need that has nerved Life to the effort of organizing itself into the human being is not the need for higher life but for a more efficient engine of destruction.

This is not a film to please Peace Marchers or Nuclear Disarmers. It does not tell what we must do to be saved. Nor is it a comfort for those who find smug superiority in irony: from the juvenile insipidities of Carl Foreman on film to the obscenity-decked verbal cartoons of Lenny Bruce in night clubs. This film says, "Ban the bomb and they'll find another way. The real Doomsday Machine is men."

The story takes place in three principal settings. (The college-humor proper names that follow are not, in my view, attempts to amuse; they are indications of amusement—derogations rather than jokes.) These settings are: the office of General Jack D. Ripper, Commander of Burpelson Air Base; the Pentagon War Room with a conference headed by President Merkin Muffley (erotica students, observe) and Chief of Staff "Buck" Turgidson (observe again), attended by the Russian Ambassador and a top US scientific advisor, Dr. Strangelove, a cripple in a wheel chair whose name originally was Dr. Merkwuerdigichliebe and who has the accent to prove it. The third setting is the interior of the one plane that, maimed, fights through to drop a bomb under the command of Major "King" Kong, a Texan to end all Texans, which—along with many others—he does. General Ripper is a kind of triple-distilled Bircher, convinced of a Communist plot to take over the country as proved by fluoridation of water. He feels that our government is laggard, that his only recourse is to launch an attack by his own group, thus forcing the US inevitably to implement the attack and thus making himself a maligned but justified savior of all things decent. On his staff is a British exchange officer, Captain Mandrake, who quickly sees that Ripper has gone mad and tries to wheedle out of him the recall code for the planes. Meanwhile, under direct presidential order, other US troops are storming the air base to capture Ripper. He commits suicide before they break in. Mandrake then puzzles out the proper code from some pet phrases of the General and telephones them to the Pentagon—with the reluctant permission of his captor, Colonel "Bat" Guano—in time to have all but one of the planes recalled.

The film bristles along on sharp points before, during, and after the events above. The President's homey telephone conversations with Premier Kissoff; the Russian Ambassador's mania for espionage with tiny cameras; Turgidson's automatic joy that one of his planes has broken through the Russian defenses; the navigator carefully correcting an error in his log as the wounded plane approaches its goal and certain end. All these are inescapably (it seems) hilarious and all are further proof, to cite Shaw's Devil again, of man's chief inventions:

> . . . of the sword and gun; above all, of justice, duty, patriotism and all the other isms by which even those who are clever enough to be humanely disposed are persuaded to become the most destructive of all destroyers.

Kubrick's films up to now have given strong evidence of his incisiveness, his mordant humor, his felicitous eye, his cool maneuver of dramatic impact. The script of *Paths of Glory* (1957) had all the simplistic and banal antiwar propaganda that *Dr. Strangelove* transcends, but it was

executed with ruthless, vivid immediacy. *Spartacus* (1960) was the best
of the post-television film spectacles, an entertaining, if mindless, show
with many well-done scenes, intimate and panoramic. *Lolita* (1962) was
tantalizingly unsatisfactory, but in such sequences as the opening murder,
it predicted the qualities that have now suavely exploded in his new film.
*Dr. Strangelove* is, first and foremost, absolutely unflinching: relentlessly
perceptive of human beings to the point of inhumanity. In technique, it
understates provocatively and comments by apposition. Kubrick's precise
use of camera angles, his uncanny sense of lighting, his punctuation with
close-ups and occasionally with zoom shots, all galvanize the picture into
macabre yet witty reality.

There are shortcomings. The casting of Sterling Hayden as Ripper   7
was, in a way, too right. The rest of the cast, because they are comedians,
comment on their parts as they play them. Hayden, evidently humorless,
presents Ripper the only way he can: as deadly realistically as he would
in any Stanley Kramer antiwar film. If George C. Scott, who is excellent
as Turgidson, had played Ripper, the fanatic would have been flayed as
well as portrayed. Even Keenan Wynn, nicely deadpan as Guano, could
have improved the part. Hayden's chief asset is that he looks exactly
right—like a famous reactionary columnist, in fact.

Peter Sellers plays three roles, Mandrake, Muffley, and the title role,   8
and differentiates them miraculously. His RAF-type is renowned and here
is extremely subtly rendered. His American and German accents are
familiar from *Lolita* and again are frighteningly accurate. Strangelove is
viciously complete; but the well-meaning President lacks points of character geography, and might have been improved with specific references
to latter-day presidents and public figures.

The "newsreel" shots of the US soldiers attacking the US base seem   9
out of place, not so much because the comedy is chilled by the sight of
actual deaths but because individual deaths are on too small a scale for
this comedy. The bomber crew are somewhat incongruously "straight" as
against their somewhat cartoon commander. The mushroom explosions
at the end, over a chorus of *We'll Meet Again*, go on about twice as long
as necessary.

But all these defects only keep the film from perfecton, not from power   10
or from blow-torch assault.

In its mode it stands alone, too much so, among recent American   11
films. In the American novel, recent work by Terry Southern himself,
Joseph Heller, J. P. Donleavy, and Elliott Baker is creating a kind of
modern Swiftian tradition. (An antecedent not lost in this film: the
plane's first target is "Laputa.") But *Dr. Strangelove* is not eminent merely
because of the flatness of surrounding movie country—it is a fine achieve-

ment: a fiery laugh at those humans down there, parochially self-righteous and self-condemned.

As expected, controversy about *Dr. Strangelove* has arisen here and abroad. To those who do not find it funny or artistically fine, I can offer only condolences and my best wishes for speedy reincarnation. To those who claim that its content is too ridiculous for credibility, I recommend the newspapers. In the same week in which the US takes economic action against nations who trade with Cuba because Castro is spreading Soviet Communism, we also sell a huge lot of wheat to Soviet Russia. Were those actions determined by Stanley Kubrick and Terry Southern or Johnson and Rusk?

But the most resounding answer to the claim that the film's parody is baseless is contained in Lewis Mumford's letter in the March 1, 1964, *New York Times*. I quote two passages for those who may have missed this important letter:

> Dr. Strangelove would be a silly, ineffective picture if its purpose were to ridicule the characters of our military and political leaders by showing them as clownish monsters—stupid, psychotic, obsessed. For we know that most of them are in fact intelligent, devoted men, with only a normal proneness to suspicion, pride, and error. What has masked the hideous nature of our demoralized strategy of total extermination is just the fact that it has been the work of otherwise well-balanced, responsible men, beginning with Henry L. Stimson.
>
> What the wacky characters in *Dr. Strangelove* are saying is precisely what needs to be said: this nightmare eventuality that we have concocted for our children is nothing but a crazy fantasy, by nature as horribly crippled and dehumanized as Dr. Strangelove himself. It is not this film that is sick: what is sick is our supposedly moral, democratic country which allowed this policy to be formulated and implemented without even the pretense of open public debate.
>
> This film is the first break in the catatonic cold war trance that has so long held our country in its rigid grip.

If that is anti-American, it is also anti-British, anti-French, anti-Russian, anti-Chinese—anti all obsolescent political solipsisms. Mr. Mumford's letter is one more item in our long debt to this civilized and civilizing man.

There were further objections, from observers more enlightened than those to whom Mr. Mumford was replying. These objections were generally of three kinds: Kubrick's ideas were too simple ("pop nihilism" was one critical phrase), his targets were too easy, and he used some glib character stereotypes. The first comment made an unwarranted assumption about this kind of art, whose function is to flay with derision. What depth have the political or social ideas in, say, Brecht's *A Man's a Man?*

The chief criteria are the aim of the work and the quality of execution. The aim of *Dr. Strangelove* is salutary, I think, and its execution first class. To the second objection, events themselves keep proposing an answer. The recent conduct of international affairs has, in some respects, outdone broad political cartoon. To insist on more subtlety in this respect than is evident in President Muffley or General Turgidson is to insist on a depth—for the sake of one's own intellectual dignity—that simply is not reflected in the facts. As for the third objection, which usually centered on the use of a German as the scientific evil genius and a Texan as the action-happy pilot, doubtless there is in life more variety than any one selection could satisfy; but Kubrick's selection does not strain credibility.

Most serious objections to this film seem to me not so much criticism    16
as an indication of the need for more films in similar vein.

QUESTIONS FOR ANALYSIS

1. What is Kauffmann's ultimate judgment of *Dr. Strangelove?* On what criteria does he base this judgment? Do you accept these criteria as appropriate for judging a film like this? Why or why not?

2. Most people expect film reviews to provide information about new films as well as judgments. Locate the places in the review where Kauffmann gives information about the film's plot and cast of characters, and put brackets around the details that you as one reader feel are necessary. On what basis did you decide which information was necessary? If possible, compare your responses with those of other readers to get a sense of the kind of information readers in general expect from film reviews.

3. In paragraph 5, Kauffmann lists several incidents from the film as "proof." What are they supposed to prove? Do you feel that you know enough about the film for these incidents to carry the weight of proof? What could Kauffmann have told you to make these incidents illustrate his point more effectively? (Chapter 1 discusses evidence.)

4. According to Kauffmann, what is the difference between comedy and satire? How would you define comedy and satire? Do you think the two differ in the way that Kauffmann suggests? Why do you suppose Kauffmann bothers to differentiate these two terms?

5. Throughout the essay, Kauffmann compares *Dr. Strangelove* to other films, books, and plays. Skim the essay, making an inventory of these comparisons and the purpose you think each serves. What do you

think Kauffmann gains by sprinkling his essay with comparisons? What does he lose? (See Taking Inventory in Chapter 1.)

6. Where in the review does Kauffmann respond to criticism of the film? What do you think are his strongest arguments? his weakest? How could these be strengthened?

7. How would you characterize the tone of this review? How is it like or unlike other film reviews with which you are familiar?

8. The sentences in the first two paragraphs are all relatively long, with only two exceptions. Find these exceptions, and conjecture about the effect of inserting two short sentences in the midst of so many longer ones. Notice also that one of the two is actually an incomplete sentence. What does Kauffmann gain by using an incomplete sentence? What does he lose?

## SUGGESTIONS FOR WRITING

1. Choose a film, play, or television program, and write a review of it. Be sure that the subject you choose is one you know very well or can study closely. If you choose a film or play, for example, try to go to more than one performance. Take thorough notes so that you can refer in your review to specific facts and details.

2. Find a newspaper or magazine review of a film, play, or television program you have seen recently, and write an essay evaluating this review. If possible, see the film or play again after you have studied the review to reaffirm your judgment and gather specific evidence for your essay. Address your essay to readers who have not read the review and are probably unfamiliar with the work it evaluates.

3. Find two reviews of the same film, play, or performance. Decide which of the two is the better review, and write an evaluative essay explaining your choice. Your evaluation of these reviews will be more detailed and authoritative if you can see the film, play, or performance again after you have read the reviews.

# Kim Marshall

An authority on education, Kim Marshall (b. 1948) was educated at Harvard and then taught sixth grade at Martin Luther King School in Boston, where he also served as curriculum coordinator. Since 1980, he has been curriculum director for the Boston public school system. In addition to teaching and developing school curricula, Marshall is a contributing editor to *Learning* magazine and has written several books on education, including *Law and Order in Grade 6E* (1972) and *The Story of Life* (1980). "The inspiration of my writing," Marshall explains, "has come from my eleven years of work in an inner-city Boston public school. I have become fascinated with classroom organization, kids, and curriculum, and have been anxious to share my experiences with others."

# *Literacy: The Price of Admission*

The following selection is a book review—another common kind of evaluation. Marshall reviews *Illiterate America* by Jonathan Kozol, also a well-known educator. (An excerpt from Kozol's book can be found in Chapter 7 of this text.) This book calls attention to the surprising fact that many Americans can neither read nor write, a situation that produces enormous problems not only for the illiterate individuals but also for the nation as a whole. Kozol does not seek merely to establish illiteracy as a major problem; he also suggests ways of solving it.

In his review, Marshall evaluates Kozol's book on the basis of how it succeeds as a proposal—how well it establishes the existence of the problem and how convincing a case it makes for the proposed solution. Marshall's review appeared in *Harvard Magazine* during the summer of 1985, shortly after Kozol's book was published.

Book reviewers, like film reviewers, usually assume that their readers are unfamiliar with the books they are evaluating and therefore describe their subjects in some detail. As you read Marshall's essay, notice how much he reveals about the contents of Kozol's book. But before you begin, ask yourself what Marshall's title, "Literacy: The Price of Admission," might mean. To what does knowing how to read and write gain admission? What happens to people in our society who don't know how to read and write? Why should illiteracy be a social as well as a personal problem?

"A third of the nation cannot read these words." So begins the first 1 chapter of Jonathan Kozol's new book, *Illiterate America,* and we are immediately skeptical of the figure. But in short order, Kozol produces a blizzard of statistics showing that 25 million adult Americans can barely read at all, while another 35 million are "semi-literate," that is, unable to read at the level demanded by our technological society. That adds up to 60 million illiterate or marginally literate adults, disproportionately black and other minority, who are "substantially excluded from the democratic process and the economic commerce of a print society." Kozol argues that even these shocking figures are conservative estimates, since the census and other surveys tend to underestimate this mute population in our midst.

Kozol acknowledges that the first category—true illiteracy—has shrunk in recent years, but the second—functional illiteracy—has grown because of the steadily increasing demands of our society. Kozol ticks off the benchmarks of literacy: a ninth-grade reading level is required to understand the antidote instructions on a bottle of corrosive kitchen lye; a tenth-grade level is needed to understand the instructions on federal income tax forms; many newspapers are written at a tenth- to twelfth-grade level; and a twelfth-grade level is required to understand life insurance forms and the national newsmagazines. He quotes the educational director of the AFL-CIO as saying that by the 1990s, anyone who doesn't have at least a twelfth-grade reading, writing, and calculating level will be absolutely lost.

None of this material is accessible to sixty million adult Americans. The illiterate do not have access to important information on nutrition, bargains, travel, safety, work, entertainment, health insurance, medical consent forms, and educational and political choices. They are unable to make intelligent decisions to better their lives. Illiterate people are easy marks for consumer fraud, and don't have the skills to catch errors and prevent themselves from being cheated.

The illiterate are also saddled with shame and self-hatred. People who emerge from schools without the ability to read have to ask themselves, as Kozol frames it, "Am I inherently deficient? Am I lacking in intelligence? in energy? in will? If the answer is yes, I am inferior. If the answer is no, I am the victim of injustice." It is an unusual person who will draw the second conclusion, and for this reason, the illiterate are less likely than any other disadvantaged group to organize politically to improve their lot.

Most devastating is the effect of illiteracy on the next generation. The children of poor and marginal readers begin school with a tremendous disadvantage, and it is a remarkable school that can make up for these deficits. In addition, illiterate parents are hesitant to visit their children's classrooms, having developed a distaste for schools from having done poorly themselves, and are often ineffective in bringing their concerns to the attention of teachers and principals.

Kozol argues that the price we pay for this extraordinary level of illit-  6
eracy includes child welfare; the costs of crime (the prison population,
Kozol says, represents the single highest concentration of adult illiterates); unemployment benefits; health costs; worker's compensation due
to damage to equipment and accidents attributable to poor reading skills;
and much more.

What is being done about illiteracy now? Kozol puts the four major  7
efforts under his analytical lens and finds them all wanting. He does give
credit to several good initiatives, and is especially complimentary of a
1983 alliance of a number of adult literacy groups with the American
Library Association and B. Dalton, the bookseller. But he feels that these
efforts are grossly underfunded and are reaching far too few people. He
calculates that present efforts to combat illiteracy are spending only $1.65
for each needy person.

Kozol finds the definition of literacy used by most programs wanting.  8
Teaching the skills needed to fill out job applications and welfare forms,
he states, is a trivialization of literacy. His list of desiderata for true
literacy aims much higher (and is, incidentally, something any public
high school curriculum should contain). This book is impressive for the
number of practical suggestions it offers for solving the illiteracy problem.
The specific ideas give credibility to Kozol's oft-repeated assertion that
we do not need another blue-ribbon commission to study this problem;
we know what to do right now. He believes that, with the proper programs and a real national commitment, we could substantially conquer
illiteracy by the year 2000.

Kozol believes that illiterate people desperately want to escape their  9
condition, and could be persuaded to participate in literacy programs that
have a number of important characteristics:

—Carefully chosen people recruiting door-to-door in target neighborhoods

—Noninstitutional settings (church basements, vacant apartments),
which students would refurbish

—Day care, potluck dinners, and other community-building devices;
concrete rewards (a bookshelf for a child, for example); and occasional
guest speakers

—Teachers who work with collegial groups of six or seven, not one-
on-one

—Active participation of the elderly, and of college and high school
students who would receive academic credit for tutoring

—"Two-way tutoring" of less skillful readers (both tutor and tutee
improve in such situations)

—Teachers from public schools, whose long-term interests are at stake

—An integrated approach to the teaching of reading, writing, and critical thinking

—The use of language experience and new oral history methods

—The use of politically charged words ("rent," "landlord," "eviction") to draw on people's experiences and engage and empower them (Kozol sees the process of motivating nonreaders as inherently political)

—The "one-way library," giving out overstock hardcover books that publishers shred by the thousands.

Kozol describes one Boston program using these ideas which in sixty    10 days of three-hours sessions in a church basement brought 250 adolescents from the third- to the sixth-grade reading level. But he is under no illusions that neighborhood barn raisings are enough to fund a nationwide network of such centers. He knows that the literacy problem must be put on a par with health care, environmental concerns, and defense. He calculates that meeting the needs of the thirty million worst-off illiterates would cost $10 billion a year and would require five million workers, as well as in-kind contributions from publishers, more action-oriented research, and universities encouraging their students to serve as volunteers. Kozol admits that none of these goals is realistic now, but thinks even a partial implementation of his proposal could make a substantial dent in the problem, reducing the number of illiterate people by one half. His book is a rousing call to arms for such a commitment.

Unfortunately, Kozol doesn't demand nearly enough of the institutions    11 responsible for teaching people to read in the first place—the public schools. Most Americans feel it is nothing short of a national scandal when children drift through school without learning to read, but Kozol throws up his hands and concentrates all his energy on adult literacy efforts. He does not mention an exciting wave of positive thinking and effective methodology in urban public school systems stemming from the work of Ronald Edmonds, Michael Rutter, and others. This research has found schools in urban areas that get excellent (and equitable) results despite the odds, and identified the factors that seem to be making a difference. Public school educators are increasingly taking responsibility for the learning of their least advantaged students, rather than making excuses for their not learning because of home environment, television, and so forth. Kozol has much to offer us in our uphill battle. I just wish there was more of a feeling in his book that we are all in this together, working toward the same goal.

Kozol's blanket indictment of computers and television as useless tools    12 for improving literacy is valid up to a point; many educators agree that most current instructional software is dreadful, and television remains a cold and one-way medium ill-suited to the needs of the illiterate. But he totally fails to mention word processing—a splendid application of computers to classrooms. There is growing evidence that the ability to edit one's writing so readily is having a very positive effect on the writing of millions of schoolchildren (as well as adults), and that in this respect computers are a liberating and empowering tool.

Kozol also minimizes the value of the rich nonprint environment in    13 which we all move—radio, television, movies, and conversation. An illiterate person *can* make reasonably intelligent voting decisions by watching speeches, press conferences, newscasts, debates, and competing advertisements, and so is not totally disenfranchised. Kozol also does not discuss the phenomenon of *aliteracy*, where millions of Americans know how to read but choose not to, and survive very well.

Kozol is a powerful and brilliant writer, but he sometimes gets carried    14 away and weakens his case. (At several points he comes dangerously close to implying that every industrial accident and billing error in the United States can be traced to illiterate workers.) He is prone to ringing words of a radical bent, and some readers who need to hear his message might close their minds because of this. (An example: "We do know this: Democracy is a mendacious term when used by one third of our electorate.") And Kozol's explanation of why we have the illiteracy problem we do hardly points toward the kind of nitty-gritty solution he proposes:

> Illiteracy among the poorest in our population is a logical consequence of the kinds of schools we run, the cities that starve them, the demogogues who segregate them, and the wealthy people who escape them altogether to enroll their kids in better funded, up-to-date, and more proficient institutions. It is a consequence, too, of economic planning which for many decades has regarded certain sectors of the population as expendable, or at least extraneous to the perpetuation of the social order.

All this notwithstanding, Kozol's is a tremendously important book    15 that deserves to make a difference. Almost twenty years ago, his first book, *Death at an Early Age*, led many idealistic young Americans to think of urban teaching as a high calling and got some of them into public education. My sense is that this tenacious visionary has again put his finger on a national issue of compelling moral importance. I only hope that *Illiterate America* will stir the current generation of latent idealists toward adult literacy action—and toward work in the beleaguered public schools. Our children deserve no less.

## QUESTIONS FOR ANALYSIS

1. Marshall begins his review by quoting a statistic from Kozol but then is "immediately skeptical of [this] figure." Skim the essay, noting other places where Marshall cites statistics from Kozol's book. How does Kozol use these statistics? Does Marshall really treat them skeptically? Should he? Why, or why not?

2. Readers unfamiliar with the book may find it hard to judge how well Marshall summarizes Kozol's argument that illiteracy is a widespread and serious problem in America. You can, however, decide whether Marshall's presentation is in itself coherent and convincing. Make an outline of the main points in the argument as Marshall presents it, and note how each point is supported. (See Analyzing an Argument in Chapter 1.) Indicate which points you find convincing, and why.

3. Kozol claims that the definition most literacy programs use trivializes the problem. How does Kozol define literacy? What are the strengths and weaknesses of this definition? How would you define it yourself?

4. From the list of characteristics of a good literacy program (paragraph 9), choose two that you think are especially important. Explain why you think each is important and what it would add to a literacy program.

5. Among the criteria for a good proposal is that the proposed solution be workable and not too expensive. What is Marshall's view of the feasibility of Kozol's proposal? What is your view?

6. What are Marshall's chief criticisms of Kozol's proposal? How does Marshall try to convince the reader that these criticisms are well taken? To what extent do Marshall's criticisms seriously undermine your confidence in Kozol's proposals?

7. Marshall suggests that literacy to Kozol has a political component. Why might Kozol think there is a connection between literacy and politics? Do you see such a connection? How does Marshall treat this idea in his evaluation of Kozol's book?

8. How would you characterize the tone of this essay? Is it consistent throughout, or does it modulate? How does Marshall's tone (or tones) contribute to or detract from the persuasiveness of his evaluation?

## SUGGESTIONS FOR WRITING

1. Choose an essay in this collection or a book you know well, and write an evaluation of the work. Select a work you can reread and analyze carefully. Address your review to readers who may not have read the text.

2. Use Kozol's criteria to evaluate your own literacy education. If his criteria do not apply to your experience, identify the criteria that do and use them in your evaluation.

3. Marshall suggests that computers, television, radio, and movies can be useful in the campaign against illiteracy. Write an essay about the value of one or more of these tools for improving literacy.

# Carlos Baker

Carlos Baker (b. 1909) is a respected literary scholar and English professor. Now retired, he held for many years the prestigious position of Woodrow Wilson Professor of Literature at Princeton University. He devoted most of his career to studying the American writer Ernest Hemingway, who won the Nobel Prize for Literature in 1954. Hemingway is probably best known for his novels *The Sun Also Rises* and *For Whom the Bell Tolls* and for his short stories. His story "A Clean, Well-Lighted Place" is reprinted in Chapter 10. Baker has written numerous articles and three books on Hemingway: the critical study *Hemingway: The Writer as Artist* (1952), the definitive biography *Ernest Hemingway: A Life Story* (1968), and the collection *Ernest Hemingway: Selected Letters* (1981). Baker is also a novelist and a poet, with two novels and one collection of poetry to his credit.

# The Way It Was

This selection opens the third chapter of *Hemingway: The Writer as Artist*. In this book, Baker analyzes Hemingway's writing and assesses his development as an artist. According to Baker, the job of the literary critic is "to separate out the elements of success and the elements of failure, and . . . finally, to recognize, what is not always immediately apparent, that each individual writer has his individual law of progress, and must be allowed to move in his own way in the performance of whatever wonders it is given him to perform."

In this excerpt, Baker focuses on Hemingway's craftsmanship, evaluating it in terms of the author's own aesthetic principles. To illustrate his judgments, Baker draws examples from two major Hemingway works: *The Sun Also Rises*, generally believed to be Hemingway's best novel, and *Death in the Afternoon*, a nonfiction treatment of bullfighting that has been called the best book on the subject in any language.

Before you begin reading, consider what the title "The Way It Was" implies. Also, skim the essay noting how often Baker quotes from other sources in this essay. You might expect a literary critic to quote from the author he is evaluating, but why might he also quote from other critics or authors?

> *"The job of the last twenty-five years was for the writer or artist to get what there was to be got (artistically) out of the world extant."*
>
> EZRA POUND

"A writer's job is to tell the truth," said Hemingway in 1942. He had     1
believed it for twenty years and he would continue to believe it as long

287

as he lived. No other writer of our time had so fiercely asserted, so pugnaciously defended, or so consistently exemplified the writer's obligation to speak truly. His standard of truth-telling remained, moreover, so high and so rigorous that he was ordinarily unwilling to admit secondary evidence, whether literary evidence or evidence picked up from other sources than his own experience. "I only know what I have seen," was a statement which came often to his lips and pen. What he had personally done, or what he knew unforgettably by having gone through one version of it, was what he was interested in telling about. This is not to say that he refused to invent freely. But he always made it a sacrosanct point to invent in terms of what he actually knew from having been there.

The primary intent of his writing, from first to last, was to seize and project for the reader what he often called "the way it was." This is a characteristically simple phrase for a concept of extraordinary complexity, and Hemingway's conception of its meaning subtly changed several times in the course of his career—always in the direction of greater complexity. At the core of the concept, however, one can invariably discern the operation of three esthetic instruments: the sense of place, the sense of fact, and the sense of scene.   2

The first of these, obviously a strong passion with Hemingway, is the sense of place. "Unless you have geography, background," he once told George Antheil, "you have nothing." You have, that is to say, a dramatic vacuum. Few writers have been more place-conscious. Few have so carefully charted out the geographical groundwork of their novels while managing to keep background so conspicuously unobtrusive. Few, accordingly, have been able to record more economically and graphically the way it is when you walk through the streets of Paris in search of breakfast at a corner café. Or when your footfalls echo among surrounding walls on the ancient cobblestones of early morning Venice, heading for the market-place beside the Adriatic. Or when, at around six o'clock of a Spanish dawn, you watch the bulls running from the corrals at the Puerta Rochapea through the streets of Pamplona towards the bullring.   3

"When I woke it was the sound of the rocket exploding that announced the release of the bulls from the corrals at the edge of town. . . . Down below the narrow street was empty. All the balconies were crowded with people. Suddenly a crowd came down the street. They were all running, packed close together. They passed along and up the street toward the bullring and behind them came more men running faster, and then some stragglers who were really running. Behind them was a little bare space, and then the bulls, galloping, tossing their heads up and down. It all went out of sight around the corner. One man fell, rolled to the gutter,   4 and lay quiet. But the bulls went right on and did not notice him. They were all running together."

This scene is as morning-fresh as a design in India ink on clean white paper. First is the bare white street, seen from above, quiet and empty. Then one sees the first packed clot of runners. Behind these are the thinner ranks of those who move faster because closer to the bulls. Then the almost comic stragglers, who are "really running." Brilliantly behind these shines the "little bare space," a desperate margin for error. Then the clot of running bulls—closing the design, except of course for the man in the gutter making himself, like the designer's initials, as inconspicuous as possible.

The earliest of his published work, descriptively speaking, shows an almost neoclassical restraint. Take a sample passage from *The Sun Also Rises*, not his earliest but fairly representative. This one concerns the Irati Valley fishing-trip of Jake Barnes and Bill Gorton.

"It was a beech wood and the trees were very old. Their roots bulked above the ground and the branches were twisted. We walked on the road between the thick trunks of the old beeches and the sunlight came through the leaves in light patches on the grass. The trees were big, and the foliage was thick but it was not gloomy. There was no undergrowth, only the smooth grass, very green and fresh, and the big gray trees were well spaced as though it were a park. 'This is country,' Bill said."

It is such country as an impressionist might paint almost exactly in the terms, and the subdued colors, which Hemingway employs. More than this, however, is the fact that in such a paragraph Dr. Samuel Johnson's Imlac could find little to criticize. Even the arrangement of the beech trees themselves, like the choice of the words, is clean and classical. The foliage is thick, but there is no gloom. Here is neither teeming undergrowth nor its verbal equivalent. The sage of Johnson's *Rasselas* advises all aspirant poets against numbering the streaks of the tulip or describing in detail the different shades of the verdure of the forest. Young Hemingway, still an aspirant poet, follows the advice. When he has finished, it is possible to say (and we supply our own inflection for Bill Gorton's words): "This is country."

For all the restraint, the avoidance of color-flaunting adjectives, and the plainsong sentences (five compound to one complex), the paragraph is loaded with precisely observed fact: beech wood, old trees, exposed roots, twisted branches, thick trunks, sun-patches, smooth green grass, foliage which casts a shade without excluding light. One cannot say that he has been given a generalized landscape—there are too many exact factual observations. On the other hand, the uniquenesses of the place receive no special emphasis. One recognizes easily the generic type of the clean and orderly grove, where weeds and brush do not flourish because of the shade, and the grass gets only enough light to rise to carpet-level. Undoubtedly, as in the neoclassical esthetic, the intent is to provide a generic frame within which the reader is at liberty to insert his own uniqueness—as many or as few as his imagination may supply.

Along with the sense of place, and as a part of it, is the sense of fact. 10 Facts march through all his pages in a stream as continuous as the refugee wagons in Thrace or the military camions on the road from the Isonzo. Speculation, whether by the author or by the characters, is ordinarily kept to a minimum. But facts, visible or audible or tangible facts, facts baldly stated, facts without verbal paraphernalia to inhibit their striking power, are the stuff of Hemingway's prose.

Sometimes, especially in the early work, the facts seem too many for 11 the effect apparently intended, though even here the reader should be on guard against misconstruing the intention of a given passage. It is hard to discover, nevertheless, what purpose beyond the establishment of the sense of place is served by Barnes's complete itinerary of his walk with Bill Gorton through the streets of Paris. The direction is from Madame Lecomte's restaurant on the Île St. Louis across to the left bank of the Seine, and eventually up the Boulevard du Port Royal to the Café Select. The walk fills only two pages. Yet it seems much longer and does not further the action appreciably except to provide Jake and Bill with healthy after-dinner exercise. At Madame Lecomte's (the facts again), they have eaten "a roast chicken, new green beans, mashed potatoes, a salad, and some apple pie and cheese." To the native Parisian, or a foreigner who knows the city, the pleasure in the after-dinner itinerary would consist in the happy shock of recognition. For others, the inclusion of so many of the facts of municipal or gastronomic geography—so many more than are justified by their dramatic purpose—may seem excessive.

Still, this is the way it was that time in Paris. Here lay the bridges 12 and the streets, the squares and the cafés. If you followed them in the prescribed order, you came to the café where Lady Brett Ashley sat on a high stool at the bar, her crossed legs stockingless, her eyes crinkling at the corners.

If an imaginative fusion of the sense of place and the sense of fact is 13 to occur, and if, out of the fusing process, dramatic life is to arise, a third element is required. This may be called the sense of scene. Places are less than geography, facts lie inert and uncoordinated, unless the imagination runs through them like a vitalizing current and the total picture moves and quickens. How was it, for example, that second day of the

San Fermin fiesta in the Pamplona bullring after Romero had killed the first bull?

"They had hitched the mules to the dead bull and then the whips cracked, the men ran, and the mules, straining forward, their legs pushing, broke into a gallop, and the bull, one horn up, his head on its side, swept a swath smoothly across the sand and out the red gate." 14

Here are a dead bull, men, mules, whips, sand, and a red gate like a closing curtain—the place and the facts. But here also, in this remarkably graphic sentence, are the seven verbs, the two adverbs, and the five adverbial phrases which fuse and coordinate the diverse facts of place and thing and set them in rapid motion. If one feels that the sentence is very satisfying as a scene, and wishes to know why, the answer might well lie where it so often lies in a successful lyric poem—that is, in our sense of difficulty overcome. Between the inertness of the dead bull when he is merely *hitched* (a placid verb) and the smooth speed with which the body finally *sweeps* across the sand and out of sight, come the verbs of sweating effort: *crack, run, strain,* and *break.* It is precisely at the verb *broke* that the sentence stops straining and moves into the smooth glide of its close. The massing, in that section of the sentence, of a half-dozen *s*'s, compounded with the *th* sounds of *swath* and *smoothly,* can hardly have been inadvertent. They ease (or grease) the path of the bull's departure. 15

The pattern in the quoted passage is that of a task undertaken, striven through, and smoothly completed: order and success. For another graphic sentence, so arranged as to show the precise opposites—total disorder and total failure—one might take the following example from *Death in the Afternoon.* The protagonist is a "phenomenon," a bullfighter who has lost his nerve. 16

"In your mind you see the phenomenon, sweating, white-faced, and sick with fear, unable to look at the horn or go near it, a couple of swords on the ground, capes all around him, running in at an angle on the bull hoping the sword will strike a vital spot, cushions sailing down into the ring and the steers ready to come in." 17

In this passage, place has become predicament. The facts, thrown in almost helter-skelter, imply the desperate inward fear which is responsible for the creation of the outward disorder. Verbs are held to a minimum, and their natural naked power is limited with qualifications. The phenomenon is *unable to look,* and *hoping to strike,* not *looking* and *striking.* He runs, but it is at a bad angle. The disorder of the swords on the ground and the capes all around is increased by the scaling-in of seat- 18 cushions from the benches, the audience's insult to gross cowardice. The author-spectator's crowning insult is the allusion to the steers, who by comparison with the enraged bull are bovine, old-womanly creatures. On being admitted to the ring, they will quiet and lead away the bull the phenomenon could not kill.

The sense of place and the sense of fact are indispensable to Hemingway's art. But the true craft, by which diversities are unified and compelled into graphic collaboration, comes about through the operation of the sense of scene. Often, moving through the Latin language countries, watching the crowd from a café table or a barrera bench, Hemingway seems like a lineal descendant of Browning's observer in *How It Strikes a Contemporary*. 19

> You saw go up and down Valladolid
> A man of mark, to know next time you saw . . .
> Scenting the world, looking it full in face.

### QUESTIONS FOR ANALYSIS

1. What do you think Hemingway means by "truth"? Is truth necessarily limited to empirical fact—firsthand observation and experience—or can it be acquired some other way? Do you agree that truth telling should be a criterion of fiction as well as nonfiction?

2. In this selection, Baker distinguishes among Hemingway's three aesthetic senses. Find the passages where Baker discusses each sense, and briefly describe it in your own words. How does he use these senses to argue for his judgment of Hemingway's style?

3. In the last paragraph, Baker claims that although the senses of place and fact are essential, Hemingway's "true craft" is conveyed through the sense of scene. Why do you think he values the sense of scene over the other two senses? Is this preference justified?

4. Several times in the essay, Baker quotes a passage from a Hemingway work and then spends a paragraph or two discussing it. Choose one such passage and its accompanying discussion. How does Baker use this passage as evidence to support his argument? To what details in the passage does he call attention in his discussion? What kinds of points does he make? How much of this discussion seems to you to be necessary or useful?

5. Baker opens and closes his essay with quotations by other writers. Look either at the opening epigraph or the closing quotation, and speculate about Baker's reasons for including these quotations. What role does each play in this essay evaluating Hemingway's writing?

6. Baker is a good stylist in his own right. Look, for instance, at paragraph 3. What patterns do you find in the sentences in this paragraph? What effect does this patterning of sentences have on you as one reader?

7. Notice Baker's use of language in this selection. Make an inventory of the figurative language, and reflect on the patterns of imagery you find. What is your impression of Baker's language? What feelings and attitudes does it convey? (See Taking Inventory in Chapter 1.)

8. Baker refers to Hemingway's "neoclassical restraint." What do you think he means by this phrase? To what extent can Baker's own style also be described in these terms?

## SUGGESTIONS FOR WRITING

1. The following paragraph appears as one of the brief sketches between the stories in Hemingway's collection *In Our Time*. Read the passage carefully, then write an essay evaluating it. Apply the same criteria that Baker uses.

> The first matador got the horn through his sword hand and the crowd hooted him. The second matador slipped and the bull caught him through the belly and he hung on to the horn with one hand and held the other tight against the place, and the bull rammed him wham against the wall and the horn came out, and he lay in the sand, and then got up like crazy drunk and tried to slug the men carrying him away and yelled for his sword but he fainted. The kid came out and had to kill five bulls because you can't have more than three matadors, and the last bull he was so tired he couldn't get the sword in. He couldn't hardly lift his arm. He tried five times and the crowd was quiet because it was a good bull and it looked like him or the bull and then he finally made it. He sat down in the sand and puked and they held a cape over him while the crowd hollered and threw things down into the bull ring.

2. Choose a passage from a writer you admire. It could be from a novel, short story, play, or essay. Write an essay evaluating this passage according to any criterion you think is appropriate. Use Baker's criteria if you like. Include the passage in your essay.

3. Write an evaluation of a notable author, performer, or film director, using representative examples from your subject's career. Write for readers generally unfamiliar with your subject's accomplishments or shortcomings.

## A Debate on the SAT

SAT is an acronym well known to high school students. The Scholastic Aptitude Test, a two-and-a-half-hour multiple-choice examination with sections on verbal and math skills, exercises awesome power over students' lives and dreams. More than a million and a half high school students take the SAT every year, and another million and a quarter take the PSAT, the Preliminary Scholastic Aptitude Test. The SAT is produced and administered by the Educational Testing Service (ETS), a private nonprofit corporation that in 1981 reported revenues of $115 million, roughly half of which came from the SAT and related college admissions tests.

The SAT has for some time been the center of controversy. Some think it has too much influence; others criticize it for being biased against minorities. The ETS claims that the test accurately reflects students' academic potential, while its critics argue that it reflects only students' test-taking ability. In 1980, a consumer advocacy group led by Ralph Nader published a 500-page report, *The Reign of the ETS*, charging the ETS with misrepresenting its tests. Earlier, in 1978, the Federal Trade Commission had taken issue with ETS's long-standing claim that the SAT cannot be coached. And researchers at the University of Michigan developed a blood test in 1967 said to be more reliable than the SAT at predicting which students would ultimately graduate from college.

The following selections present two perspectives on the value of the SAT. In the first, "The SAT," Jay Amberg defends the test against criticism of its misuse by college admissions officers, accusations of ethnic bias, and the question of whether coaching improves test scores. David Owen focuses on the coaching issue in the second selection, "Beating the Test."

# Jay Amberg

Jay Amberg (b. 1949) holds a Ph.D. in English education from Northwestern University and has taught at the high school and college levels. A resident of Glencoe, Illinois, he is currently teaching at the National College of Education as well as at a local high school where he works in the reading lab. He has authored *Verbal Review and Workbook for the SAT* (1982) and is now preparing two workbooks to prepare students for the high school equivalency test.

# *The SAT*

This selection was first published in 1982 in *The American Scholar*, a journal read mainly by college professors and administrators. When you read an evaluation, you will expect a judgment and an argument for it.

Notice how Amberg argues in support of the SAT and, in particular, how he considers others' criticism of it. Read critically, analyzing thoughtfully Amberg's defense of the SAT. Where is he convincing? unconvincing? inconsistent?

Before you begin reading, reflect for a moment on your experience with the SAT. Where did you take the exam, and what can you recall of the experience? Were you coached for the exam? What were your scores? What were your teachers', parents', and friends' attitudes toward the SAT? Can you recall anyone questioning the usefulness or fairness of the exam?

> *At any rate they keep out the half-witted.*
> — LORD BLOOMFIELD on competitive examinations

Parents at a suburban high school open house ask an English teacher  1
what he is doing to prepare their son for the Scholastic Aptitude Test—not for college, but for the SAT. A senior in high school writes in an essay, "Although being an upperclassman is often a lot of fun, taking the SAT causes tension and aggravation." Parents of high school seniors, talking at a party, compare their children's SAT scores—as though high scores certify intelligence and low scores suggest stupidity. A senior in high school who has just received average SAT scores announces to a friend that she will never amount to anything in life. A young man sues the Educational Testing Service, the creators of the SAT, because he feels he has been discriminated against by ETS. During a job interview, an employer asks a twenty-four-year-old graduate student what her SAT scores were.

Applying to American colleges is often a confusing and frustrating rite  2
of passage—perhaps *the* American rite of passage. Many students, their parents, and much of the American public believe that the SAT is the crucial factor, the gatekeeper, in this rite. Many students consider the day they receive their SAT scores the second most important day in their educational lives. (The first is the day they are actually accepted or rejected at the college of their choice.) Anyone who doubts this needs only to talk to high school seniors—or to browse through the scores of articles that appear yearly in popular magazines and in newspapers.

The current public confusion about the SAT suggests a number of  3
questions about the test itself, the Educational Testing Service, and the College Entrance Examination Board, the original creators of the SAT: How is the SAT used—and how *should* it be used—by American college admissions officers? Is the SAT a *fair* measure of scholastic aptitude? For that matter, what is the SAT—and what exactly does it attempt to measure? What, if anything, can or should young people do to prepare for the test? Why has the public concern about and criticism of the SAT

intensified in the last decade? Do ETS and the College Board have the sort of gatekeeping power attributed to them?

Much of the public concern about the SAT has focused less on the    4
test itself (most people remain confident that the test measures something akin to academic aptitude) than on the uses of the test by college ad-missions officers. Although many Americans believe that the SAT is a national gatekeeper similar to the *baccalauréat* or the Advanced Level GCE exam, neither ETS nor the College Board tells admissions officers how to use the test. Michael Kean, Midwest director of ETS, says: "ETS is not a gatekeeper. The SAT plays a role in admissions selection, in the gatekeeping process, but the term 'gatekeeper' suggests that ETS ulti-mately decides who is accepted in college. This is simply not true." What is true is that 86 percent of four-year public colleges and 90 percent of four-year private colleges consider standardized test scores an important factor in admissions. Yet only 1 percent of four-year private colleges and 2 percent of four-year public colleges claim they consider the scores "the single most important factor." In contrast, an applicant's academic per-formance in high school is considered the single most important factor in 39 percent of four-year private colleges and 43 percent of four-year public colleges. James Alexander, past president of the National Asso-ciation of College Admissions Counselors, puts these statistics into per-spective when he notes: "Admissions officers at selective colleges tend to use a variety of factors to determine who will be admitted. High school performance is the best predictor; the addition of standardized test scores, as well as other factors, will improve prediction. Very few schools will accept or reject a student on the basis of test scores alone."

How this variety of factors to determine admissions works in practice    5
is best shown through examples of particular colleges' admissions proce-dures. At Princeton University, for instance, 50 percent of the admissions decision is based on academic credentials and 50 percent on nonacademic factors. The academic portion is based on a variety of criteria: grades and rank in high school, SAT scores, achievement-test scores, and recom-mendations. Nonacademic factors include "leadership activities," school activities, sports, and personal interviews. Special attention is given to students in certain categories: prospective engineers, athletes, minorities, and alumni and faculty children. (James Wickenden, Princeton's director of admissions, admits, "We took forty-five percent of those alumni chil-dren who applied, but only twenty percent of all others.") Within this context, the SAT is used as an admission requirement that cuts across all applicants—it is the single unifying measure. A high SAT score does not, however, guarantee admission to Princeton. Less than 52 percent of the applicants for the class of 1984 with SAT verbal scores between 750–800 (the test scores are reported on a 200–800 scale) and less than

39 percent of those with similar SAT math scores were offered admission. Conversely, approximately 18 percent of those with SAT verbal scores between 550–599 and over 19 percent of those with similar SAT math scores were admitted. In fact, a few applicants with verbal and math scores below 350 were accepted. Wickenden concludes, "The SAT scores, while important, are far from being determining factors in the admission process."

At the University of Michigan, the academic part of an applicant's 6 record is most carefully evaluated. Donald Swain, assistant director of admissions, says, "We begin by looking at the academic record of an applicant as reflected by grades on a transcript. We give a little extra weight in our process to those students who have taken honors or advanced placement courses. Consistency of grades and improvement of grades are important factors." Extracurricular activities and recommendations are not strongly considered at Michigan. Alumni children and minorities receive some extra consideration, as do students who come from geographical areas not overly represented at the university. The combined SAT verbal and math scores or the composite ACT score (American College Testing Assessment published in Iowa City, Iowa) are considered important. Swain says:

> We use whatever set of scores is to the applicant's advantage. There is a tremendous range of test scores. In the liberal arts college, where we get many more applicants than we can accommodate, we hold tighter to a grade average or a test range — but there is no cutoff score. Our priority is with students who have done well day by day in class. An application that shows an outstanding record will likely, although not necessarily, counterbalance low SAT scores.

Despite what college admissions officers say about the SAT, many 7 Americans remain convinced that the Scholastic Aptitude Test measures something innate, something akin to inborn academic ability. Although "aptitude" means "a natural or acquired capacity or ability," ETS and the College Board use the term to mean only *acquired* ability. The 1981/ 82 SAT guide sent to students states: "The SAT measures developed verbal and mathematical reasoning abilities that are involved in successful academic work in college; it is not a test of some inborn and unchanging capacity." Why then the use of the ambiguous term "aptitude"? Rex Jackson of ETS writes: "The SAT is described as an aptitude test because, unlike a traditional achievement test, it is not tied to a particular course of study, and because it is designed to assist in predicting future academic performance." The SAT, then, is a test that, despite its dubious title, measures acquired academic ability unrelated to a specific course — and nothing more. It does not purport to measure motivation, creativity, or other traits generally associated with success in college and life.

The College Board and ETS recommend that SAT scores be used as 8
a supplement to students' high school records in the admissions process.
This use of the SAT is based on the assumption that it validly predicts
first-year college grades. No one at the College Board or at ETS suggests
that the test predicts success in college or in life beyond college years.
Yet, some critics, notably Warner V. Slack and Douglas Porter of Harvard Medical School, believe that the SAT does not serve even this
limited function well. In the *Harvard Education Review* (May 1980) Slack
and Porter conclude: "The validity coefficient of the [SAT] tests, together
with high school records, is, on the average, only 0.06 higher than that
of the high school record alone." Similarly, the Nader report states that
the SAT increases predictive ability over high school records alone by
only 3 to 5 percent. The College Board and ETS, using different methods, reject both the Slack and Porter and the Nader conclusions. Rex
Jackson of ETS states that the improvement in predictability of the tests
in conjunction with the high school record over the high school record
alone is 27 percent. George H. Hanford of the College Board puts the
matter more dramatically: "Thousands of validity studies prove that the
SAT increases predictive efficiency by 40 to 50 percent when it is used
in *helping* to estimate first-year college grades—not the paltry 3 to 5
percent that Ralph Nader suggests." Because the researchers use different
methods—and sometimes different figures—conclusions about the SAT's
predictive ability are likely to remain contradictory. The underlying issue,
however, is not what the exact percentage of improvement the SAT
offers is, but how the scores are used by admissions officers. As we have
seen, admissions officers at selective colleges tend to use SAT scores as
a supplementary factor that cuts across all students regardless of their
backgrounds. Used as a counterbalance to the differences in high school
curricula and the subjectivity of grades, the SAT scores, admissions officers believe, have a usefulness that transcends the argument about the
percentage of increase in predictive ability.

The fact that SAT scores are used to compare students from different 9
backgrounds, however, prompts other criticism. An ostensibly simple fact
about the SAT is that the scores of minority students are lower than
those of other students. Robert L. Williams, among other critics, makes
the point that the scores are not fair standards of comparison because
the test discriminates against blacks and other minority students, who
are not altogether familiar with mainstream American culture and with
standard written English. In an attempt to demonstrate his point, Williams wrote a test called the "Black Intelligence Scale of Cultural Homo-
geneity" (BITCH). All of the items of the BITCH were drawn exclusively
from black experience. When Williams administered the test to blacks
and whites, the scoring pattern, not surprisingly, was the reverse of the

and whites, the scoring pattern, not surprisingly, was the reverse of the SAT—blacks had higher scores. Whatever Williams' results might suggest about American culture, it is erroneous to conclude, as Williams did, that because he was capable of creating a biased test, the content of the SAT is therefore biased. Every item on the SAT is checked for bias by minority reviewers—and then checked again. Indeed, anyone familiar with the content of the SAT is aware that there are no items biased against blacks or other minorities. Any items *about* minorities are uniformly positive in nature.

Williams's point about the language of the SAT is more interesting. 10 He is perfectly correct in assuming the the test contains no black slang— or any other slang, for that matter. The language of the SAT is standard written English—the English used in most college classes, required in most college papers, and used in most American businesses. Including nonstandard English on the SAT might help minority students score better, but it would not help college admissions officers determine who would likely do well in college classes, which is, of course, what the test is designed to do. The fact that black students score well on the BITCH suggests that they know black English better than they know standard written English. Blacks and other minorities certainly have a right to their language, but such usage will not likely help them to succeed in selective American colleges or in most businesses.

Statistical evidence concerning SAT scores suggests that the argument 11 about minority discrimination is really an argument about social class in the United States. The correlation between SAT scores and family income, the critics point out, is embarrassingly high. The following table of average SAT scores for 1973/74 seniors does, in fact, show that the mean scores are higher among high income groups.

| Student's Score | Student's Mean Family Income |
|---|---|
| 750–800 | $24,124 |
| 700–749 | 21,980 |
| 650–699 | 21,292 |
| 600–649 | 20,330 |
| 550–599 | 19,481 |
| 500–549 | 18,824 |
| 450–499 | 18,122 |
| 400–449 | 17,387 |
| 350–399 | 16,182 |
| 300–349 | 14,355 |
| 250–299 | 11,428 |
| 200–249 | 8,639 |

This information leads some critics to conclude that the SAT is a substantial barrier to equal educational opportunity. Spokesmen for ETS, however, categorically deny this. An ETS pamphlet states as fact that the "use of admissions tests has also contributed to increased access of disadvantaged students to higher education," but fails to muster any evidence to support that assertion.

That students from wealthier families tend to score higher than students from poor families cannot be denied, but it is still somewhat misleading. The use of average SAT scores and median income ignores the full range of SAT scores. Many students from the highest income level have low scores, and nearly one-third of the students from the lowest income group (below $6,000) score in the upper half of the total group. Further, most other measures of educational achievement—from reading scores to college grades—show a similar relationship between achievement and family income. One should not conclude, however, that wealthy people are more intelligent than poor people. (A dim-witted *Fortune* editorial about the SAT, for example, asked rhetorically, "Are rich people smarter than poor people?" and answered, "Yes, obviously.") Rather, one has to ask what effects poverty has on learning (the SAT, after all, measures acquired ability). Implicit in this question is the assumption that wealthy people also tend to be better off educationally— an assertion that is less than shocking to anyone who has visited a variety of schools. In *College Admissions and the Public Interest*, B. Arden Thresher wrote: "Social class, which we in the United States like to ignore, or take note of only shamefacedly, plays a powerful part in access to education." James Loewen, who would agree with this appraisal, created the "Loewen Low Aptitude Test" that measures "exposure" to working-class life. The test, he says, is "designed to show my urbane white students some of the forms of test bias." And, like the BITCH, it works. Also like the BITCH, however, it, too, misses the point. The SAT test may be "biased" in favor of those "urbane" students who have had "exposure" to high culture and standard written English, but it is exactly this "bias"—in favor of culture and correct English—that colleges should be trying to preserve in our nation. Ralph W. Tyler puts the matter most succinctly: "Putting snobbism aside, the 'elite culture' is an important resource for a democratic society. . . . The scholarly heritage is a great and vital resource which schools and colleges should help students discover and learn to use."

In some ways, the most radical criticism of the SAT is that it is "coachable," that students can raise their scores by taking SAT preparation courses. Until recently ETS and the College Board have denied that coaching could improve scores at all. A 1968 College Board pamphlet, for example, stated, "Changes in scores occur in about the same degree and with the same frequency *whether or not a student is coached."* A 1977 ETS booklet asserted, "The abilities measured by the SAT develop over a student's entire academic life, so coaching—vocabulary drill, memorizing facts, or the like—can do little or nothing to raise the student's scores." Slack and Porter's survey of published research, a National Education Association study, and a Federal Trade Commission report all flatly contradict these statements. Indeed, an internal FTC memorandum suggested, "The representations of ETS and its clients regarding the susceptibility of their standardized admission examinations to coaching are false, misleading, deceptive." While there is little evidence to suggest malfeasance on the part of ETS or the College Board, there is evidence, some of it from ETS itself, that their earlier statements were incorrect. Recently ETS has begun to hedge on those earlier, unequivocal statements. In a response to Slack and Porter's conclusion that "coaching for the SAT can result in gains in scores," Rex Jackson stated: "In making their case the authors fail to draw clearly the critical distinction between programs of short-term drill and practice designed to yield quick increases in scores, and longer term educational programs designed to have lasting effects." This distinction between education and cramming is echoed throughout recent ETS publications and also by Neal Samors of ETS, who says, "With more schooling, you're likely to increase your aptitude—and your performance in college."

This distinction between long-term and short-term work is, of course, 14 educationally valid, but it still implies that short-term work is futile—an assertion that recent studies and my own experience in tutoring students would suggest is erroneous. Students I have worked with over periods of months have invariably improved their scores, but even some of those whom I have worked with for only short periods of time have improved remarkably. One girl, for example, raised her SAT math score one hundred points after only three hours of tutoring. She had understood algebra and geometry well enough, but had not known how to answer the word problems, particularly the quantitative comparisons, on the SAT. This sort of short-term work on test-taking skills, what some critics call "test-wiseness," is often beneficial to students—a point ETS concedes. In fact, each year ETS publishes a bulletin for students that includes a full practice test and advice on how to answer the various types of SAT questions. The problem is, as ETS spokesmen acknowledge, that most students do not read the bulletin, much less take the practice test. Some of the same students, however, do take short-term preparation courses, during which they learn test-taking methods—and subsequently improve their scores.

ETS spokesmen also insist that the mean scores of students taking 15
preparation courses are not significantly higher than the scores of those
who do not take such courses. The truth of this assertion is debatable
(the NEA study and the FTC report conclude that coaching does help),
but even if it were true, it is still deceptive. Just as there is a wide range
of scores despite a mean that correlates scores with family income, there
is certainly a wide range of scores despite a mean that correlates scores
with preparation courses. ETS spokesmen insist that the former range is
extremely important, but conveniently ignore the latter range. Many
students, among them those who are unfamiliar with test-taking strategies, those who suffer from "text anxiety" (and therefore need to know
exactly the kinds of questions they will be asked), and those who are not
self-motivated enough to work through ETS bulletins and SAT preparation texts, benefit from short-term coaching—even if general conclusions drawn by ETS suggest otherwise.

The fact that the SAT is susceptible to coaching does not imply that 16
it is a poor test. Students are likely to do better on any standardized test,
or for that matter on any test, if they understand the form of the test—
if they have developed test-wiseness. Further, the abilities measured by
the SAT—critical reading, vocabulary, and mathematical reasoning
skills—are, as ETS so insistently points out, *acquired.* One way to develop
test-wiseness and to acquire these abilities is to receive coaching. That
coaching helps does suggest, however, that those economically advantaged students who can afford preparation courses are likely to improve
on the cultural and educational advantages that they already have, an
instance of the rich getting, if not richer, then at least brighter. This
poses an ethical issue concerning the use of the SAT in the college
admission process. Quite simply, the SAT is not quite the unifying factor
it seems to be; it cuts differently across various ethnic and economic
groups. Again, this does not suggest that the SAT itself discriminates,
but rather that certain uses of the SAT by admissions officers at American
colleges may be discriminatory. The use of cutoff scores, for example,
quite likely discriminates against the poor and minorities, as does the use
of the scores to compare students from different economic and cultural
backgrounds. But the use of SAT scores as a supplementary item within
the context of other admissions factors and the use of scores to compare
students from similar backgrounds remain valid, indeed valuable, for admissions officers at selective American colleges. The SAT itself remains,
in the words of the College Board charter, a fair, uniform, and judiciously
administered exam.

## QUESTIONS FOR ANALYSIS

1. Describe the tone set by the epigraph and the first three paragraphs. What impression of Amberg does this opening convey? How does this opening prepare you to accept his judgment of the SAT?

2. How does Amberg attempt to allay fears that the SAT is too powerful an influence on college admissions officers? Why does he need to do this, and how successful do you think he is? What are his strongest arguments? his weakest?

3. Why does Amberg defend the ETS definition of the term *aptitude?* What is the issue here, and why is it important? How convincing is the definition?

4. In paragraph 7, Amberg quotes a representative of ETS as saying that the SAT is "designed to assist in predicting future academic performance." However, in paragraph 8, he states unequivocally: "No one at the College Board or at ETS suggests that the test predicts success in college or in life beyond the college years." Read these two paragraphs, focusing on the context in which these two quotations appear. Then comment on the apparent contradiction.

5. How convincing do you find Amberg's comment in paragraph 8 that "conclusions about the SAT's predictive ability are likely to remain contradictory. The underlying issue, however, is not what the exact percentage of improvement the SAT offers is, but how the scores are used by admissions officers"? What is the specific argument over the SAT's predictive ability? Why is it difficult to come to a satisfactory conclusion? According to Amberg, why is this failure unimportant?

6. How does Amberg rebut charges that the SAT is biased? How does reinterpreting the argument about minority discrimination as an argument about social class alter the stakes? How convincing do you find Amberg's arguments on these issues?

7. Why does Amberg regard the criticism that the SAT is coachable as "the most radical"? What is the implication if expert coaching can significantly increase test scores? How does Amberg arbitrate between the ETS position on coaching and the arguments posed by its critics? What is his own position on this issue?

## SUGGESTIONS FOR WRITING

1. If you took the SAT or an equivalent college entrance examination, like the ACT, write an essay evaluating the test. What do you think it tests? What criteria do you apply to such exams? Even though you

have to rely on memory, try to be as specific as possible. Address your essay to readers who may be unfamiliar with college entrance examinations.

2. If you were a college admissions officer, on what criteria would you evaluate students applying to your school? How much value would you give to nonacademic factors? Write an essay as if you were an admissions officer evaluating your own application. Be sure to define the criteria you use and cite specific examples from your own high school record.

3. Implied in this essay is the idea that high school should prepare students for college. Now that you have some experience of college, write an essay evaluating how well your high school prepared you for college. Address your evaluation to readers unfamiliar with your particular high school.

# David Owen

A graduate of Harvard University, David Owen (b. 1955) is an award-winning journalist whose articles have appeared in many major magazines. He has been a senior writer for *Harper's*, a visiting professor of English at Colorado College, and a Fellow of the Alicia Patterson Foundation.

Owen specializes in writing about education. In order to gather material for his first book, *High School: Undercover with the Class of '80*, he posed as a high school student. His second book, *None of the Above: Behind the Myth of the Scholastic Aptitude* (1985), Owen explains, "began as a short assignment for *Harper's*, grew into an endless article, swelled to its present form, and threatens to become a permanent obsession."

# Beating the Test

This selection is adapted from Chapter 7 of *None of the Above*. One of the myths about the SAT that Owen seeks to deflate is that it accurately reflects students' academic potential. As one of his sources, he cites the Princeton Review, an independent test-preparation course founded by John Katzman and Adam Robinson. He also refers to Bob Scheller, operator of the Pre-test Review, a school that uses the same techniques as the Princeton Review. Katzman and Robinson claim that when their students take coaching seriously, the Princeton Review course raises their SAT scores by an average of 250 points. As you read, think about what such a fact, if true, suggests about the SAT's claim to test academic potential. If coaching can be so effective, what does the SAT actually test?

ETS and the College Board have never leveled with students about     1
the content of the SAT. In order to put all students on an equal footing, they have claimed, the test is designed to be independent of any particular curriculum. The SAT, writes ETS's James Braswell, is "a broad-gauged predictive measure as opposed to a test of specialized subject matter achievement." A student studying poetry won't have an advantage over a student studying fiction, the theory goes, because the SAT will look beyond superficial content differences and focus on "reasoning." Nor will a student at one school have a necessary advantage over a student at another. The subject matter, in short, doesn't matter. The verbal SAT, Braswell says, "is completely independent of specific course content." On the math SAT, he says, "most of the mathematical content is held to topics generally taught prior to the tenth grade. By including only the subject matter to which most college-bound students have been

exposed, the test strives to measure differences in students' ability to think quantitatively."

But all of this is wrong. The SAT tests a very definite body of content    2
that changes very little from test to test. This content, as ETS says, isn't generally taught in classrooms. But it can easily be taught. Math "taught prior to the tenth grade" is much less important, in terms of doing well on the SAT, than the math tested on the SAT—and the two are not the same. The real subject matter of the test, contrary to what Braswell says, is the test itself.

The tools ETS uses to build the SAT enable the Princeton Review to    3
pick it apart. "The methods we use are aimed at the weaknesses we see in the statistical techniques used by ETS," Katzman says. By poring over old SATs and by analyzing them with computers, Katzman and Robinson have essentially deduced the SAT's specifications. ETS's obsession with consistency makes its tests extremely predictable. Katzman and Robinson don't drill students on item types they'll never see; they teach them how to put themselves inside the minds of the test-makers. One afternoon, Robinson taught me how to answer the hardest ETS analogies without looking at the stems—the words in capital letters—only at the answer choices. With a little practice, I was able to pick nine out of ten. Once you know how the test developers think, you don't always need to see the question to find the answer.

The key to Katzman, Robinson, and Scheller's method is, in a sense,    4
the biserial correlation. ETS's circular logic is meaningful after all: students who do well on the SAT really *do* do well on the SAT. And because they do, it's possible to beat the test.

In order for a test question to make it onto a real SAT, it has to have    5
certain statistical characteristics. A question is used only if high-scoring students tend to get it right and low-scoring students tend to get it wrong. If low-scoring students do as well on it as high-scoring students, then the question—unless it is intended to be easy for all—will have an unacceptably low biserial correlation, and ETS will either have to rewrite it or discard it.

On a multiple-choice test, remember, the correct answer is always right    6
there on the page. If that answer looks right to the wrong people—if low scorers pick it just as often as high scorers—then the question will wash out on the pretest and never make it to a real SAT. Imagine a math problem in which students are asked to find the square root of four. Most of the highest-scoring students know what a square root is, and they get the question right. Most of the middle-scoring students don't know what a square root is, and they get it wrong. But most of the lowest-scoring students think that the square root of any number is that number divided

by two. They do exactly as well on this item as the highest-scoring students. There are two ways to arrive at the correct answer, one of them right and one of them wrong. The question fails its biserial correlation test, and it is replaced by a question that asks students to find the square root of nine.

ETS's test-makers use this principle to help them write "effective" 7 items. They also use it to help them write appealing distractors. In order to lure the average student away from correct answers on difficult items, the test-makers try to anticipate the errors, both of logic and of computation, that he will make. Each time this student strays from the proper path, a distractor will be waiting to tempt him.

Adam Robinson calls this average test-taker Joe Bloggs. When Joe 8 Bloggs takes the SAT, he scores 450. When ETS lays a trap for him, he steps in. Princeton Review students learn how to avoid these traps by learning to understand how Joe Bloggs thinks. When Princeton Review students come to a hard question they don't understand, they ask themselves. What would Joe do here? Then they do something else.

Here's a question from a recent SAT. *Don't actually read it*; just glance 9 at the two numbers in it, then look at the answers:

25. In how many different color combinations can 3 balls be painted if each ball is painted one color and there are 3 colors available? (Order is not considered; e.g., red, blue, red is considered the same combination as red, red, blue.)
(A) 4   (B) 6   (C) 9   (D) 10   (E) 27

This is the twenty-fifth question in a twenty-five-item math section. Therefore, according to its statistics, it's the hardest question in the section. It wouldn't be here if Joe Bloggs had been able to answer it on the pretest. The correct answer, therefore, must be something that Joe didn't think of. All we have to do to find the correct answer is to eliminate everything Joe *did* think of. Doing this doesn't require any real computation.

There are two numbers in this problem, 3 and 3. Joe added them and 10 got 6. That means B is wrong. Then he multiplied them and got 9. That means C is wrong. Then he raised 3 to the third power and got 27. That means E is wrong. Now that we've narrowed it down to A and D, we can actually read the problem. Unless we're careless, we'll realize that we can easily think of more than four color combinations, so the answer can't possibly be A. That means it must be D. It is.

The verbal SAT is harder to coach than the math SAT, mostly because 11 it is, to a very great extent, a vocabulary test. This is not to say, however, that it can't be coached or even that it can't be beaten. The Princeton

Review gets excellent results on the verbal SAT. Most students improve their scores substantially.

One of the great misconceptions about the SAT is that the words on it are drawn from a pool very nearly as large as the English language. ETS promotes this misconception every time it says that an SAT score reflects a lifetime of learning and that preparing for the test over subgeologic time periods is impossible. A College Board representative once said that a student who understood every word used in the *New York Times* in a year would understand every word on the SAT. But reading the *Times* for a year would be a terribly inefficient way to prepare for the SAT. The *Times*, after all, isn't written by ETS. Why waste time studying it?

Princeton Review students learn their vocabulary from a short word list, compiled by Adam Robinson, called the Hit Parade. Conspicuously absent from it are the words that *Barron's* favors—aptitudinous tongue-twisters, like *sequacious* and *tergiversation*, that ETS's item writers never heard of. Instead, the Hit Parade contains words that tend to crop up regularly on the SAT. Discovering what these words are is easy. High school vocabularies aren't all that large. ETS can't use words that no one's heard of, because items based on such words would have terrible biserial correlations (Joe Bloggs would be as likely to get them right as anyone else). If you read enough SATs, you get a very accurate feel for the sort of words ETS likes to test. Robinson uses a computer. (The most frequently tested words on the SAT are appropriately gloomy: *enigma, apathy, indifferent.*)

Sometimes students don't even need to know what the words on the Hit Parade mean; all they need to know is that they are there. A student who is stumped for an answer looks for words from the list and limits his selection to those.

The Princeton Review uses ETS's statistics to beat the SAT. It also uses the SAT to beat ETS's statistics.

Every SAT contains six sections. One of these, the "experimental" section, doesn't count toward students' scores. It's used by ETS to pretest items for future SATs and to equate current forms of the test with past ones. Students aren't told which section is the experimental one, because ETS wants them to work just as hard on it as they do on the sections that count. If they didn't work just as hard, ETS's deltas, biserial correlations, and raw-score conversion formulas would be thrown out of whack. In order to keep students from figuring out where the experimental section is, ETS moves it around. In December of 1983 it was section 3; in May of 1984 it was section 6.

Because hard items are harder to write than easy items, the experimental section is usually quite a bit tougher than the other sections of the SAT. It's also more likely to contain miskeyed, flawed, badly written, and ambiguous items, because the pretest is the screen ETS uses to filter out defective questions (roughly 40 percent of the items in any pretest are eliminated). Encountering the experimental section unawares can throw a good test-taker completely off his stride. Some students come unglued when they hit it. Half an hour ago they were calm and doing fine; now suddenly the sun is rising in the west and setting in the east. If the experimental section comes early enough—in section 2, for instance, where it's sometimes placed—a student can lose confidence in his judgment and decimate his score on the rest of the test. 17

Warner Slack and Douglas Porter, the Harvard Medical School professors critical of the SAT, think the experimental section is unethical. "There are very strict guidelines about the use of human subjects in research," Slack told me. "If we want patients to take part in a research project, we have to have their informed consent, and the volunteers have to be told that they can withdraw from the study at any time, and they have to be told that their refusal to participate will not hinder the medical care or any other care that they receive. It's been Doug's and my position that to coerce students to participate, as ETS's research 'volunteers,' is unfair. If you want to go to Yale, you have no choice but to be their research participant—and at your own expense. As a member of the human studies committee of the Harvard Medical School, I would disapprove that project." 18

John Katzman has a simple solution to this problem. He teaches his students how to find the experimental section. When they find it, they fill it out at random, thereby saving thirty minutes of anxiety and frustration. They simply put their heads down on their desks and rest until it's time to start on the next section. (Or, if they don't mind doing a little cheating, they use their extra half-hour to work on other sections of the test. Katzman tells them explicitly not to do this.) 19

The Princeton Review's sabotage of the experimental section has a significant impact on ETS's statistics. The bigger the school becomes, the bigger this impact will be. ETS's pretest statistics are usually based on samples of fewer than 1,500 students. Depending on how the test booklets are distributed, Princeton Review students can make up a substantial percentage of the students in particular samples. When they answer the questions at random, they actually *reduce the difficulty of future SATs* by making the pretest questions look harder, statistically, than they are. 20

Katzman very graciously told ETS what he was doing. By May of 1984,   21
ETS seemed to have returned to an earlier method of arranging its SAT
booklets in hopes of making the experimental section impossible to detect. But Princeton Review students found it anyway, and with ease. As
long as ETS doesn't radically change the specifications for the SAT,
Princeton Review students will *always* be able to find it. And even if
ETS does alter the test dramatically, the Princeton Review will only be
fooled for a month at most. The section simply can't be hidden from
students who know what to look for.

Nor can ETS make the SAT uncoachable. *Any multiple-choice test built*   22
*according to a statistical model can be beaten.* The GRE, the LSAT, the
GMAT—all are susceptible to methods like the ones used by Adam
Robinson and the Princeton Review. ETS can't make its tests harder for
Princeton Review students without making them either impossible or
entirely meaningless for non–Princeton Review students. It's Joe Bloggs
who ultimately determines the content of the SAT.

Most college admissions officers I've talked to (and virtually all high   23
school guidance counselors) have seemed reasonably certain that, despite
ETS's denials, coaching does work. But they are confused about the
implications. Should they deduct points from the scores of students they
suspect of having been coached? Some do, although they have no idea
what they're doing. (James McMenamin, director of admissions at Columbia, told me that "any experienced reader of applications at a selective
college is going to be suspicious, at this point, about any big jump in
scores." The lesson: get your coaching before you take the PSAT.)
Should admissions officers add points to the scores of students who have
clearly had only limited exposure, by whatever means, to the ETS men-
tality? Should they require ETS's Achievement Tests instead of the SAT?
("That would be fine with me," says Katzman. "I can prepare a kid for
the math Achievement, English Achievement—three weeks, 200
points.") Some colleges are thinking of asking students to declare on
their applications whether they were coached.

All of this is misguided and unfair, if only because admissions officers   24
make no distinction between coaching that produces big gains and coaching that doesn't . . . . Nor do they distinguish between students who
take coaching seriously and students who don't. They look at numbers
they don't understand and make moral judgments they have no basis for
making. Students are caught in a double bind: the College Board swears
to them that coaching doesn't work, then college admissions officers
punish them if their scores go up.

Admissions officers who penalize students for trying to improve their   25
scores on the SAT are doing what ETS always accuses its critics of doing:

blaming the messenger for the message. The message in this case is that the SAT is not the test that ETS and the College Board have always claimed it to be. It's not neutral and objective. It's not curriculum-free. It's not uncoachable. It's not the same test for everyone who takes it. It's not a measure of preparation for college. Admissions officers shouldn't be upset with the Princeton Review. They should be upset with ETS and upset with the SAT.

The advantage Princeton Review students have is no different from   26 the advantage that certain privileged students—students who are test-wise, students who share the social and cultural values of the test-writers at ETS, students who have no compunction about guessing—have *always* had on the SAT. The odds have *always* been stacked against kids who aren't tuned to the ETS wavelength or who haven't spent their lives in schools where ETS tests are a way of life. Admissions officers, guidance counselors, teachers, parents, and students should stop listening to ETS and the College Board and start listening to someone who actually understands the SAT.

"The SAT," says John Katzman, "is bullshit."   27

## QUESTIONS FOR ANALYSIS

1. What is Owen evaluating in this essay?
   (a) the ETS
   (b) the SAT
   (c) the Princeton Review
   (d) Joe Bloggs
   (e) All of the above

2. Why do you think Owen devotes the entire opening paragraph to presenting the official ETS position? Look closely at his word choices, and decide whether you think he presents the ETS position fairly and objectively.

3. According to Braswell of the ETS, on what basis should the SAT be judged? On what criteria does Owen base his judgment? What criteria do you think should be applied?

4. Owen states his thesis most explicitly in the last sentence. Why do you think he waits so long? How has he prepared the reader for this judgment? Why is it still a surprise? What does Owen gain from quoting someone else instead of using his own words?

5. In your own words, summarize Owen's explanation of the role statistics plays in the SAT. "Biserial correlation" is never very clearly defined, yet it is a central concept in this selection. How does Owen

convey its meaning? Should he have defined it more explicitly? If so, how?

6. Owen quotes Warner Slack and Douglas Porter, two Harvard professors who have criticized the experimental section of the SAT as being unethical. Why do they feel this way? How might the kind of coaching done by the Princeton Review also be considered unethical? How would you evaluate the SAT and its critics in regard to this criterion of ethics?

7. In paragraphs 23–26, Owen discusses the way admissions officers of colleges and universities treat the SAT. Why should the reaction of admissions officers affect his evaluation?

8. Take inventory of Owen's uses of humor, particularly irony, in this selection. Then analyze several of his most humorous phrases. How do they work? What do you think Owen gains or loses by using humor in this way? Conjecture on the uses of humor in evaluative writing in general. What purpose can it serve?

## SUGGESTIONS FOR WRITING

1. As a student, you have experience with many kinds of tests. Select one type of test—multiple choice, essay, true or false, lab practicum—or one particular test you've recently taken, and write an essay evaluating it. Address your essay to readers who are unfamiliar with the type of test you are evaluating.

2. Look back on your career as a student and choose a teacher you've had or a particular class, team, club, or school you've been a member of or have attended. Then write an evaluative essay addressed to readers unfamiliar with your subject.

3. Write an essay evaluating this debate on the SAT or one of the other debates in this book. Address your essay to readers who have not read the essays you are evaluating. Decide who has won the debate and give the basis on which you have made this decision.

## THE DEBATE:
## ADDITIONAL QUESTIONS FOR ANALYSIS

1. How do you think David Owen would respond to Jay Amberg's uncritical acceptance of ETS's assertion that the SAT is an aptitude test that can be used to predict future academic performance? What is your own view on this issue?

2. Like Owen, Amberg raises the issue of the value of coaching students for the SAT. Compare their reasoning and conclusions on this point.

# Sissela Bok

Born in Sweden in 1934, Sissela Bok grew up in Switzerland, France, and the United States. She received her B.A. and M.A. degrees in psychology from George Washington University and her Ph.D. in philosophy from Harvard. A former member of the Ethics Advisory Board to the Secretary of Health, Education, and Welfare, Bok also teaches ethics in the Harvard-MIT division of health sciences and technology.

In addition to numerous articles on medical ethics, she has written books on two interrelated moral issues: *Lying: Moral Choice in Public and Private Life* (1978) and *Secrets: On the Ethics of Concealment and Revelation* (1983). She is concerned with what we consider to be right and wrong, and how these moral judgments affect our everyday conduct. Bok's work, as she explains in the introduction to one of her books, "aims to narrow the gap between the worlds of the moral philosopher and those confronting urgent practical moral choices."

# Intrusive Social Science Research

This selection, excerpted from *Secrets*, deals with the ethics of social science research, in particular the methodology called participant observation. A research method, participant observation involves a scientist entering a community secretly and observing from within the dynamics of community life.

In *Secrets*, Bok explores the conflict "between wanting to penetrate the secrets of others and to leave them undisturbed." For Bok, many ethical questions reside in the borderline between the right of privacy and the freedom of inquiry.

As you read, notice that Bok anticipates the arguments social scientists would make in defense of their research methods. What arguments would you expect researchers to make? What does the word "intrusive" in the title imply about Bok's attitude toward social science research? Is the term merely descriptive or is it also evaluative?

Triumphant, brooking no opposition—such was the future that Emile    1
Durkheim envisaged for the social sciences at the beginning of this century. Science, he predicted in his massive study, *The Elementary Forms of Religious Life*, would come to take over the subjects that religion and philosophy had traditionally sought to explain: nature, man, and society.[1]

Innumerable social scientists have followed his lead. They have sought    2
to probe and to describe the most intimate and secret practices. They

have studied the sacred in its manifestations across the earth, not only from the outside but from the perspective of an insider as well. By taking part in the activities of a tribe or a secret society or a religious sect, they have carried out "participant observation," collecting data and publishing their results. Few still share Durkheim's faith in the capacity of social science to allow nature, man, and society to "appear as they really are." Yet the hope lingers on in the elaborate schemes for surreptitious observation, aimed at catching human behavior unawares. As Florence Kluckhohn, an early advocate of what she called "hypocritical" participant observation, pointed out:

> There are in all groups certain kinds of data which are guarded more closely than other types. Direct questions regarding such information may be met with evasions if not outright misrepresentations. Indirect questions may also fail. Simulation of behavior made possible by participation may, however, open the door to this guarded realm.[2]

The attraction of "this guarded realm" for many researchers is not rooted in their desire for knowledge alone, nor only in their hope that it might bring insight and possible benefits. They are also drawn to it by the allure of secrecy, of boundaries, and of the forbidden. Some take pleasure in dispelling the mystery, in showing it to be "wholly superficial," in Durkheim's words. Others, on the contrary, want to get to the heart of the secret in order to partake of it, relish its intimacy. Trespassing on what is taboo attracts still others. The extraordinary amount of research into every minute aspect of sexuality or religious belief is simply not explicable on other, strictly scientific grounds.

In exploring the reasons given for probing this guarded realm—especially its most closely kept secrets—it is important to consider the legitimacy of the methods used, in particular the most surreptitious ones. The following example will convey the high interest of some such studies, and illustrate some of the methods used to carry out invasive probes without the knowledge of the individuals under investigation.

Few religious phenomena have intrigued outsiders more than messianic or millenarian beliefs that some cataclysmic event—the coming of a savior or the destruction of the world—would take place on a specific date in the near future, at a specific location. A group of European Anabaptists believed that the millennium would come in 1534 and that Muenster would be the New Jerusalem.[3] And in the seventeenth century, a large proportion of Jews throughout the world were convinced that a young rabbi from Smyrna named Sabbatai Sevi was the Messiah and that the messianic kingdom was to come at a specified, imminent date.[4] In these movements, as in the many millenarian sects in the United States, people sold their homes, gave up their jobs, and brought their families to the appointed place, only to find their prayers unanswered and their expectations unfulfilled.

What happens to faith at such times of disappointment? What happens    6
to belief in the signs that had seemed to foretell the cataclysmic event? What do members of such groups do with their lives, having previously given up all ties to ordinary existence? And how do they respond to the pity and the taunting that they encounter?

These questions could hardly fail to interest social scientists. One so-    7
ciologist, Leon Festinger, directed a study of the discrepancy—the "cog-nitive dissonance"—between the original beliefs about what was to hap-pen and the later understanding of what actually did happen.[5] He predicted that given a firm enough conviction and strong group support, members would respond to disconfirmation in an unexpected way. Rather than giving up their original belief, he argued, they would turn to pros-elytizing in order to buttress it. Signs would be re-examined, dates com-puted anew. Gaining new adherents would serve to confirm their own belief, and thus to counteract the dissonance with which they were strug-gling. Not until beset by further discouraging news would their own faith begin to waver, and the group gradually dissolve.

Festinger pointed out, however, the difficulties of proving or disproving    8
his hypothesis by looking merely at historical records; for the factor of greatest interest to him—the proselytizing after disconfirmation—might not have seemed of sufficient interest at the time to have been noticed and recorded. And then, quite by accident, he came across a newspaper report indicating that the process was about to repeat itself not far away.

> The reader can then imagine the enthusiasm with which we seized the op-portunity to collect direct observational data about a group who appeared to believe in a prediction of catastrophe to occur in the near future.

. . . One day in late September the Lake City *Herald* carried a two-    9
column story, on a back page, headlined: PROPHECY FROM PLANET. CLARION CALL TO CITY: FLEE THAT FLOOD. IT'LL SWAMP US ON DEC. 21, OUTER SPACE TELLS SUBURBANITES. The body of the story expanded somewhat on these bare facts:

> Lake City will be destroyed by a flood from Great Lake just before dawn, Dec. 21, according to a suburban housewife. Mrs. Marion Keech, of 847 West School Street, says the prophecy is not her own. It is the purport of many messages she has received by automatic writing, she says . . . sent to her by superior beings from a planet called Clarion. These beings have been visiting the earth, she says, in what we call flying saucers. During their visits, she says, they have observed fault lines in the earth's crust that foretoken the deluge.[6]

Festinger and his colleagues decided to study the group not only in the    10
remaining months before the expected calamities but on the appointed
day and for a period afterwards. A first visit with Mrs. Keech led them
to opt for a surreptitious approach.

> In our very first contact with the central members of the group, their secrecy
> and general attitude toward non-believers made it clear that the study could
> not be conducted openly.[7]

Having made such a choice, the investigators adopted a complex strat-    11
egy. They made contact with the believers by means of elaborate cover
stories designed to "obtain a quick but firm entrée into the movement."
They made false personal claims, and acted as if they were genuinely
persuaded by the evidence from outer space and interested to learn how
to avoid the flood. But still they were not allowed entry into the innermost circle of the "advanced seekers." At that point, they explain, "we
decided to equip our representative with an 'experience' with the super-
natural," borrowed from a Mexican folk tale. Similarly, another observer
told the group that she had had a dream that fitted in with their proph-
ecies:

> I was standing on the side of a hill. . . . There was a man standing on top of
> the hill with a light all around him. There were torrents of water, raging
> water all around, and the man reached down and lifted me up out of the
> water. I felt safe.[8]

The group greeted this story and the earlier one with enthusiasm. The    12
second investigator was taken to bring a message from outer space, and
was asked to record the dream on tape so that others could hear it. It
came to count as corroborating evidence—a fact that, not surprisingly,
caused the investigators some concern about their role.

As the time foreseen for the cataclysm—December 21—approached,    13
the investigators kept continuous watch over the group without letting
on that they were doing so. They saw its members grow increasingly
agitated, maintaining strict secrecy toward the curious and the reporters
who had gathered to cover the outcome. But as the day came and went,
and nothing unusual happened, the group members gave up their secrecy.
They made frantic efforts to convince outsiders, telephoning the reporters
they had so recently scorned, pressing information on every visitor. They
took to proselytizing, just as the investigators had expected them to, and
at the same time were anxiously on the lookout for signals and instructions from outer space.

Over the next few weeks, bewildered and dejected, reaching for every    14
straw and disappointed anew each time, the group finally began to fall
apart. No new converts had been made; no new signals seemed forth-

coming. It became increasingly difficult to uphold the faith. Gradually, the group scattered. The investigators left, satisfied that their hypothesis had been confirmed. In their book about these events—*When Prophecy Fails*—they concluded that their work had been "as much detective work as observation."9

Through such means, they had gained entry to what members of the 15 sect strove to keep secret. Intending to make their finding public, they had deceived the members into revealing their innermost hopes and fears as they never would have to strangers and least of all to researchers. The investigators' behavior and cover stories had led group members to become even more confident in the signals from outer space. By every definition of privacy, the investigators had invaded that of their unwitting subjects; and they had done so, not out of any desire to help these men and women, but strictly for purposes of research.

What is it about research that is thought to outweigh, at times, the 16 respect for human boundaries? Why do for its sake what one might otherwise repudiate—pry, manipulate, and lie to invade private and closely guarded realms? Do the purposes for which social scientists pursue their studies lend special legitimacy to such methods? The rationale for social science research serves . . . partly to answer, partly to deflect such questions. Four arguments—invoking the pursuit of knowledge, the benefits of research, the freedom of inquiry, and "value-free" research—defend research in general, and are extended by some to justify intrusive studies. A supportive argument concerns such studies more specifically, claiming that they are not truly invasive.

The *pursuit of knowledge* can surely justify probing that would ordinarily 17 be indiscreet or even degrading, so long as it is undertaken with the consent of those subjected to the probing, as when individuals agree to examinations by physicians, psychiatrists, and others which they would reject from other quarters. When social scientists invoke the pursuit of knowledge to justify research such as that conducted by Festinger, they likewise take it to outweigh common moral considerations. Fewer now believe in the possibility of attaining "true knowledge" than in Durkheim's time; yet research may at least push back the boundaries of ignorance and felt chaos. Perhaps it may also achieve greater insight into all that is private, exclusive, even sacred.

But how should one go about such research when people are so reluc- 18 tant to have these aspects of their existence studied, or else so unable to respond spontaneously in experimental situations? The physical world lends itself at least in part to experimental manipulation in the search for knowledge; human beings can be much more grudging. As a result, researchers have worked out ways to take people by surprise before they have a chance to resist revealing themselves, and have developed means of deceiving them in such ways that they do not know what is being studied. Under such circumstances, people may betray their "true" responses as they would not if they had been forewarned.

Yet the pursuit of knowledge cannot by itself justify deceit and intrusiveness that bypass consent. Might not Festinger justly have protested if his neighbors or local journalists had trespassed upon his most closely guarded intimacy for purposes of greater knowledge? But if that is so, what makes the difference when social scientists do so in the course of their research? [19]

Does the difference lie in the possible *benefits of research* — benefits great enough to override such protests about intrusive probing? Might researchers claim that it is one thing to pry into the religious practices of neighbors out of mere curiosity and quite another to undertake *research* into such practices? Could Festinger have argued that his study sought knowledge about conduct that seemed irrational at first glance, and that this knowledge could help individuals as well as society to cope more wisely with cognitive dissonance? [20]

The hope to provide such benefits has undoubtedly motivated many investigators. C. Wright Mills has pointed to the frequency with which social scientists state their aims as "prediction and control."[10] Through research, they seek knowledge that could help individuals and influence social policies — the treatment of welfare recipients, for example, or of schoolchildren, or the prevention of crime. But when they undertake intrusive, perhaps deceptive studies (as in all other research), social scientists have widely diverging views about the kind of influence they hope to exert. They may conduct such studies in order to predict and to influence consumer choice on behalf of companies, or apply similar techniques to voting behavior in order to swing support to the political candidates who employ them. Or they may want to shock the public into acknowledging misery and injustice. Thus social commentators have sought to penetrate and then to expose mental hospitals or camps for migrant workers, hoping to pierce the wall of public indifference even at the risk of breaching individual boundaries of reserve — as when films are made of inmates against their wishes. [21]

Anthropologists, likewise, have sought to exercise leverage of widely different and sometimes conflicting kinds. Some have studied groups and cultures that are threatened in order to speak on their behalf.[11] Any intrusiveness on their part, they argue, is minimal compared to the impact of the outside world, as one culture after another becomes extinct or is annihilated by commercial or military means.[12] Other social scientists, on the contrary, have worked to help outside groups to penetrate [22] where overt military or commercial efforts might encounter resistance. Like missionaries, they have at times been used for propaganda or infiltration, and at times in order to learn how to stifle social protest: some eager to place themselves at the service of a cause they admire, others as unwitting tools, perhaps shielding themselves from asking hard questions about the impact of their work.

With so many different aims for the "prediction and control" of social 23 science research, and with such unspecified, often disputed, benefits from this research, intrusive studies can hardly be justified merely by invoking possible benefits.[13] Those who conduct intrusive studies have not shown the links between their research and such benefits, nor explained why they think the hypothetical gains from their research should override the desires of those being studied.

The rationale for social science research may draw on an additional 24 argument that presupposes neither the value of particular studies nor the benefits to be derived from them: the claim to *freedom for scientific inquiry* no matter how inconsequential or even unpopular some lines of research may be in the eyes of critics. Such a requirement is indispensable for the protection of freedom of thought that is central to scientific inquiry; science, without such protection, is vulnerable to the many who would impose censorship, blacklists, or limitations on the study of selected topics. Scientific freedom threatens every hierarchy purporting to have access to the full truth, or to truth more important than that sought by science.

Because scientific research must be protected against such attacks, 25 many scientists have been reluctant to accept any outside criticism or restraints whatsoever. But in describing the freedom of scientific inquiry, the words "freedom" and "inquiry" can be stretched far beyond the freedom of thought. Their placid connotations can then help to ward off concern about what scientists do, and about limits to invasive or dangerous research. The concept of "inquiry" in science evokes the solitary seeker for knowledge. Freedom of such inquiry is freedom of limitless thought and unfettered speech. Steven Weinberg conveys a splendid image of the world of such a scientist:

> In the Science Museum in Kensington there is an old picture of the Octagon Room of the Greenwich Observatory, which seems to me beautifully to express the mood of science at its best: the room laid out in a cool, uncluttered, early eighteenth-century style, the few instruments standing ready for use, clocks of various sorts ticking on the walls, and from the many windows, filling the room, the clear light of day.[14]

These solitary, reflective, almost passive connotations of "scientific 26 inquiry" do not in fact correspond with many of the activities of today's scientists. These men and women are hardly solitary in their interaction with others. They are far from passive in their use of vast public funds, or in their resort to manipulative techniques for human studies. Some use electronic and chemical means to act upon human beings in ways hitherto inconceivable. Others intrude upon, and help to alter, the most fundamental beliefs individuals may hold. The freedom to do such studies is not the freedom of thought and speech that must be defended for all people, but freedom of action. The latter cannot be limitless, for scientists any more than for others, and least of all when it places unsuspecting individuals at risk.

The passive connotations of such terms as "inquiry" and "freedom" 27 may also help explain the unquestioning faith with which some social scientists have held to the notion that the conduct of their research could be "value-free." Through the 1960s, a number of researchers subscribed to a misinterpretation of Max Weber's call for *wertfrei*, or "value-free," social science. Instead of seeing it as a warning not to let values influence the interpretation of results, they came to regard any concern with ethical questions as unscientific, and to confuse the scientific ideals of disinterestedness and objectivity with a denial of the role that values play in all thinking and all work, including their own. Weber himself would have been the last to deny this role—the last, too, to refuse to acknowledge the moral dimension of research that affects human beings as research subjects or otherwise.[15]

The concept of "value-free research" is broad; but even those who 28 subscribe to it make an illegitimate leap if they deduce from it some notion of completely value-free *conduct* of research, or conjure up the specter of a value-free social scientist. Most researchers would themselves condemn egregious abuses in research, and use moral criteria in so doing; but the confused concept of "value-free research" has blunted the application of the same criteria to less egregious but nevertheless troubling cases.

Neither the shield of freedom of inquiry nor that of value-free research 29 suffices to ward off all questions about intrusive research. An additional argument is occasionally brought to its defense. . . . This argument holds that there is no need to be concerned about secrecy or about probing, since there is very little that people succeed in keeping secret in the first place. Restraints on probing by social scientists would be like locking the barn door after the cows have run away. Modern life, according to this argument, necessitates so much openness and revelation that discretion on the part of social scientists would be prudish and unnecessary. Why should social scientists be prevented from observing what everyone else is at liberty to see?

Insofar as information is thus open, the argument is surely persuasive. 30 It would be absurd to argue, for instance, that the observation of traffic patterns or of horse-racing audiences poses a problem, and that it should proceed only with the consent of all who are being observed. It would be equally uncalled-for to forbid research on what some people are willing to expose, just because others guard it closely. Rather, what is at issue is research on the private behavior of individuals without their knowledge or against their will. Of such intrusions, one can hardly claim that what is being studied is open for all to see. If it were, why would investigators regard it as necessary to employ surprise and pressure and deceit in order to penetrate what for them is so readily apparent?

Such intrusive research is not always conducted in secret. It can pro- 31 ceed openly by taking subjects by surprise and thus wrenching from them responses they might have guarded against had they been forewarned. It can also rely on pressure. Students taking courses in sociology or social psychology may have no choice but to take part as subjects of intrusive research. Such participation may be the prerequisite for taking a course, or for belonging to a department. Preadolescents in school often find it hard to refuse to answer probing questionnaires about family life or sexual matters. And welfare clients have difficulty distinguishing between the studies to which they are subjected and the many other procedures they must go through.

More often, however, intrusive research is surreptitious. Infiltration, 32 cover stories, hidden cameras, and one-way mirrors—few methods known to the world of detection and espionage are foreign to social science. The means for such covert observation grow more ingenious each year; and in some fields such methods are thought especially likely to allow examination of subjects behaving "naturally."

Consider, for example, the investigator who simulated a "lookout" 33 meant to warn homosexuals in men's rooms. He not only observed their activities covertly, but also traced the participants, took notes on their homes and their neighborhoods, and finally interviewed them, giving a false reason for doing so, without revealing to them his earlier monitoring of their actions.[16]

Or take the innumerable questionnaires and psychological tests osten- 34 sibly given for one purpose while in reality used to try to penetrate much more intimate attitudes, perhaps even ones causing the subjects great anxiety, such as sexual problems or feelings of self-hatred.

Or consider the following letter to Ruth Benedict from Jaime de An- 35 gelo, whom she had asked for help in finding an Indian informant willing to reveal sacred ceremonials:

Ruth, you have no idea how much that has hurt me. . . . Do you realize that it is just that sort of thing that kills the Indians. I mean it seriously. It kills them spiritually first, and as in their life the spiritual and the physical element are much more interdependent than our own, they soon die of it physically. . . . Don't you understand the psychological value of secrecy at a certain level of culture? . . . there are things that must not be brought to the light of day, otherwise they wither and die like uprooted plants.[17]

Whether or not the author of this letter was right in his surmise about the particular case in question, his concern points to a pattern of neglect by many early anthropologists. Because they were so interested in the knowledge they might gain, they sometimes failed to take into account the responses of those whom they studied, especially among cultures very different from their own. Some looked at the peoples they were studying much as they would have looked at exotic specimens in their laboratories. Others felt closer to them, but never imagined that the rituals and secrets they exposed in print might find their way back to the tribes they had probed to cause them embarrassment and a sense of shamed exposure.  36

None of the arguments I have examined can be stretched to justify invasive studies of the unwilling or the secretive; nor do they give such justification in the aggregate. Research lends no special legitimacy to actions otherwise disrespectful of human beings, unless they have expressly consented thereto. In that case, what conclusions should we draw with respect to research such as that of Festinger? Should social scientists leave untouched those regions of privacy and sacredness that Durkheim had singled out for future study?  37

## NOTES

1. Emile Durkheim (1858–1917), French sociologist who is considered one of the founders of modern sociology. One of his concerns was to establish a properly scientific or empirical method for the study of society. His last major work was *The Elementary Forms of Religious Life*, translated by Joseph Wardswain (Glencoe, Illinois: Free Press, 1947; first published in 1915 by G. Allen and Unwin). [eds.]

2. "The Participant-Observer Technique in Small Communities," *American Journal of Sociology* 46 (1940): 338.

3. Anabaptists are a Christian sect. An Anabaptist preacher prophesied that the millennium of Revelations, the period of a thousand years during which Christ will reign on earth, would come in 1534 and the city of Muenster would become the City of God, New Jerusalem. Anabaptists, who controlled the city, closed its gates to all nonbelievers, while Catholics and Protestants united in a siege on the city, ultimately destroying much of its population. [eds.]

4. The Messiah is the promised deliverer of the Jewish people whose coming will inaugurate the new kingdom of God. There have been many false messiahs. [eds.]

5. Leon Festinger, Henry W. Riecken, and Stanley Schachter, *When Prophecy Fails* (Minneapolis: University of Minnesota Press, 1956), chapter 1. See also Festinger, *A Theory of Cognitive Dissonance* (Evanston, Illinois: Row, Peterson, 1957). [eds.]

6. *When Prophecy Fails*, pp. 30–31.

7. *When*, p. 237.

8. *When*, p. 240.

9. *When*, p. 252.

10. "The Bureaucratic Ethics," in Maurice Stein and Arthur Vidich, eds., *Sociology on Trial* (Englewood Cliffs, N.J.: Prentice-Hall, 1963), pp. 12–25, passage quoted on p. 22.

11. See David Maybury-Lewis, "Don't Put the Blame on Anthropologists," *New York Times*, March 15, 1974.

12. "Sometimes anthropologists are even expressly requested to study materials formerly kept secret, by cultures fearing to lose their traditions. Thus the people of Telefolmin, in New Guinea, recently called in a Canadian anthropologist to collect the sacred lore from a cult center about to be sacrificed to the construction of copper mines. They had decided to do away with the site, but feared the loss of sacred lore. In that case there was, of course, no intrusiveness or deception in the research. See 'Prompt Assistance for Telefolmin,' Newsletter, *Cultural Survival* 3 (Spring, 1979)."

13. For a discussion of the uses of social science research, see Charles E. Lindblom and David K. Cohen, *Usable Knowledge: Social Science and Social Problem Solving* (New Haven, Conn.: Yale University Press, 1979).

14. Steven Weinberg, "Reflection of a Working Scientist," *Daedalus* 103 (1974):45.

15. Max Weber (1864–1920), German social scientist who had a major influence on modern sociology. His major works are *The Protestant Ethic and the Spirit of Capitalism* and *The Methodology of the Social Sciences*. [eds.]

16. Laud Humphreys, *Tearoom Trade* (Chicago: Aldine, 1970).

17. Jaime de Angelo, "Letter to Ruth Benedict," reprinted in Margaret Mead, *An Anthropologist at Work: Writings of Ruth Benedict* (Boston: Houghton Mifflin, 1959), p. 296.

## QUESTIONS FOR ANALYSIS

1. How does Bok define participant observation? Skim the selection, making an inventory of the terms she uses to characterize this kind of research. What attitudes and values do her word choices imply? (Chapter 1 offers procedures for taking inventory.)

2. Locate the section where Bok describes Festinger's research. Why is this research important to her argument? What attitudes toward this research do you think she wants to instill in her readers? How does she instill these attitudes?

3. Why do you think Bok conjectures in paragraph 3 about the motives of social science researchers? What effect do these speculations have on you?

4. Briefly summarize the arguments Bok says social scientists use to defend their research methods. Then select one of these arguments, analyze it, and evaluate Bok's rebuttal. (See Chapter 1 for how to analyze and evaluate an argument.)

5. What criteria does Bok use to condemn intrusive social science research? How do you regard these criteria?

6. Bok frames this piece by referring at the beginning and ending to Emile Durkheim. How does this framing work and what is its effect?

7. How would you characterize the tone Bok uses in this selection?

## SUGGESTIONS FOR WRITING

Although Bok limits herself to evaluating research into people's private, even religious, behavior, much of what she says can be applied more generally. Keeping what Bok has said in mind and taking your own sense of morality into account, choose one of the following situations, and write an essay evaluating the ethics involved:

Is it fair that plagiarism, the unacknowledged use of another's ideas or writing, be punished by expulsion from school?

How deeply should schools be permitted to probe into the home conditions of students with problems?

Should schools be allowed to search students' lockers or belongings?

Should undercover police sting operations be considered entrapment?

Are investigative reporters right to pursue their stories regardless of who might be hurt?

Is human subject research, such as the implementation of mechanical hearts, ethical?

Is animal research in which animals may be maimed, exposed to disease, or subjected to trauma ethical?

Is it morally acceptable to release the results of public opinion exit polls before voting is completed?

# Kevin Suto

Keven Suto (b. 1967) is a college undergraduate majoring in biology. He has played the guitar for five years and has a large record collection. By some standards, Suto is esoteric in his musical tastes. As a musician himself, he is not only interested in technique, but is also drawn to music that is original and innovative.

# A Refreshing Sound of Music

Suto wrote this review of Allan Holdsworth's album "Metal Fatigue" for his freshman writing course. Holdsworth is a guitarist who is relatively unknown. As Suto explains, Holdsworth recently formed his own group and "Metal Fatigue" is only his third album. Not only are Holdsworth's name and music likely to be unfamiliar to most readers, but the type of music he plays—a fusion of jazz and rock—is certain to be new as well. Suto, unfortunately, was so involved in the music and so out of tune with the majority of his readers that his essay leaves out some important information. As you read, ask yourself what more you as one reader need to know in order to better understand the essay. Write questions in the margins to indicate where you lack information.

Until three years ago, guitar virtuoso Allan Holdsworth was literally 1 unheard of in the music world. For years he had been doing guitar work for such critically acclaimed groups as Bill Bruford, Soft Machine, and UK, but it was only when he began doing solo work that his true genius emerged. "Metal Fatigue," his second solo album with I.O.U and his third to date, is another brilliant effort on his new Enigma label.

As in his two previous LPs, "I.O.U." and "Road Games," Holdsworth 2 combines rock and jazz to create a soothing, crisp sound original to the American recording industry. Combining jazz with a subtle dose of hard rock creates the unique Holdsworth style that guitarists and other musicians have become accustomed to in recent years. The title track "Metal Fatigue" is classic Holdsworth. Opening with a raunchy guitar intro, the piece gradually flows into a smoothly textured jazz tune. A dynamic vocal performance by Paul Williams coupled with the searing guitar of Holdsworth turns an average song into a jazz fusion delight. Add the ferocious drumming of Chad Wackerman bottomed out by the incomparable bass playing of the legendary Jeff Berlin, and it becomes a masterpiece. Such is the case with many of the cuts on "Metal Fatigue."

Produced by Holdsworth himself, the mix of the recording is one of    3
the best I've heard in a while. The balance of the instruments is superb,
each musician complementing the others. Producer Ted Templeman edited Holdsworth's first two efforts, but "Metal Fatigue" is by far the best
production of the three. You can almost hear Holdsworth's guitar weep
as they crank out "The Un-Merry-Go-Round," a fourteen-minute epi-
logue dedicated to his recently deceased father.

A performance of special note is that of Wackerman. With his in-    4
credible sense of timing, he is spectacular throughout the LP—his presence is felt every time he cracks the snare. Wackerman's efforts elevate
him to the pedestal of greatness and make the listener think of Terry
Bozio and Buddy Rich.

Although Berlin, Williams, and Wackerman add the depth and clarity    5
often lacking in many recordings, the heart of the album is Holdsworth.
His guitar work is so amazing that it opens the eyes and minds of the
harshest music critics. He soars through intricate leads troubling even to
the best musicians. His chord work is enchanting. He produces musical
sounds never before heard on guitar. As he weaves his way through eerie
passages, his work with harmonizers and the volume pedal changes his
sound into that of a chamber symphony. His leads are at times melodi-
cally slow, and at times he rips at lightning speed through complicated
structures with the precision of a Swiss watch. If you have never heard
Holdsworth before, he is in prime form here, excelling in such pieces as
"Home" and "Panic Station." In these pieces, he redefines the uses of
the electric guitar, taking over where Jimi Hendrix, Al DiMeola, and
Edward Van Halen left off. Listening to Holdsworth is like riding a roller
coaster, eagerly anticipating the next curve.

Allan Holdsworth and I.O.U. have produced a delicious blend of crea-    6
tive musicianship in an industry of glitter and gimmick. "Metal Fatigue"
is a refreshing alternative to the commercial compost commonly found
today. Only a few are as talented as the all-star members of this band.
If you wish to be turned on to an exciting new sound, I suggest that you
give this new album your attention.

## QUESTIONS FOR ANALYSIS

1. How well do you think Suto handles the disparity between his own
   and his readers' expertise? What specific additions or changes would
   you suggest he make?

2. On what criteria does Suto base his judgment of Holdsworth's album?
   Compare his criteria to the criteria you would use to evaluate a record
   album.

3. What role does comparison play in Suto's evaluation? How would this evaluation be different if Suto used as comparison some other kind of music or something else entirely? Choose one particular comparison that you think is weak and offer an alternative of your own.
4. Make an inventory of the evaluative adjectives Suto sprinkles throughout this essay. What effect do these adjectives have on you? (Chapter 1 offers guidance for taking inventory.)
5. In paragraph 5, Suto judges the value of Holdsworth's technical dexterity. How does he support this judgment?
6. How would you characterize the voice you hear in this essay? Point to passages from the essay as illustration. How effective is the tone of voice you hear in this essay?

## SUGGESTIONS FOR WRITING

1. Select an album by a musician or group you admire, and write a review of it. The album does not have to be new, but you should know it very well. Address your essay to readers who may not know the artist or be familiar with this particular album.
2. Think of something you know very well, such as music, sports, fashion, or computers. Choose a subject within that field, and use your expertise to write an essay of evaluation. Before writing, think carefully about how knowledgeable your readers will be about your subject and how much information you will need to give them.
3. Find a published review of an album with which you are familiar, and write an essay evaluating that review. When studying the review, listen to the album again to determine the accuracy of the reviewer's judgment.

# A Look at Kevin Suto's Writing Process

When his instructor assigned an evaluation paper, Suto knew immediately that he wanted to write about his own specialty, music—in particular, the guitar. The only question was what guitarist to choose. He toyed with the possibility of evaluating some well-known guitarist like Jimi Hendrix or Van Halen, but decided on Allan Holdsworth because he wanted others to know how good Holdsworth is. He knew Holdsworth was not in the musical mainstream, but felt that most people would come to appreciate him if they only knew how masterful he was on the guitar.

He spent the weekend before the essay was due immersing himself in Holdsworth's music. He listened to all three of Holdsworth's albums repeatedly, making detailed notes about what he thought was good and why. He filled up three pages of his notebook with ideas and details to back them up. Later, he reported that he never knew that researching a paper could be so much fun.

Looking back, Suto realizes that he probably got too involved in his research because he forgot to think long and hard about the central problem a writer of evaluation must face: writing as an expert for readers who are more or less ignorant about your subject. He was so sure of his own authority on the subject that he thought his readers would readily accept his judgment. He forgot that he needed to gain his readers' confidence in part by teaching them about the subject—by showing them what you know, not merely by acting as if you know it all.

## A  GUIDE  TO  EVALUATIVE  WRITING

Although all evaluations argue for a judgment, they vary a great deal in how they present the subject and how they make their argument. There may be wide variation, for example, in how much information about the subject is imparted to readers. Sometimes writers describe their subjects in detail, as Marshall and Bok do; at other times, they may assume, as Kinsley does, that readers are already familiar with the subject. Whatever you decide, don't make the mistake that Suto did of failing to think about this crucially important writing issue.

As the readings in this chapter suggest, evaluations may also differ on whether they make a case for their criteria and how they support their reasons. Whereas Bok and Suto assume that readers will accept their standards of judgment, Kauffmann argues explicitly for his. Baker constructs his argument around several reasons and provides specific evidence for each reason, while Kauffmann centers his argument on a single reason. Kinsley presents a balanced view of the subject's good and bad qualities. Bok rebuts arguments in defense of the subject.

However you finally decide to present your subject and argue for your judgment, you will need to do some thoughtful planning. The following brief guide suggests some things to consider as you plan, draft, and revise your own evaluative essay.

## *Invention*

Writing is a process of discovery—of learning what you already know about a subject and what you still need to know; of trying out ideas and arguments to see which are most effective; and of finding a voice, a tone that suits your subject and your readers. The following invention activities will help you to make these discoveries in a systematic way.

CHOOSING A SUBJECT. The readings in this chapter suggest different types of subjects you could write about—public figures, films, books, people's styles, significant contributions, ethical issues. There are also countless other possibilities, among them consumer products, sports teams, restaurants, schools, performers or their performances.

To find a subject, first list two or three specific subjects in several of these general categories. Although you may be inclined to pick the first idea that comes to mind, try to make your list as long as you can. This will ensure that you have a variety of subjects from which to choose and also encourage you to think of unique subjects.

Once you have a list of possibilities, consider the following questions as you make your final selection:

Do I already know enough about this subject, or can I get the information I need in time? If, for instance, you decide to review a film, you should have seen it recently or be able to see it soon. If you choose to evaluate a consumer product, you should already be somewhat expert about the product or have time to learn enough about it to be able to write with some authority.

Do I already have strong feelings and a firm judgment about this subject? It is always easier to write about subjects on which you have formed opinions, although it is conceivable that you could change your mind as you write. If you choose a subject that leaves you cold, your readers will probably have the same reaction. The more sure you are of your judgment, the more persuasive you are likely to be.

EXPLORING YOUR SUBJECT. Before you can go much further, you must ascertain what you already know about the subject and what additional information you may need. To do this, list everything you now know about the subject and all the questions you still have, or write about the subject for ten or fifteen minutes without stopping, putting down anything that enters your mind. If you discover that you need to gather more information, find out where you can get it and whether you have enough time for research.

ANALYZING YOUR READERS. To decide how much information about the subject to include in your essay, you will need to estimate how much your readers know about the subject and how much they need to know in order to accept your judgment. In planning your argument, you will also need to anticipate readers' attitudes and opinions. Take some time to think about the readers you will be addressing, what they might already know about the subject and what you will need to tell them, and also how they are likely to judge your subject.

A good way to analyze readers is to imagine one typical reader. It could be someone you know personally, even someone with whom you've discussed the subject—perhaps your writing instructor or a classmate. Then write an imaginary dialogue, rehearsing the points you would make and the responses you expect that this typical reader would have.

DEVELOPING YOUR ARGUMENTS.  If you have written a dialogue, you have probably already sketched out your main arguments. To develop your arguments systematically, make a chart of your criteria and the evidence you might use to support them. Divide a piece of paper into two columns. In the left-hand column, list the criteria you think are most appropriate for judging your subject; in the right-hand column, indicate the evidence you could cite—examples, illustrations, quotations, facts, authorities—to support each point.

Use this chart not only to record ideas but also to generate new ones. Thinking about your readers or the type of subject you are evaluating might suggest criteria that lead to particular examples. Thinking about your judgment might suggest details that lead to additional criteria. Instead of moving only right or left across the chart, you might also move up or down, letting one criterion suggest another.

## Drafting

After you have made a fairly detailed chart of your argument, you are probably ready to set your goals, plan the organization of your essay, and decide how to begin.

SETTING GOALS.  The decisions you make about what to include and how to order your ideas should be guided by some specific goals that reflect your purpose and your understanding of the readers' needs and expectations. Considering the following questions may help you to clarify your goals: What do I want to accomplish with this particular evaluation? Is my primary purpose to make a recommendation as Kauffmann, Marshall, and Suto do? Do I want readers to reexamine something they may have taken for granted like a famous writer's style as in Baker's essay on Hemingway? Am I trying to expose my subject's faults like Owen or weigh its good and bad points like Amberg?

How much experience evaluating a subject of this kind can I expect my readers to have? Will they share my criteria or will I have to argue for them? Kauffmann, for example, argues for his criteria against other reviewers of the film. Baker indirectly argues for his criteria by showing that they are also Hemingway's.

How much information about the subject do my readers need to understand my evaluation? Obviously, reviews of new books, films, and albums should assume little or no familiarity on the part of readers. Marshall, for instance, devotes nearly two-thirds of his essay to summarizing the book he is reviewing. Kauffmann also tells a lot about the plot, setting, characters, and key events but tries not to give too much away. Suto, on the other hand, does not tell his readers enough about jazz fusion, his esoteric subject. Other kinds of evaluation, after identifying the subject, provide information to support the argument, not for its own sake. Both Amberg and Owen, for example, only give information that relates to their argument.

PLANNING YOUR ORGANIZATION. Once you have decided how much your readers know and need to know, what criteria you will use and how best to present them, select a plan of organization that best reflects these decisions. You have many options to choose from. You can separate your description of the subject from your evaluation of it as Marshall does or weave the description into your argument as Kauffmann does. You can organize the essay around your own criteria as Baker does or around the arguments you are refuting as Bok does. You can weigh the good and bad points of the subject as Amberg does or focus your entire discussion on a single strength or shortcoming as Owen does.

BEGINNING. How you decide to begin your essay will depend on how familiar your readers are with your subject. If you are writing about something that is entirely new and unfamiliar, you will naturally want to begin with a description or summary of the subject. Amberg and Bok, for example, begin with an anecdote that dramatizes the subject. Kauffmann opens with a plot summary, but he asserts his judgment in the very first sentence. Marshall starts by quoting from the book he is reviewing in order to let readers know what it is about and also to establish his own credibility with them.

AVOIDING LOGICAL FALLACIES. Evaluative writing is particularly susceptible to certain kinds of faulty logic. To avoid these logical fallacies, ask yourself the following questions as you plan and draft your essay:

• Am I basing my argument on personal *taste* instead of general criteria (praising a story, for example, because it reminds me of my own experience)?

- Am I basing my argument on *trivial criteria* and ignoring important ones (condemning a film because it has subtitles, for example)?

- Am I guilty of *hasty generalization* (for instance, criticizing a public figure because he once said something with which I disagree)?

- Am I making *weak comparisons* (failing to acknowledge weaknesses of subjects I praise and strengths of those I criticize)?

- Am I accepting the *burden of proof* (giving reasons and citing evidence instead of merely asserting my opinions)?

- Am I guilty of *either/or thinking* (seeing only the good or only the bad in my subject)?

- Am I setting up a *straw man* (rebutting an obviously weak argument that is an easy target and ignoring stronger arguments that are harder to rebut)?

# Revising

Once you have completed a rough draft, consider how the argument might be strengthened and the writing made clearer. Begin by reading your draft in light of the critical reading questions at the beginning of this chapter. As you read, be particularly aware of how you might make your argument clearer and more convincing for your prospective readers. If possible, have someone else read your draft critically as well.

REVISING YOUR ARGUMENT. When revising, keep your purpose and your readers in mind. If necessary, add more information about the subject. Reconsider the criteria on which you have based your judgment, and decide if they are appropriate, if they need to be justified, if any are trivial. Study your reasons, looking for weak ones that should be improved or thrown out. Examine your evidence to decide whether you have provided enough support. Look at the organization of your argument—the order of reasons, the proportion of good to bad qualities, the arguments you anticipate and rebut. Listen to the voice in your draft. Is it sufficiently authoritative? Is it appropriate for your readers?

REVISING TO IMPROVE READABILITY. If any part of your essay seems confusing, add forecasts, transitions, and other orienting cues to help your readers. Look for unclear writing—words that need to be defined, language that is too abstract, sentences that are hard to read—and revise to make your writing more understandable. Finally, proofread carefully for mistakes in usage, spelling, and punctuation.

# CHAPTER SEVEN

# Analysis of Cause
# or Effect

When something surprising happens, we automatically ask, "How did that happen?" The human brain seems to demand this explanation, as though incapable of leaving a mystery unresolved. We also ask ourselves what might result, sometimes for our own safety and at other times just from natural human curiosity. From these basic human responses to events, phenomena, and trends—from our compulsion to know what *caused* them and what *effects* they might have—comes the motive for writing about causes and effects.

Analysis of cause or effect involves conjecturing about an event, phenomenon, or trend that has no obvious or certain causes or effects and arguing in support of a proposed explanation. An oceanographer in a college lecture might explain why the ocean has waves on the basis of undisputed scientific facts, for example, and a historian writing a college textbook might summarize other historians' proposed causes of the Civil War; however, neither of these scholars is conjecturing about possible but uncertain causes or presenting an argument. Both are simply reporting information.

In other writing situations, however, both the oceanographer and the historian could truly be analyzing the causes of a phenomenon or event. The oceanographer could analyze an unexplained warming trend in the ocean, while the historian could evaluate other historians' proposed causes of the Civil War in order to argue for an original but still plausible explanation. Certainly a sociologist writing a paper on the recent increase in teenage suicides would be conjecturing about possible causes, not reporting established information. This sociologist has no way of knowing for certain why more and more teenagers take their own lives but can only conjecture—and then argue with relevant facts, statistics, or anecdotes to support these conjectures.

From these examples you can see the importance of the analysis of cause or effect in academic writing. You will read many such arguments in all the college subjects you study. This kind of writing is especially prominent in the social sciences—sociology, political science, economics, anthropology, psychology, education. Much of what we want to know about ourselves, other people, and the social order can never be known definitively and unarguably, but can only be conjectured about on the basis of the best available evidence.

Analysis of cause or effect is important outside of the academic world as well. Newspaper editors and columnists often propose causes or predict the results of trends, events, or phenomena. They are quick to propose causes for a surprising election defeat, a decline in housing starts, an increase in the trade deficit with Japan, or a decline in interest rates. Sports writers might try to explain why a high school soccer team lost a game it was favored to win, why a professional team owner was unable to sign a high draft pick, or why the Pacific Ten nearly always defeats the Big Ten in the Rose Bowl.

In government, business, and education, too, causal argument plays an important part. The Secretary of State might request an analysis of the causes of terrorism in the Middle East from the State Department's Middle Eastern bureau. The chief executive officer of a computer-manufacturing firm could ask the sales manager to submit a report explaining the decline in sales of a low-priced personal computer. A school superintendent might draft a statement proposing several possible causes for falling test scores in math.

Writing your own essays analyzing causes or effects will engage you in some of the most challenging problem-solving and decision-making situations a writer can experience. You will be able to test your powers of concentration and creativity as you speculate about the causes or effects of an event, phenomenon, or trend, searching out the hidden causes behind the obvious ones, differentiating among precipitating, remote, and perpetuating causes, and attempting to discover results that are surprising and yet still plausible.

You will also have the opportunity to research the causes or effects that have been proposed by others. After evaluating their conjectures and speculations, you can experiment with strategies of integrating them into your essay, accepting some and refuting others. As in all kinds of argument, you will continue to develop your sensitivity to your readers' knowledge and attitudes, anticipating their objections to your conjectures and discovering ways to be authoritative and convincing without alienating your reader. All of the thinking, planning, and writing strategies involved in this kind of writing will make you a better writer in general and will prepare you for many reading and writing situations you will encounter in other college classes.

## A GUIDE TO READING ABOUT CAUSE OR EFFECT

Learning to recognize the basic features of writing that analyzes cause or effect will enable you to become a more confident and critical reader of this kind of writing. This section outlines these features and discusses each briefly. It also presents a sample annotated essay and a list of questions that can guide your reading of this kind of writing.

# Basic Features of Cause-Effect Analysis

Writers who conjecture about causes or speculate about results know they cannot offer definitive explanations about why something happened or what might result from it. They do, however, intend that their readers will consider their proposed causes or results to be plausible or believable. Their purpose is thus to be as convincing as possible. To this end, they include the following features: *a presentation of the event, phenomenon, or trend; a convincing argument;* and *a reasonable, authoritative voice.*

A PRESENTATION OF THE EVENT, PHENOMENON, OR TREND. Essays arguing for possible causes or effects of something must first present that something adequately to readers. If readers have witnessed the event (a disappointing loss in a basketball playoff game), then the writer may need only refer to the event before conjecturing about what its cause or causes might have been. On the other hand, if the writer is conjecturing about the causes of a historical event readers have neither witnessed nor read about (Napoleon's defeat at Waterloo), then the writer may need to describe the event in some detail. It is especially important in an essay about the causes or effects of a trend (a demonstrable increase or decrease in an activity over several years) that the writer first describe the trend and prove to readers that the trend does exist.

A CONVINCING ARGUMENT. The heart of cause or effect analysis is a convincing argument. Since there is uncertainty about what caused something or about what might result from it, the writer cannot simply list causes or results but must persuade readers that the proposed causes or results are at least as plausible as their own.

To be convincing, an essay must present causes or effects and then argue for them with facts, evidence, examples, or anecdotes. The proposed causes or effects must be arranged in an effective order, perhaps with the most convincing placed last and developed most fully. A convincing argument also anticipates readers' objections to the proposed causes or results and considers causes or effects proposed by others.

A REASONABLE, AUTHORITATIVE VOICE. Analyses of cause or effect are prompted by puzzling or inconclusive events, phenomena, or trends. There would be no need for speculations and conjecture about an event whose causes or effects were known and agreed to by everyone. Thus, in order to be believed, writers must sound reasonable. Readers are much more likely to accept an argument if it is handled competently, if they hear a voice they can trust. This voice can be serious or playful, but it must be authoritative.

## An Annotated Sample:
### *The Great Dying,* Stephen Jay Gould

Look now at the following example of an essay analyzing causes. The annotations that accompany the selection are like those that any critical reader might have produced—posing questions, defining key terms, and commenting on important features. Before you look at the annotations, be sure to read the essay all the way through. Then examine the annotations as you reread the piece.

This selection is a chapter from a recent book by the well-known geologist and historian of science Stephen Jay Gould (b. 1941). A MacArthur Prize Fellow from 1981–86, Gould is a professor at Harvard University. Among his books are *The Panda's Thumb* (1980), *The Mismeasure of Man* (1981) (for which he won the National Book Award in Science), and *The Flamingo's Smile: Reflections on Natural History* (1985).

The selection will remind you of the importance of causal analysis in the sciences. Gould considers a puzzling event in the history of the earth—the dying out of half the families of marine organisms millions of years ago—and proposes causes for it. Like many puzzling events in geology, biology, anthropology, and archaeology, this mass extinction cannot be directly researched. Gould must piece together evidence to argue for a cause that can probably never be proven beyond any further challenge or doubt. As you read, notice how he develops his argument—describing the event, considering alternative causes, explaining what readers need to know in order to understand his causes, and then arguing for his proposed causes. Gould is not writing for specialists in his field. The voice in this selection is that of an expert, informed, articulate college professor. As a college student, you will hear and read many voices like this one.

## The Great Dying

**marine: living in the ocean**

**kinds of marine organisms**

About 225 million years ago, at the end of the Permian period, fully half the families of marine organisms died out during the short span of a few million years—a prodigious amount of time by most standards, but merely minutes to a geologist. The victims of this mass extinction included all surviving trilobites, all ancient corals, all but one lineage of ammonites, and most bryozoans, brachiopods, and crinoids.

**two extinctions: Permian: 225 million years ago Cretaceous: 75 m. years ago**

**emphasizes importance of Permian extinction**

This great dying was the most profound of several mass extinctions that have punctuated the evolution of life during the past 600 million years. The late Cretaceous extinction, some 70 million years ago, takes second place. It destroyed 25 percent of all families, and cleared the earth of its dominant terrestrial animals, the dinosaurs and their kin—thus setting a stage for the dominance of mammals and the eventual evolution of man.

**paleontology: study of prehistoric life forms**

**lists causes others have proposed**

**pandemics: widespread diseases**

**familiar examples: telephone book, Disney desiccating: becoming dry**

No problem in paleontology has attracted more attention or led to more frustration than the search for causes of these extinctions. The catalog of proposals would fill a Manhattan telephone book and include almost all imaginable causes: mountain building of world wide extent, shifts in sea level, subtraction of salt from the oceans, supernovae, vast influxes of cosmic radiation, pandemics, restriction of habitat, abrupt changes in climate, and so on. Nor has the problem escaped public notice. I remember well my first exposure to it at age five: the dinosaurs of Disney's *Fantasia* panting to their deaths across a desiccating landscape to the tune of Stravinsky's *Rite of Spring*.

**event to be explained: Permian extinction**

Since the Permian extinction dwarfs all the others, it has long been the major focus of inquiry. If we could explain this greatest of all dyings, we might hold the key to understanding mass extinctions in general.

**explanation comes from (1) geology and (2) evolutionary biology**

During the past decade, important advances in both geology and evolutionary biology have combined to provide a probable answer. This solution has developed so gradually that some paleontologists scarcely realize that their oldest and deepest dilemma has been resolved.

**1. advances in geology**

Ten years ago, geologists generally believed that the

continents formed where they now stand. Large blocks of
land might move up and down and continents might

accretion: addition
"grow" by accretion of uplifted mountain chains at their

wander = drift
borders, but continents did not (wander) about the earth's
surface—their positions were fixed for all time. An alternative theory of continental (drift) had been proposed early
in the century, but the absence of a mechanism for mov-

nobody believed it
ing continents had assured its nearly universal rejection.

new theory
Now, studies of the ocean floor have yielded a mech-     7
anism in the theory of plate tectonics. The earth's surface
is divided into a small number of plates bordered by ridges
and subduction zones. New ocean floor is formed at the
ridges as older portions of the plates are pushed away. To
balance this addition, old parts of plates are drawn into

subduction: drawing
downward
the earth's interior at subduction zones.

Continents rest passively upon the plates and move      8
with them; they do not "plow" through solid ocean floor
as previous theories proposed. Continental drift, therefore, is but one consequence of plate tectonics. Other
important consequences include earthquakes at plate
boundaries (like the San Andreas Fault running past San
Francisco) and mountain chains where two plates bearing
continents collide (the Himalayas formed when the In-

relevance of plate
tectonics to Permian
extinction
dian "raft" hit Asia).

When we reconstruct the history of continental move-   9
ments, we realize that a unique event occurred in the

coalesced: came together
latest Permian: all the continents coalesced to form the
single supercontinent of Pangaea. Quite simply, the consequences of this (coalescence) caused the great Permian
extinction.

coalescence = fusion
But which consequences and why? Such a (fusion) of    10
fragments would produce a wide array of results, ranging
from changes in weather and oceanic circulation to the
interaction of previously isolated ecosystems. Here we

2. advances in
evolutionary biology and
theoretical ecology
must look to advances in evolutionary biology to theoretical ecology and our new understanding of the diversity
of living forms.

After several decades of highly descriptive and largely  11
atheoretical work, the science of ecology has been en-
livened by quantitative approaches that seek a general

organic diversity:
different kinds of
organisms
theory of organic diversity. We are gaining a better understanding of the influences of different environmental
factors upon the abundance and distribution of life. Many
studies now indicate that diversity—the numbers of different species present in a given area—is strongly influenced, if not largely controlled, by the amount of hab-
itable area itself. If, for example, we count the number

of ant species living on each of a group of islands differing only in size (and otherwise similar in such properties as climate, vegetation, and distance from the mainland), we find that, in general, the larger the island, the greater the number of species.

It is a long way from ants on tropical islands to the 12 entire marine biota of the Permian period. Yet we have good reason to suspect that area might have played a major role in the great extinction. If we can estimate organic diversity and area for various times during the Permian (as the continents coalesced), then we can test the hypothesis of control by area.

We must first understand two things about the Permian 13 extinction and the fossil record in general. First, the Permian extinction primarily affected marine organisms. The relatively few terrestrial plants and vertebrates then living were not so strongly disturbed. Second, the fossil record is very strongly biased toward the preservation of marine life in shallow water. We have almost no fossils of organisms inhabiting the ocean depths. Thus, if we want to test the theory that reduced area played a major role in the Permian extinction, we must look to the area occupied by shallow seas.

We can identify, in a qualitative way, two reasons why 14 a coalescence of continents would drastically reduce the area of shallow seas. The first is basic geometry: If each separate land mass of pre-Permian times were completely surrounded by shallow seas, then their union would eliminate all area at the sutures. Make a single square out of four graham crackers and the total periphery is reduced by half. The second reason involves the mechanics of

plate tectonics. When oceanic ridges are actively producing new sea floor to spread outward, then the ridges themselves stand high above the deepest parts of the ocean. This displaces water from the ocean basins, world sea level rises, and continents are partly flooded. Conversely, if spreading diminishes or stops, ridges begin to collapse and sea level falls.

When continents collided in the late Permian, the 15 plates that carried them "locked" together. This set a brake upon new spreading. Ocean ridges sank and shallow seas withdrew from the continents. The drastic reduction in shallow seas was not caused by a drop in sea level *per se*, but rather by the configuration of sea floor over which the drop occurred. The ocean floor does not plunge uniformly from shoreline to ocean deep. Today's continents are generally bordered by a very wide continental shelf of persistently shallow water. Seaward of the shelf lies the continental slope of much greater steepness. If sea level fell far enough to expose the entire continental shelf, then most of the world's shallow seas would disappear. This may well have happened during the late Permian.

**tentative**

Thomas Schopf of the University of Chicago has re- 16 cently tested this hypothesis of extinction by reduction in area. He studied the distribution of shallow water and terrestrial rocks to infer continental borders and extent of shallow seas for several times during the Permian as the continents coalesced. Then, by an exhaustive survey of the paleontological literature, he counted the numbers of different kinds of organisms living during each of these Permian times. Daniel Simberloff of Florida State University then showed that the standard mathematical equation relating numbers of species to area fits these data very well. Moreover, Schopf showed that the extinction did not affect certain groups differentially; its results were evenly spread over all shallow-water inhabitants. In other words, we do not need to seek a specific cause related to the peculiarities of a few animal groups. The effect was general. As shallow seas disappeared, the rich ecosystem of earlier Permian times simply lacked the space to support all its members. The bag became smaller and half the marbles had to be discarded.

**the quantitative work referred to in paragraph 11**

**\*cause of the extinction: reduced space**

Area alone is not the whole answer. Such a momentous 17 event as the fusion of a single supercontinent must have entailed other consequences detrimental to the precariously balanced ecosystem of earlier Permian time. But Schopf and Simberloff have provided persuasive evidence for granting a major role to the basic factor of space.

**persuasive evidence but not definitive—might never be possible to prove it**

It is gratifying that an answer to paleontology's out- 18 standing dilemma has arisen as a by-product of exciting advances in two related disciplines—ecology and geology. When a problem has proved intractable for more than one hundred years, it is not likely to yield to more data collected in the old way and under the old rubric. Theoretical ecology allowed us to ask the right questions and plate tectonics provided the right earth upon which to pose them.

**intractable: not easily solved**

**emphasizes importance for causal analysis of knowledge from different scientific disciplines**

# Critical Reading Questions

The following questions will enable you to read analyses of causes and effects more thoughtfully and critically. These questions can guide your reading of the selections in this chapter and of any other essays of this type. As an example of how these questions might be used, each one has been applied to the Gould selection.

1. *How does the writer present the event, trend, or phenomenon?*

Writers analyzing causes or effects have in mind a particular subject, usually an event, trend, or phenomenon. In some writing situations, the writer might safely assume that readers already know a great deal about the subject and thus simply announce the subject and immediately begin the analysis. For most subjects, however, writers must present the subject in enough detail so that readers understand fully what is to be analyzed. In some cases, the writer may even need to convince readers that the subject is important and worth analyzing.

To evaluate the writer's presentation of the subject, ask yourself whether the writer has provided enough information. Do you know all you need to know about the event, trend, or phenomenon? If you have not heard of the event, does the writer describe it adequately? If the phenomenon is a problem, has the writer demonstrated that it exists— with facts, statistics, anecdotes, or arguments about its seriousness? If the subject is a trend, has the writer presented statistics or other evidence to establish the existence of the trend?

Gould assumes that his readers have heard of the Permian extinction but do not remember many details of it and that they are unfamiliar with recent research in geology and evolutionary biology. Hence, he devotes many paragraphs to describing the extinction and providing the background information readers need in order to understand his proposed causes.

2. *What causes or effects does the writer propose?*

The proposed causes or effects are the main points, or theses, of the essay. These points can appear anywhere in the essay and are usually easy to identify. They may be listed at the beginning, or they may be introduced one at a time as the argument develops. They may also be summarized or restated at the end of the essay.

Evaluate the proposed causes or effects by first determining whether or not they are plausible. Then decide whether the writer has ignored other equally plausible causes or results. Has the writer argued only immediate or obvious causes and overlooked remote or hidden ones?

Gould first states his proposed cause of the Permian extinction toward the end of paragraph 16: "As shallow seas disappeared, the rich ecosystem of earlier Permian times simply lacked the space to support all its members. The bag became smaller, and half the marbles had to be discarded." His carefully developed argument up to that point convinces us that his thesis is plausible and should be taken seriously.

*3. How does the writer anticipate and refute objections and counterarguments?*

When the causes or consequences of an event or trend are not certain but only probable, then there is sure to be disagreement. Readers will undoubtedly be able to think of objections to the best-argued explanations. Consequently, writers try to anticipate these objections and perhaps even attempt to refute them. Although it might seem strange that writers would acknowledge a possible objection to their arguments, they in fact increase their credibility and the plausibility of their arguments by anticipating possible objections.

Locate places in the essay where the writer has anticipated possible objections. Does the writer handle these objections tactfully and convincingly? Can you think of any other objections the writer should have anticipated?

Gould does not specifically mention objections to his proposed causes, but in paragraphs 13–15 he appears to be refuting a possible objection. Since some readers might object that the coalescence of continents would not reduce the total land available to living creatures, Gould reminds readers that the Permian extinction primarily involved marine organisms in shallow seas.

*4. How does the writer consider alternative causes or effects?*

In addition to anticipating possible objections, writers may also consider alternative causes or effects that others have proposed, of which readers may or may not already be aware. Writers mention these alternatives in their essays, describing and evaluating them, accepting or refuting them. Such a strategy strengthens the writer's credibility and nearly always makes the writer's own proposed causes or effects seem more convincing. Demonstrating an awareness of the alternatives makes the writer seem more thoughtful and better informed and hence more trustworthy.

Does the writer present alternative causes or effects in the essay? If so, are they presented fairly? Does the writer incorporate them into his or her own argument or attempt to refute them? How successful is the writer in dealing with these alternatives? Can you think of alternative causes or results the writer may have overlooked?

Early in his essay (paragraph 3), Gould mentions several causes that others have proposed to explain the Permian extinction. He does not specifically refute these alternatives, but he points out (in paragraph 5) that recent research in geology and evolutionary biology has made other proposed causes obsolete.

*5. How does the writer establish an authoritative voice?*

Although there are events and trends about which there can never be any certainty, through critical reading and evaluation we do finally have to accept certain explanations. Otherwise, we would be paralyzed by indecision over important governmental, social, educational, and personal matters.

To win our trust, writers must establish their authority by appearing informed, thoughtful, and reasonable. They argue for their proposed causes or effects in a convincing way, anticipate readers' objections, and consider alternative causes or effects.

Consider how the writer establishes his or her authority in the essay. What strategies does the writer adopt to increase his or her credibility? What kind of voice do you hear in the essay? Is it consistent throughout?

Gould impresses us with his wide-ranging knowledge of paleontology. He seems knowledgeable about other attempts to explain the Permian extinction, as well as about current research that can throw new light on this perplexing event. He weaves such an informed, convincing argument that we accept his authority and his explanation.

6. *How is the essay organized?*

To discover the organization, outline the essay, listing brief phrases to indicate the sequence of the argument. Include extended considerations of objections or alternatives in your outline. Then consider whether the essay is organized as well as it might be, given the writer's purpose and argument. Would a different sequence make the argument more convincing? Could the writer have created a chain of reasoning, with each cause or effect following logically from the preceding one? Are refutations of objections or alternatives located strategically? Is the argument easy to follow, with evidence and reasoning coherently arranged? Do you find the beginning engaging and effective? Imagine alternative beginnings for the essay. Is the ending the best possible conclusion to a convincing argument? Imagine alternative endings.

Gould begins by announcing a startling and significant event in paleontology. He presents the event briefly, considers current explanations for it, and then reviews the new theories and research that will enable the reader to understand his proposed cause. This information forms the basis of the argument for his proposed explanation. Toward the end of the essay, Gould states his proposed cause explicitly and ends with a comment about the importance in science of looking at old problems in new ways.

# Victor Fuchs

Victor R. Fuchs (b. 1934) is a professor of economics at Stanford University and research associate at the National Bureau of Economic Research. He has been elected a member of the Institute of Medicine of the National Academy of Sciences and appointed a Fellow of the American Academy of Arts and Sciences. His books include *Who Shall Live? Health, Economics, and Social Choice* (1975), *The Economics of Physician and Patient Behavior* (1978), and *How We Live: An Economic Perspective on Americans from Birth to Death* (1983).

# Why Married Mothers Work

Like the Gould piece, the following selection from Fuchs's book *How We Live* is an example of causal analysis. While Gould conjectures about the causes of an event, however, Fuchs conjectures about the causes of a trend—the thirty-five-year increase in the numbers of married mothers who work.

Certain explanations and arguments, especially research reports and college textbooks, provide predictable cues to keep readers on track. For example, paragraph topics are usually announced in the first sentence of a paragraph. This sentence may also provide an obvious transition from one topic to the next. Consequently, you can usefully preview this kind of writing by skimming the selection, stopping to read only the first sentence of each paragraph. Preview the Fuchs selection in this way to learn as much as you can about it before you begin reading. Then pause to reflect on the title. Why do you think married mothers work? What reasons do you think an economist like Fuchs might give?

As you read this selection, notice how Fuchs documents the existence of the trend he discusses. You may be surprised to discover how long he waits to explain what he thinks has caused the trend. What is he doing instead?

Knowing that Fuchs is an academic, what argumentative strategies would you expect him to use? Would you expect him to rely on logical, emotional, or ethical appeals? What kind of voice would you expect to hear in this piece?

Among single women ages 25–44 four out of five work for pay, and 1 this proportion has not changed since 1950. Divorced and separated women have also traditionally worked, and their participation rates (about 75 percent) have grown only slightly. The truly astonishing changes have taken place in the behavior of married women with children, as shown in Figure 1. . . .

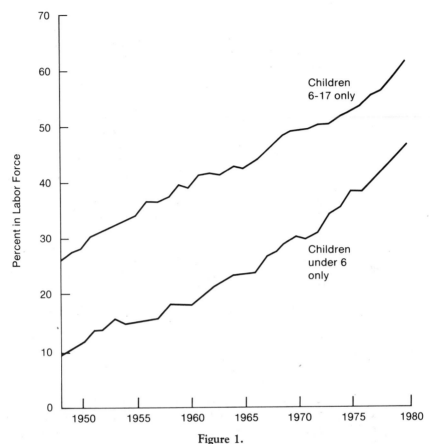

**Figure 1.**
*Labor Force Participation Rates of Married Women with Husband Present,
by Presence and Age of Own Children, 1948–1980.*
(*Sources*: Employment and Training Administration, *Employment and Training Report of the
President, 1980*, table B-4; idem, *Employment and Training Report of the President, 1981*, table
B-7.)

Why has the participation of married mothers grown so *rapidly* and so
*steadily*? Popular discussions frequently attribute this growth to changes
in attitudes that were stimulated by the feminist movement, but the time
pattern portrayed in Figure 5.1 does not lend much support to this view.
Betty Friedan's *The Feminine Mystique*, which is often credited with spark-
ing the modern feminist movement, was published in 1963, long after
the surge of married mothers into the labor force was under way. Moreover, there is no evidence of any sudden acceleration in response to this
movement. Similarly, widespread public expressions of feminism *followed*
rather than preceded the rise in the age of marriage and the fall in the
birth rate. Divorce is the one variable whose change coincided with the

burgeoning feminist movement, rising rapidly between 1965 and 1975. Thus, the feminist writings and discussion, valid as they may be in their own terms, will probably not be viewed by future historians as a basic cause of social change but primarily as a rationale and a rhetoric for changes that were already occurring for other reasons.

Government affirmative action programs are regarded by many as fostering female employment, but the timing again suggests that too much has been claimed for this explanation. These programs, which did not gain force until well into the 1960s, cannot explain the rapid rise in participation of married mothers in the 1950s—a rise that was even more rapid for older women with grown children. The timing of changes in the occupational distribution of employed married women is also contrary to what one would expect if the feminist movement or government affirmative action had a great deal of effect. The proportion who were in professional and technical occupations rose rapidly between 1948 and 1965, from 7.7 percent to 14.7 percent, but thereafter the rate of increase was more modest, only to 17.7 percent by 1979.

One of the most popular explanations for the two-earner family is that the wife's earnings are "needed to help make ends meet." This answer is the one most frequently given by women to survey researchers, and it receives some support from analytical studies that attempt to explain why, at any particular time, some wives work and some don't. There is a strong consensus among economists that, other things held constant, the higher the husband's income, the less likely it is that the wife will work for pay.

This explanation, however, does not contribute much to an understanding of changes over time. "Need," in an absolute sense, can hardly be the reason for the rapid rise in labor force participation of married mothers in the 1950s, when the real hourly earnings of their husbands were increasing at an unprecedented pace. Nathan Keyfitz (1980) observed that when women are asked why they work outside the home, they tend to reply that they need the money. "But," he writes, "the answer cannot be correct, since in earlier decades their husbands were earning less, presumably families needed money, and yet wives were content to stay home. Needing money is a universal, a constant, and a first rule of method is that one cannot explain a variable . . . with a constant."

One frequently mentioned but inadequately evaluated explanation for the surge of women into paid employment is the spread of time-saving household innovations such as clothes washers and dryers, frozen foods, and dishwashers. There is little doubt that it is easier to combine paid employment with home responsibilities now than it was fifty years ago, but it is not clear whether these time-saving innovations were the *cause* of the rise in female labor force participation or whether they were largely a *response* to meet a demand created by working women. Confusion about this point is most evident in comments that suggest that the rapid growth of supermarkets and fast-food outlets is a cause of women going to work. Similar time-saving organizations were tried at least sixty years ago, but with less success because the value of time was much lower then. The absence of supermarkets and fast-food eating places in low-income countries today also shows that their rapid growth in the United States is primarily a *result* of the rising value of time and the growth of women in the work force, not the reverse.

Within the economics profession the explanation that commands the widest consensus is that *higher wages* have attracted more married mothers into the labor force. This explanation is more firmly grounded in economic theory than many of the others and is reasonably consistent with observed behavior, both over time and among families at a given point in time. Ever since the pioneering work of Jacob Mincer (1962), numerous cross-section analyses—studies that examine differences among individual families or groups of families—uniformly report that the probability of a wife's working is *positively* related to her potential wage rate, holding constant spouse's education. This is the opposite of the previously noted *negative* effect of the husband's wage rate on the wife's labor force participation. . . .

In addition to higher wages, the rapid expansion of jobs in the service sector has contributed to the rise in female labor force participation (Fuchs 1968). The service industries (retail trade, financial service, education, health, personal services, public administration) have traditionally offered much greater employment opportunities for women than have mining, manufacturing, construction, and other branches of the industrial sector. For instance, 73 percent of nonfarm female employment was in the service sector in 1960, whereas the comparable figure for males was only 44 percent.

There are many reasons for this large differential. First, most occupations in the service sector do not place a premium on physical strength. Second, hours of work are frequently more flexible in service industries and there are many more opportunities for part-time work. Other things held constant, mothers of small children are more likely to be working in those metropolitan areas where there is large variation in the weekly hours of men (King 1978). This variation is a good indicator of the existence of part-time employment opportunities, and women are much more likely than men to seek part-time employment. Third, service sector jobs are more likely to be located in or near residential areas, thus making them more attractive to women who bear large responsibilities for child care and homemaking.

The propensity of women to seek service sector employment is partic-  10 ularly relevant because it is this sector that has provided nearly all of the additional job opportunities in the U.S. economy since the end of World War II. Between 1947 and 1980 U.S. employment expanded by 39 million; the service sector provided 33 million of these additional jobs. To be sure, some of the growth of service employment is the *result* of the increase in female labor force participation rather than the cause (Fuchs 1981a). Families with working mothers are more likely to eat out, to send their children to nursery school, and to purchase a wide range of personal and professional services. This feedback effect, however, accounts for only a part of the growth of service employment. The major explanation is that rapid increases in output per worker in agriculture and industry cut the demand for labor in those sectors and shifted employment to services. A secondary reason is that consumer demand shifted slightly toward services in response to the growth of real income.

I conclude that the growth of real wages and the expansion of the  11 service sector have been the most important reasons for the growth of female labor force participation. This participation, in turn, has had important effects on marriage, fertility, and divorce, but there is also some feedback from fertility and divorce to labor force participation. Better control of fertility makes a career in the labor market more promising to women, not only because of a reduction in the *number* of children but also because women now have better control over the *timing* of births. The increase in the *probability* of divorce contributes to the rise in female labor force participation because women recognize that complete commitment to home and husband can leave them in a perilous economic position if the marriage should dissolve. Alimony and child support payments are often inadequate, and are not paid at all in a large proportion of cases. An old song says that "diamonds are a girl's best friend," but today the ability to earn a good wage is likely to prove a more reliable asset.

## QUESTIONS FOR ANALYSIS

1. How does Fuchs demonstrate that the trend exists, that there has been a long-term increase in numbers of working married mothers? How convincing do you find this demonstration?

2. What causes would you have proposed to explain the increase in working married mothers? Does Fuchs challenge any of these expla-

nations? If so, how does he argue that they are mistaken? Are you convinced that your explanations are mistaken?

3. Fuchs argues for two causes of the increase in numbers of married mothers who work. How specifically does he argue for these two causes? What do you find most convincing and least convincing in his argument?

4. In paragraphs 7–11, Fuchs argues for his own proposed causes. What does he seem to be doing in paragraphs 2–6? What advantages or disadvantages do you see in his strategy in those paragraphs?

5. Look closely at Fuchs's strategy for rejecting the explanation that married mothers work because their families need the income (paragraphs 4 and 5). Just how does he go about rejecting this explanation? How well does he succeed?

6. Where in the essay does Fuchs assert his thesis? Why do you think he places the thesis where he does?

7. To discover how Fuchs has organized and sequenced his argument, outline the essay from beginning to end. (See Chapter 1 for a demonstration of outlining.) What advantages do you see in the way he has sequenced the parts of his argument? Can you imagine a different sequence?

8. Identify the kinds of support on which Fuchs bases the logical appeal of his argument. How would you evaluate this appeal? (Chapter 1 outlines a plan for evaluating logical appeals in an argument.)

9. In causal analysis, writers must be careful not to confuse the causes of a trend or event with the results. Notice Fuchs's discussion of this problem in paragraph 6. What can you conclude about the dangers of confusing causes with results in causal argument?

## SUGGESTIONS FOR WRITING

1. Read more about the topic of women in the work force in current periodicals and books. Identify a different trend from the one Fuchs discusses, and write an essay conjecturing about the causes of this trend. In your essay, you will need to demonstrate that the trend does exist. You may also want to discuss alternative causes proposed by others.

2. Research a completed artistic movement or historical trend—romanticism, pop art, the female suffrage movement of the nineteenth century. Write an essay, describing the trend, weighing the causes that

others have proposed, and arguing for the causes that you think are most responsible for the trend.

3. Analyze some changing pattern in leisure, entertainment, life-style, religious affiliation, political behavior, technology, or incidence of disease. Read what causes others have proposed for this changing pattern or trend. Then write an essay demonstrating that the trend exists, proposing your own causes, and considering others' proposed causes.

# Lester Thurow

Lester C. Thurow (b. 1938) is a professor of economics at Massachusetts Institute of Technology and has also taught at Harvard and at the Kennedy School of Government. A popular and influential economist, Thurow frequently testifies before Congress and appears on national television. He writes both academic and popular articles and books, among them *Generating Inequality* (1975), *The Zero Sum Society* (1980), and *Dangerous Currents: The State of Economics* (1983).

# Why Women Are Paid Less Than Men

In this selection, Thurow conjectures about possible or plausible causes of a current phenomenon—why women are paid less than men. This phenomenon is not a trend because it has not changed in over forty years. Hence, Thurow calls it a "constant."

This causal explanation of the difference between men's and women's pay originally appeared as a column in *The New York Times* in March 1981. Because its topic is timely and because it is such a fine example of arguing for the cause of a phenomenon, it has already been reprinted many times.

As you read, notice how long Thurow waits to answer the question he poses at the end of the first paragraph. Why does he not answer the question right away? What is he doing instead?

In the 40 years from 1939 to 1979 white women who work full time 1 have with monotonous regularity made slightly less than 60 percent as much as white men. Why?

Over the same time period, minorities have made substantial progress 2 in catching up with whites, with minority women making even more progress than minority men.

Black men now earn 72 percent as much as white men (up 16 per- 3 centage points since the mid-1950's) but black women earn 92 percent as much as white women. Hispanic men make 71 percent of what their white counterparts do, but Hispanic women make 82 percent as much as white women. As a result of their faster progress, fully employed black women make 75 percent as much as fully employed black men while Hispanic women earn 68 percent as much as Hispanic men.

This faster progress may, however, end when minority women finally ₄ catch up with white women. In the bible of the New Right, George Gilder's "Wealth and Poverty," the 60 percent is just one of Mother Nature's constants like the speed of light or the force of gravity.

Men are programmed to provide for their families economically while ₅ women are programmed to take care of their families emotionally and physically. As a result men put more effort into their jobs than women. The net result is a difference in work intensity that leads to that 40 percent gap in earnings. But there is no discrimination against women— only the biological facts of life.

The problem with this assertion is just that. It is an assertion with no ₆ evidence for it other than the fact that white women have made 60 percent as much as men for a long period of time.

"Discrimination against women" is an easy answer but it also has its ₇ problems as an adequate explanation. Why is discrimination against women not declining under the same social forces that are leading to a lessening of discrimination against minorities? In recent years women have made more use of the enforcement provisions of the Equal Employment Opportunities Commission and the courts than minorities. Why do the laws that prohibit discrimination against women and minorities work for minorities but not for women?

When men discriminate against women, they run into a problem. To ₈ discriminate against women is to discriminate against your own wife and to lower your own family income. To prevent women from working is to force men to work more.

When whites discriminate against blacks, they can at least think that ₉ they are raising their own incomes. When men discriminate against women they have to know that they are lowering their own family income and increasing their own work effort.

While discrimination undoubtedly explains part of the male-female ₁₀ earnings differential, one has to believe that men are monumentally stupid or irrational to explain all of the earnings gap in terms of discrimination. There must be something else going on.

Back in 1939 it was possible to attribute the earnings gap to large ₁₁ differences in educational attainments. But the educational gap between men and women has been eliminated since World War II. It is no longer possible to use education as an explanation for the lower earnings of women.

Some observers have argued that women earn less money since they ₁₂ are less reliable workers who are more apt to leave the labor force. But it is difficult to maintain this position since women are less apt to quit one job to take another and as a result they tend to work as long, or longer, for any one employer. From any employer's perspective they are more reliable, not less reliable, than men.

Part of the answer is visible if you look at the lifetime earnings profile 13 of men. Suppose that you were asked to predict which men in a group of 25-year-olds would become economically successful. At age 25 it is difficult to tell who will be economically successful and your predictions are apt to be highly inaccurate.

But suppose that you were asked to predict which men in a group of 14 35-year-olds would become economically successful. If you are successful at age 35, you are very likely to remain successful for the rest of your life. If you have not become economically successful by age 35, you are very unlikely to do so later.

The decade between 25 and 35 is when men either succeed or fail. It 15 is the decade when lawyers become partners in the good firms, when business managers make it onto the "fast track," when academics get tenure at good universities, and when blue collar workers find the job opportunities that will lead to training opportunities and the skills that will generate high earnings.

If there is any one decade when it pays to work hard and to be con- 16 sistently in the labor force, it is the decade between 25 and 35. For those who succeed, earnings will rise rapidly. For those who fail, earnings will remain flat for the rest of their lives.

But the decade between 25 and 35 is precisely the decade when women 17 are most apt to leave the labor force or become part-time workers to have children. When they do, the current system of promotion and skill acquisition will extract an enormous lifetime price.

This leaves essentially two avenues for equalizing male and female 18 earnings.

Families where women who wish to have successful careers, compete 19 with men, and achieve the same earnings should alter their family plans and have their children either before 25 or after 35. Or society can attempt to alter the existing promotion and skill acquisition system so that there is a longer time period in which both men and women can attempt to successfully enter the labor force.

Without some combination of these two factors, a substantial fraction 20 of the male-female earnings differentials are apt to persist for the next 40 years, even if discrimination against women is eliminated.

## QUESTIONS FOR ANALYSIS

1. What cause or causes would you have proposed to explain why women are paid less than men? Does Thurow mention any of these causes? What do you think of what he says?

2. Thurow clearly sees the phenomenon of lower women's pay as a serious problem (although others may not). What strategy does he adopt to present the problem in paragraphs 1–3? Given Thurow's readership and the limited space in a newspaper column, what advantages or disadvantages do you see in his strategy for presenting the problem?

3. Thurow does not begin arguing for his own proposed cause until paragraph 13. What is he doing in paragraphs 4–12? Why do you think he devotes nearly half of his limited space to something other than arguing directly for his proposed cause? How does his decision influence your response to his argument?

4. Thurow argues directly for his proposed cause in paragraphs 13–17. How convincing do you find his argument? How would you evaluate his logic? (Chapter 1 presents a plan for evaluating a logical appeal.)

5. To discover how Thurow has organized and sequenced his argument, outline his points from beginning to end. (Chapter 1 gives guidelines for outlining.) For his newspaper readers, what advantage do you see in this sequence? Can you imagine a different sequence?

6. Review carefully the general argumentative strategy, plan of organization, and appeals in the Fuchs and Thurow essays. How are the two selections alike and different? What can you conclude about causal analysis of events, trends, and phenomena? What demands does this type of writing impose on you as a thinker and as a writer?

## SUGGESTIONS FOR WRITING

1. Consider the continuing issue of discrimination against women and minorities. Choose one aspect or phenomenon of discrimination, and write a brief essay conjecturing about its causes.

2. Think about unexpected or puzzling events that have taken place in your college or community recently. Choose one of these events, and write an essay conjecturing about its causes. You may want to consider several possible causes and evaluate them carefully, perhaps rejecting some and accepting some. You may also want to anticipate readers' objections to your favored causes.

3. Select a historical event with causes that are still in dispute, and review the debate on the causes of this event. Then write an essay in which you review the debate, evaluate the proposed causes, and argue for the cause or causes you favor.

# Jonathan Kozol

A well-known critic of American schools, Jonathan Kozol (b. 1936) has been in the forefront of educational reformers during the 1970s and 1980s. He has taught in the Boston and Newton, Massachusetts, public schools, as well as at Yale University and the University of Massachusetts at Amherst. To support his writing and research, he has been awarded numerous prestigious fellowships from the Guggenheim, Ford, and Rockefeller foundations. Kozol's books include *Death at an Early Age* (1967), for which he won the National Book Award, *Free Schools* (1972), *Children of the Revolution* (1978), and *On Being a Teacher* (1981).

# The Human Cost
# of an Illiterate Society

This selection is a complete chapter from Kozol's *Illiterate America* (1985), a comprehensive study of the nature, causes, and consequences of illiteracy. In this chapter, Kozol speculates about the human (rather than the social or economic) consequences of illiteracy, outlining the limitations and dangers in the lives of adults who cannot read or write.

Kozol seeks to convince readers of his book that illiteracy is a serious problem. Appearing early in the book, this chapter provides critically important support for his larger purpose of persuading readers to accept his proposals for reducing illiteracy. Elsewhere in the book, Kozol conjectures about the causes of illiteracy, but here he concentrates on the results of the phenomenon, speculating about what life is like for an illiterate. He adopts this strategy of arguing the results of illiteracy in order to demonstrate that the human costs of the problem are great, so great as to pose a moral dilemma for our country.

PRECAUTIONS. READ BEFORE USING.    1
Poison: Contains sodium hydroxide (caustic soda-lye).
Corrosive: Causes severe eye and skin damage, may cause blindness.
Harmful or fatal if swallowed.
If swallowed, give large quantities of milk or water.
Do not induce vomiting.
Important: Keep water out of can at all times to
prevent contents from violently erupting . . .
                                  —*warning on a can of Drano*

We are speaking here no longer of the dangers faced by passengers on  2
Eastern Airlines or the dollar costs incurred by U.S. corporations and

taxpayers. We are speaking now of human suffering and of the ethical dilemmas that are faced by a society that looks upon such suffering with qualified concern but does not take those actions which its wealth and ingenuity would seemingly demand.

Questions of literacy, in Socrates' belief, must at length be judged as matters of morality. Socrates could not have had in mind the moral compromise peculiar to a nation like our own. Some of our Founding Fathers did, however, have this question in their minds. One of the wisest of those Founding Fathers (one who may not have been most compassionate but surely was more prescient than some of his peers) recognized the special dangers that illiteracy would pose to basic equity in the political construction that he helped to shape.                        3

"A people who mean to be their own governors," James Madison wrote, "must arm themselves with the power knowledge gives. A popular government without popular information or the means of acquiring it, is but a prologue to a farce or a tragedy, or perhaps both."                        4

Tragedy looms larger than farce in the United States today. Illiterate citizens seldom vote. Those who do are forced to cast a vote of questionable worth. They cannot make informed decisions based on serious print information. Sometimes they can be alerted to their interests by aggressive voter education. More frequently, they vote for a face, a smile, or a style, not for a mind or character or body of beliefs.                        5

The number of illiterate adults exceeds by 16 million the entire vote cast for the winner in the 1980 presidential contest. If even one third of all illiterates could vote, and read enough and do sufficient math to vote in their self-interest, Ronald Reagan would not likely have been chosen president. There is, of course, no way to know for sure. We do know this: Democracy is a mendacious term when used by those who are prepared to countenance the forced exclusion of one third of our electorate. So long as 60 million people are denied significant participation, the government is neither of, nor for, nor by, the people. It is a government, at best, of those two thirds whose wealth, skin color, or parental privilege allows them opportunity to profit from the provocation and instruction of the written word.                        6

The undermining of democracy in the United States is one "expense" that sensitive Americans can easily deplore because it represents a contradiction that endangers citizens of all political positions. The human price is not so obvious at first.                        7

Since I first immersed myself within this work I have often had the following dream: I find that I am in a railroad station or a large department store within a city that is utterly unknown to me and where I cannot understand the printed words. None of the signs or symbols is                        8 familiar. Everything looks strange: like mirror writing of some kind. Gradually I understand that I am in the Soviet Union. All the letters on the walls around me are Cyrillic. I look for my pocket dictionary but I find that it has been mislaid. Where have I left it? Then I recall that I forgot to bring it with me when I packed my bags in Boston. I struggle to remember the name of my hotel. I try to ask somebody for directions. One person stops and looks at me in a peculiar way. I lose the nerve to ask. At last I reach into my wallet for an ID card. The card is missing. Have I lost it? Then I remember that my card was confiscated for some reason, many years before. Around this point, I wake up in a panic.

This panic is not so different from the misery that millions of adult   9
illiterates experience each day within the course of their routine existence in the U.S.A.

Illiterates cannot read the menu in a restaurant.   10

They cannot read the cost of items on the menu in the *window* of the   11
restaurant before they enter.

Illiterates cannot read the letters that their children bring home from   12
their teachers. They cannot study school department circulars that tell them of the courses that their children must be taking if they hope to pass the SAT exams. They cannot help with homework. They cannot write a letter to the teacher. They are afraid to visit in the classroom. They do not want to humiliate their child or themselves.

Illiterates cannot read instructions on a bottle of prescription medicine.   13
They cannot find out when a medicine is past the year of safe consumption; nor can they read of allergenic risks, warnings to diabetics, or the potential sedative effect of certain kinds of nonprescription pills. They cannot observe preventive health care admonitions. They cannot read about "the seven warning signs of cancer" or the indications of blood-sugar fluctuations or the risks of eating certain foods that aggravate the likelihood of cardiac arrest.

Illiterates live, in more than literal ways, an uninsured existence. They   14
cannot understand the written details on a health insurance form. They cannot read the waivers that they sign preceding surgical procedures. Several women I have known in Boston have entered a slum hospital with the intention of obtaining a tubal ligation and have emerged a few days later after having been subjected to a hysterectomy. Unaware of their rights, incognizant of jargon, intimidated by the unfamiliar air of fear and atmosphere of ether that so many of us find oppressive in the confines even of the most attractive and expensive medical facilities, they have signed their names to documents they could not read and which nobody, in the hectic situation that prevails so often in those

overcrowded hospitals that serve the urban poor, had even bothered to explain.

Childbirth might seem to be the last inalienable right of any female 15 citizen within a civilized society. Illiterate mothers, as we shall see, already have been cheated of the power to protect their progeny against the likelihood of demolition in deficient public schools and, as a result, against the verbal servitude within which they themselves exist. Surgical denial of the right to bear that child in the first place represents an ultimate denial, an unspeakable metaphor, a final darkness that denies even the twilight gleamings of our own humanity. What greater violation of our biological, our biblical, our spiritual humanity could possibly exist than that which takes place nightly, perhaps hourly these days, within such overburdened and benighted institutions as the Boston City Hospital? Illiteracy has many costs; few are so irreversible as this.

Even the roof above one's head, the gas or other fuel for heating that 16 protects the residents of northern city slums against the threat of illness in the winter months become uncertain guarantees. Illiterates cannot read the lease that they must sign to live in an apartment which, too often, they cannot afford. They cannot manage check accounts and therefore seldom pay for anything by mail. Hours and entire days of difficult travel (and the cost of bus or other public transit) must be added to the real cost of whatever they consume. Loss of interest on the check accounts they do not have, and could not manage if they did, must be regarded as another of the excess costs paid by the citizen who is excluded from the common instruments of commerce in a numerate society.

"I couldn't understand the bills," a woman in Washington, D.C., 17 reports, "and then I couldn't write the checks to pay them. We signed things we didn't know what they were."

Illiterates cannot read the notices that they receive from welfare offices 18 or from the IRS. They must depend on word-of-mouth instruction from the welfare worker—or from other persons whom they have good reason to mistrust. They do not know what rights they have, what deadlines and requirements they face, what options they might choose to exercise. They are half-citizens. Their rights exist in print but not in fact.

Illiterates cannot look up numbers in a telephone directory. Even if 19 they can find the names of friends, few possess the sorting skills to make use of the yellow pages; categories are bewildering and trade names are beyond decoding capabilities for millions of nonreaders. Even the emergency numbers listed on the first page of the phone book—"Ambulance," "Police," and "Fire"—are too frequently beyond the recognition of nonreaders.

Many illiterates cannot read the admonition on a pack of cigarettes. 20 Neither the Surgeon General's warning nor its reproduction on the package can alert them to the risks. Although most people learn by word of mouth that smoking is related to a number of grave physical disorders, they do not get the chance to read the detailed stories which can document this danger with the vividness that turns concern into determination to resist. They can see the handsome cowboy or the slim Virginia lady lighting up a filter cigarette; they cannot heed the words that tell them that this product is (not "may be") dangerous to their health. Sixty million men and women are condemned to be the unalerted, high-risk candidates for cancer.

Illiterates do not buy "no-name" products in the supermarkets. They 21 must depend on photographs or the familiar logos that are printed on the packages of brand-name groceries. The poorest people, therefore, are denied the benefits of the least costly products.

Illiterates depend almost entirely upon label recognition. Many labels, 22 however, are not easy to distinguish. Dozens of different kinds of Campbell's soup appear identical to the nonreader. The purchaser who cannot read and does not dare to ask for help, out of the fear of being stigmatized (a fear which is unfortunately realistic), frequently comes home with something which she never wanted and her family never tasted.

Illiterates cannot read instructions on a pack of frozen food. Packages 23 sometimes provide an illustration to explain the cooking preparations; but illustrations are of little help to someone who must "boil water, drop the food—*within* its plastic wrapper—in the boiling water, wait for it to simmer, instantly remove."

Even when labels are seemingly clear, they may be easily mistaken. A 24 woman in Detroit brought home a gallon of Crisco for her children's dinner. She thought that she had bought the chicken that was pictured on the label. She had enough Crisco now to last a year—but no more money to go back and buy the food for dinner.

Recipes provided on the packages of certain staples sometimes tempt 25 a similiterate person to prepare a meal her children have not tasted. The longing to vary the uniform and often starchy content of low-budget meals provided to the family that relies on food stamps commonly leads to ruinous results. Scarce funds have been wasted and the food must be thrown out. The same applies to distribution of food-surplus produce in emergency conditions. Government inducements to poor people to "explore the ways" by which to make a tasty meal from tasteless noodles, surplus cheese, and powdered milk are useless to nonreaders. Intended as benevolent advice, such recommendations mock reality and foster deeper feelings of resentment and of inability to cope. (Those, on the

other hand, who cautiously refrain from "innovative" recipes in preparation of their children's meals must suffer the opprobrium of "laziness,"
"lack of imagination . . .")

Illiterates cannot travel freely. When they attempt to do so, they   26
encounter risks that few of us can dream of. They cannot read traffic
signs 'and, while they often learn to recognize and to decipher symbols,
they cannot manage street names which they haven't seen before. The
same is true for bus and subway stops. While ingenuity can sometimes
help a man or woman to discern directions from familiar landmarks,
buildings, cemeteries, churches, and the like, most illiterates are virtually
immobilized. They seldom wander past the streets and neighborhoods
they know. Geographical paralysis becomes a bitter metaphor for their
entire existence. They are immobilized in almost every sense we can
imagine. They can't move up. They can't move out. They cannot see
beyond. Illiterates may take an oral test for drivers' permits in most
sections of America. It is a questionable concession. Where will they go?
How will they get there? How will they get home? Could it be that some
of us might like it better if they stayed where they belong?

Travel is only one of many instances of circumscribed existence.   27
Choice, in almost all its facets, is diminished in the life of an illiterate
adult. Even the printed TV schedule, which provides most people with
the luxury of preselection, does not belong within the arsenal of options
in illiterate existence. One consequence is that the viewer watches only
what appears at moments when he happens to have time to turn the
switch. Another consequence, a lot more common, is that the TV set
remains in operation night and day. Whatever the program offered at
the hour when he walks into the room will be the nutriment that he
accepts and swallows. Thus, to passivity, is added frequency—indeed,
almost uninterrupted continuity. Freedom to select is no more possible
here than in the choice of home or surgery or food.

"You don't choose," said one illiterate woman. "You take your wishes   28
from somebody else." Whether in perusal of a menu, selection of highways, purchase of groceries, or determination of affordable enjoyment,
illiterate Americans must trust somebody else: a friend, a relative, a
stranger on the street, a grocery clerk, a TV copywriter.

"All of our mail we get, it's hard for her to read. Settin' down and   29
writing a letter, she can't do it. Like if we get a bill . . . we take it over
to my sister-in-law . . . My sister-in-law reads it."

Billing agencies harass poor people for the payment of the bills for   30
purchases that might have taken place six months before. Utility companies offer an agreement for a staggered payment schedule on a bill past
due. "You have to trust them," one man said. Precisely for this reason,

you end up by trusting no one and suspecting everyone of possible deceit. A submerged sense of distrust becomes the corollary to a constant need to trust. "They are cheating me . . . I have been tricked . . . I do not know . . ."

*Not knowing:* This is a familiar theme. Not knowing the right word for 31 the right thing at the right time is one form of subjugation. Not knowing the world that lies concealed behind those words is a more terrifying feeling. The longitude and latitude of one's existence are beyond all easy apprehension. Even the hard, cold stars within the firmament above one's head begin to mock the possibilities for self-location. Where am I? Where did I come from? Where will I go?

"I've lost a lot of jobs," one man explains. "Today, even if you're a 32 janitor, there's still reading and writing . . . They leave a note saying, 'Go to room so-and-so . . .' You can't do it. You can't read it. You don't know."

"The hardest thing about it is that I've been places where I didn't 33 know where I was. You don't know where you are . . . You're lost."

"Like I said: I have two kids. What do I do if one of my kids starts 34 choking? I go running to the phone . . . I can't look up the hospital phone number. That's if we're at home. Out on the street, I can't read the sign. I get to a pay phone. 'Okay, tell us where you are. We'll send an ambulance.' I look at the street sign. Right there, I can't tell you what it says. I'd have to spell it out, letter for letter. By that time, one of my kids would be dead . . . These are the kinds of fears you go with, every single day . . ."

"Reading directions, I suffer with. I work with chemicals . . . That's 35 scary to begin with . . ."

"You sit down. They throw the menu in front of you. Where do you 36 go from there? Nine times out of ten you say, 'Go ahead. Pick out something for the both of us.' I've eaten some weird things, let me tell you!"

Menus. Chemicals. A child choking while his mother searches for a 37 word she does not know to find assistance that will come too late. Another mother speaks about the inability to help her kids to read: "I can't read to them. Of course that's leaving them out of something they should have. Oh, it matters. You *believe* it matters! I ordered all these books. The kids belong to a book club. Donny wanted me to read a book to him. I told Donny: 'I can't read.' He said: 'Mommy, you sit down. I'll read it to you.' I tried it one day, reading from the pictures. Donny looked at me. He said, 'Mommy, that's not right.' He's only five. He knew I couldn't read . . ."

A landlord tells a woman that her lease allows him to evict her if her   38
baby cries and causes inconvenience to her neighbors. The consequence
of challenging his words conveys a danger which appears, unlikely as it
seems, even more alarming than the danger of eviction. Once she admits
that she can't read, in the desire to maneuver for the time in which to
call a friend, she will have defined herself in terms of an explicit impo-
tence that she cannot endure. Capitulation in this case is preferable to
self-humiliation. Resisting the definition of oneself in terms of what one
cannot do, what others take for granted, represents a need so great that
other imperatives (even one so urgent as the need to keep one's home
in winter's cold) evaporate and fall away in face of fear. Even the loss of
home and shelter, in this case, is not so terrifying as the loss of self.

"I come out of school. I was sixteen. They had their meetings. The   39
directors meet. They said that I was wasting their school paper. I was
wasting pencils . . ."

Another illiterate, looking back, believes she was not worthy of her   40
teacher's time. She believes that it was wrong of her to take up space
within her school. She believes that it was right to leave in order that
somebody more deserving could receive her place.

Children choke. Their mother chokes another way: on more than   41
chicken bones.

People eat what others order, know what others tell them, struggle   42
not to see themselves as they believe the world perceives them. A man
in California speaks about his own loss of identity, of self-location, definition:

"I stood at the bottom of the ramp. My car had broke down on the   43
freeway. There was a phone. I asked for the police. They was nice. They
said to tell them where I was. I looked up at the signs. There was one
that I had seen before. I read it to them: ONE WAY STREET. They thought
it was a joke. I told them I couldn't read. There was other signs above
the ramp. They told me to try. I looked around for somebody to help.
All the cars was going by real fast. I couldn't make them understand that
I was lost. The cop was nice. He told me: 'Try once more.' I did my
best. I couldn't read. I only knew the sign above my head. The cop was
trying to be nice. He knew that I was trapped. 'I can't send out a car to
you if you can't tell me where you are.' I felt afraid. I nearly cried. I'm
forty-eight years old. I only said: 'I'm on a one-way street . . .' "

Perhaps we might slow down a moment here and look at the realities   44
described above. This is the nation that we live in. This is a society that
most of us did not create but which our President and other leaders have
been willing to sustain by virtue of malign neglect. Do we possess the

character and courage to address a problem which so many nations, poorer than our own, have found it natural to correct?

The answers to these questions represent a reasonable test of our belief 45 in the democracy to which we have been asked in public school to swear allegiance.

## QUESTIONS FOR ANALYSIS

1. Kozol relies on a strategy of enumerating, or listing, results. Count the results to discover just how many he lists. Instead of arguing at length the importance of a few results, he lists many results, pausing to argue a few of them briefly. What effect does this enumerating strategy have on you? Given Kozol's purpose in this chapter and its importance in his book, what advantages or disadvantages do you see in his strategy of enumeration?

2. List the results in order, identifying each with a word or brief phrase. Why do you think Kozol sequenced the results in just this way? Do they form related clusters? Do they form a chain of reasoning, with one result leading to the next? Why do you think Kozol begins with certain results and concludes with others?

3. To what extent does Kozol rely on logical, emotional, and ethical appeals? (Chapter 1 provides guidelines for evaluating appeals in an argument.) How do you evaluate his reliance on various appeals?

4. What kinds of evidence does Kozol select to argue for particular results of illiteracy? What do you suppose is the source of this evidence? How effectively does Kozol present this evidence?

5. Identify the one result of illiteracy that you find most convincing. Within the context of Kozol's argument, what seems to you especially convincing about this result?

6. Kozol insists that illiteracy is a moral problem. What does he mean by this claim, and how does he go about establishing it? Given his purpose and readers, what advantages do you see in his linking of illiteracy with morality? Are you convinced of this link?

7. Why do you think Kozol opened this chapter with instructions from a can of Drano (a chemical for unclogging bathroom or kitchen drains)?

8. Writers often frame an essay or book chapter by referring at the end to something from the beginning. How does Kozol use framing in this selection? What advantages do you see in this framing?

## SUGGESTIONS FOR WRITING

1. Identify a social problem that concerns you, and write an essay speculating about the results of this problem. You may rely only on your own speculations, or you may research what others have said about the problem, evaluating the results they suggest and proposing your own. You do not need to propose a solution to this problem, but only to argue its results convincingly.

2. Think about recent controversial decisions made by leaders in your community or college. Choose one of these decisions, and write an essay speculating about the results of this decision.

3. Identify a crucial decision that you will be making soon. Describe the situation, explain the decision you will make, and speculate about the results of your decision.

# William Kowinski

William Kowinski is a free-lance writer who has been the book review editor and managing arts editor of the Boston *Phoenix*. He has written articles for many newspapers and magazines, including *Esquire* and the *New York Times Magazine*. He lives in Greensburg, Pennsylvania.

# Mallaise: How to Know If You Have It

This selection is taken from *The Malling of America* (1985), a wide-ranging study of the history, architecture, and social significance of shopping malls. In this chapter, Kowinski speculates about the effects of malls on people who visit them, speculations based on seven years of visiting malls and interviewing people there. Since you too have probably repeatedly visited malls, you will be in a good position to evaluate Kowinski's speculations. As you begin reading, notice how he engages readers' interest. Then, as you read further, pay special attention to the proposed effects of malls. Kowinski's title is a pun on the word *malaise*, which refers to a feeling of discomfort or uneasiness.

Malls make some people sick. Literally, sometimes. They feel feverish, 1 their eyes glaze, their stomachs tumble, they fall down, they throw up.

Some people are just annoyed by one or another aspect of a mall, or 2 a nonspecific quality of a particular mall, or malls in general. "That mall makes me *sick*!" they say. Or "I don't like malls—I *hate* them." Malls make people angry. Some of these people are shoppers, but some are people who work in malls or even own mall stores.

Malls affect people. They're designed to. But in some ways, either by 3 their nature or by a side effect caused by their main ingredients, they do things to people that people are unaware of or don't understand, but if they knew or understood, they probably wouldn't like it.

There are other more obvious things that happen to people in malls 4 that they don't or wouldn't like. Crime, for instance.

This section of *The Malling of America* is about some of the negative 5 aspects of malls that affect people and that people perceive. Does the mall make you tired? Set your nerves on edge? Do you find it difficult to concentrate? Do you feel the absence of certain phenomena—weather, for example, or civil liberties? Do you sometimes wonder if you are really as safe as mall management would like you to believe?

If you're a parent, do you fear for your children's ability to survive    6
outside comfort control because they spend so much time in the mall?
And if you're an adolescent, do you feel your horizons becoming limited
to a hundred chain-store outlets and three anchor department stores? Or
are you worried that this is precisely the world your parents do live in,
and where they want you always to remain?

These are some of the symptoms of mallaise. Perhaps you have one or    7
two, or know someone who does, or perhaps you want to be prepared,
just in case. Then perhaps you should read on.

I had my first attack of *mal de mall* in Columbia, Maryland. I was in    8
a restaurant in the Columbia Mall having coffee. The attack was characterized by feverishness, sudden fatigue, and high anxiety, all recurring
whenever I glanced out at the mall itself. The thought of going out there
again made me sweat and swoon, and I had to fight the hallucinatory
certainty that when I left the restaurant I would be in Greengate mall,
or maybe Woodfield, or Tysons Corner. Or *all* of them.

*Mal de mall*, or mall sickness, is one of the classifications of mallaise,    9
the general term for physical and psychological disturbances caused by
mall contact. I know because I made them all up. Among the symptoms
I have personally observed or heard about from their victims are these:

*Dismallcumbobulation:* "I don't like to go to malls because I always get    10
lost," a woman told me, "and that's embarrassing. I feel stupid. It makes
me mad." The hyped-up overabundance of similar products plus the bland
sameness of many mall environments make people feel lost even when
they aren't. Even familiar malls relocate stores and reconfigure themselves, which adds to the feeling of a continuous featureless space. And
the similarity of one mall to another is disorienting. You walk out of the
Stuft Potato and you not only don't remember which way your car is,
you might not remember what mall this is. There are other kinds of
dismallcumbobulation: the loss of a sense of time as well as place, and
forgetting one's purpose in coming to the mall—all of which can lead to
apathy and hopelessness, loss of consciousness, or fainting. Some victims
recommend deep-breathing exercises every fifteen minutes while at the
mall.

*Inability to Relate to Others:* "It's impossible to talk to someone when    11
you're shopping at the mall," a friend told me, explaining why she prefers
to shop alone. "I notice it at the mall all the time—you see two people
together but they aren't really talking to each other. They're talking, but
they're staring off in different directions, and pretty soon they just wander
away from each other." Among the possible effects of this symptom are
disenchantment and divorce.

*Plastiphobia*, or the fear of being enclosed in a cocoon of blandness.  12
"Suddenly I just stood still and looked around," a young man said. "I
saw all the people and what we were all doing there, what we were
spending our day doing, and I suddenly just couldn't wait to get out. I
was in a plastic place with plastic people buying plastic products with
plastic charge cards. I had to escape." Sometimes this reaction is accompanied by severe anxiety, alienation from the human race, and in at least
one very severe case I know of, by all the usual manifestations of a drug
overdose.

All of these, and their variations, are unfortunate side effects (or per-  13
haps just extreme cases) of the main psychological effects that the mall
intends. Excitement may become overstimulation; relaxation may drift
into confusion and torpor. The combination is what I call the Zombie
Effect.

There is, in fact, a fine line between the ideal mall shopper and the  14
dismayed mall shopper, between mall bliss and mallaise, between the
captivated shopper and the Zombie Effect. The best description of the
Zombie Effect I've heard was Barbara Lambert's, which she imparted
while we toured the malls of Chicagoland.

It hits you, Barbara said, when you're standing there naked, looking  15
in the mirror of the dressing room. Your clothes are in a pile on the floor
or draped over a chair. Maybe it's just a little cubicle with a curtain, and
you can still hear the hum and buzz of the mall and the tiny timbres of
Muzak. You're about to try something on, in an effortless repetition of
what you've been doing since you came to the mall. And suddenly you
realize *you've been here all day*. Time has in fact been passing while you've
been gliding through store after store in a tender fuzz of soft lights and
soft music. The plash of fountains, the glow of people, but almost no
intrusive sound has broken your floating—no telephone, no demands,
nothing to dodge or particularly watch out for. Just a gentle visual parade
of clothes, fabric tags, and washing instructions. Racks, displays, cos-
metics, brisk signs, flowing greenery, and spasms of color in the dream
light. An ice-cream cone, a cup of coffee. Other figures have glided by:
walking models of the mall's products, or walking models of the weird.
An old man who reminds you of your grandfather, sitting on a blond-
wood bench under a potted palm. A woman who may or may not have
been your best friend's other best friend in high school, striding by on
strange shoes—or maybe that's a new style and yours are strange? You're
looking at your naked image in a bare little room, and a little breeze
touches you. Whatever you actually came here for is in the distant past.
You've been floating here . . . for hours.

But that's the whole idea of this psychological structure: to turn off    16
your mind and let you float; to create a direct and unfettered connection
between eyeing and buying; and the more you do, the easier it becomes.
Malls make for great eye/hand-on-credit-card coordination.

The way it's done is with a combination of peacefulness and stimula-    17
tion. The environment bathes you in sweet neutrality with soft light,
candied music, and all the amenities that reassure and please without
grabbing too much individual attention. At the same time, the stores
and products dance for you with friendly smiles and colorful costumes.
The sheer number of products and experiences you pay for and their
apparent variety are in themselves factors that excite and focus.

Once again, it's all a lot like television. TV lulls and stimulates si-    18
multaneously. The medium itself is familiar and comfortable and friendly;
the programs can be interesting but it is not really by accident that they
are not as compact, colorful, dramatic, or insistent as the commercials.
Watching television we are everywhere and nowhere in particular, just
as at the mall. Suddenly you might realize that you've been watching it
all day, just floating for hours. And if you look at people watching television—especially their eyes—they look pretty much like mall shoppers:
the Zombie Effect.

But these effects are all supposed to be pleasant and unconscious.    19
When either the lulling or stimulating quality—or especially the combination and conflict between them—is strongly felt, then it's no longer
pleasant. Overstimulation causes anxiety, and sometimes an intense focus
on heavy-duty, no-nonsense, get-out-of-my-way shopping, or else a fren-
zied need to get out of there, fast and forever. The lulling and sense
deprivation cause listlessness and confusion, and occasionally rebellion
at being Muzaked into implacable mushy madness. The conflict of both
going on at the same time can cause the sense of dislocation and exhaustion that is the clearest indicator of the Zombie Effect. The victim
shuffles and mumbles, is distant or unduly preoccupied, doesn't listen,
acts automatically, and not only can't remember where the car is parked
but often doesn't care.

There are ancillary symptoms and causes as well: headaches caused by    20
guilt at buying too much; depression at not being able to buy everything;
the walking emptiness caused by consistently emphasized, endless greed.

The cure for all forms of mallaise is theoretically simple: The victim    21
leaves the mall. There are no laws requiring people to stay in the mall,
or even to go there in the first place. It isn't anyone's civic, moral,
spiritual, or intellectual duty. The mall may be the best place—or even
the only place—to shop for certain products, but that doesn't mean the

shopper has to stay there for hours. Nevertheless, it isn't always easy to leave.

For that is another aspect of the Zombie Effect: Victims stay for no 22 good or apparent reason, and even beyond their conscious desire to be there. Shoppers mallinger partly because of the mall's psychological apparatus, its implicit promise of safety, sanctuary, and salvation. Of Nirvana! The Crystal City! A New Heaven on a New Earth! The mall hasn't become the most successful artificial environment in America for nothing.

With its real walls and psychological illusions, the mall protects against 23 so many hazards and uncertainties that the mallaise sufferer may well mallinger a little longer to ponder the consequences of walking out. Such a person may fear trading the malladies of the Zombie Effect for the perils of mall withdrawal, which is characterized by shaking in downtown areas, fear of crossing streets, inordinate terror in the presence of rain or sunshine, confusion when actual travel is required between purchases, and the feeling of estrangement when wearing a coat.

I wish I could say that medical science is on top of this new set of 24 malladies, but the truth is that it is scandalously behind the times. Right now, there may be many thousands of Zombie Effect sufferers, untreated and undiagnosed. If you find this hard to believe—well, have you been to the mall lately?

## QUESTIONS FOR ANALYSIS

1. How would you describe Kowinski's attitude toward his subject and readers? What voice or tone do you hear in this selection? Point to particular passages that reveal his attitude.

2. Contrast Kowinski's and Kozol's attitudes toward their subjects. If their attitudes seem different to you, decide what accounts for this difference.

3. Reread carefully Kowinski's introduction to his speculations (paragraphs 1–7). What strategies does he use to engage readers' interest and draw them into his chapter? How did his introduction influence the way you read the chapter?

4. In paragraphs 9 through 14, Kowinski presents the main effect of malls, along with its symptoms. How does Kowinski organize this section? What advantages or disadvantages do you see in this strategy?

5. Throughout the chapter, Kowinski contrasts the intended effects of malls with the unintended side effects. Skim the essay, looking for

places where he makes this contrast explicit. Given his purpose, why do you think he relies on this contrast?

6. What kind of evidence for the Zombie Effect does Kowinski offer? Why do you think he chose this kind of evidence?

7. Writers speculating about results often use analogies, which can be quite tricky to use convincingly because they may not stand up under critical analysis. Analyze Kowinski's analogy comparing mall visits to TV watching (paragraph 18). What are the points of comparison in the analogy? How successful do you think it is?

8. Kowinski concludes his speculations about the effects of malls in paragraph 20. What does he decide to do in the remaining paragraphs? What advantages or disadvantages do you see in his decision?

## SUGGESTIONS FOR WRITING

1. Kowinski speculates about the effects of a familiar activity—visiting shopping malls. Choose some other familiar activity not generally considered harmful, and write an essay speculating about its ill effects. You might consider activities like studying, praying, jogging, napping, vacationing, or dancing. If possible, participate in the activity again, observing closely what goes on and talking to others who participate. Your essay may be serious or humorous.

2. Think about common public or commercial institutions with which you are familiar, such as golf courses, sports stadiums, churches, schools, colleges, swimming pools, or summer camps. Choose one of these, and write a humorous essay speculating about its unexpected harmful effects on those who visit it.

# Carl Sagan

Carl Sagan (b. 1934) is an unusually well-known American scientist because of the popularity of his television series "Cosmos." An astronomer and director of Cornell University's Laboratory for Planetary Studies, he is a Fellow of the American Academy of Arts and Sciences. Among his many books are *Intelligent Life in the Universe* (1966), *The Cosmic Connection* (1973), and *The Dragons of Eden* (1980), for which he was awarded the Pulitzer Prize. Sagan has been honored repeatedly for distinguished work in astronomy.

# *Nuclear War and Climatic Catastrophe: A Nuclear Winter*

This essay appeared in *Parade* magazine, October 30, 1983. Aimed at a newspaper audience, it is a brief version of a longer and much more technical report that was prepared by Sagan and a number of other scientists concerned about the dangers of the nuclear arms race. This technical report was entitled "Global Atmospheric Consequences of Nuclear War."

Sagan writes here about the possible results of even a limited nuclear war, but he does not begin discussing these results immediately. As you begin reading, notice what he does instead. How does he prepare readers for his argument?

1    Except for fools and madmen, everyone knows that nuclear war would be an unprecedented human catastrophe. A more or less typical strategic warhead has a yield of 2 megatons, the explosive equivalent of 2 million tons of TNT. But 2 million tons of TNT is about the same as all the bombs exploded in World War II—a single bomb with the explosive power of the entire Second World War but compressed into a few seconds of time and an area 30 or 40 miles across . . .

2    In a 2-megaton explosion over a fairly large city, buildings would be vaporized, people reduced to atoms and shadows, outlying structures blown down like matchsticks and raging fires ignited. And if the bomb were exploded on the ground, an enormous crater, like those that can be seen through a telescope on the surface of the Moon, would be all that remained where midtown once had been. There are now more than 50,000 nuclear weapons, more than 13,000 megatons of yield, deployed in the arsenals of the United States and the Soviet Union—enough to obliterate a million Hiroshimas.

But there are fewer than 3000 cities on the Earth with populations of   3
100,000 or more. You cannot find anything like a million Hiroshimas to
obliterate. Prime military and industrial targets that are far from cities
are comparatively rare. Thus, there are vastly more nuclear weapons than
are needed for any plausible deterrence of a potential adversary.

Nobody knows, of course, how many megatons would be exploded in   4
a real nuclear war. There are some who think that a nuclear war can be
"contained," bottled up before it runs away to involve much of the
world's arsenals. But a number of detailed analyses, war games run by
the U.S. Department of Defense, and official Soviet pronouncements all
indicate that this containment may be too much to hope for: Once the
bombs begin exploding, communications failures, disorganization, fear,
the necessity of making in minutes decisions affecting the fates of millions, and the immense psychological burden of knowing that your own
loved ones may already have been destroyed are likely to result in a
nuclear paroxysm. Many investigations, including a number of studies
for the U.S. government, envision the explosion of 5000 to 10,000
megatons—the detonation of tens of thousands of nuclear weapons that
now sit quietly, inconspicuously, in missile silos, submarines and long-
range bombers, faithful servants awaiting orders.

The World Health Organization, in a recent detailed study chaired by   5
Sune K. Bergstrom (the 1982 Nobel laureate in physiology and medicine), concludes that 1.1 billion people would be killed outright in such
a nuclear war, mainly in the United States, the Soviet Union, Europe,
China and Japan. An additional 1.1 billion people would suffer serious
injuries and radiation sickness, for which medical help would be unavailable. It thus seems possible that more than 2 billion people—almost
half of all the humans on Earth—would be destroyed in the immediate
aftermath of a global thermonuclear war. This would represent by far the
greatest disaster in the history of the human species and, with no other
adverse effects, would probably be enough to reduce at least the Northern
Hemisphere to a state of prolonged agony and barbarism. Unfortunately,
the real situation would be much worse.

In technical studies of the consequences of nuclear weapons explo-   6
sions, there has been a dangerous tendency to underestimate the results.
This is partly due to a tradition of conservatism which generally works
well in science but which is of more dubious applicability when the lives
of billions of people are at stake. In the Bravo test of March 1, 1954, a
15-megaton thermonuclear bomb was exploded on Bikini Atoll. It had
about double the yield expected, and there was an unanticipated last-
minute shift in the wind direction. As a result, deadly radioactive fallout
came down on Rongelap in the Marshall Islands, more than 200 kilo-

meters away. Almost all the children on Rongelap subsequently developed thyroid nodules and lesions, and other long-term medical problems, due to the radioactive fallout.

Likewise, in 1973, it was discovered that high-yield airbursts will chemically burn the nitrogen in the upper air, converting it into oxides of nitrogen; these, in turn, combine with and destroy the protective ozone in the Earth's stratosphere. The surface of the Earth is shielded from deadly solar ultraviolet radiation by a layer of ozone so tenuous that, were it brought down to sea level, it would be only 3 millimeters thick. Partial destruction of this ozone layer can have serious consequences for the biology of the entire planet.

These discoveries, and others like them, were made by chance. They were largely unexpected. And now another consequence—by far the most dire—has been uncovered, again more or less by accident.

The U.S. Mariner 9 spacecraft, the first vehicle to orbit another planet, arrived at Mars in late 1971. The planet was enveloped in a global dust storm. As the fine particles slowly fell out, we were able to measure temperature changes in the atmosphere and on the surface. Soon it became clear what had happened:

The dust, lofted by high winds off the desert into the upper Martian atmosphere, had absorbed the incoming sunlight and prevented much of it from reaching the ground. Heated by the sunlight, the dust warmed the adjacent air. But the surface, enveloped in partial darkness, became much chillier than usual. Months later, after the dust fell out of the atmosphere, the upper air cooled and the surface warmed, both returning to their normal conditions. We were able to calculate accurately, from how much dust there was in the atmosphere, how cool the Martian surface ought to have been.

Afterwards, I and my colleagues, James B. Pollack and Brian Toon of NASA's Ames Research Center, were eager to apply these insights to the Earth. In a volcanic explosion, dust aerosols are lofted into the high atmosphere. We calculated by how much the Earth's global temperature should decline after a major volcanic explosion and found that our results (generally a fraction of a degree) were in good accord with actual measurements. Joining forces with Richard Turco, who has studied the effects of nuclear weapons for many years, we then began to turn our attention to the climatic effects of nuclear war.

We knew that nuclear explosions, particularly groundbursts, would lift an enormous quantity of fine soil particles into the atmosphere (more than 100,000 tons of fine dust for every megaton exploded in a surface burst). Our work was further spurred by Paul Crutzen of the Max Planck Institute for Chemistry in Mainz, West Germany, and by John Birks of the University of Colorado, who pointed out that huge quantities of smoke would be generated in the burning of cities and forests following a nuclear war.

Groundbursts—at hardened missile silos, for example—generate fine    13
dust. Airbursts—over cities and unhardened military installations—make fires and therefore smoke. The amount of dust and soot generated depends on the conduct of the war, the yields of the weapons employed and the ratio of groundbursts to airbursts. So we ran computer models for several dozen different nuclear war scenarios. Our baseline case, as in many other studies, was a 5000-megaton war with only a modest fraction of the yield (20 percent) expended on urban or industrial targets. Our job, for each case, was to follow the dust and smoke generated, see how much sunlight was absorbed and by how much the temperatures changed, figure out how the particles spread in longitude and latitude, and calculate how long before it all fell out of the air back onto the surface. Since the radio-activity would be attached to these same fine particles, our calculations also revealed the extent and timing of the subsequent radioactive fallout.

Some of what I am about to describe is horrifying. I know, because it    14
horrifies me. There is a tendency—psychiatrists call it "denial"—to put it out of our minds, not to think about it. But if we are to deal intelligently, wisely, with the nuclear arms race, then we must steel ourselves to contemplate the horrors of nuclear war.

The results of our calculations astonished us. In the baseline case, the    15
amount of sunlight at the ground was reduced to a few percent of normal—much darker, in daylight, than in a heavy overcast and too dark for plants to make a living from photosynthesis. At least in the Northern Hemisphere, where the great preponderance of strategic targets lies, an unbroken and deadly gloom would persist for weeks.

Even more unexpected were the temperatures calculated. In the base-    16
line case, land temperatures, except for narrow strips of coastline, dropped to minus 25° Celsius (minus 13° Fahrenheit) and stayed below freezing for months—even for a summer war. (Because the atmospheric structure becomes much more stable as the upper atmosphere is heated and the lower air is cooled, we may have severely *under*estimated how long the cold and the dark would last.) The oceans, a significant heat reservoir, would not freeze, however, and a major ice age would probably not be triggered. But because the temperatures would drop so catastrophically, virtually all crops and farm animals, at least in the Northern Hemisphere, would be destroyed, as would most varieties of uncultivated or domesticated food supplies. Most of the human survivors would starve.

In addition, the amount of radioactive fallout is much more than    17
expected. Many previous calculations simply ignored the intermediate

time-scale fallout. That is, calculations were made for the prompt fall-out—the plumes of radioactive debris blown downwind from each tar-get—and for the long-term fallout, the fine radioactive particles lofted into the stratosphere that would descend about a year later, after most of the radioactivity had decayed. However, the radioactivity carried into the upper atmosphere (but not as high as the stratosphere) seems to have been largely forgotten. We found for the baseline case that roughly 30 percent of the land at northern midlatitudes could receive a radioactive dose greater than 250 rads, and that about 50 percent of northern mid-latitudes could receive a dose greater than 100 rads. A 100-rad dose is the equivalent of about 1000 medical X-rays. A 400-rad dose will, more likely than not, kill you.

The cold, the dark and the intense radioactivity, together lasting for 18 months, represent a severe assault on our civilization and our species. Civil and sanitary services would be wiped out. Medical facilities, drugs, the most rudimentary means for relieving the vast human suffering, would be unavailable. Any but the most elaborate shelters would be useless, quite apart from the question of what good it might be to emerge a few months later. Synthetics burned in the destruction of the cities would produce a wide variety of toxic gases, including carbon monoxide, cya-nides, dioxins and furans. After the dust and soot settled out, the solar ultraviolet flux would be much larger than its present value. Immunity to disease would decline. Epidemics and pandemics would be rampant, especially after the billion or so unburied bodies began to thaw. More-over, the combined influence of these severe and simultaneous stresses on life are likely to produce even more adverse consequences—biologists call them synergisms—that we are not yet wise enough to foresee.

So far, we have talked only of the Northern Hemisphere. But it now 19 seems—unlike the case of a single nuclear weapons test—that in a real nuclear war, the heating of the vast quantities of atmospheric dust and soot in northern midlatitudes will transport these fine particles toward and across the Equator. We see just this happening in Martian dust storms. The Southern Hemisphere would experience effects that, while less severe than in the Northern Hemisphere, are nevertheless extremely ominous. The illusion with which some people in the Northern Hemi-sphere reassure themselves—catching an Air New Zealand flight in a time of serious international crisis, or the like—is now much less tenable, even on the narrow issue of personal survival for those with the price of a ticket.

But what if nuclear wars *can* be contained, and much less than 5000 20 megatons is detonated? Perhaps the greatest surprise in our work was that even small nuclear wars can have devastating climatic effects. We considered a war in which a mere 100 megatons were exploded, less than one percent of the world arsenals, and only in low-yield airbursts over cities. This scenario, we found, would ignite thousands of fires, and the smoke from these fires alone would be enough to generate an epoch of cold and dark almost as severe as in the 5000-megaton case. The threshold for what Richard Turco has called The Nuclear Winter is very low.

Could we have overlooked some important effect? The carrying of dust 21 and soot from the Northern to the Southern Hemisphere (as well as more local atmospheric circulation) will certainly thin the clouds out over the Northern Hemisphere. But, in many cases, this thinning would be insufficient to render the climatic consequences tolerable—and every time it got better in the Northern Hemisphere, it would get worse in the Southern.

Our results have been carefully scrutinized by more than 100 scientists 22 in the United States, Europe and the Soviet Union. There are still arguments on points of detail. But the overall conclusion seems to be agreed upon: There are severe and previously unanticipated global consequences of nuclear war—subfreezing temperatures in a twilit radioactive gloom lasting for months or longer.

Scientists initially underestimated the effects of fallout, were amazed 23 that nuclear explosions in space disabled distant satellites, had no idea that the fireballs from high-yield thermonuclear explosions could deplete the ozone layer and missed altogether the possible climatic effects of nuclear dust and smoke. What else have we overlooked?

Nuclear war is a problem that can be treated only theoretically. It is 24 not amenable to experimentation. Conceivably, we have left something important out of our analysis, and the effects are more modest than we calculate. On the other hand, it is also possible—and, from previous experience, even likely—that there are further adverse effects that no one has yet been wise enough to recognize. With billions of lives at stake, where does conservatism lie—in assuming that the results will be better than we calculate, or worse?

Many biologists, considering the nuclear winter that these calculations 25 describe, believe they carry somber implications for life on Earth. Many species of plants and animals would become extinct. Vast numbers of surviving humans would starve to death. The delicate ecological relations that bind together organisms on Earth in a fabric of mutual dependency would be torn, perhaps irreparably. There is little question that our global civilization would be destroyed. The human population would be reduced to prehistoric levels, or less. Life for any survivors would be extremely hard. And there seems to be a real possibility of the extinction of the human species.

It is now almost 40 years since the invention of nuclear weapons. We 26
have not yet experienced a global thermonuclear war—although on more
than one occasion we have come tremulously close. I do not think our
luck can hold forever. Men and machines are fallible, as recent events
remind us. Fools and madmen do exist, and sometimes rise to power.
Concentrating always on the near future, we have ignored the long-term
consequences of our actions. We have placed our civilization and our
species in jeopardy.

Fortunately, it is not yet too late. We can safeguard the planetary 27
civilization and the human family if we so choose. There is no more
important or more urgent issue.

## QUESTIONS FOR ANALYSIS

1. What would you say is the thesis of this essay? How convincingly
   argued do you find this thesis? What do you think is the most convincing part of the argument?

2. Sagan waits until paragraph 15 to begin discussing the results of a
   nuclear war. Outline paragraphs 1–13 in order to discover Sagan's
   strategy of preparing readers for these results. (Chapter 1 presents a
   plan for outlining a selection.) How many different things does he do
   in these paragraphs? How successful do you think he has been in
   preparing newspaper readers for the results he proposes?

3. What do you think of Sagan's "baseline case" strategy? Do you see
   any problems with his basing the argument on such a case?

4. List the results of nuclear war Sagan proposes. Why do you think he
   sequences the results as he does? Can you see any advantages to this
   sequence?

5. In paragraphs 20–24, Sagan's argument takes a different turn. What
   seems to be his strategy in these paragraphs? What advantages do you
   see in this strategy?

6. Writers often frame an essay by repeating at the end some element
   from the beginning. How does Sagan frame this essay?

7. Analyze the appeals in this essay—logical, emotional, ethical. (Chapter 1 offers guidelines for evaluating appeals in arguments.) How
   would you evaluate the appropriateness and effectiveness of these appeals?

8. What kind of reader might be very skeptical about Sagan's argument
   or antagonistic toward his purpose? Just how and why would such a
   reader object to this essay?

9. Did you find this essay easy or difficult to read? Decide what made it easy or difficult. In general, what factors make some readings more difficult for you than others?

## SUGGESTIONS FOR WRITING

1. Identify an ominous college or community problem, the consequences of which you suspect people underestimate. Write an essay about this problem, speculating about its dire results.

2. Imagine a potential national or international catastrophe, and write an essay speculating about its results. You might need to research the nature of the catastrophe (what would actually happen) in order to present it believably to your readers. You might also want to consider in your essay results others have already proposed for such a catastrophe.

3. Write an essay speculating about the immediate and long-term results of a recent scientific discovery.

4. Think of a significant change you would like to see in the rules for a particular sport. Write an essay explaining this change, establishing its significance, and speculating about the results of the change for both players and fans.

# Lori Weichenthal

A resident of Los Gatos, California, Lori Weichenthal is a biology major planning to become a doctor. She has been an avid theatergoer since the eighth grade, when she attended the Oregon Shakespeare Festival in Ashland with her English class. As a high school student, she was a summer intern at the San Jose (California) Repertory Theater. Besides her interest in theater, she enjoys horseback riding and going to the beach.

# The Rise of Regional Theater

Weichenthal's essay is ambitious, well argued, and carefully documented. As serious an effort as it is, it began with her personal interest in regional theaters in Ashland and San Jose. Writing the essay enabled her to combine personal experience (memory, reflection), reporting (interviews with regional theater directors), and library research.

As you begin reading the essay, notice how she demonstrates that the trend does exist. Then notice how many different kinds of causes she proposes to explain the trend.

In 1956, theater lovers in San Jose, California, and Cleveland, Ohio, 1 had something in common: a long and often futile wait to see professionally produced plays. The dramatic world of the United States was centered in the theaters along New York's Broadway. Few quality theater companies existed elsewhere. The only opportunities most Americans had to see a polished production was when the Broadway companies traversed the country with the top shows of the season. Even then, many theatergoers were left without a ticket: the tours usually covered only major cities; and many regions of the country, especially in the Northwest, were entirely overlooked. In the mid-sixties, however, permanent professional theaters began to appear in places as diverse as Miami, Florida, and Anchorage, Alaska. Today, in 1986, this movement has developed into a thriving trend, and audiences in San Jose and Cleveland have to wait no more. Each city now possesses its own professional theater, which produces upwards of six plays a year. Both cities have benefited from the trend toward new regional theaters.

The rise of regional theater was at first very slow. In 1956, *Theatre* 2 *World*, the yearbook of the theatrical industry, recognized only two professional theaters beyond the boundaries of New York City, although in actuality a few more existed (Blums 6). Most were small, struggling

379

companies, attempting to maintain a limited summer session on a shoe-string budget. In 1965, however, a call went forth to establish a National Endowment for the Arts. The Ford Foundation and the federal govern-ment responded, allocating a substantial sum of money to advance re-gional theater and to deal with the "theatrical wilderness" that existed in many parts of the country, especially in the Northwestern and South-ern states (Ross ix). With this money, new companies slowly began to emerge, and existing companies grew stronger. In 1968, twenty-eight professional theaters outside of New York were recorded in *Theatre World* (Willis vol. 25).[1] In 1974, the number doubled, reaching fifty-nine (Wil-lis vol. 31). In addition, interesting notes began to appear in the once Broadway-monopolized book, commenting on the possible values of the emerging companies:

> The importance of these regional companies for experimental purposes, and for developing new talent and audiences is obvious. They are deserving indeed of any encouragement that may be given them. Perhaps the future of the Broadway theater may depend upon their continuing productivity. (Willis 6 vol. 31)

The established dramatic community was beginning to take notice that professional theater no longer existed only within the confines of New York City.

With the arrival of the eighties, the number of regional theaters took    3 an amazing leap, rising to a recorded 152 (Zeisler iv). This number continued to increase throughout the early eighties, even as Broadway began to experience a decline. As the number of new regional theaters increased on an average of ten per year, the number of Broadway pro-ductions declined by ten. Attendance at Broadway theaters decreased by 5 percent, as the number of individuals attending regional productions climbed to twelve million (all data are from Willis). Broadway, it seemed, could no longer be considered the center of the dramatic universe. Re-gional theater had risen and was taking some of the glow from the Broad-way sun. What caused this change? What force fueled and maintained the ascent of regional theater?

The most apparent explanation for the appearance of local professional    4 theaters is the establishment of the National Endowment for the Arts (NEA). Before the NEA's founding, financial support simply was not available for dramatic pursuits beyond Broadway. Theater was an invest-ment into which producers put money in order to extract profits. Regional theaters presented little chance for monetary gain and, consequently, attracted few investors. The few companies that existed before the En-dowment did so through "great determination, a tight budget, and a great deal of begging" (Ruben 94).

With the money from NEA, however, regional theater could develop 5
and expand. It is no surprise that the first jump in the number of regional
theaters corresponds directly with the establishment of NEA. In addition,
NEA allocated money to establish communication and exchange net-
works among the isolated companies throughout the country. This increased the growth potential of new companies, who could now rely on
the experience of more established theatrical groups. Thus, NEA was
vital to the original establishment of the trend toward regional theater.
Money alone, however, cannot explain the increase in local companies;
money does not ensure success or the existence of an audience, a necessity
for theatrical survival. Yet, most of the theaters founded with the assistance of the Endowment have survived, developed significant audiences
and even managed to make a profit. A more intensive search, then, is
necessary to explain properly the trend toward regional theater.

One deeper cause for the rise of regional theater is that, in recent 6
decades, there has been a general increase in demand for live entertainment. In 1982, the amount of income that the average United States
citizen spent on live entertainment increased 5 percent over 1973 (Census Bureau 205). In the category of live entertainment, theater was a
major contributor, behind only rock concerts. Thus, regional theater has
benefited from people's increasing interest in live entertainment. Even
as technology brings inexpensive electronic media into the home, the
special exchange between audience and performer that constitutes live
theater is growing in importance. Paul Barnes, director of educational
outreach at the Oregon Shakespearean Festival (OSF), noted that the
young especially are excited by live theater and the many levels of response it provides: "They are not just sitting in front of a sterile tube.
They are sitting with a group of vibrant people, watching fellow humans
act. The possibilities are limitless" (Barnes).

Regional theater is uniquely capable of fulfilling the need for live en- 7
tertainment. Many theaters, including OSF, have even experimented
with participatory plays, further servicing their audiences' desire for live
interaction. Such plays have become increasingly popular, playing to sell-
out audiences in many local theaters throughout the country. Thus, the
modern need for personal involvement in entertainment, so naturally
fulfilled by theatrical productions, has encouraged the rise of regional
companies in the United States. A purely economic explanation for the
success of permanent professional theaters is also available: regional theaters are more financially feasible than the Broadway-centered system. For
less money, regional theater reaches more people than Broadway and its
touring companies could ever manage. In 1980, the 152 regional theaters
reached 12 million theatergoers at an average cost of $2.53 (Zeisler iv).

For a touring company to reach only a tenth of this audience cost an average of $4.61 (Willis 5 vol. 37).[2]

This great price gap is largely due to the fact that regional theaters are   8
more cost effective. As mostly nonprofit organizations, they stick to tight budgets and rarely run into the overexpenditures that are legendary on Broadway. In 1983, OSF had a budget of $2,354,000 for the production of eleven plays, an average cost of $214,000 a play. The company took in $2,476,000 that year, leaving a profit of $122,000 to reinvest (Ross 105). The same year, it cost $5,000,000 to produce one Broadway play (*My One and Only*), and investment returns were not good (Brustein 23).

This difference in fiscal responsibility ultimately shows up in ticket   9
prices. The average ticket price to a Broadway production in 1983 was $25; the high was $50 (Willis 5). In contrast, a subscription for five plays at one newly formed regional theater, the San Jose Repertory, cost $36, an obvious savings (Isenberg 95). Such differences in price make regional theater far more consumer attractive. As a New York critic put it, Broadway is "trying to sell a million Cadillacs when only a fraction of the populace has the means to buy them!" (Brustein 26). Many theatergoers are choosing the economy model provided by regional theater and are discovering a much smoother ride.

Beyond economics, the success of regional theater can be attributed   10
to its early realization of its role in the community. Beyond providing quality performances, a Broadway company has no commitment to the cities at which it stops on tour. This is not true of a local permanent theater, which, in order to survive, must maintain positive relations within the region it serves. From the start, many local companies realized their calling to be more than just producers of plays; they took on some extra responsibility and established outreach programs to tap unfound audiences and to develop new audiences and artists for the future.

OSF has maintained an outreach program almost from its founding.   11
Originally simply a service where actors traveled to surrounding colleges to teach Shakespeare, the program expanded in 1975 to involve two actor teams that traverse the Pacific Coast from Alaska to central California, instructing school-age students and getting them "into Shakespeare." In addition, the festival offers specials to all its audiences, including backstage tours and round-table discussions with actors and production stage hands. Paul Barnes, the director of these outreach programs, says that they are all ways to provide for the theater of the future. He believes the positive effects of the program are already traceable. People from new areas, tapped by the traveling actors, have begun attending the festival; and young theatergoers have increased markedly,

adding to the total audience gain of 100,000 over ten years (all data are from Barnes interview).

Newer regional theaters have also established outreach programs. The 12 San Jose Repertory, in its first year of existence, established a magnet program with a local high school to encourage artistic talent. It also established a touring program visiting local schools, to introduce young children to theater. The initial expense drained their limited funds; however, director David Lemos called it an investment that paid off. Such programs made the public aware of the theater and helped to triple audience size, as well as serving to develop fresh talent that has already appeared in several company productions (Lemos).

OSF and San Jose Repertory are the rule, not the exception. Almost 13 all regional theaters today have some type of outreach program, and the dividends they have received have been many. The programs have found the audience to maintain the theaters now, as well as the audience and actors of tomorrow. Regional theaters' realization of the necessity of their outreach role has contributed significantly to their survival.

Another possible cause of the increasing numbers of regional theaters 14 is that these companies can design their productions to meet the specific interests of the local citizenry. In 1984, OSF produced a play, *Dreamhouse*, about California life (located in Ashland, Oregon, near the California border, the festival draws largely a California clientele). The play, which probably would not have sold well in Ohio, had a 96 percent box office return, largely because it was a play that dealt with immediate issues important to Californians (Ruben 96). Similarly, the San Jose Repertory produced a play, *Yup!*, about the lives of Yuppies, young urban professionals in the surrounding Silicon Valley. The show was sold out throughout the summer while a Broadway musical in town at the same time attracted only half an audience (Lemos). Such productions meet the needs of the local audiences and have made regional theaters popular with wide ranges of audiences. This popularity has helped to maintain the regional theaters and has convinced many communities to establish their own theaters, furthering the trend of regional theater in the United States.

All of these causes help explain the trend toward regional theater. The 15 establishment of NEA clearly contributed to the initial stages of the movement, and the economic advantages and unique service capacity of regional companies have helped in their development and maintenance. However, even all these aspects together do not provide a complete picture as to why regional theater has risen, and they certainly do not explain the sudden surge in the trend during the eighties. There must still be a deeper, more fundamental, explanation of the ascent of regional companies. Taking into account the proverbial saying that "art mirrors life," a look at the nation as a whole provides a clue: this theatrical movement is merely a part of a larger, more general, trend toward decentralization.

In his popular book *Megatrends*, John Naisbitt documents this trend as 16 it affects every aspect of American life from politics to television. The main aspect of the trend is that now and in the future important movements will come from the grass roots. The rise of regional theater fits perfectly into this megatrend, taking the power away from the center of Broadway and giving it to the regions, just as important political activity is now centered in the states, not the nation's capital. In addition, the megatrend of decentralization explains the sudden rise in regional theater in the eighties, as this is when Naisbitt documents the real force of the trend beginning.

Thus, the best explanation of the rise of regional theater is that it is 17 part of the larger movement toward decentralization that the country is undergoing. All the other causes contributed toward regional theaters' rise, and probably other causes too, but it is this single cause which gives the theatrical movement meaning. The strength of the local theaters does not mean the death of Broadway as some critics may contend. Rather, it signals a new age, where the vitality and talent will come from the regions to Broadway and other national centers.

### NOTES

1. Data cited with no page number were obtained by counting the entries contained within one volume.
2. These costs are based on data from the cited text, calculated using the formula (cost of production)/(total audience attendance).

### WORKS CITED

Barnes, Paul. [Personal interview]. 3 May and 6 May 1986.

Blums, Daniel, ed. *Theatre World*. New York: Grenburg, 1957.

Brustein, Robert. "The Broadway Slump." *The New Republic* (7 March 1983): 25–26.

Census Bureau. *Census of Sports and Leisure*. Washington, D.C.: Census, 1982.

Isenberg, Barbara, ed. *California Theatre Annual*. California: Performing Arts Network, 1982.

Lemos, David. [Personal interview]. 3 May 1986.

Naisbitt, John. *Megatrends: Ten New Directions Transforming Our Lives*. New York: Warner Books, 1982.

Ross, Laura, ed. *Theatre Profiles 5*. New York: Theatre Communications, 1982.

Rubin, Margaret, ed. *Ashland, Oregon, Shakespearean Festival.* Ashland: Oregon Shakespearean Festival, 1984.

Willis, John, ed. *Theatre World.* Vols. 25–39. New York: Crown, 1984.

Zeisler, Peter. *Theatre Profiles 3.* New York: Theatre Communications, 1980.

## QUESTIONS FOR ANALYSIS

1. Do you find Weichenthal's explanation for the increase in regional theaters convincing? What part of her argument do you find most convincing? least convincing?

2. How does Weichenthal demonstrate that the trend exists, that there has indeed been an increase in the number of regional theaters? What do you find convincing or unconvincing about this demonstration?

3. List in order the causes Weichenthal proposes to explain the rise of regional theaters. What kinds of causes does she propose, and how does she argue for each one? Can you imagine a better order for the causes? Can you think of any causes she has overlooked?

4. Which, if any, of the causes Weichenthal proposes might also be considered effects?

5. Examine Weichenthal's documentation closely. How much diversity do you find in these sources? How convincing do you find the documentation?

6. Writers often have difficulty integrating sources smoothly into their essays. Choose one paragraph in which Weichenthal cites several outside sources. How successfully does she integrate these sources into the paragraph?

7. Analyze the causal arguments in the Gould, Fuchs, Thurow, and Weichenthal selections. Pay particular attention to the ways in which these authors support their proposed causes and anticipate readers' possible objections. From your analysis, what can you conclude about the nature of causal argument?

## SUGGESTIONS FOR WRITING

1. Consider recent trends in entertainment and the arts, and write an essay about one of these trends. In your essay, demonstrate that you have identified a trend (which continues over a period of time), not a fad (which lasts for no more than a year or two). Document that the trend is increasing or decreasing over time, and argue for possible causes of the trend. Try to anticipate readers' objections to your proposed causes and consider alternative causes in your essay.

2. Read recent magazine articles on educational change, and identify a trend in secondary or college education that interests you. Write an essay about this trend, documenting that it exists and proposing possible causes of it.

# A Look at Lori Weichenthal's Writing Process

Weichenthal's instructor asked students to identify some trend, to document it, and then to argue for some possible causes of the trend. Weichenthal hoped that she would be able to write about some aspect of theater, her favorite form of entertainment. Every summer for several years she had seen plays at the Ashland, Oregon, Shakespeare Festival. During her high school years, she had participated in an internship program with the San Jose, California, Repertory Theater and had seen nearly all the plays produced in San Jose. Although she loved theater and had a great deal to say about it, the only trend she could immediately identify was a possible increase in the number of internship programs with schools.

Weichenthal's first inquiries at the library led her to periodicals reporting on professional theater. Examining books on theater shelved near these periodicals, she discovered a book on regional theater. Here, she learned of the dramatic increase in numbers and influence of regional theaters over the last twenty years. She realized immediately that the increase in internships was a sustaining cause (and perhaps also an effect) of the larger trend of the increasing numbers of regional theaters. She was then able to document this larger trend convincingly from several periodicals reporting annually on American theater.

Reading about this trend, she discovered several plausible causes for it. Programs of the National Endowment for the Arts seemed the obvious precipitating cause. Several writers stressed the relatively low operating and ticket costs of regional theaters, while others mentioned the importance of community programs and local play themes. She incorporated all of these causes into her essay, arguing in part from her own experience with the Ashland and San Jose companies and from what she learned in phone calls to the directors of these companies. John Naisbitt's book *Megatrends*, which had been assigned in her writing class, contributed the "deeper, more fundamental" cause of decentralization (itself a trend, as well). A student who read Weichenthal's first draft suggested the possible cause of increasing interest in live entertainment; after finding statistics to support this cause, Weichenthal incorporated it into her revision.

## A GUIDE TO WRITING
## ABOUT CAUSE OR EFFECT

From the readings in this chapter, you have learned a great deal about writing that analyzes causes or effects and are in a good position to understand the problems and possibilities of this kind of writing. This section offers guidance for writing an essay of this type. You will find activities to help you identify a topic and discover what to say about it, organize your ideas and plan the essay, and revise your draft to strengthen your argument and improve readability.

# *Invention*

The following activities can help to get you started and enable you to explore your subject fully. A few minutes spent completing each of these writing activities will improve your chances of producing a detailed and convincing first draft. You can decide on a subject for your essay, review what you presently know about the subject, conjecture about possible causes or effects, evaluate others' proposed causes or effects, and analyze how you might convince readers that you have a plausible argument.

CHOOSING A SUBJECT. The subject of a cause or effect essay may be a trend, an event, or a phenomenon. All of these possibilities are illustrated by the readings in this chapter. Before considering a subject for your essay, you might want to review the suggestions for writing that follow each reading. These varied possibilities for cause or effect essays may suggest an essay you would like to write.

After reviewing the suggestions for writing, you may still need to identify an appropriate subject for an essay. A good way to begin is to list as many possibilities as you can think of. List making generates ideas: as soon as you start a list, you will think of possibilities you cannot imagine now.

Even if you feel confident that you already have a subject, listing other possibilities will help you to test your choice. Make separate lists for *trends, events,* or *phenomena.* List specific subjects suggested by the possibilities included here for each category.

For *trends,* consider the following possibilities:

changes in men's or women's roles and opportunities in marriage, education, or work

changing patterns in leisure, entertainment, life style, religious life, health, technology

completed artistic or historical trends (various art movements or historical changes)

long-term changes in economic conditions or political behavior

For *events*, these possibilities might help you to get your own list under
way:

a recent college, community, national, or international event about
which there is puzzlement or controversy

a major event in your own life that you would like to understand better
or a decision you will make soon that will have results you cannot
fully predict

a historical event about which there is still some dispute as to its causes
or effects

For *phenomena*, there are many possibilities:

social problems like discrimination, homeless people, child abuse, illiteracy, high school dropouts, youth suicides, unwed mothers

various aspects of college life like libraries too noisy to study in, classes
too large, lack of financial aid, difficulties in scheduling the classes
you want, shortcomings in student health services, unavailability of
housing (in this essay you will not need to solve these problems,
but only to analyze their causes or effects)

human traits like anxiety, selfishness, fear of success, fear of failure,
leadership, jealousy, lack of confidence, envy, opportunism, curiosity, openness, health or fitness

After you have completed your lists, reflect on the possibilities you
have compiled. Since an authoritative essay analyzing causes or effects
requires sustained thinking, drafting, revising, and possibly even research, you will want to choose a subject to which you can commit
yourself enthusiastically for a week or two. Choose a subject that interests
you, even if you feel uncertain about how to approach it. The writing
and research activities that follow will enable you to test your subject
choice and to discover what you have to say about it.

EXPLORING YOUR SUBJECT. You may discover you know more about your
topic than you suspected if you write about it for a few minutes without
stopping. This brief sustained writing stimulates memory search, helps
you probe your interest in the subject, and enables you to test your subject
choice. As you write, consider questions such as these: What interests
me in this subject? What is there about it that might interest readers?

What do I already know about it? Why don't we already have an accepted explanation for this subject? What causes or effects have people already suggested for this subject? How can I learn more about it?

CONSIDERING CAUSES OR EFFECTS. Before you research your subject (should you need to), you will want to discover what causes (or effects) of it you can already imagine. Make a list of possible causes or effects. Consider background, immediate, and perpetuating causes; consider effects that are immediate and those that are long-term. Try to think not only of obvious causes or effects, but also of ones that are likely to be overlooked in a superficial analysis of your subject.

Reflect on your list, identifying the most convincing causes or effects. Do you have enough to make a strong argument? Could a friend help you to extend your list? Imagine how you might convince readers of the plausibility of some of these causes or effects.

RESEARCHING YOUR SUBJECT. When developing an essay analyzing causes or effects, you can often gain great advantage by researching your subject. (See the appendix to this book for library research strategies.) You can review and evaluate others' proposed causes or effects, in case you want to present any of these alternatives in your own essay. Reviewing others' causes or effects may suggest to you plausible causes or effects you have overlooked. You may also find evidence and arguments to use in your own counterarguments to readers' objections.

ANALYZING YOUR READERS. Your purpose is to convince readers with a plausible argument for your proposed causes or effects. To succeed, you will need to choose causes or effects, evidence, and arguments that will convince your particular readers. You will want to anticipate objections these readers may have to any of your proposed causes or effects and to identify alternatives they may favor.

To analyze your readers, you might find it helpful to write for a few minutes, identifying who they are, what they know about the subject, and how they can be convinced by your proposed causes or effects.

REHEARSING YOUR ARGUMENT. The heart of your essay will be the argument you make for the plausibility of your proposed causes or effects. Like a ballet dancer or baseball pitcher warming up for a performance, you can prepare for your first draft by rehearsing the argument you will make. Write for a few minutes about each cause or effect, trying out an argument for your particular readers. This writing activity will focus your thinking and encourage you to keep discovering new arguments up until the time you start drafting. It may also lead you to search for additional evidence to support your arguments.

# Drafting

Review the lists, writings, and notes you produced in the preceding invention activities. Note the most promising material. You may realize that you need further information, a deeper analysis, or a better understanding of your readers. If you have the time, stop now to fill in these gaps. If you feel reasonably confident about your material, however, you may be ready to begin drafting. Remember that you will solve some problems and make further discoveries as you draft. The following guidelines will help you to set goals for your draft and to plan your organization.

SETTING GOALS.  If you establish goals for your draft before you begin writing, you will find that you can move ahead more quickly. With general goals in mind, you can make particular writing decisions more confidently. Consider these questions now and keep them in mind as you draft in order to maintain your focus:

How will I convince my readers that my proposed causes or effects are plausible? Shall I marshal scientific evidence like Gould, quote authorities and give several reasons like Fuchs, include personal anecdotes and cases like Kozol, or present an elaborate scenario like Sagan?

How should I anticipate readers' objections to my argument? What should I do about alternative causes or effects? Shall I merely list alternative causes and then dismiss them as obsolete like Gould, consider alternative causes carefully and refute each one like Fuchs and Thurow, or review alternative causes and incorporate all of them into my own explanation like Weichenthal?

How much will my readers need to know about my subject—the event, trend, or phenomenon? Will I need to describe my subject in some detail in the way that Sagan documents the nuclear threat, or can I assume that my readers have personal experience with my subject just as Weichenthal seems to assume that her readers have all seen a play at some regional theater. Like Gould, who must review for his readers recent advances in geology and evolutionary biology, must I provide background information so that readers can follow my argument for my proposed causes or effects? If my subject is a trend, can I demonstrate that the trend exists with a chart like Fuchs or by quoting authoritative sources like Weichenthal?

How can I begin engagingly and end conclusively? Shall I begin by emphasizing the importance or timeliness of my subject like Gould, Kozol, and Sagan? Might I begin with a personal anecdote in the way that Kozol relates his recurring dream of being in Russia and unable to read the Cyrillic alphabet?

How will I establish my authority to argue the causes or effects of my subject? Shall I do this by citing personal experience and presenting a carefully researched consideration of others' proposed causes like Weichenthal, by showing a comprehensive understanding of the effects of a phenomenon like illiteracy as does Kozol, or by displaying a breadth of scientific knowledge like Gould and Sagan?

PLANNING YOUR ORGANIZATION. With goals in mind and invention notes at hand, you are ready to make a tentative outline of your draft. The sequence of proposed causes or effects will be at the center of your outline, but you may also want to plan where you will consider alternatives or counterargue objections. Notice that all the writers in this chapter who conjecture about causes (Gould, Fuchs, Thurow, and Weichenthal) consider alternative causes—evaluating, refuting, or accepting them—before they present their own. Much of an essay analyzing causes may be devoted to considering alternatives. Both writers who conjecture about causes and writers who speculate about effects usually consider readers' possible objections to their causes or effects along with the argument for each cause or effect. If you must provide readers with a great deal of information about your subject as context for your argument, you may want to outline this information carefully. For your essay, this part of the outline may be a major consideration. Notice how prominent background information is in Gould's essay about the Permian extinction or Sagan's essay on nuclear winter. Your plan should make the information readily accessible to your readers. Remember that this outline is merely tentative; you may decide to change it once you start drafting.

# Revising

Once you have a complete first draft, you will almost certainly be able to find ways to improve it. With your purpose and readers in mind, read your draft critically, using the critical reading questions at the beginning of this chapter. (If possible, have someone else read your draft critically, too.) As you revise, you will be primarily concerned with strengthening your argument and improving the readability of your essay.

REVISING TO STRENGTHEN THE ARGUMENT. Decide whether you have adequately considered your readers' needs. Your argument should be aimed at particular readers, not to manipulate them, but to convince them that your conjectures or speculations are plausible. Make sure that your readers will not feel that you have ignored obvious alternatives or failed to anticipate predictable objections. Be certain, too, that you have not assumed readers know more about your subject than they in fact do. Try to develop and strengthen the argument for each proposed cause or effect, adding further evidence or anecdotes. Or perhaps you should drop a weakly argued cause or effect entirely and rearrange the sequence in which you present the causes or effects. You may even find that you want to do further research on your subject in order to gain a better understanding and to discover still other possible causes or effects.

REVISING TO IMPROVE READABILITY. Reconsider your beginning and ending. Can you think of another beginning that would more effectively orient your readers and draw them into your essay? Can you improve your ending so that it brings your argument to a more emphatic and memorable close? Examine each sentence closely to ensure that it says what you intend it to say. Cut any unnecessary words or phrases. Try to improve the flow from sentence to sentence, and consider adding transitions or other cues and signals to keep the reader on track.

Once you have completed your revision, proofread your essay with extreme care in order to catch any errors of mechanics, usage, punctuation, or style. Try to have someone else proofread the essay as well.

# CHAPTER EIGHT

# *Proposal*

Proposals, one of the most common kinds of writing in the workplace and in government, are written every day to analyze problems and to recommend practical solutions. Some of these proposals have immediate pragmatic ends, particularly those written in the workplace. Several engineering firms, for example, might write proposals to compete for a contract to build an intraurban rail system. The business manager of a small firm might write a memo to the company president proposing a new word-processing department to replace the archaic typing pool. Seeking funding to support her research on the American poet Walt Whitman, a university professor might write a proposal to the National Endowment for the Humanities.

Other proposals address social problems and have more long-range ends in that they attempt to influence the direction of public policy. The United Nations, for instance, might form a task force to recommend ways to eliminate acid rain. The National Education Association might sponsor a commission to suggest how the decline in Scholastic Aptitude Test (SAT) scores could be reversed. A private institution such as the Carnegie Foundation might ask a group of respected academic, government, and business leaders to propose ways to reduce the budget deficit.

Still other proposals are written by individuals who want to solve problems plaguing communities or groups to which they belong. A student living in a college dormitory might make a proposal to reduce the noise level at certain hours so that students can study. Another student might propose that an escort service be created to prevent rape on campus. A sorority member might recommend rescheduling rush week so that it will not interfere with midterm exams.

When writing proposals about local problems that we can investigate firsthand, we usually feel confident about our ability to analyze these problems and propose workable solutions. When we try to write about public policy, however, we may feel inadequate and uninformed. As citizens, it is important that we all learn how to inform ourselves about public issues and develop confidence in our own ideas.

One way to gain confidence and ability is by studying proposal writing—learning to read proposals critically and write them effectively. This kind of writing helps you learn how to find the information you need, develops your capacity to analyze and argue persuasively, and teaches you to detect manipulative and faulty reasoning. Most important, it can give you a voice in the decision-making process.

## A GUIDE TO READING PROPOSALS

You can become a more effective reader of proposals by learning to recognize their basic features and by asking analytical and evaluative questions as you read. This section presents the basic features of proposals, illustrates these features with a sample annotated proposal, and offers a list of questions that will help you read this kind of writing more critically.

## *Basic Features of Proposals*

Proposals are not hard to identify because they are always concerned with problems and how to solve them. Proposal writers seek to exert influence by making their environment more responsive to their needs and desires. Proposals thus include the following basic features: *a clearly defined problem, a proposed solution, a convincing argument, comparison of the proposed solution with alternatives,* and *a reasonable tone.*

A CLEARLY DEFINED PROBLEM. A proposal cannot exist without a problem, but the problem must be one that can be pointed to and not some vague complaint. The problem usually needs to be defined in some detail to convince readers of its existence and seriousness. To define the problem, writers often provide concrete evidence—facts, statistics, testimony of witnesses and authorities. They may also include general information indicating the type of problem it is, how it came about, who is affected by it, and what its consequences might be.

A PROPOSED SOLUTION. Beyond establishing that a problem exists and is serious, a proposal must also suggest a way to solve that particular problem. The assertion of this solution is the proposal's thesis. Proposal writers usually offer original ideas, but they may also support the ideas of others, perhaps ideas that have been suggested but not taken seriously.

A CONVINCING ARGUMENT. Readers need to be convinced that the proposed solution is the best way of solving the problem. Therefore, proposal writers must present the case for their solution, using all or only some of the following strategies to convince readers to accept their solution:

*Arguing That the Proposed Solution Will Solve the Problem.* To make this case, writers provide reasons and supporting evidence to prove that the proposed solution will actually solve the problem. This may involve analyzing the problem's causes and showing how the proposed solution will eliminate these causes.

*Arguing That the Proposed Solution Is Feasible.* To demonstrate that the proposed solution is a feasible way of solving the problem, the writer must show how easily it can be put into practice. The easier the proposed solution is to implement, the more likely it is to win readers' support. Therefore, writers carefully set out the steps needed to implement the solution, attempting to convince readers that implementation will be neither too hard nor too costly.

*Arguing That Objections to the Proposed Solution Should Not Undermine Confidence in It.* In advancing their argument, proposal writers try to be convincing without being combative. Above all, they seek to accommodate readers, to find a basis of agreement upon which to build. Often they anticipate how readers might object to their argument and then attempt to allay fears. Careful not to condescend to readers or dismiss their concerns lightly, they show that readers' objections are unfounded.

COMPARISON OF THE PROPOSED SOLUTION WITH ALTERNATIVES. As part of the effort to accommodate their readers, proposal writers seldom claim that their solution is the only one possible, but they do argue that theirs is the best. By comparing their own solution to the alternatives, writers reveal the advantages of their own proposal and the disadvantages of the others. They may make a point-by-point comparison, showing that their solution is strong where the others are weak; or they may show that all the possibilities have their strengths and weaknesses, but that the proposed solution's strengths outweigh its weaknesses.

A REASONABLE TONE.  Since the aim of all proposals is to get readers to agree, proposal writers never adopt a querulous or quarrelsome tone. They always strive to be perceived as reasonable and accommodating. Even when they criticize other people's proposals or refute objections, they avoid attacking people personally or unfairly. Proposal writers also try to impress readers with their command of the subject. By appearing knowledgeable, they hope to win readers' confidence in their authority.

## An Annotated Sample:
### *Grant Bachelor's Degrees by Examination,* Mark Kleiman

People usually read proposals because they are troubled by a problem and want to solve it. Occasionally, proposals alert them to new problems. They delight in reading proposals that are thoughtful, thorough, and innovative. They especially admire the creativity displayed in a proposal that reconceives an old problem in an altogether new way or finds solutions no one has considered.

The following sample proposal, which you should read in its entirety before looking at the annotations, takes an iconoclastic view of higher education. Mark Kleiman, a research fellow at Harvard University, argues that since getting a college degree represents a problem for some people, it should be possible to receive a degree without the education. Before you begin reading, think about why and for whom the traditional means of getting a college degree might be a problem.

Kleiman did not address his proposal to educators but published it in the *Wall Street Journal,* a daily newspaper primarily for business people. To accept this proposal, readers must change their way of thinking about college education. Kleiman attempts to affect this change by describing the college degree in language associated with business rather than with education. As you read, notice how he is able to make his proposal seem quite reasonable and practical.

### *Grant Bachelor's Degrees by Examination*

**PROBLEM: college too expensive**
**Really a problem?**
**For whom?**

Colleges and universities offer their undergraduate students <u>two distinct commodities</u>: an <u>education</u> (or rather the opportunity for one) and a <u>degree.</u> The offer is what    1 antitrust lawyers call a "tie sale": They won't sell you the diploma unless you buy the whole package.

As fall approaches and parents dig into their pockets (or apply to their banks) for the $15,000 a year it now costs to send a child to a "prestige" institution such as the one where I work, it's time to ask why the education-and-degree package shouldn't be unbundled. If a student can achieve on his own, and demonstrate to the faculty, knowledge and competence higher than, say, the median of a school's graduating class, why shouldn't he be able to buy a certificate testifying as much?

Such a certificate—a B.A. by examination—would qualify its holder for employment, or for graduate or professional study, without costing him four years of for-gone earnings plus the cash price of a small house.

Rather than thinking of this proposal as unbundling credential-granting from education, one might prefer to consider it as substituting a performance standard for a technical-specification standard in the award of degrees.

There are three arguments for such a proposal.

First, it would save resources.

Second, it would make a valuable credential available to some who cannot now afford it, thus contributing to social mobility. (In addition to those earning their first degrees in this way, B.A.-by-exam programs at high-prestige schools might attract students who feel, often correctly, that their obscure sheepskins are holding them back.)

Third, and more speculatively, it might free high-powered but unconventional high-school graduates to pursue a self-education more useful to them than any pre-packaged education, without shutting themselves out of jobs and advanced-degree programs.

There are two obvious objections. Those who took their B.A.s by examination might miss out on the opportunities college provides for social interaction and other forms of personal and intellectual development. It might also be said that, since no examination could capture the richness of an undergraduate education, B.A.s by exam would have incentives to become, and would in fact be, narrower and shallower than their eight-semesters-in-residence counterparts.

The first objection is probably true but not conclusive. Some who would choose the exam route over the regular undergraduate course would probably be wise not to buy the nonacademic attributes of college for four years' in-

**Margin notes:**

Is education a commodity? don't usually think of colleges as businesses

broken up into its components, each component offered separately
middle number

SOLUTION: buy a BA
Advantage: same benefit for less money
good idea!
given up

Jargon
ARGUMENTS
1. money

2. social mobility

Effect: High cost prevents poor from going to college. What about loans and scholarships? Also some colleges are cheap.

3. usefulness

OBJECTIONS
1. miss out

2. exams narrow

RESPONSES TO OBJECTIONS
1. choice

How do you know whether college is for you?

2. make exam hard

be enough ——

come plus $60,000; others will not, in fact, choose the more expensive option, even if it is the only one offered.

To the second objection there are two solutions: high standards and resource-intensive examinations. A process lasting a month and costing $3,000 to administer and score, testing both general knowledge and competence in a major field, and involving written, oral and practical components and the preparation of a thesis or the equivalent, should suffice to evaluate breadth and depth at least as well as the current system does. The interests of the group running an examination program would run parallel with those of the rest of the institution in keeping standards high, and the social and moral pressure to award degrees in borderline cases ought to be much less for exam students than for ordinary undergraduates. By setting standards for examination B.A.s above the median of the eight-semester graduates, an institution could ensure that the exam program raised the average educational level of its degree-holders.

Exams might be too hard. Or BA wouldn't be worth much in job market

IMPLEMENTATION

The price to candidates could reflect fully loaded cost plus a substantial contribution to overhead and still look like a bargain. To deal with the unwillingness of potential candidates to gamble several thousand dollars on their chances of success, it might make sense to administer a fairly cheap ($200) screening test and give anyone who passed a money-back guarantee on the more thorough (and expensive) degree exam. The failure rate could be built into the price, or some insurance company might be willing to administer the screening test and sell failure insurance.

Those who fail would waste money

MODIFICATION OF PROPOSAL

This proposal should not be confused with college credit for "life experience," "urban semesters" or other moves to substitute the pragmatic for the scholarly in undergraduate education. The point is to tie the degree more rather than less tightly to specific academic competence, to certify the result—an educated person—rather than the *process* leading to that result.

sums up

could be done easily

If this idea required a consensus in order to be tried out, it would never stand a chance. Fortunately, no such consensus is needed. All it takes is one undeniably first-rate institution willing to break the credential cartel.

# Critical Reading Questions

As a critical reader, you should ask yourself certain key questions as you read proposals. These questions focus attention on the central issues, helping you to determine both what is being said and how to evaluate it. To demonstrate how these questions can guide your reading, we have applied each one to Kleiman's essay.

1. *How well defined is the problem? Does the proposal establish that the problem is real and serious?*

As you read a proposal, pay special attention to how the problem is defined. Proposals dealing with commonly acknowledged problems may not need to define the problem in detail, but all proposals should describe the problem to some extent. In cases where the problem is new or defined in an unusual way, the need for definition is especially great. Notice too how the writer classifies and analyzes the problem. Finally, consider how the writer explains the causes of the problem.

Because most people do not imagine alternative means of getting a college degree, Kleiman must be especially careful to establish the problem. He classifies the problem as an economic one, which enables him to propose an economic solution. By separating the education from the degree, he lays the groundwork for his proposal. Critical readers may find it hard to accept this problem analysis. Although Kleiman does not directly address the causes of the problem, he does point out the high cost of college education. However, his proposal fails to consider alternative solutions that would reduce the cost of education, such as scholarships or relatively inexpensive but equally prestigious public colleges.

2. *What exactly is the proposed solution, and what is your initial reaction to it?*

The proposed solution should not be hard to find since it is usually restated several times. Kleiman introduces his solution in the title and refers to it throughout the essay. Summarizing the proposed solution, particularly if it seems complicated, can be a useful critical reading strategy. Noting your first reaction to the solution enables you to anticipate objections and judge the argument.

3. *How successfully does the writer demonstrate that the proposed solution will actually solve the problem without causing even more serious problems?*

Proposal writers usually offer several reasons to prove that their solution will solve the problem. Kleiman argues that since the problem is an economic one, it needs an economic solution. By qualifying an individual for employment, he reasons, a degree granted by examination would have the same effect as a regular degree and would also be economically advantageous—saving four years of tuition and enabling the individual to earn money during the four years that would have been spent in college. If you disagree that the problem is primarily economic, you will undoubtedly think this solution is inadequate. Even if you acknowledge it is an economic problem, you may decide that this proposal does not offer a less costly education, only a cheaper degree.

4. *How does the writer argue that the proposed solution is feasible and can be easily implemented?*

Not all proposals need to demonstrate how the proposed solution would work, but as a critical reader you should consider whether such an explanation is necessary and, if it is provided, whether it is adequate. Begin by determining whether the proposal outlines specific actions for implementing the proposed solution. If it does, ask yourself how workable the plan seems. If the proposal does not set out a specific plan, ask yourself whether such a plan should have been spelled out or if you can imagine how the solution could be put into effect.

Kleiman sets out a fairly complicated plan to implement his solution. You might, however, think of some shortcomings: the exam might be too hard to study for; people would take exam prep courses and wind up getting an inferior education; only those who could afford to take the exam (and the preparation courses) would take the exam, thus setting up another inequity.

5. *How well does the writer anticipate possible objections to the proposed solution?*

Since writers of proposals want to accommodate their readers, they usually handle objections without criticizing those who might raise them. They also take such objections seriously, trying to be balanced and fair in dismissing them.

Kleiman considers two objections to his proposed solution. He agrees that the first may be true, although it is not conclusive; he responds to the second objection by modifying his solution. Treating objections in this way is calculated to allay readers' fears by showing that the writer is sensitive to their concerns and to promote the proposed solution by making it generally acceptable.

6. *How successfully does the writer demonstrate that the proposed solution has more advantages and fewer disadvantages than the alternative solutions do?*

Although proposals do not have to consider alternative solutions, most writers compare such alternatives unfavorably to their own. Kleiman, for example, notes that his solution makes available the benefit of college without the cost. Critical readers, however, might question whether the diploma is really the most important benefit of college and whether his proposal would benefit the poor, as he claims.

7. *How reasonable and trustworthy does the writer seem to be?*

Proposal writers need to instill confidence that they fully understand the problem and have no personal interest in the outcome. If the proposed solution will be of personal benefit to the writer, readers are likely to be distrustful and suspicious.

Kleiman seems to have nothing at stake in making his proposal. He is not a student seeking a degree, but an educator trying to reform the system.

8. *How effectively are the parts of the proposal arranged?*

Because proposals contain many parts and are often complicated, they should be clearly organized and easy to follow.

Kleiman makes his proposal readable by clearly distinguishing different parts—the problem and proposed solution, arguments for the proposal, possible objections and responses to the arguments, a plan to implement the solution, and advantages of the proposed solution over the alternatives.

# Gary Hart

After graduating from Yale Divinity School, Gary Hart (b. 1936) changed career goals and enrolled in Yale Law School, eventually becoming an attorney for the Justice Department. He first became involved in politics in 1968 as a volunteer for Robert F. Kennedy. Four years later, he gained national prominence as George McGovern's campaign director. Although both these presidential campaigns failed, Hart was not disillusioned with politics but was inspired to run for public office himself. In 1974, he successfully ran for the Senate in Colorado and was later reelected to a second term. He failed in 1984 to win the Democratic nomination for president, but is planning to run again in 1988.

Following his experience as McGovern's campaign director, Hart wrote a chronicle of the campaign entitled *Right from the Start* (1973). As he was preparing his own bid for the presidency, Hart wrote a book outlining his political philosophy, *The New Democracy* (1983). He has recently published a third book (co-written with William S. Lind) called *America Can Wait: The Case for Military Reform* (1986). The following selection, one of many articles Hart has written, appeared in the May 1985 issue of *USA Today*, a magazine published by the Society for the Advancement of Education and read primarily by policymakers.

# The Case for National Service

Hart wrote this proposal to support legislation he was sponsoring in the Senate. The idea of a program of national service is not new. As Hart reminds us in the opening paragraphs of his essay, Franklin D. Roosevelt instituted the Civilian Conservation Corps during the Depression and John F. Kennedy developed both the Peace Corps and VISTA. Before reading Hart's proposal, try to remember what you know about these national service programs. What kinds of service did they involve? What problems were they designed to address? How successful were they? Then spend a few minutes conjecturing on what a new system of national service might accomplish. Specifically, what would you want to do if you were asked to serve your nation?

Fifty-two years ago, Franklin D. Roosevelt established the Civilian Conservation Corps (CCC)—a program designed to help America work its way out of the Depression. The achievements of the CCC over its nine and one-half years were astounding. Three million young Americans planted more than 2,000,000,000 trees, beautified over 3,000,000 square miles of land, and built over 126,000 miles of roads and trails.

1

The CCC did much more than transform America's landscape. The program saved a whole generation of American youth from the despair and the hardship of the Depression. The voices of those who served in the CCC tell the story best:

"Bewildered, we faced the grey dawn of this depression. Our President and his colleagues saw the problem and decided to challenge the youth of America . . . we pushed forward toward a wilderness that would test our courage."

"I am thankful that I belong to a [nation] that has a President like FDR who made possible such an organization for the boys who were on the down and out."

Similarly, when the men and women of my generation were just beginning our careers, we were inspired by a president—John F. Kennedy—who challenged us to ask what we could do for our country, not what our country could do for us. Hundreds of thousands responded to that call by seeking public service, joining the Peace Corps to assist emerging democracies abroad, and, later, by joining VISTA to aid the disadvantaged here in our own nation.

Today, America's leaders need to challenge the idealism of our young people once again with the opportunity for national service. America currently faces a crisis among our young people as unemployment, teenage pregnancy, drug abuse, and simple boredom all plague too many of America's youth. At the same time, our nation has severe, unmet needs—elderly Americans who need help shopping, parks that need guides, and a potential shortage of military personnel during the remainder of this century. A system of national service could help America meet all these needs, while inspiring the idealism of America's young people once again.

How would a system of national service be established and how would it work? Earlier this year, Rep. Robert G. Torricelli (D.-N.J.) and I introduced legislation to create a Select Commission on National Service Opportunities. This Commission—which would include representatives from labor, business, education, the military, and young people—would recommend the best ways to structure and administer a national service system. Among the questions that the Commission would answer are:

*What kind of service opportunities should be available to participants?* I favor a system that would offer young people both military and non-military opportunities. The Commission would identify the tasks that would be most useful both to the national service participants and to the nation.

*Who would participate, and under what conditions?* Some studies have concluded that, at least in its initial stages, a national service system would need to be voluntary; the Commission would recommend whether a mandatory system would ever be feasible. It would also recommend what age groups would serve and for how long. In any case, women as well as men must be fully involved.

*What would the cost be?* For a national service system to be successful, 10 the costs of the program would need to be kept to a minimum. The Commission would examine past and existing service programs at the Federal, state, and local levels, as well as in other countries, and recommend how to administer the program in the most efficient and effective manner.

There are many other details and questions the Commission would 11 need to address, but the case for some form of national service is clear. That case is based on two sets of urgent needs currently facing America— the personal, educational, and employment needs of our young people and the social needs of our nation.

America needs national service for our young people. A national 12 service program would tap their idealism, communicate America's democratic values, and develop their sense of citizenship and a feeling of true patriotism.

Some say today's generation of young people lack idealism and a sense 13 of responsibility. They portray youth as materialistic, selfish, and un-idealistic, insulated from the problems of our country and the world—a group that cares more about Honda Civics than about civic duty.

I refuse to believe this caricature of America's youth. No one who has 14 watched young people working to fight famine in Ethiopia and hunger here in America can believe this generation lacks idealism. No one who has marched with students protesting racism in South Africa can believe today's young people lack high values.

Today's young people have not rejected the call to idealism and 15 service. They simply have not heard it yet. Too many of our national leaders indulge in self-congratulatory rhetoric, rather than challenging the best in America—as Presidents Roosevelt and Kennedy did.

The importance of issuing this challenge can not be overstated. Social 16 theorists, from Socrates to Thomas Jefferson, have long recognized that the education and training of young people is one of the most fundamental duties of any society. As the great American educator Horace Mann once noted, "Republics, one after another . . . have perished from a want of intelligence and virtue in the masses of people. If we do not prepare children to become good citizens . . . then our republic must go down to destruction."

Unfortunately, today, America is failing to provide training and civic 17 education for too many of our youth, with disastrous results for our society. America's young people are idealistic and energetic at heart, but too many of them are hampered by a lack of opportunity and a lack of hope. For example:

- Youth unemployment nationally is nearly 20%; for minority urban youth, the rate is almost 50%.
- Nearly one-fourth of American youth do not graduate from high school.
- Out-of-wedlock births among American teenage girls 15–19 have quadrupled since 1950; there are 263,000 illegitimate children born to mothers in that age group each year.
- Since 1960, the suicide rate among American teenagers has more than doubled; there are approximately 5,000 suicides in the 15–24 age group each year.

My colleague, Daniel Patrick Moynihan (D.-N.Y.), has underscored  18 the need for an American family policy. I believe that America also needs a youth policy to combat the problems plaguing our young and to give our young people all the opportunities they deserve. Indeed, most other industrialized democracies already have youth policies for these purposes.

A system of national service should be at the center of America's youth  19. policy. National service could:

- Show the majesty of America's parklands to an 18-year-old from the South Bronx who has only seen the inner city.
- Challenge a bored suburban teenager from Skokie with the task of weatherizing low-income housing in downtown Chicago.
- Give real work experience in a modern hospital to a young girl from rural Appalachia.
- Give an unemployed teenager from Houston the chance to work on the newest radar technology while serving his country in the Navy.
- Teach teenagers from a Los Angeles barrio and from Beverly Hills who are working together on a conservation project that they aren't as different from each other as they once thought.

National service would be an important part of a teenager's education.  20 Some 75 years ago, philosopher William James argued for a system of national service for youth in order to "get the childishness knocked out of them, and to come back into society with healthier sympathies and soberer ideas." A national service system would complement the traditional classroom experience and would complete the education of our young people.

National service can challenge our youth. It can supplement the ed- 21
ucation of America's young in the best way and teach them the duties
of citizenship. It can introduce them to the beauty of our nation and
give them pride in helping their fellow Americans.

National service would help meet not just the needs of the young, but 22
the needs of our broader society as well. Today, there is a renewed pride
in our country. After the social unrest of the 1960's and the economic
disruptions of the 1970's, many Americans now feel that we can once
again overcome our nation's problems and create a better future. However, we also live at a time of over $200,000,000,000 Federal deficits,
state tax revolts, and pinched municipal budgets—all of which make it
difficult to meet many of our most crying national needs.

National service could provide America with an invaluable army in 23
the fight against unmet social needs. We don't have to look far to see
fellow Americans in need of assistance.

There are millions of elementary and secondary school students who 24
could greatly benefit from tutoring and counseling by national service
participants.

There are some 7,000,000 "latch-key" children who must care for 25
themselves while their parents are at work. National service participants
could help supervise them in day camps and day care facilities.

There are 3,000,000 elderly who can not shop, prepare meals, or do 26
chores without help. National service participants could provide companionship and assistance to these senior citizens.

The list of such needs is nearly endless. There are millions of acres of 27
Federal lands that need improvement, low-income homes that need to
be insulated, lakes and streams with acid rain problems that need to be
monitored.

In all, several studies estimate there is a need for some 3–5,000,000 28
national service participants in efforts to improve life in America. A
national service program would go far in meeting those needs without
displacing adult workers from existing or potential jobs.

Finally, national service would help America meet some unmet mili- 29
tary needs as well. Since 1974, the all-volunteer force has done an excellent job of recruiting and meeting our military manpower needs. However, as the baby boom generation ages and the number of 18–22-year-
olds declines, there is a serious question as to whether the all-volunteer
force can meet future military manpower needs. One manpower study
suggests that, if we needed to increase forces by 25% over five years—in
response to a foreign threat, for example—the volunteer force would have
great difficulty filling the need. If we do need manpower beyond what
the all-volunteer force can provide, national service might be the most
fair and effective way to help meet those needs.

Many people of my generation remember the unfairness of the Selec- 30
tive Service draft during the Vietnam War. That system disproportionately asked the least advantaged of America's youth to show the "last
full measure" of their devotion to their country, while those who could
afford college were often able to escape the draft. There is no reason why
income should ever again determine who will—and who will not—bear
the burden of defending America's freedom.

National service could help provide a larger pool of manpower for the 31
armed forces. Moreover, by making military service an attractive opportunity to rich as well as poor, college-bound as well as job-bound, a
national service system could make our military forces more representative of our society as a whole.

A final reason I support a system of national service comes from my 32
experience during the presidential campaign of 1984. During the last
election—perhaps during every election—the rhetoric and symbolism of
patriotism were everywhere. Rallies were draped with red, white, and
blue bunting, the national conventions of both parties were filled with
waving flags, and candidates paraded Olympic gold medalists and honored
war heroes.

This is all as it should be. These are all grand symbols of the pride 33
and greatness which is America. Yet, I believe true patriotism demands
more. True patriots understand that, as Americans, we must serve our
nation in times of peace as well as war, in calm as well as crisis. There
are always needs to meet, people to help, problems to solve, new vistas
to reach. No matter how well we are doing individually or collectively,
the true patriot always believes America can do better. It is time America's national leadership tried to inspire a deeper level of patriotism as
well.

Ultimately, the questions are: Does the opportunity of being an Amer- 34
ican carry certain obligations? Does patriotism carry a price? Too many
of our leaders say no. I say yes.

As Thomas Jefferson said nearly two centuries ago: "A debt of service 35
is due from every man to his country proportioned to the bounties which
nature and fortune have measured to him." This is a message America's
young—and all Americans—need to hear again today.

## QUESTIONS FOR ANALYSIS

1. The theme of Hart's presidential campaign was that he was the candidate with new ideas, yet he opens this proposal by showing that his
   idea is not original. Given what he hopes to accomplish with this
   proposal, what advantages or disadvantages do you see in this way of
   beginning?

2. Hart identifies one of the problems his solution will solve as "a crisis among our young people." How does he define this crisis, and how does he attempt to establish that it exists and is serious? To what extent are you persuaded by Hart's argument?

3. The other problem Hart identifies involves certain "unmet needs." What are these needs? How do you think working to meet such unmet needs would challenge a young person's idealism? How does including this second problem strengthen or weaken the proposal?

4. According to Hart, young people are commonly caricatured as "materialistic, selfish, and unidealistic." What is implied by Hart's use of the term *caricature*? Does Hart himself avoid caricature in his own discussion of young people?

5. Hart apparently agrees with William James about youth's need to "get the childishness knocked out of them." How does Hart's use of the word *childishness* color your reception of his argument?

6. Although Hart clearly favors making national service mandatory, he proposes that a commission be formed to study the feasibility of a mandatory national service system. Why do you suppose he proposes such a commission instead of simply arguing for his own idea?

7. In your view, what is the most successful part of Hart's proposal? the least successful? Would you have any qualms about joining his proposed national service?

## SUGGESTIONS FOR WRITING

1. How else might the "unmet needs" Hart identifies be met? Write a letter to the editor of your local or college newspaper suggesting how any one of these problems might be solved. Consider such questions as the following:

   Should business play a role in meeting these needs? Does government have a responsibility? How could community groups be encouraged to help? In the next proposal, "Broken Connections," Mackey and Appleman suggest that high schools ought to give students credit for volunteer work. What do you think? If you would like to learn more about these unmet needs, you could do some library research.

2. Hart also identifies several problems plaguing young people—unemployment, unwanted pregnancy, drug abuse, suicide, boredom. What other problems would you add to this list? Write a proposal suggesting a solution to any one of the problems on your list. Address your

proposal to any individual or group of people you think could be of help in solving the problem.

3. Think of an organization or a club to which you belong and the problems it has. Select one of these problems, and write a proposal that defines the problem and indicates how it could be solved. Address your proposal to the other members of the group.

# James Mackey and Deborah Appleman

James Mackey and Deborah Appleman, social scientists specializing in education at the University of Minnesota, have done considerable research on adolescent alienation. In 1984, Mackey published his research findings in *A Twelve-Year Study of Adolescent Alienation*. In that same year, "Broken Connections: The Alienated Adolescent in the 80s" appeared in *Curriculum Review*, a journal for teachers and school administrators.

# *Broken Connections: The Alienated Adolescent in the 80s*

Anticipating this proposal, how do you expect social scientists and high school principals to view alienated adolescents? What assumptions do you have about the way they will understand the problem of alienation among adolescents? Looking back on your own high school experience, how were rebellious or disenchanted students treated? How do you think they should be treated? In titling their essay "Broken Connections," Mackey and Appleman imply that alienation has something to do with the severing of connections. What kinds of connections are important in adolescence? What was important to you when you were a teenager?

Although the hallways and classrooms of our public schools look no 1 different than they did a generation ago, some of the current inhabitants of the schools differ significantly from their predecessors in appearance and in attitude. Wan, bleary-eyed faces more frequently greet today's teachers. Heads resting on desks from physical exhaustion as well as from boredom are unfortunately commonplace.

In many schools, the ranks of "spirit clubs" have dwindled as students 2 display less interest in extracurricular activities. Throughout the country, sports teams have fewer participants as good athletes opt to work instead of to play sports. In one midwestern school, only 10 girls tried out for 20 cheerleading spots, positions that their mothers' generation coveted. Both the yearbook and the school newspaper of a suburban high school nearly folded last year after the advisors were unable to find a sufficient student staff. Another high school cancelled senior class elections when only two students volunteered to run for office.

Faculty lounges buzz with descriptions of cynical pupils who are disil- 3
lusioned with school and immersed in the drug culture. Many teachers
are unable to motivate these students, who seem more interested in
financing their auto insurance than in mastering algebraic equations.
Such signs of disaffection are symptomatic of a larger dilemma which our
schools must face. It is a phenomenon we call adolescent alienation, an
attitude which seems to be becoming alarmingly prevalent.

Since the beginning of man's awareness of "self" and "other," alien- 4
ation has frayed the fabric of social institutions. In recent decades the
term has become a euphemism for every kind of aberrant behavior from
drug use to rejection of the political system. Adolescents are especially
affected by this malaise. Let us consider the case of John Kelly, for
example.

> When John Kelly was 10, he was curious and energetic, the mascot of his
> family. His inquisitiveness led him to railroad yards, museums, and bus ad-
> ventures downtown alone. In school, he was charming, cooperative, and
> interested. At 13, John suddenly changed. His agreeable nature vanished as
> he quarreled endlessly with his older brothers. He became moody and sullen,
> constantly snapping at his parents. He began to skip school and disrupt class
> when he did attend. When he was finally expelled, his parents enrolled him
> in another junior high school, hoping the change would solve some of John's
> problems. Instead, his difficulties intensified as he dropped his boyhood
> friends, stopped communicating with his parents, and withdrew into himself.
> Now, 16-year-old John bears little resemblance to the loving, active child his
> family once knew. He has been suspended from yet another school, hangs out
> with an older crowd, and comes home only to sleep. His parents feel hurt,
> bewildered, frustrated, and frightened.

As John Kelly's case makes clear, adolescent alienation is a teenager's 5
inability to connect meaningfully with other people. At its root is aloneness, a feeling that no one else is quite like you, that you are not what
other people want you to be.

The senior author of this article began research on adolescent alien- 6
ation 12 years ago in an attempt to illuminate this widely used but poorly
defined concept. The primary purpose of the research was to construct a
theoretical framework that isolated and defined the dimensions of adolescent alienation. In addition, the research sought to develop a reliable
and valid instrument to measure this phenomenon.

Our effort to define alienation consisted of three parts. First, we gath- 7
ered from the literature a set of descriptions of alienation. Second, we
established a series of propositions regarding subgroups of alienated adolescents. Third, we developed a 40-item Likert-type attitude scale which
we administered to 500 adolescents and analyzed to provide an empir-
ically grounded definition of adolescent alienation.

Subsequently, surveys have examined how the patterns of adolescent 8
alienation have shifted with the tides of social change. In all, surveys
involving over 4600 adolescents were conducted in 1971, 1976, and
during a period extending from the spring of 1980 to the fall of 1982.

Teenagers who feel alienated are often not interested in the things 9
that other adolescents care about. Frequently these teenagers believe that
predominant adult values are shallow, materialistic, and meaningless.
Increasingly many teenagers are bored by their parents' and teachers' goals
and expectations. They feel that most of the things they learn in school
are a waste of time. It frightens them to hear adults say that these are
the "best times of your life" when fun is the last word they use to describe
their teenage years.

Given its deleterious effects on schools and other social institutions, 10
it is essential that teachers understand adolescent alienation. What are
its dimensions? Is there one kind or many?

Our research has etched a clear profile of adolescent alienation. This 11
profile shows three distinct varieties:

- The Personally Incapacitated Adolescents. They want to succeed but 12
  feel they do not possess the skills necessary to do so. They feel bewildered by the complexity of their social world and regard the information they possess as inadequate. This type of alienated adolescent is often shy and withdrawn and does poorly in school.

- The Guideless Adolescents. They reject socially acceptable means 13
  for achieving goals. Although they accept most of their parents' goals
  and values, they are disillusioned with conventional social rules because they block their route to success. They resent society because
  it fails to provide them with enough opportunity to achieve their
  desires. This sort of alienation might manifest itself, for example, in
  lying, cheating, or stealing.

- The Culturally Estranged Adolescents. They deliberately disavow 14
  predominant cultural values. Although they have full knowledge of
  both the values and the way to achieve them, they reject them. They
  withdraw from any active pursuit of success, money, possessions, and
  other "middle class" goals. This particular kind of alienated adolescent frequently does well in school and is quite verbal about his or
  her disaffection.

Analysis of the data gathered from our surveys, in addition to revealing 15
the profiles described above, also showed that different groups of adolescents had different profiles of alienation. More importantly, the degree
and type of alienation could generally be inferred from the affluence of
the adolescent's community. For example, because they are more likely

to have the knowledge, skills, role models, and encouragement for success, adolescents in more advantaged communities feel less Personal Incapacity and Guidelessness. Rather, these adolescents are more inclined to develop a critical stance toward conventional beliefs—more Cultural Estrangement—because they see them at closer hand, and because their privileged status allows them the luxury of deviance.

The portrait of alienation which emerged from the turbulent 1960s 16 has generally held up into the more placid 1980s, but with some distinct exceptions. One notable change—echoed by political observers and students of adolescents alike—has been a general decline in overall social concerns. In addition, feelings of incapacity among young women seem to have increased, perhaps a reflection of heightened expectations due to the women's movement.

In the early 1970s adolescents were very critical toward middle class 17 values. By the middle 70s, this cultural estrangement had lessened somewhat. Currently the facile rejection of mainstream middle class values seems on the rise, but it is more diffuse and difficult to pinpoint precisely. This is due in large part to the fact that repudiation of middle class values is no longer a part of a particular ideological orientation, but is more idiosyncratic in motive.

More adolescents are alienated today because the world has grown 18 increasingly complex and difficult for teenagers to fathom. They are assailed from all directions by social forces that isolate and bewilder them. The increasing possibility of nuclear war makes them feel that the world will not last, fixates them in the present, and convinces them that it makes no sense to plan for the future. Computers and other electronic technology entrance and bedevil them simultaneously. While they mindlessly amuse themselves with video games, music videos, and Walkmans, they secretly fear the spectre of unemployment and personal uselessness. Family disruptions such as divorce, frequently absent working parents, and even child abuse enhance adolescents' feeling that no one cares about them.

It is not surprising that adolescents commonly perceive the world as 19 so complex that it is impossible to figure out. The results of increasing adolescent alienation have profound social consequences. Bewildered by complexity, immobilized by powerlessness, and sometimes dulled by drugs, adolescents—in ever-increasing numbers—display widespread public resignation.

Although there are many ways to demonstrate their resignation, one 20 of the most obvious mechanisms is by retreating from the school. Recently, adolescents have employed three principal means of retreat.

The first of these retreats is "vocationalism," as witnessed by the enor- 21
mous increase in the number of adolescents who work. According to the
most recent statistics, 42 percent of all high school sophomores were
employed part-time. For seniors, the number of working students has
increased to 3 out of 5. While some benefits derive from an increase in
adolescent employment, these benefits are not, for the most part, reaped
by the schools. Large scale employment probably places the public school,
with its somewhat abstract subject matter, in a position of secondary
importance. Indeed, 51 percent of high school seniors agree that their
jobs are more enjoyable than school.

A second retreat for today's alienated adolescents is their increasing 22
involvement in the drug culture. During the past five years, the structure
of adolescent drug use has changed. Once confined to specific and iden-
tifiable groups in school, drug use is becoming more of a cross-clique
phenomenon. Even social groups such as athletes, who formerly looked
down on drug users, now use drugs in their recreational activities.

Increased drug use clearly affects academic performance. The more 23
time adolescents spend under the influence of drugs, the less time they
have to learn. Other effects of drugs are more ominous. While no evidence suggests that marijuana use results in permanent brain damage, it
does inhibit short term memory, decreases creativity, shortens attention
span, and reduces energy and motivation. All of these factors, of course,
harm the adolescent's academic performance, which in a kind of vicious
circle, results in increased alienation from the school.

The third example of retreatism is a pronounced increase in a kind of 24
apoliticalism which extends beyond the realm of the political process
into adolescent perceptions of American life. This disposition involves
a narrowing of the adolescent vision of the American dream, a profound
disinterest in and distrust of all forms of political activity, and a parochial
attitude toward the world beyond the narrow adolescent horizon. This
apoliticalism is fueled by a lack of spurs to action, feelings of powerlessness, and general feelings of the futility of political action. These feelings
of futility and cynicism about political activity seem to echo down the
corridors of the adolescent social world and include a disinterest in participation in other areas, including social activities.

Given the current nature of our society, it is no wonder that adoles- 25
cents have retreated into work, apoliticalism, and drugs. Living under
the shadow of nuclear war, in the midst of a largely materialistic and
somewhat cynical world, it is no wonder that many of today's adolescents
feel confused and perhaps a bit frightened. Because many of them have
not developed the coping skills necessary to deal with adult challenges,
they pull away from society by retreating into part-time jobs, escaping

with drugs, and refusing to participate in the political system. Sometimes they even estrange themselves from their own families and seem to be alarmingly isolated.

Although adolescent alienation is cause for concern, the situation is  26 not hopeless. Instead of helplessly watching these students float farther away, educators can help pull them back into the mainstream of school life. There are several ways this can be done:

- Recognize that alienation is a natural consequence of serious reflec-  27 tion on the complexities and seeming absurdities of life. Let students know that, ironically, they are not alone in their alienation. It has plagued philosophers and other intellectuals for years. At the same time, young people and educators need to be able to discriminate between normal feelings of estrangement and pathological ones. It is normal to demand independence and desire privacy. It is not normal to withdraw entirely from social involvements.

- Incorporate the topic of alienation into the curriculum when appro-  28 priate. In literature, the theme of alienation permeates novels as diverse as *Steppenwolf* and *The Outsiders*. Studies of the evolution of political systems and economic theory are bound to scrutinize Marx's writings on the subject of alienation. By discovering the common thread of alienation in different classes, students will at once feel more connected to the learning material and less "different" from their peers as well.

- Provide positive channels for the expression of students' feelings of  29 isolation or estrangement through writing topics as well as small-group discussions.

- Become more aware of the potentially alienating aspects of large,  30 comprehensive high schools. Fred Newman of the University of Wisconsin-Madison has examined the problem of adolescent alienation in terms of the structure of the school system. In a 1981 paper entitled "Reducing Student Alienation," he suggests that major structural changes in the school can help reduce student alienation.

  He advocates the creation of school units that are small with clear  31 limited goals; the encouragement of students and parents to openly participate in school governance; and the opportunity for students and staff to engage in cooperative endeavors that contribute to the school's operation. Although these suggestions require long-term structural change, the principles of participation and cooperation can be woven into the fabric of school life with little immediate change.

  An advisor/advisee program, where students have at least one con-  32 tinuous supportive relationship with a faculty member, is but one example of a positive change that is easy to incorporate into the existing school structure.

- Address the drug issue constructively. Teachers can deal with the 33 use of drugs in several ways. First, part of their classroom expectations should be to make students accountable for staying straight in school. Teachers must abandon the "I'm here to teach biology and student drug use is not my problem" ideology. The drug problem is shared by all who work with adolescents. Educators must become aware of the symptoms and causes of drug use and learn to refer students with drug problems to sources of assistance in a positive and appropriate manner. Finally, teachers must accept the sad fact that the only thing we teach students who are high during school is that they can get away with being high in school.

Adolescent alienation is not a fad destined to fade in a year or two. It is 34 an authentic and serious consequence of the ever-increasing complexities of life in the modern world. While adolescence by its very nature has always been fraught with turmoil, the increasing instability of the outside world makes adolescence even more precarious. As the media ominously reminds us, we are losing a significant number of our young people to drugs, cults, and suicide — the second leading cause of death among adolescents. While not all young adults are overtly self-destructive, many do find themselves afflicted by a malaise of apathy and apoliticalism.

If we wish to reclaim the many adolescents who seem to have drifted 35 away from us, we must understand the sources of their disaffection. While we do not pretend that the above suggestions will eradicate alienation, they do provide some helpful ways in which we can rekindle young adults' interests in family, friends, school, and society.

As the 1983 Carnegie Report "High School" suggests, high schools must 36 reconnect themselves to society as a whole by having students participate as volunteers in social service agencies as well as continuing their involvements in work/study programs. Positive and productive connections to the world that exists outside the school grounds will not only improve school/community relationships, but will serve to ground students in the daily life of the community. This participation in the "real" world may help the alienated adolescent to feel less estranged and disinterested.

## QUESTIONS FOR ANALYSIS

1. Since this is a rather long and complicated essay, begin by making a brief outline and then summarizing its main points. (Chapter 1 offers procedures for outlining and summarizing.)

2. Reflect on what you think Mackey and Appleman mean by the key term *alienation*. Then take inventory of the words and phrases they associate with it, such as *disaffection* and *disillusioned*. To what extent are the writers redefining or reevaluating this term for their readers? What attitudes do they assume readers have about alienation? What attitudes do they themselves appear to have? (See Taking Inventory in Chapter 1.)

3. According to Mackey and Appleman, today's high school students are not very interested in extracurricular activities. On the basis of your own experience and observation, do you think this statement is accurate? If so, what does it imply about adolescent alienation? What implications do Mackey and Appleman draw from their observation?

4. Mackey and Appleman suggest that adolescent alienation is a growing trend, that more adolescents are alienated today than in the past. What reasons do they give for this increase in alienation? How convincing do you find their reasoning, and what does it add to their proposal?

5. How much confidence do you have in Mackey and Appleman's authority? What suggests that they are experts and should be relied upon?

6. Why do you think Mackey and Appleman cite the example of John Kelly? Do you find it convincing? Why or why not?

7. Mackey and Appleman propose various ways to bring alienated students back into "the mainstream of school life." What are these proposed solutions? Which do you think has the best chance of solving the problem? In weighing the solutions, consider Mackey and Appleman's use of the term *mainstream*. What does it imply? Do you think a good solution should involve changing the mainstream itself as well as changing the alienated adolescents? Why or why not?

8. Near the end of the essay, Mackey and Appleman suggest that alienation may be "an authentic and serious consequence of the ever-increasing complexities of life in the modern world." If the problem of alienation is a natural outgrowth of modern life, how seriously should their solutions be regarded?

9. What do you learn from this essay about the way social scientists study social problems? What advantages and disadvantages do you see in their methods?

## SUGGESTIONS FOR WRITING

1. If you agree that many high school and college students feel alienated, how do you think alienation should be combated? Write a proposal of your own suggesting a solution to the problem of alienation among

students. Imagine that your proposal will be published in the campus newspaper and that your readers are familiar with the Mackey and Appleman proposal. Indicate where you agree and disagree with Mackey and Appleman.

2. One of the characteristics of adolescent alienation, according to Mackey and Appleman, is "apoliticalism," the "refusal to participate in the political system" Write a proposal of your own suggesting a solution to this problem. Consider such questions as the following: Would young people become more involved in the political system if they knew more about its inner workings? Should internships in local government be given high school credit? Should a course in current affairs be made part of the curriculum? Should political parties send representatives to high school campuses to drum up student interest? Address your proposal to any individual or group you think could do something practical to remedy the problem.

3. Identify a problem in your campus community that needs to be solved. Write a proposal suggesting a solution to this problem and address it to members of the college administration or student body. Try to make it a practical proposal, one that could actually be implemented.

# Carol Bly

Born in Duluth, Minnesota, and educated at Wellesley and the University of Minnesota, Carol Bly (b. 1930) considers herself something of an authority on contemporary rural life in America, having lived for more than twenty-five years in a town with a population of only 2,242. Bly has had a varied career. She has managed a literary magazine and has written poetry, short fiction, essays, and a humanities handbook called *Common Ground* (1981). Some of her writing has been published in the Minnesota Public Radio magazine and in prestigious journals like *Ploughshares* and *The New Yorker*. In addition, she has lectured at Carleton College, the University of Wisconsin, and other midwestern colleges. As consultant for the National Endowment for the Humanities, Bly served in the American Farm Project and as director of a humanities project called "A Lifeline to High School Students." She also worked as a visiting writer in the Duluth school system. In a *New York Times* book review of her collected essays, *Letters from the Country* (1981), the reviewer summed up Bly's personal quest: she "wants the farmers and small town merchants of America to live with passion, to have a sense of greatness in their lives, to take themselves as seriously as a Beethoven or a Thoreau."

# *Enemy Evenings*

Originally written for a local magazine called *Minnesota Monthly*, "Enemy Evenings" directly addresses people's reluctance to speak openly about serious issues. Bly herself is unafraid to challenge her neighbors. In another essay, she writes that we are too "wedded to saying-nice-things-or-nothing-at-all." This desire to be nice and to avoid conflict is so strong, Bly suggests in "Enemy Evenings," that the only conversation people engage in is small talk.

As Bly knows, many of her readers are less inclined than she to view small talk as a problem. Before reading her essay, consider for a moment what small talk means to you and how it might become a problem for a community. Then, as you read the proposal, notice how Bly carefully defines the problem and forcefully argues that it is serious.

In Minnesota towns one sometimes has the feeling of moving among ghosts, because we don't meet and talk to our local opponents on any question. We know, for example, that somewhere in our town of 2,242, there live people who believe that the preservatives sodium nitrite, sodium nitrate, and BHA variously threaten future health, and also in town live the local staff of the Agricultural Extension Division, who have just

1

419

published an essay saying the advantages of these preservatives outweigh the disadvantages. Yet these two sets of people don't meet each other on open panels, and scarcely at all even privately, thus providing another major American issue which small-town people are left out of.

The case is always made that to keep a town from flying apart you 2 must discuss only matters in which there is little conflict. That means that whenever a woman physician enters a room in which a few people are urging, intriguingly enough, that the man should be head of the woman (St. Paul), the topic must automatically be changed to whether or not we are getting that hard winter they kept talking about last fall.

There is nothing much wrong with weather talk except that far from 3 preventing people from feeling "threatened" it is in fact the living proof that you don't care about those people: you haven't any interest in their thoughts; you don't want to hear them out.

There is little lonelier than small-town life when small talk is the 4 principal means of peace. Sherwood Anderson illustrated it long ago, but people who still read Anderson seem to do so in a mist of nostalgia rather than for any revelation we can put to use. Also, I'm not content with the usual explanations for small-town citizens' being so uneasy around intense feelings. The question is: why are thousands and thousands of lively and feeling people who live in the countryside willing to give up, for their whole lives, the kind of friendship people enjoy who deliberately, curiously, and civilly draw out one another's views on serious subjects?

The reason generally offered, of course, is that airing last night's hassle 5 at the church council will curtail this morning's sale of advertising space in the paper. This reason presupposes that serious exchange is a *hassle*, and must be the result of gaucherie. I don't believe it. Another commonly offered explanation is that less-informed or less-intelligent people will feel unequal to frank self-expression in the presence of more-informed or more-intelligent people. That is abundantly untrue. I have heard extremely strong opinions plentifully and bravely offered by people including myself who could hardly have been less informed or less gifted about the subject.

We simply need experience in taking an interest in the other side and 6 doing so with the proponents of the other side present. If we could get this habit going I think we could reduce one of the most dismal characteristics of small-town life—the loneliness. Of course human loneliness is general, but this particular source of it, exercised in hypocrisy, could be ended.

Therefore, I propose that small community groups develop panels for 7 Enemy Evenings. Obviously some much better word has to be used, but

I like the pure madness of this one: it reminds me of that fantastic creation of Nixon, Ehrlichman, and Haldeman—the enemies list. Enemy Evenings would definitely need two things: a firm master of ceremonies in whom general affection for human beings would be paramount, not a chill manner or a childish desire to get the fur flying; second, it would need very just panel representation. An example of unjust panel representation would be a four-person panel to discuss the defense budget made up of a leader of American Writers vs. the Vietnam War; a director of Episcopal Community Services, Minneapolis; Senator Mondale; and (the chump) an American Party spokesman. It would be helpful too, if controversial panels were conducted with humor, but that isn't essential.

In discussing this notion at a Cultural Affairs Committee meeting in my town, we observed with interest the 1974–75 policy of the Minnesota Humanities Commission, emphasizing the relation between private concerns and public policies. Also, the National Endowment for the Humanities (through the Upper Midwest Council) has supported a series of television dialogues this winter, covering controversial subjects. All that is interesting, but for the common viewer what is seen on television is irrevocably "something they had on television." Seeing one's own neighbor speak out passionately (and having the chance to respond) is immediately engaging.

Here is a suggested rough list of seldom-discussed subjects with strongly opposed participants:

1. The emphasis on technical training at the high school level
   Suggested participants:
   > Local painters, writers, and musicians
   > Vocational center director and staff
   > Visiting college humanities division members
   > Visiting Vo-Tech schools' faculty members

2. Fertilizing methods
   Suggested participants:
   > County agent
   > Anhydrous ammonia dealers
   > Bag fertilizer dealers
   > Soil Conservation Service Experiment station personnel
   > Members of the Soil Improvement Association
   > Local subscribers to Department of Natural Resources publications and *Organic Gardening*, and readers of U.S. Agricultural yearbooks

3. Competition vs. cooperation, as taught in U.S. elementary schools
   Suggested participants:

Angry parents on both sides
School counselor
Fifth- or sixth-grade faculty members
Psychology faculty from neighboring community colleges

4. Defense Department budget of the United States
Suggested participants:
VFW or Legion Auxiliary officers
VFW or Legion Post officers
Local members, Women's League for Peace and Freedom
Local members, Common Cause
National Guard unit officers

5. St. Paul's stand on man as the head of woman
Suggested participants:
Fundamentalist church representatives
Local Charismatic Christians—who tend to be nicely divided
on this, providing an interesting confusion
Local members of Business and Professional Women's Clubs
Local Officers of American Federation of Women's Clubs
Grain elevator managers

A painful fact of American life is that people from small towns are 10
afraid of directness. Small-town kids, unlike suburban kids, can't take
much from the shoulder. Example: A suburban Minneapolis child with
a first-rate music instructor goes off to her piano lesson. She is working
up a small piece of Mozart, she hasn't done her homework, and she
smears the counting. The music instructor tells her it's an irresponsible
job, sloppy phrasing, whatever she tells her—in any case, it won't do.
The child returns home and works the piece up much more conscien-
tiously next time, having learned that music is a disciplined pleasure.

A rural piano student cannot be spoken to so plainly. It is hard for 11
her to be stirred into being responsible to the music at hand because the
instant a teacher tries to correct her directly her soul sags into mere self-
condemnation. Our style, in the countryside, is not to criticize children
at all: we very seldom tell them the plane model was glued carelessly and
the sleeve set in without enough easing. (The counterpart of this is that
we seldom praise them much for anything either. "You played a real good
game against Dawson"; "You did a real good job of that speech contest"—
not "I knew you'd do well at the speech thing: I didn't know that I would
cry—in fact, I'm *still* moved by what you said!") So the children develop
neither stamina about criticism nor the imagination to picture to themselves gigantic praise if they excel. They live lightly handed into a middle
world of little comment, and therefore little incitement to devotion.

Should a music teacher try to explain Mozart's involvement in the mu-sic—what *he* had in mind for this or that phrase—the student wouldn't hear over the ground noise of dismay in her own feelings. "I'm being attacked! I'm being attacked!" is all her inexperienced soul can take in. Piranhas when you're out swimming, mean music teachers when you're taking piano—it's all the same to her. On a psychological ladder, she is rungs below being able to move from self to Mozart.

What we need in rural life is more Serious Occasion. By the time a   12 child is ten, he or she should have heard, at least a few hundreds of times, "I loved that dying cowboy routine. Do it again. Do be quiet, Uncle Malcolm. Noah's going to do his dying cowboy routine." And adults would have shut up, listened, and praised. That moment would have been a Serious Occasion. Then a child is caught lying. It is horrible to lie—the notice of it should be serious and major. Then lying—whether or not one did it—is the subject of a Serious Occasion. Then, after some hundreds of such occasions, one can take in a conversation about music—what does Mozart want out of this piece? Remember: we are not now talking about you or yourself. We are talking about someone *other*—a musician long dead—and he is making a demand on us, and we are going to meet that demand! We are not going to scream and flee, because discipline is not the same thing as piranhas in the river.

I think we will surge into twice as much life through Serious Occasion.   13 . . . I commend frank panel evenings with opponents taking part: let's try that for a change of air, after years of chill and evasive tact.

## QUESTIONS FOR ANALYSIS

1. How does Bly establish that small talk is a problem? Briefly summarize and then react to Bly's definition of the problem. What difficulties does she anticipate readers will have with her definition? How well does she anticipate and respond to your own difficulties with it?

2. Bly uses examples extensively throughout this proposal. Skim the essay, noting the examples. Then conjecture on the role of these particular examples. What do they add to the proposal?

3. Bly seems to think there is a difference between small-town life and urban life. Take inventory of the words and phrases she uses in con-nection with this opposition and reflect on what values and attitudes they suggest. From your own experience and reading, do you think people in small towns differ from people in cities? How do you think distinguishing between small-town people and others furthers her ar-gument?

4. Look carefully at the list of possible subjects and participants for En-emy Evenings. What advantages or disadvantages do you see in Bly's inserting such a list in the middle of her essay?

5. What is the connection between Serious Occasions and Enemy Eve-nings? How could Bly have made the connection clearer? How does the idea of Serious Occasions contribute to the proposal for Enemy Evenings?

6. Why does Bly say that young people are unable to "move from self to Mozart"? What does this statement imply, and how does it support her argument? From your own experience and observation, how ac-curate is Bly's description?

7. Bly occasionally combines informal words like *hassle* with more formal ones like *gaucherie*. Skim the essay, noting other instances of informal and formal language. Then conjecture on how Bly's language affects her tone and credibility.

8. Bly opens her proposal with this statement: "In Minnesota towns one sometimes has the feeling of moving among ghosts, because we don't meet and talk to our local opponents on any question." Similarly, she concludes by saying that people "will surge into twice as much life through Serious Occasion." Reread the essay, making an inventory of other references to this opposition between vital living and a ghost-like death-in-life. How does such an opposition serve Bly's purpose? (See Inventory of Oppositions in Chapter 1.)

## SUGGESTIONS FOR WRITING

1. In her proposal, Bly suggests that people in small towns do not relate honestly to one another. Is there any problem with the way people you know interrelate? If so, how would you define the problem and what solution would you propose? Write a proposal addressed to the people involved that explains the problem and argues for your solution.

2. In order to teach children to be unafraid of criticism, Bly argues parents should take their children more seriously. Think about the relationships between parents and children you know. Is there any problem in these relationships to which you could propose a solution? Write a proposal defining the problem and arguing for your solution.

3. Bly identifies a problem that most people would overlook, one that she must prove actually exists. Can you think of a problem in your own neighborhood or city that most people would deny exists? Write a proposal addressed to your neighbors arguing that the problem exists and explaining how it could be solved.

## A Debate on Nuclear Disarmament

Proposals commonly debate important matters of public policy and provide forums that allow people to air their differences and to find common ground. Since writing a proposal requires definition and analysis of the problem, proposals often lead to new ways of seeing old problems and therefore to innovative solutions. The next two selections are part of an ongoing debate on the most important problem we face today: the threat of nuclear war.

In the first selection, George Kennan defines the problem in a new way, arguing that the weapons stockpile each side has built to deter the other from starting a war is itself a major problem and threat to world peace. The second proposal, by Charles Krauthammer, defends nuclear stockpiling because he believes it is an effective deterrent.

Kennan and Krauthammer both present long, carefully reasoned arguments that deserve close, critical reading. You will probably find many points on each side with which you can agree and disagree. These provocative documents are intended as much to involve people in this crucial debate as to offer specific proposals for resolving the problem.

# George Kennan

George Kennan (b. 1904) is a highly respected political scientist and statesman whose career in the Foreign Service spanned four decades, including ambassadorial posts to the Soviet Union in the early fifties and Yugoslavia in the sixties. He received his education at Princeton and returned years later as a professor in the Institute for Advanced Study.

The author of many books and articles, Kennan won both the National Book Award and the Pulitzer Prize twice—once for history with *Russia Leaves the War* (1957), and a second time for biography with *Memoirs, 1925–1950* (1968). He is probably best known for *American Diplomacy* (1951), a book that is still required reading in most colleges today. Kennan's most recent work is *The Nuclear Delusion* (1982), a collection of essays from which the following selection is taken.

# A Proposal for International Disarmament

Kennan is recognized as an authority on the Soviet Union, yet it is still possible, as John Kenneth Galbraith once remarked, "to argue with this most brilliant and civilized of students of the public scene." Kennan does not assume that people will accept his argument on authority. In fact, he tries to be contentious, to rekindle the debate on disarmament by offering a new perspective on the problem. He wrote this proposal in 1981 after Congress had failed to ratify the SALT II treaty, which had been negotiated by former president Carter at the Strategic Arms Limitation Talks. President Reagan opposed the SALT negotiations and had no new peace initiative to offer at that time. As you read his proposal, pay special attention to the way Kennan tries to stir up the debate and inspire people to seek a viable solution.

Notice also that Kennan originally delivered this proposal as a speech when he was awarded the Albert Einstein Peace Prize. Before reading the selection, consider for a moment what writing strategies you might expect to find in a speech that you would not find in an essay written to be read. Then, as you read, see if you can detect these or any other speech-writing strategies.

Adequate words are lacking to express the full seriousness of our present   1
situation. It is not just that we are for the moment on a collision course politically with the Soviet Union, and that the process of rational communication between the two governments seems to have broken down completely; it is also—and even more importantly—the fact that the ultimate sanction behind the conflicting policies of these two governments is a type and volume of weaponry which could not possibly be used without utter disaster for us all.

For over thirty years, wise and far-seeing people have been warning us   2
about the futility of any war fought with nuclear weapons and about the dangers involved in their cultivation. Some of the first of these voices to be raised were those of great scientists, including outstandingly that of Albert Einstein himself. But there has been no lack of others. Every president of this country, from Dwight Eisenhower to Jimmy Carter, has tried to remind us that there could be no such thing as victory in a war fought with such weapons. So have a great many other eminent persons.

When one looks back today over the history of these warnings, one   3
has the impression that something has now been lost of the sense of urgency, the hopes, and the excitement that initially inspired them, so many years ago. One senses, even on the part of those who today most acutely perceive the problem and are inwardly most exercised about it, a certain discouragement, resignation, perhaps even despair, when it comes to the question of raising the subject again. The danger is so obvious. So much has already been said. What is to be gained by reiteration? What good would it now do?

Look at the record. Over all these years the competition in the de-   4
velopment of nuclear weaponry has proceeded steadily, relentlessly, without the faintest regard for all these warning voices. We have gone on

piling weapon upon weapon, missile upon missile, new levels of destructiveness upon old ones. We have done this helplessly, almost involuntarily: like the victims of some sort of hypnotism, like men in a dream, like lemmings heading for the sea, like the children of Hamlin marching blindly along behind their Pied Piper. And the result is that today we have achieved, we and the Russians together, in the creation of these devices and their means of delivery, levels of redundancy of such grotesque dimensions as to defy rational understanding.

I say redundancy. I know of no better way to describe it. But actually,  5 the word is too mild. It implies that there could be levels of these weapons that would not be redundant. Personally, I doubt that there could. I question whether these devices are really weapons at all. A true weapon is at best something with which you endeavor to affect the behavior of another society by influencing the minds, the calculations, the intentions, of the men that control it; it is not something with which you destroy indiscriminately the lives, the substance, the hopes, the culture, the civilization, of another people.

What a confession of intellectual poverty it would be—what a bank-  6 ruptcy of intelligent statesmanship—if we had to admit that such blind, senseless acts of destruction were the best use we could make of what we have come to view as the leading elements of our military strength!

To my mind, the nuclear bomb is the most useless weapon ever in-  7 vented. It can be employed to no rational purpose. It is not even an effective defense against itself. It is only something with which, in a moment of petulance or panic, you commit such fearful acts of destruction as no sane person would ever wish to have upon his conscience.

There are those who will agree, with a sigh, to much of what I have  8 just said, but will point to the need for something called deterrence. This is, of course, a concept which attributes to others—to others who, like ourselves, were born of women, walk on two legs, and love their children, to human beings, in short—the most fiendish and inhuman of tendencies.

But all right: accepting for the sake of argument the profound iniquity  9 of these adversaries, no one could deny, I think, that the present Soviet and American arsenals, presenting over a million times the destructive power of the Hiroshima bomb, are simply fantastically redundant to the purpose in question. If the same relative proportions were to be preserved, something well less than 20 percent of those stocks would surely suffice for the most sanguine concepts of deterrence, whether as between the two nuclear superpowers or with relation to any of those other governments that have been so ill-advised as to enter upon the nuclear path. Whatever their suspicions of each other, there can be no excuse on the part of these two governments for holding, poised against each other and poised in a sense against the whole Northern Hemisphere, quantities of these weapons so vastly in excess of any rational and demonstrable requirements.

How have we got ourselves into this dangerous mess?    10

Let us not confuse the question by blaming it all on our Soviet adversaries. They have, of course, their share of the blame, and not least in their cavalier dismissal of the Baruch Plan so many years ago. They too have made their mistakes; and I should be the last to deny it.    11

But we must remember that it has been we Americans who, at almost every step of the road, have taken the lead in the development of this sort of weaponry. It was we who first produced and tested such a device; we who were the first to raise its destructiveness to a new level with the hydrogen bomb; we who introduced the multiple warhead; we who have declined every proposal for the renunciation of the principle of "first use"; and we alone, so help us God, who have used the weapon in anger against others, and against tens of thousands of helpless noncombatants at that.    12

I know that reasons were offered for some of these things. I know that others might have taken this sort of a lead, had we not done so. But let us not, in the face of this record, so lose ourselves in self-righteousness and hypocrisy as to forget our own measure of complicity in creating the situation we face today.    13

What is it then, if not our own will, and if not the supposed wickedness of our opponents, that has brought us to this pass?    14

The answer, I think, is clear. It is primarily the inner momentum, the independent momentum, of the weapons race itself—the compulsions that arise and take charge of great powers when they enter upon a competition with each other in the building up of major armaments of any sort.    15

This is nothing new. I am a diplomatic historian. I see this same phenomenon playing its fateful part in the relations among the great European powers as much as a century ago. I see this competitive buildup of armaments conceived initially as a means to an end but soon becoming the end itself. I see it taking possession of men's imagination and behavior, becoming a force in its own right, detaching itself from the political differences that initially inspired it, and then leading both parties, invariably and inexorably, to the war they no longer know how to avoid.    16

This is a species of fixation, brewed out of many components. There are fears, resentments, national pride, personal pride. There are misreadings of the adversary's intentions—sometimes even the refusal to consider them at all. There is the tendency of national communities to idealize themselves and to dehumanize the opponent. There is the blink-    17 ered, narrow vision of the professional military planner, and his tendency to make war inevitable by assuming its inevitability.

Tossed together, these components form a powerful brew. They guide 18 the fears and the ambitions of men. They seize the policies of governments and whip them around like trees before the tempest.

Is it possible to break out of this charmed and vicious circle? It is 19 sobering to recognize that no one, at least to my knowledge, has yet done so. But no one, for that matter, has ever been faced with such great catastrophe, such inalterable catastrophe, at the end of the line. Others, in earlier decades, could befuddle themselves with dreams of something called "victory." We, perhaps fortunately, are denied this seductive prospect. We have to break out of the circle. We have no other choice.

How are we to do it? 20

I must confess that I see no possibility of doing this by means of 21 discussions along the lines of the negotiations that have been in progress, off and on, over this past decade, under the acronym of SALT. I regret, to be sure, that the most recent SALT agreement has not been ratified. I regret it, because if the benefits to be expected from that agreement were slight, its disadvantages were even slighter; and it had a symbolic value which should not have been so lightly sacrificed.

But I have, I repeat, no illusion that negotiations on the SALT pat- 22 tern—negotiations, that is, in which each side is obsessed with the chimera of relative advantage and strives only to retain a maximum of the weaponry for itself while putting its opponent to the maximum disadvantage—I have no illusion that such negotiations could ever be adequate to get us out of this hole. They are not a way of escape from the weapons race; they are an integral part of it.

Whoever does not understand that when it comes to nuclear weapons 23 the whole concept of relative advantage is illusory—whoever does not understand that when you are talking about absurd and preposterous quantities of overkill the relative sizes of arsenals have no serious meaning—whoever does not understand that the danger lies, not in the possibility that someone else might have more missiles and warheads than we do, but in the very existence of these unconscionable quantities of highly poisonous explosives, and their existence, above all, in hands as weak and shaky and undependable as those of ourselves or our adversaries or any other mere human beings: whoever does not understand these things is never going to guide us out of this increasingly dark and menacing forest of bewilderments into which we have all wandered.

I can see no way out of this dilemma other than by a bold and sweeping 24 departure, a departure that would cut surgically through the exaggerated anxieties, the self-engendered nightmares, and the sophisticated mathematics of destruction in which we have all been entangled over these recent years, and would permit us to move, with courage and decision, to the heart of the problem.

President Reagan recently said, and I think very wisely, that he would   25 "negotiate as long as necessary to reduce the numbers of nuclear weapons to a point where neither side threatens the survival of the other."

Now that is, of course, precisely the thought to which these present   26 observations of mine are addressed. But I wonder whether the negotiations would really have to be at such great length. What I would like to see the president do, after due consultation with the Congress, would be to propose to the Soviet government an immediate across-the-boards reduction by 50 percent of the nuclear arsenals now being maintained by the two superpowers; a reduction affecting in equal measure all forms of the weapon, strategic, medium-range, and tactical, as well as all means of their delivery: all this to be implemented at once and without further wrangling among the experts, and to be subject to such national means of verification as now lie at the disposal of the two powers.

Whether the balance of reduction would be precisely even—whether   27 it could be construed to favor statistically one side or the other—would not be the question. Once we start thinking that way, we would be back on the same old fateful track that has brought us where we are today. Whatever the precise results of such a reduction, there would still be plenty of overkill left—so much so that if this first operation were successful, I would then like to see a second one put in hand to rid us of at least two-thirds of what would be left.

Now I have, of course, no idea of the scientific aspects of such an   28 operation; but I can imagine that serious problems might be presented by the task of removing, and disposing safely of, the radioactive contents of the many thousands of warheads that would have to be dismantled. Should this be the case, I would like to see the president couple his appeal for a 50 percent reduction with the proposal that there be established a joint Soviet-American scientific committee, under the chairmanship of a distinguished neutral figure, to study jointly and in all humility the problem not only of the safe disposal of these wastes but also of how they could be utilized in such a way as to make a positive contribution to human life, either in the two countries themselves or— perhaps preferably—elsewhere. In such a joint scientific venture we might both atone for some of our past follies and lay the foundation for a more constructive relationship.

It will be said this proposal, whatever its merits, deals with only a part   29 of the problem. This is perfectly true. Behind it there would still lurk the serious political differences that now divide us from the Soviet government. Behind it would still lie the problems recently treated, and still to be treated, in the SALT forum. Behind it would still lie the great question of the acceptability of war itself, any war, even a conventional one, as a means of solving problems among great industrial powers in this age of high technology.

What has been suggested here would not prejudice the continued treatment of these questions just as they might be treated today, in whatever forums and under whatever safeguards the two powers find necessary. The conflicts and arguments over these questions could all still proceed to the heart's content of all those who view them with such passionate commitment. The stakes would simply be smaller; and that would be a great relief to all of us.   30

What I have suggested is, of course, only a beginning. But a beginning has to be made somewhere; and if it has to be made, is it not best that it should be made where the dangers are the greatest, and their necessity the least? If a step of this nature could be successfully taken, people might find the heart to tackle with greater confidence and determination the many problems that would still remain.   31

It will also be argued that there would be risks involved. Possibly so. I do not see them. I do not deny the possibility. But if there are, so what? Is it possible to conceive of any dangers greater than those that lie at the end of the collision course on which we are now embarked? And if not, why choose the greater—why choose, in fact, the greatest— of all risks, in the hopes of avoiding the lesser ones?   32

We are confronted here, my friends, with two courses. At the end of the one lies hope—faint hope, if you will, uncertain hope, hope surrounded with dangers, if you insist. At the end of the other lies, so far as I am able to see, no hope at all.   33

Can there be—in the light of our duty not just to ourselves (for we are all going to die sooner or later) but of our duty to our own kind, our duty to the continuity of the generations, our duty to the great experiment of civilized life on this rare and rich and marvelous planet—can there be, in the light of these claims on our loyalty, any question as to which course we should adopt?   34

In the final week of his life, Albert Einstein signed the last of the collective appeals against the development of nuclear weapons that he was ever to sign. He was dead before it appeared. It was an appeal drafted, I gather, by Bertrand Russell. I had my differences with Russell at the time as I do now in retrospect; but I would like to quote one sentence from the final paragraph of that statement, not only because it was the   35

last one Einstein ever signed, but because it sums up, I think, all that I
have to say on the subject. It reads as follows:

> We appeal, as human being to human beings: Remember your humanity, and
> forget the rest.

## QUESTIONS FOR ANALYSIS

1. How does Kennan set the stage for his proposed solution? Examine
   the opening paragraphs to see how he prepares readers to accept his
   argument. How effective do you find this opening?

2. What does Kennan mean by "redundancy"? How does Kennan help
   you to understand the concept? What role does this concept play in
   the essay?

3. Why do you think Kennan reminds us that "there is no such thing
   as victory" in a war fought with nuclear weapons? Why does Kennan
   treat this notion as fact when some would regard it as opinion?

4. What alternative solution does Kennan bring up and argue against?
   How does he use this strategy of rebutting alternatives as a way of
   arguing for his own solution?

5. Kennan suggests that one of the causes of the problem is "the inner
   momentum, the independent momentum, of the weapons race itself."
   How do the images in paragraph 4 reinforce this idea of momentum?

6. On what basis does Kennan dismiss the SALT negotiations? How
   convincing is his argument, and how does it further his own proposed
   solution?

7. Kennan suggests that some readers would object that his proposal
   carries "risks." What risks might his proposal carry? How does he try
   to allay his readers' fears?

8. At the beginning of his proposal, Kennan acknowledges feelings of
   "discouragement, resignation, perhaps even despair." Yet he wants
   his proposal to be hopeful and inspiring. How convincing is his hope-
   fulness? How would you characterize the tone of his essay?

9. Every sentence in paragraph 17 has the same structure, beginning
   with either "There is" or "There are." Take inventory of the essay,
   noting other instances where sentence patterns are repeated. Kennan
   is a skilled writer certainly capable of varying his sentences. What
   does repeating sentence patterns in this essay accomplish?

## SUGGESTIONS FOR WRITING

1. Kennan claims that "there is a tendency of national communities to idealize themselves and to dehumanize their opponent." This tendency probably exists on all levels of human interaction, even interaction of the most trivial kind, such as card games and family squabbles. Identify one particular situation in which this human tendency creates a problem. Write a proposal defining the problem and offering a way to remedy or lessen it.

2. Kennan's proposal takes a problem of long standing, redefines it, and finds a new and promising solution. Think of a problem that has troubled a group to which you belong, and develop a new way of defining this problem. Then write a proposal redefining the problem and suggesting how it might be solved.

# Charles Krauthammer

At a relatively young age, Charles Krauthammer (b. 1950) has already achieved success in two different careers. First, he studied medicine at Harvard Medical School and specialized in psychiatry, later serving as chief resident of the Psychiatric Consultation Service at Massachusetts General Hospital. Krauthammer was awarded the Edwin Dunlop Prize for his psychiatric research.

Wedding his fascination with politics and his love of writing, Krauthammer worked in the late 1970s as a speechwriter for then Vice President Walter Mondale. This experience launched his second career—as a political writer for *Time* magazine and *The New Republic*, where he became a senior editor. Krauthammer has won the National Magazine Award for Essays and Criticism; his latest book, *Cutting Edges: Making Sense of the 80s* (1985), is a collection of his writings.

# In Defense of Deterrence

When this essay was originally published in the *The New Republic*, it bore the title "The Real Way to Prevent Nuclear War." When he included it in *Cutting Edges*, Krauthammer changed the title to "In Defense of Deterrence." What would you say is the significance of this change in title? What tone is implied in each of the titles? The essay, as you will see, is pugnacious in its criticism of the alternative solutions proposed by statesmen like George Kennan and nuclear freeze advocates like Jonathan Schell. In another essay, Krauthammer defended deterrence as "the only responsible attitude toward nuclear weapons that has so far been conceived." As you read this selection, pay special attention to the way Krauthammer anticipates and argues against alternative solutions.

"Safety will be the sturdy child of terror, and survival the twin brother of annihilation." That was Winston Churchill's description of what he called "the balance of terror." Each superpower has the ability to incinerate the defenseless population of the other many times over; each refrains from attacking because it fears retaliation in kind; each knows that aggression is tantamount to suicide. That is deterrence. Sometimes deterrence is called MAD, mutual assured destruction. By whatever name, deterrence has prevented the outbreak of nuclear war, indeed any war, between the United States and the Soviet Union for a generation.

Living in a world of deterrence is very uncomfortable. Every American and Soviet city dweller knows that he is targeted for destruction by nuclear weapons five thousand miles away. But the physical danger is only part of the problem. The world of deterrence is a world of paradoxes. Weapons are built in order never to be used. Weapons purely for defense of helpless populations, like the antiballistic missile systems, become the greatest threat to peace. Weapons aimed at people lessen the risk of war; weapons aimed at weapons, increase it.

The strains of living in such a world are enormous. A vast antinuclear movement is now rising in the U.S., animated principally by weariness and revulsion with this arrangement. Why now? Ronald Reagan is much of the answer. He helped defeat the SALT II treaty before his election, and has been reluctant to engage the Soviets in strategic arms talks since. For the first time in more than a decade, the U.S. and the Soviet Union are not engaged in negotiations to control strategic nuclear weapons. Worse, Mr. Reagan and some of his advisers have spoken in frighteningly offhand ways about "limited nuclear war" and nuclear warning shots. The Carter Administration's mobile MX plan played a part, too. It appeared such an enormously cumbersome and expensive contrivance that people began to wonder if the experts had not lost touch with reality. So millions of Americans have decided it is time for them to take the problem into their own hands, and an antinuclear grass-roots crusade has emerged.

Like all crusades, it has its bible: Jonathan Schell's . . . *The Fate of the Earth* . . . and its banner: "the freeze." Recently it even acquired an auxiliary brigade, four members of the American foreign policy establishment who opened a wholly new front by calling for a U.S. renunciation of any first use of nuclear weapons. The bible, the banner, and the brigade approach the nuclear dilemma from different directions, but they all challenge the established doctrines of deterrence. The brigade wants to limit deterrence; the freeze proponents want to ignore it; and Jonathan Schell wants to abolish it. Each deserves the closest scrutiny.

Jonathan Schell flatly rejects deterrence. That is the source of his originality. Otherwise his three-part thesis is unremarkable. Part I restates, albeit elegantly, the awful details of a nuclear holocaust, and concludes that it would lead to the extinction of the human race. (That is the view of some scientists, though not of the National Academy of Sciences' study which Schell used in reaching many of his conclusions.) Part II, an interminable rumination on the meaning of human extinction, comes to the unsurprising conclusion that extinction would be monstrous.

"From the foregoing it follows," Schell writes, after delivering his message in a reiterative style that constitutes its own kind of overkill, "that there can be no justification for extinguishing mankind." The real interest in Schell's book lies in Part III, "The Choice." Here he argues that traditional approaches to nuclear peril, like strategic arms limitation treaties, are mere gestures, aspirin given to a dying patient. He argues that deterrence is a logical fraud because the leaders of a country that had sustained a first strike would have no reason to retaliate, indeed, no country in whose name to retaliate.

What Schell refuses to acknowledge is that any potential aggressor   7 would be deterred—and for over thirty years has been deterred—from striking first because he must anticipate not only the logical responses of the victim, but all possible human responses. Revenge, for example, is one motive to launch a second strike. Paul Warnke, President Carter's arms control chief, gives another. He argues that "our moral commitment" would "require that the leaders who had perpetrated this enormity not be allowed to inherit the earth and bend its people to their will." Soviet leaders reading Warnke (a nuclear dove and a supporter of the freeze) are highly unlikely to calculate that a first strike would meet with no response because that would be "illogical." Furthermore, no one knows what would happen in the confused, unimaginably strained atmosphere of a nuclear crisis. To act—to attack—under the assumption that the other side is constrained to follow purely "logical" courses of action is itself totally illogical. It is precisely because of these calculations that nuclear deterrence has succeeded in preventing nuclear war. That is not to say that deterrence can never fail, but the argument from history is a powerful one. An even more powerful one is the absence of an alternative.

Not that Schell shies away from providing one: a world graced by total   8 disarmament (nuclear and conventional), the abolition of violence, the eradication of national boundaries, the renunciation of sovereignty, and the founding of a new world political order for the peaceful settlement of international disputes. How does he propose to bring this about? That is a detail he could not work into his 231-page treatise. That "awesome, urgent task," he graciously concedes, "I have left to others."

Although he does not explain how we are to bring about a lion-and-   9 lamb scenario which even Isaiah had the audacity only to predict and not to mandate, he does give us a clue as to what the operating principle of his post-messianic world will be. Here we come directly to the critical center of Schell's thinking, to the force that not only underlies his passion today but will save mankind tomorrow—fear. In his world, Schell writes, "Fear would no longer dictate particular decisions, such as whether or not the Soviet Union might place missiles in Cuba; rather, it would be a moving force behind the establishment of a new system by which every decision was made. And, having dictated the foundation of the system, it would stand guard over it forever after, guaranteeing that the species did not slide back toward anarchy and doom." I have my doubts.

Fear is not just the saving principle of Schell's new world order; it is 10 the animating force behind a new mass movement—the freeze campaign. The movement demands a mutual halt in the development, production, and deployment of all nuclear weapons, "because," as the campaign slogan puts it, "no one wants a nuclear war." Like Schell, freeze proponents are deeply concerned, and rightly so, about the prospect of living in a world in which we have the capacity to blow ourselves to bits at any moment. The freeze crusade has enlisted hundreds of thousands of Americans by showing what happens if the Sword of Damocles ever drops. Thus the graphic stills of Hiroshima victims and the maps with concentric circles radiating from ground zero in everyone's hometown. Schell recognizes that removing this sword requires renunciation not just by overkill, but of minimal deterrence, of the simple capacity to destroy the other side *once*. But very few freeze proponents advocate reducing levels below "sufficiency," because they recognize that in a pre-messianic world this would destabilize the nuclear balance and increase the chances of war. Under a freeze—indeed, under even the most radical of arms proposals, such as former Ambassador George Kennan's proposal to cut nuclear levels in half—the superpowers would still retain the capacity for the total destruction of the other society. Insofar as people support the freeze because they can't stand the thought of being a target for Soviet missiles, they have joined the wrong movement. The freeze offers no solution to that problem. They should be with Jonathan Schell's total disarmament movement, working on the "awesome, urgent task" of remaking human nature.

Some might argue that there is another way, short of universal broth- 11 erhood, to remove the Sword of Damocles. That is unilateral disarmament. But quite apart from the fact that such a move would mean the surrender of our values, it would do little to secure our survival. The historical record does not support the proposition that helplessness is a guarantee of safety. There has been one nuclear war on record; in it a nonnuclear Japan lost Hiroshima and Nagasaki. So far there has been only one biological war, the one going on today in Laos and Cambodia. These weapons, now used against helpless tribesmen, were never used against American troops fighting the same Vietnamese forces in the same place. The Hmong, unlike the Americans, lack the capacity to retaliate in kind.

The freeze is not unilateralist, nor do many of its advocates reject 12 deterrence. They say they reject overkill. "Enough is enough," they say. "Why waste billions on useless weapons if all they will do, as Churchill said, is to make the rubble bounce?" (It is sometimes also argued, somewhat anomalously, that having useless, rubble-bouncing weapons is at the same time dangerous.)

The problem is that in their zeal to curb overkill, freeze advocates 13 ignore the requirements of deterrence and, in particular, the requirement for survivability of the deterrent. Our weapons must be able to withstand a first strike and penetrate Soviet defenses in a retaliatory strike (and vice versa). If either side finds the survivability of its weapons systems declining, the world becomes less safe. In an international crisis, each side, particularly the more vulnerable side, has incentive to strike first: the invulnerable side to use its advantage, the vulnerable side to strike before it is too late.

What would happen under a freeze? The U.S. retaliatory capacity 14 depends on the three legs of its strategic triad: the land-based ICBMs, the bomber force, and submarines. Because of the increasing accuracy, power, and numbers of Soviet missiles, the U.S. land-based missile force will soon become vulnerable to a first strike. (It is precisely to eliminate that vulnerability that President Carter proposed hiding the MX in multiple shelters, a scheme now abandoned.) That leaves the bomber and submarine forces. The bomber force consists of aging B-52s that are increasingly vulnerable to attack while still on the ground, and to being shot down while trying to penetrate Soviet air space. Hence President Carter's decision to deploy air-launched cruise missiles, which would be better able to penetrate Soviet defenses and would allow the B-52s to remain outside Soviet air space. The freeze proposal would prevent deployment of these missiles. It would also prevent production and development of a new bomber, either the B-1 or the Stealth, which would be better able to elude destruction on the ground and Soviet defenses in the air. Note that the B-1 or the Stealth would not be any more destructive than the B-52. They would not make the rubble bounce any higher. They would simply be more likely to get to the target, and therefore present the Soviets with a very good reason never to launch a first strike.

That leaves the submarine force, which the U.S. is now in the process 15 of modernizing to make more survivable. The new Tridents are quieter than existing subs, and because they have longer-range missiles they can hide in larger areas of the ocean. The freeze would stop their deployment.

The freeze, a proposal devised for its simplicity, does not deal very 16 well with paradox. It is one of the paradoxes of deterrence that defensive weapons (the ABM, for example) can be more destabilizing and therefore more dangerous to peace than offensive weapons. The freeze fixates on nuclear weapons because they appear more terrible than others. And indeed they are. But they are not necessarily more destabilizing. As former Under Secretary of the Navy James Woolsey points out, the freeze does nothing to prevent nonnuclear antisubmarine and antiaircraft advances, which weaken deterrence. But it does prevent modernization of nuclear systems designed for survivability, which enhances deterrence.

What exactly does it mean to say that if survivability declines, war 17 becomes more likely? One quick fix for a vulnerable deterrent is to adopt a policy of launch-on-warning: as soon as we detect enemy missiles leaving their silos, we launch our missiles before they can be destroyed. (Some officials unsuccessfully urged President Carter to adopt launch-on-warning as an alternative to building the mobile MX.) But this creates a hairtrigger situation, where the time for the world's most important decision is not a matter of minutes but of seconds, too short to check out a faulty radar reading or a misinterpretation of data. That's the price of ignoring deterrence.

This analysis looks simply at what would happen if the freeze were 18 already a reality. But however fervently American citizens may wish it, they cannot vote a "mutual verifiable freeze" into existence. Unfortunately, that must be negotiated with the Soviets. And bad as a freeze would be as an end point, it would be worse as a U.S. negotiating position—which is exactly what it would be if, say, the Kennedy-Hatfield amendment were adopted. First, it is certain to delay other arms control initiatives. The freeze appeals to American voters because of its simplicity, but a mutual freeze would involve complex negotiations with the Soviets. What exactly would be frozen? At what stage? How would it be verified? The production, stockpiling, and qualitative upgrading of nuclear weapons cannot be detected by satellite, and the Russians have always refused on-site inspection. That problem alone turns the freeze into either a nonstarter or a source of interminable negotiation.

Ironically, there does exist an arms control proposal which, though 19 very complicated, poorly understood by the American people, and unsuited for two-hour ratification by town meetings, is very well understood by the Soviets: SALT II. They have already signed it. If the aim of the freeze movement is a quick, simple, bold move in arms control that would allow us to proceed to real reductions, then the answer is not a freeze, but SALT II. Representative Les Aspin has already pointed out with dismay the American penchant for reinventing the arms control wheel every four years. In 1977 President Carter rejected the Vladivostok Accords negotiated by President Ford and proposed drastic reductions instead. The Soviets rejected his proposal out of hand. It took more than two years to renegotiate SALT II on the original lines of Vladivostok. President Reagan in turn rejected SALT II and called for as yet unspecified START talks. The freeze proponents are doing precisely the same thing. It simply makes no sense to propose a freeze that would require years of negotiations when SALT II is at hand, has already been approved by the Soviets, and could be adjusted in small details and ratified quickly. Of course, SALT is not as catchy a slogan as the freeze. But it is certainly a better, quicker, and more serious path to arms control.

Another aim of the freeze campaign is to move to real reductions. But to arm a U.S. negotiating team with a freeze offer is to ensure that it will have no leverage with which to bargain the Soviets into reductions. We will have unilaterally announced our willingness to forgo all our modernization programs, like the Trident, the cruise missile, and the Stealth bomber. The theory is that this gesture will elicit from the Soviets a more conciliatory negotiating position. The theory is in conflict with history. The Soviets do not have a good record of responding to unilateral gestures. At the Glassboro Summit in 1967, President Johnson tried to interest Premier Kosygin in ABM negotiations. Kosygin demurred. A year later, the Senate defeated an amendment to deny funds for an American ABM system. Three days later Soviet Foreign Minister Andrei Gromyko announced the Soviets' willingness to negotiate arms control. Eventually they agreed to an almost total ban on ABMs. We are using the same strategy today in Geneva, offering systems that we propose to build as bargaining chips. We offer to forgo deployment of the Pershing II and ground-launched cruise missiles in Europe if the Soviets dismantle their SS-20s. Under a freeze, our position in Geneva would collapse and the SS-20s would remain in place. (Brezhnev calls *that* arrangement a freeze.) In strategic arms talks, any attempts on our part to, say, bargain away one of our new systems against the Soviets' destabilizing silo-killing ICBMs would fail.

The freeze is not a plan; it is a sentiment. (Montana's proposed freeze resolution, for example, opposes "the production, development and deployment of nuclear weapons by any nation." It will unfortunately not be binding on President Zia of Pakistan.) The freeze reflects the deeply felt and wholly laudable wish of millions of Americans that something be done to control nuclear weapons. But when taken seriously as a plan, the freeze continually fails on its own terms. It seeks safety, but would jeopardize deterrence; it seeks quick action, but would delay arms control; it seeks real reductions, but removes any leverage we might have to bring them about.

Finally, it mistakes the most likely cause of an outbreak of nuclear war. In its fixation on numbers, the freeze assumes that somehow high weapons levels *in themselves* make war more likely. True, an uncontrolled arms race breeds suspicion between the superpowers and can increase the risk of war; but arms control measures (like SALT I or II) can allow higher levels, and still decrease the risk by building confidence on both sides and letting each know precisely what the other is doing. If nuclear war ever comes, it most likely will be not because the weapons fire themselves, but because some national leader, in order to preserve some national interest, orders them fired. When did we come closest to nuclear war in the last thirty-six years? In October 1962, when President Kennedy decided to threaten Khrushchev with war unless he obeyed our ultimatum on the Cuban missiles. In 1962 the level of nuclear arms was much lower than it is today. And when was the chance of nuclear war smallest? Probably at the height of detente, during the Apollo-Soyuz love fest, when U.S.-Soviet relations were good, even though each side had the capacity for multiple overkill.

The absolute level of nuclear weapons is only one factor, and a rela- 23 tively small one at that, in determining the likelihood of nuclear war breaking out. (It is certainly less important than the balance of vulnerabilities on each side, i.e., the stability of deterrence.) The most likely source of nuclear war is from a regional conflict between the superpowers, where one or the other has important interests, but finds itself at a conventional disadvantage. That is the American situation today in Europe and in the Persian Gulf. To prevent the Soviets from taking advantage of their superiority in conventional arms, the U.S. has reserved the option of using nuclear weapons to respond to a nonnuclear Soviet attack. This policy of extending nuclear deterrence to conventional conflicts has kept the peace. But it is dangerous. It blurs the line between conventional and nuclear war, and by threatening "limited" nuclear war it opens the door to a nuclear holocaust since no one knows whether a limited nuclear war can be kept limited. The most effective way to eliminate that danger, and thus eliminate the greatest existing risk of nuclear war, is to make this kind of extended deterrence unnecessary: to right the conventional balance by radically bolstering allied forces, particularly on the West European frontier. NATO could then deter a conventional attack without having to threaten to wage nuclear war.

One of Schell's dictums is that compared to the peril of a nuclear 24 holocaust, all other human values pale into insignificance, indeed, lose their meaning because they lose their context. If the antinuclear crusaders really believe that, they should be clamoring for increased conventional forces to reduce the European imbalance. They aren't. The reason is that the freeze crusade, which springs from deeply felt antiwar and antiarmament sentiments, is not comfortable with the thought that preventing nuclear war may require a radically enlarged conventional defense. Furthermore, one of the major appeals of the antinuclear movement is the promise to halt the economic drain caused by "useless" nuclear weapons and to redirect resources to human needs. But a shift away from strategic to conventional weapons would be very expensive. Our reliance on nuclear weapons—and the current conventional balance in Europe—results in large part from a desire to *reduce* defense spending. In the 1950s we decided to buy defense in Europe on the cheap. Rather than match the vast armies and tank forces of the Warsaw Pact, we decided to go nuclear, because, as John Foster Dulles put it, it offered "more bang for the buck."

But the European defense balance has become more unstable since 25 Dulles's day. In the 1950s the U.S. threatened "massive retaliation." If the Soviets crossed into Western Europe, we would attack the Russian homeland with a strategic nuclear strike. When the Russians acquired the same capacity against the U.S., that threat lost its credibility. The Kennedy Administration adopted a new policy of "flexible response," a euphemism for a limited nuclear war. Under the new doctrine, the U.S. reserved the right to use theater nuclear weapons on the battlefield to thwart a conventional Soviet attack. That has been our policy ever since. (Ronald Reagan did not invent it, although he has the habit of throwing it around more casually and publicly than other Presidents.) This doctrine has troubled many Americans, but as long as the U.S. was not prepared to challenge the Soviet conventional superiority in Europe, nor prepared to abandon its European allies, there seemed no other choice.

Enter the auxiliary brigade of the antinuclear movement: four former 26 high Administration officials, two of whom, under President Kennedy, gave us "limited nuclear war" (Robert McNamara and McGeorge Bundy); one of whom gave us "containment" (George Kennan); and one of whom gave us SALT I (Gerard Smith). Two weeks ago they opened an entirely new front in the crusade. They called for the adoption of a "no-first-use" policy on nuclear weapons. It was a renunciation of "flexible response" and of "extended deterrence." (They would retain extended deterrence in one restricted sense: as a retaliation for a Soviet *nuclear* attack on Western Europe, an unlikely possibility since the Soviets are prepared to renounce first use, and since with their conventional advantage they have no reason to attack with nuclear weapons.)

The problem with folding our nuclear umbrella, as the four wise men 27 themselves acknowledged, is that, unaccompanied by conventional rearmament, it means the end of the Western alliance and the abandonment in particular of West Germany to Soviet intimidation and blackmail. The other problem with a no-first-use policy is that it might paradoxically increase the chances of nuclear war. Today a war between the U.S. and the Soviets is deterred at its origin: since even the slightest conventional conflict between them carries the threat of escalating into a nuclear one, neither happens. The no-first-use policy moves the "firebreak" from the line dividing war from peace to the line dividing conventional war from nuclear war. It trades the increased chance of conventional war (because now less dangerous and more "thinkable") for a decreased chance of such a war becoming nuclear. But no one can guarantee that *in extremis*, faced with a massive Soviet invasion of Western Europe, the U.S. would stick to its no-first-use pledge. Thus, by making a European war thinkable, this policy could, whatever its intentions, lead to a nuclear war.

Unless, that is, we have the conventional forces to preserve the orig- 28 inal firebreak between war and peace. Thus, to prevent both political and (possibly) nuclear calamity, a no-first-use pledge must be accompanied, indeed preceded, by a serious conventional buildup of Western forces on the European frontier. The problem with McNamara et al. is that although they acknowledge this need, they treat it very casually— certainly with nothing like the urgency with which they call for abandoning extended deterrence. They speak only vaguely of the need for "review" and "study" of conventional military needs, of whether the political will exists in the West for such a buildup, and of "whether we Americans have a durable and effective answer to our military manpower needs in the present all-volunteer active and reserve forces" (they cannot quite bring themselves to say the word "draft"). Their eagerness to be the first off the blocks with a no-first-use policy is obvious. Their reluctance to urge on their antinuclear allies the only responsible and safe (and costly) means of achieving it is lamentable. The result of their highly publicized, grossly unbalanced proposal is predictable: another support in the complex and highly vulnerable structure of deterrence has been weakened. The world will be no safer for it.

Despite the prophesies of Schell, the pandering of the freeze-riding 29 politicians, and the posturing of the four wise men—and the good intentions of millions of concerned Americans caught up in the antinuclear maelstrom—there is no need to reinvent nuclear policy. There *is* a need for arms control: SALT II is the best transition to real reductions. There *is* a need to avoid limited nuclear war: rebuilding our conventional strength and perhaps reintroducing the draft would reduce that risk. These proposals are neither new nor exciting. Unlike Schell's crusade, they don't promise to restore "the wholeness and meaning of life." They don't suggest that "the passion and will that we need to save ourselves would flood into our lives. Then the walls of indifference, inertia, and coldness that now isolate each of us from others, and all of us from the past and future generations, would melt, like snow in the spring." They don't promise to set right "our disordered instinctual life." That is because working to reduce the chances of nuclear war is not an exercise in psychotherapy. It is not a romance. It is mundane work in pursuit of mundane objectives: a modest program of nuclear modernization, SALT II, and a bigger conventional defense. These measures will not cure anomie, but will help to maintain deterrence, that difficult abstraction on which our values and our safety depends.

## QUESTIONS FOR ANALYSIS

1. "In Defense of Deterrence" is a long and complicated proposal. In order to analyze Krauthammer's argument, make a brief outline of his major claims and supports. (See Analyzing an Argument in Chapter 1.)

2. Krauthammer opens his proposal with a quotation from Winston Churchill: "Safety will be the sturdy child of terror, and survival the twin brother of annihilation." What are the advantages of beginning the proposal with this quotation? the disadvantages?

3. Summarize Krauthammer's psychological explanation of the nuclear freeze movement. What is the effect of explaining an alternative solution in this way? If you were sympathetic to the freeze movement, how would you react to Krauthammer's explanation of its motives?

4. Krauthammer uses sarcasm to ridicule his opponents. Take inventory of the instances of sarcasm, and conjecture about the advantages and disadvantages of using sarcasm in this way. How effective a strategy do you think it is?

5. In responding to Jonathan Schell's objection that "deterrence is a logical fraud," Krauthammer notes that potential aggressors may act illogically. How well does this point support his own proposal?

6. To Krauthammer's claim that the "argument from history" is the best support for deterrence, one reader offered this rejoinder: "There is no assurance that retaliatory capacity is the real deterrent. Global winds of massive radiation, radical climatic change, or the collapse of the international economy may be deterrence enough." How might Krauthammer respond to this objection? What is your own response?

7. What kinds of evidence does Krauthammer cite? How does he use this evidence most effectively?

8. How authoritative does Krauthammer seem to be? Does he instill confidence? Describe your impression of him from the voice you hear in this essay.

## SUGGESTIONS FOR WRITING

1. In addition to ratifying SALT II, Krauthammer mentions two additional solutions: rebuilding our conventional weapons arsenal and reintroducing the military draft. Which of these solutions could you support, or do you have any other solutions to offer? Write a proposal of your own, arguing that your solution would help to lessen the threat of nuclear war.

2. Krauthammer is at his best finding fault with other solutions to the problem. Recall solutions to problems in your school, work, or social life of which you have been highly critical. Choose one of these solutions, and write a proposal criticizing that solution and arguing for your own.

3. Even though the threat of nuclear war is abstract, as Krauthammer suggests, it puts immense pressure on our daily existence. Can you think of any other problem that affects you every day? How might that problem be solved? Write a proposal defining the problem and arguing for your solution to it.

## THE DEBATE: ADDITIONAL QUESTIONS FOR ANALYSIS

1. On the basis of your analysis of these two selections, how would you compare the way Kennan and Krauthammer present themselves to their readers? How do their tones and styles of writing differ? How appropriate are their respective tones to the circumstances in which the proposals were first presented (Kennan's was a speech upon acceptance of an award, Krauthammer's an article in a liberal news magazine)?

2. Contrast the ways in which Kennan and Krauthammer deal with alternative solutions. What do their respective ways of treating alternatives suggest about their understanding of their readers and the situations in which they are writing?

3. Krauthammer calls Kennan's proposal to reduce nuclear levels by half "the most radical of arms proposals." Even under this proposal, however, "the superpowers would still retain the capacity for the total destruction of the other society." Therefore, according to Krauthammer, Kennan's proposal "offers no solution to the problem." How do you think Kennan would respond to this criticism? How do you respond?

4. The major alternative solution Kennan considers is deterrence. On what grounds does Kennan dismiss deterrence? How do you think he would respond to Krauthammer's defense of it?

5. How do you think Krauthammer would respond to Kennan's assertion that "the nuclear bomb is the most useless weapon ever invented. It can be employed to no rational purpose"?

# Jonathan Swift

Jonathan Swift (1667–1745) is best known as the author of *Gulliver's Travels* (1726), a book that is often regarded as a children's story but which is actually a sweeping satire of the age. As befits a clergyman—Swift was dean of an Anglican church in Dublin, Ireland—the butt of much of Swift's satire is moral obtuseness. Born in Ireland of English parents, he was also particularly sensitive to injustices resulting from British rule of Ireland. The situation in Ireland at the time was grim. The Irish Catholic peasants, charged excessive rents by the British absentee landlords, were desperately poor. With the exception of Swift, few spoke out on behalf of the Irish, and the British Parliament simply ignored the problem. Swift is still revered in Ireland for his series of letters opposing England's plan to impose new coins, a plan that would have further debased the value of Irish currency and worsened the already extreme poverty in Ireland.

# A Modest Proposal

"A Modest Proposal (For Preventing the Children of Poor People in Ireland from Being a Burden to Their Parents or Country, and for Making Them Beneficial to the Public)" was originally published as an anonymous pamphlet in 1729. At the time, some readers took it at face value, thinking it was a serious proposal to solve the problem of poverty in Ireland. It is not hard to see how readers could have been duped since it is a textbook example of proposal writing—defining and establishing the problem with a multitude of facts and systematically expounding the advantages of the proposed solution over the alternatives. But it is also a masterful piece of irony. Conjecture, as you read, how readers could have mistaken the tone. What does Swift do to make his voice believable at the same time that he is making such an outrageous proposal?

It is a melancholy object to those who walk through this great town[1] or travel in the country, when they see the streets, the roads, and cabin doors, crowded with beggars of the female sex, followed by three, four, or six children, all in rags and importuning every passenger for an alms. These mothers, instead of being able to work for their honest livelihood, are forced to employ all their time in strolling to beg sustenance for their helpless infants, who, as they grow up, either turn thieves for want of

---

[1]Dublin.

work, or leave their dear native country to fight for the Pretender in Spain, or sell themselves to the Barbados.[2]

I think it is agreed by all parties that this prodigious number of children    2
in the arms, or on the backs, or at the heels of their mothers, and frequently of their fathers, is in the present deplorable state of the kingdom a very great additional grievance; and therefore whoever could find out a fair, cheap, and easy method of making these children sound, useful members of the commonwealth would deserve so well of the public as to have his statue set up for a preserver of the nation.

But my intention is very far from being confined to provide only for    3
the children of professed beggars; it is of a much greater extent, and shall take in the whole number of infants at a certain age who are born of parents in effect as little able to support them as those who demand our charity in the streets.

As to my own part, having turned my thoughts for many years upon    4
this important subject, and maturely weighed the several schemes of other projectors,[3] I have always found them grossly mistaken in their computation. It is true, a child just dropped from its dam may be supported by her milk for a solar year, with little other nourishment; at most not above the value of two shillings, which the mother may certainly get, or the value in scraps, by her lawful occupation of begging; and it is exactly at one year that I propose to provide for them in such a manner as instead of being a charge upon their parents or the parish, or wanting food and raiment for the rest of their lives, they shall on the contrary contribute to the feeding, and partly to the clothing, of many thousands.

There is likewise another great advantage in my scheme, that it will    5
prevent those voluntary abortions, and that horrid practice of women murdering their bastard children, alas, too frequent among us, sacrificing the poor innocent babes, I doubt, more to avoid the expense than the shame, which would move tears and pity in the most savage and inhuman breast.

The number of souls in this kingdom being usually reckoned one mil-    6
lion and a half, of these I calculate there may be about two hundred thousand couples whose wives are breeders; from which number I subtract thirty thousand couples who are able to maintain their own children, although I apprehend there cannot be so many under the present distress of the kingdom; but this being granted, there will remain an hundred

---

[2]Rebellious Irishmen had joined an army to help James Stuart, the Pretender, reclaim the throne of England. Many others had gone to Barbados as indentured servants because they could find no other way to emigrate to the new world.

[3]Planners or those making proposals.

and seventy thousand breeders. I again subtract fifty thousand for those women who miscarry, or whose children die by accident or disease within the year. There only remain an hundred and twenty thousand children of poor parents annually born. The question therefore is, how this number shall be reared and provided for, which, as I have already said, under the present situation of affairs, is utterly impossible by all the methods hitherto proposed. For we can neither employ them in handicraft or agriculture; we neither build houses (I mean in the country) nor cultivate land. They can very seldom pick up a livelihood by stealing till they arrive at six years old, except where they are of towardly parts;[4] although I confess they learn the rudiments much earlier, during which time they can however be looked upon only as probationers, as I have been informed by a principal gentleman in the country of Cavan, who protested to me that he never knew above one or two instances under the age of six, even in a part of the kingdom so renowned for the quickest proficiency in that art.

I am assured by our merchants that a boy or girl before twelve years old is no salable commodity; and even when they come to this age they will not yield above three pounds, or three pounds and half a crown at most on the Exchange; which cannot turn to account either to the parents or the kingdom, the charge of nutriment and rags having been at least four times that value. 7

I shall now therefore humbly propose my own thoughts, which I hope will not be liable to the least objection. 8

I have been assured by a very knowing American of my acquaintance in London, that a young healthy child well nursed is at a year old a most delicious, nourishing, and wholesome food, whether stewed, roasted, baked, or boiled; and I make no doubt that it will equally serve in a fricassee or a ragout.[5] 9

I do therefore humbly offer it to public consideration that of the hundred and twenty thousand children, already computed, twenty thousand may be reserved for breed, whereof only one fourth part to be males, which is more than we allow to sheep, black cattle, or swine; and my reason is that these children are seldom the fruits of marriage, a circumstance not much regarded by our savages, therefore one male will be sufficient to serve four females. That the remaining hundred thousand may at a year old be offered in sale to the persons of quality and fortune through the kingdom, always advising the mother to let them suck plentifully in the last month, so as to render them plump and fat for a good 10

---

[4]Innate abilities.
[5]Stew.

table. A child will make two dishes at an entertainment for friends; and when the family dines alone, the fore or hind quarter will make a reasonable dish, and seasoned with a little pepper or salt will be very good boiled on the fourth day, especially in winter.

I have reckoned upon a medium that a child just born will weigh 11 twelve pounds, and in a solar year if tolerably nursed increaseth to twenty-eight pounds.

I grant this food will be somewhat dear, and therefore very proper for 12 landlords, who, as they have already devoured most of the parents, seem to have the best title to the children.

Infant's flesh will be in season throughout the year, but more plentiful 13 in March, and a little before and after. For we are told by a grave author, an eminent French physician,[6] that fish being a prolific diet, there are more children born in Roman Catholic countries about nine months after Lent than at any other season; therefore, reckoning a year after Lent, the markets will be more glutted than usual, because the number of popish infants is at least three to one in this kingdom; and therefore it will have one other collateral advantage, by lessening the number of Papists among us.

I have already computed the charge of nursing a beggar's child (in 14 which list I reckon all cottagers, laborers, and four-fifths of the farmers) to be about two shillings per annum, rags included; and I believe no gentleman would repine to give ten shillings for the carcass of a good fat child, which, as I have said, will make four dishes of excellent nutritive meat, when he hath only some particular friend or his own family to dine with him. Thus the squire will learn to be a good landlord, and grow popular among the tenants; the mother will have eight shillings net profit, and be fit for work till she produces another child.

Those who are more thrifty (as I must confess the times require) may 15 flay the carcass; the skin of which artificially[7] dressed will make admirable gloves for ladies, and summer boots for fine gentlemen.

As to our city of Dublin, shambles[8] may be appointed for this purpose 16 in the most convenient parts of it, and butchers we may be assured will not be wanting; although I rather recommend buying the children alive, and dressing them hot from the knife as we do roasting pigs.

A very worthy person, a true lover of his country, and whose virtues 17 I highly esteem, was lately pleased in discoursing on this matter to offer a refinement upon my scheme. He said that many gentlemen of his

---

[6]The French humorist, François Rabelais.
[7]Artfully.
[8]Slaughterhouses.

kingdom, having of late destroyed their deer, he conceived that the want of venison might be well supplied by the bodies of young lads and maidens, not exceeding fourteen years of age nor under twelve, so great a number of both sexes in every country being now ready to starve for want of work and service; and these to be disposed of by their parents, if alive, or otherwise by their nearest relations. But with due deference to so excellent a friend and so deserving a patriot, I cannot be altogether in his sentiments; for as to the males, my American acquaintance assured me from frequent experience that their flesh was generally tough and lean, like that of our schoolboys, by continual exercise, and their taste disagreeable; and to fatten them would not answer the charge. Then as to the females, it would, I think with humble submission, be a loss to the public, because they soon would become breeders themselves; and besides, it is not improbable that some scrupulous people might be apt to censure such a practice (although indeed very unjustly) as a little bordering upon cruelty; which, I confess, hath always been with me the strongest objection against any project, how well soever intended.

But in order to justify my friend, he confessed that this expedient was  18 put into his head by the famous Psalmanazar,[9] a native of the island Formosa, who came from thence to London above twenty years ago, and in conversation told my friend that in his country when any young person happened to be put to death, the executioner sold the carcass to persons of quality as a prime dainty; and that in his time the body of a plump girl of fifteen, who was crucified for an attempt to poison the emperor, was sold to his Imperial Majesty's prime minister of state, and other great mandarins of the court, in joints from the gibbet, at four hundred crowns. Neither indeed can I deny that if the same use were made of several plump young girls in this town, who without one single groat to their fortunes cannot stir abroad without a chair, and appear at the playhouse and assemblies in foreign fineries which they never will pay for, the kingdom would not be the worse.

Some persons of a desponding spirit are in great concern about that  19 vast number of poor people who are aged, diseased, or maimed, and I have been desired to employ my thoughts what course may be taken to ease the nation of so grievous an encumbrance. But I am not in the least pain upon that matter, because it is very well known that they are every day dying and rotting by cold and famine, and filth and vermin, as fast as can be reasonably expected. And as to the younger laborers, they are now in almost as hopeful a condition. They cannot get work, and con-

---

[9]Frenchman George Psalmanazar wrote a fictional description of Formosa and duped London society into believing he was Japanese.

sequently pine away for want of nourishment to a degree that if any time they are accidentally hired to common labor, they have not strength to perform it; and thus the country and themselves are happily delivered from the evils to come.

I have too long digressed, and therefore shall return to my subject. I think the advantages by the proposal which I have made are obvious and many, as well as of the highest importance. 20

For first, as I have already observed, it would greatly lessen the number of Papists, with whom we are yearly overrun, being the principal breeders of the nation as well as our most dangerous enemies; and who stay at home on purpose to deliver the kingdom to the Pretender, hoping to take their advantage by the absence of so many good Protestants, who have chosen rather to leave their country than to stay at home and pay tithes against their conscience to an Episcopal curate. 21

Secondly, the poorer tenants will have something valuable of their own, which by law may be made liable to distress,[10] and help to pay their landlord's rent, their corn and cattle being already seized and money a thing unknown. 22

Thirdly, whereas the maintenance of an hundred thousand children, from two years old and upwards, cannot be computed at less than ten shillings a piece per annum, the nation's stock will be thereby increased fifty thousand pounds per annum, besides the profit of a new dish introduced to the tables of all gentlemen of fortune in the kingdom who have any refinement in taste. And the money will circulate among ourselves, the goods being entirely of our own growth and manufacture. 23

Fourthly, the constant breeders, besides the gain of eight shillings sterling per annum by the sale of their children, will be rid of the charge of maintaining them after the first year. 24

Fifthly, this food would likewise bring great custom to taverns, where the vintners will certainly be so prudent as to procure the best receipts for dressing it to perfection, and consequently have their houses frequented by all the fine gentlemen, who justly value themselves upon their knowledge in good eating; and a skillful cook, who understands how to oblige his guests, will contrive to make it as expensive as they please. 25

Sixthly, this would be a great inducement to marriage, which all wise nations have either encouraged by rewards or enforced by laws and penalties. It would increase the care and tenderness of mothers toward their children, when they were sure of a settlement for life to the poor babes, 26

---

[10]Open to repossession by creditors.

provided in some sort by the public, to their annual profit instead of expense. We should see an honest emulation among the married women, which of them could bring the fattest child to the market. Men would become as fond of their wives during the time of their pregnancy as they are now of their mares in foal, their cows in calf, or sows when they are ready to farrow; nor offer to beat or kick them (as is too frequent a practice) for fear of a miscarriage.

Many other advantages might be enumerated. For instance, the addition of some thousand carcasses in our exportation of barreled beef, the propagation of swine's flesh, and improvements in the art of making good bacon, so much wanted among us by the great destruction of pigs, too frequent at our tables, which are no way comparable in taste or magnificence to a well-grown, fat, yearling child, which roasted whole will make a considerable figure at a lord mayor's feast or any other public entertainment. But this and many others I omit, being studious of brevity. 27

Supposing that one thousand families in this city would be constant customers for infants' flesh, besides others who might have it at merry meetings, particularly weddings and christenings, I compute that Dublin would take off annually about twenty thousand carcasses, and the rest of the kingdom (where probably they will be sold somewhat cheaper) the remaining eighty thousand. 28

I can think of no one objection that will possibly be raised against this proposal, unless it should be urged that the number of people will be thereby much lessened in the kingdom. This I freely own, and it was indeed one principal design in offering it to the world. I desire the reader will observe, that I calculate my remedy for this one individual kingdom of Ireland and for no other that ever was, is, or I think ever can be upon earth. Therefore let no man talk to me of other expedients: of taxing our absentees at five shillings a pound: of using neither clothes nor household furniture except what is of our own growth and manufacture: of utterly rejecting the materials and instruments that promote foreign luxury: of curing the expensiveness of pride, vanity, idleness, and gaming in our women: of introducing a vein of parsimony, prudence, and temperance: of learning to love our country, in the want of which we differ even from Laplanders and the inhabitants of Topinamboo:[11] of quitting our animosities and factions, nor acting any longer like the Jews, who were murdering one another at the very moment their city was taken:[12] 29

---

[11]In Brazil.

[12]During the Roman siege of Jerusalem (70 A.D.), some Jews were murdered for conspiring with the enemy.

of being a little cautious not to sell our country and conscience for nothing: of teaching landlords to have at least one degree of mercy toward their tenants: lastly, of putting a spirit of honesty, industry, and skill into our shopkeepers; who, if a resolution could now be taken to buy only our native goods, would immediately unite to cheat and exact upon us in the price, the measure, and the goodness, nor could ever yet be brought to make one fair proposal of just dealing, though often and earnestly invited to it.[13]

Therefore I repeat, let no man talk to me of these and the like expedients, till he hath at least some glimpse of hope that there will ever be some hearty and sincere attempt to put them in practice. 30

But as to myself, having been wearied out for many years with offering vain, idle, visionary thoughts, and at length utterly despairing of success, I fortunately fell upon this proposal, which, as it is wholly new, so it hath something solid and real, of no expense and little trouble, full in our own power, and whereby we can incur no danger in disobliging England. For this kind of commodity will not bear exportation, the flesh being of too tender a consistence to admit a long continuance in salt, although perhaps I could name a country which would be glad to eat up our whole nation without it.[14] 31

After all, I am not so violently bent upon my own opinion as to reject any offer proposed by wise men, which shall be found equally innocent, cheap, easy, and effectual. But before something of that kind shall be advanced in contradiction to my scheme, and offering a better, I desire the author or authors will be pleased maturely to consider two points. First, as things now stand, how they will be able to find food and raiment for an hundred thousand useless mouths and backs. And secondly, there being a round million of creatures in human figure throughout this kingdom, whose sole subsistence put into a common stock would leave them in debt two millions of pounds sterling, adding those who are beggars by profession to the bulk of farmers, cottagers, and laborers, with their wives and children who are beggars in effect; I desire those politicians who dislike my overture, and may perhaps be so bold to attempt an answer, that they will first ask the parents of these mortals whether they would not at this day think it a great happiness to have been sold for food at a year old in this manner I prescribe, and thereby have avoided such a perpetual scene of misfortunes as they have since gone through by the oppression of landlords, the impossibility of paying rent without money or trade, the want of common sustenance, with neither house nor clothes 32

---

[13]Swift made these proposals in other pamphlets.
[14]England.

to cover them from the inclemencies of the weather, and the most inevitable prospect of entailing the like or greater miseries upon their breed forever.

I profess, in the sincerity of my heart, that I have not the least personal interest in endeavoring to promote this necessary work, having no other motive than the public good of my country, by advancing our trade, providing for infants, relieving the poor, and giving some pleasure to the rich. I have no children by which I can propose to get a single penny; the youngest being nine years old, and my wife past childbearing. 33

## QUESTIONS FOR ANALYSIS

1. Briefly summarize this proposal, describing the problem and the proposed solution. (A discussion of summarizing appears in Chapter 1.)

2. What impression do you have of the person making this proposal? How authoritative and reasonable does he seem to be? What values and attitudes does he appeal to?

3. Like the other proposals in this chapter, this one is written in the first person. Unlike the others, however, it seems doubtful that the author could seriously propose such a solution to the problem. How do you know that Swift is being ironic? Where do you detect Swift's own voice?

4. At one point, Swift characterizes Americans as cannibals. What other groups does he satirize? What do these attacks contribute to the essay?

5. A characteristic of this proposal is its overwhelming use of statistics. What are these statistics used to prove? How convincing are they?

6. How are alternative solutions handled in this proposal? Why do you suppose Swift treats them this way?

7. Skim the essay, taking inventory of instances in which human beings are referred to in terms usually used for livestock. What does such labeling of people imply? (Chapter 1 gives guidance for taking inventory.)

## SUGGESTIONS FOR WRITING

1. Although this proposal was written many years ago, the problems it addresses—poverty, hunger, moral stupidity—unfortunately remain. How would you awaken your neighbors to the plight of the less fortunate? Write a proposal suggesting a way to increase the awareness of people in your own community about a specific social problem.

2. Swift uses irony to ridicule attitudes held by some of his contemporaries. Irony lets him carry these attitudes to their logical extreme and thereby expose them for what they really are. Think of opinions and attitudes you find repellent, and use irony and exaggeration to write your own "modest proposal."

# Elizabeth Lantry

Elizabeth Lantry (b. 1966) is an economics major who plans to get a master's degree in business administration and eventually to own a small business. To earn some money and at the same time to learn about business, Lantry took a job in a local frozen yogurt store. She worked part time during the school year and full time during the summer. Recently, Lantry was offered the job of manager in another of the yogurt company's stores. With the understanding that she could not work more than twenty hours a week during school, Lantry accepted the promotion because "it was a wonderful opportunity to get management experience."

# Wanted: Shift Managers

Lantry wrote this proposal for her composition course shortly after becoming a manager. As her title suggests, Lantry's proposal calls for the hiring of shift managers to assist the store manager. Reading critically, you should be sensitive to the rhetorical situation in which Lantry was writing. She had just accepted a job as manager and was now asking that shift managers be hired to help her do her job. How do you imagine Lantry's employers would respond to her proposal? How could she argue convincingly for hiring assistant managers without leading her employers to conclude that she could not handle her new responsibilities? Keep these questions in mind as you read and analyze Lantry's proposal.

I have been working for the California Yogurt Company for over a 1 year and, as you know, have recently accepted the position of manager of the Del Mar store. Now I am faced with my first managerial problem and would appreciate your support for this proposal.

Let me begin by admitting that my inexperience is part of the problem. 2 I find it hard to manage sixteen- and seventeen-year-olds who don't work responsibly and who treat me more as a friend than as an authority. Many of the fourteen counter employees confide in me about personal as well as work problems. Although I enjoy having a personal relationship with them and think that maintaining good rapport is part of my job, I feel awkward managing people I am friendly with. This problem is exacerbated by the fact that they sometimes take advantage of my friendliness. On more than one occasion, I have walked into the store to find counter personnel talking to each other instead of waiting on customers, or serving customers too casually. Things are also not kept as clean as I like or the company expects.

In fact, I have noticed that most of the counter employees work well   3
only when I am present—and even then some fool around too much.
Perhaps they are too immature. They seem to forget what they are supposed to do unless they are constantly reminded. Many are shy and
uncomfortable waiting on strangers and would rather talk with one another than attend to customers. They also lack initiative. Instead of
simply getting containers from the storeroom when they run low, for
example, they wait for me to order them to do so.

I know that I need to learn to draw a line between being a friend and   4
being a manager, but I think the problem goes deeper. Possibly the former
manager did not train them well or clarify what was expected. Being so
young, unfocused, and unserious, they are sometimes very hard to manage. They need guidance, but would balk at anything too heavy-handed.
If they felt harassed, they would not become more outgoing and efficient,
but more morose and lackadaisical.

Whatever the reasons for employees' letting down when the manager   5
is not around, it is a serious problem not only for me personally but also
for the company as a whole. Obviously my employees' performance reflects on my ability to hire and manage people. But more important,
customers might be unhappy with the service and not return. My store
is blessed with hundreds of regular customers who come in several times
a week for their frozen yogurt "fix." If they were unhappy with us, they
could easily take their patronage to Froglanders, the yogurt store nearby.
Also, someone interested in buying a franchise who stopped by unan-
nounced when I am not there might decide against owning a store for
fear it would require too much time and effort.

The counter employees themselves probably suffer most from their own   6
bad work habits. They get caught up in a vicious cycle. When customers
get annoyed with their gruffness and inefficiency, for example, they get
discouraged and more careless. When they do not keep busy or keep the
store clean, they get demoralized and even lazier. Working responsibly
in a clean, friendly environment promotes integrity and a positive self-
image. It would be unfortunate if these fine young people were to go
away from their first work experience feeling that they had failed and
that work was boring and unsatisfying.

I've struggled to find a solution to this complicated problem. One   7
solution I've considered is to spy on the employees to see who is working
and who isn't when I'm not around. Spying, however, shows I don't trust
them and would be sure to ruin the friendly feeling I've tried hard to
develop in the store. Another possible solution would be to fire those
whose performance is substandard, but that seems too rash for a correct-
able problem and would likely destroy the others' motivation. Firing

employees seems appropriate only when they have been forewarned and failed to improve.

The best solution would be to have a manager on every shift to en- 8 courage counter employees to do their best and to monitor their performance. Not only would the shift manager be a model of good work habits, but he or she could also give employees immediate positive—and negative—reinforcement. A shift manager behind the counter maintaining company standards would, I think, increase employees' morale. Shift managers would help clarify what is expected of each employee and could make sure that each person gets a diversity of tasks. By clarifying expectations and reducing the monotony of doing a single task repeatedly, shift managers would help increase job satisfaction. Having an authority present at all times will lead to quicker resolution of petty conflicts and give employees less opportunity to hold grudges against one another, helping to maintain the friendly atmosphere.

If the best and most responsible counter staff could be promoted to 9 shift manager, the increase in morale and efficiency would far outweigh the added salary costs. It would not cost very much: a fair pay raise might be twenty-five to fifty cents per hour. I think those with leadership potential and drive would go after the promotion. It might not mean much money, but with only a few additional duties they would gain immensely in status and self-esteem. Only three shift managers would be needed for each store, but the possibility of a future promotion would give added incentive to the rest of the counter employees. Because so few employees think of their jobs as long term, we have not been able to use promotion as an incentive. I am one of only a handful of people who have moved up from counter employee to store manager. The possibility of becoming a shift manager with its additional salary, but without the heavy responsibility of being store manager, might encourage some of our best people to stay on after the summer.

Unlike the store manager, who has to do a great deal of paperwork, 10 shift managers would be able to work next to the counter staff all the time. Their supervision would seem natural, not punitive. Each shift would work together as a team, with the shift manager serving as captain. We might even set up a friendly competition among the shifts to help build morale.

To make this plan work, we would not have to give shift managers 11 extra training. As expert counter workers, they already know the routine and company standards. They would be able to train new people and supervise the others immediately. They could get advice on how to handle recalcitrant employees from regularly scheduled meetings with the other shift managers and the general store manager. At these meetings, we would identify problem workers and figure out how to deal with them. Since counter employees are always rearranging their schedules, the shift managers will probably have had a chance to work with nearly everyone. This arrangement will also allow me to maintain a friendly but business-like relationship with the counter personnel. I would mediate between counter employees and shift managers, but not have to make my presence felt all the time.

For a small amount of money, the California Yogurt Company could    12 gain a great deal. Efficiency would be improved, standards of cleanliness upheld, morale increased, and our tradition of friendly service continued.

## QUESTIONS FOR ANALYSIS

1. Why do you think Lantry begins her proposal by admitting she is inexperienced? What advantage or disadvantage do you see in this way of beginning? Specifically, what effect might it have on her credibility?

2. Lantry is only a few years older than her employees, yet she talks about them as if they were a different generation. Take inventory of the language she uses to describe her teenage employees. What attitudes and values are implied by her word choices? Why might she view her employees in this way?

3. How successfully does Lantry explain the causes and effects of the problem to her employer? Drawing on your own experience with teen-agers in comparable situations, how would you amend Lantry's explanation?

4. Before proposing her own solution, Lantry dismisses two alternative solutions. How does rejecting these particular alternatives increase the likelihood that her employer will adopt her solution? What other solutions can you think of that Lantry might have anticipated?

5. Evaluate Lantry's argument for her proposed solution. How well does she anticipate her employer's objections?

6. Lantry apparently did no research for this proposal, but relied totally on her own observation and understanding. What kinds of research could she have done? How would this research have strengthened her argument?

## SUGGESTIONS FOR WRITING

1. Identify a problem where you work and write a letter to your employer explaining the problem and proposing a solution. You will probably have to convince your employer that the problem is serious and that

your solution can be easily and inexpensively implemented. Employers often give rewards for creative solutions to problems, no matter how small or insignificant they may seem.

2. Identify a problem on your campus and write a proposal on how it could be solved. Address your proposal either to a particular person in a position of authority or to the campus community at large by writing a letter to the college newspaper.

# A Look at Elizabeth Lantry's Writing Process

Unlike some of her classmates, Lantry had no difficulty choosing a subject for her proposal. She had just taken a job managing a frozen yogurt store and was having a hard time getting the counter crew to do their jobs responsibly when she was not present. She decided to write a proposal in class that she could later give to her employer.

Initially, she could not decide how much to explain about the workings of the store, her own job, and the duties of the counter staff. In her first draft, she did not include much detail of this sort, but the two classmates who read her draft told her that they needed more background information. To accommodate them, Lantry added a lot of detail to the draft before handing it in to her instructor.

When the essay was returned to her, Lantry was disappointed with the grade and confused by the instructor's concluding question: "Who are you addressing in this proposal?" Lantry went to see her instructor and they discussed her essay. She realized that she had had two conflicting readers in mind—her classmates and her employer. The information needed by her classmates was not necessarily the same information needed by her employer. Lantry understood that she had to choose between these different audiences and that the right choice for her was the employer. Her instructor assured her that if she revised the essay, he would reread it as if he were her employer. His judgment would be determined by how convincingly she analyzed the problem and argued for her solution.

Not quite sure how much rewriting she would need to do, Lantry looked over her invention notes and made some new notes about her reader. For each point she raised, she tried to anticipate what her employer would say. If she could not imagine his response, she thought how she would respond if she were the employer and her store manager came to her with this proposal.

Lantry was so pleased with the changes she made—and with her instructor's reaction to her revision—that she gave the proposal to her employer. He was delighted that she had gone to the trouble to write it and promised to give it serious consideration.

## A  GUIDE  TO  PROPOSAL  WRITING

As the proposals in this chapter illustrate, a proposal has two basic features: the problem and the solution. To establish that the problem exists and is serious, the proposal writer usually offers a detailed analysis of the problem, including facts, examples, and statistics. To convince readers to accept the solution offered, the writer presents an argument, often anticipating possible objections, rejecting alternative solutions, and demonstrating how the proposed solution can be easily implemented.

Proposal writing requires careful planning. The writer must not only determine exactly what the problem is and how to solve it, but must also consider how readers will respond to the argument. The following guide to invention, drafting, and revising divides this complex writing task into smaller, more manageable parts and leads you systematically through each stage of the process.

# *Invention*

Invention refers to the process of discovery and planning by which you generate something to say. The following invention activities will help you to choose a problem to write about, analyze it and identify a solution, consider your readers, develop an argument for your proposed solution, and research your proposal.

CHOOSING A PROBLEM. The readings in this chapter offer solutions to a range of challenging social problems, and various suggestions for writing follow each one. Unless you have either special knowledge of a social or political problem or adequate time to conduct research, you should choose a problem that concerns a local group in which you now participate.

Begin the selection process by listing several groups to which you presently belong—for instance, your neighborhood, film society, dormitory, sports team, biology class, or church group. For each group, list as many problems facing it as you can. If you cannot think of any problems for a particular organization, consult with other members. Then reflect on your list of problems, and choose the one for which you would most like to find a solution. It can be a problem that everyone already knows about or one that only you are aware of.

ANALYZING THE PROBLEM AND IDENTIFYING A SOLUTION. You can profitably analyze the problem by exploring it in writing. Jot down what you now know about the problem, how you know it is a problem, and why you think it is serious. Compare this problem to others you know about. Consider how it came about and what ill effects it produces by remaining unsolved.

This analysis of the problem will probably lead you to possible solutions. If no solution is apparent, one of the following creative problem-solving procedures may help:

Solve one small aspect of the problem.

Find out how a comparable problem has been solved.

Develop a solution that eliminates one or more of the problem's causes.

Think of another way to categorize the problem.

Envision the problem in another medium or context.

Consider how another person you respect (someone you know personally or a historical or fictional figure) might solve the problem.

If you cannot think of an original solution, investigate ones that others have proposed. At some point, you will need to consider alternative solutions anyway and how they compare to your own. Remember that your solution does not have to be original, but it should be one you feel strongly about.

To test the feasibility of your solution, try listing the steps that would be necessary in order to implement it. Such an outline of steps might be used later to convince readers that the solution will indeed work.

CONSIDERING YOUR READERS. Since you want your proposal to be persuasive, you first need to have some idea of who your readers will be and what they will find convincing. Will you be writing to other members of your group, to an outside committee, to an individual in a position of authority? Once you have particular readers in mind, you can decide how much they already know about the problem and what solutions they might prefer. Consider what values and attitudes you share with your readers and how they have responded in the past to similar problems.

DEVELOPING AN ARGUMENT. In order for your proposal to succeed, it must present a convincing argument based on sound reasoning and evidence. Begin constructing an argument by listing reasons and evidence—facts, statistics, examples, testimony from witnesses or authorities—supporting each reason. Try to imagine how your prospective readers will respond. If it helps, pretend to be one particular person (real or imaginary) responding to each reason. Defend your solution against objections such as these: it won't really solve the problem, we can't afford it, there isn't enough time, no one will cooperate, it's already been tried, I don't see how to even get started, you're making this proposal because it will benefit you personally.

As part of your argument, compare your solution to alternative solutions by weighing the strengths and weaknesses of each. Then, demonstrate to readers that your solution has more advantages and fewer disadvantages. Also, show readers how relatively easy it will be to implement your solution.

RESEARCHING YOUR PROPOSAL. If you are writing about a problem in a group to which you belong, talk to other members of the group to learn more about their understanding of the problem. You might even try out your solution on one or two people; their objections and questions will help you sharpen your own ideas.

If you are writing about a larger social or political problem, you should do research in order to confirm what you remember and to learn more about the problem. You can probably locate all the information you need in a good research library; you could also interview an expert on the problem. Readers will not take you seriously unless you seem well informed.

# *Drafting*

Once you have completed the invention activities, you can use your exploratory writing and the notes you have compiled as the basis for a rough draft. Before you begin writing, however, you should set goals and decide on a tentative plan for your draft.

SETTING GOALS. Before writing you should set some goals for your essay that reflect your readers' concerns and your purpose for writing. Consider, for example, how your readers are likely to view the problem. If they are unfamiliar with it, you will have to inform them, as Hart does in citing statistics. If they are vaguely aware of the problem but not inclined to take it seriously, you will have to demonstrate its seriousness, as Mackey and Appleman do by reporting their research into the problem. If readers have a narrow understanding of the problem, you may have to redefine it for them, as Kennan does in showing that the solution we have been following has itself become a problem. Consider also, in arguing for your proposed solution, how you can acknowledge your readers' legitimate concerns. Notice how Hart, recognizing that many readers would oppose making a military draft part of a mandatory national service, modifies his own proposal.

Given your readers and purpose, you should also consider what tone to adopt. Lantry, like Mackey and Appleman, takes a businesslike tone. Hart and Kennan try to by inspirational. Krauthammer adopts a sarcastic tone in order to undermine the alternative solutions others have proposed. Swift uses irony to get readers to see the horrific dimensions of the problem and the false beneficence of some would-be problem solvers.

PLANNING YOUR ORGANIZATION. Determining what your readers presently think and what you want them to think will help you not only formulate goals but also determine how to organize your proposal. If your readers are already familiar with the problem, for example, you may need only to refer to it in passing. If, however, they have never thought about the problem or have not perceived it in the way you want them to, you should probably spend some time right away explaining the problem.

Here is a general plan you might follow if your prospective readers have already considered other solutions to the problem:

Identify the problem.

Describe your proposed solution.

Discuss the advantages of your solution as compared to other solutions.

Restate the primary advantage of your proposed solution.

Swift, Kennan, and Hart follow this basic outline, while Krauthammer centers his essay around his refutation of alternative solutions and Mackey and Appleman devote most of their essay to an analysis of the problem.

BEGINNING. Most proposal writers begin by presenting the problem. They may, like Kennan, assert its seriousness. They usually describe the problem in vivid detail to impress readers. Mackey and Appleman, Bly, and Swift all present examples to dramatize the problem. Krauthammer opens his essay with an arresting quote that calls attention to the paradoxical nature of the problem. Among our selections, only Hart begins with the solution. This is an appropriate strategy because he argues that his proposal will solve not one but two different problems.

AVOIDING LOGICAL FALLACIES. As you plan and draft your proposal, be particularly careful to avoid these logical fallacies:

Am I committing an *either/or fallacy* by presenting my solution as the only possible solution (ignoring or dismissing alternative solutions out of hand)?

Am I setting up alternative solutions or objections to my proposal as *straw men* (mentioning only the weak alternatives or objections that are easy to knock down)?

Am I guilty of *oversimplifying* (suggesting that the problem is less complicated and easier to solve than it really is)?

Am I making an *ad hominem* (Latin for "to the man") attack (criticizing or satirizing my opponents instead of addressing their ideas and arguments)?

# Revising

No amount of invention and planning can ensure that a draft will be complete and well organized. In fact, as you draft you are likely to discover new and important points and also to encounter problems that you could not have anticipated. Therefore, you should be prepared to do some rethinking and restructuring of your draft, particularly when you are writing a proposal or any other complicated essay.

Begin by reading your draft thoughtfully and critically, using the critical reading questions at the beginning of this chapter. If possible, try to have someone else read your draft too.

REVISING TO STRENGTHEN YOUR ARGUMENT. When revising, keep in mind the dual purpose of your proposal: to inform readers about the problem and to convince them to accept your solution. Try to be even more specific in presenting the problem, demonstrating that it exists and explaining why it is serious. Always keep your readers in mind as you work to strengthen your argument. Show that your solution really solves the problem, and describe in detail how it can be implemented. Compare the proposed solution to alternative solutions in order to argue the advantages of your own. Reconsider your assumptions. Identify your underlying values and beliefs and determine whether your readers share them. If they do, try to make this bond even stronger by stating the assumptions directly. If they do not share your values, determine the values and beliefs you do share and try to build your argument on these.

REVISING TO IMPROVE READABILITY. Make an outline of your draft in order to see its organization more objectively. If you think readers will find the structure too complicated or confusing, reorganize your points or make the connections between one part and the next more obvious. Rewrite any unclear writing—language that is too abstract, indirect, or garbled. Finally, proofread your draft carefully; check for any mistakes in usage, spelling, and punctuation.

# CHAPTER NINE

## Position Paper

Chapter 8 focused on proposals, a pragmatic kind of writing used to solve problems and to get things accomplished. This chapter introduces the position paper, a related kind of writing that plays a central role in civic life. While the proposal solves problems, the position paper debates opinions on controversial issues. Proposals have a specific, practical purpose; position papers tend to be more general and philosophical. If you were concerned, for example, about the problem of drug abuse on high school campuses, you might write a proposal recommending that students' lockers be searched. If, however, you were concerned about the issue of whether schools have the right to infringe on students' privacy by searching their lockers without permission, you would write a position paper instead. Debating such issues produces many of the laws that govern our lives, determine the kinds of schools we attend, the sort of medical care we receive, the quality of life we enjoy. Entering the debate on these issues is a sign of full, responsible citizenship.

Position papers are written on issues that are controversial, issues upon which reasonable people disagree, sometimes vehemently. Simply gathering information will not settle these disputes, although the more that is known about an issue, the more informed the opinions on the issue will be. What is needed is an airing of the arguments on all sides of the issue. Only when debate is open and vigorous can we fully understand what is at stake and hope to reach a consensus of opinion.

As citizens in a democracy, we have a duty to inform ourselves about the issues and to participate actively in the public debate over them. As college students, you can expect to read and write position papers in many of your courses, particularly in philosophy, history, and political science. Even in biology, you may have the opportunity to explore the issue of creationism or animal experimentation. By arguing for your opinion and defending it against possible objections, you learn to think critically. You not only examine the opinions and reasoning of others but also look objectively at your own values and assumptions. Writing position papers brings you into communication with other people. It leads you to discover ways to bridge the gap between yourself and others, to recognize where you disagree and where there might be common ground for agreement.

## A GUIDE TO READING POSITION PAPERS

Although reading position papers can be intellectually challenging, the task will become easier if you are familiar with some of the basic features and strategies of this kind of writing. This section describes these features, illustrates them with a brief, annotated position paper, and provides a list of key questions to help you read position papers critically.

# Basic Features of Position Papers

Writers of position papers usually feel strongly about the issues they write about, and they strive to convince readers to accept their opinions as valid and reasonable. To achieve this end, position papers typically include the following features: *a well-defined, controversial issue; a clear position on the issue; a convincing argument;* and *a reasonable tone.*

A WELL-DEFINED, CONTROVERSIAL ISSUE. Although the issue addressed in the position paper may be complex, it should be carefully defined so that readers understand exactly what is at stake and why the issue is important. Moreover, the issue must be not only controversial but also arguable. Some issues upon which there is considerable debate are not arguable because they can either be resolved by fact or are so deeply rooted in belief that they are impervious to fact or reason. For example, arguing over which river is the longest in the world is pointless because the answer is a simple matter of fact that can be easily demonstrated. Arguing over matters of faith is just as pointless, for somewhat more subtle reasons. The issue of whether abortion should be legal, for example, is not arguable for those who oppose abortion on religious grounds. The best issues for position papers are matters of opinion—judgments rather than certainties. Fact and beliefs should be brought to bear on these issues but cannot easily resolve them.

A CLEAR POSITION ON THE ISSUE. A position paper makes explicit the opinion it advocates by announcing it directly in a thesis statement, which may appear at any point in the essay. In long, complicated essays, the thesis may even be restated several times. Although it should be stated emphatically, the thesis can be modified in the course of the argument. In fact, qualifying a position to accommodate objections or limiting the conditions under which it is true strengthens rather than weakens an argument. What writers should avoid is equivocation, backing away or hedging so much that readers cannot determine what position is being taken. The thesis must be clear—neither ambiguous nor vague.

A CONVINCING ARGUMENT. A position paper does not merely assert an opinion; it also presents an argument designed to persuade readers that the opinion is valid and reasonable. Ideally, readers should be so impressed by the argument that they willingly give up their own opinions and adopt the writer's. Arguments are rarely that convincing, however. It is more realistic to expect that readers might be persuaded to accept the legitimacy of the writer's position on the issue and to adjust their own opinion to accommodate what they have learned.

Writers argue persuasively primarily by appealing to the reader's sense of logic. An argument is convincing when it supports its claim with reasons and evidence—facts, statistics, testimony of authorities, and examples. Since opinions are also based on values and assumptions, however, a convincing argument must appeal to readers' feelings in addition to their reason. This does not mean that good arguments should be manipulative but that they should be responsive to readers' needs and feelings. To be effective, an argument addresses the whole person.

A REASONABLE TONE. In debating controversial issues, writers naturally assume that their readers will either disagree with them or be skeptical. Because they seek to build bridges between their own opinions and those of others, writers of position papers typically adopt a tone that will be perceived as reasonable and trustworthy. Even when challenging their readers' basic assumptions about deeply felt issues, writers try to inspire respect and confidence. They attempt to demonstrate their good will and understanding by anticipating objections to their argument and, whenever possible, by making concessions and qualifying their position to accommodate objections. Even when they cannot agree with readers' objections, writers of proposal papers nonetheless acknowledge these objections as legitimate and explain their reasons for rejecting them.

An Annotated Reading:
### *When Rights Collide*, Amitai Etzioni

A position paper deals with an important issue. People who are undecided about the issue might read to learn more about it, while those who already have a strong opinion might read to hear it defended or to find out how convincing a case can be made for the opposing viewpoint. Even those who are relatively uninterested in the issue might read a position paper for the sheer intellectual pleasure, testing their reasoning powers by trying to find gaps in logic, expose hidden assumptions, or reveal subtle ways in which the writer is trying to manipulate them.

Look now at a sample position paper, with annotations that might have been produced by any critical reader. As you read, consider how you would have annotated the essay differently.

This selection was written by Amitai Etzioni (b. 1929), a professor of sociology at Columbia University and director of the Center for Policy Research. Born in Germany in 1929, Etzioni was educated at Hebrew University and the University of California. He has written three books, all dealing with war: *A Diary of a Commando Soldier*, *The Hard Way to Peace*, and *Winning Without War*. This essay, "When Rights Collide," concerns the conflict between individual rights and the rights of society.

### *When Rights Collide*

| | |
|---|---|
| **Identifies opposing position: profreedom** | The viewpoint, now gaining momentum, that would allow individuals to "make up their own minds" about smoking, air bags, safety helmets, Laetrile, and the like ignores some elementary social realities. The ill-informed nature of this viewpoint is camouflaged by the appeal to values that are dear to most Americans. The essence of |
| **Etzioni's judgment** | the argument is that what individuals wish to do with their lives and limbs, foolhardy though it might be, is their own business, and that any interference would abridge their rights. |
| **Quotes authorities** | Mr. Gene Wirwahn, the legislative director of the American Motorcyclist Association, which is lobbying |

1

2

against laws requiring riders to wear helmets put it squarely: "The issue that we're speaking about is not the voluntary use of helmets. It's the question of whether or not there should be laws telling people to wear them."

**Agree on issue: individual freedom vs. government regulation**

State representative Anne Miller, a liberal Democrat in Illinois, favors legalization of Laetrile. She explains that she is aware that this apricot-pit extract is useless, but insists that "the government shouldn't protect people from bad judgment. They might as well bar holy water."

**Analogy comparing laetrile (disputed anticancer drug) to holy water; "useless" but gives hope**

U.S. representative Louis Wyman recently invoked much the same argument in leading the brigade that won adoption in the House of a resolution making seat belts voluntary. The 1974-model cars had been engineered not to start unless the seat belt was buckled. Wyman, a New Hampshire Republican, called the buckle-up system un-American, saying it made the government a Big Brother to auto drivers. Representative Abraham Kazen, Texas Democrat, summed it all up: "It is wrong to tell the individual what is good for him. . . . These are some of the things that the American people want to judge for themselves. Give them the equipment if they so desire, *and if they do not, let them do whatever they want.*"

**Allusion to *1984***

**Issue crosses party lines**

No civil society can survive if it permits each person to maximize his or her freedoms without concern for the consequences of one's act on others. If I choose to drive without a seat belt or air bag, I am greatly increasing my chances, in case of accident, of being impaled on the steering wheel or exiting via the windshield. It is not just my body that is jeopardized; my careening auto, which I cannot get back under control, will be more likely to injure people in other autos, pedestrians, or riders in my car. (Yes, my passengers choose their own fate when they decide to ride with me, but what about the infants who are killed and injured because they are not properly protected?)

**Asserts his own position & reasons**

**Reason #1: Individual acts have consequences for others.**

**Example—True?**

**Concession: adults different from kids**

American institutions were fashioned in an era of vast unoccupied spaces and preindustrial technology. In those days, collisions between public needs and individual rights may have been minimal. But increased density, scarcity of resources, and interlocking technologies have now heightened the concern for "public goods," which belong to no one in particular but to all of us jointly. Polluting a lake or river or the air may not directly damage any one person's private property or living space. But it destroys a good that all of us—including future generations—benefit from and have a title to. Our public goods are entitled to a measure of protection.

**Historical perspective**

**Reason #2: Individual acts might harm public goods.**

**Example: pollution**

**Reason #3: Taxpayer pays for individual's acts;** *irresponsible—* **needs definition**

The individual who chooses to act irresponsibly is playing a game of heads I win, tails the public loses. All too often, the unbelted drivers, the smokers, the unvaccinated, the users of quack remedies draw on public funds to pay for the consequences of their unrestrained freedom of choice. Their rugged individualism rapidly becomes dependency when cancer strikes, or when the car overturns, sending the occupants to hospitals for treatment

**Example: subsidies to hospitals and medical schools**

paid for at least in part by the public, through subsidies for hospitals and medical training. But the public till is not bottomless, and paying for these irresponsible acts leaves other public needs without funds.

**Concession**

True, totalitarian regimes often defend their invasions of individual liberties by citing public need or "national interest." One difference is that they are less concerned with protecting public goods than they are with building national power or new world orders. Instead of insisting on protection for *some* public rights, such regimes seek to

**Insists on moderation**

put the national interest above all individual rights. The lesson is that we must not allow any claim of public or

**Examine every suspect claim**

national need to go unexplained. But at the same time,

**Accuses opposition of name-calling**

we cannot allow simpleminded sloganeering (from "creeping Communism" to "Big Brother") to blind us to the fact that there are needs all of us share as a community.

**Reason #4: People don't always act in their own best interests.**

Last but not least, we must face the truth about ourselves. Are we the independent, self-reliant individuals the politicians like to tell us we are? Or are we a human combination of urges and self-controls, impulses and ra-

**True? Do adults need guidance?**

tional judgments? Can we trust ourselves to make wise judgments routinely, or do we at times have to rely on the laws our elected representatives have fashioned, with our consent, to help guide us? The fact is that driving slowly saves lives, lots of lives; but until we are *required* to do so, most of us drive too fast. The same holds true for buckling our seat belts, buying air bags, and so on. Similarly, we need protection from quack cures. It sounds

*libertarian:* **advocates liberty—naive**

very libertarian to argue that each person can make up his or her own mind about Laetrile. But the fact is that

**Comes back to laetrile Why it should be banned**

when confronted with cancer and fearful of surgery, thousands of Americans are tempted to try a "painless medication" first, often delaying surgery until it is too late.

**Summarizes argument**

All in all it is high time the oversimplifications about individual freedom versus Big Brother government were replaced by a social philosophy that calls for a balance

balance: key word but
appears at end for first
time

among the rights of *various* individuals, between individuals rights and *some* public rights, and that acknowledges the support we fallible individuals need from the law.

# Critical Reading Questions

These questions will help you to analyze and evaluate position papers on any issue. Refer to these questions as you read the selections in this chapter, and as you draft and revise your own position paper. To illustrate how these questions might be used, each has been applied to the sample position paper.

1. *How does the writer define the issue? Is it clearly arguable? What is at stake?*

This question might be difficult to answer since you may be inclined to view the issue somewhat differently than the writer does. Remember that the writer defines the issue not only to inform readers but also to convince them that it is important and ought to be seen in a particular way. In addition, writers often redefine issues that are already familiar, and they may do so in radically new terms. Even though you may eventually decide that the writer's definition of the issue is too narrow or simplistic, you should delay making a judgment until you have fully analyzed the argument and understand what the writer is trying to accomplish.

Etzioni assumes that most of his readers will regard regulations on such things as smoking, auto safety, and medication as isolated issues. He therefore must convince readers to accept his way of redefining the issue — that these particular issues are actually interrelated and that the more fundamental issue of government regulation versus individual freedom underlies and unites them. To do this, he quotes several authorities who have spoken out on these issues, demonstrating that he is not alone in redefining the issue in this way. By quoting these figures with whom he disagrees but whom he apparently respects, Etzioni strengthens his own credibility. This strategy also allows him to emphasize the importance of the issue. What is basically at stake, according to Etzioni, is our society's ability to function while at the same time maintaining respect for individual liberty. Defined in this way, the issue is not only controversial but also clearly arguable. It cannot be resolved by facts or faith alone.

2. *What exactly is the writer's position on this issue? How well is it distinguished from opposing positions? Are the opposing positions presented fairly?*

Writers of position papers typically set forth only two positions—one pro and the other con. Occasionally, however, an issue is so complicated that the writer's position must be placed in the context of several different positions. As a critical reader, you must first identify where the writer stands on the issue and the relation of the writer's position to the opposing positions. Then, decide whether the writer has represented the range of opinion on this issue fairly. If the opposing position is exaggerated or oversimplified, for example, the writer may have set up the opposition as a straw man, an unfair target established simply because it is so easily knocked down.

Etzioni sets up a debate between those who favor complete freedom for the individual and those who, like Etzioni, think some restrictions on individual freedom are necessary. Some readers might accuse Etzioni of exaggerating the opposing viewpoint, particularly in paragraph 6 when he speaks of "unrestrained freedom of choice." In fact, he accuses the opposition of oversimplifying the issue by defining it in either/or terms: either we have complete freedom or we have "Big Brother" totalitarianism. In your role as a critical reader, you will want to examine how Etzioni represents the opposing position and decide for yourself whether his credibility is in question or whether his criticism is well taken.

3. *How effectively does the writer argue for the position? What are the main reasons, and how well are they supported?*

To read a position paper critically, you must examine the reasoning to determine whether it is logical and convincing. Chapter 1 offers a strategy for analyzing and evaluating arguments that begins with outlining the main reasons and supporting evidence. An outline of Etzioni's argument might look like this:

Thesis: Individual freedom should have some restrictions

A. Because individual acts have consequences that affect others (car accidents)

B. Because individual acts may harm public goods (water and air pollution)

C. Because individual acts can cost the taxpayer (subsidies to hospitals and medical schools)

D. Because individuals do not always act in their own best interest
   1. Unsafe driving habits
   2. Inability to cope with serious illness

Once you have outlined the argument, evaluate how well each reason is developed and explained and determine whether it is adequately supported by the evidence. Some readers of Etzioni's argument might find fault with his third reason—that careless drivers in fact infringe on the rights of taxpayers, who wind up footing the hospital bill. A critical reader might have difficulty making this connection. Taxes may help subsidize hospitals and doctors' education, but does that really mean that the public is paying careless drivers' hospital bills? Don't they have to pay their own bills? Or is Etzioni referring to people who cannot afford to pay their own bills, in which case the issue is not individual rights versus government regulation but something else altogether?

4. *How effectively does the writer handle objections? Are valid objections acknowledged and invalid ones rebutted?*

Because the primary purpose of the position paper is to convince readers, writers typically try to anticipate objections that might be made to their argument. In reading critically, you must decide how well the writer anticipates possible objections and either accommodates or rebuts them. You must also determine whether these objections are represented fairly and whether any important objections have been left out. The way in which a writer handles possible objections affects not only the logical appeal of the argument but also the writer's credibility. If you feel that valid objections have been slighted or ignored altogether, your confidence in the writer's fairness will likely suffer. If, on the other hand, you think the writer has made every effort to acknowledge and accommodate reasonable objections, then you are more likely to respect and therefore accept the writer's opinion.

Etzioni acknowledges several objections to his argument. In paragraph 4, for example, he addresses an objection about the free choice of automobile passengers, although he does not state the objection explicitly. Notice that while he concedes that adult passengers are responsible for their own fate, he makes an exception in the case of infants, who must be taken care of by others. Similarly, in paragraph 7 Etzioni acknowledges that "national interest" is sometimes used as an excuse for the invasion of individual liberty. To prevent this abuse, he concedes that claims of national interest over individual freedom must be routinely examined.

5. *What tone does the writer adopt? How appropriate is this tone for the subject and audience?*

The tone of a position paper reflects the writer's attitude toward the subject and readers. If a position paper treats a serious issue with levity, readers might think the writer does not take it—or them—seriously. If, on the other hand, it is overly solemn, readers could think this earnestness is false or that the writer is being stuffy. Striking the right tone is surely the most difficult part of writing. As a critical reader, try to become more sensitive to the tone of a selection. Read passages aloud and with feeling to detect the writer's voice. Pay special attention to the words the writer chose to use and what other words could have been used. Why do you think the writer chose those particular words? Reflect on the overall impression the essay conveys and your image of the writer as a person.

From the beginning, Etzioni tries to impress readers with his directness. In the opening paragraph, he calls the opposing position "ill-informed" and asserts that it "ignores some elementary social realities." Notice that he is careful to avoid committing an *ad hominem* fallacy (attacking an opponent instead of the opponent's argument). He does not say his opponents are "ill informed," but that their viewpoint is. Moreover, rather than implying they are callous, he suggests that they may be naive. In this way, he represents himself as thoughtful and moderate.

6. *How well organized is the essay?*

Since position papers tend to be fairly complicated and the reasoning somewhat hard to follow, it is particularly important that they be carefully organized and provide cues to keep readers on track. Most position papers forecast their argument by listing the main reasons for the position taken before developing them. They also usually separate the parts of the argument—distinguishing the definition of the issue from the arguments pro and con—and offer transitions to label the divisions clearly. In especially complex arguments, writers may number the points or summarize before going on to the next part of the argument.

Etzioni's essay is so brief and relatively uncomplicated that he does not bother forecasting, although he does conclude with a sentence summary of his main points. By treating each major reason in a paragraph of its own, he makes the argument easy to follow. To avoid making the argument seem mechanical, he omits unnecessary transitions (except for "Last but not least" in the penultimate paragraph).

# A Debate on Liberal Education

Liberal education has long been a Western ideal, one that dates back to the ancient Greeks. Plato espoused the idea in *The Republic*, claiming that the essence of education is love "not of a part of wisdom only, but of the whole." Over the centuries, however, people have argued that liberal education is, among other things, elitist, ethnocentric, and irrelevant.

The value of knowing a little about everything has become especially questionable in an age of increasing specialization. As a college student, you will find this issue particularly significant because it affects how you will spend the next four years. Students at some schools are required to complete a core curriculum of courses in the liberal arts—history, literature, philosophy, and foreign language—before specializing in a major, while students at other schools may begin work on their majors from the start.

The two selections that follow take up radically different positions on the value of a liberal arts education. In the first piece, Robert C. Solomon defends liberal education as a remedy for the widespread ignorance of today's college students. Caroline Bird, in the second essay, criticizes people like Solomon who, she feels, set up the liberal arts as a religion and place themselves in the position of high priests.

# Robert C. Solomon

Robert C. Solomon (b. 1942) is a philosopher and a college professor who has had firsthand experience at public and private college across the nation. As an undergraduate, he studied at the University of Pennsylvania and received his Ph.D. from the University of Michigan. Before assuming his present position at the University of Texas at Austin, he taught at Princeton University, the University of Southern California, and the University of Pittsburgh.

Solomon has written many books on the history of philosophy, including *Nietzsche* (1973), *Introducing Philosophy* (1977), and *History and Human Nature: A Philosophical Review of European History and Culture, 1750–1850* (1979). His experience as a student and a teacher, together with his study of philosophy, led him to conclude that the average college student of the eighties desperately needs a broad liberal education. Because he felt the issue should be of interest to the general public and not just to academics, Solomon published his essay "Culture Gives Us a Sense of Who We Are" (1981) in the *Los Angeles Times*, a newspaper read by over a million people.

# Culture Gives Us
## a Sense of Who We Are

Solomon wrote this essay for a broad general audience in order to raise people's awareness of the issue. Knowing Solomon's audience and his purpose for writing should lead you as a critical reader to anticipate his writing strategies. What tone will he adopt? What assumptions will he make about his readers and their knowledge of liberal arts education?

As the title indicates, Solomon uses the idea of culture as the crux of his argument. Obviously, he will have to define what he means by this central term. Before you begin reading, take a moment to define the term for yourself. What do *you* mean by *culture*? How important is culture to you? Then, as you read the essay, pay close attention to the way Solomon uses the word. How does he define *culture*? Does he assume there is only one culture or several subcultures? Can culture really be taught by a liberal arts education? Should it?

In our aggressively egalitarian society, "culture" has always been a suspect word, suggesting the pretentions of an effete and foolish leisure class, like the grand dames spoofed in Marx Brothers' films. But the pretentions of a self-appointed cultural elite notwithstanding, "culture" actually refers to nothing more objectionable than a system of shared symbols and examples that hold a society together. Within a culture we are kindred spirits, simply because we understand one another.

A recent and somewhat frightening Rockefeller Foundation study on the state of the humanities in American life reported that the vast majority of even our most educated citizens are ignorant of the common literature and history that reinforce not only cultural identity but also moral choices. Doctors, lawyers and business executives are in positions of great responsibility, but often have little or no training in the ethical background that makes their critical choices meaningful.

Across our society in general, we find ourselves increasingly fragmented, split into factions and "generation gaps"—which now occur at two- or three-year intervals—just because the once-automatic assumption of a shared culture, something beyond shared highways, television programming and economic worries, is no longer valid.

In our schools, according to the Rockefeller report, the problem lies largely in what has recently been hailed as the "back to basics" movement, which includes no cultural content whatsoever, just skills and techniques. Reading is taught as a means of survival in the modern world, not as a source of pleasure and of shared experience. The notion of "great books" is viewed by most educators as an archaic concept, relegated to

480

the museum of old teaching devices, such as the memorization in Greek of passages from Homer.

But are "great books" (and legends, poems, paintings and plays) indeed   5
the only conduit of culture, or have they been replaced by more accessible and effortless media of transmission—television, for example, and films?

Films, to be sure, have entered into our cultural identity in an ex-   6
tremely powerful way; indeed, it is not clear that a person who knows nothing of Bogart or Chaplin, who has never seen (young) Brando or watched a Western could claim to be fully part of American culture. But these are classics, and they have some of the same virtue as great books; their symbols, characters and moral examples have been around long enough to span generations and segments of our population, and to provide a shared vocabulary, shared heroes and shared values. No such virtue is to be found in television series that disappear every two years (or less), films that survive but a season or "made-for-TV" movies with a lifetime of two hours minus commercial breaks.

"Television culture" is no culture at all, and it is no surprise that,   7
when kids change heroes with the season, their parents don't (and couldn't possibly) keep up with them. The symbolism of *Moby Dick* and *The Scarlet Letter*, however much we resented being force-fed them in school, is something we can all be expected to share. The inanities of *The Dukes of Hazzard*, viewed by no matter how many millions of people, will not replace them.

The same is true of our musical heritage. The Beatles are only a name   8
to most 12-year-olds. Beethoven, by contrast, continues to provide the musical themes we can assume (even if wrongly) that all of us have heard, time and time again. This isn't snobbery; it's continuity.

A professor recently wrote in the *Wall Street Journal* that he had men-   9
tioned Socrates in class (at a rather prestigious liberal arts college) and had drawn blanks from more than half the students. My colleagues and I at the University of Texas swap stories about references that our students don't catch. Even allowing generous leeway for our own professional prejudices and misperceptions of what is important, the general picture is disturbing. We are becoming a culture without a culture, lacking fixed points of reference and a shared vocabulary.

It would be so easy, so inexpensive, to change all that; a reading list   10
for high school students; a little encouragement in the media; a bit more enlightenment in our college curricula.

With all of this in mind, I decided to see just what I could or could   11
not assume among my students, who are generally bright and better educated than average (given that they are taking philosophy courses, hardly an assumed interest among undergraduates these days). I gave

them a name quiz, in effect, of some of the figures that, on most people's list, would rank among the most important and often referred to in Western culture. Following are some of the results, in terms of the percentage of students who recognized them:

Socrates, 87%; Louis XIV, 59%; Moses, 90%; Hawthorne, 42%; John 12 Milton, 35%; Trotsky, 47%; Donatello, 8%; Copernicus, 47%; Puccini, 11%; Charlemagne, 40%; Virginia Woolf, 25%; Estes Kefauver, 8%; Debussy, 14%; Giotto, 4%; Archduke Ferdinand, 21%; Lewis Carroll, 81%; Charles Dodgson, 5%; Thomas Aquinas, 68%; Spinoza, 19%; Moliere, 30%; Tchaikovsky, 81%; Darwin, 56%; Karl Marx, 65%; Faulkner, 43%; George Byron, 18%; Goethe, 42%; Raphael, 17%; Euripides, 8%; Homer, 39%; T.S. Eliot, 25%; Rodin, 24%; Mozart, 94%; Hitler, 97%; Wagner, 34%; Dante, 25%; Louis XVI, 25%; Kafka, 38%; Stravinsky, 57%; John Adams, 36%.

A friend who gave the same quiz to his English composition class got 13 results more than 50% lower on average.

I suppose that many people will think the quiz too hard, the names 14 often too obscure—but that, of course, is just the point. The students, interestingly enough, did not feel this at all—not one of them. They "sort of recognized" most of the names and felt somewhat embarrassed at not knowing exactly who these people were. There was no sense that the quiz was a "trivia" contest (as in, "What's the name of Dale Evans' horse?") and there were no accusations of elitism or ethnocentrism. The simple fact was that they knew these names were part of their culture, and in too many cases they knew that they weren't—but should be—conversant with them. Maybe that, in itself, is encouraging.

### QUESTIONS FOR ANALYSIS

1. Solomon opens his essay by suggesting that *culture* is a "suspect word" in our society. What advantages do you see in beginning the essay this way? What disadvantages?

2. What do you think constitutes our "common literature and history"? Make a list of literary works and historical events you think each member of society should be familiar with, and then compare your list to those made by your classmates. How do these lists compare with one another and with Solomon's list in paragraph 12? What can you conclude from comparing these lists?

3. Solomon asserts that this common literature and history should influence people's moral decisions. What do you think he means? Choose a single literary work or historical event from your list and conjecture about what moral training this particular work or event conveys.

4. Solomon refers to the notion of "great books." What are these books? Why are they considered great by some but "archaic" or outmoded by others? Why does Solomon think they still have value? Do you agree?

5. Summarize Solomon's argument about television, film, and music as conduits of culture. Then identify the weakest link in his argument, explaining why you think it is weak and how it might be strengthened.

6. In the last paragraph, Solomon suggests three possible objections to his argument. What are these objections? Select one of these objections, and build a case for it.

7. In paragraph 10, Solomon offers the barest outlines of a proposal. What role does this abbreviated proposal play in his position paper? Why do you suppose he merely hints at a proposal rather than presenting a fully elaborated one?

8. Solomon draws a distinction between the cultural values of film versus those of television. Examine this difference in depth, bringing your own experience to bear upon it. Do you agree with Solomon's preference for film? Given that he was writing for a general audience, why do you think he disparages television?

9. How would you characterize Solomon's tone in this essay? Does he seem elitist? If so, point to specific examples of elitism. If not, use evidence from the essay to defend him against charges of elitism.

### SUGGESTIONS FOR WRITING

1. Critical readers might argue that what Solomon (and Bird, in the next essay) is addressing is not whether a liberal or general education is valuable but whether the humanities—philosophy, literature, the arts, and history—should have an equal place with the sciences in our increasingly technological society. Write a position paper on this subject, clearly defining the central issue and stating your opinion about it.

2. Solomon characterizes television programs like *The Dukes of Hazzard* as "inane"; others go farther and call such programs harmful because they teach young, impressionable children that it is fun to disobey the law. At the heart of the controversy is the question of whether parents should limit or censor their children's television watching. Consider the pros and cons of this issue, and then write a position paper arguing for your own position.

3. Another controversy embedded in Solomon's essay involves the concept of "great books." Although he is willing to extend the concept

to include certain films and music, some may still find this idea limited and elitist. Write a position paper on the issue of "great books." What books, films, and music do you consider great? What are your criteria for including these particular works and excluding others? Do you think everyone should study the works you consider great? Why or why not?

# Caroline Bird

Caroline Bird (b. 1915) graduated from Vassar College and did graduate work in sociology at the University of Toledo and the University of Wisconsin. A member of the American Sociological Association, Bird was Froman Distinguished Professor at Russell Sage College. She is a strong advocate of women's rights, serving on the national advisory committee of NOW (the National Organization for Women) and as a director of the Equity Action League.

Bird began her writing career as a researcher for *Newsweek* and *Fortune* magazines. Since then, she has contributed many articles to national magazines and written numerous books, including *The Crowding Syndrome* (1972), *Everything a Woman Needs to Know to Get Paid What She's Worth* (1973), and *The Case Against College* (1975).

# The Liberal Arts Religion

This selection is a chapter in *The Case Against College*, a book which aims to provide potential college students and their parents with "some realistic help in deciding whether the promotional claims" for college are justified. Read the selection with this purpose and audience in mind. But before beginning, ask yourself what is implied in the title "The Liberal Arts Religion." What can you infer about Bird's attitude and tone from this title?

The academic dean of a famous old college lowered her voice, glanced 1 apprehensively around her office, and confessed: "I just wish I had the guts to tell parents that when you get out of this place you aren't prepared to *do anything*."

Actually, it did not take much guts. The "best" colleges are the liberal 2 arts schools which are the most "academic"—they don't teach students anything useful in particular. Even after they have to face the world, alumni expect no more. In a study intended to probe what graduates seven years out of college thought their colleges should have given them, the Carnegie Commission found overwhelming preference for "liberal" over "vocational" goals.[1]

What does anyone mean by "a liberal education"? People shift their 3 ground when they try to explain what it is and why it is so important. It's hard to tell whether they're talking about *subjects* that can be studied in school, such as philosophy and literature; a *process* of learning or thinking; or a *personal transformation* ("college opened my eyes"); or a *value system* to which the wise and honest can repair.

The *subject matter* of the liberal arts used to be the classics. If not the   4
ancients, then newer books on history, sociology, economics, science, and other products of the minds of men. As we near the twenty-first century, however, most educators have given up the attempt to pass on the "great tradition of Western man" in a four-year core curriculum. It's not *what* you study, they say, it's *how* you study it.

"A liberal education is an experience that is philosophical in the broad-   5
est sense," David Truman, dean of Columbia and later president of Mount Holyoke, has said. "The particular subjects do not so much contain this quality as provide jointly a possible means of approaching it. The liberal arts, then, include those subjects that can most readily be taught so as to produce an understanding of the modes of thought, the grounds of knowledge, and their interrelations, established and to be discovered."

In plainer language alumni say, "College taught me how to think for   6
myself." If you ask people what they mean by thinking and how college teaches it, they recoil from the implication that the kind of thinking they mean is a specific skill, such as the art of rhetoric, but start talking about a "whole new way of looking at the world"—a personal transformation.

Personal transformation, not only in how one's mind works but in how   7
one views the world and oneself, is the most cherished expectation— and sometimes it is achieved. "College changed me inside," one alumnus told us. Some wax poetic. "The liberal arts education aspires to expand the imaginative space and time in which a person lives." Others talk about the "broadening" that occurs when a young woman from a Midwest farming town encounters adults who don't regret the fact that MacArthur was not elected President, or when the son of a city plumber learns that the police are not always right and that some people on welfare aren't cheating. Discoveries like this are valuable, alumni say, because they force students to "formulate the values and goals of my life," as the Carnegie Commission puts it.

And this turns out to be the hidden agenda of a liberal arts education.   8
A value system, a standard, a set of ideals to keep you pointed in the right direction, even if you can't get there. "Like Christianity, the liberal arts are seldom practiced and would probably be hated by the majority of the populace if they were," said one defender.

The analogy is apt. The fact is, of course, that the liberal arts are a   9
religion in every sense of that term. When people talk about them, their

language becomes elevated, metaphorical, extravagant, theoretical, and reverent.

In answering a black student who charged the Kirkland College cur- 10 riculum with "irrelevance," President Samuel F. Babbitt remonstrated that her liberal arts education aimed to expose her "to the values, the successes, the failures of great minds, great men and women engaged in every conceivable endeavor through the study of history and literature and art and the other disciplines that man has formed in order to un- derstand where he has been and how to order his world."

"The purpose of the liberal arts is not to teach businessmen business," 11 Alfred Whitney Griswold, former president of Yale, told an alumni gath- ering. Rather, he went on, it is to "awaken and develop the intellectual and spiritual powers in the individual before he enters upon his chosen career, so that he may bring to that career the greatest possible assets of intelligence, resourcefulness, judgment, and character."

These thickets of verbal foliage are embarrassing to the more sensitive 12 spokesmen for higher education. John T. Retalliata, president of the Illinois Institute of Technology, told an audience of parents in 1973, "I suppose a generalized goal is to have your sons and daughters, somehow, become 'educated' and, with that education, become well-employed and happy." Clark Kerr, notable as the embattled president of the University of California during the 1960s, told a 1972 television audience that "generally, the studies show that people who've been to college, oh, enjoy life more, they have more varied interests, they participate more in com- munity activities." On another occasion, he told Alan Pifer, president of the Carnegie Corporation, that "with all that has happened in the world of knowledge in recent years, it is really impossible for people in higher education to come to agreement on what constitutes a liberal education."

Intellectuals have trouble describing the benefits of a liberal education 13 because the liberal arts are a religion, the established religion of the ruling class. The exalted language, the universal setting, the ultimate value, the inability to define, the appeal to personal witness, the indirectness, the aphorisms—these are all the familiar modes of religious discourse.

As with religion, no proof is required, only faith. You don't have to 14 prove the existence of God. You don't have to understand the Virgin Birth. You don't have to prove that Camus is better than Jacqueline Susann. Camus is sacred, so Camus is better and so are the people who dig him. If you don't dig Camus, the trouble is not with Camus, but with you.

Faith in personal salvation by the liberal arts is professed in a creed 15 intoned on ceremonial occasions such as commencements. It is blasphemy to take the promises literally, and if you don't understand what the words mean, you are only admitting your lack of grace.

Take, for instance, the goal of college most fervently sought by the 16 alumni queried by the Carnegie Commission, "development of my abilities to think and express myself." Only the captious dare to ask, "What do you mean by your ability to think?" If you inquire, it very quickly develops that those who value this objective aren't talking about what the Swiss educator Jean Piaget, the semanticist Noam Chomsky, or the Harvard psychologist Jerome Bruner mean when they talk about "thinking."[2] The kind of "thinking" the cognitive psychologists are talking about has to be acquired long before you are old enough to go to college, and if Piaget is right, most of it has to be learned before a child is old enough to go to school. What the alumni and employers expect college to teach is the habit of logical analysis and the conventions of rhetoric that make it possible to resolve differences of view on human affairs by debate and discussion. Colleges with very small classes try to give their students practice in the art of dialogue, but the students who speak up in class are usually the ones who have already learned how at the dinner table at home and in bull sessions with friends.

If the liberal arts are a religious faith, the professors are its priests. 17 Professors are not accountable to the laity they serve. They themselves define the boundaries of their authority and choose their own successors. Their authority is unassailable, because by definition they know best. As such, they are invulnerable to lay criticism. One of the educators with whom I talked dismissed the doubts of students out of hand. "I am not convinced that eighteen-year-olds can or should be expected to know what college will ultimately do for them."

The professors disclaim arbitrary personal power. They go by rules. 18 They contend that right is not what they think but what the sacred scriptures or the ecclesiastical courts decree. Professors say that truth is what comes out when you subject data to a process called the scientific method, and it is this process, rather than its product, that is written in the stars. But the process itself, this very scientific method, is also a product of the mind of man, and it may not be the only process the mind of man can devise. Other processes may produce other kinds of truth. No one, for instance, would suggest that the visions of William Blake could be "disproved" by the scientific method.

Colleges govern themselves by their own rules and sometimes confront 19 civil authority. Only during the 1960s, when the students were out of control, did college administrators admit the right of the local police to "invade" the campus. And, like the church, American colleges have used their credibility to exercise political, economic, and social power in an irresponsible way. Along with access to heaven, they don't mind controlling access to the good things of this world. So long as the diploma is a credential for good jobs, giving or withholding it determines the fate of students here on earth. The colleges do not claim that they are preparing candidates for executive work, for instance, but they do not renounce their role as gatekeeper of the best jobs. As one professor told us, "We can't help it that the big companies like to hire our graduates."

To be blunt, the colleges have been as willing as the church to grab 20 the power the faithful thrust upon them. Through their power to issue the diploma, they decide the fate of individuals. Through their power to determine who shall be admitted to college, they select as "naturally better" those who manipulate abstract symbols and unwittingly consign to the damnation of dead-end, second-class role, those whose intelligence is manual, visual, or artistic. The power we allow them to have makes our society more vulnerable to words and abstractions than it would otherwise be, and it is not necessary to have a settled opinion on whether this is good or bad to recognize the danger of subjecting young people during their formative years to control by authorities who are pursuing objectives that leave most of the population cold. We think they are benign, therefore we accept their rule over our young. Imagine the outcry at the very idea of turning our surplus young people over to the military for safekeeping!

Americans have always been sensitive to the attempts of their armed 21 forces to use military competence as a basis for exercising political power. But we do not distrust the same kind of bid when it comes from the professoriate. Through their control of research, they decide what frontiers of knowledge shall be pushed back. Through their interpretation of the scientific method, if not the sacred writings of "the great Western tradition," they decide what shall be accepted as good, or true, or even beautiful.

But just as technical progress threatened the various monopolies of the 22 church at the end of the Middle Ages, so the information explosion today threatens the monopoly of college over knowledge.

Of all the forms in which ideas are disseminated, the college professor 23 lecturing his class is the slowest and the most expensive. The culturally deprived for whom college is supposedly so broadening are in the best position to see this. "I can read a book just as good as the man can talk," a black woman student told us. "Nine chances out of ten that's all you get—a professor who's just reading out of the book."

A better college experience would, no doubt, have provided more 24 stimulation than students encountered in the overloaded colleges of the 1960s. But this begs the issue.

Today you don't have to go to college to read the great books. You 25
don't have to go to college to learn about the great ideas of Western
man. If you want to learn about Milton, or Camus, or even Margaret
Mead, you can find them. In paperbacks. In the public library. In museum
talks. In the public lectures most colleges offer for free. In adult education
courses given by local high schools. People don't storm these sources
because they aren't interested, and there's no particular reason why they
should be. Forcing people to "learn" about them by all sorts of social and
economic carrots and sticks implies that those who have had contact
with "high culture" are somehow better than other people.

And if you do want to learn, it isn't always necessary to go to the 26
original source. I say this knowing that I am stamping myself as an
academic heretic. But the culture consumer should be able to decide for
himself exactly why, when, how much, and in what form he would like
to partake of Daniel Defoe's *Robinson Crusoe*, or Milton's *Areopagitica*,
or Simone de Beauvoir's *The Second Sex*. When I was in high school
during the 1920s, the whole English class took a month to read *Ivanhoe*,
Sir Walter Scott's novel about the crusades. In 1969 my eight-year-old
son zipped through a Classic Comic version in fifteen minutes, and I
don't think the original warranted the extra time it would have taken
him. If you are not interested in the development of the English novel,
*Robinson Crusoe* can be an exasperating, slow-moving yarn, significant
only because the name has become a symbol of lone adventure and one
of the passwords recognized by all men who consider themselves educated. Milton's *Areopagitica* is another password, important for what it
says and when it was said. There's a benefit in knowing about these
works, but the benefit to any particular person at a particular time may
not justify the cost of taking them raw. For many people, and many
purposes, it makes more sense to read a summary, an abstract, or even
listen to a television critic.

The problem is no longer how to provide access to the broadening 27
ideas of the great cultural tradition, nor even how to liberate young
people so that they can adopt a different life-style than the one in which
they were reared. The problem is the other way around: how to choose
among the many courses of action proposed to us, how to edit the stim-
ulations that pour into our eyes and ears every waking hour. A college
experience that piles option on option and stimulation on stimulation
merely adds to the contemporary nightmare. Increasingly, overloaded
undergraduates give up the attempt to reason and flirt, half seriously,
with the occult, which leaves vexing decisions to fate.

In order to deal with options, you need values. When Morris Keeton 28
and Conrad Hilberry attempted to define a liberal education in their

book *Struggle and Promise: A Future for Colleges*, they found that one of the recurrent themes was that it provides "an integrated view of the world which can serve as an inner guide,"[3] and more than four-fifths of the alumni queried by the Carnegie Commission said they expected that their college should have "helped me to formulate values and goals of my life." The formation of values may not be the first goal mentioned in discussions of a liberal education, but it tends to be the final ground on which hard-pressed defenders take their stand.

How does a student acquire a standard of values? The liberally educated are forbidden, by their own creed, from any procedure so simple as telling students what is right and good. In theory a student is taught how to decide for himself, but in practice it doesn't work quite that way. All but the wayward and the saints take their values of the good, the true, and the beautiful from the people around them. When we speak of students acquiring "values" in college, we often mean that they will acquire the values—and sometimes we mean only the tastes—of their professors. 29

The values of professors may well be "higher" than many students can expect to encounter elsewhere, but often those values aren't relevant to the situations in which students find themselves in college or later. Too many academics systematically overvalue symbols and abstractions. Historians will recall that it was a professor of history, President Woodrow Wilson, who sent American soldiers abroad to "make the world safe for democracy." 30

In addition to a distressing confusion of symbol and thing, professors are sometimes painfully ignorant of many essential facts of life. A lot of them know very little about the economic structure of the United States, and their notions of what goes on inside major corporations are based on books written forty years ago about conditions prevailing fifty years ago. And they may also be partially responsible for some of the "alienation" of the young because they have encouraged the belief that transactions of power and money are to be avoided as a dirty business. 31

In so doing, of course, they are intuitively defending the legitimacy of their own power. A poor boy who wanted to make good in the Middle Ages had to become a priest and at least profess to see the world in spiritual terms. A poor boy who wants to make good in twentieth-century America has to get a liberal education and at least profess to see the world in intellectual terms. 32

The academic elite are the self-proclaimed guardians of what's right. Who's to tell them when they are wrong? Academics pride themselves on introducing students to a free marketplace of ideas, but they are the ones who make the rules, and the rules themselves can perpetuate dangerous distortions of reality. Not so long ago, for instance, no painter 33 who drew pubic hair on a nude figure could expect to be taken seriously as an artist. It would have been vulgar to see it. The oversight is amusing now, but it was not trivial. Victorian prudery was hard to combat because it was a convention of the "best people." It's easy to laugh, but harder to be sure that we are not overlooking some other facts of life today.

A liberal arts education does, of course, transmit standards of value, and those in charge assume, almost as self-confidently as that great Victorian, Matthew Arnold, that "the best that has been known and thought in the world" is what they say it is. Intellectual leaders today worry about sounding snobbish, but they are just as sure as the great eighteenth-century English essayist Richard Steele that "it is the great aim of education to raise ourselves above the vulgar." And those who have been so educated are happy to accept the distinction. At Harvard commencements there is an audible sigh of emotion when the president, as he has done for 300 years, welcomes the new graduates into "the fellowship of educated men." (Since 1970, it has been "the fellowship of educated men and women.") 34

## NOTES

1. "When alumni were forced to choose between a general education and a career-oriented education, they overwhelmingly endorsed the idea of a general education," Joe L. Spaeth and Andrew M. Greeley reported in *Recent Alumni and Higher Education*, a Carnegie Commission study published by McGraw-Hill, New York, in 1970. The study queried 40,000 graduates of the class of 1961 in 135 colleges in 1961, 1962, 1963, 1964, and 1968.

2. For a quick introduction to the slippery concepts involved in thinking about thinking, see the section "The Elements and Vehicles of Thought," pp. 188–237, in Berelson & Steiner, *Human Behavior, An Inventory of Scientific Findings*, Harcourt Brace, New York, 1964.

3. A dogged attempt to cope with the verbal foliage surrounding definitions of a liberal education appears in Morris Keeton and Conrad Hilberry's *Struggle and Promise: A Future for Colleges*, McGraw-Hill, New York, 1969, p. 260. They identify several common elements including cultivation of the intellect; encouragement of "independent judgment" or "critical thought"; liberating the individual so that he can see the world in perspectives other than his own; evoking an integrated view of the world which can serve as an inner guide; equipping the individual to serve his society.

## QUESTIONS FOR ANALYSIS

1. How does Bird use the opening paragraphs to establish that the issue is controversial and important?

2. Beginning with paragraph 3, Bird discusses several ways in which people have attempted to define a liberal education. What are these

definitions? Why do you think she spends so much time examining others' efforts to define the term?

3. How does Bird organize her argument? To answer this question, make a brief outline of her argument, indicating its main points and supporting evidence. (See the discussion of outlining an argument in Chapter 1.)

4. How does Bird develop the analogy between the liberal arts and religion? Considering how Bird uses analogy to support her argument, why do you suppose arguing by analogy is usually regarded as a weak argumentative strategy?

5. Another argumentative strategy Bird relies upon in this selection is citing authorities. Annotate the essay, noting each authority she refers to or quotes. Then take inventory of the different ways she uses authorities to support her argument. Does she ever misuse authorities either by setting them up as straw men (easy targets) or by making an *ad hominem* (unfairly personal) attack on them? From your analysis of Bird's use of authorities, what would you say are the strengths and weaknesses of this strategy?

6. What does Bird say is the role college professors play in making the liberal arts a religion? How much of Bird's attack on professors is based on an emotional appeal and how much is based on logic? Point to examples of both appeals to support your answer.

7. How does Bird attempt to redefine the issue in paragraphs 27 and 28? Do you agree or disagree that "a college experience that piles option on option and stimulation on stimulation merely adds to the contemporary nightmare"? What does this statement imply about the role of education?

8. Most of the sentences in this selection are long and fairly complicated, but a few are quite short. Find these short sentences. Why do you think Bird chose to put these ideas in sentences by themselves rather than combining them with other ideas in longer sentences?

9. What is Bird's tone, and how effective do you think it is? Does she come across as reasonable and trustworthy?

## SUGGESTIONS FOR WRITING

1. Bird quotes the former president of Yale University as saying that the purpose of the liberal arts is to "awaken and develop the intellectual and spiritual powers in the individual before he enters upon his chosen career, so that he may bring to that career the greatest possible assets

of intelligence, resourcefulness, judgment, and character." Should education prepare individuals for their careers even in this remote and indirect way? If the aim of education is career preparation, why is a liberal education preferable to vocational training? Write a position paper addressing this issue. Refer to relevant passages from "Culture Gives Us a Sense of Who We Are" and "The Liberal Arts Religion," but do not merely repeat Solomon's or Bird's arguments. Present your own opinion and your reasons for holding it.

2. In paragraph 13, Bird claims that the liberal arts are "the established religion of the ruling class." Some would argue further that all education—from elementary school through college—indoctrinates rather than educates. Write a position paper on some aspect of this issue. Be careful to define the issue before presenting your argument.

3. Bird raises another controversial issue in paragraph 26, claiming that "if you do want to learn, it isn't always necessary to go to the original source." Are Cliff Notes on Shakespeare or the Classic Comic versions of his plays really adequate substitutes for the firsthand, though difficult and time-consuming, experience of reading the originals? On the basis of your own experience, write a position paper arguing for your opinion on this issue.

## THE DEBATE:
## ADDITIONAL QUESTIONS FOR ANALYSIS

1. Apply Bird's analogy between the liberal arts and religion to Solomon's essay. In what ways do you think Solomon uses religious language in his defense of culture?

2. Contrast Solomon's and Bird's ideas about great books. Does Solomon expect people to accept the great books on faith, or does he offer reasons for their lasting value?

3. Both Solomon and Bird discuss the need for students to acquire a standard of values. Compare their views. Where should these values come from? What should they be? Why are they necessary?

4. How do you think Solomon would respond to Bird's argument that "today you don't have to go to college to read the great books" (paragraph 25)? How would you reply to Bird?

## A Debate on Capital Punishment

In 1972, the Supreme Court struck down existing laws that made it possible to sentence men and women to death. The Court, however, did not abolish capital punishment; it merely declared existing laws unconstitutional because they applied the death penalty arbitrarily. In fact, the ruling encouraged lawmakers in each of the fifty states to write new legislation. Since then the court system on both the state and federal levels has been busy adjudicating the constitutionality of these new laws. Despite innumerable legal challenges and delays, roughly 2,000 people have been sentenced to death and nearly seventy have been executed so far. In the next few years, many more executions may take place as the courts clarify what makes capital punishment legally acceptable.

Opinion on the issue of capital punishment understandably remains strongly divided. Many proponents of the death penalty claim that it deters potential murderers from committing murder and that it is a valid form of punishment. Opponents often argue that life imprisonment without the possibility of parole should be enough and that capital punishment is nothing more than unnecessarily cruel and socially demoralizing retribution.

The following selections represent three voices on this highly charged issue. The first selection is by Edward Koch, the mayor of New York City, who holds that the death penalty paradoxically "affirms life." In rebuttal, David Hoekema, a philosophy professor, argues that the death penalty has the contrary effect of legitimating murder. The concluding selection is by Margaret Mead, the respected anthropologist, who urges us to take a different perspective on the issue, to place it "within the context of our way of living and our view of human values."

# Edward Koch

Edward Koch (b. 1924) has been mayor of New York City since 1978. Educated at City College of New York, Koch received his law degree from New York University. He soon entered politics and served as a city councilman, state representative, and member of Congress before being elected mayor. An outspoken man, Koch often writes articles for local and national newspapers and magazines. Recently, with the aid of William Rauch, Koch wrote an autobiography entitled *Mayor* (1984), which focuses on New York City politics and his life in government.

# *Death and Justice*

In this selection, originally published in 1985 in *The New Republic*, Koch entered the public debate on capital punishment with an elaborate argument in favor of the death penalty. Koch naturally assumed that he would have some credibility with readers by virtue of his position as mayor. As you read, notice how he reminds readers of his position and tries to build on his authority. Also consider how knowing that Koch is an attorney and a politician influences your reading. Are you more or less critical of his reasoning?

Before reading, preview the title of the essay. What do the words *death* and *justice* mean to you? Why do you suppose Koch links them with *and* instead of *or*? What would be the difference?

Last December a man named Robert Lee Willie, who had been con-  1
victed of raping and murdering an 18-year-old woman, was executed in the Louisiana state prison. In a statement issued several minutes before his death, Mr. Willie said: "Killing people is wrong. . . . It makes no difference whether it's citizens, countries, or governments. Killing is wrong." Two weeks later in South Carolina, an admitted killer named Joseph Carl Shaw was put to death for murdering two teenagers. In an appeal to the governor for clemency, Mr. Shaw wrote: "Killing is wrong when I did it. Killing is wrong when you do it. I hope you have the courage and moral strength to stop the killing."

It is a curiosity of modern life that we find ourselves being lectured on  2
morality by cold-blooded killers. Mr. Willie previously had been con-victed of aggravated rape, aggravated kidnapping, and the murders of a Louisiana deputy and a man from Missouri. Mr. Shaw committed another murder a week before the two for which he was executed, and admitted mutilating the body of the 14-year-old girl he killed. I can't help won-dering what prompted these murderers to speak out against killing as they entered the death-house door. Did their newfound reverence for life stem from the realization that they were about to lose their own?

Life is indeed precious, and I believe the death penalty helps to affirm  3
this fact. Had the death penalty been a real possibility in the minds of these murderers, they might well have stayed their hand. They might have shown moral awareness before their victims died, and not after. Consider the tragic death of Rosa Velez, who happened to be home when a man named Luis Vera burglarized her apartment in Brooklyn. "Yeah, I shot her," Vera admitted. "She knew me, and I knew I wouldn't go to the chair."

During my 22 years in public service, I have heard the pros and cons  4
of capital punishment expressed with special intensity. As a district leader, councilman, congressman, and mayor, I have represented con-stituencies generally thought of as liberal. Because I support the death penalty for heinous crimes of murder, I have sometimes been the subject of emotional and outraged attacks by voters who find my position repre-hensible or worse. I have listened to their ideas. I have weighed their

objections carefully. I still support the death penalty. The reasons I maintain my position can be best understood by examining the arguments most frequently heard in opposition.

(1) *The death penalty is "barbaric."* Sometimes opponents of capital punishment horrify with tales of lingering death on the gallows, of faulty electric chairs, or of agony in the gas chamber. Partly in response to such protests, several states such as North Carolina and Texas switched to execution by lethal injection. The condemned person is put to death painlessly, without ropes, voltage, bullets, or gas. Did this answer the objections of death penalty opponents? Of course not. On June 22, 1984, *The New York Times* published an editorial that sarcastically attacked the new "hygienic" method of death by injection, and stated that "execution can never be made humane through science." So it's not the method that really troubles opponents. It's the death itself they consider barbaric.

Admittedly, capital punishment is not a pleasant topic. However, one does not have to like the death penalty in order to support it any more than one must like radical surgery, radiation, or chemotherapy in order to find necessary these attempts at curing cancer. Ultimately we may learn how to cure cancer with a simple pill. Unfortunately, that day has not yet arrived. Today we are faced with the choice of letting the cancer spread or trying to cure it with the methods available, methods that one day will almost certainly be considered barbaric. But to give up and do nothing would be far more barbaric and would certainly delay the discovery of an eventual cure. The analogy between cancer and murder is imperfect, because murder is not the "disease" we are trying to cure. The disease is injustice. We may not like the death penalty, but it must be available to punish crimes of cold-blooded murder, cases in which any other form of punishment would be inadequate and, therefore, unjust. If we create a society in which injustice is not tolerated, incidents of murder—the most flagrant form of injustice—will diminish.

(2) *No other major democracy uses the death penalty.* No other major democracy—in fact, few other countries of any description—are plagued by a murder rate such as that in the United States. Fewer and fewer Americans can remember the days when unlocked doors were the norm and murder was a rare and terrible offense. In America the murder rate climbed 122 percent between 1963 and 1980. During that same period, the murder rate in New York City increased by almost 400 percent, and the statistics are even worse in many other cities. A study at M.I.T. showed that based on 1970 homicide rates a person who lived in a large American city ran a greater risk of being murdered than an American soldier in World War II ran of being killed in combat. It is not surprising

that the laws of each country differ according to differing conditions and traditions. If other countries had our murder problem, the cry for capital punishment would be just as loud as it is here. And I daresay that any other major democracy where 75 percent of the people supported the death penalty would soon enact it into law.

(3) *An innocent person might be executed by mistake.* Consider the work    8
of Adam Bedau, one of the most implacable foes of capital punishment in this country. According to Mr. Bedau, it is "false sentimentality to argue that the death penalty should be abolished because of the abstract possibility that an innocent person might be executed." He cites a study of the 7,000 executions in this country from 1893 to 1971, and concludes that the record fails to show that such cases occur. The main point, however, is this. If government functioned only when the possibility of error didn't exist, government wouldn't function at all. Human life de-serves special protection, and one of the best ways to guarantee that protection is to assure that convicted murderers do not kill again. Only the death penalty can accomplish this end. In a recent case in New Jersey, a man named Richard Biegenwald was freed from prison after serving 18 years for murder; since his release he has been convicted of committing four murders. A prisoner named Lemuel Smith, who, while serving four life sentences for murder (plus two life sentences for kidnap-ping and robbery) in New York's Green Haven Prison, lured a woman corrections officer into the chaplain's office and strangled her. He then mutilated and dismembered her body. An additional life sentence for Smith is meaningless. Because New York has no death penalty statute, Smith has effectively been given a license to kill.

But the problem of multiple murder is not confined to the nation's    9
penitentiaries. In 1981, 91 police officers were killed in the line of duty in this country. Seven percent of those arrested in the cases that have been solved had a previous arrest for murder. In New York City in 1976 and 1977, 85 persons arrested for homicide had a previous arrest for murder. Six of these individuals had two previous arrests for murder, and one had four previous murder arrests. During those two years the New York police were arresting for murder persons with a previous arrest for murder on the average of one every 8.5 days. This is not surprising when we learn that in 1975, for example, the median time served in Massa-chusetts for homicide was less than two-and-a-half years. In 1976 a study sponsored by the Twentieth Century Fund found that the average time served in the United States for first-degree murder is ten years. The median time served may be considerably lower.

(4) *Capital punishment cheapens the value of human life.* On the contrary,    10

it can be easily demonstrated that the death penalty strengthens the value of human life. If the penalty for rape were lowered, clearly it would signal a lessened regard for the victims' suffering, humiliation, and personal integrity. It would cheapen their horrible experience, and expose them to an increased danger of recurrence. When we lower the penalty for murder, it signals a lessened regard for the value of the victim's life. Some critics of capital punishment, such as columnist Jimmy Breslin, have suggested that a life sentence is actually a harsher penalty for murder than death. This is sophistic nonsense. A few killers may decide not to appeal a death sentence, but the overwhelming majority make every effort to stay alive. It is by exacting the highest penalty for the taking of human life that we affirm the highest value of human life.

(5) *The death penalty is applied in a discriminatory manner.* This factor   11
no longer seems to be the problem it once was. The appeals process for a condemned prisoner is lengthy and painstaking. Every effort is made to see that the verdict and sentence were fairly arrived at. However, assertions of discrimination are not an argument for ending the death penalty but for extending it. It is not justice to exclude everyone from the penalty of the law if a few are found to be so favored. Justice requires that the law be applied equally to all.

(6) *Thou Shalt Not Kill.* The Bible is our greatest source of moral   12
inspiration. Opponents of the death penalty frequently cite the sixth of the Ten Commandments in an attempt to prove that capital punishment is divinely proscribed. In the original Hebrew, however, the Sixth Commandment reads, "Thou Shalt Not Commit Murder," and the Torah specifies capital punishment for a variety of offenses. The biblical viewpoint has been upheld by philosophers throughout history. The greatest thinkers of the 19th century—Kant, Locke, Hobbes, Rousseau, Montesquieu, and Mill—agreed that natural law properly authorizes the sovereign to take life in order to vindicate justice. Only Jeremy Bentham was ambivalent. Washington, Jefferson, and Franklin endorsed it. Abraham Lincoln authorized executions for deserters in wartime. Alexis de Tocqueville, who expressed profound respect for American institutions, believed that the death penalty was indispensable to the support of social order. The United States Constitution, widely admired as one of the seminal achievements in the history of humanity, condemns cruel and inhuman punishment, but does not condemn capital punishment.

(7) *The death penalty is state-sanctioned murder.* This is the defense with   13
which Messrs. Willie and Shaw hoped to soften the resolve of those who sentenced them to death. By saying in effect, "You're no better than I am," the murderer seeks to bring his accusers down to his own level. It is also a popular argument among opponents of capital punishment, but

a transparently false one. Simply put, the state has rights that the private individual does not. In a democracy, those rights are given to the state by the electorate. The execution of a lawfully condemned killer is no more an act of murder than is legal imprisonment an act of kidnapping. If an individual forces a neighbor to pay him money under threat of punishment, it's called extortion. If the state does it, it's called taxation. Rights and responsibilities surrendered by the individual are what give the state its power to govern. This contract is the foundation of civilization itself.

Everyone wants his or her rights, and will defend them zealously. Not  14 everyone, however, wants responsibilities, especially the painful responsibilities that come with law enforcement. Twenty-one years ago a woman named Kitty Genovese was assaulted and murdered on a street in New York. Dozens of neighbors heard her cries for help but did nothing to assist her. They didn't even call the police. In such a climate the criminal understandably grows bolder. In the presence of moral cowardice, he lectures us on our supposed failings and tries to equate his crimes with our quest for justice.

The death of anyone—even a convicted killer—diminishes us all. But  15 we are diminished even more by a justice system that fails to function. It is an illusion to let ourselves believe that doing away with capital punishment removes the murderer's deed from our conscience. The rights of society are paramount. When we protect guilty lives, we give up innocent lives in exchange. When opponents of capital punishment say to the state: "I will not let you kill in my name," they are also saying to murderers: "You can kill in your *own* name as long as I have an excuse for not getting involved."

It is hard to imagine anything worse than being murdered while neigh-  16 bors do nothing. But something worse exists. When those same neighbors shrink back from justly punishing the murderer, the victim dies twice.

## QUESTIONS FOR ANALYSIS

1. To discover how Koch organizes his argument, make a brief outline of the essay. Notice that he begins by quoting two men who were executed under the death penalty and that he returns to them near the end of the essay. What effect does repeating this reference have? What do you think Koch is trying to accomplish with this framing device? How effective is it?

2. Outline Koch's argument. Why do you think Koch examines the opposing arguments in the order that he does? Does one set the stage for another? Are they all of equal importance? Which arguments re-

ceive the greatest emphasis? Can you suggest a better order? (See Chapter 1 for advice on outlining an argument.)

3. Annotate the essay, noting the various ways in which Koch supports his argument. Then take inventory of your annotations, categorizing the different kinds of evidence he uses. Which kinds of evidence does he use most effectively? least effectively?

4. Koch argues by analogy in several places, and at one point he calls his analogy "imperfect." Analyze his use of analogy. Why does he use it? What advantages or disadvantages do you see in arguing from analogy as Koch does?

5. Why does Koch quote Adam Bedau? Another Bedau study found that of the thousands of murder convictions since 1900, error was eventually admitted to have occurred in at least 400 of the cases. How would Koch's argument be affected if he had cited the results of this study?

6. Since capital punishment is such an emotional issue, it is natural to expect that an author would appeal to readers' emotions. Describe the way Koch makes this appeal by pointing to specific instances in the text. Also, decide whether you think Koch is being manipulative at any point. If so, what effect does this manipulation have on the outcome of his argument? (Chapter 1 discusses evaluating an argument's emotional appeal.)

7. Arguments in position papers are often based on general principles. On what principles does Koch base his argument? Summarize his reasoning based on these principles.

8. How convincing do you find this essay? On reflection, what do you think is Koch's strongest argument? his weakest?

## SUGGESTIONS FOR WRITING

1. Write a position paper of your own rebutting or extending Koch's argument. Refer to specific points or evidence in Koch's essay to develop your own argument.

2. In paragraph 14 Koch writes: "Everyone wants his or her rights, and will defend them zealously. Not everyone, however, wants responsibilities." Do you think this statement is true? What responsibilities, for example, accompany such constitutional rights as the right to pursue happiness and the right to a free press? Write a position paper addressing this general issue, using examples of any rights and responsibilities about which you feel strongly. Before writing, consider how your opponent would argue for the opposing position.

3. Do you agree with Koch that "if government functioned only when the possibility of error didn't exist, government wouldn't function at all" (paragraph 8)? What does this statement imply? Should the government ever be held accountable for its errors? For example, should the families of the astronauts who died in the 1986 Challenger space shuttle disaster be able to sue NASA and other government agencies? Should the government be held responsible for soldiers' deaths in questionable military operations? Write a position paper on this general issue, citing whatever specific examples you choose.

# David Hoekema

Formerly a philosophy professor at St. Olaf College in Minnesota, David Hoekema is currently the executive secretary of the American Philosophical Association. Hoekema has written extensively on the ethical dimension of contemporary social issues such as apartheid, hunger, and nuclear war. In 1979, he addressed the issue of capital punishment in a speech delivered at a forum sponsored by the Citizens' Committee for Criminal Justice. This selection is a revised version that appeared in a journal called *The Christian Century*.

# Capital Punishment: The Question of Justification

In this essay, Hoekema addresses the issue of capital punishment with the objectivity one might expect from a philosopher. What other expectations do you have about his argument? How does the fact that it was published in *The Christian Century* influence your expectations? What do you think might be a "Christian" position on this issue? What kind of argument might support this position?

In 1810 a bill introduced in the British Parliament sought to abolish   1
capital punishment for the offense of stealing five shillings or more from a shop. Judges and magistrates unanimously opposed the measure. In the House of Lords, the chief justice of the King's Bench, Lord Ellenborough, predicted that the next step would be abolition of the death penalty for stealing five shillings from a house; thereafter no one could "trust himself for an hour without the most alarming apprehension that, on his return, every vestige of his property [would] be swept away by the hardened robber" (quoted by Herbert B. Ehrmann in "The Death Penalty and the Administration of Justice," in *The Death Penalty in America*, edited by Hugo Adam Bedau [Anchor, 1967], p. 415).

During the same year Parliament abolished the death penalty for pick-   2
ing pockets, but more than 200 crimes remained punishable by death. Each year in Great Britain more than 2,000 persons were being sentenced to die, though only a small number of these sentences were actually carried out.

I

In this regard as in many others, the laws of the English colonies in   3
North America were much less harsh than those of the mother country.

At the time of the Revolution, statutes in most of the colonies prescribed hanging for about a dozen offenses—among them murder, treason, piracy, arson, rape, robbery, burglary, sodomy and (in some cases) counterfeiting, horse theft and slave rebellion. But by the early nineteenth century a movement to abolish the death penalty was gaining strength.

The idea was hardly new: czarist Russia had eliminated the death    4
penalty on religious grounds in the eleventh century. In the United States the movement had been launched by Benjamin Rush in the eighteenth century, with the support of such other distinguished citizens of Philadelphia as Benjamin Franklin and Attorney General William Bradford. By the 1830s, bills calling for abolition of capital punishment were being regularly introduced, and defeated, in several state legislatures. In 1846 Michigan voted effectively to abolish the death penalty—the first English-speaking jurisdiction in the world to do so.

In the years since, twelve states have abolished capital punishment    5
entirely. Although statutes still in effect in some states permit the death penalty to be imposed for a variety of offenses—ranging from statutory rape to desecration of a grave to causing death in a duel—murder is virtually the only crime for which it has been recently employed. There are about 400 persons in U.S. prisons under sentence of death, but only one execution (Gary Gilmore's) has been carried out in this country in the past eleven years.

However, the issue of whether capital punishment is justifiable is by    6
no means settled. Since the Supreme Court, in the case of *Furman* v. *Georgia* in 1972, invalidated most existing laws permitting capital punishment, several states have enacted new legislation designed to meet the court's objections to the Georgia law. And recent public-opinion surveys indicate that a large number, possibly a majority, of Americans favor imposing the death penalty for some crimes. But let us ask the ethical question: Ought governments to put to death persons convicted of certain crimes?

## II

First, let us look at grounds on which capital punishment is defended.    7
Most prominent is the argument from *deterrence*. Capital punishment, it is asserted, is necessary to deter potential criminals. Murderers must be executed so that the lives of potential murder victims may be spared.

Two assertions are closely linked here. First, it is said that convicted    8
murderers must be put to death in order to protect the rest of us against those individuals who might kill others if they were at large. This argument, based not strictly on deterrence but on incapacitation of known

offenders, is inconclusive, since there are other effective means of protecting the innocent against convicted murderers—for example, imprisonment of murderers for life in high-security institutions.

Second, it is said that the example of capital punishment is needed to    9
deter those who would otherwise commit murder. Knowledge that a crime is punishable by death will give the potential criminal pause. This second argument rests on the assumption that capital punishment does in fact reduce the incidence of capital crimes—a presupposition that must be tested against the evidence. Surprisingly, none of the available empirical data shows any significant correlation between the existence or use of the death penalty and the incidence of capital crimes.

When studies have compared the homicide rates for the past fifty years    10
in states that employ the death penalty and in adjoining states that have abolished it, the numbers have in every case been quite similar; the death penalty has had no discernible effect on homicide rates. Further, the shorter-term effects of capital punishment have been studied by examining the daily number of homicides reported in California over a ten-year period to ascertain whether the execution of convicts reduced the number. Fewer homicides were reported on days immediately following an execution, but this reduction was matched by an increase in the number of homicides on the day of execution and the preceding day. Executions had no discernible effect on the weekly total of homicides. (Cf. "Death and Imprisonment as Deterrents to Murder," by Thorsten Sellin, in Bedau, op. cit., pp. 274–284, and "The Deterrent Effect of Capital Punishment in California," by William F. Graves, in Bedau, op. cit., pp. 322–332.)

The available evidence, then, fails to support the claim that capital    11
punishment deters capital crime. For this reason, I think, we may set aside the deterrence argument. But there is a stronger reason for rejecting the argument—one that has to do with the way in which supporters of that argument would have us treat persons.

Those who defend capital punishment on grounds of deterrence would    12
have us take the lives of some—persons convicted of certain crimes—because doing so will discourage crime and thus protect others. But it is a grave moral wrong to treat one person in a way justified solely by the needs of others. To inflict harm on one person in order to serve the purposes of others is to use that person in an immoral and inhumane way, treating him or her not as a person with rights and responsibilities but as a means to other ends. The most serious flaw in the deterrence argument, therefore, is that it is the wrong *kind* of argument. The execution of criminals cannot be justified by the good which their deaths may do the rest of us.

## III

A second argument for the death penalty maintains that some crimes, 13
chief among them murder, *morally require* the punishment of death. In
particular, Christians frequently support capital punishment by appeal to
the Mosaic code, which required the death penalty for murder. "The law
of capital punishment," one writer has concluded after reviewing relevant
biblical passages, "must stand as a silent but powerful witness to the
sacredness of God-given life" ("Christianity and the Death Penalty," by
Jacob Vellenga, in Bedau, op. cit., pp. 123–130).

In the Mosaic code, it should be pointed out, there were many capital 14
crimes besides murder. In the book of Deuteronomy, death is prescribed
as the penalty for false prophecy, worship of foreign gods, kidnapping,
adultery, deception by a bride concerning her virginity, and disobedience
to parents. To this list the laws of the book of Exodus add witchcraft,
sodomy, and striking or cursing a parent.

I doubt that there is much sentiment in favor of restoring the death 15
penalty in the United States for such offenses. But if the laws of Old
Testament Israel ought not to govern our treatment of, say, adultery,
why should they govern the penalty for murder? To support capital punishment by an appeal to Old Testament law is to overlook the fact that
the ancient theocratic state of Israel was in nearly every respect profoundly different from any modern secular state. For this reason, we
cannot simply regard the Mosaic code as normative for the United States
today.

But leaving aside reference to Mosaic law, let me state more strongly 16
the argument we are examining. The death penalty, it may be urged, is
the only just penalty for a crime such as murder; it is the only fair
*retribution*. Stated thus, the argument at hand seems to be the right *kind*
of argument for capital punishment. If capital punishment can be justified
at all, it must be on the basis of the *seriousness of the offense* for which it
is imposed. Retributive considerations *should* govern the punishment of
individuals who violate the law, and chief among these considerations
are the principle of proportionality between punishment and offense and
the requirement that persons be punished only for acts for which they
are truly responsible. I am not persuaded that retributive considerations
are sufficient to set a particular penalty for a given offense, but I believe
they do require that in comparative terms we visit more serious offenses
with more severe punishment.

Therefore, the retributive argument seems the strongest one in support 17
of capital punishment. We ought to deal with convicted offenders not
as we want to, but as they deserve. And I am not certain that it is wrong

to argue that a person who has deliberately killed another person deserves to die.

But even if this principle is valid, should the judicial branch of our 18 governments be empowered to determine whether individuals deserve to die? Are our procedures for making laws and for determining guilt sufficiently reliable that we may entrust our lives to them? I shall return to this important question presently. But consider the following fact: During the years from 1930 to 1962, 466 persons were put to death for the crime of rape. Of these, 399 were black. Can it seriously be maintained that our courts are administering the death penalty to all those and only to those who deserve to die?

## IV

Two other arguments deserve brief mention. It has been argued that, 19 even if the penalty of life imprisonment were acceptable on other grounds, our society could not reasonably be asked to pay the cost of maintaining convicted murderers in prisons for the remainder of their natural lives.

This argument overlooks the considerable costs of retaining the death 20 penalty. Jury selection, conduct of the trial, and the appeals process become extremely time-consuming and elaborate when death is a possible penalty. On the other hand, prisons should not be as expensive as they are. At present those prisoners who work at all are working for absurdly low wages, frequently at menial and degrading tasks. Prisons should be reorganized to provide meaningful work for all able inmates; workers should be paid fair wages for their work and charged for their room and board. Such measures would sharply reduce the cost of prisons and make them more humane.

But these considerations—important as they are—have little relevance 21 to the justification of capital punishment. We should not decide to kill convicted criminals only because it costs so much to keep them alive. The cost to society of imprisonment, large or small, cannot justify capital punishment.

Finally, defenders of capital punishment sometimes support their case 22 by citing those convicted offenders—for example, Gary Gilmore—who have asked to be executed rather than imprisoned. But this argument, too, is of little relevance. If some prisoners would prefer to die rather than be imprisoned, perhaps we should oblige them by permitting them to take their own lives. But this consideration has nothing to do with the question of whether we ought to impose the punishment of death on certain offenders, most of whom would prefer to live.

## V

Let us turn now to the case *against* the death penalty. It is sometimes    23
argued that capital punishment is unjustified because those guilty of
crimes cannot help acting as they do: the environment, possibly inter-
acting with inherited characteristics, causes some people to commit
crimes. It is not moral culpability or choice that divides law-abiding
citizens from criminals—so Clarence Darrow argued eloquently—but the
accident of birth or social circumstances.

If determinism of this sort were valid, not only the death penalty but    24
all forms of punishment would be unjustified. No one who is compelled
by circumstances to act deserves to be punished. But there is little reason
to adopt this bleak view of human action. Occasionally coercive threats
compel a person to violate the law; and in such cases the individual is
rightly excused from legal guilt. Circumstances of deprivation, hardship
and lack of education—unfortunately much more widely prevalent—
break down the barriers, both moral and material, which deter many of
us from breaking the law. They are grounds for exercising extreme caution
and for showing mercy in the application of the law, but they are not
the sole causes of crimes: they diminish but do not destroy the responsibility of the individual. The great majority of those who break the law
do so deliberately, by choice and not as a result of causes beyond their
control.

Second, the case against the death penalty is sometimes based on the    25
view that the justification of punishment lies in the reform which it
effects. Those who break the law, it is said, are ill, suffering either from
psychological malfunction or from maladjustment to society. Our responsibility is to treat them, to cure them of their illness, so that they
become able to function in socially acceptable ways. Death, obviously,
cannot reform anyone.

Like the deterrence argument for capital punishment, this seems to be    26
the wrong *kind* of argument. Punishment is punishment and treatment
is treatment, and one must not be substituted for the other. Some persons
who violate the law are, without doubt, mentally ill. It is unreasonable
and inhumane to punish them for acts which they may not have realized
they were doing; to put such a person to death would be an even more
grievous wrong. In such cases treatment is called for.

But most persons who break the law are not mentally ill and do know    27
what they are doing. We may not force them to undergo treatment in
place of the legal penalty for their offenses. To confine them to mental
institutions until those put in authority over them judge that they are
cured of their criminal tendencies is far more cruel than to sentence them

to a term of imprisonment. Voluntary programs of education or vocational training, which help prepare prisoners for noncriminal careers on release, should be made more widely available. But compulsory treatment for all offenders violates their integrity as persons; we need only look to the Soviet Union to see the abuses to which such a practice is liable.

## VI

Let us examine a third and stronger argument, a straightforward moral   28
assertion; the state ought not to take life unnecessarily. For many reasons—among them the example which capital punishment sets, its effect on those who must carry out death sentences and, above all, its violation of a basic moral principle—the state ought not to kill people.

The counterclaim made by defenders of capital punishment is that in   29
certain circumstances killing people is permissible and even required, and that capital punishment is one of those cases. If a terrorist is about to throw a bomb into a crowded theater, and a police officer is certain that there is no way to stop him except to kill him, the officer should of course kill the terrorist. In some cases of grave and immediate danger, let us grant, killing is justified.

But execution bears little resemblance to such cases. It involves the   30
planned, deliberate killing of someone in custody who is not a present threat to human life or safety. Execution is not necessary to save the lives of future victims, since there are other means to secure that end.

Is there some vitally important purpose of the state or some funda-   31
mental right of persons which cannot be secured without executing convicts? I do not believe there is. And in the absence of any such compelling reason, the moral principle that it is wrong to kill people constitutes a powerful argument against capital punishment.

## VII

Of the arguments I have mentioned in favor of the death penalty, only   32
one has considerable weight. That is the retributive argument that murder, as an extremely serious offense, requires a comparably severe punishment. Of the arguments so far examined against capital punishment, only one, the moral claim that killing is wrong, is, in my view, acceptable.

There is, however, another argument against the death penalty which   33
I find compelling—that based on the imperfection of judicial procedure. In the case of *Furman* v. *Georgia*, the Supreme Court struck down existing legislation because of the arbitrariness with which some convicted offenders were executed and others spared. Laws enacted subsequently in

several states have attempted to meet the court's objection, either by making death mandatory for certain offenses or by drawing up standards which the trial jury must follow in deciding, after guilt has been established, whether the death penalty will be imposed in a particular case. But these revisions of the law diminish only slightly the discretion of the jury. When death is made the mandatory sentence for first-degree murder, the question of death or imprisonment becomes the question of whether to find the accused guilty as charged or guilty of a lesser offense, such as second-degree murder.

When standards are spelled out, the impression of greater precision is 34 often only superficial. A recent Texas statute, for example, instructs the jury to impose a sentence of death only if it is established "beyond a reasonable doubt" that "there is a probability that the defendant would commit criminal acts of violence that would constitute a continuing threat to society" (Texas Code of Criminal Procedure, Art. 37.071; quoted in *Capital Punishment: The Inevitability of Caprice and Mistake,* by Charles L. Black, Jr. [Norton, 1974], p. 58). Such a law does not remove discretion but only adds confusion.

At many other points in the judicial process, discretion rules, and 35 arbitrary or incorrect decisions are possible. The prosecutor must decide whether to charge the accused with a capital crime, and whether to accept a plea of guilty to a lesser charge. (In most states it is impossible to plead guilty to a charge carrying a mandatory death sentence.) The jury must determine whether the facts of the case as established by testimony in court fit the legal definition of the offense with which the defendant is charged—a definition likely to be complicated at best, incomprehensible at worst. From a mass of confusing and possibly conflicting testimony the jury must choose the most reliable. But evident reliability can be deceptive: persons have been wrongly convicted of murder on the positive identification of eyewitnesses.

Jurors must also determine whether at the time of the crime the accused 36 satisfied the legal definition of insanity. The most widely used definition—the McNaghten Rules formulated by the judges of the House of Lords in 1843—states that a person is excused from criminal responsibility if at the time of his act he suffered from a defect of reason which arose from a disease of the mind and as a result of which he did not "know the nature and quality of his act," or "if he did know it . . . he did not know he was doing what was wrong" (quoted in *Punishment and Responsibility,* by H. L. A. Hart [Oxford University Press, 1968], p. 189). Every word of this formula has been subject to legal controversy in interpretation, and it is unreasonable to expect that juries untrained in law will be able to apply it consistently and fairly. Even after sentencing, some offenders escape the death penalty as a result of appeals, other technical legal challenges, or executive clemency.

Because of all these opportunities for arbitrary decision, only a small 37 number of those convicted of capital crimes are actually executed. It is hardly surprising that their selection has little to do with the character of their crimes but a great deal to do with the skill of their legal counsel. And the latter depends in large measure on how much money is available for the defense. Inevitably, the death penalty has been imposed most frequently on the poor, and in this country it has been imposed in disproportionate numbers on blacks.

To cite two examples in this regard: All those executed in Delaware 38 between 1902 and the (temporary) abolition of the state's death penalty in 1958 were unskilled workers with limited education. Of 3,860 persons executed in the United States between 1930 and the present, 2,066, or 54 percent, were black. Although for a variety of reasons the per capita rate of conviction for most types of crime has been higher among the poor and the black, that alone cannot explain why a tenth of the population should account for more than half of those executed. Doubtless prejudice played a part. But no amount of goodwill and fair-mindedness can compensate for the disadvantage to those who cannot afford the highly skilled legal counsel needed to discern every loophole in the judicial process.

## VIII

Even more worrisome than the discriminatory application of the death 39 penalty is the possibility of mistaken conviction and its ghastly consequences. In a sense, any punishment wrongfully imposed is irrevocable, but none is so irrevocable as death. Although we cannot give back to a person mistakenly imprisoned the time spent or the self-respect lost, we can release and compensate him or her. But we cannot do anything for a person wrongfully executed. While we ought to minimize the opportunities for capricious or mistaken judgments throughout the legal system, we cannot hope for perfect success. There is no reason why our mistakes must be fatal.

Numerous cases of erroneous convictions in capital cases have been 40 documented; several of those convicted were put to death before the error was discovered. However small their number, it is too large. So long as the death penalty exists, there are certain to be others, for every judicial procedure—however meticulous, however compassed about with safeguards—must be carried out by fallible human beings.

One erroneous execution is too many, because even lawful executions 41 of the indisputably guilty serve no purpose. They are not justified by the need to protect the rest of us, since there are other means of restraining persons dangerous to society, and there is no evidence that executions deter the commission of crime. A wrongful execution is a grievous injustice that cannot be remedied after the fact. Even a legal and proper execution is a needless taking of human life. Even if one is sympathetic—as I am—to the claim that a murderer deserves to die, there are compelling reasons not to entrust the power to decide who shall die to the persons and procedures that constitute our judicial system.

## QUESTIONS FOR ANALYSIS

1. Outline Hoekema's essay to see how he organizes his argument. Why do you think he divides it into parts? What seem to you to be the advantages and disadvantages of organizing the essay as he does? (See the discussion of outlining under Analyzing an Argument in Chapter 1.)

2. Hoekema begins by telling the history of the issue. What do you think would be lost—or gained—if he had begun instead with paragraph 6 or 7?

3. Hoekema says he takes up the deterrence argument first because it is the "most prominent" defense for capital punishment. Why then should he examine this argument before he has even established his credibility with his readers? How fair is his representation of the opposition's argument, and how convincing do you find his rebuttal?

4. In paragraph 17 Hoekema concedes that he is "not certain that it is wrong to argue that a person who has deliberately killed another person deserves to die." Why does he make this concession? In saying this, has he forfeited the argument?

5. If, as Hoekema says, financial considerations are irrelevant, why do you suppose he mentions them? Do you agree that they are irrelevant?

6. If Hoekema opposes capital punishment, why does he spend so much time systematically refuting arguments that have been made to support his own position? How does this part of his essay contribute to his credibility?

7. The retributive argument, according to Hoekema, is the strongest one on the pro side, while the moral claim that killing is wrong is the strongest argument for the con side. Contrast these two arguments. Taking Hoekema's discussion into account, which do you think is the more convincing of the two arguments?

8. At various points in the essay, Hoekema quotes from publications on capital punishment. Find these references, and determine what the advantages or disadvantages of this argumentative strategy are.

9. Describe how Hoekema concludes the essay. Why is this an effective ending?

## SUGGESTIONS FOR WRITING

1. Hoekema dismisses most of the arguments on both sides of the issue. Choose one of these arguments for or against capital punishment, and write a position paper responding to Hoekema. Write as if you were addressing Hoekema directly.

2. Hoekema asserts that punishment ought to be meted out on the basis of "fair retribution," in other words, that the punishment should fit the crime. How do we decide what is fair retribution? Is it fair for a student who commits plagiarism to be dismissed from school? Is it fair for a student to be suspended for a year for possession of drugs? Write a position paper on the general issue, citing any examples you wish.

3. Hoekema refutes Clarence Darrow's deterministic argument that it is not "moral culpability or choice that divides law-abiding citizens from criminals . . . but the accident of birth or social circumstances." Develop this argument in a position paper of your own, either defending or refuting it.

# Margaret Mead

Educated at Barnard College and Columbia University as an anthropologist, Margaret Mead (1901–1978) gained worldwide recognition with the publication of her first book, *Coming of Age in Samoa* (1928). Focusing her research on primitive South Pacific societies, Mead sought to study the relationship between individual development and socialization. Although some of her early research is now being questioned, Mead's contribution to anthropology remains firm. She served for many years as director of the prestigious Center for Research in Contemporary Culture at Columbia University and also had a lifelong position as curator for the American Museum of Natural History.

In the 1940s, Mead turned her attention to national and international affairs. She undertook a study of contemporary American character and became involved in a number of reform movements. One of the few intellectual women of her age to attain international prominence, Mead supported the feminist movement. She wrote this piece on capital punishment shortly before she died.

# A Life for a Life: What That Means Today

Writing this essay, Mead could assume that her name would be recognized by most readers and also that her voice would carry substantial weight. As you read, pay close attention to Mead's tone. To what extent does she appear to assume that she has credibility with her readers? What does she do to win her readers' confidence? Also notice that Mead is speaking directly to women in this essay. How does targeting this particular audience affect her argument? Does it limit the argument's general effectiveness?

The struggle for and against the abolition of capital punishment has 1 been going on in our country and among enlightened peoples everywhere for well over a century. In the years before the Civil War the fight to end the death penalty was led in America by men like Horace Greeley, who also was fighting strongly to abolish slavery, and by a tiny handful of active women like New England's Dorothea Dix, who was fighting for prison reform. In those years three states—Michigan in 1847, Rhode Island in 1852 and Wisconsin in 1853—renounced the use of capital punishment, the first jurisdictions in the modern world to do so.

Both sides claim a primary concern for human rights. Those who de-  2
mand that we keep—and carry out—the death penalty speak for the
victims of capital crimes, holding that it is only just that murderers,
kidnapers, rapists, hijackers and other violent criminals should suffer for
the harm they have done and so deter others from committing atrocious
crimes.

In contrast, those who demand that we abolish capital punishment  3
altogether are convinced that violence breeds violence—that the death
penalty carried out by the State against its own citizens in effect legiti-
mizes willful killing. Over time, their concern has been part of a much
more inclusive struggle for human rights and human dignity. They were
among those who fought against slavery and they have been among those
who have fought for the civil rights of Black Americans, of immigrants
and of ethnic minorities and Native Americans, for the rights of prisoners
of war as well as for the prisoners in penitentiaries, for the rights of the
poor, the unemployed and the unemployable, for women's rights and for
the rights of the elderly and of children.

Now, I believe, we can—if we will—put this all together and realize  4
that in our kind of civilization "a life for a life" need not mean destructive
retribution, but instead the development of new forms of community in
which, because all lives are valuable, what is emphasized is the prevention of crime and the protection of all those who are vulnerable.

The first step is to realize that in our society we have permitted the  5
kinds of vulnerability that characterize the victims of violent crime and
have ignored, where we could, the hostility and alienation that enter
into the making of violent criminals. No rational person condones violent crime, and I have no patience with sentimental attitudes toward
violent criminals. But it is time that we open our eyes to the conditions
that foster violence and that ensure the existence of easily recognizable
victims.

Americans respond generously—if not always wisely—to the occur-  6
rence of natural catastrophes. But except where we are brought face to
face with an unhappy individual or a family in trouble, we are turned off
by the humanly far more desperate social catastrophes of children who
are trashed by the schools—and the local community—where they should
be learning for themselves what it means and how it feels to be a valued
human being. We demean the men and women who are overwhelmed
by their inability to meet their responsibilities to one another or even to
go it alone, and we shut our awareness of the fate of the unskilled, the
handicapped and the barely tolerated elderly. As our own lives have
become so much more complex and our social ties extraordinarily fragile,

we have lost any sense of community with others whose problems and difficulties and catastrophes are not our own.

We do know that human lives are being violated—and not only by criminals. But at least we can punish criminals. That is a stopgap way. But it is not the way out of our dilemma.    7

We also know that in any society, however organized, security rests on accepted participation—on what I have called here a sense of community in which everyone shares.    8

Up to the present, the responsibility for working out and maintaining the principles on which any code of law must depend and for the practical administration of justice has been primarily a male preoccupation. At best, women working within this framework have been able sometimes to modify and sometimes to mitigate the working of the system of law.    9

Now, however, if the way out is for us to place the occurrence of crime and the fate of the victim and of the criminal consciously within the context of our way of living and our view of human values, then I believe liberated women have a major part to play and a wholly new place to create for themselves in public life as professional women, as volunteers and as private citizens concerned with the quality of life in our nation. For it is women who have constantly had to visualize in personal, human terms the relationships between the intimate details of living and the setting in which living takes place. And it is this kind of experience that we shall need in creating new kinds of community.    10

Women working in new kinds of partnership with men should be able to bring fresh thinking into law and the administration of justice with a greater awareness of the needs of individuals at different stages of life and the potentialities of social institutions in meeting those needs. What we shall be working toward is a form of deterrence based not on fear of punishment—which we know is ineffective, even when the punishment is the threat of death—but on a shared way of living.    11

It will be a slow process at best to convince our fellow citizens that justice and a decline in violence can be attained only by the development of communities in which the elderly and children, families and single persons, the gifted, the slow and the handicapped can have a meaningful place and live with dignity and in which rights and responsibilities are aspects of each other. And I believe that we can make a start only if we have a long view, but know very well that what we can do today and tomorrow and next year will not bring us to utopia. We cannot establish instant security; we can only build for it step by step.    12

We must also face the reality that as far as we can foresee there will always be a need for places of confinement—prisons of different kinds,    13 to be frank—where individuals will have to be segregated for short periods, for longer periods or even, for some, for a whole lifetime. The fear that the violent person will be set free in our communities (as we all know happens all too often under our present system of law) is an important component in the drive to strengthen—certainly not to abolish—the death penalty. For their own protection as well as that of others, the few who cannot control their violent impulses and, for the time being, the larger number who have become hopelessly violent must be sequestered. . . .

The tasks are urgent and difficult. Realistically we know we cannot 14 abolish crime. But we can abolish crude and vengeful treatment of crime. We can abolish—as a nation, not just state by state—capital punishment. We can accept the fact that prisoners, convicted criminals, are hostages to our own human failures to develop and support a decent way of living. And we can accept the fact that we are responsible to them, as to all living beings, for the protection of society, and especially responsible for those among us who need protection for the sake of society.

## QUESTIONS FOR ANALYSIS

1. What other social issues does Mead connect to opposition to capital punishment? Why do you think she makes this connection? Do you think it is a good way to begin a position paper? Why or why not?

2. In paragraph 2 Mead defines the common ground that she thinks opponents and proponents of capital punishment both share. What, in your own words, is this common ground? How does Mead try to build agreement on this common ground? How successful do you think she is?

3. Why does Mead insert into her argument this statement: "No rational person condones violent crime, and I have no patience with sentimental attitudes toward violent criminals"?

4. What is Mead saying in paragraph 5? How effectively does she support her point? What kind of additional information would make her argument here more convincing?

5. In this essay, Mead sets up an opposition between the state and the community. Take inventory of these two terms and of any related terms. What does she mean by this opposition? Where do these terms fit into her argument on capital punishment? (See Chapter 1 for procedures on taking inventory of opposites.)

6. At the end of this position paper, Mead proposes a fundamental change in society as a way to solve what she perceives as the problem underlying the capital punishment issue. Summarize her proposal— her definition of the problem and her proposed solution. How convincing do you find this proposal? Reflect more generally on the role this proposal plays in her position paper. It is appropriate to make such a proposal in a position paper? What effect does it have on the persuasiveness of her argument?

7. Why do you think paragraphs 7 and 8 are notably shorter than others in the essay? Are they underdeveloped, or are they short for some particular reason?

### SUGGESTIONS FOR WRITING

1. Write a position paper in which you respond to Mead's essay. Do not simply restate her point if you agree, but extend and support it further. If you disagree, refute her argument.

2. Select any of the issues other than capital punishment to which Mead alludes—civil rights, the plight of the poor, or immigration, for example—and write a position paper on some aspect of this issue. Be sure to define the specific issue clearly and to consider opposing positions in your essay.

3. This essay is, in a sense, a call for women to become more involved in politics. Do you think that women should play a larger role in the civic life of the nation? Is it even reasonable to address women as a monolithic group? Write a position paper on this issue, defining it for yourself and for your readers.

### THE DEBATE:
### ADDITIONAL QUESTIONS FOR ANALYSIS

1. Both Koch and Hoekema refer to the Bible. Contrast their arguments that are based on religious beliefs. How important do you think this kind of argument is likely to be for the general reader?

2. How do you think Hoekema and Mead would respond to Koch's claim that "assertions of discrimination [in the application of the death penalty] are not an argument for ending the death penalty but for extending it"? What is your response?

3. How do you think Koch and Mead would respond to Hoekema's claim that "the most serious flaw in the deterrence argument . . . is that it is the wrong *kind* of argument"? How do you react?

4. How do you think Koch and Hoekema would respond to Mead's claim that "we have permitted the kinds of vulnerability that characterize the victims of violent crime and have ignored, where we could, the hostility and alienation that enter into the making of violent criminals"? How do you react?

# A Debate on Civil Disobedience

Like the debate on liberal education, the debate on civil disobedience dates back to the ancient Greeks. It was addressed by Plato in *The Apology of Socrates* and *Crito*, by Sophocles in *Antigone*, by the seventeenth-century British philosopher Thomas Hobbes in *The Leviathan*, by the nineteenth-century American writer Henry David Thoreau in "Civil Disobedience," by the twentieth-century Indian political and spiritual leader Mohandas Gandhi in *Nonviolent Resistance*, and most recently by the 1960s civil rights leader Martin Luther King, Jr., in "Letter from Birmingham Jail."

In recent years, civil disobedience has become a highly charged issue on college campuses. In the past, students have protested racial segregation and American involvement in the Vietnam War. Today students are protesting apartheid, experimentation on animals, and America's growing involvement in the politics of Central America. Shanty towns are springing up on campuses throughout the country, students are sitting in and marching—some are even raiding science laboratories.

The debate centers on the question of whether disobeying the law can be justified. Socrates, who was accused of corrupting youth through his teachings, declares in *The Apology* that to conform to the wishes of the state "would be a disobedience to God." This justification, generally referred to as the "higher-law argument," has become the clarion call of civil disobedients. In response, opponents usually invoke the argument developed by Hobbes that because social order is founded on a "social contract" everyone must follow the laws of the state. The reasoning goes that if each individual followed the dictates of conscience, anarchy would result.

Yet the debate, as the following selections show, is much more complicated and subtle. In the first essay, a distinguished jurist, Lewis H. Van Dusen, Jr., attacks civil disobedience as a threat to the rule of law upon which this nation is founded. In the second selection, the respected civil rights leader Martin Luther King, Jr., defends civil disobedience as "standing up for what is best in the American dream and for the most sacred values in our Judaeo-Christian heritage."

# Lewis H. Van Dusen, Jr.

Lewis H. Van Dusen, Jr. (b. 1910) is a Rhodes Scholar and a graduate of Harvard Law School. He practices law in Philadelphia and has served as the chancellor of the Philadelphia Bar Association. Van Dusen has also been active in the American Bar Association as chairman of the Committee on Ethics and Professional Responsibility, and as a member of the Committee on the Federal Judiciary.

# Civil Disobedience:
## Destroyer of Democracy

Since this essay was originally published in the *American Bar Association Journal*, you might expect it to be full of technical terminology and esoteric legal arguments. But skimming it, you will see that Van Dusen is addressing a more general audience and also providing readers with cues to help them follow his argument.

In his title, Van Dusen announces explicitly where he stands on this issue. Yet you might try to anticipate his argument by asking yourself how civil disobedience might undermine democracy. Specifically, what assumptions are made in a democratic system about obedience to the law?

As Charles E. Wyzanski, Chief Judge of the United States District 1 Court in Boston, wrote in the February, 1968, *Atlantic:* "Disobedience is a long step from dissent. Civil disobedience involves a deliberate and punishable breach of legal duty." Protesters might prefer a different definition. They would rather say that civil disobedience is the peaceable resistance of conscience.

The philosophy of civil disobedience was not developed in our American 2 democracy, but in the very first democracy of Athens. It was expressed by the poet Sophocles and the philosopher Socrates. In Sophocles's tragedy, Antigone chose to obey her conscience and violate the state edict against providing burial for her brother, who had been decreed a traitor. When the dictator Creon found out that Antigone had buried her fallen brother, he confronted her and reminded her that there was a mandatory death penalty for this deliberate disobedience of the state law. Antigone nobly replied, "Nor did I think your orders were so strong that you, a mortal man, could overrun the gods' unwritten and unfailing laws."

Conscience motivated Antigone. She was not testing the validity of 3 the law in the hope that eventually she would be sustained. Appealing to the judgment of the community, she explained her action to the chorus. She was not secret and surreptitious—the interment of her brother was open and public. She was not violent; she did not trespass on another citizen's rights. And finally, she accepted without resistance the death sentence—the penalty for violation. By voluntarily accepting the law's sanctions, she was not a revolutionary denying the authority of the state. Antigone's behavior exemplifies the classic case of civil disobedience.

Socrates believed that reason could dictate a conscientious disobedi- 4 ence of state law, but he also believed that he had to accept the legal sanctions of the state. In Plato's *Crito*, Socrates from his hanging basket accepted the death penalty for his teaching of religion to youths contrary to state laws.

The sage of Walden, Henry David Thoreau, took this philosophy of  5
nonviolence and developed it into a strategy for solving society's injustices. First enunciating it in protest against the Mexican War, he then turned it to use against slavery. For refusing to pay taxes that would help pay the enforcers of the fugitive slave law, he went to prison. In Thoreau's words, "If the alternative is to keep all just men in prison or to give up slavery, the state will not hesitate which to choose."

Sixty years later, Gandhi took Thoreau's civil disobedience as his strat-  6
egy to wrest Indian independence from England. The famous salt march against a British imperial tax is his best-known example of protest.

But the conscientious law breaking of Socrates, Gandhi and Thoreau  7
is to be distinguished from the conscientious law testing of Martin Luther King, Jr., who was not a civil disobedient. The civil disobedient withholds taxes or violates state laws knowing he is legally wrong, but believing he is morally right. While he wrapped himself in the mantle of Gandhi and Thoreau, Dr. King led his followers in violation of state laws he believed were contrary to the Federal Constitution. But since Supreme Court decisions in the end generally upheld his many actions, he should not be considered a true civil disobedient.

The civil disobedience of Antigone is like that of the pacifist who  8
withholds paying the percentage of his taxes that goes to the Defense Department, or the Quaker who travels against State Department regulations to Hanoi to distribute medical supplies, or the Vietnam war protester who tears up his draft card. This civil disobedient has been nonviolent in his defiance of the law; he has been unfurtive in his violation; he has been submissive to the penalties of the law. He has neither evaded the law nor interfered with another's rights. He has been neither a rioter nor a revolutionary. The thrust of his cause has not been the might of coercion but the martyrdom of conscience.

### Was the Boston Tea Party Civil Disobedience?

Those who justify violence and radical action as being in the tradition  9
of our Revolution show a misunderstanding of the philosophy of democracy.

James Farmer, former head of the Congress of Racial Equality, in de-  10
fense of the mass action confrontation method, has told of a famous organized demonstration that took place in opposition to political and economic discrimination. The protesters beat back and scattered the law

enforcers and then proceeded to loot and destroy private property. Mr. Farmer then said he was talking about the Boston Tea Party and implied that violence as a method for redress of grievances was an American tradition and a legacy of our revolutionary heritage. While it is true that there is no more sacred document than our Declaration of Independence, Jefferson's "inherent right of rebellion" was predicated on the tyrannical denial of democratic means. If there is no popular assembly to provide an adjustment of ills, and if there is no court system to dispose of injustices, then there is, indeed, a right to rebel.

The seventeenth century's John Locke, the philosophical father of the   11 Declaration of Independence, wrote in his *Second Treatise on Civil Government*: "Wherever law ends, tyranny begins . . . and the people are absolved from any further obedience. Governments are dissolved from within when the legislative [chamber] is altered. When the government [becomes] . . . arbitrary disposers of lives, liberties and fortunes of the people, such revolutions happen. . . ."

But there are some sophisticated proponents of the revolutionary re-   12 dress of grievances who say that the test of the need for radical action is not the unavailability of democratic institutions but the ineffectuality of those institutions to remove blatant social inequalities. If social injustice exists, they say, concerted disobedience is required against the constituted government, whether it be totalitarian or democratic in structure.

Of course, only the most bigoted chauvinist would claim that America   13 is without some glaring faults. But there has never been a utopian society on earth and there never will be unless human nature is remade. Since inequities will mar even the best-framed democracies, the injustice rationale would allow a free right of civil resistance to be available always as a shortcut alternative to the democratic way of petition, debate and assembly. The lesson of history is that civil insurgency spawns far more injustices than it removes. The Jeffersons, Washingtons and Adamses resisted tyranny with the aim of promoting the procedures of democracy. They would never have resisted a democratic government with the risk of promoting the techniques of tyranny.

### Legitimate Pressures and Illegitimate Results

There are many civil rights leaders who show impatience with the   14 process of democracy. They rely on the sit-in, boycott or mass picketing to gain speedier solutions to the problems that face every citizen. But we must realize that the legitimate pressures that won concessions in the past can easily escalate into the illegitimate power plays that might extort demands in the future. The victories of these civil rights leaders must not shake our confidence in the democratic procedures, as the pressures of demonstration are desirable only if they take place within the limits allowed by law. Civil rights gains should continue to be won by the persuasion of Congress and other legislative bodies and by the decision of courts. Any illegal entreaty for the rights of some can be an injury to the rights of others, for mass demonstrations often trigger violence.

Those who advocate taking the law into their own hands should reflect 15 that when they are disobeying what they consider to be an immoral law, they are deciding on a possibly immoral course. Their answer is that the process for democratic relief is too slow, that only mass confrontation can bring immediate action, and that any injuries are the inevitable cost of the pursuit of justice. Their answer is, simply put, that the end justifies the means. It is this justification of any form of demonstration as a form of dissent that threatens to destroy a society built on the rule of law.

Our Bill of Rights guarantees wide opportunities to use mass meetings, 16 public parades and organized demonstrations to stimulate sentiment, to dramatize issues and to cause change. The Washington freedom march of 1963 was such a call for action. But the rights of free expression cannot be mere force cloaked in the garb of free speech. As the courts have decreed in labor cases, free assembly does not mean mass picketing or sit-down strikes. These rights are subject to limitations of time and place so as to secure the rights of others. When militant students storm a college president's office to achieve demands, when certain groups plan rush-hour car stalling to protest discrimination in employment, these are not dissent, but a denial of rights to others. Neither is it the lawful use of mass protest, but rather the unlawful use of mob power.

Justice Black, one of the foremost advocates and defenders of the right 17 of protest and dissent, has said:

> . . . Experience demonstrates that it is not a far step from what to many seems to be the earnest, honest, patriotic, kind-spirited multitude of today, to the fanatical, threatening, lawless mob of tomorrow. And the crowds that press in the streets for noble goals today can be supplanted tomorrow by street mobs pressuring the courts for precisely opposite ends.

Society must censure those demonstrators who would trespass on the 18 public peace, as it must condemn those rioters whose pillage would destroy the public peace. But more ambivalent is society's posture toward the civil disobedient. Unlike the rioter, the true civil disobedient commits no violence. Unlike the mob demonstrator, he commits no trespass on others' rights. The civil disobedient, while deliberately violating a law, shows an oblique respect for the law by voluntarily submitting to its sanctions. He neither resists arrest nor evades punishment. Thus, he breaches the law but not the peace.

But civil disobedience, whatever the ethical rationalization, is still an 19
assault on our democratic society, an affront to our legal order and an
attack on our constitutional government. To indulge civil disobedience
is to invite anarchy, and the permissive arbitrariness of anarchy is hardly
less tolerable than the repressive arbitrariness of tyranny. Too often the
license of liberty is followed by the loss of liberty, because into the desert
of anarchy comes the man on horseback, a Mussolini or a Hitler.

### Violations of Law Subvert Democracy

Law violations, even for ends recognized as laudable, are not only 20
assaults on the rule of law, but subversions of the democratic process.
The disobedient act of conscience does not ennoble democracy; it erodes
it.

First, it courts violence, and even the most careful and limited use of 21
nonviolent acts of disobedience may help sow the dragon-teeth of civil
riot. Civil disobedience is the progenitor of disorder, and disorder is the
sire of violence.

Second, the concept of civil disobedience does not invite principles 22
of general applicability. If the children of light are morally privileged to
resist particular laws on grounds of conscience, so are the children of
darkness. Former Deputy Attorney General Burke Marshall said: "If the
decision to break the law really turned on individual conscience, it is
hard to see in law how [the civil rights leader] is better off than former
Governor Ross Barnett of Mississippi who also believed deeply in his
cause and was willing to go to jail."

Third, even the most noble act of civil disobedience assaults the rule 23
of law. Although limited as to method, motive and objective, it has the
effect of inducing others to engage in different forms of law breaking
characterized by methods unsanctioned and condemned by classic theories of law violation. Unfortunately, the most patent lesson of civil disobedience is not so much nonviolence of action as defiance of authority.

Finally, the greatest danger in condoning civil disobedience as a per- 24
missible strategy for hastening change is that it undermines our democratic processes. To adopt the techniques of civil disobedience is to assume that representative government does not work. To resist the
decisions of courts and the laws of elected assemblies is to say that democracy has failed.

There is no man who is above the law, and there is no man who has 25
a right to break the law. Civil disobedience is not above the law, but
against the law. When the civil disobedient disobeys one law, he invariably subverts all law. When the civil disobedient says that he is above

the law, he is saying that democracy is beneath him. His disobedience shows a distrust for the democratic system. He is merely saying that since democracy does not work, why should he help make it work. Thoreau expressed well the civil disobedient's disdain for democracy:

> As for adopting the ways which the state has provided for remedying the evil, I know not of such ways. They take too much time and a man's life will be gone. I have other affairs to attend to. I came into this world not chiefly to make this a good place to live in, but to live in it, be it good or bad.

Thoreau's position is not only morally irresponsible but politically reprehensible. When citizens in a democracy are called on to make a profession of faith, the civil disobedients offer only a confession of failure. Tragically, when civil disobedients for lack of faith abstain from democratic involvement, they help attain their own gloomy prediction. They help create the social and political basis for their own despair. By foreseeing failure, they help forge it. If citizens rely on antidemocratic means of protest, they will help bring about the undemocratic result of an authoritarian or anarchic state.   26

How far demonstrations properly can be employed to produce political and social change is a pressing question, particularly in view of the provocations accompanying the National Democratic Convention in Chicago last August and the reaction of the police to them. A line must be drawn by the judiciary between the demands of those who seek absolute order, which can lead only to a dictatorship, and those who seek absolute freedom, which can lead only to anarchy. The line, wherever it is drawn by our courts, should be respected on the college campus, on the streets and elsewhere.   27

Undue provocation will inevitably result in overreaction, human emotions being what they are. Violence will follow. This cycle undermines the very democracy it is designed to preserve. The lesson of the past is that democracies will fall if violence, including the intentional provocations that will lead to violence, replaces democratic procedures, as in Athens, Rome and the Weimar Republic. This lesson must be constantly explained by the legal profession.   28

We should heed the words of William James:   29

> Democracy is still upon its trial. The civic genius of our people is its only bulwark and . . . neither battleships nor public libraries nor great newspapers nor booming stocks: neither mechanical invention nor political adroitness, nor churches nor universities nor civil service examinations can save us from degeneration if the inner mystery be lost.
>
> That mystery, at once the secret and the glory of our English-speaking race, consists of nothing but two habits. . . . One of them is habit of trained and

disciplined good temper towards the opposite party when it fairly wins its innings. The other is that of fierce and merciless resentment toward every man or set of men who break the public peace. (James, *Pragmatism* 1907, pages 127–128)

## QUESTIONS FOR ANALYSIS

1. How useful for you as a reader is Van Dusen's strategy of dividing his argument into sections and giving each a subheading? To answer this question, begin by outlining the argument. (See the discussion of outlining an argument in Chapter 1.)

2. Van Dusen begins his essay by defining the central term, civil disobedience. Summarize this definition. Why does he claim in paragraph 7 that Martin Luther King, Jr., "should not be considered a true civil disobedient"? Assuming that he is representing King accurately, how convincing do you find the distinction he draws between King and the other civil disobedients he cites?

3. How does Van Dusen answer his own rhetorical question, "Was the Boston Tea Party Civil Disobedience?" How does he use the case of the Boston Tea Party to support his argument against what he calls in paragraph 13 "the injustice rationale" for civil disobedience?

4. Van Dusen asserts at the end of paragraph 10 that civil disobedience is justified only if there is "no popular assembly" or "court system." Consider each of the following hypothetical situations, explaining how you think Van Dusen would respond and how you would respond: (a) In a democratic society with a duly elected assembly and a court system, would civil disobedience be justified if a minority of the people were prevented from voting on laws that governed their own lives, as was the case in some southern states and is currently the case in South Africa under apartheid? (b) In a democratic society with a duly elected assembly and a court system, would civil disobedience be justified if the government pursued a heinous policy such as using chemical warfare or committing genocide?

5. In paragraphs 14–19 Van Dusen distinguishes between "legitimate" and "illegitimate" kinds of demonstrations. Take inventory of the acts he includes under each heading. Then explain his distinction, indicating why you do or do not accept it. (Chapter 1 has procedures for taking inventory.)

6. Examine the list of reasons why civil disobedience erodes democracy. Select a reason you think is weak and write a paragraph refuting it. If you do not think any of Van Dusen's reasons is weak, write a paragraph defending one of them against possible criticism.

7. How would you characterize the tone of the last few paragraphs? Is this tone consistent throughout the essay, or does it vary? Point to specific passages to illustrate your answer.

8. Van Dusen frames this essay with quotations from respected authorities, and throughout the essay he alludes to and sometimes quotes other important historical figures. How does this writing strategy contribute to his credibility?

9. Evaluate the logic of Van Dusen's argument. Why do you think he argues in the beginning that Martin Luther King, Jr., is not a "true civil disobedient" if in the end he intends to criticize all forms of civil disobedience? (See Chapter 1 for advice on evaluating an essay's logic.)

## SUGGESTIONS FOR WRITING

1. Write a position paper arguing for your own definition of civil disobedience. You may want to explain how your definition corresponds with or diverges from Van Dusen's definition.

2. Write an essay agreeing or disagreeing with Van Dusen's judgment about the Boston Tea Party. Was it an act of civil disobedience? To prepare your essay, you will probably have to do some library research. (See the appendix for advice on using the library.)

3. In the opening of his essay, Van Dusen refers to famous documents on civil disobedience by Plato, Sophocles, and Thoreau. Read one of these authors and then write a position paper, explaining why you agree or disagree with him.

# Martin Luther King, Jr.

Martin Luther King, Jr. (1929–1968) is a modern American hero for many people in this country and around the world. His birthday was recently made a national holiday to commemorate both the man and the movement he led. A Baptist minister who became leader of the civil rights movement, King was awarded the Nobel Peace Prize in 1964 and was assassinated in 1968.

King graduated from Morehouse College and Grozer Theological Seminary and earned a Ph.D. from Boston University. He was pastor at a Montgomery, Alabama, church in 1955 when he first advocated civil disobedience, a citywide bus boycott protesting segregated seating on public transportation. In 1957 King organized the Southern Christian Leadership Conference, and a year later he moved the headquarters to Atlanta, Georgia, where he became pastor with his father of the Ebenezer Baptist Church.

King carried his campaign of civil disobedience throughout the South. In 1963 he went to Birmingham, Alabama, to lead protestors in a demonstration against segregation of restaurants, hotels, and department stores. Violence escalated and a black church was bombed, killing four little girls. King was arrested and jailed. In prison, he wrote the following selection, an expression of his moral philosophy and a justification of civil disobedience.

## *Letter from Birmingham Jail*

King wrote this essay in response to a public statement published in a local newspaper. In fact, he began writing his reaction in the margins of the newspaper and eventually made it public. The statement, reprinted on page 6, was signed by eight clergymen, and although it does not explicitly mention King or the Southern Christian Leadership Conference, it criticizes him for exporting civil disobedience to Birmingham. Before reading King's letter, look back at the clergymen's statement. Then ask yourself how you would have responded if you were in King's place. How would you defend King's actions?

MY DEAR FELLOW CLERGYMEN:

While confined here in the Birmingham city jail, I came across your 1 recent statement calling my present activities "unwise and untimely." Seldom do I pause to answer criticism of my work and ideas. If I sought to answer all the criticisms that cross my desk, my secretaries would have little time for anything other than such correspondence in the course of the day, and I would have no time for constructive work. But since I feel that you are men of genuine good will and that your criticisms are sincerely set forth, I want to try to answer your statement in what I hope will be patient and reasonable terms.

I think I should indicate why I am here in Birmingham, since you have been influenced by the view which argues against "outsiders coming in." I have the honor of serving as president of the Southern Christian Leadership Conference, an organization operating in every southern state, with headquarters in Atlanta, Georgia. We have some eighty-five affiliated organizations across the South, and one of them is the Alabama Christian Movement for Human Rights. Frequently we share staff, educational, and financial resources with our affiliates. Several months ago the affiliate here in Birmingham asked us to be on call to engage in a nonviolent direct-action program if such were deemed necessary. We readily consented, and when the hour came we lived up to our promise. So I, along with several members of my staff, am here because I was invited here. I am here because I have organizational ties here.

But more basically, I am in Birmingham because injustice is here. Just as the prophets of the eighth century B.C. left their villages and carried their "thus saith the Lord" far beyond the boundaries of their home towns, and just as the Apostle Paul left his village of Tarsus and carried the gospel of Jesus Christ to the far corners of the Greco-Roman world, so am I compelled to carry the gospel of freedom beyond my own home town. Like Paul, I must constantly respond to the Macedonian call for aid.

Moreover, I am cognizant of the interrelatedness of all communities and states. I cannot sit idly by in Atlanta and not be concerned about what happens in Birmingham. Injustice anywhere is a threat to justice everywhere. We are caught in an inescapable network of mutuality, tied in a single garment of destiny. Whatever affects one directly, affects all indirectly. Never again can we afford to live with the narrow, provincial "outside agitator" idea. Anyone who lives inside the United States can never be considered an outsider anywhere within its bounds.

You deplore the demonstrations taking place in Birmingham. But your statement, I am sorry to say, fails to express a similar concern for the conditions that brought about the demonstrations. I am sure that none of you would want to rest content with the superficial kind of social analysis that deals merely with effects and does not grapple with underlying causes. It is unfortunate that demonstrations are taking place in Birmingham, but it is even more unfortunate that the city's white power structure left the Negro community with no alternative.

In any nonviolent campaign there are four basic steps: collection of 6
the facts to determine whether injustices exist; negotiation; self-purification; and direct action. We have gone through all these steps in Birmingham. There can be no gainsaying the fact that racial injustice engulfs
this community. Birmingham is probably the most thoroughly segregated
city in the United States. Its ugly record of brutality is widely known.
Negroes have experienced grossly unjust treatment in the courts. There
have been more unsolved bombings of Negro homes and churches in
Birmingham than in any other city in the nation. These are the hard,
brutal facts of the case. On the basis of these conditions, Negro leaders
sought to negotiate with the city fathers. But the latter consistently
refused to engage in good-faith negotiation.

Then, last September, came the opportunity to talk with leaders of 7
Birmingham's economic community. In the course of the negotiations,
certain promises were made by the merchants—for example, to remove
the stores' humiliating racial signs. On the basis of these promises, the
Reverend Fred Shuttlesworth and the leaders of the Alabama Christian
Movement for Human Rights agreed to a moratorium on all demonstrations. As the weeks and months went by, we realized that we were the
victims of a broken promise. A few signs, briefly removed, returned; the
others remained.

As in so many past experiences, our hopes had been blasted, and the 8
shadow of deep disappointment settled upon us. We had no alternative
except to prepare for direct action, whereby we would present our very
bodies as a means of laying our case before the conscience of the local
and the national community. Mindful of the difficulties involved, we
decided to undertake a process of self-purification. We began a series of
workshops on nonviolence, and we repeatedly asked ourselves: "Are you
able to accept blows without retaliating?" "Are you able to endure the
ordeal of jail?" We decided to schedule our direct-action program for the
Easter season, realizing that except for Christmas, this is the main shopping period of the year. Knowing that a strong economic-withdrawal
program would be the by-product of direct action, we felt that this would
be the best time to bring pressure to bear on the merchants for the needed
change.

Then it occurred to us that Birmingham's mayoral election was coming 9
up in March, and we speedily decided to postpone action until after
election day. When we discovered that the Commissioner of Public
Safety, Eugene "Bull" Connor, had piled up enough votes to be in the
run-off, we decided again to postpone action until the day after the run-
off so that the demonstrations could not be used to cloud the issues. Like
many others, we wanted to see Mr. Connor defeated, and to this end

we endured postponement after postponement. Having aided in this community need, we felt that our direct-action program could be delayed no longer.

You may well ask, "Why direct action? Why sit-ins, marches, and so forth? Isn't negotiation a better path?" You are quite right in calling for negotiation. Indeed, this is the very purpose of direct action. Nonviolent direct action seeks to create such a crisis and foster such a tension that a community which has constantly refused to negotiate is forced to confront the issue. It seeks so to dramatize the issue that it can no longer be ignored. My citing the creation of tension as part of the work of the nonviolent-resister may sound rather shocking. But I must confess that I am not afraid of the word "tension." I have earnestly opposed violent tension, but there is a type of constructive, nonviolent tension which is necessary for growth. Just as Socrates felt that it was necessary to create a tension in the mind so that individuals could rise from the bondage of myths and half-truths to the unfettered realm of creative analysis and objective appraisal, so must we see the need for nonviolent gadflies to create the kind of tension in society that will help men rise from the dark depths of prejudice and racism to the majestic heights of understanding and brotherhood. 10

The purpose of our direct-action program is to create a situation so crisis-packed that it will inevitably open the door to negotiation. I therefore concur with you in your call for negotiation. Too long has our beloved Southland been bogged down in a tragic effort to live in monologue rather than dialogue. 11

One of the basic points in your statement is that the action that I and my associates have taken in Birmingham is untimely. Some have asked: "Why didn't you give the new city administration time to act?" The only answer that I can given to this query is that the new Birmingham administration must be prodded about as much as the outgoing one, before it will act. We are sadly mistaken if we feel that the election of Albert Boutwell as mayor will bring the millennium to Birmingham. While Mr. Boutwell is a much more gentle person than Mr. Connor, they are both segregationists, dedicated to maintenance of the status quo. I have hoped that Mr. Boutwell will be reasonable enough to see the futility of massive resistance to desegregation. But he will not see this without pressure from devotees of civil rights. My friends, I must say to you that we have not made a single gain in civil rights without determined legal and nonviolent pressure. Lamentably, it is an historical fact that privileged groups seldom give up their privileges voluntarily. Individuals may see the moral light and voluntarily give up their unjust posture; but, as Reinhold Niebuhr has reminded us, groups tend to be more immoral than individuals. 12

We know through painful experience that freedom is never voluntarily 13 given by the oppressor; it must be demanded by the oppressed. Frankly, I have yet to engage in a direct-action campaign that was "well timed" in the view of those who have not suffered unduly from the disease of segregation. For years now I have heard the word "Wait!" It rings in the ear of every Negro with piercing familiarity. This "Wait" has almost always meant "Never." We must come to see, with one of our distinguished jurists, that "justice too long delayed is justice denied."

We have waited for more than 340 years for our constitutional and 14 God-given rights. The nations of Asia and Africa are moving with jetlike speed toward gaining political independence, but we still creep at horse-and-buggy pace toward gaining a cup of coffee at a lunch counter. Perhaps it is easy for those who have never felt the stinging darts of segregation to say, "Wait." But when you have seen vicious mobs lynch your mothers and fathers at will and drown your sisters and brothers at whim; when you have seen hate-filled policemen curse, kick, and even kill your black brothers and sisters; when you see the vast majority of your twenty million Negro brothers smothering in an airtight cage of poverty in the midst of an affluent society; when you suddenly find your tongue twisted and your speech stammering as you seek to explain to your six-year-old daughter why she can't go to the public amusement park that has just been advertised on television, and see tears welling up in her eyes when she is told that Funtown is closed to colored children, and see ominous clouds of inferiority beginning to form in her little mental sky, and see her beginning to distort her personality by developing an unconscious bitterness toward white people; when you have to concoct an answer for a five-year-old son who is asking, "Daddy, why do white people treat colored people so mean?"; when you take a cross-country drive and find it necessary to sleep night after night in the uncomfortable corners of your automobile because no motel will accept you; when you are humiliated day in and day out by nagging signs reading "white" and "colored"; when your first name becomes "nigger," your middle name becomes "boy" (however old you are) and your last name becomes "John," and your wife and mother are never given the respected title "Mrs."; when you are harried by day and haunted by night by the fact that you are a Negro, living constantly at tiptoe stance, never quite knowing what to expect next, and are plagued with inner fears and outer resentments; when you are forever fighting a degenerating sense of "nobodiness"—then you will understand why we find it difficult to wait. There comes a time when the cup of endurance runs over, and men are no longer willing to be plunged into the abyss of despair. I hope, sirs, you can understand our legitimate and unavoidable impatience.

You express a great deal of anxiety over our willingness to break laws. 15
This is certainly a legitimate concern. Since we so diligently urge people
to obey the Supreme Court's decision of 1954 outlawing segregation in
the public schools, at first glance it may seem rather paradoxical for us
consciously to break laws. One may well ask: "How can you advocate
breaking some laws and obeying others?" The answer lies in the fact that
there are two types of laws: just and unjust. I would be the first to
advocate obeying just laws. One has not only a legal but a moral responsibility to obey just laws. Conversely, one has a moral responsibility
to disobey unjust laws. I would agree with St. Augustine that "an unjust
law is no law at all."

Now, what is the difference between the two? How does one determine 16
whether a law is just or unjust? A just law is a man-made code that
squares with the moral law or the law of God. An unjust law is a code
that is out of harmony with the moral law. To put it in the terms of St.
Thomas Aquinas: An unjust law is a human law that is not rooted in
eternal law and natural law. Any law that uplifts human personality is
just. Any law that degrades human personality is unjust. All segregation
statutes are unjust because segregation distorts the soul and damages the
personality. It gives the segregator a false sense of superiority and the
segregated a false sense of inferiority. Segregation, to use the terminology
of the Jewish philosopher Martin Buber, substitutes an "I-it" relationship
for an "I-thou" relationship and ends up relegating persons to the status
of things. Hence segregation is not only politically, economically, and
sociologically unsound, it is morally wrong and sinful. Paul Tillich has
said that sin is separation. Is not segregation an existential expression of
man's tragic separation, his awful estrangement, his terrible sinfulness?
Thus it is that I can urge men to obey the 1954 decision of the Supreme
Court, for it is morally right; and I can urge them to disobey segregation
ordinances, for they are morally wrong.

Let us consider a more concrete example of just and unjust laws. An 17
unjust law is a code that a numerical or power majority group compels a
minority group to obey but does not make binding on itself. This is
*difference* made legal. By the same token, a just law is a code that a
majority compels a minority to follow and that it is willing to follow
itself. This is *sameness* made legal.

Let me give another explanation. A law is unjust if it is inflicted on 18
a minority that, as a result of being denied the right to vote, had no part
in enacting or devising the law. Who can say that the legislature of
Alabama which set up that state's segregation laws was democratically
elected? Throughout Alabama all sorts of devious methods are used to
prevent Negroes from becoming registered voters, and there are some

counties in which, even though Negroes constitute a majority of the population, not a single Negro is registered. Can any law enacted under such circumstances be considered democratically structured?

Sometimes a law is just on its face and unjust in its application. For instance, I have been arrested on a charge of parading without a permit. Now, there is nothing wrong in having an ordinance which requires a permit for a parade. But such an ordinance becomes unjust when it is used to maintain segregation and to deny citizens the First-Amendment privilege of peaceful assembly and protest. [19]

I hope you are able to see the distinction I am trying to point out. In no sense do I advocate evading or defying the law, as would the rabid segregationist. That would lead to anarchy. One who breaks an unjust law must do so openly, lovingly, and with a willingness to accept the penalty. I submit that an individual who breaks a law that conscience tells him is unjust, and who willingly accepts the penalty of imprisonment in order to arouse the conscience of the community over its injustice, is in reality expressing the highest respect for law. [20]

Of course, there is nothing new about this kind of civil disobedience. It was evidenced sublimely in the refusal of Shadrach, Meshach, and Abednego to obey the laws of Nebuchadnezzar, on the ground that a higher moral law was at stake. It was practiced superbly by the early Christians, who were willing to face hungry lions and the excruciating pain of chopping blocks rather than submit to certain unjust laws of the Roman Empire. To a degree, academic freedom is a reality today because Socrates practiced civil disobedience. In our own nation, the Boston Tea Party represented a massive act of civil disobedience. [21]

We should never forget that everything Adolf Hitler did in Germany was "legal" and everything the Hungarian freedom fighters did in Hungary was "illegal." It was "illegal" to aid and comfort a Jew in Hitler's Germany. Even so, I am sure that, had I lived in Germany at the time, I would have aided and comforted my Jewish brothers. If today I lived in a Communist country where certain principles dear to the Christian faith are suppressed, I would openly advocate disobeying that country's antireligious laws. [22]

I must make two honest confessions to you, my Christian and Jewish brothers. First, I must confess that over the past few years I have been gravely disappointed with the white moderate. I have almost reached the regrettable conclusion that the Negro's great stumbling block in his stride toward freedom is not the White Citizen's Counciler or the Ku Klux Klanner, but the white moderate, who is more devoted to "order" than to justice; who prefers a negative peace which is the absence of tension to a positive peace which is the presence of justice; who constantly says, "I [23] agree with you in the goal you seek, but I cannot agree with your methods of direct action"; who paternalistically believes he can set the timetable for another man's freedom; who lives by a mythical concept of time and who constantly advises the Negro to wait for a "more convenient season." Shallow understanding from people of good will is more frustrating than absolute misunderstanding from people of ill will. Lukewarm acceptance is much more bewildering than outright rejection.

I had hoped that the white moderate would understand that law and  24
order exist for the purpose of establishing justice and that when they fail in this purpose they become the dangerously structured dams that block the flow of social progress. I had hoped that the white moderate would understand that the present tension in the South is a necessary phase of the transition from an obnoxious negative peace, in which the Negro passively accepted his unjust plight, to a substantive and positive peace, in which all men will respect the dignity and worth of human personality. Actually, we who engage in nonviolent direct action are not the creators of tension. We merely bring to the surface the hidden tension that is already alive. We bring it out in the open, where it can be seen and dealt with. Like a boil that can never be cured so long as it is covered up but must be opened with all its ugliness to the natural medicines of air and light, injustice must be exposed, with all the tension its exposure creates, to the light of human conscience and the air of national opinion, before it can be cured.

In your statement you assert that our actions, even though peaceful,  25
must be condemned because they precipitate violence. But is this a logical assertion? Isn't this like condemning a robbed man because his possession of money precipitated the evil act of robbery? Isn't this like condemning Socrates because his unswerving commitment to truth and his philosophical inquiries precipitated the act by the misguided populace in which they made him drink hemlock? Isn't this like condemning Jesus because his unique God-consciousness and never-ceasing devotion to God's will precipitated the evil act of crucifixion? We must come to see that, as the federal courts have consistently affirmed, it is wrong to urge an individual to cease his efforts to gain his basic constitutional rights because the quest may precipitate violence. Society must protect the robbed and punish the robber.

I had also hoped that the white moderate would reject the myth con-  26
cerning time in relation to the struggle for freedom. I have just received a letter from a white brother in Texas. He writes: "All Christians know that the colored people will receive equal rights eventually, but it is possible that you are in too great a religious hurry. It has taken Christianity almost two thousand years to accomplish what it has. The teach-

ings of Christ take time to come to earth." Such an attitude stems from a tragic misconception of time, from the strangely irrational notion that there is something in the very flow of time that will inevitably cure all ills. Actually, time itself is neutral; it can be used either destructively or constructively. More and more I feel that the people of ill will have used time much more effectively than have the people of good will. We will have to repent in this generation not merely for the hateful words and actions of the bad people, but for the appalling silence of the good people. Human progress never rolls in on wheels of inevitability; it comes through the tireless efforts of men willing to be co-workers with God, and without this hard work, time itself becomes an ally of the forces of social stagnation. We must use time creatively, in the knowledge that the time is always ripe to do right. Now is the time to make real the promise of democracy and transform our pending national elegy into a creative psalm of brotherhood. Now is the time to lift our national policy from the quicksand of racial injustice to the solid rock of human dignity.

You speak of our activity in Birmingham as extreme. At first I was rather disappointed that fellow clergymen would see my nonviolent efforts as those of an extremist. I began thinking about the fact that I stand in the middle of two opposing forces in the Negro community. One is a force of complacency, made up in part of Negroes who, as a result of long years of oppression, are so drained of self-respect and a sense of "somebodiness" that they have adjusted to segregation; and in part of a few middle-class Negroes who, because of a degree of academic and economic security and because in some ways they profit by segregation, have become insensitive to the problems of the masses. The other force is one of bitterness and hatred, and it comes perilously close to advocating violence. It is expressed in the various black nationalist groups that are springing up across the nation, the largest and best-known being Elijah Muhammad's Muslim movement. Nourished by the Negro's frustration over the continued existence of racial discrimination, this movement is made up of people who have lost faith in America, who have absolutely repudiated Christianity, and who have concluded that the white man is an incorrigible "devil." 27

I have tried to stand between these two forces, saying that we need emulate neither the "do-nothingism" of the complacent nor the hatred and despair of the black nationalist. For there is the more excellent way of love and nonviolent protest. I am grateful to God that, through the influence of the Negro church, the way of nonviolence became an integral part of our struggle. 28

If this philosophy had not emerged, by now many streets of the South would, I am convinced, be flowing with blood. And I am further con- 29 vinced that if our white brothers dismiss as "rabblerousers" and "outside agitators" those of us who employ nonviolent direct action, and if they refuse to support our nonviolent efforts, millions of Negroes will, out of frustration and despair, seek solace and security in black-nationalist ideologies—a development that would inevitably lead to a frightening racial nightmare.

Oppressed people cannot remain oppressed forever. The yearning for freedom eventually manifests itself, and that is what has happened to the American Negro. Something within has reminded him of his birthright of freedom, and something without has reminded him that it can be gained. Consciously or unconsciously, he has been caught up by the *Zeitgeist*, and with his black brothers of Africa and his brown and yellow brothers of Asia, South America, and the Caribbean, the United States Negro is moving with a sense of great urgency toward the promised land of racial justice. If one recognizes this vital urge that has engulfed the Negro community, one should readily understand why public demonstrations are taking place. The Negro has many pent-up resentments and latent frustrations, and he must release them. So let him march; let him make prayer pilgrimages to the city hall; let him go on freedom rides— and try to understand why he must do so. If his repressed emotions are not released in nonviolent ways, they will seek expression through violence; this is not a threat but a fact of history. So I have not said to my people, "Get rid of your discontent." Rather, I have tried to say that this normal and healthy discontent can be channeled into the creative outlet of nonviolent direct action. And now this approach is being termed extremist.

But though I was initially disappointed at being categorized as an extremist, as I continued to think about the matter I gradually gained a measure of satisfaction from the label. Was not Jesus an extremist for love: "Love your enemies, bless them that curse you, do good to them that hate you, and pray for them which despitefully use you, and persecute you." Was not Amos an extremist for justice: "Let justice roll down like waters and righteousness like an ever-flowing stream." Was not Paul an extremist for the Christian gospel: "I bear in my body the marks of the Lord Jesus." Was not Martin Luther an extremist: "Here I stand; I cannot do otherwise, so help me God." And John Bunyan: "I will stay in jail to the end of my days before I make a butchery of my conscience." And Abraham Lincoln: "This nation cannot survive half slave and half free." And Thomas Jefferson: "We hold these truths to be self-evident, that all men are created equal. . . ." So the question is not whether we will be extremists, but what kind of extremists we will be. Will we be extremists for hate or for love? Will we be extremists for the preservation of injustice or for the extension of justice? In that dramatic scene on Calvary's hill three men were crucified. We must never forget that all three were crucified for the same crime—the crime of extremism. Two were extremists for immorality, and thus fell below their environment. The other, Jesus Christ, was an extremist for love, truth, and goodness, and thereby rose above his environment. Perhaps the South, the nation, and the world are in dire need of creative extremists.

I had hoped that the white moderate would see this need. Perhaps I 32 was too optimistic; perhaps I expected too much. I suppose I should have realized that few members of the oppressor race can understand the deep groans and passionate yearnings of the oppressed race, and still fewer have the vision to see that injustice must be rooted out by strong, persistent, and determined action. I am thankful, however, that some of our white brothers in the South have grasped the meaning of this social revolution and committed themselves to it. They are still all too few in quantity, but they are big in quality. Some—such as Ralph McGill, Lillian Smith, Harry Golden, James McBride Dabbs, Ann Braden, and Sarah Patton Boyle—have written about our struggle in eloquent and prophetic terms. Others have marched with us down nameless streets of the South. They have languished in filthy, roach-infested jails, suffering the abuse and brutality of policemen who view them as "dirty niggerlovers." Unlike so many of their moderate brothers and sisters, they have recognized the urgency of the moment and sensed the need for powerful "action" antidotes to combat the disease of segregation.

Let me take note of my other major disappointment. I have been so 33 greatly disappointed with the white church and its leadership. Of course, there are some notable exceptions. I am not unmindful of the fact that each of you has taken some significant stands on this issue. I commend you, Reverend Stallings, for your Christian stand on this past Sunday, in welcoming Negroes to your worship service on a nonsegregated basis. I commend the Catholic leaders of this state for integrating Spring Hill College several years ago.

But despite these notable exceptions, I must honestly reiterate that I 34 have been disappointed with the church. I do not say this as one of those negative critics who can always find something wrong with the church. I say this as a minister of the gospel, who loves the church; who was nurtured in its bosom; who has been sustained by its spiritual blessings and who will remain true to it as long as the cord of life shall lengthen.

When I was suddenly catapulted into the leadership of the bus protest 35 in Montgomery, Alabama, a few years ago, I felt we would be supported by the white church. I felt that the white ministers, priests, and rabbis of the South would be among our strongest allies. Instead, some have been outright opponents, refusing to understand the freedom movement and misrepresenting its leaders; all too many others have been more cautious than courageous and have remained silent behind the anesthetizing security of stained glass windows.

In spite of my shattered dreams, I came to Birmingham with the hope    36 that the white religious leadership of this community would see the justice of our cause and, with deep moral concern, would serve as the channel through which our just grievances could reach the power structure. I had hoped that each of you would understand. But again I have been disappointed.

I have heard numerous southern religious leaders admonish their wor-    37 shipers to comply with a desegregation decision because it is the law, but I have longed to hear white ministers declare: "Follow this decree because integration is morally right and because the Negro is your brother." In the midst of blatant injustices inflicted upon the Negro, I have watched white churchmen stand on the sideline and mouth pious irrelevancies and sanctimonious trivialities. In the midst of a mighty struggle to rid our nation of racial and economic injustice, I have heard many ministers say: "Those are social issues, with which the gospel has no real concern." And I have watched many churches commit themselves to a completely otherworldly religion which makes a strange, un-Biblical distinction between body and soul, between the sacred and the secular.

I have traveled the length and breadth of Alabama, Mississippi, and    38 all the other southern states. On sweltering summer days and crisp autumn mornings I have looked at the South's beautiful churches with their lofty spires pointing heavenward. I have beheld the impressive outlines of her massive religious-education buildings. Over and over I have found myself asking: "What kind of people worship here? Who is their God? Where were their voices when the lips of Governor Barnett dripped with words of interposition and nullification? Where were they when Governor Wallace gave a clarion call for defiance and hatred? Where were their voices of support when bruised and weary Negro men and women decided to rise from the dark dungeons of complacency to the bright hills of creative protest?"

Yes, these questions are still in my mind. In deep disappointment I    39 have wept over the laxity of the church. But be assured that my tears have been tears of love. There can be no deep disappointment where there is not deep love. Yes, I love the church. How could I do otherwise? I am in the rather unique position of being the son, the grandson, and the great-grandson of preachers. Yes, I see the church as the body of Christ. But, oh! How we have blemished and scarred that body through social neglect and through fear of being nonconformists.

There was a time when the church was very powerful—in the time 40 when the early Christians rejoiced at being deemed worthy to suffer for what they believed. In those days the church was not merely a thermometer that recorded the ideas and principles of popular opinion; it was a thermostat that transformed the mores of society. Whenever the early Christians entered a town, the people in power became disturbed and immediately sought to convict the Christians for being "disturbers of the peace" and "outside agitators." But the Christians pressed on, in the conviction that they were "a colony of heaven," called to obey God rather than man. Small in number, they were big in commitment. They were too God-intoxicated to be "astronomically intimidated." By their effort and example they brought an end to such ancient evils as infanticide and gladiatorial contests.

Things are different now. So often the contemporary church is a weak, 41 ineffectual voice with an uncertain sound. So often it is an archdefender of the status quo. Far from being disturbed by the presence of the church, the power structure of the average community is consoled by the church's silent—and often even vocal—sanction of things as they are.

But the judgment of God is upon the church as never before. If today's 42 church does not recapture the sacrificial spirit of the early church, it will lose its authenticity, forfeit the loyalty of millions, and be dismissed as an irrelevant social club with no meaning for the twentieth century. Every day I meet young people whose disappointment with the church has turned into outright disgust.

Perhaps I have once again been too optimistic. Is organized religion 43 too inextricably bound to the status quo to save our nation and the world? Perhaps I must turn my faith to the inner spiritual church, the church within the church, as the true *ekklesia* and the hope of the world. But again I am thankful to God that some noble souls from the ranks of organized religion have broken loose from the paralyzing chains of conformity and joined us as active partners in the struggle for freedom. They have left their secure congregations and walked the streets of Albany, Georgia, with us. They have gone down the highways of the South on tortuous rides for freedom. Yes, they have gone to jail with us. Some have been dismissed from their churches, have lost the support of their bishops and fellow ministers. But they have acted in the faith that right defeated is stronger than evil triumphant. Their witness has been the spiritual salt that has preserved the true meaning of the gospel in these troubled times. They have carved a tunnel of hope through the dark mountain of disappointment.

I hope the church as a whole will meet the challenge of this decisive 44 hour. But even if the church does not come to the aid of justice, I have no despair about the future. I have no fear about the outcome of our struggle in Birmingham, even if our motives are at present misunderstood. We will reach the goal of freedom in Birmingham and all over the nation, because the goal of America is freedom. Abused and scorned though we may be, our destiny is tied up with America's destiny. Before the pilgrims landed at Plymouth, we were here. Before the pen of Jefferson etched the majestic words of the Declaration of Independence across the pages of history, we were here. For more than two centuries our forebears labored in this country without wages; they made cotton king; they built the homes of their masters while suffering gross injustice and shameful humiliation—and yet out of a bottomless vitality they continued to thrive and develop. If the inexpressible cruelties of slavery could not stop us, the opposition we now face will surely fail. We will win our freedom because the sacred heritage of our nation and the eternal will of God are embodied in our echoing demands.

Before closing I feel impelled to mention one other point in your 45 statement that has troubled me profoundly. You warmly commended the Birmingham police force for keeping "order" and "preventing violence." I doubt that you would have so warmly commended the police force if you had seen its dogs sinking their teeth into unarmed, nonviolent Negroes. I doubt that you would so quickly commend the policemen if you were to observe their ugly and inhumane treatment of Negroes here in the city jail; if you were to watch them push and curse old Negro women and young Negro girls; if you were to see them slap and kick old Negro men and young boys; if you were to observe them, as they did on two occasions, refuse to give us food because we wanted to sing our grace together. I cannot join you in your praise of the Birmingham police department.

It is true that the police have exercised a degree of discipline in han- 46 dling the demonstrators. In this sense they have conducted themselves rather "nonviolently" in public. But for what purpose? To preserve the evil system of segregation. Over the past few years I have consistently preached that nonviolence demands that the means we use must be as pure as the ends we seek. I have tried to make clear that it is wrong to use immoral means to attain moral ends. But now I must affirm that it is just as wrong, or perhaps even more so, to use moral means to preserve immoral ends. Perhaps Mr. Connor and his policemen have been rather nonviolent in public, as was Chief Pritchett in Albany, Georgia, but they have used the moral means of nonviolence to maintain the immoral end of racial injustice. As T. S. Eliot has said, "The last temptation is the greatest treason: To do the right deed for the wrong reason."

I wish you had commended the Negro sit-inners and demonstrators of 47 Birmingham for their sublime courage, their willingness to suffer, and their amazing discipline in the midst of great provocation. One day the South will recognize its real heroes. They will be the James Merediths, with the noble sense of purpose that enables them to face jeering and hostile mobs, and with the agonizing loneliness that characterizes the life of the pioneer. They will be old, oppressed, battered Negro women, symbolized in a seventy-two-year-old woman in Montgomery, Alabama, who rose up with a sense of dignity and with her people decided not to ride segregated buses, and who responded with ungrammatical profundity to one who inquired about her weariness: "My feets is tired, but my soul is at rest." They will be the young high school and college students, the young ministers of the gospel and a host of their elders, courageously and nonviolently sitting in at lunch counters and willingly going to jail for conscience' sake. One day the South will know that when these disinherited children of God sat down at lunch counters, they were in reality standing up for what is best in the American dream and for the most sacred values in our Judaeo-Christian heritage, thereby bringing our nation back to those great wells of democracy which were dug deep by the founding fathers in their formulation of the Constitution and the Declaration of Independence.

Never before have I written so long a letter. I'm afraid it is much too 48 long to take your precious time. I can assure you that it would have been much shorter if I had been writing from a comfortable desk, but what else can one do when he is alone in a narrow jail cell, other than write long letters, think long thoughts, and pray long prayers?

If I have said anything in this letter that overstates the truth and 49 indicates an unreasonable impatience, I beg you to forgive me. If I have said anything that understates the truth and indicates my having a patience that allows me to settle for anything less than brotherhood, I beg God to forgive me.

I hope this letter finds you strong in the faith. I also hope that cir- 50 cumstances will soon make it possible for me to meet each of you, not as an integrationist or a civil-rights leader but as a fellow clergyman and a Christian brother. Let us all hope that the dark clouds of racial prejudice will soon pass away and the deep fog of misunderstanding will be lifted from our fear-drenched communities, and in some not too distant tomorrow the radiant stars of love and brotherhood will shine over our great nation with all their scintillating beauty.

Yours for the cause of Peace and Brotherhood,
MARTIN LUTHER KING, JR.

## QUESTIONS FOR ANALYSIS

1. We can see from the clergymen's statement and can also infer from the letter that four objections were made against King. Separate the strands of his response to each of these criticisms. Then briefly summarize each criticism and King's response.

2. King refers to many biblical and historical figures. Identify three of these allusions and explain how each works in the essay. From this analysis, what can you conclude about the advantages or disadvantages of using allusion in a position paper? (See Chapter 1 for advice on summarizing.)

3. In paragraphs 5–9 King narrates the events that led him to Birmingham. Examine this narrative carefully, and then describe how he uses it as an argumentative strategy. How effective do you think it is?

4. Why does King differentiate between just and unjust laws? Examine his distinction closely. How do just laws differ from unjust laws? Do you accept his assertion that we have a "moral responsibility to disobey unjust laws"? Why or why not?

5. How does King move from his disappointment at being labeled an extremist to the idea that he should be proud of the description? In what ways does he regard himself as a moderate? as an extremist?

6. From the salutation of this letter we know that King is specifically addressing clergymen. What other evidence can you find in the text to suggest that he framed his argument particularly for religious leaders? As a general reader, do you feel that the essay is not addressed to you? How does King make his writing accessible?

7. Where in this essay does King appeal to his readers' emotions? How effective is this appeal? (Analyzing an Argument in Chapter 1 discusses the emotional appeal.)

8. Characterize the tone of this essay. Is it consistent throughout? What can you conclude about King's use of tone as an argumentative strategy? (See the discussion of ethical appeal in Chapter 1.)

## SUGGESTIONS FOR WRITING

1. Write a position paper in which you respond to this claim: Civil disobedience is a threat to the order and stability of society. In writing your essay, refer to King's essay as well as Van Dusen's.

2. Van Dusen accuses King of letting the end justify the means (paragraph 15). The issue of whether ends justify means has long been debated and comes up repeatedly in both formal and informal argu-

ments. Write an essay in which you argue your opinion on this issue. You may refer to related issues of civil disobedience and capital punishment as examples, but keep your focus on the larger philosophical question of ends justifying means.

3. In his essay King suggests that religious leaders should play an active role in politics. In recent years the Moral Majority, under the direction of the Reverend Jerry Falwell, has had a major role in politics, and a minister—Pat Robertson—has announced as a contender for the Republican presidential nomination. Does the participation of religious leaders in politics contradict the idea of separation of church and state? Write an essay arguing for your position on this issue.

THE DEBATE:
ADDITIONAL QUESTIONS FOR ANALYSIS

1. In paragraph 7 Van Dusen claims that Martin Luther King, Jr., "was not a civil disobedient." What is your opinion? Why do you think King was or was not a true civil disobedient?

2. At the end of paragraph 10 Van Dusen declares: "If there is no popular assembly to provide an adjustment of ills, and if there is no court system to dispose of injustices, then there is, indeed, a right to rebel." Given that America had both a popular assembly and a court system, how would King justify his actions to Van Dusen?

3. Do you agree with Van Dusen that King believes that the end justifies the means? What evidence is there either way? Why does it matter?

4. King and Van Dusen both mention that the democratic process of relieving social injustice is often too slow. Contrast their responses to this problem. What does each think should be done? What do you think?

# Sam Job

Sam Job (b. 1955) works as a technical services librarian at a community college. Occasionally, he returns to the classroom to study a subject he is interested in, as was the case when he wrote the following essay. Job has many diverse interests. He does genealogical research and plans to write a history of his family. He also plays the guitar and studies folk music, is an expert gardener, and has mastered Spanish, which he taught in a bilingual elementary school classroom.

# 55 M.P.H.: An Outdated Law

While some people feel that the 55 m.p.h. speed limit is a nuisance, they obey it because it is law. Many others, however, consciously exceed the speed limit. In this essay, Job argues that the law is outdated, that changes have taken place that render it obsolete. Before reading the essay, try to imagine what these changes could be. Also, try to recall why the law was put into effect in the first place.

Tension filled the air as the cars revved their engines on the morning 1 of May 25, 1979. Record-breaking speeds had become commonplace on this 7.85-mile closed-circuit track in Nardo, Italy. Dr. Hans Liebold waited anxiously at the starting line in his Mercedes-Benz CIII-IV experimental coupe. Then the checkered flag dropped. A whir of squealing wheels blackened the pavement with friction-burned rubber as the roaring engine catapulted the sleek automobile down the track and into the first curve. Car and driver were one machine. The steering wheel turned left and right, the gears shifted up and down, and the car accelerated and decelerated to accommodate the turns and straightaways on the track. Liebold crossed the finish line with a lap time of 1 minute and 52.67 seconds for a new world record of 250.958 m.p.h. (*Guinness*, 1985, p. 343).

The technology used to design Liebold's Mercedes Benz has become 2 common knowledge within the last seven years. The cars on the road today are designed to cruise safely at high speeds, and the freeways are constructed like modern raceways to handle speeds in excess of 100 m.p.h. And yet, when the engine revs, the gear box whines, and the sleek new economy car pulls onto the freeway, it soon settles into a boring hum as the driver settles back for a long ride at 55 m.p.h.

As unreasonable as it may seem, the United States continues with an  3
outdated speed law—the 55 m.p.h. maximum speed restriction passed
on January 2, 1974. The government then justified it on the grounds
that it would conserve fuel and cut down traffic fatalities. The nation
was facing a feigned fuel-supply shortage at the time, and gas prices
climbed above $1.50 a gallon to meet the economic law of supply and
demand. Large gas-eating cars lined up for miles to get their weekly fuel
rations. Prices might have continued to rise, but a government investigation of the oil industry found that there was no fuel shortage after all
(Osborne, 1984, p. 89). During the oil industry investigation, however,
researchers confirmed the federal government's belief that lowering the
maximum speed limit to 55 m.p.h. would decrease the number of traffic
accidents and lower the fatality rate (Powell & Sheler, 19 May 1986, p.
27). When the fuel-shortage scandal was finally settled, a few states
wanted to reinstate the 65 m.p.h. maximum speed law. But the federal
government threatened to cut off all federal funding for road construction
and repair to any state that raised its maximum speed limit above 55
m.p.h. (Powell, 1986, p. 27).

Proponents of the 55 m.p.h. speed law proclaim that driving at 55  4
m.p.h. conserves energy, but they also declare that fossil fuel supplies
are limited. They fail to acknowledge that the gas shortage no longer
exists—if anything, the nation is suffering from an oil glut that has
lowered gas prices to less than a dollar a gallon (Osborne, 1984, p. 89).
They also fail to point out that within the last twelve years the United
States has become the largest nation of economy car owners in the world.
Some economy cars are getting better gas mileage than motorcycles—55
miles per gallon (Ceppos, 1984, p. 27). With the strides being made in
exploiting solar and other energy sources, the chances are great that some
other form of energy will be used to run automobiles long before fossil
fuel resources are exhausted (Tholstrup & Perkins, 1983, November, p.
600).

Advocates of the 55 m.p.h. speed law claim that motorists control  5
their cars better at slower speeds, which results in fewer accidents and
lower fatality rates. Logically, driving at slower speeds seems safer because
there is more time to observe, judge, act on pedestrian and traffic errors,
and stop when necessary to avoid accidents. Nevertheless, the proponents fail to inform us that the freeways in America are constructed to
handle speeds in excess of 100 m.p.h. New economy cars are designed
to cruise at speeds above 65 m.p.h. Road and weather conditions are
favorable for high-speed traffic in most states for at least six months of
the year. Special speed zones across long stretches of isolated rural valleys,
mountains, and deserts could eliminate boredom and better fit our fast-

paced society's needs (Powell, 1986, p. 27). Special speed zones on inner-city freeways during the late night and early morning hours could also accommodate commodity transportation vehicles, which have important deadlines to meet.

Those who favor the 55 m.p.h. speed law say that the new economy 6 cars are plastic coffins on wheels because plastic does not provide the protection that metal does. Nevertheless, these new economy cars are better equipped to prevent and survive an accident. They maneuver better, turn more easily and in less space, stop faster, and are replete with safety devices. Their bumpers are reinforced with rubber to cushion the impact of front- and rear-end collisions; their windows are made of safety glass to prevent serious cuts; many cars will not even start unless the seat belts are fastened.

A recent California Highway Patrol report stated that the average 7 motorist (69.6%) drives at 57.6 m.p.h. Another small group (14.8%) consistently drives over 65 m.p.h. (*San Bernardino Sun*, 18 May 1986, p. D 1). The 55 m.p.h. speed law is being disregarded by a large majority of licensed motorists. The numbers are increasing each year, in spite of the exorbitant fees being collected on over one million traffic citations issued each year in California alone (*San Bernardino Sun*, 1986, p. D 2). Now is the time to release this nation from bondage by abolishing an outdated law and giving power back to the individual states to enact reasonable maximum speed laws tailored to their specific needs and road conditions.

## BIBLIOGRAPHY

Ceppos, Rich. (1984, January). Top ten fuelers, 1984: winners and losers in the battle for more mpg. *Car and Driver, 29,* 27.

Cooper, Steve. (1986, May 18). Speeding, lying: The California way of life. *San Bernardino Sun,* pp. D 1–2.

*Guinness Book of World Records.* (1985). New York: Sterling Publishing.

Osborne, David. (1984, March). America's plentiful energy resource. *The Atlantic Monthly, 253,* 3, 86–102.

Powell, Stewart, & Sheler, Jeffery L. (1986, May 19). Americans itch to step on the gas. *U.S. News & World Report, 100,* 19, 27.

Tholstrup, Hans, & Perkins, Larry. (1983, November). Across Australia by sun-power. *National Geographic, 164,* 2, 600–607.

## QUESTIONS FOR ANALYSIS

1. How would this essay be different if it began with paragraph 3? What would be lost or gained?

2. How does Job anticipate and respond to possible counterarguments? What advantages or disadvantages do you see in this argumentative strategy?

3. Summarize Job's argument about energy conservation. How important to this argument is his assertion that the fuel shortage was feigned? How convincing do you find the argument?

4. Take one of Job's arguments and write a paragraph debating the point with him.

5. What values and concerns does Job assume his readers have? As one reader, how successfully does his essay appeal to your basic values and concerns?

6. Why does Job conclude the essay with statistics showing how many motorists drive faster than 55 miles per hour? How would you make Job's argument here more explicit?

7. How does Job establish credibility with the reader?

8. Look back at Amitai Etzioni's essay "When Rights Collide" at the beginning of this chapter. Which of Etzioni's arguments on government regulation apply to Job's essay? How well does Job anticipate Etzioni's argument?

## SUGGESTIONS FOR WRITING

1. Write an essay agreeing or disagreeing with Job. If you disagree, debate with him. If you agree, do not simply restate his arguments but extend them and supply new arguments of your own.

2. Are motorists who break the speed limit performing an act of civil disobedience? Write a position paper on this issue. If you have read the King and Van Dusen essays on civil disobedience, refer to their arguments in your own essay.

# A Look at
# Sam Job's Writing Process

Job remembers that he got the idea to write on the controversial 55 m.p.h. speed limit from another student in his writing class. Everyone was asked to bring to class a list of ten possible position paper topics. Job made a list containing general issues as well as some closer to his own experience: censorship, the American military, nuclear war, compulsory seat belts, smoking in public places, victims' rights, the arms race, year-round schools, the energy crisis, and ecology. He had a position on some, but not all, these issues. For a few, he didn't even have a clear understanding of what the controversy was about. He also realizes now that he repeated himself by including nuclear war and the arms race—after all, who is for nuclear war?

In class a secretary was appointed to write the students' topics on the board. Job made a note of some of these additional topics that he thought had promise: male/female roles, Central America, creationism/evolution, capital punishment, drunk driving, corporal punishment in schools, population control, euthanasia, on the job drug abuse, the lottery, and the 55 m.p.h. speed limit. Then the class broke into small groups. Students were told to select three topics each and discuss why they liked them, what they thought was the controversy, and which position they were inclined to take. Job preferred topics like the 55 m.p.h. speed limit, compulsory seat belts, and smoking in public places, whereas the other group members were drawn to the more abstract and, as he said, "earth-shaking" topics.

Upon reflection, Job admits he felt overwhelmed by the broader, more philosophical and political topics since he felt that he didn't know enough to take positions on them or have time to do sufficient research. He settled for a topic that he knew personally. He felt he could fairly represent the opposing positions and argue forcefully for his own. As he had predicted, the essay was fairly easy to write. The research went quickly, and by exploring the pros and cons of the issue, he developed a strategy that he used throughout the essay of making small concessions before arguing each point.

## A GUIDE TO WRITING POSITION PAPERS

As the selections in this chapter indicate, the position paper can be quite an intricate piece of writing or it can be simple and direct. The complexity of a particular essay will depend on how complicated the issue is and how the argument is constructed. Writers of position papers must be very much aware of their readers. Since they may be writing to people with whom they disagree on the issue, they must make a special effort to gain their confidence and respect. Probably the best way of doing this is by presenting a coherent, well-reasoned argument. The following brief guide suggests activities to help you invent, draft, and revise a position paper of your own.

# *Invention*

Invention is especially important in writing a position paper because there are so many things to consider as you write: how you might define— or redefine—the issue, what other opinions you should discuss and how you should represent them, what reasons and evidence you could offer to support your opinion and in what order, and what tone would be most appropriate for the particular subject and audience. These invention activities will help you to focus your thinking on these writing issues.

CHOOSING A CONTROVERSIAL ISSUE. Most authors of position papers choose issues about which they feel strongly and already know a good deal. If you do not have a specific issue in mind, you might want to consider the issues that appear in the writing suggestions that follow each reading in this chapter. You can discover other possibilities by reading newspapers or newsmagazines.

Make a list of the possibilities you are considering, indicating what you think each issue involves and what position you are presently inclined to take on it. The ideal issue will be one about which you have already formed an opinion; in writing about this issue you will have an opportunity to examine your own point of view critically. Also, your writing task will be easier if you can choose an issue upon which there is a clear division of opinion.

Once you have selected an issue, you may need to do some background research on it, particularly if the issue is one that you have not thought very much about until now. If you think you need more information at this point, go to the library or interview some people. You should not get too caught up in the process of doing research, however, until you are fairly sure of your audience, because knowledge of your readers will influence the kind of information you decide to use in your paper. Remember too that you are planning to write a persuasive essay, not a report of what others think about the issue. You can certainly cite authorities, but the essay should represent your best thinking on the subject, not someone else's.

ANALYZING YOUR READERS. Most position papers are set up as a debate in which the writer addresses readers who hold the opposing position.

You may, however, choose to address your essay to readers who are undecided about the issue. At this stage in your planning, you should try to identify your prospective audience. Write a few sentences profiling your readers. What are their views on the issue? What reasons do they most often give for their opinions? What kinds of information and evidence do they use to support their opinions? What basic assumptions or values underlie their opinions? What are the historical, political, or ideological dimensions to their opinions? What kinds of personal experiences and beliefs are you likely to have in common with these readers? On what basis might you build a bridge of shared concerns with them? What kinds of arguments might carry weight with them?

STATING YOUR THESIS. Having identified the issue and audience, try stating what you now think will be the thesis of your position paper. You will undoubtedly need to refine this statement as you clarify your position and explore your argument, but stating it tentatively here will help focus the rest of your invention.

EXPLORING YOUR REASONS. Now that you have chosen a promising issue and analyzed your prospective readers, you should devote your energies to exploring your own reasons for holding your position. Do this with your readers in mind, setting up a debate between yourself and your readers.

Divide a page in half vertically and list your reasons in the left-hand column and your readers' responses to each reason in the right-hand column. You may not know how your readers will respond to every point you make, of course, but you should try to put yourself in their place and decide whether there are any objections they could make or on what grounds they might accept the point. Leave a space of about five lines between each of your reasons. Then use that space to develop the reason and to indicate what kinds of evidence you might use to support it. Planning an argument this way is likely to be messy, particularly if you move frequently from one column to the other. Although it may seem chaotic, this can be a very productive invention activity. These notes may serve later as a rough outline after you have decided which are your best arguments and in what order you should arrange them.

DEVELOPING YOUR BEST REASONS. This activity is really an extension of the previous one. It involves reviewing your notes and selecting the reasons you now think are the most promising. These should be reasons that might actually persuade your readers, reasons that you believe in and that you can support with specific evidence. Take each reason in turn and try to develop it as fully as you can. You may need more information, and you can either locate it now or make a note to do so later. The important thing is to clarify for yourself how this particular reason justifies your position. In addition, you should identify the kinds of evidence you can use to support each reason. Do you have examples? facts? statistics? authorities you can quote? anecdotes you can relate? Instead of simply listing possible evidence, try actually drafting a few sentences.

For each of your reasons, you should also acknowledge any strong objections readers might make. If you can accommodate any of these objections by making concessions or qualifying your position, it's a good idea to do so. If not, rehearse your rebuttal, explaining why you must disagree.

RESTATING YOUR THESIS. Look back at your earlier tentative thesis statement and revise it to conform with what you have discovered in exploring your argument. You may only need to make minor revisions to signal how you have modified or qualified your position. Or you may need to rewrite the entire statement to account for your new understanding of the issue.

# *Drafting*

After a thoughtful and thorough invention process, you are ready to set goals for drafting, plan your organization, and consider how to begin the essay and avoid logical fallacies.

SETTING GOALS. Before writing, reorient yourself by setting goals that reflect your purpose and audience. Ask yourself specifically what you want to accomplish by writing to these readers about this issue. Are you chiefly interested in presenting your opinion, or do you want to change your readers' minds? If your goal is the latter, consider whether you are being realistic. Remember that some issues—capital punishment, for example—are so deeply rooted in values and beliefs that it is very hard to get people to change their minds. The most you can hope to do is either present your own best argument as Koch does or get readers to reexamine the issue from a more objective point of view as Hoekema and Mead try to do.

Consider how familiar your readers already are with the issue. If you think it is new to them, you will need to help them understand why it is important. Because Solomon assumes that his readers have not thought deeply about the liberal arts, he tries to demonstrate their importance. Bird makes the same assumption but takes the opposite position. If, on the other hand, you assume readers are familiar with the issue, you might, like Job, try to get them to see it in a new light. It is usually safe to assume that your readers have not explored the issue as thoroughly as you, and you will therefore need to identify the main issues at stake and define the key terms.

Consider also which of your readers' values and assumptions correspond to your own. If, for example, you are writing about something your readers are likely to fear or detest, acknowledge their feelings as legitimate and show that you share their concerns. All three writers on capital punishment, for instance, align themselves with readers by voicing their repugnance at the taking of life. Mead also acknowledges the common "fear that the violent person will be set free in our communities" when she advocates assuring that murderers be kept in prison and not paroled.

Finally, think of the kinds of arguments that would be most likely to convince your particular readers on this issue. Will they respect the judgment of authorities or expert witnesses on this issue, as Solomon and Bird seem to think? Do they need facts and statistics to better understand the dimensions of the issue, as Koch and Hoekema apparently assume? Will they be especially responsive to arguments based on principle, as King believes?

PLANNING YOUR ORGANIZATION. With these goals in mind, reread the invention writing you did under the exploring and developing your reasons sections. They should give you the perspective to order your reasons and outline your argument. Writers often begin and end with the strongest reasons, putting weaker ones in the middle. This organization gives the best reasons the greatest emphasis. Koch, Hoekema, and Job more or less follow this pattern. Another common plan is to begin with a definition like Van Dusen and Solomon, letting the definition carry most of the argument's weight. Koch and King also organize their essays around a point-by-point rebuttal of their opponents' arguments, while Hoekema systematically examines the arguments raised by both sides.

BEGINNING. The opening of a position paper sets the tone, identifies the issue, and usually establishes the writer's position. In deciding how to begin, think again about your readers and their attitudes toward the issue. Solomon, for example, must get over two obstacles—his readers' ignorance of the liberal arts and their pejorative associations with the word *culture*. Assuming his readers are bored by debates about the 55 m.p.h. speed law and need a reason to read about it, Job presents a dramatic narrative to draw them in. To get readers as agitated as he is about capital punishment, Koch begins by quoting convicted murderers lecturing us about the morality of killing. To give readers a longer perspective on the same issue, Hoekema and Mead both begin by recounting some of its history.

AVOIDING LOGICAL FALLACIES.   Arguing about controversial issues demands probably the most difficult kind of reasoning because emotions run high and issues tend to be extremely complex. To avoid making errors in your argument, ask yourself the following questions as you plan and draft your essay:

> Am I making *sweeping generalizations* (for instance, assuming that if killing is morally wrong, then state-licensed murder must also be wrong)?
>
> Am I committing an *ad hominem* attack on my opponents (criticizing their intelligence or motives rather than their arguments)?
>
> Am I *distorting the facts* (for instance, selecting only those facts that support my argument and ignoring all others)?
>
> Am I *oversimplifying* the issue (making a complex issue seem simple)?
>
> Am I guilty of *either-or reasoning* (assuming that there are only two positions on an issue, the right one and theirs)?

# Revising

Even the most experienced writers revise their drafts. No amount of invention and planning can ensure that a draft will be complete and perfectly organized. In fact, as you draft you are likely to discover new and important points to make. You may also encounter unanticipated problems that require radical rethinking or restructuring of your essay. This is particularly true for a complicated essay like a position paper.

Begin your revision by reading your draft critically, using the critical reading questions at the beginning of this chapter. In addition, try to get someone else to read your draft critically. Following are suggestions for revising to strengthen your argument and to improve readability.

REVISING TO STRENGTHEN YOUR ARGUMENT.   As you revise, keep in mind your purpose: to persuade readers that your opinion is valid and reasonable. Consider how well you have managed your tone and accommodated your readers. Look for places where you might modify your language or provide more information. If you can make any concessions without renouncing your position, try to do so. Also, examine closely how you represent and react to opposing opinions. Are you fair and objective? Could you explain your objections any better? Can you emphasize the areas where you and your readers agree rather than where you disagree? How might this strategy strengthen your argument?

Focus on your reasons and supporting evidence. Is each reason developed sufficiently, or can you add more detail for your readers? Ask yourself why your readers should be convinced by each reason. Then consider how you might bring the point home more dramatically. Study the evidence you provide to see whether it is as convincing as you had hoped. How else might you support your point? What other examples or facts could you mention? What authorities could you cite?

Look again at your definition of the issue, and try to modify this definition so as to win readers to your side. Remember that defining the issue is part of your argument, and that it establishes the way the argument might be resolved. Does your definition polarize opinion unnecessarily? Could it be less extreme and more conciliatory?

REVISING TO IMPROVE READABILITY. Begin by outlining your draft to determine whether your argument is coherent and well organized. Consider inserting forecasting statements, summaries, or transitions to make the organization clearer. Look for any unclear writing. Be especially critical of abstract and indirect language. Long, convoluted sentences do not impress readers; they depress and confuse them. Finally, proofread your draft carefully, and correct any errors in usage, punctuation, and spelling.

# *Literary Analysis*

It is fitting that the last chapter of a book called *Reading Critically, Writing Well* be about literature, for in reading literature we see what writing well truly means and garner the fruits of critical reading. From reading literature and writing about our reading, we learn about others and about ourselves. We explore values, ideas, experiences, deriving both pleasure and insight. Some would even say that through this process we become most fully human.

From earliest childhood, stories and nursery rhymes draw us irresistibly into their web of words. Literary images, like images in our dreams, reverberate with meaning, touching deep chords in us. As we analyze a work of literature, we often see reflections of our own experience. But literature is not simply a mirror held up to nature. It invents life in the medium of language, creating its own verbal structure. As we read critically, we examine this structure, sculpting our own meanings out of it. This does not suggest, however, that literary meaning is arbitrary. Rather it means that literary meaning is rich and various, that it shifts as contexts and perspectives shift. Although the words on the page remain forever the same, our interpretation of these words depends on the assumptions we bring to them, the significances we choose to highlight. Consequently, as interpreters, we half-perceive and half-create the work, fulfilling what was, until then, only potential.

## A GUIDE TO READING LITERATURE

This chapter discusses critical reading of two kinds of texts: literature and essays about literature. Of the three basic literary genres or types— fiction, poetry, and drama—this section focuses on fiction, particularly the short story. Short stories present literary experience in microcosm. They entertain us with their sequence of events, fascinate us with their insight into human values and behavior, and educate us with their intriguing commentary on the human situation. Furthermore, they ensnare us in their web of words, entice us with their verbal patterning. Because of the form's compactness, "almost every word," as William Faulkner put it, "has got to be almost exactly right." Like poetry, short stories maximize the metaphoric and symbolic resources of the language.

# Basic Features of the Short Story

We experience stories much as we experience life—as it washes over us. Yet when we come to describe our experience of reading stories and share our interpretations, we refer to such things as character and theme. That is, we analyze the story, discussing its constituent elements in order to see how it works as a whole. The more carefully we examine these elements, the better we understand how the story comes to have meaning for us. Although there are also many extrinsic approaches to literature that relate the literary text to such topics as society, myth, history, the human psyche, the relations between men and women, generic expectations, and other texts, all of these approaches benefit from consideration of the following intrinsic features of a literary work: *plot, characterization, point of view, setting, language,* and *theme.*

PLOT. Plot is a narrative of events arranged in a time sequence. However, it is more than just a story line ("The king died, and then the queen died," to use E. M. Forster's famous example). Plot has causality ("The king died, and then the queen died of grief"), which means that a plot can be explained as well as described. A critical reader, therefore, does not simply recount the plot, telling what happens in it, but also analyzes the plot, conjecturing about why things happen as they do and interpreting what they mean. Thus, every plot detail carries significance for the active reader.

CHARACTERIZATION. Characterization, the creation of a fictional person, lies at the heart of realistic fiction (though it may be only a secondary element in romance or fantasy). Characters are revealed by their actions, speech, thoughts, physical appearance, the setting, and what we learn from the narrator or other characters. Not only does character generate plot and plot result from character, but character is the center of meaning and interest for the reader. Conflict takes place within a character or between characters. Whereas "flat characters" have but a single dimension, "rounded characters" are complex, contradictory, and capable of growth—much as real people are. What motivates characters and causes them to change gives us insight into human nature. In realistic fiction, a character's change of heart or increase in understanding can be a momentous event.

POINT OF VIEW. A story's point of view is the narrative voice in which the events are related. There are many variations, but two basic points of view predominate: first-person and third-person. In first-person narration, the author creates a character (who may be the central protagonist or just a bystander) and uses that character's voice to tell the story. Readers may be privy to the character's stream of consciousness or may know only what the character chooses to reveal. First-person narrators are often reliable, but not always; they are sometimes stupid or naive, and occasionally they even lie. It is up to the reader to decide into which category a narrator falls.

When a story is told in the third person, the narrator does not participate in the action, and the narrative voice is not that of any of the characters. This voice may be omniscient—all-knowing, with free access to the motives, thoughts, and feelings of the characters—or it may be limited—with access to only one character's mind. It may also be journalistically objective, limiting itself to descriptions of external actions and events.

SETTING. The locale and period in which the action of a story takes place is its setting. The setting can make the story seem real or interesting, and it can also add to our understanding of the story's meaning. The setting may influence a character's behavior or reflect his or her state of mind. It may foreshadow events yet to happen or reinforce events that have already occurred. Often the language of the setting is highly evocative and even symbolic.

LANGUAGE. The language of literature, the words chosen to create a fictional world, is richly connotative or suggestive. Connotative words have an intricate texture of associations and implications. The various shadings of implications often make the meaning of a particular word ambiguous or uncertain. Some literary critics view ambiguous words as having multiple meanings that ultimately work together to reinforce a single, unified pattern of meaning; others see ambiguous words as wedges that reveal conflicting meanings within a text and expose the indeterminacy of its meaning.

Literary language tends also to be highly figurative. Using language figuratively—as in metaphor and simile—involves departing from normal usage in order to extend or change a word's meaning. Here is a brief list of literary terms to describe some common figurative uses of language:

—An image (a red rose) evokes sensory impressions to suggest a resemblance between the fictional and the phenomenal world.

—Metaphor (my love is a red rose) and simile (my love is like a red rose) both use images to compare or transfer meaning from one object to another.

—Metonymy (the rose that my love picked in the garden wilted in the heat) names one object (the literal rose) to throw light on another (the lover) with which it is associated.

—Symbols are more general terms used to extend the range of meaning of a word beyond its immediate, literal meaning. In the following poem by William Blake, for example, the rose is used symbolically to refer to the destructions of love by hyprocrisy and deceit (among other possible meanings):

O Rose, thou art sick!
The invisible worm
That flies in the night,
In the howling storm,

Has found out thy bed
Of crimson joy,
And his dark secret love
Does thy life destroy.

THEME. Theme refers to the general ideas conveyed by the story through its language, plot, characterization, point of view, and setting. Themes may concern such abstractions or universals as life and death, illusion and reality, alienation and communion, money and greed, heroism and egotism, fate and free will.

To find a story's themes is to be analytical and creative at the same time. As we read, we infer a story's meanings; we read between the lines, making connections and drawing out implications. As we find our critical, interpretive voices, we approach conversation with the text; in that dialogue, meaning is forged and we discover what the story is about.

A Sample Short Story:
## A Clean, Well-Lighted Place, Ernest Hemingway

Here is a sample short story to read and enjoy. As you analyze the story, think about its basic features—plot, characterization, point of view, setting, language, and theme—and how they contribute to your enjoyment and understanding of it. Following the sample is a discussion of literary analysis and several essays analyzing this story.

Written by Ernest Hemingway, one of America's foremost writers and winner of the Nobel Prize for Literature in 1954, "A Clean, Well-Lighted Place" has been praised by many critics and called "one of Mr. Hemingway's most perfect and most touching stories." It originally appeared in the March 1933 issue of *Scribner's Magazine* and was reprinted that same year in the collection *Winner Take Nothing*. Since then, it has been anthologized frequently and commented upon in numerous articles and books.

Like most of Hemingway's fiction, "A Clean, Well-Lighted Place" is misleadingly simple. Its plot can be briefly summarized, but its meaning cannot be easily explicated. Reading this story requires that the reader engage in interpretation. And, as Hemingway himself wrote in a letter, no single reading will exhaust its many possibilities for meaning: "In truly good writing no matter how many times you read it you do not know how it is done. That is because there is a mystery in all great writing and that mystery does not dis-sect out. It continues and it is always valid. Each time you re-read you see or learn something new."

## A Clean, Well-Lighted Place

It was late and every one had left the café except an old man who sat in the shadow the leaves of the tree made against the electric light. In the day time the street was dusty, but at night the dew settled the dust and the old man liked to sit late because he was deaf and now at night it was quiet and he felt the difference. The two waiters inside the café knew that the old man was a little drunk, and while he was a good client they knew that if he became too drunk he would leave without paying, so they kept watch on him.

"Last week he tried to commit suicide," one waiter said.

"Why?"

"He was in despair."

"What about?"

"Nothing."

"How do you know it was nothing?"

"He has plenty of money."

They sat together at a table that was close against the wall near the door of the café and looked at the terrace where the tables were all empty except where the old man sat in the shadow of the leaves of the tree that moved slightly in the wind. A girl and a soldier went by in the street. The street light shone on the brass number on his collar. The girl wore no head covering and hurried beside him.

"The guard will pick him up," one waiter said.

"What does it matter if he gets what he's after?"

"He had better get off the street now. The guard will get him. They went by five minutes ago."

The old man sitting in the shadow rapped on his saucer with his glass. The younger waiter went over to him.

"What do you want?"

The old man looked at him. "Another brandy," he said.

"You'll be drunk," the waiter said. The old man looked at him. The waiter went away.

"He'll stay all night," he said to his colleague. "I'm sleepy now. I never get into bed before three o'clock. He should have killed himself last week."

The waiter took the brandy bottle and another saucer from the counter inside the café and marched out to the old man's table. He put down the saucer and poured the glass full of brandy.

"You should have killed yourself last week," he said to the deaf man. The old man motioned with his finger. "A little more," he said. The waiter poured on into the glass so that the brandy slopped over and ran down the stem into the top saucer of the pile. "Thank you," the old man said. The waiter took the bottle back inside the café. He sat down at the table with his colleague again.

"He's drunk now," he said.

"He's drunk every night."

"What did he want to kill himself for?"

"How should I know."

"How did he do it?"

"He hung himself with a rope."

"Who cut him down?"

"His niece."

"Why did they do it?"

"Fear for his soul."

"How much money has he got?"

"He's got plenty."

"He must be eighty years old."

"Anyway I should say he was eighty."

"I wish he would go home. I never get to bed before three o'clock. What kind of hour is that to go to bed?"

"He stays up because he likes it."

"He's lonely. I'm not lonely. I have a wife waiting in bed for me."

"He had a wife once too."

"A wife would be no good to him now."

"You can't tell. He might be better with a wife."

"His niece looks after him."

"I know. You said she cut him down."

"I wouldn't want to be that old. An old man is a nasty thing."

"Not always. This old man is clean. He drinks without spilling. Even now, drunk. Look at him."

"I don't want to look at him. I wish he would go home. He has no regard for those who must work."

The old man looked from his glass across the square, then over at the waiters.

"Another brandy," he said, pointing to his glass. The waiter who was in a hurry came over.

"Finished," he said, speaking with that omission of syntax stupid people employ when talking to drunken people or foreigners. "No more tonight. Close now."

"Another," said the old man.

"No. Finished." The waiter wiped the edge of the table with a towel and shook his head.

The old man stood up, slowly counted the saucers, took a leather coin purse from his pocket and paid for the drinks, leaving half a peseta tip.

The waiter watched him go down the street, a very old man walking unsteadily but with dignity.

"Why didn't you let him stay and drink?" the unhurried waiter asked. They were putting up the shutters. "It is not half-past two."

"I want to go home to bed."

"What is an hour?"

"More to me than to him."

"An hour is the same."

"You talk like an old man yourself. He can buy a bottle and drink at home."

"It's not the same."

"No, it is not," agreed the waiter with a wife. He did not wish to be unjust. He was only in a hurry.

"And you? You have no fear of going home before your usual hour?"

"Are you trying to insult me?"

"No, hombre, only to make a joke."

"No," the waiter who was in a hurry said, rising from pulling down the metal shutters. "I have confidence. I am all confidence."

"You have youth, confidence, and a job," the older waiter said. "You have everything."

"And what do you lack?"

"Everything but work."

"You have everything I have."

"No. I have never had confidence and I am not young."

"Come on. Stop talking nonsense and lock up."

"I am one of those who like to stay late at the café," the older waiter said. "With all those who do not want to go to bed. With all those who need a light for the night."

"I want to go home and into bed."

"We are of two different kinds," the older waiter said. He was now dressed to go home. "It is not only a question of youth and confidence although those things are very beautiful. Each night I am reluctant to close up because there may be some one who needs the café."

"Hombre, there are bodegas open all night long."

"You do not understand. This is a clean and pleasant café. It is well lighted. The light is very good and also, now, there are shadows of the leaves."

"Good night," said the younger waiter.

"Good night," the other said. Turning off the electric light he continued the conversation with himself. It is the light of course but it is necessary that the place be clean and pleasant. You do not want music. Certainly you do not want music. Nor can you stand before a bar with dignity although that is all that is provided for these hours. What did he fear? It was not fear or dread. It was a nothing that he knew too well. It was all a nothing and a man was nothing too. It was only that and light was all it needed and a certain cleanness and order. Some lived in it and never felt it but he knew it all was nada y pues nada* y pues nada. Our nada who art in nada, nada be thy name thy kingdom nada thy will be nada in nada as it is in nada. Give us this nada our daily nada and nada us our nada as we nada our nadas and nada us not into nada but deliver us from nada; pues nada. Hail nothing full of nothing, nothing is with thee. He smiled and stood before a bar with a shining steam pressure coffee machine.

"What's yours?" asked the barman.

---

*y pues nada: and then nothing

"Nada."

"Otro loco mas," said the barman and turned away.

"A little cup," said the waiter.

The barman poured it for him.

"The light is very bright and pleasant but the bar is unpolished," the waiter said.

The barman looked at him but did not answer. It was too late at night for conversation.

"You want another copita?" the barman asked.

"No, thank you," said the waiter and went out. He disliked bars and bodegas. A clean, well-lighted café was a very different thing. Now, without thinking further, he would go home to his room. He would lie in the bed and finally, with daylight, he would go to sleep. After all, he said to himself, it is probably only insomnia. Many must have it.

## A GUIDE TO READING LITERARY ANALYSIS

Now that you have read Hemingway's story, you can test your interpretation by comparing it to the following written analyses of the story. First, however, let us examine the basic features of literary analysis, present an annotated sample, and discuss some critical reading questions to keep in mind as you study the essays that follow.

# Basic Features of Literary Analysis

Literary analysis essentially involves interpreting a literary work and arguing for a particular way of understanding it. A literary critic does what any critical reader does—actively analyzes the text in search of coherent meanings while also being alert to discontinuities and contradictions. The written analysis usually includes the following features: *a brief presentation of the literary work, a coherent interpretation, a reasonable argument supported by textual evidence, and a clear pattern of organization.*

A BRIEF PRESENTATION OF THE LITERARY WORK. Literary analysis nearly always begins by identifying the work and its author. The essay might also place the work in the context of the author's other writing or in a more general literary or historical context. Since literary critics generally assume their readers already know the works they are discussing, they seldom summarize the plot. Whatever description they do offer serves primarily to orient readers and to support their interpretation.

A COHERENT INTERPRETATION. Interpretation is the crux of literary analysis. It is the central idea the writer is trying to communicate and is usually stated explicitly in a thesis statement. Without this focal point, the essay would be just an accumulation of ideas about the work, rather than a coherent, reasoned analysis of it.

A REASONABLE ARGUMENT SUPPORTED BY TEXTUAL EVIDENCE. Although it is called an analysis, writing about literature is essentially an argument. Literary critics argue for their interpretation not so much to convince readers to adopt it, but rather to convince them that it makes sense. The argument basically justifies the writer's way of reading the work by pointing to important details in the work and explaining their significance. Although they may assume their readers are familiar with the work, literary critics never expect readers to see it as they do or automatically to understand—let alone accept—their interpretation.

The primary source of evidence for a literary critic's argument is the work itself. Critics quote from the work, describe it, summarize it, and paraphrase it. They do more than just refer to specific passages in the work, however: they analyze the word choices and point to particular patterns of meaning. Since the language of literature is so suggestive, critics must demonstrate to readers how they arrived at their understanding of the work by pointing to specific words in the text and explaining what these words mean to them.

In addition to offering textual evidence, literary critics may also find ideas and evidence to support their interpretation from outside sources— other critics, biographical information about the author, historical facts. Such evidence can give insight into the work, and it may also increase the writer's authority and credibility. Writers may cite other critics not only to support their own interpretation but also to disagree with the interpretations of others. Disagreements over interpretations are productive, often leading to clearer insights and deeper understanding of the work.

A CLEAR PATTERN OF ORGANIZATION. Although literary critics want their analysis to account for subtleties in the work, they do not want their readers to have difficulty understanding their interpretation or following their argument. They strive to make their writing clear and direct, therefore, and provide forecasting and transition statements to keep readers oriented.

An Annotated Literary Analysis:
## The Nada-Concept in "A Clean, Well-Lighted Place,"
### Carlos Baker

Literary analysis is usually read to enhance the enjoyment of literature by allowing active readers to engage in lively conversation and debate with other readers. Testing their own interpretations against others' interpretations, readers often gain new insights. Reading a new interpretation can unlock a work's mysteries, making what seemed flat and uninviting suddenly full of life and meaning. It can also be intellectually stimulating, challenging readers to find fault with another's argument or leading them to appreciate the unfolding of a particularly well-reasoned or well-supported argument.

Look now at one brief literary analysis, which has been annotated in light of the critical reading questions that follow the selection. This piece of criticism was excerpted from Carlos Baker's book *Hemingway: The Writer as Artist*. Baker is a respected Hemingway authority who has also written a biography of Hemingway, *Ernest Hemingway: A Life Story* (1968), and edited his correspondence, *Ernest Hemingway: Selected Letters* (1981). A prolific writer, Baker also writes poetry and novels.

In this selection, Baker argues that the story's meaning can be discovered by analyzing the relationships among the characters. He uses what he calls a "triangulation-process," which, as you will see, allows him to explore systematically the relationships among the three characters in the story. As you read, notice particularly how Baker keeps readers on track as he examines the pattern of interrelationships in the story.

## The Nada-Concept in
## "A Clean, Well-Lighted Place"

| | |
|---|---|
| **Subject: Hemingway's story named at outset** | The ultimate horror gets its most searching treatment 1 in "A Clean, Well-Lighted Place," a superb story and quite properly one of Hemingway's favorites. It shows |
| **Naturalism: mode of fiction like realism but with a deterministic view of life** | once again that remarkable union of the naturalistic and the symbolic which is possibly his central triumph in the realm of practical esthetics. The "place" of the title is a |
| **Thesis: the clean, well-lighted place opposes chaos, or *nada*** | Spanish café. Before the story is over, this place has come to stand as an image of light, cleanness, and order against the dark chaos of its counter-symbol in the story: the idea of *nada*, or nothingness. The *nada*-concept is located and |
| **Forecast: will discuss the relationships among the characters** | pinned to the map by a kind of triangulation-process. The three elements consist in the respective relationships of an old waiter and a young waiter to an elderly man who |

sits drinking brandy every night in their clean, well-lighted café.

**1. Relationship between old and young waiter**

**Topic sentence: explains how they are opposites**

The old waiter and the young waiter are in opposition. They stand (by knowledge, temperament, experience, and insight) on either side of one of the great fences which exist in the world for the purpose of dividing sheep from goats. The young waiter would like to go home to bed, and is impatient with the old drinker of brandy. The old waiter, on the other hand, knows very well why the old patron comes often, gets drunk, stays late, and leaves only when he must. For the old waiter, like the old patron, belongs to the great brotherhood: all those "who like to stay late at the café . . . all those who do not want to go to bed . . . all those who need a light for the night." He is reluctant to see his own café close—both because he can sympathize with all the benighted brethren and for the very personal reason that he, too, needs the cleanness, the light, and the order of the place as an insulation against the dark.

**Quotes to support idea about brotherhood**

**benighted: unenlightened**

**Returns to thesis idea here**

**2. Relationship between the two old men**

**Topic sentence: identifies relationship between old men**

**Why "careless" and "unspecialized"? What does Baker mean here? confrère: colleague, brother**
**Indented quotation**

**Baker changes text by identifying the speakers. Is this OK? Shouldn't he say what he's doing?**

**Extended analysis of the quotation**

**Understatement: irony**

**Idea of holding *nada* at bay related to thesis idea of the place as a "counter-symbol" to nada**

**Repeated reference to "brotherhood"—Why?**

The unspoken brotherly relationship between the old waiter and the old patron is dramatized in the opening dialogue, where the two waiters discuss the drinker of brandy as he sits quietly at one of the tables. The key notion here is that the young and rather stupid waiter has not the slightest conception of the special significance which the old waiter attaches to his young confrère's careless and unspecialized use of the word *nothing*.

Young Waiter: Last week he tried to commit suicide.
Old Waiter: Why?
Young Waiter: He was in despair.
Old Waiter: What about?
Young Waiter: Nothing.
Old Waiter: How do you know it was nothing?
Young Waiter: He has plenty of money.

They are speaking in Spanish. For the old waiter, the word *nothing* (or *nada*) contains huge actuality. The great skill displayed in the story is the development, through the most carefully controlled understatement, of the young waiter's mere *nothing* into the old waiter's Some-thing—a Something called Nothing which is so huge, terrible, overbearing, inevitable, and omnipresent that, once experienced, it can never be forgotten. Sometimes in the day, or for a time at night in a clean, well-lighted place, it can be held temporarily at bay. What links the old waiter and the old patron most profoundly is their brotherhood in arms against this beast in the jungle.

# Critical Reading Questions

The following questions call attention to the key features of essays analyzing works of literature and can enable you to read such essays critically. To suggest how these questions might be used to guide your reading of literary analysis, each has been applied to the Baker selection.

1. *What literary work is being analyzed, and is it described in adequate detail?*

The subject of a literary analysis is seldom difficult to identify. Literary critics often identify the work they are discussing in their title and usually refer to it somewhere in the opening paragraphs. This is precisely what Baker does.

The issue of whether there is too much or too little plot summary depends on how familiar readers are with the work. Many writers assume that their readers will know the works they are discussing and may even return to them with the analysis in hand, but that may not always be the case. On occasion, particularly if the work is rare and not frequently discussed, readers' memories need to be refreshed. Most writers, however, give very little extraneous information about the story. Nearly everything Baker says, for example, serves primarily to support his point, and only secondarily to remind readers about the story.

2. *What is the thesis?*

Since readers of literary criticism anticipate directness, writers normally state their thesis explicitly. Although they may introduce the thesis by giving a context for their interpretation, they usually place the thesis statement early in the essay. There is no invariable rule that a thesis must be stated in a single sentence, but readers have come to expect that the main idea will be encapsulated in a fairly brief statement and that the rest of the essay will support and develop this kernel idea.

Baker states his thesis directly in the first paragraph. The marginal annotations label and briefly summarize the thesis, noting too that Baker returns to this idea at the end of the second paragraph. By keeping track of the main idea in this way, critical readers can see how the thesis is developed and determine whether it is argued for convincingly.

3. *Is the organization clear and easy to follow?*

Literary criticism should be clear and direct to enable readers to follow the organization and keep track of the way the thesis is being developed. Baker provides a forecasting statement indicating his organizational plan, along with topic sentences identifying the focus of each paragraph. Although readers of a short piece such as Baker's may not need this much orientation, signposts like these are crucial for longer, more complex essays.

### 4. *How convincing is the argument?*

To judge the argument, look closely at the interpretive statements the writer makes and the evidence offered to support these assertions. Baker, for instance, sets up an opposition between old and young. In doing so, he makes some judgments about the young waiter that some critical readers may not feel are warranted.

In trying to define *nada*, Baker cites the younger and older waiters' uses of the word "nothing." He not only quotes but also attempts to explain the lines he has quoted. Baker's distinction between the young waiter's "mere *nothing*" and the older waiter's "Something" might seem quite vague to some readers.

Finally, as the annotations note, Baker changes the original text by labelling the speakers. For the purpose of clarifying who the speakers are, altering quoted material in this way would not be an issue except that, as you will read in the next essay, there is an important critical debate over which lines should be attributed to each speaker.

# Annette Benert

Annette Benert (b. 1941) is an associate professor at Allentown College of St. Francis de Sales in Pennsylvania. She teaches American literature and composition as well as courses in women's studies and film. In much of her work Benert tries "to center art in the surrounding culture." She is interested, for example, in the novelist Henry James as a social critic. She has published several essays on James, including "Monsters, Bagmen, and Little Old Ladies: Henry James and the Un-Making of America," to be published in *Arizona Quarterly* in 1987.

# Survival Through Irony: Hemingway's "A Clean, Well-Lighted Place"

Written when Benert was still a graduate student for a class in American literature, this selection was originally published in a professional journal entitled *Studies in Short Fiction*. In contrast to Baker's rather brief and undeveloped analysis of "A Clean, Well-Lighted Place," Benert's essay is long and fully developed. It also contains many references to other literary critics, including Baker.

Although Benert is not the authority on Hemingway that Carlos Baker is, her essay has a tone of assurance. She achieves this tone by painstakingly building a case to support her interpretation. As you read, notice Benert's tone and how she develops her argument. Since she mentions irony in the title, you should spend a few moments before reading the essay to think about your understanding of this concept and how it might apply to "A Clean, Well-Lighted Place."

"A Clean, Well-Lighted Place" has with justice been considered an archetypal Hemingway story, morally and aesthetically central to the Hemingway canon. But its crystalline structure and sparse diction have led many critics to judge the story itself a simple one, either about nothingness, "a little *nada* story," or about the author's positive values, a story "lyric rather than dramatic."[1] I would like to suggest that it is in neither sense simple, but that the feelings and ideas which lie behind it are complex and are expressed dramatically, chiefly through the characterization of the older waiter. The latter is a man of enormous awareness continually torn between what might be called religious idealism and intellectual nihilism, a combination that surfaces in irony in several places in the story. This tension between two modes of viewing the world is developed through imagery that functions as a setting, through characterization, and, more abstractly, through a theme which I take to be the barriers against *nada*.

The most obvious source of imagery is the words of the title, the qualities of light and cleanness, to which one may add quietness. These terms admirably illustrate what Richard K. Peterson calls the "use of apparently objective words to express values";[2] they may be followed with profit throughout Hemingway's stories, novels, and non-fiction. But in this story each of these qualities exists also in its negative aspect, its shadow side.

Light provides the most striking image pattern. The café has an "electric light" that the older waiter eventually turns off. A street light is picked up by the brass number on a passing soldier's collar. The older waiter is "with all those who need a light for the night." The café where he works is "well lighted"; its "light is very good." In the bodega where he buys coffee "the light is very bright and pleasant." After going home he would be able to sleep "with daylight." Obviously, light is not only the antithesis of darkness but an effective barrier against it, or, rather, as Randall Stewart puts it, the light "at any rate, must be made to do."[3]

But it is stated twice that the patron, the old man, "sat in the shadow of the leaves," and the older waiter likes the café not only because its light is good but because "now there are shadows of the leaves." Further, the old man particularly liked sitting in the café at night because "the dew settled the dust" of the day and "it was quiet and he felt the difference," though he was deaf. Here shadow clearly has a positive connotation, in the sense of shade, of protection from the glare of the light, perhaps because the light is artificial but more likely because any direct light hurts the eyes and exposes the person. In addition, the night is clean and quiet, positive values contrasted to the day's dirt and noise.

The older waiter is equally concerned that his "place" be clean. He contradicts the younger waiter's remark that "an old man is a nasty thing" with "this old man is clean. He drinks without spilling. Even now, drunk." In contrast to the younger waiter, who wipes "the edge of the table with a towel" to emphasize that the old man should leave, but earlier had poured brandy so that it "slopped over and ran down the stem into the top saucer of the pile," the older waiter emphasizes several times the necessity of cleanness. Bars and bodegas are open all night, and they have light, but one cannot "stand before a bar with dignity, with correctness."

Its natural occurrence, however, is at night, when "the dew settled the dust." Its negative aspect is even more evident in that statement of the younger waiter that "an old man is a nasty thing," which, as a generalization, the older waiter does not contradict. Since age, as opposed to youth, is specifically associated in this story with greater awareness and sensitivity, in Hemingway terms "imagination," cleanness may be linked with ignorance and insensitivity.

The third positive quality of the café is its quietness; the old man, in addition, is deaf. There is the suggestion that another thing wrong with bars is that they may have music, but, in any case, "you do not want music. Certainly you do not want music." Any form of noise, then, like darkness and dirt, is to be avoided.

In this quality is the negative side of all three most evident. The old patron not only cannot tolerate direct light and can be classified with "nasty things," but also he is actually deaf so that no sound even has relevance for him. That the shadow side of quietness is its extreme, in the form of a negation of one whole sense faculty and a major art form, reminds the reader that all three qualities are in some sense negations. Light functions as an absence of darkness, cleanness as an absence of dirt, quietness as an absence of sound. Yet all three are posited as barriers against the ultimate negation, against Nothingness itself—perhaps, for once in literature, a genuine paradox, but certainly a major source of irony in this story.

Other images are less important but function in the same way. Liquor, the "giant killer" of other stories, is a weapon against the darkness, but it also impairs physical functioning, making the old man walk "unsteadily," so that the older waiter notices with pride that he can drink "without spilling. Even now, drunk," walk "with dignity." The younger waiter is "not lonely" because he has "a wife waiting in bed," but for the old man who "had a wife once" now "a wife would be no good," making women, a relationship to a woman, a material, but very temporary and thus illusory, protection against nothingness. All Hemingway's sleepless heroes desire sleep, but the old waiter, acutely conscious of the darkness lurking behind the light, cannot allow himself to lose that consciousness until he has light to protect him. There is a synonymity between being aware and being awake that overrides the psychologically negative connotations of insomnia. Thus, the man who can sleep is unaware and insensitive.

But in "A Clean, Well-Lighted Place" characterization is even more important than imagery. Though the old patron is the main topic of conversation between the two waiters, he is less important as a character than either of them. He functions more as part of the setting, a demonstration of the way things are, and as an indirect means for the characterization of the other two men. The younger waiter, also called "the waiter who was in a hurry" and "the waiter with a wife," is not the villain he is often cast to be; he after all "did not wish to be unjust." He is merely *l'homme moyen sensuel*,[4] lacking that moral and aesthetic sensibility Hemingway calls "imagination." He alone should serve as a refutation of the "locker-room" Hemingway, if such is still needed, but he is much less important than his co-worker, indeed serving as a kind of foil for him.[5]

That the older waiter is also called "the unhurried waiter" makes evident    11 the pun in the appellation. The younger man is "waiting" impatiently to go home and the older is "waiting" patiently or has transcended "waiting" altogether, has gone one step beyond Beckett's tramps,[6] having learned that there is nothing to wait for. As Joseph Gabriel has it, he "must bear at the same time his intense spiritual hunger and the realization of the impossibility of its fulfillment."[7] His alienation is dramatized, as Robert Weeks has noted, by his being "in the presence of others who either do not even notice him, or if they do are unaware of his ordeal and of the gallantry with which he endures it."[8] But he is also something more, and something more complex, than these tragic, heroic qualities would suggest.

He first appears in that initial dialogue, which, by its lack of speech    12 tags and the ensuing possible mis-assignment of them, has plagued so many readers. The second long dialogue makes clear that the older waiter provides the younger with information concerning the old patron's attempted suicide, and that the older man possesses the greater degree of sensitivity and awareness. This characterization is then read back into the first dialogue, making the younger waiter tell about the old man's act, so that he may be given the line "Nothing" to describe the old man's despair.[9] That Hemingway, nothing if not a craftsman of the first rank, could have made such a major error is simply beyond belief. The passage surely must be read as follows:

> Older waiter: "Last week he tried to commit suicide."
> Younger waiter: "Why?"
> Older waiter: "He was in despair." [as he of all men would understand]
> Younger waiter: "What about?"
> Older waiter: "Nothing." [that is, *nada*, Nothingness]
> Younger waiter: "How do you know it was nothing?" [that is, nothing tangible or material]
> Older waiter: "He has plenty of money." [that is, his despair must have had metaphysical, rather than physical, grounds]

Ambiguity exists, not as Joseph Gabriel would have it, in that the speeches may be assigned either way,[10] but, in addition to the above, in the possibility of the older waiter's sarcastic response to a man after all incapable of understanding either old man anyway. Perhaps he means also something like "of course, what could any man possibly despair over—he has plenty of money?" This possibility is underscored by his response later to the query, "What did he want to kill himself for?" with the abrupt "How should I know."

The older waiter manifests this kind of double vision repeatedly. He 13 remarks that the old patron "might be better with a wife"; yet he clearly knows the transitory nature of such a comfort. He has just informed his colleague that, like the latter, the old man "had a wife once too," implying that she is dead, and later hints in jest that wives may be unfaithful. As they close up the café, the older waiter states that the younger has "everything," meaning "youth, confidence, and a job"; yet such attributes are temporary and at best can counteract only the young man's "nothing," not the old man's "nothingness." With some justice does the former accuse the latter of "talking nonsense" after the remark, but without sensing its latent sardonic quality.

The strongest evidence of the older waiter's double awareness is of 14 course the long paragraph of the two parodic prayers.[11] *It* is used eleven times with references varying from the café, to the merely grammatical subject of the verb *is*, to the anguish he tries to define, to the world, to nothingness itself. The fragments of the two prayers follow naturally from the catechetical dialogues at the beginning of the story and from the repetitions of *it* and *nothing*.[12] Like the world and man himself, religious form is hollow at the core, filled with "nothing," or, rather, "nothingness," in existential terms, the abyss. Though there is "nothing" to be gained, the older waiter does profit by thus saying his prayers. Such a vision—of lost "everything" and of realized "nothing"—does not send him into Byronic heroics.[13] We read instead that "he smiled and stood before a bar with a shining steam pressure coffee machine." He could smile and remain upright because he knew that the world and himself, even his prayer, were "nothing," and by that act of awareness could survive with dignity, could transcend "it."

This hyper-consciousness, of course, keeps him awake at night. Thus 15 perhaps his definitive act of self-perspective is the observation, "After all, it is probably only insomnia. Many must have it." Calling his condition "insomnia" is an act of humility eliminating the last possibility of error, of assuming himself, by his consciousness, to be more than "nothing." Even as an act of reassurance, a whistling in the dark, it forestalls the dangers of pride by an admission of uncertainty even about the existence of "*nada*." It is an act of merciless self-consistency, thus liberating him from messianic responsibilities,[14] and enabling him to continue to smile at himself and to keep that café open at night. The older waiter, then, can look at the world both ways—as a mean of deep religious sensibility he can see the Nothingness of existence, and as a man who "knew it all was nada" he can make jokes and, above all, smile.

Perhaps belatedly, but at least on the evidence of imagery and char- 16 acterization, we may now discuss the theme of the story. Most readers take the latter to be *nada*, making "A Clean, Well-Lighted Place," despite the title, a story about Nothingness and the pessimism and despair of the human response to it.[15] This view ignores both the definition of *nada* inferable from the story and the nature of the old waiter's response to it.

Despite Hemingway's manipulation of the pronoun *it*, the reader must 17 not confuse Nothingness with the responses it produces, nor the response of the older waiter with that of the old man. *Nada* is depicted primarily spatially, as an objective reality, out there beyond the light; it is a final hard fact of human existence, though "some lived in it and never felt it," e.g., the younger waiter. In addition, it becomes temporal with the older waiter's repetition of *"y pues nada"* before the prayer. Though Carlos Baker, with great sensitivity, calls it "a Something called Nothing which is so huge, terrible, overbearing, inevitable, and omnipresent that, once experienced it can never be forgotten,"[16] which "bulks like a Jungian Shadow,"[17] its mythic qualities are perhaps not even that well defined.

More important, the response of the old patron—the search for obliv- 18 ion through drunkenness or suicide—is not the only one, and certainly not the one of the older waiter. John Killinger observes that "the only entity truly capable of defying the encroachments of Nothingness is the individual,"[18] and Cleanth Brooks that "the order and the light are supplied by *him*,"[19] the old waiter, the individual. Carrying this affirmation one step further, Wayne Booth notes "a mood of bitterness against darkness combined with a determination to fight the darkness with light—if only the clean, well-lighted place of art itself."[20] But, as we have seen, all the positive imagery, including light, is ironically undercut by the presence of a shadow side, and the "darkness" is counteracted on more levels than that simply of "light."

The older waiter in fact acts in various ways against Nothingness. He 19 expresses solidarity with the old patron, and would willingly keep the café open as long as anyone wants it; he is instrumental in keeping the lights on. But his acquaintance with *nada* is intimate enough to keep him awake all night, every night; yet this hyper-awareness leads him neither toward self-destruction nor toward egocentricity. He can fuse religious sensibility with existential anxiety into a parodic prayer, after which he can smile. Turning off the light in the café and going home to bed is a daily act of courage done silently, without complaint. His sensitivity to places which make dignity possible gives us the verbal clue that his life is one of survival with dignity.

Thematically, then, the older waiter actively demonstrates that life [20] against *nada* is achieved by awareness, sensitivity, human solidarity, ritual (verbal and physical), humor, and courage. Together these qualities make dignity, or, to use Jamesian terms, style or form;[21] we encounter them also in the good bullfighters in *Death in the Afternoon*,[22] which may amplify that book's moral as well as aesthetic relevance. Such attributes also lead to a double vision and a mode of expression which may be called irony, a potent antidote to both despair and pride. The older waiter, against the heaviest odds, is a man in control.

"A Clean, Well-Lighted Place" is, without cheating, a totally affir- [21] mative story, one of the very few in our literature. It assumes a world without meaning, life on the edge of the abyss, but that is not what it is about. It assumes a protagonist of acute awareness and minor characters of lesser consciousness, but it is not about that difference. It is, rather, a dramatization of the possibility, given the above conditions, of man continuing to act, to feel even for others, to think even about metaphysics, to create (with a smile), to control and thereby to humanize both himself and his environment. The older waiter is neither a hero nor a saint, but, to borrow from Camus,[23] that more ambitious being, a man.

## NOTES

1. Cleanth Brooks, *The Hidden God* (New Haven: Yale University Press, 1963), p. 10.

2. *Hemingway: Direct and Oblique* (The Hague: Mouton, 1969), p. 26.

3. *American Literature and Christian Doctrine* (Baton Rouge: Louisiana State University Press, 1958), p. 135.

4. *l'homme moyen sensuel*: sensual man (Eds.)

5. William Bache, "Craftsmanship in 'A Clean, Well-Lighted Place,' " *Personalist*, 37 (1956), 64, calls the older waiter "the truest symbol of modern man . . . caught on the horns of the selfish and cruel materialism of youth and the insomnious nihilism of old age." The story seems to me to dramatize instead three responses to the modern world, none as simple as Bache's description would imply.

6. Allusion to characters in Samuel Beckett's play *Waiting for Godot*. (Eds.)

7. "The Logic of Confusion in Hemingway's 'A Clean, Well-Lighted Place,' " *College English*, 22 (1961), 541.

8. "Introduction" to Robert F. Weeks, ed., *Hemingway: A Collection of Critical Essays* (Englewood Cliffs, New Jersey: Prentice-Hall, 1962), p. 12.

9. See the debate in *College English*: Frederick P. Kroeger, "The Dialogue in 'A Clean, Well-Lighted Place,' " 20 (1959), 240–241; William E. Colburn, "Confusion in 'A Clean, Well-Lighted Place,' " 20 (1959), 241–242; Otto Reinert, "Hemingway's Waiter Once More," 20 (1959), 417–418; also Edward Stone, "Hemingway's Waiters Once More," *American Speech*, 37 (1962), 239–240.

10. "The Logic of Confusion," pp. 542–543. I disagree, however, that "the structure of the dialogue symbolically represents the theme of chaos," p. 545; neither dialogue nor theme seems to me to be chaotic.

11. parodic: imitative for purposes of satire and ridicule (Eds.)

12. catechetical: teaching by question and answer, as in the Christian catechism (Eds.)

13. Allusion to Lord Byron (1788–1824), English Romantic poet whose heroes are noted for their melancholy and melodramatic energy. (Eds.)

14. messianic: pertaining to the Messiah or a deliverer (Eds.)

15. See Ray B. West, *The Short Story in America, 1900–1950* (Chicago: Gateway Editions, 1952), p. 93; Joseph DeFalco, *The Hero in Hemingway's Short Stories* (Pittsburgh: University of Pittsburgh Press, 1963), p. 216; Sheridan Baker, *Ernest Hemingway: An Introduction and Interpretation* (New York: Holt, Rinehart and Winston, 1967), p. 86.

16. *Hemingway: The Writer as Artist* (Princeton: Princeton University Press, 1963; rpt. 1970), p. 124.

17. Baker, p. 132.

18. *Hemingway and the Dead Gods: A Study in Existentialism* (Lexington: University of Kentucky Press, 1960), p. 14.

19. *The Hidden God*, p. 10.

20. *The Rhetoric of Fiction* (Chicago: University of Chicago Press, 1961), p. 299. Sean O'Faolain, "A Clean, Well-Lighted Place," in Weeks, ed., *Hemingway*, p. 113, comments likewise that Hemingway's "art is, in fact, a very clean, well-lighted place."

21. Allusion to Henry James (1843–1916), the American novelist and short story writer. (Eds.)

22. A book by Hemingway on bullfighting. (Eds.)

23. Albert Camus (1913–1960), French existentialist novelist, playwright, and essayist who won the Nobel Prize in 1957. (Eds.)

## QUESTIONS FOR ANALYSIS

1. Benert begins her essay by quoting two other critics of "A Clean, Well-Lighted Place." She refers to critics throughout her essay for a variety of purposes. Take inventory of her references to other critics. What role does each play in her argument? Identify any patterns you see. (Taking Inventory is discussed in Chapter 1.)

2. Locate the sentence in which Benert forecasts her essay. Then outline the essay to determine just how her forecasting statement, combined

with other orienting cues, helps to keep the reader on track. (See Chapter 1 for a discussion of outlining.)

3. In paragraph 12, Benert quotes the same passage that Baker quoted in his discussion of this story. Compare their treatments of this passage: How do they differ? Why does each quote the passage? Which analysis do you find more convincing?

4. Benert pays a great deal of attention to word choice. In paragraph 14, for instance, she counts the number of times the word *it* is used. What other evidence can you find of her focus on language? Why do you suppose she pays so much attention to word choice?

5. In her title, Benert uses the term *irony*, and she refers to "double vision" or "double awareness" at several places in the essay. What do you think she means by these terms? What role do these ideas play in her analysis of Hemingway's story?

6. Benert concludes that " 'A Clean, Well-Lighted Place' is, without cheating, a totally affirmative story." How well does she convince you that this is so? (Chapter 1 offers advice on evaluating an argument.)

## SUGGESTIONS FOR WRITING

1. As the Benert and Baker essays show, critical readers disagree on how to attribute parts of the dialogue in "A Clean, Well-Lighted Place." Reread the story to decide which lines belong to the older waiter and which to the younger waiter. Then write an essay justifying your decision.

2. Another interpretation of "A Clean, Well-Lighted Place" is that it is about art and the artist's attempt to create order and beauty in this world. Reread the story with this idea in mind and write an essay either supporting or refuting this interpretation.

# Lisa Farnum

Lisa Farnum (b. 1967) began college with the intention of becoming a biomed major, but was disenchanted by the extraordinary competition among students. Although she had not been very interested in, or very good at, English in high school, she enjoyed freshman composition. She especially liked the second semester, which focused on writing about literature. During that class, Farnum wrote the following selection and first considered becoming an English major. As she explained, interpreting literature interests her because it is both "an intellectual challenge and a chance to be imaginative."

# The Light of Life

As you skim this essay, you will immediately see that, unlike Benert, Farnum does not refer to other critics. Her instructor wanted students to arrive at their own interpretations without being influenced by the authoritative voices of published writers. Since you have already read Baker and Benert on "A Clean, Well-Lighted Place," it would be difficult to read Farnum's interpretation as if you did not know what other critics have written. Therefore, as you read this selection, consider how knowing these two critics might have helped Farnum clarify or extend her ideas. Look particularly for places where Baker or Benert would disagree with Farnum's analysis.

In the story "A Clean, Well-Lighted Place" by Ernest Hemingway, 1 images of light and dark accompany the action. To understand fully the meaning of the story, and particularly to understand the "prayer" at the end, we must discover the significance of this pattern of light and dark imagery.

Hemingway contrasts light and hope, on the one hand, and dark and 2 hopelessness, on the other. But the contrast is not simply one of polar opposites; the story contains subtle and meaningful variations between light and dark, including the dark of the night, the shadows of the leaves, the absence of light caused by the shutters, the street light, the electric light inside the cafe, and the promise of daylight. Daylight is traditionally associated with hope and, in this story, the older waiter waits through the night, unable to sleep, until the dawn. He describes himself as "one of those who like to stay late at the cafe. With all those who do not want to go to bed. With all those who need a light for the night." Not only does he need light to get through the night, but giving others light in the darkness also gives him a reason to go on.

In addition, light is associated with the potential for new life. The 3 street light illuminates the brass on the soldier's collar. Since soldiers personify youth and strength, and this one accompanies a girl, the light shining on him suggests the possibility of new life coming into this world.

The older waiter needs the assurance of the light, but recognizes that 4 the shadows are necessary for his cafe to be perfect. The shadows can be seen as standing for the human condition because they are dark places playing off against the light. Shadows are associated with the old man who sits by himself "in the shadow of the leaves of the tree." The old man has tried to kill himself, but his attempt was aborted by his niece. Now neither alive nor dead, he sits in the shadows. Drinking frees him temporarily, but he will never completely be in the dark until he dies. The shadows suggest a limbo between life and death, a kind of death-in-life.

The older waiter is also in a spiritual limbo. Afraid to sleep and face 5 the darkness within, he clings to the artificial, electric light and dares to sleep only when daylight arrives. He tries to convince himself that "it is probably only insomnia," but at a deeper level he knows that this is the way life is and that his experience is not unique—"Many must have it." As he confesses to the young waiter, he has never had "confidence and [is] not young."

His prayer best expresses this state of hopelessness and resignation. 6 The "light" has just been turned off, and he is walking alone in the dark. Depression has set in, and as a response to it, he revises "The Lord's Prayer" by inserting the word *nada*, which shows that his life means nothing to him. But one also gets the sense when reading the prayer that *nada* itself loses all meaning. It is repeated until the other words merge into the background as "nada . . . nada . . . nada" is thrust rhythmically at us.

The tone of this story is reflective. The older waiter has in a real sense 7 already given up, but he still clings to life and to the light. It is as if knowing the worst there is to know—namely, that "it was all a nothing and a man [is] nothing too"—cannot diminish his will to live.

## QUESTIONS FOR ANALYSIS

1. Look closely at the way Farnum opens her essay. Instead of stating her thesis, she describes her plan for analyzing the story. What advantages or disadvantages do you see with this way of starting a literary analysis? How else could she have begun her essay?

2. Farnum explains in the opening paragraph that an understanding of the story's theme depends on analyzing the imagery. Summarize her argument. What does she say the theme is? How does she relate the pattern of imagery to the theme?

3. Take inventory of Farnum's use of language from the story. Compare the way Farnum uses language from the story with the way that Baker and Benert do. Do they primarily use quotation or paraphrase? Do they discuss Hemingway's word choices or simply restate them?

4. In paragraph 3, Farnum makes some assertions about what the soldier stands for. Do you find her interpretation convincing? Why or why not?

5. Farnum describes the older waiter as being in a state of "spiritual limbo." How does she arrive at this idea, and how does she then use it to explain the significance of the prayer?

6. Why do you suppose Farnum calls the story's tone "reflective"? What does she mean by this term? How might she have further developed and supported this idea?

7. Look back over the essay to determine how Farnum keeps the reader on track. Then briefly explain how she does it and whether the essay needs more orienting cues.

### SUGGESTIONS FOR WRITING

1. Select another story by Hemingway or by some other author, and write an essay analyzing it. Do not read other critics but depend solely on your own reading to come up with an original interpretation of the story. Address your essay to readers who do not know the story very well.

2. Choose a story that has been analyzed in print by other critics. Study the story and the critics before writing your own interpretation. In your own essay, refer to critics with whom you disagree as well as those with whom you agree. Address your essay to readers unfamiliar with the critical debate on this particular story.

# A Look at Lisa Farnum's Writing Process

After Lisa Farnum's composition class had read and discussed several short stories, her instructor asked the class to write about one of these stories. Farnum chose Hemingway's story "A Clean, Well-Lighted Place" because, as she told her instructor later, she found it more puzzling than the other stories. She compared analyzing the story to doing jigsaw puzzles, an activity she had always enjoyed: "You have to figure out which pieces fit together and then try to understand the meaning of the pattern you have found."

What puzzled Farnum most was the prayer at the end. Not only did she find it hard to understand what it meant, but she was not at all sure how the earlier part of the story led to it. She began by carefully rereading and annotating the story, eventually reading it three or four times and seeing something new each time. When this painstaking process was done, Farnum felt disappointed because she still did not have a clear idea of what the prayer meant.

At this point, Farnum visited her instructor during office hours. Her instructor encouraged Farnum to make an inventory of her annotations to find patterns in the story, to write a tentative thesis based on one of these patterns, and then to do some exploratory writing to see what she might discover.

After she had made her inventory, Farnum found that many of her annotations centered around the light and dark imagery. Once she had identified this pattern, planning the essay became easier, although it still took her some time to understand how the imagery pattern related to the prayer. Once she realized the central role of the older waiter, however, she was able to see the connection. During this stage, she had written two pages of exploratory paragraphs and stray ideas.

She drafted the essay in one sitting, following a rough outline based on her exploratory writing. Then she let the draft sit for a day or two before revising and typing it. Most of her revision involved sharpening her points to make them clearer and more direct and adding topic sentences and other orienting cues.

## A GUIDE TO WRITING LITERARY ANALYSIS

At the heart of all writing about literature is analysis of the literary text. Whether you decide to focus solely on the text or to refer also to other critics, you will need to read the work closely and critically and sort through your various impressions systematically. The following brief guide to composing essays about literature should help you understand the writing process and solve some of the special problems involved.

# *Invention*

Writing about literature entails determining what you want to say about the work and finding evidence to support your idea. Literary analysis invites original interpretation as long as it is grounded in a perceptive reading. The burden of proof rests with the writer, who must not only explain the interpretation but also convince readers that it is justified. The following invention activities—choosing a work, analyzing it, deciding on a tentative thesis, considering your readers, researching other critics, and finding evidence for your thesis—should simplify somewhat the complicated task of interpreting literary texts.

CHOOSING A WORK. Your instructor may assign a particular story or ask you to choose from a selected list of stories. If you are given a choice, read a few stories before selecting the one you want to write about. Choose one that excites your interest and imagination, one that intrigues you because you cannot quite figure it out. It will probably take some time and effort before you feel you understand the work well enough to write about it, but writing about a story that snaps shut the first time you read it can actually be unsatisfying as well as unproductive. Like reading, writing should be a voyage of discovery; knowing the destination at the outset can make writing dull and mechanical.

ANALYZING THE WORK. There are many routes to interpreting a literary work. Some critics begin with an idea or a vague feeling. Others start with a problem or a puzzle. Whatever the point of origin, everyone returns to an analysis of the text. Many students and teachers find useful the two-step process of annotating and taking inventory. You are probably quite expert by this time at using these critical reading strategies. Chapter 1 explains how to annotate various features of a text and then analyze them by taking inventory. To apply these strategies to a work of literature, begin by annotating the work's basic features: its plot, characterization, point of view, setting, language, and theme. Note, for example, distinctive words or images, surprising events or statements. Identify the point of view and mark passages that characterize it including evaluative terms or attitudes. Examine the language used to describe the setting or characters' moods and actions.

Then take inventory of selected annotations to figure out what they might mean. Look for patterns of every kind—similarities and dissimilarities, consistencies and inconsistencies, parallels and contradictions. Repetitions of word choice, for instance, are usually significant. Group related words—synonyms as well as antonyms. Juxtapose different features: compare language used to describe the setting to language describing characters' moods and actions; contrast the point of view from which the story is told to the way the events are laid out; relate characterization to the language choices. Experiment with different ways of grouping your ideas and observations, and expect to be surprised by the new meanings you discover.

DECIDING ON A TENTATIVE THESIS. Your preliminary analysis of the work should lead you to a tentative thesis with which you can further explore the text. The thesis that results from your initial analysis will probably undergo some revision as you continue to think about the story. You may even find you have to replace your initial idea with another, more promising one. Nevertheless, it's advisable to make a tentative decision at this point.

To help you decide, try out several ideas by asking yourself questions and doing some exploratory writing about a few of them. Here are a few questions to get you started.

If the principal character undergoes some kind of change, how is this change significant?

If the story seems to be about a relationship between characters, what makes this relationship significant?

If the story calls particular attention to the characters' different values, motives, or beliefs, or if a single character embodies contradictory values, motives, or beliefs, what is the significance of these differences or contradictions?

If you notice a pattern in the language of the story—images, symbols, metaphors, ironies, multiple meanings, paradoxes—what does this pattern suggest about the meaning of the story?

If you detect a parallel between the setting and the characters' actions, values, or moods, how is this parallel significant?

Is the narrative point of view significant? Is the story told from the point of view of a particular character? Does the narrator seem reliable, or is he or she a poor judge?

If the story focuses on a particular theme, how is its theme conveyed in the plot, characterization, and language patterns?

CONSIDERING YOUR READERS. After deciding on a tentative thesis, you should pause in your analysis of the literary work to consider your readers. Write a brief profile of your prospective readers answering some of these questions: Who will read your essay? How familiar do you expect these readers to be with the work you are analyzing? Are they likely to know the published criticism and to expect you to know it as well? How surprising do you think your interpretation will be for them? What interpretations do you assume they will favor? What point do you expect will be hardest to get across? Why? What point will be easiest?

RESEARCHING OTHER CRITICS.  If you think your readers expect you to cite other critics in your essay, or if your instructor invites you to do so, this is a good time to do some library research. Reading what others have to say about the story will probably challenge your ideas and also suggest new ways of looking at the story. Although studying other critics may expand your understanding and help you to anticipate objections to your argument, it may sometimes make you feel that your own ideas don't measure up. Remember that you have as much right as anyone else to interpret the story. With that right, however, comes the responsibility to support your interpretation with solid evidence and reasonable analysis. The appendix, Strategies for Research and Documentation, offers advice on finding critics and referring to them in your essay.

FINDING TEXTUAL EVIDENCE.  Once you have settled on a tentative thesis and understand your readers, you need to marshal evidence from the story to support your thesis. To do this, you will want to review your annotations and inventory, any exploratory writing you have done, and notes on critics you may have read. Most of all, you will want to return to the text itself and read it over again, this time with an eye for anything that could support or undermine your thesis. This process should lead you to clarify and refocus your thesis. It may also lead you to decide that you do not have enough evidence to support that particular thesis. If so, you will need to find another thesis for your essay by returning to the text for another close reading and studying your annotations, inventory, and exploratory writing.

# *Drafting*

If your analysis of the work has been thoughtful and imaginative, you should have a fairly good idea of what your thesis will be and how well you can support it with textual evidence. Before drafting, you will want to set some goals for your writing, prepare a tentative outline, plan your organization, decide how to begin your essay, and determine how to avoid logical fallacies.

SETTING GOALS.  Before you start to draft your essay, consider the following questions, which will help you establish goals for yourself that reflect your purpose and readers' needs. How much plot summary, if any, do my readers need? You will notice that none of the critics in this chapter assumes the readers are so unfamiliar with the story that they need a summary of it. Whenever they refer to elements of the plot, they do so primarily to make a point, not to remind readers of the story. When Farnum, for example, tells about the old man's aborted suicide attempt, she is developing her idea that he represents a shadow state between life and death.

Should I establish a critical context for my interpretation? If you think your readers expect you to relate your ideas to other critics' ideas, then like Benert you should place your analysis in relation to other interpretations. You do not need to cite only critics who support your argument. Disagreeing with critics shows you have considered alternative arguments.

Should I forecast my argument? All three writers explain at the outset how they propose to develop their argument. At the end of the opening paragraph, for instance, Baker explains he will use what he calls "a kind of triangulation-process" to locate the *nada*-concept.

What other orienting cues should I provide? The answer to this question depends on how long and complicated your argument is. Benert provides many transitions, whereas Baker provides very few.

How can I make my tone authoritative? For writers with little experience analyzing literary works, this is perhaps the hardest question to answer. Authority comes with confidence, which comes, in turn, with practice. But you can also gain confidence in your ideas by finding support for them in the text. For most readers, the most authoritative writers are those who argue most persuasively, supporting insight with specific evidence.

OUTLINING THE ESSAY. Making an outline at this stage helps you to organize your thoughts and select the evidence you think you will want to use in your essay. Think of this outline as flexible rather than binding. As you draft the essay, you will inevitably find that some things work and others do not. The act of writing will lead you to discover new ideas and to develop old ones. It will alert you to problems and help you find solutions. An outline should not short-circuit the creative process, just make it a little more orderly.

PLANNING YOUR ORGANIZATION. To support their interpretations, literary critics typically construct their arguments around one or more of the work's basic components. To support his idea of what *nada* means, for instance, Baker discusses characterization, focusing particularly on the pattern of relationships. Similarly, Benert systematically examines the story's imagery, characterization, and theme to substantiate her assertions about the story.

Most writers develop a working outline based on their invention. This outline, though only tentative, gives direction to their draft. Although they want to remain open to new ideas, they also want to give the ideas they already have thorough and systematic development.

BEGINNING.   Most literary critics begin in the same way. They identify the work by title and the author by name right away, often in the opening sentence. Then they forecast their essay, often stating the thesis and indicating how the argument will develop. Baker, for example, gives his opinion of the story, states his thesis, and forecasts his argument in the opening paragraph. Benert's opening is a little more complex. She begins by summarizing the critical judgment of the story and suggesting how her analysis diverges from the general opinion. Then she forecasts her argument. Benert really does not explicitly state her thesis until the last paragraph of the essay. Farnum also saves her thesis till the end, indicating in the opening paragraph what her general purpose and strategy will be.

AVOIDING LOGICAL FALLACIES.   In writing literary analysis, you must be particularly careful to avoid certain logical fallacies. As you plan and draft your essay, ask yourself these questions:

> Will I be committing an *either/or fallacy* by presenting my interpretation and not discussing other possible interpretations?
>
> How can I show that I have accepted the *burden of proof*? Will I cite enough evidence to convince readers that my argument is grounded in the text?
>
> Can I avoid *hasty generalization* by offering adequate evidence for the general statements I make about the work?
>
> How can I avoid making a *straw man* of other interpretations or misrepresenting them to make my interpretation seem stronger?

# Revising

Literary critics typically make so many discoveries as they draft their essays that they expect to substantially revise the draft when they are done. Because they have a firmer grasp of their interpretation after presenting their case, for example, they can make their thesis more explicit and forecast the development of their argument more accurately. When revising your literary analysis, pay special attention to the specificity and logic of your argument as well as the readability and correctness of your writing.

REVISING TO STRENGTHEN YOUR ARGUMENT. When revising, reconsider your interpretation of the story. Consider whether your thesis is focused enough and clear or whether it needs to be refined. Can you add more evidence or explain more specifically how your evidence supports your thesis? Look closely at the transitions connecting your ideas. Are they logical? Can you make them more explicit? If you cite other critics, do you represent their ideas fairly? Do you depend on them too much to make your points for you? Reread your argument with your readers in mind. Have you fully acknowledged the possibility that they might interpret the story in some other way and that therefore you need to show them not only how you interpret the story but also why you see it as you do? Reconsider the order of your ideas. Do they make a coherent case or should you reorder them?

REVISING TO IMPROVE READABILITY. Outline the points you make to see how clearly they follow from one another. If you need to make the organization more explicit, provide transitions between sentences and paragraphs. Consider whether there are any places where you present more detail than necessary. Reconsider the opening to see if you can better prepare readers to follow your argument. Check to see if your thesis and forecasting statements are clear and direct. Reconsider the ending to see whether it reduces or oversimplifies your interpretation. If possible, end by suggesting the implications of your analysis.

No essay is complete without a careful proofreading for usage, punctuation, and spelling errors. Reread the essay again in order to find errors you habitually make. If possible, you might also exchange your essay with a classmate to give each other's essays a final proofreading.

# FURTHER STORIES FOR ANALYSIS

The following selections by some of America's best storytellers focus upon the common themes of love and relationships. In "The Diary of Adam and Eve," Mark Twain (1835–1910) begins at the beginning, presenting a humorous look at the relations between men and women. The author of *The Adventures of Huckleberry Finn* (1885), one of the great American novels, Twain wrote short stories and journalistic sketches as well as novels. Defending his humorous stories, Twain admitted that they "may be spun out to great length, and may wander around as much as [they please], and arrive nowhere in particular" but they are nevertheless works of "high and delicate art."

A less humorous but equally ironic piece, "The Story of an Hour" by Kate Chopin (1851–1904), follows. This very brief short story concerns a woman's innermost feelings about her marriage. A widow with six young children, Chopin published her first novel at the age of forty. She also published two collections of stories, but is best known for her brilliant last novel, *The Awakening* (1899). Because her fiction deals frankly with sex and marriage, it elicited a storm of controversy that cut short her career.

"Wakefield" is a provocative story by the dean of American short story writers, Nathaniel Hawthorne (1804–1864). It tells about a husband who cannot live with his wife but also cannot live without her. Hawthorne wrote many classic stories including "Young Goodman Brown" and "Ethan Brand," as well as everyone's favorite novel of adultery, *The Scarlet Letter* (1850).

The last piece, "My Man Bovanne," is a powerful story by the contemporary author Toni Cade Bambara. Full of humor and gentleness, this story shows a woman caring for a man despite her grown children's disapproval. Bambara has published two collections of stories, *Gorilla, My Love* (1972) and *The Sea Birds Are Still Alive* (1977), and a novel called *The Salt Eaters* (1980). "Stories are important," Bambara tells us, because "they keep us alive. In the ships, in the camps, in the quarters, in the fields, prisons, on the road, on the run, underground, under siege, in the throes, on the verge—the storyteller snatches us back from the edge."

# Mark Twain

# *The Diary of Adam and Eve*

### Part I—Extracts from Adam's Diary

*Monday*  This new creature with the long hair is a good deal in the way. It is always hanging around and following me about. I don't like this; I am not used to company. I wish it would stay with the other animals. . . . Cloudy today, wind in the east; think we shall have rain. . . . *We?* Where did I get that word?—I remember now—the new creature uses it.

*Tuesday*   Been examining the great waterfall. It is the finest thing on the estate, I think. The new creature calls it Niagara Falls—why, I am sure I do not know. Says it *looks* like Niagara Falls. That is not a reason, it is mere waywardness and imbecility. I get no chance to name anything myself. The new creature names everything that comes along, before I can get in a protest. And always that same pretext is offered—it *looks* like the thing. There is the dodo, for instance. Says the moment one looks at it one sees at a glance that it "looks like a dodo." It will have to keep that name, no doubt. It wearies me to fret about it, and it does no good, anyway. Dodo! It looks no more like a dodo than I do.

*Wednesday*   Built me a shelter against the rain, but could not have it to myself in peace. The new creature intruded. When I tried to put it out it shed water out of the holes it looks with, and wiped it away with the back of its paws, and made a noise such as some of the other animals make when they are in distress. I wish it would not talk; it is always talking. That sounds like a cheap fling at the poor creature, a slur; but I do not mean it so. I have never heard the human voice before, and any new and strange sound intruding itself here upon the solemn hush of these dreaming solitudes offends my ear and seems a false note. And this new sound is so close to me; it is right at my shoulder, right at my ear, first on one side and then on the other, and I am used only to sounds that are more or less distant from me.

*Friday*   The naming goes recklessly on, in spite of anything I can do. I had a very good name for the estate, and it was musical and pretty— Garden of Eden. Privately, I continue to call it that, but not any longer publicly. The new creature says it is all woods and rocks and scenery, and therefore has no resemblance to a garden. Says it *looks* like a park, and does not look like anything *but* a park. Consequently, without consulting me, it has been new-named—Niagara Falls Park. This is sufficiently high-handed, it seems to me. And already there is a sign up:

KEEP OFF
THE GRASS

My life is not as happy as it was.

*Saturday*   The new creature eats too much fruit. We are going to run short, most likely. "We" again—that is *its* word; mine, too, now, from hearing it so much. Good deal of fog this morning. I do not go out in the fog myself. The new creature does. It goes out in all weathers, and stumps right in with its muddy feet. And talks. It used to be so pleasant and quiet here.

*Sunday*   Pulled through. This day is getting to be more and more trying. It was selected and set apart last November as a day of rest. I had already six of them per week before. This morning found the new creature trying to clod apples out of that forbidden tree.

*Monday*    The new creature says its name is Eve. That is all right, I have no objections. Says it is to call it by, when I want it to come. I said it was superfluous, then. The word evidently raised me in its respect; and indeed it is a large, good word and will bear repetition. It says it is not an It, it is a She. This is probably doubtful; yet it is all one to me; what she is were nothing to me if she would but go by herself and not talk.

*Tuesday*    She has littered the whole estate with execrable names and offensive signs:

> THIS WAY TO THE WHIRLPOOL
>
> THIS WAY TO GOAT ISLAND
>
> CAVE OF THE WINDS THIS WAY

She says this park would make a tidy summer resort if there was any custom for it. Summer resort—another invention of hers—just words, without any meaning. What is a summer resort? But it is best not to ask her, she has such a rage for explaining.

*Friday*    She has taken to beseeching me to stop going over the Falls. What harm does it do? Says it makes her shudder. I wonder why; I have always done it—always like the plunge, and coolness. I supposed it was what the Falls were for. They have no other use that I can see, and they must have been made for something. She says they were only made for scenery—like the rhinoceros and the mastodon.

I went over the Falls in a barrel—not satisfactory to her. Went over in a tub—still not satisfactory. Swam the Whirlpool and the Rapids in a fig-leaf suit. It got much damaged. Hence, tedious complaints about my extravagance. I am too much hampered here. What I need is change of scene.

*Saturday*    I escaped last Tuesday night, and traveled two days, and built me another shelter in a secluded place, and obliterated my tracks as well as I could, but she hunted me out by means of a beast which she has tamed and calls a wolf, and came making that pitiful noise again, and shedding that water out of the places she looks with. I was obliged to return with her, but will presently emigrate again when occasion offers. She engages herself in many foolish things; among others, to study out why the animals called lions and tigers live on grass and flowers, when, as she says, the sort of teeth they wear would indicate that they were intended to eat each other. This is foolish, because to do that would be to kill each other, and that would introduce what, as I understand it, is called "death"; and death, as I have been told, has not yet entered the Park. Which is a pity, on some accounts.

*Sunday* Pulled through.

*Monday* I believe I see what the week is for: it is to give time to rest up from the weariness of Sunday. It seems a good idea. . . . She has been climbing that tree again. Clodded her out of it. She said nobody was looking. Seems to consider that a justification for chancing any dangerous thing. Told her that. The word justification moved her admiration—and envy, too, I thought. It is a good word.

*Tuesday* She told me she was made out of a rib taken from my body. This is at least doubtful, if not more than that. I have not missed any rib. . . . She is in much trouble about the buzzard; says grass does not agree with it; is afraid she can't raise it; thinks it was intended to live on decayed flesh. The buzzard must get along the best it can with what it is provided. We cannot overturn the whole scheme to accommodate the buzzard.

*Saturday* She fell in the pond yesterday when she was looking at herself in it, which she is always doing. She nearly strangled, and said it was most uncomfortable. This made her sorry for the creatures which live in there, which she calls fish, for she continues to fasten names on to things that don't need them and don't come when they are called by them, which is a matter of no consequence to her, she is such a num-skull, anyway; so she got a lot of them out and brought them in last night and put them in my bed to keep warm, but I have noticed them now and then all day and I don't see that they are any happier there than they were before, only quieter. When night comes I shall throw them outdoors. I will not sleep with them again, for I find them clammy and unpleasant to lie among when a person hasn't anything on.

*Sunday* Pulled through.

*Tuesday* She has taken up with a snake now. The other animals are glad, for she was always experimenting with them and bothering them; and I am glad because the snake talks, and this enables me to get a rest.

*Friday* She says the snake advised her to try the fruit of that tree, and says the result will be a great and fine and noble education. I told her there would be another result, too—it would introduce death into the world. That was a mistake—it had been better to keep the remark to myself; it only gave her an idea—she could save the sick buzzard, and furnish fresh meat to the despondent lions and tigers. I advised her to keep away from the tree. She said she wouldn't. I foresee trouble. Will emigrate.

*Wednesday* I have had a variegated time. I escaped last night, and rode a horse all night as fast as he could go, hoping to get clear out of the Park and hide in some other country before the trouble should begin; but it was not to be. About an hour after sun-up, as I was riding through a flowery plain where thousands of animals were grazing, slumbering, or playing with each other, according to their wont, all of a sudden they broke into a tempest of frightful noises, and in one moment the plain was a frantic commotion and every beast was destroying its neighbor. I knew what it meant—Eve had eaten that fruit, and death was come into the world. . . . The tigers ate my horse, paying no attention when I ordered them to desist, and they would have eaten me if I had stayed— which I didn't, but went away in much haste. . . . I found this place, outside the Park, and was fairly comfortable for a few days, but she has found me out. Found me out, and has named the place Tonawanda— says it *looks* like that. In fact I was not sorry she came, for there are but meager pickings here, and she brought some of those apples. I was obliged to eat them, I was so hungry. It was against my principles, but I find that principles have no real force except when one is well fed. . . . She came curtained in boughs and bunches of leaves, and when I asked her what she meant by such nonsense, and snatched them away and threw them down, she tittered and blushed. I had never seen a person titter and blush before, and to me it seemed unbecoming and idiotic. She said I would soon know how it was myself. This was correct. Hungry as I was, I laid down the apple half-eaten—certainly the best one I ever saw, considering the lateness of the season—and arrayed myself in the dis- carded boughs and branches, and then spoke to her with some severity and ordered her to go and get some more and not make such a spectacle of herself. She did it, and after this we crept down to where the wild- beast battle had been, and collected some skins, and I made her patch together a couple of suits proper for public occasions. They are uncom- fortable, it is true, but stylish, and that is the main point about clothes. . . . I find she is a good deal of a companion. I see I should be lonesome and depressed without her, now that I have lost my property. Another thing, she says it is ordered that we work for our living hereafter. She will be useful. I will superintend.

*Ten Days Later*    She accuses *me* of being the cause of our disaster! She says, with apparent sincerity and truth, that the Serpent assured her that the forbidden fruit was not apples, it was chestnuts. I said I was innocent, then, for I had not eaten any chestnuts. She said the Serpent informed her that "chestnut" was a figurative term meaning an aged and moldy joke. I turned pale at that, for I have made many jokes to pass the weary time, and some of them could have been of that sort, though I had honestly supposed that they were new when I made them. She asked me if I had made one just at the time of the catastrophe. I was obliged to admit that I had made one to myself, though not aloud. It was this. I was thinking about the Falls, and I said to myself, "How wonderful it is to see that vast body of water tumble down there!" Then in an instant a bright thought flashed into my head, and I let it fly, saying, "It would be a deal more wonderful to see it tumble *up* there!"— and I was just about to kill myself with laughing at it when all nature broke loose in war and death and I had to flee for my life. "There," she said, with triumph, "that is just it; the Serpent mentioned that very jest, and called it the First Chestnut, and said it was coeval with the creation." Alas, I am indeed to blame. Would that I were not witty; oh, that I had never had that radiant thought!

*Ten Years Later*  After all these years, I see that I was mistaken about Eve in the beginning; it is better to live outside the Garden with her than inside it without her. At first I thought she talked too much; but now I should be sorry to have that voice fall silent and pass out of my life. Blessed be the chestnut that brought us near together and taught me to know the goodness of her heart and the sweetness of her spirit!

## Part II—Eve's Diary

### (Translated from the original)

*Saturday*  I am almost a whole day old, now. I arrived yesterday. That is as it seems to me. And it must be so, for if there was a day-before-yesterday I was not there when it happened, or I should remember it. It could be, of course, that it did happen, and that I was not noticing. Very well; I will be very watchful now, and if any day-before-yesterdays happen I will make a note of it. It will be best to start right and not let the record get confused, for some instinct tells me that these details are going to be important to the historian some day. For I feel like an experiment, I feel exactly like an experiment; it would be impossible for a person to feel more like an experiment than I do, and so I am coming to feel convinced that is what I *am*—an experiment; just an experiment, and nothing more.

Then if I am an experiment, am I the whole of it? No, I think not; I think the rest of it is part of it. I am the main part of it, but I think the rest of it has its share in the matter. Is my position assured, or do I have to watch it and take care of it? The latter, perhaps. Some instinct tells me that eternal vigilance is the price of supremacy. (That is a good phrase, I think, for one so young.)

Everything looks better to-day than it did yesterday. In the rush of finishing up yesterday, the mountains were left in a ragged condition, and some of the plains were so cluttered with rubbish and remnants that the aspects were quite distressing. Noble and beautiful works of art should not be subjected to haste; and this majestic new world is indeed a most noble and beautiful work. And certainly marvelously near to being perfect, notwithstanding the shortness of the time. There are too many stars in some places and not enough in others, but that can be remedied presently, no doubt. The moon got loose last night, and slid down and fell out of the scheme—a very great loss; it breaks my heart to think of it. There isn't another thing among the ornaments and decorations that is comparable to it for beauty and finish. It should have been fastened better. If we can only get it back again—

But of course there is no telling where it went to. And besides, whoever gets it will hide it; I know it because I would do it myself. I believe I can be honest in all other matters, but I already begin to realize that the core and center of my nature is love of the beautiful, a passion for the beautiful, and that it would not be safe to trust me with a moon that belonged to another person and that person didn't know I had it. I could give up a moon that I found in the daytime, because I should be afraid some one was looking; but if I found it in the dark, I am sure I should find some kind of an excuse for not saying anything about it. For I do love moons, they are so pretty and so romantic. I wish we had five or six; I would never go to bed; I should never get tired lying on the moss-bank and looking up at them.

Stars are good, too. I wish I could get some to put in my hair. But I suppose I never can. You would be surprised to find how far off they are, for they do not look it. When they first showed, last night, I tried to knock some down with a pole, but it didn't reach, which astonished me; then I tried clods till I was all tired out, but I never got one. It was because I am left-handed and cannot throw good. Even when I aimed at the one I wasn't after I couldn't hit the other one, though I did make some close shots, for I saw the black blot of the clod sail right into the midst of the golden clusters forty or fifty times, just barely missing them, and if I could have held out a little longer maybe I could have got one.

So I cried a little, which was natural, I suppose, for one of my age, and after I was rested I got a basket and started for a place on the extreme rim of the circle, where the stars were close to the ground and I could get them with my hands, which would be better, anyway, because I could gather them tenderly then, and not break them. But it was farther than I thought, and at last I had to give it up; I was so tired I couldn't drag my feet another step; and besides, they were sore and hurt me very much.

I couldn't get back home; it was too far and turning cold; but I found some tigers and nestled in among them and was most adorably comfortable, and their breath was sweet and pleasant, because they live on strawberries. I had never seen a tiger before, but I knew them in a minute by the stripes. If I could have one of those skins, it would make a lovely gown.

To-day I am getting better ideas about distances. I was so eager to get hold of every pretty thing that I giddily grabbed for it, sometimes when it was too far off, and sometimes when it was but six inches away but seemed a foot—alas, with thorns between! I learned a lesson; also I made an axiom, all out of my own head—my very first one: *The scratched Experiment shuns the thorn.* I think it is a very good one for one so young.

I followed the other Experiment around, yesterday afternoon, at a distance, to see what it might be for, if I could. But I was not able to make it out. I think it is a man. I had never seen a man, but it looked like one, and I feel sure that that is what it is. I realize that I feel more curiosity about it than about any of the other reptiles. If it is a reptile, and I suppose it is; for it has frowsy hair and blue eyes, and looks like a reptile. It has no hips; it tapers like a carrot; when it stands, it spreads itself apart like a derrick; so I think it is a reptile, though it may be architecture.

I was afraid of it at first, and started to run every time it turned around, for I thought it was going to chase me; but by and by I found it was only trying to get away, so after that I was not timid any more, but tracked it along, several hours, about twenty yards behind, which made it nervous and unhappy. At last it was a good deal worried, and climbed a tree. I waited a good while, then gave it up and went home.

To-day the same thing over. I've got it up the tree again.

*Sunday* It is up there yet. Resting, apparently. But that is a subterfuge: Sunday isn't the day of rest; Saturday is appointed for that. It looks to me like a creature that is more interested in resting than in anything else. It would tire me to rest so much. It tires me just to sit around and watch the tree. I do wonder what it is for; I never see it do anything.

They returned the moon last night, and I was *so* happy! I think it is very honest of them. It slid down and fell off again, but I was not distressed; there is no need to worry when one has that kind of neighbors; they will fetch it back. I wish I could do something to show my appreciation. I would like to send them some stars, for we have more than we can use. I mean I, not we, for I can see that the reptile cares nothing for such things.

It has low tastes, and is not kind. When I went there yesterday evening in the gloaming it had crept down and was trying to catch the little speckled fishes that play in the pool, and I had to clod it to make it go up the tree again and let them alone. I wonder if *that* is what it is for? Hasn't it any heart? Hasn't it any compassion for those little creatures?

Can it be that it was designed and manufactured for such ungentle work? It has the look of it. One of the clods took it back of the ear, and it used language. It gave me a thrill, for it was the first time I had ever heard speech, except my own. I did not understand the words, but they seemed expressive.

When I found it could talk I felt a new interest in it, for I love to talk; I talk, all day, and in my sleep, too, and I am very interesting, but if I had another to talk to I could be twice as interesting, and would never stop, if desired.

If this reptile is a man, it isn't an *it*, is it? That wouldn't be grammatical, would it? I think it would be a *he*. I think so. In that case one would parse it thus: nominative, *he*; dative, *him*; possessive, *his'n*. Well, I will consider it a man and call it he until it turns out to be something else. This will be handier than having so many uncertainties.

*Next week Sunday*    All the week I tagged around after him and tried to get acquainted. I had to do the talking, because he was shy, but I didn't mind it. He seemed pleased to have me around, and I used the sociable "we" a good deal, because it seemed to flatter him to be included.

*Wednesday*    We are getting along very well indeed, now, and getting better and better acquainted. He does not try to avoid me any more, which is a good sign, and shows that he likes to have me with him. That pleases me, and I study to be useful to him in every way I can, so as to increase his regard. During the last day or two I have taken all the work of naming things off his hands, and this has been a great relief to him, for he has no gift in that line, and is evidently very grateful. He can't think of a rational name to save him, but I do not let him see that I am aware of his defect. Whenever a new creature comes along I name it before he has time to expose himself by an awkward silence. In this way I have saved him many embarrassments. I have no defect like his. The minute I set eyes on an animal I know what it is. I don't have to reflect a moment; the right name comes out instantly, just as if it were an inspiration, as no doubt it is, for I am sure it wasn't in me half a minute before. I seem to know just by the shape of the creature and the way it acts what animal it is.

When the dodo came along he thought it was a wildcat—I saw it in his eye. But I saved him. And I was careful not to do it in a way that could hurt his pride. I just spoke up in a quite natural way of pleased surprise, and not as if I was dreaming of conveying information, and said, "Well, I do declare, if there isn't the dodo!" I explained—without seeming to be explaining—how I knew it for a dodo, and although I thought maybe he was a little piqued that I knew the creature when he didn't, it was quite evident that he admired me. That was very agreeable, and I thought of it more than once with gratification before I slept. How little a thing can make us happy when we feel that we have earned it!

*Thursday*  My first sorrow. Yesterday he avoided me and seemed to wish I would not talk to him. I could not believe it, and thought there was some mistake, for I loved to be with him, and loved to hear him talk, and so how could it be that he could feel unkind toward me when I had not done anything? But at last it seemed true, so I went away and sat lonely in the place where I first saw him the morning that we were made and I did not know what he was and was indifferent about him; but now it was a mournful place, and every little thing spoke of him, and my heart was very sore. I did not know why very clearly, for it was a new feeling; I had not experienced it before, and it was all a mystery, and I could not make it out.

But when night came I could not bear the lonesomeness, and went to the new shelter which he has built, to ask him what I had done that was wrong and how I could mend it and get back his kindness again; but he put me out in the rain, and it was my first sorrow.

*Sunday*  It is pleasant again, now, and I am happy; but those were heavy days; I do not think of them when I can help it.

I tried to get him some of those apples, but I cannot learn to throw straight. I failed, but I think the good intention pleased him. They are forbidden, and he says I shall come to harm; but so I come to harm through pleasing him, why shall I care for that harm?

*Monday*  This morning I told him my name, hoping it would interest him. But he did not care for it. It is strange. If he should tell me his name, I would care. I think it would be pleasanter in my ears than any other sound.

He talks very little. Perhaps it is because he is not bright, and is sensitive about it and wishes to conceal it. It is such a pity that he should feel so, for brightness is nothing; it is in the heart that values lie. I wish I could made him understand that a loving good heart is riches, and riches enough, and that without it intellect is poverty.

Although he talks so little, he has quite a considerable vocabulary. This morning he used a surprisingly good word. He evidently recognized, himself, that it was a good one, for he worked it in twice afterward, casually. It was not good casual art, still it showed that he possesses a certain quality of perception. Without a doubt that seed can be made to grow, if cultivated.

Where did he get that word? I do not think I have ever used it.

No, he took no interest in my name. I tried to hide my disappointment, but I suppose I did not succeed. I went away and sat on the moss-bank with my feet in the water. It is where I go when I hunger for companionship, some one to look at, some one to talk to. It is not enough—that lovely white body painted there in the pool—but it is something, and something is better than utter loneliness. It talks when I talk; it is sad when I am sad; it comforts me with its sympathy; it says, "Do not be downhearted, you poor friendless girl; I will be your friend." It *is* a good friend to me, and my only one; it is my sister.

That first time that she forsook me! Ah, I shall never forget that— never, never. My heart was lead in my body! I said, "She was all I had, and now she is gone!" In my despair I said, "Break, my heart; I cannot bear my life any more!" and hid my face in my hands, and there was no solace for me. And when I took them away, after a little, there she was again, white and shining and beautiful, and I sprang into her arms!

That was perfect happiness; I had known happiness before, but it was not like this, which was ecstasy. I never doubted her afterward. Some- times she stayed away—maybe an hour, maybe almost the whole day, but I waited and did not doubt; I said, "She is busy, or she is gone a journey, but she will come." And it was so: she always did. At night she would not come if it was dark, for she was a timid little thing; but if there was a moon she would come. I am not afraid of the dark, but she is younger than I am; she was born after I was. Many and many are the visits I have paid her; she is my comfort and my refuge when my life is hard—and it is mainly that.

*Tuesday*    All the morning I was at work improving the estate; and I purposely kept away from him in the hope that he would get lonely and come. But he did not.

At noon I stopped for the day and took my recreation by flitting all about with the bees and the butterflies and reveling in the flowers, those beautiful creatures that catch the smile of God out of the sky and preserve it! I gathered them, and made them into wreaths and garlands and clothed myself in them while I ate my luncheon—apples, of course; then I sat in the shade and wished and waited. But he did not come.

But no matter. Nothing would have come of it, for he does not care for flowers. He calls them rubbish, and cannot tell one from another, and thinks it is superior to feel like that. He does not care for me, he does not care for flowers, he does not care for the painted sky at even- tide—is there anything he does care for, except building shacks to coop himself up in from the good clean rain, and thumping the melons, and sampling the grapes, and fingering the fruit on the trees, to see how those properties are coming along?

I laid a dry stick on the ground and tried to bore a hole in it with another one, in order to carry out a scheme that I had, and soon I got an awful fright. A thin, transparent bluish film rose out of the hole, and I dropped everything and ran! I thought it was a spirit, and I *was* so frightened! But I looked back, and it was not coming; so I leaned against a rock and rested and panted, and let my limbs go on trembling until they got steady again; then I crept warily back, alert, watching, and ready to fly if there was occasion; and when I was come near, I parted the branches of a rose-bush and peeped through—wishing the man was about, I was looking so cunning and pretty—but the spirit was gone. I went there, and there was a pinch of delicate pink dust in the hole. I put my finger in, to feel it, and said *ouch!* and took it out again. It was a cruel pain. I put my finger in my mouth; and by standing first on one foot and then the other, and grunting, I presently eased my misery; then I was full of interest, and began to examine.

I was curious to know what the pink dust was. Suddenly the name of it occurred to me, though I had never heard of it before. It was *fire!* I was as certain of it as a person could be of anything in the world. So without hesitation I named it that—fire.

I had created something that didn't exist before; I had added a new thing to the world's uncountable properties; I realized this, and was proud of my achievement, and was going to run and find him and tell him about it, thinking to raise myself in his esteem—but I reflected, and did not do it. No—he would not care for it. He would ask what it was good for, and what could I answer? for if it were not *good* for something, but only beautiful, merely beautiful—

So I sighed, and did not go. For it wasn't good for anything; it could not build a shack, it could not improve melons, it could not hurry a fruit crop; it was useless, it was a foolishness and a vanity; he would despise it and say cutting words. But to me it was not despicable; I said, "Oh, you fire, I love you, you dainty pink creature, for you are *beautiful*—and that is enough!" and was going to gather it to my breast. But refrained. Then I made another maxim out of my own head, though it was so nearly like the first one that I was afraid it was only a plagiarism: *"The burnt Experiment shuns the fire."*

I wrought again; and when I had made a good deal of fire-dust I emptied it into a handful of dry brown grass, intending to carry it home and keep it always and play with it; but the wind struck it and it sprayed up and spat out at me fiercely, and I dropped it and ran. When I looked back the blue spirit was towering up and stretching, and rolling away like a cloud, and instantly I thought of the name of it—*smoke!*—though, upon my word, I had never heard of smoke before.

Soon, brilliant yellow and red flares shot up through the smoke, and I named them in an instant—*flames*—and I was right, too, though these were the very first flames that had ever been in the world. They climbed the trees, they flashed splendidly in and out of the vast and increasing volume of tumbling smoke, and I had to clap my hands and laugh and dance in my rapture, it was so new and strange and so wonderful and so beautiful!

He came running, and stopped and gazed, and said not a word for many minutes. Then he asked what it was. Ah, it was too bad that he should ask such a direct question. I had to answer it, of course, and I did. I said it was fire. If it annoyed him that I should know and he must ask, that was not my fault; I had no desire to annoy him. After a pause he asked:

"How did it come?"

Another direct question, and it also had to have a direct answer.

"I made it."

The fire was traveling farther and farther off. He went to the edge of the burned place and stood looking down, and said:

"What are these?"

"Fire-coals."

He picked up one to examine it, but changed his mind and put it down again. Then he went away. *Nothing* interests him.

But I was interested. There were ashes, gray and soft and delicate and pretty—I knew what they were at once. And the embers; I knew the embers, too. I found my apples, and raked them out, and was glad; for I am very young and my appetite is active. But I was disappointed; they were all burst open and spoiled. Spoiled apparently; but it was not so; they were better than raw ones. Fire is beautiful; some day it will be useful, I think.

*Friday*   I saw him again, for a moment, last Monday at nightfall, but only for a moment. I was hoping he would praise me for trying to improve the estate, for I had meant well and had worked hard. But he was not pleased, and turned away and left me. He was also displeased on another account: I tried once more to persuade him to stop going over the Falls. That was because the fire had revealed to me a new passion—quite new, and distinctly different from love, grief, and those others which I had already discovered—*fear*. And it is horrible!—I wish I had never discovered it; it gives me dark moments, it spoils my happiness, it makes me shiver and tremble and shudder. But I could not persuade him, for he has not discovered fear yet, and so he could not understand me.

*Friday*   Tuesday—Wednesday—Thursday—and to-day: all without seeing him. It is a long time to be alone; still, it is better to be alone than unwelcome.

I *had* to have company—I was made for it, I think—so I made friends with the animals. They are just charming, and they have the kindest disposition and politest ways; they never look sour, they never let you feel that you are intruding, they smile at you and wag their tail, if they've got one, and they are always ready for a romp or an excursion or anything you want to propose. I think they are perfect gentlemen. All these days we have had such good times, and it hasn't been lonesome for me, ever. Lonesome! No, I should say not. Why, there's always a swarm of them around—sometimes as much as four or five acres—you can't count them; and when you stand on a rock in the midst and look out over the furry expanse it is so mottled and splashed and gay with color and frisking sheen and sun-flash, and so rippled with stripes, that you might think it was a lake, only you know it isn't; and there's storms of sociable birds, and hurricanes of whirring wings; and when the sun strikes all that feathery commotion, you have a blazing up of all the colors you can think of, enough to put your eyes out.

We have made long excursions, and I have seen a great deal of the world; almost all of it, I think; and so I am the first traveler, and the only one. When we are on the march, it is an imposing sight—there's nothing like it anywhere. For comfort I ride a tiger or a leopard, because it is soft and has a round back that fits me, and because they are such pretty animals; but for long distance or for scenery I ride the elephant. He hoists me up with his trunk, but I can get off myself; when we are ready to camp, he sits and I slide down the back way.

The birds and animals are all friendly to each other, and there are no disputes about anything. They all talk, and they all talk to me, but it must be a foreign language, for I cannot make out a word they say; yet they often understand me when I talk back, particularly the dog and the elephant. It makes me ashamed. It shows that they are brighter than I am, and are therefore my superiors. It annoys me, for I want to be the principal Experiment myself—and I intend to be, too.

I have learned a number of things, and am educated, now, but I wasn't at first. I was ignorant at first. At first it used to vex me because, with all my watching, I was never smart enough to be around when the water was running uphill; but now I do not mind it. I have experimented and experimented until now I know it never does run uphill, except in the dark. I know it does in the dark, because the pool never goes dry, which it would, of course, if the water didn't come back in the night. It is best to prove things by actual experiment; then you *know*; whereas if you depend on guessing and supposing and conjecturing, you will never get educated.

Some things you *can't* find out; but you will never know you can't by
guessing and supposing: no, you have to be patient and go on experimenting until you find out that you can't find out. And it is delightful
to have it that way, it makes the world so interesting. If there wasn't
anything to find out, it would be dull. Even trying to find out and not
finding out is just as interesting as trying to find out and finding out, and
I don't know but more so. The secret of the water was a treasure until I
*got* it; then the excitement all went away, and I recognized a sense of
loss.

By experiment I know that wood swims, and dry leaves, and feathers,
and plenty of other things; therefore by all that cumulative evidence you
know that a rock will swim; but you have to put up with simply knowing
it, for there isn't any way to prove it—up to now. But I shall find a
way—then *that* excitement will go. Such things make me sad; because
by and by when I have found out everything there won't be any more
excitements, and I do love excitements so! The other night I couldn't
sleep for thinking about it.

At first I couldn't make out what I was made for, but now I think it
was to search out the secrets of this wonderful world and be happy and
thank the Giver of it all for devising it. I think there are many things
to learn yet—I hope so; and by economizing and not hurrying too fast I
think they will last weeks and weeks. I hope so. When you cast up a
feather it sails away on the air and goes out of sight; then you throw up
a clod and it doesn't. It comes down, every time. I have tried it and
tried it, and it is always so. I wonder why it is? Of course it *doesn't* come
down, but why should it *seem* to? I suppose it is an optical illusion. I
mean, one of them is. I don't know which one. It may be the feather,
it may be the clod; I can't prove which it is, I can only demonstrate that
one or the other is a fake, and let a person take his choice.

By watching, I know that the stars are not going to last. I have seen
some of the best ones melt and run down the sky. Since one can melt,
they can all melt; since they can all melt, they can all melt the same
night. That sorrow will come—I know it. I mean to sit up every night
and look at them as long as I can keep awake; and I will impress those
sparkling fields on my memory, so that by and by when they are taken
away I can by my fancy restore those lovely myriads to the black sky and
make them sparkle again, and double them by the blur of my tears.

### After the Fall

When I look back, the Garden is a dream to me. It was beautiful,
surpassingly beautiful, enchantingly beautiful; and now it is lost, and I
shall not see it any more.

The Garden is lost, but I have found *him*, and am content. He loves me as well as he can; I love him with all the strength of my passionate nature, and this, I think, is proper to my youth and sex. If I ask myself why I love him, I find I do not know, and do not really much care to know; so I suppose that this kind of love is not a product of reasoning and statistics, like one's love for other reptiles and animals. I think that this must be so. I love certain birds because of their song; but I do not love Adam on account of his singing—no, it is not that; the more he sings the more I do not get reconciled to it. Yet I ask him to sing, because I wish to learn to like everything he is interested in. I am sure I can learn, because at first I could not stand it, but now I can. It sours the milk, but it doesn't matter; I can get used to that kind of milk.

It is not on account of his brightness that I love him—no, it is not that. He is not to blame for his brightness, such as it is, for he did not make it himself; he is as God made him, and that is sufficient. There was a wise purpose in it, *that* I know. In time it will develop, though I think it will not be sudden; and besides, there is no hurry; he is well enough just as he is.

It is not on account of his gracious and considerate ways and his delicacy that I love him. No, he has lacks in these regards, but he is well enough just so, and is improving.

It is not on account of his industry that I love him—no, it is not that. I think he has it in him, and I do not know why he conceals it from me. It is my only pain. Otherwise he is frank and open with me, now. I am sure he keeps nothing from me but this. It grieves me that he should have a secret from me, and sometimes it spoils my sleep, thinking of it, but I will put it out of my mind; it shall not trouble my happiness, which is otherwise full to overflowing.

It is not on account of his education that I love him—no, it is not that. He is self-educated, and does really know a multitude of things, but they are not so.

It is not on account of his chivalry that I love him—no, it is not that. He told on me, but I do not blame him; it is a peculiarity of sex, I think, and he did not make his sex. Of course I would not have told on him, I would have perished first; but that is a peculiarity of sex, too, and I do not take credit for it, for I did not make my sex.

Then why is it that I love him? *Merely because he is masculine*, I think.

At bottom he is good, and I love him for that, but I could love him without it. If he should beat me and abuse me, I should go on loving him. I know it. It is a matter of sex, I think.

He is strong and handsome, and I love him for that, and I admire him and am proud of him, but I could love him without those qualities. If he were plain, I should love him; if he were a wreck, I should love him; and I would work for him, and slave over him, and pray for him, and watch by his bedside until I died.

Yes, I think I love him merely because he is *mine* and is *masculine*. There is no other reason, I suppose. And so I think it is as I first said: that this kind of love is not a product of reasonings and statistics. It just *comes*—none knows whence—and cannot explain itself. And doesn't need to.

It is what I think. But I am only a girl, and the first that has examined this matter, and it may turn out that in my ignorance and inexperience I have not got it right.

### Forty Years Later

It is my prayer, it is my longing, that we may pass from this life together—a longing which shall never perish from the earth, but shall have place in the heart of every wife that loves, until the end of time; and it shall be called by my name.

But if one of us must go first, it is my prayer that it shall be I; for he is strong. I am weak, I am not so necessary to him as he is to me—life without him would not be life; how could I endure it? This prayer is also immortal, and will not cease from being offered up while my race continues. I am the first wife; and in the last wife I shall be repeated.

### At Eve's Grave

ADAM: Wheresoever she was, *there* was Eden.

# Kate Chopin

---

# *The Story of an Hour*

Knowing that Mrs. Mallard was afflicted with a heart trouble, great care was taken to break to her as gently as possible the news of her husband's death.

It was her sister Josephine who told her, in broken sentences, veiled hints that revealed in half concealing. Her husband's friend Richards was there, too, near her. It was he who had been in the newspaper office when intelligence of the railroad disaster was received, with Brently Mallard's name leading the list of "killed." He had only taken the time to assure himself of its truth by a second telegram, and had hastened to forestall any less careful, less tender friend in bearing the sad message.

She did not hear the story as many women have heard the same, with a paralyzed inability to accept its significance. She wept at once, with sudden, wild abandonment, in her sister's arms. When the storm of grief had spent itself she went away to her room alone. She would have no one follow her.

There stood, facing the open window, a comfortable, roomy armchair. Into this she sank, pressed down by a physical exhaustion that haunted her body and seemed to reach into her soul.

She could see in the open square before her house the tops of trees that were all aquiver with the new spring life. The delicious breath of rain was in the air. In the street below a peddler was crying his wares. The notes of a distant song which some one was singing reached her faintly, and countless sparrows were twittering in the eaves.

There were patches of blue sky showing here and there through the clouds that had met and piled above the other in the west facing her window.

She sat with her head thrown back upon the cushion of the chair, quite motionless, except when a sob came up into her throat and shook her, as a child who has cried itself to sleep continues to sob in its dreams.

She was young, with a fair, calm face, whose lines bespoke repression and even a certain strength. But now there was a dull stare in her eyes, whose gaze was fixed away off yonder on one of those patches of blue sky. It was not a glance of reflection, but rather indicated a suspension of intelligent thought.

There was something coming to her and she was waiting for it, fearfully. What was it? She did not know; it was too subtle and elusive to name. But she felt it, creeping out of the sky, reaching toward her through the sounds, the scents, the color that filled the air.

Now her bosom rose and fell tumultuously. She was beginning to recognize this thing that was approaching to possess her, and she was striving to beat it back with her will—as powerless as her two white slender hands would have been.

When she abandoned herself a little whispered word escaped her slightly parted lips. She said it over and over under her breath: "Free, free, free!" The vacant stare and the look of terror that had followed it went from her eyes. They stayed keen and bright. Her pulses beat fast, and the coursing blood warmed and relaxed every inch of her body.

She did not stop to ask if it were or were not a monstrous joy that held her. A clear and exalted perception enabled her to dismiss the suggestion as trivial.

She knew that she would weep again when she saw the kind, tender hands folded in death; the face that had never looked save with love upon her, fixed and gray and dead. But she saw beyond that bitter moment a long procession of years to come that would belong to her absolutely. And she opened and spread her arms out to them in welcome.

There would be no one to live for her during those coming years; she would live for herself. There would be no powerful will bending her in that blind persistence with which men and women believe they have a right to impose a private will upon a fellow-creature. A kind intention or a cruel intention made the act seem no less a crime as she looked upon it in that brief moment of illumination.

And yet she had loved him—sometimes. Often she had not. What did it matter! What could love, the unsolved mystery, count for in face of this possession of self-assertion which she suddenly recognized as the strongest impulse of her being!

"Free! Body and soul free!" she kept whispering.

Josephine was kneeling before the closed door with her lips to the keyhole, imploring for admission. "Louise, open the door! I beg; open the door—you will make yourself ill. What are you doing, Louise? For heaven's sake open the door."

"Go away. I am not making myself ill." No; she was drinking in a very elixir of life through that open window.

Her fancy was running riot along those days ahead of her. Spring days, and summer days, and all sorts of days that would be her own. She breathed a quick prayer that life might be long. It was only yesterday she had thought with a shudder that life might be long.

She arose at length and opened the door to her sister's importunities. There was a feverish triumph in her eyes, and she carried herself unwittingly like a goddess of Victory. She clasped her sister's waist, and together they descended the stairs. Richards stood waiting for them at the bottom.

Some one was opening the front door with a latchkey. It was Brently Mallard who entered, a little travel-stained, composedly carrying his gripsack and umbrella. He had been far from the scene of accident, and did not even know there had been one. He stood amazed at Josephine's piercing cry; at Richards' quick motion to screen him from the view of his wife.

But Richards was too late.

When the doctors came they said she had died of heart disease—of joy that kills.

# Nathaniel Hawthorne

## *Wakefield*

In some old magazine or newspaper I recollect a story, told as truth, of a man—let us call him Wakefield—who absented himself for a long time from his wife. The fact, thus abstractedly stated, is not very uncommon, nor—without a proper distinction of circumstances—to be condemned either as naughty or nonsensical. Howbeit, this, though far from the most aggravated, is perhaps the strangest, instance on record, of marital delinquency; and, moreover, as remarkable a freak as may be found in the whole list of human oddities. The wedded couple lived in London. The man, under pretence of going a journey, took lodgings in the next street to his own house, and there, unheard of by his wife or friends, and without the shadow of a reason for such self-banishment, dwelt upwards of twenty years. During that period, he beheld his home every day, and frequently the forlorn Mrs. Wakefield. And after so great a gap in his matrimonial felicity—when his death was reckoned certain, his estate settled, his name dismissed from memory, and his wife, long, long ago, resigned to her autumnal widowhood—he entered the door one evening, quietly, as from a day's absence, and became a loving spouse till death.

This outline is all that I remember. But the incident, though of the purest originality, unexampled, and probably never to be repeated, is one, I think, which appeals to the generous sympathies of mankind. We know, each for himself, that none of us would perpetrate such a folly, yet feel as if some other might. To my own contemplations, at least, it has often recurred, always exciting wonder, but with a sense that the story must be true, and a conception of its hero's character. Whenever any subject so forcibly affects the mind, time is well spent in thinking of it. If the reader choose, let him do his own meditation; or if he prefer to ramble with me through the twenty years of Wakefield's vagary, I bid him welcome; trusting that there will be a pervading spirit and a moral, even should we fail to find them, done up neatly, and condensed into the final sentence. Thought has always its efficacy, and every striking incident its moral.

What sort of a man was Wakefield? We are free to shape out our own idea, and call it by his name. He was now in the meridian of life; his matrimonial affections, never violent, were sobered into a calm, habitual sentiment; of all husbands, he was likely to be the most constant, because a certain sluggishness would keep his heart at rest, wherever it might be placed. He was intellectual, but not actively so; his mind occupied itself in long and lazy musings, that ended to no purpose, or had not vigor to attain it; his thoughts were seldom so energetic as to seize hold of words. Imagination, in the proper meaning of the term, made no part of Wakefield's gifts. With a cold but not depraved nor wandering heart, and a mind never feverish with riotous thoughts, nor perplexed with originality, who could have anticipated that our friend would entitle himself to a foremost place among the doers of eccentric deeds? Had his acquaintances been asked, who was the man in London the surest to perform nothing to-day which should be remembered on the morrow, they would have thought of Wakefield. Only the wife of his bosom might have hesitated. She, without having analyzed his character, was partly aware of a quiet selfishness, that had rusted into his inactive mind; of a peculiar sort of vanity, the most uneasy attribute about him; of a disposition to craft, which had seldom produced more positive effects than the keeping of petty secrets, hardly worth revealing; and, lastly, of what she called a little strangeness, sometimes, in the good man. This latter quality is indefinable, and perhaps non-existent.

Let us now imagine Wakefield bidding adieu to his wife. It is the dusk of an October evening. His equipment is a drab greatcoat, a hat covered with an oilcloth, top-boots, an umbrella in one hand and a small portmanteau in the other. He has informed Mrs. Wakefield that he is to take the night coach into the country. She would fain inquire the length of his journey, its object, and the probable time of his return; but, indulgent to his harmless love of mystery, interrogates him only by a look. He tells her not to expect him positively by the return coach, nor to be alarmed should he tarry three or four days; but, at all events, to look for him at supper on Friday evening. Wakefield himself, be it considered, has no suspicion of what is before him. He holds out his hand, she gives her own, and meets his parting kiss in the matter-of-course way of a ten years' matrimony; and forth goes the middle-aged Mr. Wakefield, almost resolved to perplex his good lady by a whole week's absence. After the door has closed behind him, she perceives it thrust partly open, and a vision of her husband's face, through the aperture, smiling on her, and gone in a moment. For the time, this little incident is dismissed without a thought. But, long afterwards, when she has been more years a widow than a wife, that smile recurs, and flickers across all her reminiscences of Wakefield's visage. In her many musings, she surrounds the original smile with a multitude of fantasies, which make it strange and awful: as, for instance, if she imagines him in a coffin, that parting look is frozen on his pale features; or, if she dreams of him in heaven, still his blessed spirit wears a quiet and crafty smile. Yet, for its sake, when all others have given him up for dead, she sometimes doubts whether she is a widow.

But our business is with the husband. We must hurry after him along the street, ere he lose his individuality, and melt into the great mass of London life. It would be vain searching for him there. Let us follow close at his heels, therefore, until, after several superfluous turns and doublings, we find him comfortably established by the fireside of a small apartment, previously bespoken. He is in the next street to his own, and at his journey's end. He can scarcely trust his good fortune, in having got thither unperceived—recollecting that, at one time, he was delayed by the throng, in the very focus of a lighted lantern; and, again, there were footsteps that seemed to tread behind his own, distinct from the multitudinous tramp around him; and, anon, he heard a voice shouting afar, and fancied that it called his name. Doubtless, a dozen busybodies had been watching him, and told his wife the whole affair. Poor Wakefield! Little knowest thou thine own insignificance in this great world! No mortal eye but mine has traced thee. Go quietly to thy bed, foolish man; and, on the morrow, if thou wilt be wise, get thee home to good Mrs. Wakefield, and tell her the truth. Remove not thyself, even for a little week, from thy place in her chaste bosom. Were she, for a single moment, to deem thee dead, or lost, or lastingly divided from her, thou wouldst be wofully conscious of a change in thy true wife forever after. It is perilous to make a chasm in human affections; not that they gape so long and wide—but so quickly close again!

Almost repenting of his frolic, or whatever it may be termed, Wakefield lies down betimes, and starting from his first nap, spreads forth his arms into the wide and solitary waste of the unaccustomed bed. "No,"—thinks he, gathering the bedclothes about him, —"I will not sleep alone another night."

In the morning he rises earlier than usual, and sets himself to consider what he really means to do. Such are his loose and rambling modes of thought that he has taken this very singular step with the consciousness of a purpose, indeed, but without being able to define it sufficiently for his own contemplation. The vagueness of the project, and the convulsive effort with which he plunges into the execution of it, are equally characteristic of a feeble-minded man. Wakefield sifts his ideas, however, as minutely as he may, and finds himself curious to know the progress of matters at home—how his exemplary wife will endure her widowhood of a week; and, briefly, how the little sphere of creatures and circumstances, in which he was a central object, will be affected by his removal. A morbid vanity, therefore, lies nearest the bottom of the affair. But, how is he to attain his ends? Not, certainly, by keeping close in this comfortable lodging, where, though he slept and awoke in the next street to his home, he is as effectually abroad as if the stage-coach had been whirling him away all night. Yet, should he reappear, the whole project is knocked in the head. His poor brains being hopelessly puzzled with this dilemma, he at length ventures out, partly resolving to cross the head of the street, and send one hasty glance towards his forsaken domicile. Habit—for he is a man of habits—takes him by the hand, and guides him, wholly unaware, to his own door, where, just at the critical moment, he is aroused by the scraping of his foot upon the step. Wakefield! whither are you going?

At that instant his fate was turning on the pivot. Little dreaming of the doom to which his first backward step devotes him, he hurries away, breathless with agitation hitherto unfelt, and hardly dares turn his head at the distant corner. Can it be that nobody caught sight of him? Will not the whole household—the decent Mrs. Wakefield, the smart maid servant, and the dirty little footboy—raise a hue and cry, through London streets, in pursuit of their fugitive lord and master? Wonderful escape! He gathers courage to pause and look homeward, but is perplexed with a sense of change about the familiar edifice, such as affects us all, when, after a separation of months or years, we again see some hill or lake, or work of art, with which we were friends of old. In ordinary cases, this indescribable impression is caused by the comparison and contrast between our imperfect reminiscences and the reality. In Wakefield, the magic of a single night has wrought a similar transformation, because, in that brief period, a great moral change has been effected. But this is a secret from himself. Before leaving the spot, he catches a far and momentary glimpse of his wife, passing athwart the front window, with her face turned towards the head of the street. The crafty nincompoop takes to his heels, scared with the idea that, among a thousand such atoms of mortality, her eye must have detected him. Right glad is his heart, though his brain be somewhat dizzy, when he finds himself by the coal fire of his lodgings.

So much for the commencement of this long whimwham. After the initial conception, and the stirring up of the man's sluggish temperament to put it in practice, the whole matter evolves itself in a natural train. We may suppose him, as the result of deep deliberation, buying a new wig, of reddish hair, and selecting sundry garments, in a fashion unlike his customary suit of brown, from a Jew's old-clothes bag. It is accomplished. Wakefield is another man. The new system being now established, a retrograde movement to the old would be almost as difficult as the step that placed him in his unparalleled position. Furthermore, he is rendered obstinate by a sulkiness occasionally incident to his temper, and brought on at present by the inadequate sensation which he conceives to have been produced in the bosom of Mrs. Wakefield. He will not go back until she be frightened half to death. Well; twice or thrice has she passed before his sight, each time with a heavier step, a paler cheek, and more anxious brow; and in the third week of his non-appearance he detects a portent of evil entering the house, in the guise of an apothecary. Next day the knocker is muffled. Towards nightfall comes the chariot of a physician, and deposits its big-wigged and solemn burden at Wakefield's door, whence, after a quarter of an hour's visit, he emerges, perchance the herald of a funeral. Dear woman! Will she die? By this time, Wakefield is excited to something like energy of feeling, but still lingers away from his wife's bedside, pleading with his conscience that she must not be disturbed at such a juncture. If aught else restrains him, he does not know it. In the course of a few weeks she gradually recovers; the crisis is over; her heart is sad, perhaps, but quiet; and, let him return soon or late, it will never be feverish for him again. Such ideas glimmer through the mist of Wakefield's mind, and render him indistinctly conscious that an almost impassable gulf divides his hired apartment from his former home. "It is but in the next street!" he sometimes says. Fool! it is another world. Hitherto, he has put off his return from one particular day to another; henceforward, he leaves the precise time undetermined. Not to-morrow—probably next week—pretty soon. Poor man! The dead have nearly as much chance of revisiting their earthly homes as the self-banished Wakefield.

Would that I had a folio to write, instead of an article of a dozen pages! Then might I exemplify how an influence beyond our control lays its strong hand on every deed which we do, and weaves its consequences into an iron tissue of necessity. Wakefield is spell-bound. We must leave him, for ten years or so, to haunt around his house, without once crossing the threshold, and to be faithful to his wife, with all the affection of which his heart is capable, while he is slowly fading out of hers. Long since, it must be remarked, he had lost the perception of singularity in his conduct.

Now for a scene! Amid the throng of a London street we distinguish a man, now waxing elderly, with few characteristics to attract careless observers, yet bearing, in his whole aspect, the handwriting of no common fate, for such as have the skill to read it. He is meagre; his low and narrow forehead is deeply wrinkled; his eyes, small and lustreless, sometimes wander apprehensively about him, but oftener seem to look inward.

He bends his head, and moves with an indescribable obliquity of gait, as if unwilling to display his full front to the world. Watch him long enough to see what we have described, and you will allow that circumstances—which often produce remarkable men from nature's ordinary handiwork—have produced one such here. Next, leaving him to sidle along the footwalk, cast your eyes in the opposite direction, where a portly female, considerably in the wane of life, with a prayer-book in her hand, is proceeding to yonder church. She has the placid mien of settled widowhood. Her regrets have either died away, or have become so essential to her heart, that they would be poorly exchanged for joy. Just as the lean man and well-conditioned woman are passing, a slight obstruction occurs, and brings these two figures directly in contact. Their hands touch; the pressure of the crowd forces her bosom against his shoulder; they stand, face to face, staring into each other's eyes. After a ten years' separation, thus Wakefield meets his wife!

The throng eddies away, and carries them asunder. The sober widow, resuming her former pace, proceeds to church, but pauses in the portal, and throws a perplexed glance along the street. She passes in, however, opening her prayer-book as she goes. And the man! with so wild a face that busy and selfish London stands to gaze after him, he hurries to his lodgings, bolts the door, and throws himself upon the bed. The latent feelings of years break out; his feeble mind acquires a brief energy from their strength; all the miserable strangeness of his life is revealed to him at a glance: and he cries out, passionately, "Wakefield! Wakefield! You are mad!"

Perhaps he was so. The singularity of his situation must have so moulded him to himself, that, considered in regard to his fellow-creatures and the business of life, he could not be said to possess his right mind. He had contrived, or rather he had happened, to dissever himself from the world—to vanish—to give up his place and privileges with living men, without being admitted among the dead. The life of a hermit is nowise parallel to his. He was in the bustle of the city, as of old; but the crowd swept by and saw him not; he was, we may figuratively say, always beside his wife and at his hearth, yet must never feel the warmth of the one nor the affection of the other. It was Wakefield's unprecedented fate to retain his original share of human sympathies, and to be still involved in human interests, while he had lost his reciprocal influence on them. It would be a most curious speculation to trace out the effect of such circumstances on his heart and intellect, separately, and in unison. Yet, changed as he was, he would seldom be conscious of it, but deem himself the same man as ever; glimpses of the truth, indeed, would come, but only for the moment; and still he would keep saying, "I shall soon go back!"—nor reflect that he had been saying so for twenty years.

I conceive, also, that these twenty years would appear, in the retrospect, scarcely longer than the week to which Wakefield had at first limited his absence. He would look on the affair as no more than an interlude in the main business of his life. When, after a little while more, he should deem it time to reënter his parlor, his wife would clap her hands for joy, on beholding the middle-aged Mr. Wakefield. Alas, what a mistake! Would Time but await the close of our favorite follies, we should be young men, all of us, and till Doomsday.

One evening, in the twentieth year since he vanished, Wakefield is taking his customary walk towards the dwelling which he still calls his own. It is a gusty night of autumn, with frequent showers that patter down upon the pavement, and are gone before a man can put up his umbrella. Pausing near the house, Wakefield discerns, through the parlor windows of the second floor, the red glow and the glimmer and fitful flash of a comfortable fire. On the ceiling appears a grotesque shadow of good Mrs. Wakefield. The cap, the nose and chin, and the broad waist, form an admirable caricature, which dances, moreover, with the up-flickering and down-sinking blaze, almost too merrily for the shade of an elderly widow. At this instant a shower chances to fall, and is driven, by the unmannerly gust, full into Wakefield's face and bosom. He is quite penetrated with its autumnal chill. Shall he stand, wet and shivering here, when his own hearth has a good fire to warm him, and his own wife will run to fetch the gray coat and small-clothes, which, doubtless, she has kept carefully in the closet of their bed chamber? No! Wakefield is no such fool. He ascends the steps—heavily!—for twenty years have stiffened his legs since he came down—but he knows it not. Stay, Wakefield! Would you go to the sole home that is left you? Then step into your grave! The door opens. As he passes in, we have a parting glimpse of his visage, and recognize the crafty smile, which was the precursor of the little joke that he has ever since been playing off at his wife's expense. How unmercifully has he quizzed the poor woman! Well, a good night's rest to Wakefield!

This happy event—supposing it to be such—could only have occurred at an unpremeditated moment. We will not follow our friend across the threshold. He has left us much food for thought, a portion of which shall lend its wisdom to a moral, and be shaped into a figure. Amid the seeming confusion of our mysterious world, individuals are so nicely adjusted to a system, and systems to one another and to a whole, that, by stepping aside for a moment, a man exposes himself to a fearful risk of losing his place forever. Like Wakefield, he may become, as it were, the Outcast of the Universe.

# Toni Cade Bambara

## *My Man Bovanne*

Blind people got a hummin jones[1] if you notice. Which is understandable completely once you been around one and notice what no eyes will force you into to see people, and you get past the first time, which seems to come out of nowhere, and it's like you in church again with fat-chest ladies and old gents gruntin a hum low in the throat to whatever the preacher be saying. Shakey Bee bottom lip all swole up with Sweet Peach[2] and me explainin how come the sweet-potato bread was a dollar-quarter this time stead of dollar regular and he say un hunh he understand, then he break into this *thizzin* kind of hum which is quiet, but fiercesome just the same, if you ain't ready for it. Which I wasn't. But I got used to it and the onliest time I had to say somethin bout it was when he was playin checkers on the stoop one time and he commenst to hummin quite churchy seem to me. So I says, "Look here Shakey Bee, I can't beat you and Jesus too." He stop.

So that's how come I asked My Man Bovanne to dance. He ain't my man mind you, just a nice ole gent from the block that we all know cause he fixes things and the kids like him. Or used to fore Black Power got hold their minds and mess em around till they can't be civil to ole folks. So we at this benefit for my niece's cousin who's runnin for somethin with this Black party somethin or other behind her. And I press up close to dance with Bovanne who blind and I'm hummin and he hummin, chest to chest like talkin. Not jammin my breasts into the man. Wasn't bout tits. Was bout vibrations. And he dug it and asked me what color dress I had on and how my hair was fixed and how I was doin without a man, not nosy but nice-like, and who was at this affair and was the canapés dainty-stingy or healthy enough to get hold of proper. Comfy and cheery is what I'm tryin to get across. Touch talking like the heel of the hand on the tambourine or on a drum.

---

[1] A compelling need.
[2] A brand of dipping snuff.

But right away Joe Lee come up on us and frown for dancin so close to the man. My own son who knows what kind of warm I am about; and don't grown men all call me long distance and in the middle of the night for a little Mama comfort? But he frown. Which ain't right since Bovanne can't see and defend himself. Just a nice old man who fixes toasters and busted irons and bicycles and things and changes the lock on my door when my men friends get messy. Nice man. Which is not why they invited him. Grass roots you see. Me and Sister Taylor and the woman who does heads at Mamies and the man from the barber shop, we all there on account of we grass roots. And I ain't never been souther than Brooklyn Battery and no more country than the window box on my fire escape. And just yesterday my kids tellin me to take them countrified rags off my head and be cool. And now can't get Black enough to suit em. So everybody passin sayiñ My Man Bovanne. Big deal, keep steppin and don't even stop a minute to get the man a drink or one of them cute sandwiches or tell him what's goin on. And him standin there with a smile ready case someone do speak he want to be ready. So that's how come I pull him on the dance floor and we dance squeezin past the tables and chairs and all them coats and people standin round up in each other face talkin bout this and that but got no use for this blind man who mostly fixed skates and skooters for all these folks when they was just kids. So I'm pressed up close and we touch talkin with the hum. And here come my daughter cuttin her eye[3] at me like she do when she tell me about my "apolitical" self like I got hoof and mouf disease and there ain't no hope at all. And I don't pay her no mind and just look up in Bovanne shadow face and tell him his stomach like a drum and he laugh. Laugh real loud. And here come my youngest, Task, with a tap on my elbow like he the third grade monitor and I'm cuttin up on the line to assembly.

"I was just talkin on the drums," I explained when they hauled me into the kitchen. I figured drums was my best defense. They can get ready for drums what with all this heritage business. And Bovanne stomach just like that drum Task give me when he come back from Africa. You just touch it and it hum thizzm, thizzm. So I stuck to the drum story. "Just drummin that's all."

"Mama, what are you talkin about?"

"She had too much to drink," say Elo to Task cause she don't hardly say nuthin to me direct no more since that ugly argument about my wigs.

---

[3] Giving a sharp look.

"Look here Mama," say Task, the gentle one. "We just tryin to pull your coat. You were makin a spectacle of yourself out there dancing like that."

"Dancin like what?"

Task run a hand over his left ear like his father for the world and his father before that.

"Like a bitch in heat," say Elo.

"Well uhh, I was goin to say like one of them sex-starved ladies gettin on in years and not too discriminating. Know what I mean?"

I don't answer cause I'll cry. Terrible thing when your own children talk to you like that. Pullin me out the party and hustlin me into some stranger's kitchen in the back of a bar just like the damn police. And ain't like I'm old old. I can still wear me some sleeveless dresses without the meat hangin off my arm. And I keep up with some thangs through my kids. Who ain't kids no more. To hear them tell it. So I don't say nuthin.

"Dancin with that tom," say Elo to Joe Lee, who leanin on the folks' freezer. "His feet can smell a cracker a mile away and go into their shuffle number post haste. And them eyes. He could be a little considerate and put on some shades. Who wants to look into them blown-out fuses that—"

"Is this what they call the generation gap?" I say.

"Generation gap," spits Elo, like I suggested castor oil and fricassee possum in the milk-shakes or somethin. "That's a white concept for a white phenomenon. There's no generation gap among Black people. We are a col—"

"Yeh, well never mind," says Joe Lee. "The point is Mama . . . well, it's pride. You embarrass yourself and us too dancin like that."

"I wasn't shame." Then nobody say nuthin. Them standin there in they pretty clothes with drinks in they hands and gangin up on me, and me in the third-degree chair and nary a olive to my name. Felt just like the police got hold to me.

"First of all," Task say, holdin up his hand and tickin off the offenses, "the dress. Now that dress is too short, Mama, and too low-cut for a woman your age. And Tamu's going to make a speech tonight to kick off the campaign and will be introducin you and expecting you to organize the council of elders—"

"Me? Didn nobody ask me nuthin. You mean Nisi? She change her name?"

"Well, Norton was supposed to tell you about it. Nisi wants to introduce you and then encourage the older folks to form a Council of the Elders to act as an advisory—"

"And you going to be standing there with your boobs out and that wig on your head and that hem up to your ass. And people'll say, 'Ain't that the horny bitch that was grindin with the blind dude?' "

"Elo, be cool a minute," say Task, gettin to the next finger. "And then there's the drinkin. Mama, you know you can't drink cause next thing you know you be laughin loud and carryin on," and he grab another finger for the loudness. "And then there's the dancin. You been tattooed on the man for four records straight and slow draggin even on the fast numbers. How you think that look for a woman your age?"

"What's my age?"

"What?"

"I'm axin you all a simple question. You keep talkin bout what's proper for a woman my age. How old am I anyhow?" And Joe Lee slams his eyes shut and squinches up his face to figure. And Task run a hand over his ear and stare into his glass like the ice cubes goin calculate for him. And Elo just starin at the top of my head like she goin rip the wig off any minute now.

"Is your hair braided up under that thing? If so, why don't you take it off? You always did do a neat cornroll."[4]

"Uh huh," cause I'm thinkin how she couldn't undo her hair fast enough talking bout cornroll so countrified. None of which was the subject. "How old, I say?"

"Sixtee-one or—"

"You a damn lie Joe Lee Peoples."

"And that's another thing," say Task on the fingers.

"You know what you all can kiss," I say, gettin up and brushin the wrinkles out my lap.

"Oh, Mama," Elo say, puttin a hand on my shoulder like she hasn't done since she left home and the hand landin light and not sure it supposed to be there. Which hurt me to my heart. Cause this was the child in our happiness fore Mr. Peoples die. And I carried that child strapped to my chest till she was nearly two. We was close is what I'm tryin to tell you. Cause it was more me in the child than the others. And even after Task it was the girlchild I covered in the night and wept over for no reason at all less it was she was a chub-chub like me and not very pretty, but a warm child. And how did things get to this, that she can't put a sure hand on me and say Mama we love you and care about you and you entitled to enjoy yourself cause you a good woman?

---

[4] Cornrow, a hairstyle in which all the hair is interwoven from the scalp into small braids.

"And then there's Reverend Trent," say Task, glancin from left to right like they hatchin a plot and just now lettin me in on it. "You were suppose to be talking with him tonight, Mama, about giving us his basement for campaign headquarters and—"

"Didn nobody tell me nuthin. If grass roots mean you kept in the dark I can't use it. I really can't. And Reven Trent a fool anyway the way he tore into the widow man up there on Edgecomb cause he wouldn't take in three of them foster children and the woman not even comfy in the ground yet and the man's mind messed up and—"

"Look here," say Task. "What we need is a family conference so we can get all this stuff cleared up and laid out on the table. In the meantime I think we better get back into the other room and tend to business. And in the meantime, Mama, see if you can't get to Reverend Trent and—"

"You want me to belly rub with the Reven, that it?"

"Oh damn," Elo say and go through the swingin door.

"We'll talk about all this at dinner. How's tomorrow night, Joe Lee?" While Joe Lee being self-important I'm wonderin who's doin the cooking and how come no body ax me if I'm free and do I get a corsage and things like that. Then Joe nod that it's O.K. and he go through the swingin door and just a little hubbub come through from the other room. Then Task smile his smile, lookin just like his daddy, and he leave. And it just me in this stranger's kitchen, which was a mess I wouldn't never let my kitchen look like. Poison you just to look at the pots. Then the door swing the other way and it's My Man Bovanne standin there sayin Miss Hazel but lookin at the deep fry and then at the steam table, and most surprised when I come up on him from the other direction and take him on out of there. Pass the folks pushin up towards the stage where Nisi and some other people settin and ready to talk, and folks gettin to the last of the sandwiches and the booze fore they settle down in one spot and listen serious. And I'm thinkin bout tellin Bovanne what a lovely long dress Nisi got on and the earrings and her hair piled up in a cone and the people bout to hear how we all gettin screwed and gotta form our own party and everybody there listenin and lookin. But instead I just haul the man on out of there, and Joe Lee and his wife look at me like I'm terrible, but they ain't said boo to the man yet. Cause he blind and old and don't nobody there need him since they grown up and don't need they skates fixed no more.

"Where we goin, Miss Hazel?" Him knowin all the time.

"First we gonna buy you some dark sunglasses. Then you comin with me to the supermarket so I can pick up tomorrow's dinner, which is goin to be a grand thing proper and you invited. Then we goin to my house."

"That be fine. I surely would like to rest my feet." Bein cute, but you got to let men play out they little show, blind or not. So he chat on bout how tired he is and how he appreciate me takin him in hand this way. And I'm thinkin I'll have him change the lock on my door first thing. Then I'll give the man a nice warm bath with jasmine leaves in the water and a little Epsom salt on the sponge to do his back. And then a good rubdown with rose water and olive oil. Then a cup of lemon tea with a taste in it. And a little talcum, some of that fancy stuff Nisi mother sent over last Christmas. And then a massage, a good face massage round the forehead which is the worryin part. Cause you gots to take care of the older folks. And let them know they still needed to run the mimeo machine and keep the spark plugs clean and fix the mailboxes for folks who might help us get the breakfast program goin, and the school for the little kids and the campaign and all. Cause old folks in the nation. That what Nisi was sayin and I mean to do my part.

"I imagine you are a very pretty woman, Miss Hazel."

"I surely am," I say just like the hussy my daughter always say I was.

# Strategies for Research and Documentation

Many of the selections in this text are based on field and library research: writers have visited places and interviewed people, and have gone to the library to gather necessary information. Critical readers are often called upon to do research, following up on ideas or claims, looking firsthand at a source mentioned by the writer, or finding more information about a writer they admire. Writers also have occasion to do research: unless they write solely from memory, writers will rely in part on research for their essays, reports, and books.

Many of the writing suggestions in this text invite field or library research. As a writer at work using this text—and for writing you do for many of your college courses—you have to do research. You will often need to document your sources, indicating precisely where you found certain information. This appendix offers some strategies and guidelines for field and library research, along with instructions for documenting your sources.

## FIELD RESEARCH

In universities, government agencies, and the business world, field research can be as important as library research or experimental research. In specialties such as sociology, political science, anthropology, polling, advertising, and news reporting, field research is the basic means of gathering information.

This appendix is a brief introduction to two of the major kinds of field research: observations and interviews. The writing activities involved are central to several academic specialties. If you major in education, journalism, or one of the social sciences, you probably will be asked to do writing based on observations and interviews. You will also read large amounts of information based on these ways of learning about people, groups, and institutions.

All the suggestions for writing in Chapter 4, "Observation," require these two kinds of research.

# *Observation*

## Planning the Observational Visit

GETTING ACCESS. If the place you propose to visit is public, you probably will have easy access to it. If everything you need to see is within view of anyone passing by or using the place, you can make your observations without any special arrangements. Indeed, you may not even be noticed. If you require special access, you will need to arrange your visit, calling ahead or making a get-acquainted visit, in order to introduce yourself and state your purpose. Find out the times you may visit, and be certain you can get to the place easily.

ANNOUNCING YOUR INTENTIONS. State your intentions directly and fully. Say who you are, where you are from, and what you hope to do. You may be surprised at how receptive people can be to a student on assignment from a college course. Not every place you wish to visit will welcome you, however. A variety of constraints on outside visitors exist in private businesses as well as public institutions. But generally, if people know your intentions, they may be able to tell you about aspects of a place or activity you would not have thought to observe.

TAKING YOUR TOOLS. Take a notebook with a firm back so that you will have a steady writing surface, perhaps a small stenographer's notebook with a spiral binding across the top. Remember to take a writing instrument. Some observers dictate their notes into portable tape recorders, a method you may wish to try.

## Observing and Taking Notes

OBSERVING. Some activities invite multiple vantage points, whereas others seem to limit the observer to a single perspective. Take advantage of every perspective available to you. Come in close, take a middle position, and stand back. Study the scene from a stationary position and also try to move around it. The more varied your perspectives, the more you are likely to observe.

Your purpose in observing is both to describe the activity and to analyze it. You will want to look closely at the activity itself, but you will also want to think about what makes this activity special, what seems to be the point of it.

Try to be an innocent observer: pretend you have never seen anything like this activity before. Look for typical features of the activity as well as unusual features. Look at it from the perspective of your readers. Ask what details of the activity would surprise and inform and interest them.

TAKING NOTES. You undoubtedly will find your own style of note-taking, but here are a few pointers. (1) Write only on one side of the page. Later, when you organize your notes, you may want to cut up the pages and file notes under different headings. (2) Take notes in words, phrases, or sentences. Draw diagrams or sketches, if they help you see and understand the place. (3) Note any ideas or questions that occur to you. (4) Use quotation marks around any overheard conversation you take down.

Since you can later reorganize your notes quite easily, you do not need to take notes in any planned or systematic way. You might, however, want to cover these possibilities:

*The Setting.* The easiest way to begin is to name objects you see. Just start by listing objects. Then record details of some of these objects — color, shape, size, texture, function, relation to similar or dissimilar objects. Although your notes probably will contain mainly visual details, you might also want to record sounds and smells. Be sure to include some notes about the shape, dimensions, and layout of the place. How big is it? How is it organized?

*The People.* Record the number of people, their activities, their movements and behavior. Describe their appearance or dress. Record parts of overheard conversations. Note whether you see more men than women, more of one racial group rather than of another, more older than younger people. Most important, note anything surprising and unusual about people in the scene.

*Your Personal Reactions.* Include in your notes any feelings you have about what you observe. Also record, as they occur to you, any hunches or ideas or insights you have.

## Reflecting on What You Saw

Immediately after your visit (within just a few minutes, if possible), find a quiet place to reflect on what you saw, review your notes, and add to them. Give yourself at least a half hour for quiet thought.

What you have in your notes and what you recall on reflection will suggest many more images and details from your observations. Add these to your notes.

Finally, review all your notes, and write a few sentences about your main impressions of the place. What did you learn? How did this visit change your preconceptions about the place? What surprised you most? What is the dominant impression you get from your notes?

# *Interviews*

Interviewing tends to involve four basic steps: (1) planning and setting up the interview, (2) note-taking, (3) reflecting on the interview, and (4) writing up your notes.

## Planning and Setting Up the Interview

CHOOSING AN INTERVIEW SUBJECT. The first step is to decide whom to interview. If you are writing about something in which several people are involved, choose subjects representing a variety of perspectives—a range of different roles, for example. If you are profiling a single person, most, if not all, of your interviews will be with that person.

You should be flexible because you may be unable to speak to the person you targeted and may wind up with someone else—the person's assistant, perhaps. You might even learn more from an assistant than you would from the person in charge.

ARRANGING AN INTERVIEW. You may be nervous about calling up a busy person and asking for some of his or her time. Indeed, you may get turned down. But if so, do ask if someone else might talk to you.

Do not feel that just because you are a student you do not have the right to ask for people's time. People are often delighted to be asked about themselves. And, since you are a student on assignment, some people may feel that they are doing a form of public service to talk with you.

When introducing yourself to arrange the interview, give a short and simple description of your project. If you say too much, you could prejudice or limit the person's response. It is a good idea to exhibit some enthusiasm for your project, of course.

Keep in mind that the person you are interviewing is donating time to you. Be certain that you call ahead to arrange a specific time for the interview. Be on time. Bring all the materials you need, and express your thanks when the interview is over.

PLANNING FOR THE INTERVIEW. Make any necessary observational visits and do any essential background reading before the interview. Consider your objectives. Do you want an orientation to the place (the "big picture") from this interview? Do you want this interview to lead you to other key people? Do you want mainly facts or information? Do you need clarification of something you have heard in another interview or observed or read? Do you want to learn more about the person, or learn about the place through the person, or both? Should you trust or distrust this person?

The key to good interviewing is flexibility. You may be looking for facts, but your interview subject may not have any to offer. In that case, you should be able to shift gears and go after whatever your subject has to discuss.

*Prepare Some Questions in Advance.* Take care in composing these questions; they can be the key to a successful interview. Bad questions rarely yield useful answers. A bad question places unfair limits on respondents. Two specific types to avoid are forced-choice questions and leading questions.

*Forced-choice questions* are bad because they impose your terms on your respondents. Consider this example: "Do you think rape is an expression of sexual passion or of aggression?" A person may think that neither sexual passion nor aggression satisfactorily explains rape. A better way to phrase the question would be to ask, "People often fall into two camps on the issue of rape. Some think it is an expression of sexual passion, while others argue it is really not sexual but aggressive. Do you think it is either of these? If not, what is your opinion?" This form of questioning allows you to get a reaction to what others have said at the same time it gives the person freedom to set the terms.

*Leading questions* are bad because they assume too much. An example of this kind of question is this: "Do you think the increase in the occurrence of rape is due to the fact that women are perceived as competitors in a severely depressed economy?" This question assumes that there is an increase in the occurrence of rape, that women are perceived (apparently by rapists) as competitors, and that the economy is severely depressed.

A better way of asking the question might be to make the assumptions more explicit by dividing the question into its parts: "Do you think there is an increase in the occurrence of rape? What could have caused it? I've heard some people argue that the economy has something to do with it. Do you think so? Do you think rapists perceive women as competitors for jobs? Could the current economic situation have made this competition more severe?"

Good questions come in many different forms. One way of considering them is to divide them into two types: open and closed. *Open questions* give the respondent range and flexibility. They also generate anecdotes, personal revelations, and expressions of attitudes. The following are examples of open questions:

- I wonder if you would take a few minutes to tell me something about your early days in the business. I'd be interested to hear about how it got started, what your hopes and aspirations were, what problems you faced and how you dealt with them.
- Tell me about a time you were (name an emotion).
- What did you think of (name a person or event)?
- What did you do when (name an event) happened?

The best questions are those that allow the subject to talk freely but to the point. If the answer strays too far from the point, a follow-up question may be necessary to refocus the talk. Another tack you may want to try is to rephrase the subject's answer, to say something like: "Let me see if I have this right," or "Am I correct in saying that you feel. . . ." Often, a person will take the opportunity to amplify the original response by adding just the anecdote or quotation you've been looking for.

*Closed questions* usually request specific information. For example:

- How do you do (name a process)?
- What does (name a word) mean?
- What does (a person, object, or place) look like?
- How was it made?

## Taking Your Tools

As for an observational visit, you will need a notebook with a firm back so that you can write on it easily without the benefit of a table or desk. We recommend a full-size (8½ × 11) spiral or ring notebook.

In this notebook, divide several pages into two columns with a line drawn vertically from a distance of about one third of the width of the page from the left margin. Use the left-hand column to note details about the scene, the person, the mood of the interview, other impressions. Head this column DETAILS AND IMPRESSIONS. At the top of the right-hand column, write several questions. You may not use them, but they will jog your memory. This column should be titled INFORMATION. In this column you will record what you learn from answers to your questions.

## Taking Notes During the Interview

Because you are not taking a verbatim transcript of the interview (if you wanted a literal account, you would use a tape recorder or shorthand), your goals are to gather information and to record a few good quotations and anecdotes. In addition, because the people you interview may be unused to giving interviews and so will need to know you are listening, it is probably a good idea to do more listening than note-taking. You may not have much confidence in your memory, but, if you pay close attention, you are likely to recall a good deal of the conversation afterward. During the interview, you should take some notes: a few quotations; key words and phrases to jog your memory; observational jottings about the scene, the person, and the mood of the interview. Remember that *how* something is said is as important as *what* is said. Pick up material that will give the interview write-up texture—gesture, physical appearance, verbal inflection, facial expression, dress, hair-style, body language, anything that makes the person an individual.

## Reflecting on the Interview

As soon as you finish the interview, find a quiet place to reflect on it, and review your notes. This reflection is essential because so much happens in an interview that you cannot record at the time. You need to spend at least a half hour, maybe longer, adding to your notes and thinking about what you learned.

At the end of this time, write a few sentences about your main impressions from the interview. What did you learn? What surprised you most? How did the interview change your attitude or understanding about the person or place? How would you summarize your main impressions of the person? How did this interview influence your plans to interview others or to reinterview this person? What do you want to learn from these next interviews?

## LIBRARY RESEARCH

Library research involves a variety of diverse activities: checking the card catalog, browsing in the stacks, possibly consulting the *Readers' Guide to Periodical Literature,* asking the reference librarian for help. Although librarians are there to help in time of need, all college students should nevertheless learn basic library research skills. Here we present the search strategy, a systematic and efficient way of doing library research.

The search strategy was developed by librarians to make library research manageable and productive. Although specific search strategies will vary to fit the needs of individual research problems, the general process will be demonstrated here: how to get started; where to find sources; what types of sources are available and what sorts of information they provide; how to evaluate these sources; and, most important, how to go about this process of finding and evaluating sources *systematically.*

Library research can be useful at various stages of the writing process. How you use the library depends on the kind of essay you are writing and the special needs of your subject. You may, for example, need to do research immediately to choose a subject. Or you may choose a topic without the benefit of research but then use the library to find specific information to support your thesis. But no matter when you use library research, you will need to have a search strategy. This search strategy

*Overview of a Search Strategy*

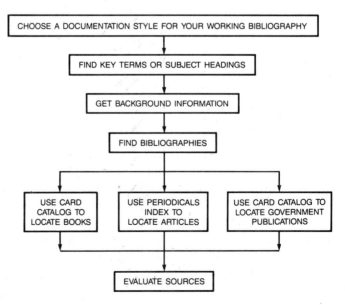

will guide you in setting up a working bibliography and a documentation style, in searching for key words or subject headings, in seeking background information, in finding bibliographies, and in using the card catalog and specialty indexes. Finally, it will help you evaluate the sources that you will use in your writing.

# A *Working Bibliography*

A working bibliography is a preliminary, ongoing record of books, articles, pamphlets—all the sources of information you discover as you research your subject. (A final bibliography, on the other hand, lists only sources actually used in your paper.) Some of the sources in your working bibliography may turn out to be irrelevant, while others simply will be unavailable. In addition, you can use your working bibliography as a means of keeping track of any encyclopedias, bibliographies, and indexes you consult, even though you may not list these resources in your final bibliography.

Because you probably may have to cite many different sources, you must decide on a documentation style before you write. The next section presents the documentation styles sponsored by the Modern Language Association (MLA) and the American Psychological Association (APA). Other disciplines often have their own preferred styles of documentation, which your instructor may wish you to use. Decide on a style to use at the beginning, when you are constructing a working bibliography, as well as later, when you compile a final bibliography.

Practiced researchers keep their working bibliography either in a notebook or on index cards. They make a point of keeping bibliographical information separate from notes they take on the sources listed in their bibliography.

Many researchers find index cards more convenient because they are so easily alphabetized. Others find them too easy to lose and prefer, instead, to keep everything—working bibliography, notes, and drafts—in one notebook. Whether you use cards or a notebook, the important thing is to make your entries accurate and complete.

# Key *Subject Headings*

To research a subject, you need to know how it is classified, what key words are used as subject headings in encyclopedias, bibliographies, and the card catalog. As you learn more about your subject, you will discover how other writers refer to it, how it usually is subdivided, and also what subjects are related to it. To begin your search, you should consult the *Library of Congress Subject Headings*. This reference book lists the standard subject headings used in card catalogs and in many encyclopedias and bibliographies. It usually can be found near the card catalog.

Sometimes, the words you think would be used for subject headings are not the ones actually used. For example, if you look up "World War I," you will find a cross-reference to "European War, 1914–1918." But, if you look up "bulimia," you will find neither a heading nor a cross-reference. Since many people call bulimia an "eating disorder," you might try that heading. But again you would draw a blank. If you tried "appetite," however, you would be referred to "anorexia," a related disorder. Here is the entry for "appetite":

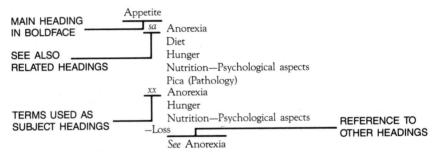

If you then look up "anorexia," you still will not find "bulimia," but you can expect some of the publications on anorexia to deal also with bulimia. In this process of trying possible headings and following up cross-references, you also will find related headings such as "nutrition," "obesity," and "psychological."

## Background Information

Once you have decided on the form and style of a working bibliography and have found promising subject headings, your search strategy will lead you to the gathering of background sources of information. Such sources will give you a general understanding of the nature and scope of your research subject. They may also provide a historical perspective on the subject, helping you grasp its basic principles and ideas, suggesting what its major divisions or aspects might be, and identifying important people associated with it.

Encyclopedias are the best sources of background information. You have no doubt heard of the *Encyclopaedia Britannica*, probably the best-known general encyclopedia. But there are many specialized encyclopedias. To use encyclopedias effectively, you need to know what subject headings you are looking for. Check each encyclopedia's subject index to locate your subject.

## General Encyclopedias

General encyclopedias are usually multivolume works that contain articles on all areas of knowledge. Written by experts, the articles frequently conclude with a list of important works and bibliographies. Most encyclopedias arrange their subjects alphabetically. Standard general encyclopedias include *Encyclopaedia Britannica*, *Encyclopedia Americana*, *Collier's Encyclopedia*, and *World Book Encyclopedia*.

## Specialized Encyclopedias

Specialized encyclopedias focus on a single area of knowledge. To find specialized encyclopedias, look in the subject card catalog under the appropriate subject heading. Encyclopedias usually are catalogued under the subheading "Dictionaries" and are kept in the reference section of the library. Here is a partial list of specialized encyclopedias:

*Encyclopedia of Education*
*Encyclopedia of Philosophy*
*Grove's Dictionary of Music and Musicians*
*International Encyclopedia of the Social Sciences*
*Harvard Encyclopedia of American Ethnic Groups*
*McGraw-Hill Dictionary of Art*
*McGraw-Hill Encyclopedia of Science and Technology*
*Oxford Classical Dictionary*
*Oxford Companion to American History*

# *Bibliographies*

A bibliography is simply a list of publications on a given subject. Whereas an encyclopedia gives you background information on your subject, a bibliography gives an overview of what has been published on the subject. Its scope may be broad or narrow. Some bibliographers try to be exhaustive, including every title they can find, while most are selective. To discover how selections were made, check the bibliography's preface or introduction. Occasionally, bibliographies are annotated; that is, they provide brief summaries of the entries and, sometimes, also evaluate them. Bibliographies may be found in a variety of places: in encyclopedias, in the card catalog, and in secondary sources. The best way to locate a comprehensive, up-to-date bibliography on your subject is to use the *Bibliographic Index*, a master list of bibliographies with fifty or more titles. It includes bibliographies from articles, books, and government publications. A new volume of *Bibliographic Index* is published every year. Because this index is not cumulative, you should check back over several years, beginning with the most current volume.

## The Card Catalog

The card catalog tells you what books are in the library. Books are listed on three separate cards—by author, subject, and title. Author, subject, and title cards all give the same basic information. Each card includes a *call number* in the upper left-hand corner. You will want to take extreme care in copying down this number, for it guides you to the source you seek.

## Periodicals Indexes and Abstracts

The most up-to-date information on a subject usually is not found in books, but in recently published articles that appear in journals and serials, or periodicals, as they often are called. Periodicals appear daily, weekly, quarterly, or annually (hence the name *periodical*). Articles in such publications usually are not listed in the card catalog; to find them, you must instead use periodicals indexes and abstracts. Indexes will only list articles, whereas abstracts summarize as well as list them. Like encyclopedias, periodicals indexes and abstracts exist in both general and specialized forms.

### General Indexes

General indexes list articles in nontechnical, general interest publications. They cover a broad range of subjects. Most have separate author and subject listings as well as a list of book reviews. Following are some general indexes:

*Readers' Guide to Periodical Literature* (1905–present) covers more than 180 popular periodicals.

*Humanities Index* (1974–present) covers archaeology, history, classics, literature, performing arts, philosophy, and religion.

*Social Sciences Index* (1974–present) covers economics, geography, law, political science, psychology, public administration, and sociology.

*Public Affairs Information Service Bulletin* [PAIS] (1915–present) covers articles and other publications by public and private agencies on economic and social conditions, international relations, and public administration. Subject listing only.

## Specialized Indexes

Specialized indexes list articles in periodicals devoted to technical or scholarly research reports. Following is a list of some specialized indexes:

*Almanac of American Politics* (1972–present)
*American Statistics Index* (1973–present)
*Applied Science and Technology Index* (1958–present)
*Biological and Agricultural Index* (1964–present)
*Congressional Digest* (1921–present)
*Congressional Quarterly Weekly Reports* (1956–present)
*Education Index* (1929–present)
*Historical Abstracts* (1955–present)
*MLA International Bibliography of Books and Articles in the Modern Languages and Literature* (1921–present)
*Philosopher's Index* (1967–present)
*Psychology Abstracts* (1927–present)
*Statistical Abstracts of the United States* (annual)
*Statistical Yearbook* (1949–present)

## Newspaper Indexes

Newspapers often provide information unavailable elsewhere, especially accounts of current events, analyses of recent trends, texts of important speeches by public officials, obituaries, and film and book reviews. Libraries usually miniaturize newspapers and store them on microfilm (reels) or microfiche (cards), which must be placed in viewing machines in order to be read. Following are some general and specialized newspaper indexes:

### General news indexes

*Facts on File* (1941–present)
*Keesing's Contemporary Archives* (1931–present)

**Indexes to particular newspapers**

*Christian Science Monitor Index* (1960–present)
(London) *Times Index* (1785–present)
*New York Times Index* (1851–present)
*Wall Street Journal Index* (1972–present)

**Computerized newspaper and periodical indexes**

The *National Newspaper Index*—lists items in the *New York Times, Wall Street Journal*, and *Christian Science Monitor*.

*Magazine Index*—lists articles in nearly 400 general periodicals.

# Government Publications

The countless documents published by agencies of the United States government and by state governments and United Nations organizations may be an additional source of useful information. Most college research libraries have a government publications collection, usually catalogued and housed separately. The collection should include agency publications, statistics, research reports, and public service pamphlets. Following are some indexes of government publications:

The *Monthly Index to the United States Government Publications* (1895–present)—separate cumulative index is published annually.

*CIS Index* and *CIS Abstracts* (1970–present)—Congressional Committee documents.

*Public Affairs Information Service Bulletin* [PAIS] (1915–present)—PAIS indexes government documents as well as books on political and social issues.

*International Bibliography, Information, Documentation* (1973–present)— indexes selected documents published by the United Nations and other international organizations.

*United Nations Documents Index* (1950–present)—comprehensive index to documents published by the United Nations.

## ACKNOWLEDGING SOURCES

Much of the writing you will do in college requires you to use outside sources in combination with your own firsthand observation and reflection. When you get information and ideas from reading, lectures, and interviews, you are using sources. In college, using sources is not only acceptable, it is expected. Educated people nearly always base their original thought on the work of others. In fact, most of your college education is devoted to teaching you two things: (1) what Matthew Arnold called "the best that has been thought and said," and (2) the way to analyze the thoughts of others, integrate them into your own thinking, and effectively convey what you think to others.

Although there is no universally agreed-upon system for acknowledging sources, there is agreement on both the need for documentation and the items that should be included. Writers should acknowledge sources for two reasons—to give credit to those sources and to enable readers to consult the sources for further information. This information should be included when documenting sources: (1) name of author, (2) title of publication, and (3) publication source, date, and page.

Most documentation styles combine some kind of citation in the text with a separate list of references keyed to the textual citations. There are basically two ways of acknowledging sources: (1) citing sources within the essay, enclosing the citation in parentheses, and (2) footnotes (or endnotes) plus a bibliography. The Modern Language Association (MLA), a professional organization of English instructors, has until very recently endorsed the footnote style of documentation. But, with the 1984 revision of the *MLA Handbook*, the MLA has gone over to the simpler parenthetical citation method. The new MLA style is similar to the style endorsed by the American Psychological Association (APA)— the style used by many social and natural science instructors.

If you have any questions, consult the *MLA Handbook for Writers of Research Papers*, Second Edition (1984), or the *Publication Manual of the American Psychological Association*, Third Edition (1983). The *MLA Handbook* includes both the new and old MLA styles.

## Citing Sources Within Your Essay

The MLA and APA styles both advocate parenthetical citations within an essay keyed to a works-cited list at the end. However, they differ on what should be included in the parenthetical citation. Whereas the MLA uses an author-page citation, the APA uses an author-year-page citation.

MLA  Dr. James is described as a "not-too-skeletal Ichabod Crane" (Simon 68).

APA  Dr. James is described as a "not-too-skeletal Ichabod Crane" (Simon, 1982, p. 68).

Notice that the APA style uses a comma between author, year, and page as well as "p." for page (Simon, 1982, p. 68), whereas the MLA puts nothing but space between author and page (Simon 68). For a block quotation, put the citation after the final period; otherwise, put the citation before the final period.

If the author's name is cited in the essay, put the page reference in parentheses as close as possible to the borrowed material, but without disrupting the flow of the sentence. For the APA style, cite the year in parentheses directly following the author's name, and place the page reference in parentheses before the period ending the sentence. In the case of block quotations for both MLA and APA, put the page reference in parentheses two spaces after the period ending the sentence.

MLA    Simon describes Dr. James as a "not-too-skeletal Ichabod Crane" (68).

APA    Simon (1982) describes Dr. James as a "not-too-skeletal Ichabod Crane" (p. 68).

To cite a source by two or more authors, the MLA uses all the authors' last names, unless the entry in the works-cited list gives the first author's name followed by "et al." The APA uses all the authors' last names the first time the reference occurs and the last name of the first author followed by "et al." subsequently.

MLA    Dyal, Corning, and Willows identify several types of students, including the "Authority-Rebel" (4).

APA    Dyal, Corning, and Willows (1975) identify several types of students, including the "Authority-Rebel" (p. 4).

MLA    The Authority-Rebel "tends to see himself as superior to other students in the class" (Dyal, Corning, and Willows 4).

APA    The Authority-Rebel "tends to see himself as superior to other students in the class" (Dyal et al., 1975, p. 4).

To cite one of two or more works by the same author(s), the MLA uses the author's last name, a shortened version of the title, and the page. The APA uses the author's last name plus the year and page.

MLA    When old paint becomes transparent, it sometimes shows the artist's original plans: "a tree will show through a woman's dress" (Hellman, *Pentimento* 1).

APA    When old paint becomes transparent, it sometimes shows the artist's original plans: "a tree will show through a woman's dress" (Hellman, 1973, p. 1).

To cite a work listed only by its title, both the MLA and the APA use a shortened version of the title.

MLA    Lillian Hellman calls Dashiell Hammett: "my closest, my most beloved friend" (*Woman* 224).

APA    Lillian Hellman (1969) calls Dashiell Hammett: "my closest, my most beloved friend" (*Woman* p. 224).

To quote material taken not from the original but from a secondary source that quotes the original, both the MLA and the APA give the secondary source in the works-cited list, and cite both the original and secondary sources within the essay.

MLA    E. M. Forster says "the collapse of all civilization, so realistic for us, sounded in [Matthew Arnold's] ears like a distant and harmonious cataract" (qtd. in Trilling 11).

APA    E. M. Forster says "the collapse of all civilization, so realistic for us, sounded in [Matthew Arnold's] ears like a distant and harmonious cataract" (cited in Trilling, 1955, p. 11).

# Citing Sources at the End of Your Essay

Keyed to the parenthetical citations in the text, the list of works cited identifies all the sources your essay used. Every source cited in the text must refer to an entry in the works-cited list. And, conversely, every entry in the works-cited list must correspond to at least one parenthetical citation in the text.

Whereas the MLA style manual uses the title "Works Cited," the APA prefers "References." Both alphabetize the entries according to the first author's last name. When several works by an author are listed, the APA recommends these rules for arranging the list:

- Same-name single-author entries precede multiple-author entries:
  Aaron, P. (1985).
  Aaron, P., & Zorn, C. R. (1982).
- Entries with the same first author and different second author should be alphabetized according to the second author's last name:
  Aaron, P., & Charleston, W. (1979).
  Aaron, P., & Zorn, C. R. (1982).
- Entries by the same authors should be arranged by year of publication, in chronological order:
  Aaron, P., & Charleston, W. (1979).
  Aaron, P., & Charleston, W. (1984).
- Entries by the same author(s) with the same publication year should be arranged alphabetically by title (excluding *A, An, The*), and low-

ercase letters (*a, b, c,* and so on) should follow the year in parentheses:

Aaron, P. (1985a). Basic . . . .
Aaron, P. (1985b). Elements . . . .

The essential difference between the MLA and APA styles of listing sources is the order in which the information is presented. The MLA follows this order: author's name; title; publication source, year, and page. The APA puts the year after the author's name. The examples that follow indicate other minor differences in capitalization and arrangement between the two documentation styles.

# Books

### A book by a single author

MLA    Simon, Kate. *Bronx Primitive.* New York: Harper, 1982.

APA    Simon, Kate. (1982). *Bronx primitive.* New York: Harper and Row.

### A book by an agency or corporation

MLA    Association for Research in Nervous and Mental Disease. *The Circulation of the Brain and Spinal Cord: A Symposium on Blood Supply.* New York: Hafner, 1966.

APA    Association for Research in Nervous and Mental Disease. (1966). *The circulation of the brain and spinal cord: A symposium on blood supply.* New York: Hafner Publishing Co.

### A book by two authors

MLA    Strunk, W., Jr., and E. B. White. *The Elements of Style.* 4th ed. New York: Macmillan, 1983.

APA    Strunk, W., Jr., & White, E. B. (1983). *The elements of style.* (4th ed.). New York: Macmillan.

### A book by three or more authors

MLA    Dyal, James A., William C. Corning, and Dale M. Willows. *Readings in Psychology: The Search for Alternatives.* 3rd ed. New York: McGraw-Hill, 1975.

OR    Dyal, James A., et al. *Readings in Psychology: The Search for Alternatives.* 3rd ed. New York: McGraw-Hill, 1975.

APA    Dyal, James A., Corning, William C., & Willows, Dale M. (1975). *Readings in psychology: The search for alternatives.* (3rd ed.). New York: McGraw-Hill.

## A book by an unknown author

Use title in place of author.

MLA    *College Bound Seniors.* Princeton, NJ: College Board Publications, 1979.

APA    *College bound seniors.* (1979). Princeton, NJ: College Board Publications.

## An edition prepared by a named editor

APA    Arnold, Matthew. *Culture and anarchy.* (J. Dover Wilson, Ed.). Cambridge: Cambridge University Press, 1966. (Originally published, 1869.)

If you refer to the text itself, begin with the author:

MLA    Arnold, Matthew. *Culture and Anarchy.* Ed. J. Dover Wilson, Cambridge: Cambridge UP, 1966.

If you cite the editor in your text, begin with the editor:

MLA    Wilson, J. Dover, ed. *Culture and Anarchy.* By Matthew Arnold. Cambridge: Cambridge UP, 1966.

## An anthology

MLA    Dertouzos, Michael L., and Joel Moses, eds. *The Computer Age: A Twenty-Year View.* Cambridge, MA: MIT, 1979.

APA    Dertouzos, Michael L., & Moses, Joel. (Eds.). (1979). *The computer age: A twenty-year view.* Cambridge, MA: MIT Press.

## A translation

APA    Tolstoy, Leo. (1972). *War and Peace.* (Constance Garnett, Trans.). London: Pan Books. (Originally published 1868–1869).

If you are referring to the work itself, begin with the author:

MLA    Tolstoy, Leo. *War and Peace.* Trans. Constance Garnett. London: Pan, 1972.

If you cite the translator in your text, begin the entry with the translator's name:

MLA    Garnett, Constance, trans. *War and Peace.* By Leo Tolstoy. London: Pan, 1972.

## A work in an anthology

MLA    Faulkner, William. "Dry September." *Literature: The Human Experience.* Ed. Richard Abcarian and Marvin Klotz. New York: St. Martin's, 1983. 549–557.

OR    Bell, Daniel. "The Social Framework of the Information Society." In *The Computer Age: A Twenty-Year View.* Ed. Michael L. Dertouzos and Joel Moses. Cambridge, MA: MIT, 1979. 163–211.

APA    Bell, Daniel. (1979). The social framework of the information society. In Michael L. Dertouzos and Joel Moses (Eds.), *The computer age: A twenty-year view* (pp. 163–211). Cambridge, MA: MIT.

## An essay in an anthology by the same author

MLA    Weaver, Richard. "The Rhetoric of Social Science." In his *Ethics of Rhetoric.* South Bend, Indiana: Gateway, 1953, 186–210.

APA    Weaver, Richard. (1953). The rhetoric of social science. In Weaver, Richard, *Ethics of rhetoric* (pp. 186–210). South Bend, Indiana: Gateway Editions.

# Articles

## An article in a journal with continuous annual pagination

MLA    Dworkin, Ronald. "Law as Interpretation." *Critical Inquiry* 9 (1982): 179–200.

APA    Dworkin, Ronald. (1982). Law as interpretation. *Critical Inquiry, 9,* 179–200.

## An article in a journal that paginates each issue separately

MLA    Festinger, Leon. "Cognitive Dissonance." *Scientific American* 2 (Oct. 1962): 93–102.

APA    Festinger, Leon. (1962, October). Cognitive dissonance. *Scientific American, 2,* 93–102.

## An article from a daily newspaper

MLA    Lubin, J. S. "On Idle: The Unemployed Shun Much Mundane Work, at Least for a While." *The Wall Street Journal* 5 December 1980: 1, 25.

APA    Lubin, J. S. (1980, December 5). On idle: The unemployed shun much mundane work, at least for a while. *The Wall Street Journal,* pp. 1, 25.

# Other Sources

## Computer software

MLA    Hogue, Bill. *Miner 2049er.* Computer Software. Big Five Software.

OR    *Microsoft Word.* Computer Software. Microsoft, 1984.

APA    Hogue, Bill. (1982). *Miner 2049er.* [Computer program.]. Van Nuys, CA: Big Five Software.

OR    *Microsoft Word.* (1984). [Computer program.]. Bellevue, WA: Microsoft.

## Records and tapes

MLA    Beethoven, Ludwig van. *Violin Concerto in D Major, op. 61.* Cond. Alexander Gauk. U.S.S.R. State Orchestra. David Oistrakh, violinist. Allegro, ACS 8044, 1980.

OR    Springsteen, Bruce. "Dancing in the Dark." *Born in the U.S.A.* Columbia, QC 38653, 1984.

APA    Beethoven, Ludwig van. (Composer). (1980). *Violin Concerto in D Major, op. 61.* (Cassette Recording No. ACS 8044). New York: Allegro.

OR    Springsteen, Bruce. (Singer and Composer). (1984). "Dancing in the Dark." *Born in the U.S.A.* (Record No. QC 38653). New York: Columbia.

## Interviews

MLA    Lowell, Robert. "Robert Lowell." With Frederick Seidel. *Paris Review* 25 (Winter-Spring): 56–95.

OR    Franklin, Anna. Personal Interview. 3 September 1983.

APA    Lowell, Robert. [Interview with Frederick Seidel.]. *Paris Review, 25* (Winter-Spring), pp. 56–95.

OR    Franklin, Anna. [Personal Interview.]. 3 September 1983.

Brodie, M. Fawn, "The Semi-Transparent Shadows," reprinted from *Thomas Jefferson: An Intimate History* by Fawn M. Brodie, by permission of W. W. Norton & Company, Inc. Copyright © by Fawn M. Brodie.

Didion, Joan, "On Self-Respect," from *Slouching Toward Bethlehem* by Joan Didion. Copyright © 1961, 1968 by Joan Didion. Reprinted by permission of Farrar, Straus and Giroux, Inc.

Dillard, Annie, "Solar Eclipse," from pp. 89–93, 102–103 of *Teaching a Stone to Talk: Expeditions and Encounters* by Annie Dillard. Copyright © 1982 by Annie Dillard. Reprinted by permission of Harper & Row, Publishers, Inc.

Etzioni, Amitai, "When Rights Collide," *Psychology Today*. Copyright © 1977 by Ziff Davis Publishing Co. Reprinted with permission from the author.

Feynman, Richard P., "He Fixes Radios by Thinking," reprinted from *"Surely You're Joking, Mr. Feynman!" Adventures of a Curious Character*, Richard P. Feynman. As told to Ralph Leighton. Edited by Edward Hutchings. Copyright © 1985 by Richard P. Feynman and Ralph Leighton.

FitzGerald, Frances, "Fire in the Lake," excerpt from the last chapter of *Fire in the Lake* by Frances FitzGerald. Copyright © 1972 by Frances FitzGerald. Reprinted by permission of Little, Brown & Company in association with the Atlantic Monthly Press.

Forster, E. M., "My Wood," from *Arbinger Harvest*, copyright 1936, 1964 by Edward Morgan Forster. Reprinted by permission of Harcourt Brace Jovanovich, Inc.

Fuchs, Victor R., "Why Married Mothers Work," from *How We Live* by Victor R. Fuchs, Harvard University Press, 1983. Copyright © 1983 by the President and Fellows of Harvard College.

Goleman, Daniel, "The Intelligent Filter," from *Vital Lies, Simple Truths: The Psychology of Self-Deception*. Copyright © 1985 by Daniel Goleman, Ph.D.

Gould, Stephen Jay, "The Great Dying." Reprinted from *Ever Since Darwin, Reflections in Natural History* by Stephen Jay Gould, by permission of W. W. Norton & Company, Inc. Copyright © 1977 by Stephen Jay Gould. Copyright © 1973, 1974, 1975, 1976, 1977 by The American Museum of Natural History.

Halberstam, David, "Tiff Wood, Sculler," from Chapter 6 of *The Amateurs* by David Halberstam. Copyright © 1985 by David Halberstam. By permission of William Morrow Company.

Hemingway, Ernest, "A Clean Well-Lighted Place," from *Winner Take Nothing*. Copyright 1933 Charles Scribner's Sons; copyright renewed © 1961 Ernest Hemingway. Reprinted with the permission of Charles Scribner's Sons.

Hoekema, David, "Capital Punishment: The Question of Justification." Copyright 1979 Christian Century Foundation. Reprinted by permission from the March 28, 1979, issue of the Christian Century.

Kauffmann, Stanley, "Dr. Strangelove." Reprinted by permission of *The New Republic*, © 1964, The New Republic, Inc.

Kennan, George, "A Proposal for International Disarmament," from *The Nuclear Delusion* by George Kennan. Copyright © 1976, 1980, 1981, 1982 by George F. Kennan. Reprinted by permission of Pantheon Books, a division of Random House, Inc.

King, Martin Luther, Jr., "Letter from Birmingham Jail" (April 16, 1963) from *Why We Can't Wait* by Martin Luther King, Jr. Copyright © 1963 by Martin Luther King Jr. Reprinted by permission of Harper & Row, Publishers, Inc.

Kinsley, Michael ("TRB") "Saint Ralph." Reprinted by permission of *The New Republic*, © 1985, The New Republic, Inc.

Kleiman, Mark, "Grant Bachelor's Degrees by Examination." Copyright 1985, Mark. A. R. Kleiman. Reprinted from *The Wall Street Journal*.

Koch, Edward, "Death and Justice." Reprinted by permission of *The New Republic*, © 1982, The New Republic, Inc.

Kowinski, William S., "Mallaise: How To Know If You Have It," from *The Malling of America* by William Severini Kowinski. Copyright © 1985 by William Severini Kowinski. By permission of William Morrow and Company.

Kozol, Jonathan, "The Human Cost of an Illiterate Society," from *Illiterate America* by Jonathan Kozol. Copyright © 1985 by Jonathan Kozol. Reprinted by permission of Doubleday & Company, Inc.

Krauthammer, Charles, "In Defense of Deterrence." Reprinted by permission of *The New Republic*, © 1982, The New Republic, Inc.

Leakey, Richard E. and Roger Lewin, "People of the Lake" by Richard E. Leakey and Roger Lewin from *People of the Lake*. Copyright © 1978 by Richard E. Leakey and Roger Lewin. Reprinted by permission of Doubleday & Company, Inc.

Mackey, James and Deborah Appleman, "Broken Connections: The Alienated Adolescent in the 80s." Reprinted with permission from Sept./Oct. 1984 issue of *Curriculum Review*, Chicago, Illinois.

McPhee, John, excerpt retitled "The New York Pickpocket Academy" from *Giving Good Weight* by John McPhee. Copyright © 1975, 1976, 1978, 1979 by John McPhee. Reprinted by permission of Farrar, Straus and Giroux, Inc.

Marshall, Kim, "Literacy: The Price of Admission." Copyright © 1985 Harvard Magazine. Reprinted by permission.

Mead, Margaret, "A Life for a Life." From pp. 286–290 "Crime: A Life for a Life" (June 1978), in *Aspects of the Present* by Margaret Mead and Rhoda Metraux. Copyright © 1980 by Mary Catherine Bateson Kassarjian and Rhoda Metraux. By permission of William Morrow and Company.

Miller, Jon D., "Scientific Literacy: A Conceptual and Empirical Review." Reprinted or reproduced by permission of *Daedalus*, Journal of the American Academy of Arts and Sciences, Spring 1983, Cambridge, MA.

Owen, David, "Beating the Test," from *None of the Above* by David Owen. Copyright © 1985 by David Owen. Reprinted by permission of Houghton Mifflin Company.

Petrunkevitch, Alexander, excerpt from "The Spider and the Wasp," by Alexander Petrunkevitch. Copyright © 1952 by Scientific American, Inc. All rights reserved.

Rodriguez, Richard, "Gains and Losses," from *Hunger of Memory* by Richard Rodriguez. Copyright 1982 by Richard Rodriguez. Reprinted by permission of David R. Godine, Publisher, Boston.

Sagan, Carl, "Nuclear War and Climatic Catastrophe: A Nuclear Winter." Reprinted by permission of the author's agents, Scott Meredith Literary Agency, Inc., 845 Third Ave., NY, NY 10022.

Shames, Laurence, "The Eyes of Fear." Reprinted with permission from *Esquire*. Copyright © 1982 by Esquire Associates.

Solomon, Robert C., "Culture Gives Us a Sense of Who We Are," from *The Los Angeles Times*, Jan. 25, 1981. Reprinted with permission from the author.

Theroux, Phyllis, "Fear of Families," from pp. 94–96 of *Peripheral Visions* by Phyllis Theroux. Copyright © 1982 by Phyllis Theroux. By permission of William Morrow & Company.

Thomas, Lewis, "On Natural Death," from *The Medusa and the Snail: More Notes of a Biology Watcher* by Lewis Thomas. Copyright © 1979 by Lewis Thomas. Reprinted by permission of Viking Penguin, Inc.

Thurow, Lester, "Why Women Are Paid Less Than Men." Copyright © 1981 by The New York Times Company. Reprinted by permission.

Toth, Susan Allen, "Blaine's Pool," from *Blooming: A Small Town Childhood* by Susan Allen Toth. Copyright © 1978, 1981 by Susan Allen Toth. Reprinted by permission of Little, Brown & Company.

Van Deusen, Lewis H., Jr., "Civil Disobedience: Destroyer of Democracy." Reprinted with permission from the ABA *Journal*, the Lawyer's Magazine.

Walker, Alice, "Beauty: When the Other Dancer Is the Self." Copyright © 1983 by Alice Walker. Reprinted from her volume *In Search of Our Mothers' Gardens* by permission of Harcourt Brace Jovanovich, Inc.

Wallerstein, Judith S. and Joan B. Kelly, "California's Children of Divorce." Adapted from *Surviving the Breakup: How Children and Parents Cope with Divorce* by Judith S. Wallerstein and Joan Berlin Kelly. Copyright © 1980 by Judith S. Wallerstein and Joan Berlin Kelly. Reprinted by permission of Basic Books, Inc., Publishers.

Welty, Eudora, "Miss Duling," reprinted by permission of the publishers from *One Writer's Beginnings* by Eudora Welty, Cambridge, Mass.: Harvard University Press, Copyright © 1983, 1984 by Eudora Welty.

White, E. B., "The Ring of Time," pp. 142–145 of "The Ring of Time" in *Essays of E. B. White.* Copyright © 1956, renewed 1984 by E. B. White. Reprinted by permission of Harper & Row, Publishers, Inc.

Woolf, Virginia, "The Death of the Moth," from *The Death of the Moth and Other Essays* by Virginia Woolf, copyright 1942 by Harcourt Brace Jovanovich, Inc.; renewed 1970 by Marjorie T. Parsons. Reprinted by permission of the publisher, the author's estate, and Hogarth Press.

Zukav, Gary, "Heisenberg's Uncertainty Principle," from pp. 132–136 of *The Dancing Wu Li Masters* by Gary Zukav. Copyright © 1979 by Gary Zukav. By permission of William Morrow & Co.

# Topical Index

This index classifies readings by topics in order to facilitate topic-centered discussions and special writing assignments.

# Index of Authors, Titles, and Terms

N 3971